BEST OF
EASTERN
EUROPE
2005

Rick Steves & Cameron Hewitt

EASTERN EUROPE OVERVIEW

See following pages for detail areas shown below.

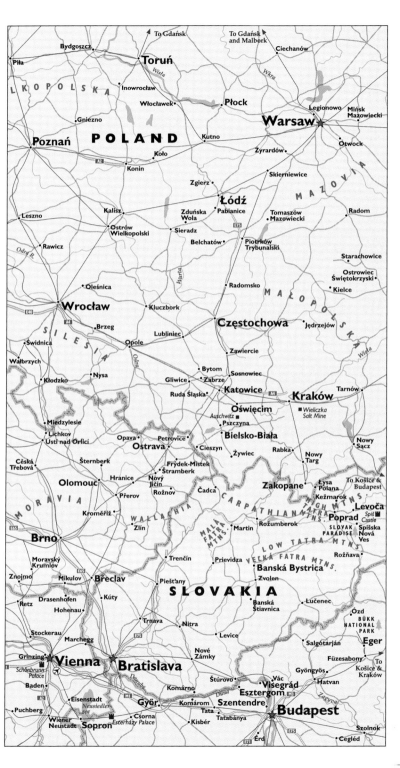

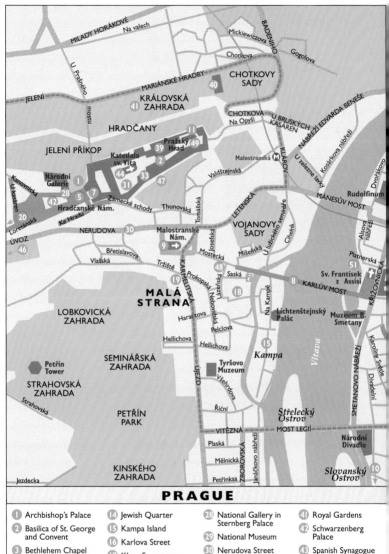

PRAGUE

1. Archbishop's Palace
2. Basilica of St. George and Convent
3. Bethlehem Chapel
4. Black Light Theater (2 locations)
5. Castle Square
6. Ceremonial Hall
7. Changing of the Guard
8. Charles Bridge
9. Church of St. Nicholas (in Malá Strana)
10. To Dancing House
11. Golden Lane
12. Havelská Market
13. Hus Memorial
14. Jewish Quarter
15. Kampa Island
16. Karlova Street
17. Klaus Synagogue
18. Lennon Wall
19. Little Quarter
20. To Loreto Shrine
21. Entrance to Lucerna Gallery
22. Maisel Synagogue
23. Memorial to Victims of Communism
24. Mucha Museum
25. Municipal House
26. Museum of Communism
27. Na Příkopě Street
28. National Gallery in Sternberg Palace
29. National Museum
30. Nerudova Street
31. Obelisk
32. Old Jewish Cemetery
33. Old Royal Palace
34. Old Town Hall, Astronomical Clock, Tower & Chapel
35. Old Town Square
36. Old-New Synagogue
37. Pinkas Synagogue
38. Powder Tower
39. Prague Castle
40. Queen Anne's Summer Palace
41. Royal Gardens
42. Schwarzenberg Palace
43. Spanish Synagogue
44. St. Vitus Cathedral
45. St. Wenceslas Statue
46. To Strahov Monastery & Library
47. Terraced Gardens
48. Torture Museum
49. Toy and Barbie Museum
50. Týn Church
51. Vltava River Cruises
52. Wenceslas Square

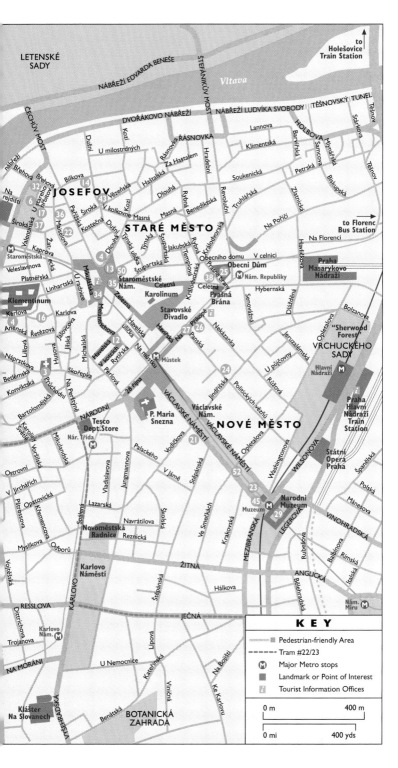

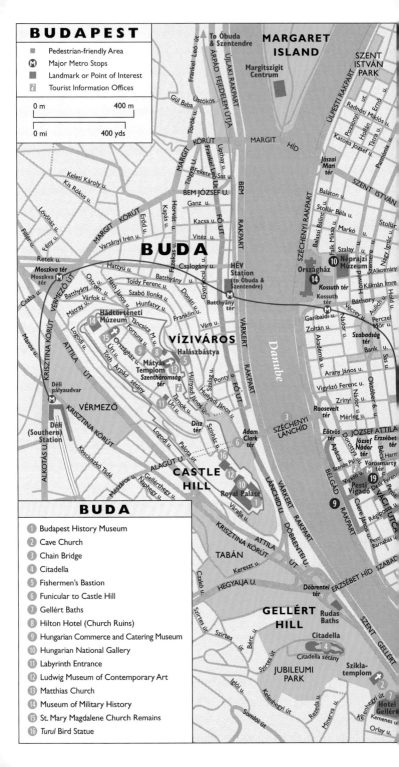

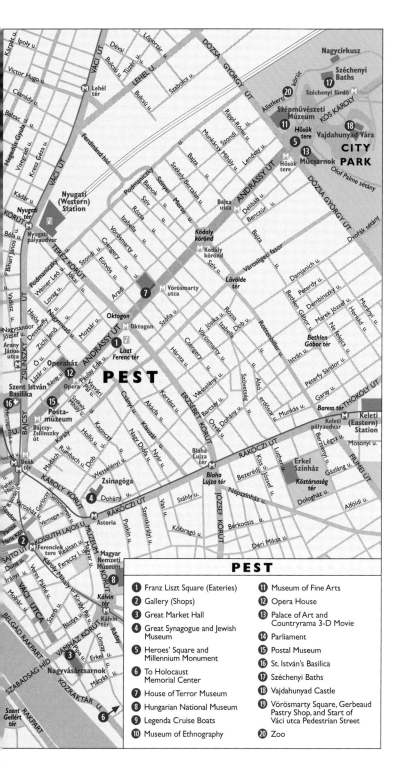

PEST

1. Franz Liszt Square (Eateries)
2. Gallery (Shops)
3. Great Market Hall
4. Great Synagogue and Jewish Museum
5. Heroes' Square and Millennium Monument
6. To Holocaust Memorial Center
7. House of Terror Museum
8. Hungarian National Museum
9. Legenda Cruise Boats
10. Museum of Ethnography
11. Museum of Fine Arts
12. Opera House
13. Palace of Art and Countryrama 3-D Movie
14. Parliament
15. Postal Museum
16. St. István's Basilica
17. Széchenyi Baths
18. Vajdahunyad Castle
19. Vörösmarty Square, Gerbeaud Pastry Shop, and Start of Váci utca Pedestrian Street
20. Zoo

Rick Steves'

BEST OF
EASTERN
EUROPE

2005

AVALON
TRAVEL

CONTENTS

Top Destinations in Eastern Europe

INTRODUCTION

Until 1989, Eastern Europe was a foreboding place—a gloomy corner of the "Evil Empire." Now the obligatory grays and preachy reds of communism live only in history books, museums, and kitschy theme restaurants. Today's Eastern Europe is a traveler's delight, with low prices, friendly locals, lively squares, breathtaking sights, fascinating history, and a sense of pioneer excitement. For the experienced traveler, the East feels like the West once did: unpredictable, challenging, and rewarding.

This book breaks Eastern Europe into its top big-city, small-town, and back-to-nature destinations. It then gives you all the information and opinions necessary to wring the maximum value out of your limited time and money. If you're planning for a month or less in this region, this book is all you need.

Experiencing Europe's culture, people, and natural wonders economically and hassle-free has been my goal for more than 25 years of traveling, tour guiding, and travel writing. With this book, I pass on to you the lessons I've learned, researched (in mid-2004) for 2005.

Rick Steves' Best of Eastern Europe is a personal tour guide in your pocket. Better yet, it's actually two tour guides in your pocket: My co-author and researcher for this guidebook is Cameron Hewitt, who leads Eastern Europe tours at Rick Steves' Europe Through the Back Door. Inspired by his Polish roots, Cameron has a powerful passion for Eastern Europe. Together, we will keep this book up-to-date and accurate (though for simplicity, from this point "we" will shed our respective egos and become "I").

Americans approach Eastern Europe expecting grouchy, monolingual service; crumbling, communist-era infrastructure; and grimy, depressing landscapes dotted with rusting factories. Many Westerners seem to think that independent travel in the East is reckless—or even dangerous. But those who visit are pleasantly surprised at the beauty, friendliness, safety, and ease of travel in these countries. You'll be amazed at how quickly Eastern European countries have Western-ized. Travel in Eastern Europe is nearly as smooth as travel in the West. Any remaining rough edges simply add to the charm and car-bonate the experience. The language barrier is tiny—English is even more widely spoken here than in much of Western Europe. And, more important, the delightful villages, cosmopolitan cities, and exciting museums are welcoming and world-class.

To today's Eastern Europeans, the Soviet regime is old news, Cold War espionage is the stuff of movies, and oppressive Stalin sculptures are a distant memory. A decade and a half after the fall of the Iron Curtain, Eastern Europeans think about communism only when tourists bring it up. Freedom is a generation old, and—for better or for worse—McDonald's, MTV, and mobile phones are every bit as entrenched as in the West. The Czech Republic, Slovakia, Poland, Hungary, and Slovenia all joined the European Union in 2004—and all of them now have fast-growing economies.

You'll wander among Prague's dreamy, fairytale spires, bask in the energy of Kraków's market square, and soak with chess players in a Budapest bath. Ponder Europe's most moving Holocaust memorial at Auschwitz. Enjoy nature as you stroll on boardwalks through the Plitvice Lakes' waterfall wonderland or glide across Lake Bled to a church-topped island in the shadow of the Julian Alps. Taste a proud Hungarian vintner's wine in an Eger cave, and say, *"Egészségedre!"* (or stick with "Cheers!").

I've been selective, including only the top destinations and sights. For example, Croatia has dozens of island getaways. I take you to the quaintest: Korčula. Poland has plenty of big cities—but Kraków, Warsaw, and Gdańsk are clearly the most worthwhile and interesting.

The best is, of course, only my opinion. But after spending half my life researching Europe, I've developed a sixth sense for what stokes the traveler's wanderlust. Just thinking about the places fea-tured in this book makes me want to polka.

This Information is Accurate and Up-to-Date

Most publishers of guidebooks that cover a region from top to bottom can afford an update only every two or three years, and even then, the research is often by letter or e-mail. Since this book is selective, covering only the places I think make the top month of sightseeing in Eastern Europe, I can update it in person each summer. The information in this book is accurate as of mid-2004—but, especially in fast-changing Eastern Europe, I know you'll under-stand that guidebooks begin to yellow even before they're printed. Still, if you're traveling with the current edition of this book, I guar-antee you're using the most up-to-date information available in

What is "Eastern Europe"?

"Eastern Europe" means different things to different people. To most Americans, Eastern Europe includes any place that was once behind the Iron Curtain, from the former East Germany to Moscow. But people who actually live in many of these countries consider themselves "Central Europeans," and think of "Eastern Europe" as nations located farther east: Russia, Ukraine, Belarus, and Romania.

In this book, I use the term "Eastern Europe" to describe the **Czech Republic, Slovakia, Poland, Hungary, Slovenia,** and **Croatia.** I've also annexed a trio of worth-a-visit gateway cities in Germany and Austria, each of which has important cultural and historic ties to these nations: **Vienna** was the imperial capital of Eastern Europe for centuries, and **Berlin** and **Dresden** share a more recent communist history with the region.

So what do my six "Eastern European" countries have in common? All of these destinations fell under communist control during the last half of the 20th century. More importantly, for hundreds of years leading up to World War I, they were all part of the Austrian Hapsburg Empire. Before the Hapsburgs, the kings and emperors of these countries also frequently governed their neighbors. And all of these countries (except Hungary) are populated by people of Slavic heritage.

I hope that natives, sticklers, and historians will understand the liberties I've taken with the title of this book—after all, would you buy a book called *Rick Steves' Best of the Former Hapsburg Empire?*

print. For the latest, see www.ricksteves.com/update. Also at my Web site, check my Graffiti Wall (select "Rick Steves' Guidebooks," then "Eastern Europe") for a huge, valuable list of reports and experiences—good and bad—from fellow travelers.

Use this year's edition. If you're packing an old book, you'll understand the seriousness of your mistake...in Europe. Your trip costs about $10 per waking hour. Your time is valuable. This guidebook saves lots of time.

About This Book

This book is organized by destination. Each destination is covered as a mini-vacation on its own, filled with exciting sights and convenient, affordable places to stay. In each chapter, you'll find:

Planning Your Time, a suggested schedule with thoughts on how best to use your limited time.

Orientation, including tourist information, city transportation, and an easy-to-read map designed to make the text clear and your arrival smooth.

Sights with ratings: ▲▲▲—Worth getting up early and skipping breakfast for; ▲▲—Worth getting up early for; ▲—Worth seeing if it's convenient; No rating—Worth knowing about.

Sleeping and Eating, with addresses and phone numbers of my favorite budget hotels and restaurants.

Transportation Connections, covering the most common train routes to help you lace together your trip.

Country Introductions give you an overview of each country's culture, customs, history, food, language, and other useful practicalities.

The chapter on **Understanding Yugoslavia,** which sorts out the various countries and conflicts, gives you a good picture of why Yugoslavia was formed, and why it broke up.

The **appendix** contains a telephone calling chart, a list of U.S. embassies, a summary of national holidays, and a climate chart.

Browse through this book, choose your favorite destinations, and link them together. Then have a great trip! You'll travel like a temporary local, getting the absolute most out of every mile, minute, and dollar. You won't waste time on mediocre sights because, unlike other guidebook authors, I cover only the best. Since lousy, expensive hotels are a major financial pitfall, I've worked hard to assemble the best accommodations values for each stop. As you travel the route I know and love, I'm happy you'll be meeting some of my favorite Europeans.

PLANNING

Trip Costs

Traveling in Eastern Europe is cheap. Generally speaking, things that natives buy—such as food, transportation, and museum tickets—are affordable (in line with the local economy). Hotels, on the other hand, are expensive—often surpassing even Western prices for comparable comfort. Still, if you avoid restaurants with inflated prices on the main tourist drag, and if you use my listings to stay only at the best-value hotels, a trip to the East is substantially cheaper than a trip to the West.

Five components make up your trip cost: airfare, surface transportation, room and board, sightseeing/entertainment, and shopping/miscellany. The prices I've listed below are more or less average for all of the destinations in this book. In general, things are cheaper in Hungary, Poland, and Slovakia, and costlier in Croatia and Slovenia (and the gateway cities of Vienna, Berlin, and Dresden). Big cities (such as Prague and Warsaw) are more expensive than smaller destinations (like Český Krumlov and Eger).

Airfare: Don't try to sort through the mess. Get and use a good travel agent. A basic round-trip flight from the United States to

Prague should cost $600 to $1,200 (even cheaper in winter), depending on where you fly from and when. Always consider saving time and money in Europe by flying "open jaw" (into one city and out of another). The additional cost of flying into Prague and out of Dubrovnik could be cheaper than the added expense and trouble of a two-day overland return trip to Prague.

Surface Transportation: For the three-week whirlwind trip described on page 6, allow $300 per person for public transportation (train, bus, and boat tickets) or $800 per person (based on 2 people sharing the car) for a three-week car rental, parking, gas, and insurance. Car rental is cheapest when reserved from the United States. Train travelers will probably save money by simply buying tickets along the way, rather than purchasing a railpass (see "Transportation," page 21).

Room and Board: You can thrive in Eastern Europe on an average of $70 a day per person for room and board. A $70-a-day budget per person allows $10 for lunch, $15 for dinner, and $45 for lodging (based on 2 people splitting the cost of a $90 double room that includes breakfast). That's doable. Students and tightwads do it on $40 a day ($20 per bed, $20 for meals and snacks). Budget sleeping and eating require the skills and information covered later in this chapter (and in much more depth in my book *Rick Steves' Europe Through the Back Door*).

Sightseeing and Entertainment: Sightseeing is cheap here. Major sights generally cost around $2 to $5, with some more expensive sights at around $10. Figure $10 to $25 for splurge experiences (e.g., going to concerts, taking a twilight cruise on the Danube, watching Slovenia's Lipizzaner stallions, or soaking in a Budapest bath). You can hire a private guide for about $60 for four hours. An overall average of $20 a day works for most. Don't skimp here. After all, this category directly powers most of the experiences all the other expenses are designed to make possible.

Shopping and Miscellany: Figure $1 per postcard, coffee, beer, and ice-cream cone. Shopping can vary in cost from nearly nothing to a small fortune. Good budget travelers find that this category has little to do with assembling a trip full of lifelong and wonderful memories.

When to Go

The "tourist season" runs roughly from May through September.

Summer has its advantages: the best weather, very long days (light until after 21:00), and the busiest schedule of tourist fun.

In spring and fall—May, June, September, and early October—travelers enjoy fewer crowds, milder weather, and the ability to grab a room almost whenever and wherever they like.

Winter travelers find concert season in full swing, with absolutely no tourist crowds (except in always-packed Prague), but

Eastern Europe: Best Three-Week Trip (By Train)

Day	Plan	Sleep in
1	Arrive in Prague	Prague
2	Prague	Prague
3	Prague, maybe day trip to Kutná Hora or Český Krumlov; night train to Kraków	Night train
4	Kraków	Kraków
5	Kraków, day trip to Auschwitz	Kraków
6	Kraków, maybe day trip to Wieliczka Salt Mine or Warsaw; night train to Eger	Night train
7	Eger	Eger
8	Early to Budapest	Budapest
9	Budapest	Budapest
10	Budapest, maybe day trip to Danube Bend	Budapest
11	To Ljubljana (catch early, direct 8.5-hr train; no handy night-train option)	Ljubljana
12	Ljubljana	Ljubljana
13	To Bled	Bled
14	Day trips around Julian Alps	Bled
15	To Zagreb, sightseeing, then early evening bus to Plitvice Lakes National Park	Plitvice
16	Plitvice hike in morning, then afternoon bus to Split	Split
17	Split	Split
18	Boat to Korčula	Korčula
19	Korčula	Korčula
20	Boat to Dubrovnik	Dubrovnik
21	Dubrovnik	Dubrovnik
22	Dubrovnik and fly home	

This speedy, far-reaching itinerary works best by public transportation. Most of the time, you'll take the train. Exceptions: Bled and Ljubljana are better connected by bus. To get from Bled to Plitvice, take the bus to Ljubljana, the train to Zagreb, then the bus to Plitvice. To get from Plitvice to the coast, take an afternoon bus to Split, or take the bus back to Zagreb to catch a cheap flight. The Dalmatian Coast destinations are best connected to each other by boat or bus (no trains). A cheap one- or two-day car rental makes sense in countries, such as Slovenia, that offer inviting day-trip destinations difficult to reach by public transit.

By **car,** this is a tiring itinerary, with lots of long road days. Instead, connect long-distance destinations by night train (e.g., Prague to Kraków, Kraków to Eger/Budapest), then strategically rent cars for a day or two in areas that merit having wheels (e.g., the Czech or Slovenian countryside).

Germanic Addendum: If you want to add the German gateway cities to this tour, begin with two days in Berlin, and spend a few hours in Dresden on the way to Prague. Vienna (which is well worth 2 days) is out of the way for the above itinerary (fitting best between Budapest and Ljubljana; it also makes sense if you're going directly between Budapest and Prague).

some accommodations and sights are either closed or run on a limited schedule. Croatian coastal towns are completely dead in winter. Confirm your sightseeing plans locally, especially when traveling off-season. The weather can be cold and dreary, and night will draw the shades on your sightseeing before dinnertime. You may find the climate chart in the appendix helpful.

Sightseeing Priorities

Depending on the length of your trip, here are my recommended priorities. Assuming you're traveling by public transportation, I've taken geographical proximity into account.

3 days:	Prague
5 days, add:	Budapest
7 days, add:	Kraków and Auschwitz
9 days, add:	Český Krumlov
12 days, add:	Ljubljana and Bled
16 days, add:	Dubrovnik and Split
22 days, add:	Plitvice Lakes, Gdańsk and Malbork Castle, Eger, Korčula, Danube Bend
More time:	Choose from among Warsaw, Toruń, Zagreb, Slovakia's Spiš Region, and Bratislava... and slow down.

(The map on page 7 and the 3-week itinerary on page 6 include most of the stops in the first 22 days.)

Berlin, Dresden, and Vienna: These three gateway cities make for great destinations. But since the focus of this book is Eastern Europe, I've included them mostly for the convenience of readers who will pass through them on their way to or from Eastern Europe. On a tour of Germany and Austria, they rate higher on the list of priorities (see *Rick Steves' Germany & Austria* guidebook for more information). But if your focus is Eastern Europe, there's plenty to keep you busy in the Czech Republic, Slovakia, Poland, Hungary, Slovenia, and Croatia.

Itinerary Specifics

As you read through this book, note days when sights are closed, and plan your itinerary accordingly. Saturday morning feels like any bustling weekday morning, but at lunchtime, many shops close down through Sunday. Sundays have pros and cons, as they do for travelers in the United States (special events, limited hours, shops and banks closed, limited public transportation, no rush hours). Popular places are even more popular on weekends.

Plan ahead for banking, laundry, postal chores, and picnics. To maximize rootedness, minimize one-night stands. Mix intense and relaxed periods. Every trip (and every traveler) needs at least a few slack days. Pace yourself. Assume you will return.

RESOURCES

Eastern European Tourist Offices in the United States

Each country's national tourist office in the United States is a wealth of information. Before your trip, get the free general information packet and request any specifics you may want (such as regional and city maps and festival schedules).

Czech Tourist Authority: 1109 Madison Ave., New York, NY 10028, tel. 212/288-0830, fax 212/288-0971, www.czechcenter.com, info@czechcenter.com. To get a weighty information package (1–2 lbs., no advertising), send a check for $4 to cover postage and specify trip dates and places of interest. Basic information and map are free.

Polish National Tourist Office: 5 Marine View Plaza #208, Hoboken, NJ 07030-5722, tel. 201/420-9910, fax 201/584-9153, www.polandtour.org, pntonyc@polandtour.org. Warsaw and Kraków information, regional brochures, and maps.

Hungarian National Tourist Office: 150 E. 58th St., 33rd floor, New York, NY 10155, tel. 212/355-0240, fax 212/207-4103, www.gotohungary.com, hnto@gotohungary.com. *Routes to your Roots* booklet for those of Hungarian descent, *Budapest Guide*, and horseback riding info.

Slovenian Tourist Office: 2929 E. Commercial Blvd. Suite 201, Fort Lauderdale, FL 33308, tel. 954/491-0112, fax 954/771-9841, www.slovenia-tourism.si, slotouristboard@kompas.net. *Welcome to Slovenia* brochure, map, information on various regions, hiking, biking, winter travel, and farm stays.

Croatian National Tourist Office: 350 Fifth Ave. #4003, New York, NY 10118, tel. 800/829-4416 or 212/279-8672, fax 212/279-8683, www.croatia.hr, cntony@earthlink.net. Free brochures and maps.

German National Tourist Office: 122 E. 42nd St., 52nd floor, New York, NY 10168, tel. 212/661-7200, fax 212/661-7174, www.cometogermany.com, gntonyc@d-z-t.com. Maps, Rhine schedules, castles, biking, and city and regional information.

Austrian Tourist Office: P.O. Box 1142, New York, NY 10108-1142, tel. 212/944-6880, fax 212/730-4568, www.austria-tourism.com, travel@austria.info. Ask for their *Austria Kit* with map. Fine hikes and city information.

Rick Steves' Books and Public Television Shows

Rick Steves' Europe Through the Back Door 2005 gives you budget travel tips on minimizing jet lag, packing light, planning your itinerary, traveling by car or train, finding budget beds, avoiding rip-offs, using mobile phones, hurdling the language barrier, staying healthy, using your bidet, taking great photographs, and lots more.

Rick Steves' Guidebooks

Rick Steves' Europe Through the Back Door
Rick Steves' Best European City Walks & Museums
Rick Steves' Easy Access Europe

Country Guides
Rick Steves' Best of Europe
Rick Steves' Best of Eastern Europe
Rick Steves' France
Rick Steves' Germany & Austria
Rick Steves' Great Britain
Rick Steves' Ireland
Rick Steves' Italy
Rick Steves' Portugal
Rick Steves' Scandinavia
Rick Steves' Spain
Rick Steves' Switzerland

City and Regional Guides
Rick Steves' Amsterdam, Bruges & Brussels
Rick Steves' Florence & Tuscany
Rick Steves' London
Rick Steves' Paris
Rick Steves' Prague & the Czech Republic*
Rick Steves' Provence & the French Riviera
Rick Steves' Rome
Rick Steves' Venice

*New in 2005

(Avalon Travel Publishing)

The book also includes chapters on 38 of Rick's favorite Back Doors, three of which are in Eastern Europe.

Rick Steves' Country Guides, an annually updated series that covers Europe, offer you the latest on the top sights and destinations, with tips on how to make your trip efficient and fun.

Rick Steves' City and Regional Guides, freshly updated every year, focus on Europe's most compelling destinations. Along with specifics on sights, restaurants, hotels, and nightlife, you'll get self-guided, illustrated tours of the outstanding museums and most characteristic neighborhoods.

Rick Steves' Easy Access Europe, written for travelers with limited mobility, covers London, Paris, Bruges, Amsterdam, and the Rhine River.

Rick Steves' Europe 101: History and Art for the Traveler (with Gene Openshaw) gives you the story of Europe's people, history, and art. Written for smart people who were sleeping in their history and art classes before they knew they were going to Europe, *101* really helps Europe's sights come alive. However, *Europe 101* has far more information on Western Europe than on the East.

Rick's public television series, *Rick Steves' Europe,* keeps churning out shows. Of 95 episodes (the new series, plus *Travels in Europe with Rick Steves*), six shows cover Eastern Europe (including new episodes on Poland and Budapest), and three others feature the gateway cities of Berlin and Vienna.

Rick Steves' Postcards from Europe, Rick's autobiographical book, packs more than 25 years of travel anecdotes and insights into the ultimate 2,000-mile European adventure.

Other Guidebooks

You may want some supplemental information if you'll be traveling beyond my recommended destinations. When you consider the improvements they'll make in your $3,000 vacation, $25 or $35 for extra maps and books is money well spent. Especially for several people traveling by car, the weight and expense are negligible.

The Rough Guides (individually covering the countries in this book) are packed with historical and cultural insight, but not updated annually. Lonely Planet guides are well-researched (also not updated annually); their far-ranging *Eastern Europe* overview book gives you little to go on in each destination, but their country- and city-specific guides are more thorough.

Students, backpackers, and nightlife-seekers should consider the Let's Go guides (by Harvard students, the best hostel listings, updated annually). Dorling Kindersley publishes snazzy Eyewitness Guides covering Prague, Budapest, Kraków, Warsaw, Poland, Croatia, Berlin, and Vienna. While pretty to look at, these books weigh a ton and are skimpy on actual content.

In Your Pocket publishes regularly updated magazines on major Eastern European cities (including Prague, Budapest, Kraków, Warsaw, Gdańsk, and Zagreb). These handy guides are especially good for their up-to-date hotel and restaurant recommendations (available locally, usually for a few dollars, but often free; condensed versions available free online at www.inyourpocket.com).

If your exploration of Germanic countries takes you beyond Vienna, Berlin, and Dresden, consider *Rick Steves' Germany & Austria 2005*. If your Czech travels include destinations outside Prague and Český Krumlov, pick up *Rick Steves' Prague & the Czech Republic 2005*.

More Recommended Reading and Movies

For information on Eastern Europe past and present, consider these books and films:

Begin Your Trip at www.ricksteves.com

At ricksteves.com, you'll find a wealth of **free information** on destinations covered in this book, including fresh European travel and tour news every month and helpful "Graffiti Wall" tips from thousands of fellow travelers.

While you're visiting the site, Rick Steves' **online Travel Store** is a great place to save money on travel bags and accessories specially designed by Rick Steves to help you travel smarter and lighter. These include Rick's popular carry-on bags (wheeled and rucksack versions), money belts, day bags, totes, toiletries kits, packing cubes, clotheslines, locks, clocks, sleep sacks, adapters, and a wide selection of guidebooks, planning maps, and *Rick Steves' Europe* DVDs.

Traveling through Europe by rail is a breeze, but choosing the right railpass for your trip (amidst hundreds of options) can drive you nutty. At ricksteves.com you'll find **Rick Steves' Annual Guide to European Railpasses**—the best way to convert chaos into pure travel energy. Buy your railpass from Rick, and you'll get a bunch of free extras to boot.

Travel agents will tell you about mainstream tours of Europe, but they won't tell you about **Rick Steves' tours**. Rick Steves' Europe Through the Back Door travel company offers more than two dozen itineraries and 250+ departures reaching the best destinations in this book...and beyond. You'll enjoy the services of a great guide, a fun bunch of travel partners (with group sizes in the mid-20s), and plenty of room to spread out in a big, comfy bus. You'll find tours to fit every vacation size, from week-long city getaways (Paris, London, Venice, Florence, Rome) to 12- to 18-day country tours to three-week "Best of Europe" adventures. For details, visit www.ricksteves.com or call 425/771-8303, ext. 217.

Non-Fiction: Lonnie Johnson's *Central Europe: Enemies, Neighbors, Friends* is the best overview history of the countries in this book. Croatian journalist Slavenka Drakulić has written a pair of insightful essay collections: *Café Europa: Life After Communism* and *How We Survived Communism and Even Laughed.* Timothy Garton Ash has written several good "eyewitness" books analyzing the transition in Eastern Europe over the last 20 years, including *History of the Present* and *The Magic Lantern.* For information on Eastern European Roma (Gypsies), consider *Bury Me Standing* by Isabel Fonseca. Tina Rosenberg's dense but thought-provoking *The Haunted Land* asks how those who actively supported communism in Central Europe should be treated in the post-communist age.

Fiction: Among great Czech works of fiction, consider *Utz* (Bruce Chatwin), *I Served the King of England* (Bohumil Hrabal), and *The Good Soldier Švejk* (Jaroslav Hašek). The Czech existential-ist writer Franz Kafka wrote many well-known novels, including *The Trial* and *The Metamorphosis*. Joseph Roth's *The Radetzky March* details the decline of an aristocratic family in the Austro-Hungarian Empire. *Zlateh the Goat* (Isaac Bashevis Singer) includes seven folk-tales of Jewish Eastern Europe.

Films: Czech Republic—*Kolya* (1996); *The Trial* (1993); *Kouř* (*Smoke*, 1991); *The Unbearable Lightness of Being* (1988); *The Firemen's Ball* (1967); *Closely Watched Trains* (1966); *The Loves of a Blonde* (1965). Poland—*The Pianist* (2002); *Schindler's List* (1993); *The Wedding* (1972). Hungary—*Csinibaba* (1997); *Time Stands Still* (1981); *The Witness* (1969). Croatia—*How the War Started on My Island* (1996); *Underground* (1995); *Tito and Me* (1992); *When Father Was Away on Business* (1985). Slovenia—*No Man's Land* (2002, Slovenian-produced, but deals with Bosnia; Oscar winner for Best Foreign Film).

Maps

The black-and-white maps in this book, drawn by Dave Hoerlein, are concise and simple. Dave, who is well-traveled in Eastern Europe, has designed the maps to help you locate recommended places and get to the tourist offices, where you can pick up a more in-depth map of the city or region (usually free). Better maps are sold at newsstands and bookstores—take a look before you buy to be sure the map has the level of detail you want.

European bookstores, especially in touristy areas, have good selections of maps. For drivers, I'd recommend a 1:200,000- or 1:300,000-scale map for each country. Train travelers usually manage fine with the freebies they get with their railpass and from the local tourist offices.

PRACTICALITIES

Red Tape: Currently, Americans and Canadians need only a pass-port, but no visa or shots, to travel in the countries covered in this book.

Borders: You'll have to show your passport when you cross a border. Americans get needlessly edgy at Eastern European borders, their imaginations fueled by years of Cold War espionage flicks. A Czech friend of mine remembers crossing borders in the early 1980s and having long needles poked into his back seat to reveal any unwel-come cargo. Scary legends—about greedy, bribe-hungry border guards and passports held hostage—run rampant among travelers.

Relax! Even if any of these stories were once true, they've long since gone the way of the hammer and sickle. Borders, whether by car or by train, are generally a non-event—flash your passport, maybe wait a few minutes, and move on. You'll be quickly checked as many as

EU Membership and the "New Europe"

On May 1, 2004, the Czech Republic, Slovakia, Poland, Hungary, Slovenia, and five other countries joined the European Union. Each of these countries had a referendum, allowing residents to vote on whether to join the EU. In every case, the referendum passed, but sometimes by a narrow margin. EU membership—and investment—is certain to benefit these countries' economies (as it has in Ireland). But Eastern Europeans still have their doubts.

Take Poland as an example. Poles have a strong agricultural heritage. During the communist era, the Soviets collectivized small family farms in most of its satellite states—but Poland managed to preserve its traditional plots. After a half-century of successfully fighting for the rights of independent small farmers, EU-member Poland now...has to collectivize small farms. (For more on Polish cold feet, see page 150.)

Another prickly issue keeps the Czech Republic Czech. After World War II, many German families living in the so-called "Sudetenland"—on the fringes of today's Czech Republic—were forced into Germany. Since then, Germans have not been able to return. But now that the Czech Republic and Germany belong to the same European Union, Germans are able to buy back their family homesteads in the Czech countryside...and they are likely to win any bidding war against the poorer Czechs.

Traditional Czech cuisine is also in jeopardy. EU hygiene standards dictate that cooked food can't be served more than two hours old. My Czech friend complained, "This makes many of our best dishes illegal." Czech specialties, often simmered, taste better the next day.

four times—by the customs and immigration officers of the country you're leaving and, sometimes after continuing ahead a few yards, the one you're entering. On international night trains, you'll likely be woken up at each border for a check (though sometimes your conductor will take your passport overnight to handle the red tape for you).

The procedure at every border is different. Usually, it's just a quick glance at the passport, the clunk of a stamp, and you're on your way. If there is a delay, don't panic. There may be a red-tape backup, or the guards might just be particularly thorough (or grouchy) that day. While I have occasionally seen the offer of a cold beer help speed things along, bribery is generally not necessary—and I've never been asked outright for a bribe (even when I've got a tour bus full of 24 antsy Americans).

The worst thing you can do is get impatient or pushy. The angrier you get, the longer it'll take. A polite smile will speed things along just as fast as a cold beer.

Even as borders fade, when you change countries, you must still change telephone cards and postage stamps.

Time: Eastern Europe is six/nine hours ahead of the East/West

A wise Czech grandmother put it best. In her lifetime, she had lived in a country ruled from Vienna (Hapsburgs), Berlin (Nazis), and Moscow (communists). She said, "Now that we're finally ruled from Prague, why would we want to turn our power over to Brussels?"

Existing EU members were also skeptical about adding on more countries. Wealthy nations have already seen funds taken from them to improve the floundering economies of poorer countries (like Portugal, Greece, and Ireland). This issue is especially dicey in Germany, where people living in the former West already loudly complain about the financial burden of pulling up the East.

All of this controversy was only exacerbated in February 2003, when, at the peak of the international debate about going to war in Iraq, U.S. Secretary of Defense Donald Rumsfeld called these Eastern countries the "New Europe." Though he meant it as an insult to Western European countries (such as France and Germany), the term has caught on—and it does capture the complicated circumstances of today's Europe. The East looks to the future, eager to distance itself from its painful recent history, while the West is more comfortable living in the past, when its power was at its peak (and French, not English, was the world's language). As Eastern Europe joins the EU, and the geographical center of Europe shifts from Brussels to Prague, the power of existing EU members—especially Germany and France—is diluted. In this "New Europe," the Czech Republic or Poland might emerge with a leading role.

Coasts of the United States. In Europe—and throughout this book—you'll be using the 24-hour clock. After 12:00 noon, keep going—13:00, 14:00, and so on. For anything over 12, subtract 12 and add P.M. (14:00 is 2:00 P.M.)

Discounts: While discounts for sightseeing and transportation are not listed in this book, youths (under 18) and students (only with International Student Identity Cards) sometimes get discounts—but only by asking.

Watt's up? If you're bringing electrical gear, you'll need a two-prong adapter plug and a converter. Travel appliances often have convenient built-in converters; look for a voltage switch marked 120V (U.S.) and 240V (Europe).

MONEY

Exchange Rates

Whenever possible, I've priced things throughout this book in local currencies. Some vendors—especially hotels—prefer to set their prices in euros, and only in these cases I've followed suit. Even if places list prices in euros, they'll happily accept the local currency.

Germany and Austria use the euro. Although the Czech Republic, Slovakia, Poland, Hungary, and Slovenia joined the European Union in 2004, it'll take another few years before they officially adopt the euro. These countries, along with Croatia, still use their traditional currencies:

> 25 Czech crowns (*koruna*, Kč) = about $1
> 30 Slovak crowns (*koruna*, Sk) = about $1
> 3.5 Polish złoty (zł, or PLN) = about $1
> 200 Hungarian forints (Ft, or HUF) = about $1
> 200 Slovenian tolars (SIT) = about $1
> 6 Croatian kuna (HRK) = about $1
> 1 euro (€) = about $1.20

To roughly convert prices in Czech crowns into dollars, multiply by four and drop the last two digits (e.g., 1,000 Kč = about $40). For Slovak crowns, divide by three and drop the last digit (e.g., 750 Sk = about $25). To roughly go from Hungarian forints or Slovenian tolars into dollars, divide by two and drop the last two digits (e.g., 10,000 Ft or SIT = about $50). To very roughly convert Polish prices into dollars, divide by four (e.g., 80 zł = about $20). To convert Croatian kuna into dollars, divide by six (e.g., 70 kuna = about $11).

So, that 20-zł Polish woodcarving is about $5, the 5,000-Ft Hungarian dinner is around $25, and the 2,000-Kč taxi ride through Prague is...uh-oh.

Banking

Bring a debit card (or ATM card) and a credit card, along with a couple hundred dollars in cash as a backup. The best and easiest way to get local cash is to use the omnipresent bank machines (always open, low fees, and quick processing). You'll need a PIN code—numbers only, no letters—to use with your Visa or MasterCard. Before you go, verify with your bank that your card will work and alert them that you'll be making withdrawals in Europe; otherwise, the bank may not approve transactions if it perceives unusual spending patterns. Bring two cards in case one gets damaged. The universal word for "cash machine" in all of these countries is *Bankomat*.

Note that ATMs are likely to give you high-denomination bills, which can be difficult to break (especially at odd hours). My strategy: Go immediately to a bank to break the big bills, or request an odd amount of money from the ATM (such as 2,800 Kč instead of 3,000 Kč; it's not always successful, but it's worth a try).

Just like at home, credit or debit cards work easily at larger hotels, restaurants, and shops. Visa and MasterCard are more commonly accepted than American Express. Smaller businesses prefer payment in local currency. Smart travelers function with hard cash and plastic.

Traveler's checks are expensive and time-consuming, but if you bring some, you'll find that regular banks have the best rates for cashing them (except in Poland, where *kantors*, or money-changing kiosks, generally offer good rates—check several to find the best). Many banks charge a fee per check cashed, so rather than cashing five $100 checks, cash one $500 check. For a large exchange, it pays to compare rates and fees. Post offices (business hours) and train stations (long hours) usually change money if you can't get to a bank.

Note that although the Czech Republic, Slovakia, Poland, Hungary, Slovenia, and Croatia haven't officially adopted the euro, many hotels, restaurants, and shops in these countries (especially in touristy areas) accept euros—but you'll often get bad rates (and your change back in the local currency). If you're just passing through the country, your euros will probably get you by—and can actually be helpful in an emergency in any of these countries. But if you're staying awhile, go with the local currency.

Because each country still has its own currency, and you'll likely be crossing several borders throughout your trip, you may wind up with leftover cash from a previous stop. Coins can't be exchanged in other countries—try to spend them before you cross the border. But bills are easy to convert to the "new" country's currency.

Keep your credit and debit cards and most of your money hidden away in a money belt (a cloth pouch worn around your waist and tucked under your clothes). Thieves target tourists. A money belt provides peace of mind and allows you to carry lots of cash safely. Don't be petty about getting money. Withdraw a week's worth of cash, stuff it in your money belt, and travel!

Tipping

Tipping in Eastern Europe isn't as automatic and generous as it is in the United States—but for special service, tips are appreciated, if not expected. As in the United States, the proper amount depends on your resources, tipping philosophy, and the circumstance, but some general guidelines apply.

Restaurants: Tipping is an issue only at restaurants that have waiters and waitresses. If you order your food at a counter, don't tip. At Eastern European restaurants that have a waitstaff, service is generally included, although it's common to round up the bill after a good meal (usually 5–10 percent, e.g., for a 380-Kč meal, pay 400 Kč). All too often, American travelers, feeling guilty for paying so little for such a fine meal, are tempted to overtip. But please believe me—it's not necessary. A tip of 10 percent is already overly generous, and 15 percent verges on extravagant.

Taxis: To tip the cabbie, round up about five percent. If the

Damage Control for Lost or Stolen Cards

You can stop thieves from using your ATM, debit, or credit card by reporting the loss immediately to the proper company. Call these 24-hour U.S. numbers collect: Visa (tel. 410/581-9994), MasterCard (tel. 636/722-7111), and American Express (tel. 336/393-1111).

Providing the following information will help expedite the process: the name of the financial institution that issued you the card, full card number, the cardholder's name as printed on the card, billing address, home phone number, circumstances of the loss or theft, and identification verification including a Social Security number or birth date and your mother's maiden name. (Packing along a photocopy of the front and back of your cards helps you answer the harder questions.) If you are the secondary cardholder, you'll also need to provide the primary cardholder's identification verification details. You can generally receive a temporary card within two or three business days in Europe.

If you promptly report your card lost or stolen, you typically won't be responsible for any unauthorized transactions on your account, although many banks charge a liability fee of $50.

cabbie hauls your bags and zips you to the airport to help you catch your flight, you might want to toss in a little more. But if you feel like you're being driven in circles or otherwise ripped off, skip the tip.

Hotels: I don't tip at hotels, but if you do, give the porter the local equivalent of $0.50 for carrying bags, and, at the end of your stay, leave a dollar's worth of local cash for the maid if the room was kept clean.

Special Services: Tour guides at public sites sometimes hold out their hands for tips after they give their spiels. If I've already paid for the tour, I don't tip extra. In general, if someone in the service industry does a super job for you, a small tip (the equivalent of a dollar) is appropriate...but not required.

When in Doubt, Ask. If you're not sure whether (or how much) to tip for a service, ask your hotelier or the local tourist information office; they'll fill you in on how it's done on their turf.

VAT Refunds for Shoppers

Wrapped into the purchase price of your souvenirs is a Value Added Tax (VAT) that varies per country. If you make a purchase of a minimum amount—which also differs per country—at a store that participates in the VAT refund scheme, you're entitled to get most of that tax back (see chart for VAT rates and minimum amounts). Personally, I've never felt that VAT refunds are worth the hassle, but if you do, here's the scoop.

VAT Rates and Minimum Purchases Required to Qualify for Refunds

Country of Purchase	VAT rate*	Minimum in Local Currency	Minimum in U.S. Dollars**
Austria	20%	€75.01	$98
Croatia	18.5%	501 kn	$90
Czech Rep.	22%	2,500 Kč	$105
Germany	16%	€30	$39
Hungary	25%	50,000 Ft	$267
Poland	22%	200 zł	$61
Slovakia	20%	5,000 Sk	$166
Slovenia	20%	15,001 SIT	$83

*VAT Rate indicates the percentage of the total purchase price that is VAT
** Exchange rate as of November 17, 2004

Source: HOTREC (Hotels, Restaurants & Cafes in Europe). Please note that figures are subject to change. For more information, visit www.hotrec.org or www.globalrefund.com.

If you're lucky, the merchant will subtract the tax when you make your purchase (this is more likely to occur if the store ships the goods to your home). Otherwise, you'll need to do all this:

- **Get the Paperwork:** Have the merchant completely fill out the necessary refund document, called a "cheque." You'll have to present your passport at the store.

- **Get Your Stamp at the Border:** Process your cheque(s) at your last stop in the EU with the customs agent who deals with VAT refunds. It's best to keep your purchases in your carry-on for viewing, but if they're too large or dangerous (such as knives) to carry on, then track down the proper customs agent to inspect them before you check your bag. You're not supposed to use your purchased goods before you leave. If you show up at customs wearing your chic Czech shirt, officials might look the other way—or deny you a refund.

- **Collect Your Refund:** You'll need to return your stamped documents to the retailer or its representative. Many merchants work with services such as Global Refund or Premier Tax Free, which have offices at major airports, ports, or border crossings. These services, which extract a 4 percent fee, can refund your money immediately in your currency of choice or credit your card (within 2 billing cycles). If you have to deal directly with the retailer, mail the store your stamped documents, and then wait. It could take months.

Customs Regulations

You can take home $800 in souvenirs per person duty-free. The next $1,000 is taxed at a flat 3 percent. After that, you pay the individual item's duty rate. You can also bring in duty-free a liter of alcohol (slightly more than a standard-size bottle of wine), a carton of cigarettes, and up to 100 cigars. As for food, anything in cans or sealed jars is acceptable. Skip dried meat, cheeses, and fresh fruits and veggies. To check customs rules and duty rates, visit www.customs.gov.

TRAVEL SMART

Your trip is like a complex play—easier to follow and really appreciate on a second viewing. While no one does the same trip twice to gain that advantage, reading this book in its entirety before your trip accomplishes much the same thing. As a practical matter (to avoid redundancy), many cultural or historic details are explained for one sight and not repeated for another—even if they would increase your understanding and appreciation of that second sight.

Reread entire chapters as you travel, and visit local tourist information offices. Upon arrival in a new town, lay the groundwork for a smooth departure. Buy a phone card and use it for reservations and confirmations. Enjoy the hospitality of Eastern Europeans. Ask questions. Most locals are eager to point you in their idea of the right direction. Wear your money belt, pack along a pocket-size notebook to organize your thoughts, and practice the virtue of simplicity. Those who expect to travel smart, do.

Tourist Information

The tourist information office is your best first stop in any new city. Try to arrive, or at least telephone, before it closes. In this book, I'll refer to a tourist information office as a **TI**. Throughout Eastern Europe, you'll find TIs are usually well-organized and have an English-speaking staff. Most local tourist offices in Eastern Europe are run by the government, which means their information isn't colored by a drive for profit.

Unlike in Western Europe, TIs often don't have a room-booking service—though they can almost always give you a list of local hotels, and if they're not too busy, can call around for you to check on availability. Every town has at least one travel agency with a room-booking service. Even if there's no "fee," you'll pay more for the room than if you book direct, using the listings in this book.

Museum Tips

Eastern Europe's dusty museums don't quite rank with the Louvre or the Prado. The best attractions here are the warm, generous people, the breathtaking public spaces (such as Prague's Charles

Bridge or Kraków's Main Market Square), and new, modern museums that chronicle the communist regime and celebrate its demise (like Budapest's House of Terror and Statue Park, Berlin's Checkpoint Charlie Museum, and Gdańsk's "Roads to Freedom" exhibit at the Solidarity shipyard).

But the region does have its museums, and many of them are quite good. I've carefully evaluated the best to help you decide which to visit. Generally, you'll follow a confusing, one-way tour route through a maze of rooms with squeaky parquet floors. While many museums label exhibits in English, most don't post full explanations; you'll have to buy a book or borrow laminated translations. In some cases, neither option is available. Audioguides are still rare.

TRANSPORTATION

By Car or Train?

The train (with buses or short-term car rentals to fill in the gaps) is best for single travelers; those who'll be spending more time in big cities; those with an ambitious, multi-country itinerary; and those who don't want to drive in Europe. While a car gives you more freedom—enabling you to search for hotels more easily and carrying your bags for you—the train zips you effortlessly from city to city, usually dropping you in the center, near the tourist office. Cars are great in the Czech or Slovenian countryside, but a worthless headache in places like Prague, Budapest, and Dubrovnik. If you're lacing the big cities together, the last thing you want is a car. Save lots of stress and money by taking the train (and even hiring local guides with cars for your side-trips).

Trains

Trains are punctual and cover cities well, but frustrating schedules make a few out-of-the-way recommendations not worth the time and trouble for the less determined (such as Croatia's Plitvice Lakes National Park, accessible only by bus). For timetables, visit Germany's excellent all-Europe timetable at http://bahn.hafas.de/bin/query .exe/en (expanded Czech train and bus schedules at www.vlak-bus.cz). You'll rarely need a reservation, except for night trains.

Night Trains: To cover the long distances between the major destinations in this book, use night trains as often as possible (remember, each night on the train saves a day for sightseeing). Fortunately, most of Eastern Europe's big cities are connected by night trains, even if the timing sometimes isn't ideal (e.g., arrival very early in the morning). The biggest problem night-trainers encounter is being woken up each time they cross a border to show their passports (unless the conductor offers to take your passport to deal with the red tape while you sleep).

Public Transportation in Eastern Europe

No matter how many times you hear "totally true" stories of train cars being "gassed" with a sleep-inducing drug by thieves, it's a legend, most likely invented by travelers who felt foolish for sleeping through a theft. But as on Western European night trains, thefts do occur, so lock the door and secure your belongings (to make it difficult—or at least noisy—for thieves to rip you off). When sleeping on a night train, I wear my money belt.

Railpasses: While railpasses can be a good deal in Western Europe, they usually aren't the best option in the East for two reasons: Point-to-point tickets are cheap and simple here, and most railpasses don't conveniently combine Eastern European countries. For example, with the Eurail Selectpass, you can buy unlimited travel for up to 10 travel days (within a 2-month period) in three adjacent countries; but of the countries in this book, only Hungary, Germany, Austria, and Slovenia/Croatia are eligible. Another option is the European East Pass, covering the Czech Republic, Hungary, Poland, Slovakia, and Austria—but not Slovenia, Croatia, or Germany. Three brand-new combo-passes combine various countries: one for Austria and the Czech Republic; another for Austria, Slovenia, and Croatia; and another for Hungary, Slovenia, and Croatia. If one of these passes matches your itinerary, give it a look—but again, in most cases, point-to-point tickets are the better deal. For all of the options, see the charts on pages 24 and 25.

The Czech Republic, Hungary, Germany, and Austria have their own individual railpasses—valid for trips limited to their country—but the only pass offering exciting savings is Germany's; a German Flexipass can save you money in just a couple of long trips (find our Railpass Guide online at www.ricksteves.com/rail).

Language Barrier: For tips on buying train tickets from monolingual staff in Eastern European stations, see "Hurdling the Language Barrier" on page 29.

Car Rental

It's cheaper to arrange your car rental in advance from the United States than to wait until you get to Europe. You'll want a weekly rate with unlimited mileage. For three weeks or longer, leasing is cheaper, because it saves you money on taxes and insurance. Comparison-shop through your agent. DER, a German company, often has the best rates (U.S. tel. 800/782-2424, www.dertravel.com).

Allow about $800 per person (based on 2 people sharing the car) to rent a small economy car for three weeks with unlimited mileage, including gas, parking, and insurance. I normally rent a small, inexpensive model like a Ford Fiesta. For a bigger, roomier, more powerful but still inexpensive car, move up to a Ford Escort or Volkswagen Polo. If you drop your car off early or keep it longer, you'll be credited or charged at a fair, prorated price.

Eastern Europe Railpasses

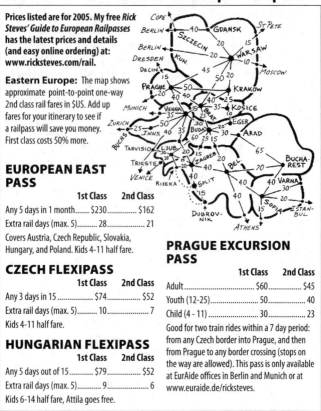

Prices listed are for 2005. My free *Rick Steves' Guide to European Railpasses* has the latest prices and details (and easy online ordering) at: www.ricksteves.com/rail.

Eastern Europe: The map shows approximate point-to-point one-way 2nd class rail fares in $US. Add up fares for your itinerary to see if a railpass will save you money. First class costs 50% more.

EUROPEAN EAST PASS

	1st Class	2nd Class
Any 5 days in 1 month	$230	$162
Extra rail days (max. 5)	28	21

Covers Austria, Czech Republic, Slovakia, Hungary, and Poland. Kids 4-11 half fare.

CZECH FLEXIPASS

	1st Class	2nd Class
Any 3 days in 15	$74	$52
Extra rail days (max. 5)	10	7

Kids 4-11 half fare.

HUNGARIAN FLEXIPASS

	1st Class	2nd Class
Any 5 days out of 15	$79	$52
Extra rail days (max. 5)	9	6

Kids 6-14 half fare, Attila goes free.

PRAGUE EXCURSION PASS

	1st Class	2nd Class
Adult	$60	$45
Youth (12-25)	50	40
Child (4 - 11)	30	23

Good for two train rides within a 7 day period: from any Czech border into Prague, and then from Prague to any border crossing (stops on the way are allowed). This pass is only available at EurAide offices in Berlin and Munich or at www.euraide.de/ricksteves.

For peace of mind, consider CDW insurance (Collision Damage Waiver, about 25 percent extra). In case of an accident, CDW insurance lowers your deductible (generally up to around $1,200, rather than the standard value-of-the-car deductible). Some companies sell additional coverage to buy down the deductible when you pick up the car. Increasingly, it's a better deal to waive the car rental company's CDW insurance entirely and opt instead for the coverage that comes with many "gold" credit cards (often with a zero deductible). Ask your credit-card company how it works, and quiz them about deductibles and worst-case scenarios (for example, they may only cover damage up to the credit limit of your card). Another alternative is to buy CDW coverage from a third party, such as Travel Guard ($7/day, U.S. tel. 800/826-4919, www.travelguard .com; often not honored by car rental companies in Italy and the Republic of Ireland).

For driving in Eastern Europe, it's wise to get an international

Eastern Europe Railpasses

EURAIL SELECTPASSES

This pass covers travel in three adjacent "Western European" countries such as Germany, Austria & Hungary. Can also choose Slovenia/Croatia as one "country." Please visit www.ricksteves.com/rail or see the railpass guide for four- and five-country options.

	1st class Selectpass	1st class Saverpass	2nd class Youthpass
5 days in 2 months	$370	$316	$241
6 days in 2 months	410	348	267
8 days in 2 months	488	414	317
10 days in 2 months	564	480	367

Saverpass: Price is per person for 2 or more adults traveling together at all times.
Youthpasses: Under age 26 only. Kids 4-11 pay half adult fare; under 4: free.

HUNGARY+ROMANIA OR HUNGARY/SLOVENIA/CROATIA

	1st Class Individual	1st Class Saverpass	2nd Class Youthpass
Any 5 days in 2 months	$200	$170	$140
Any 6 days in 2 months	220	188	159
Any 8 days in 2 months	260	222	189
Any 10 days in 2 months	300	256	209

Youth passes are for travelers under age 26 and fares vary slightly depending on countries selected. Saver prices are per person for 2 or more traveling together. Children 4-11 pay half of First Class or Saver Fare, under 4 free.

AUSTRIA+CZECH REP OR AUSTRIA/SLOVENIA/CROATIA

	1st Class Individual	1st Class Saverpass	2nd Class Youthpass
Any 4 days in 2 months	$230	$200	$167
Extra days (max 6)	35	30	24

Youth passes are for travelers under age 26. Saver prices are per person for 2 or more traveling together. Children 4-11 pay half of First Class or Saver Fare, under 4 free.

driver's license ahead of time at your local AAA office ($10 plus 2 passport-type photos).

Crossing borders with a rental car into, out of, and within Eastern Europe can be tricky. Though these countries are safe to travel in, some popular destinations (like Prague) are notorious for sky-high car-theft rates (especially of rentals). And, since American companies still think of the former Eastern Bloc as a single unit, the car thieves of Prague make it hard to drive a Western rental even into super-safe Slovenia.

Generally speaking, if you rent a car in Eastern Europe, you can cross borders within the East. But you might get hassled if you're going between Eastern and Western Europe. No matter where you're going, state your travel plans up front to the rental company. Some won't allow any of their rental cars to enter Eastern Europe, and some restrict certain types of cars: BMWs, Mercedes, and convertibles. Ask about extra fees—some companies automatically tack on theft and collision coverage for an Eastern European excursion. To avoid hassles at the borders, ask the rental agent to mark your contract with the company's permission to cross. For more on borders, see "Borders," page 13.

Driving

During the communist era, Eastern Europe's infrastructure lagged far behind the West's. Now that the Iron Curtain is long gone, super-highways are being rolled out like crazy. The Czech Republic, Hungary, Slovenia, Croatia, and eastern Germany all have new free-ways, but it's not unusual to find that a still-under-construction freeway ends, requiring a transfer to an older, slower road. Likewise, you'll sometimes discover that a much faster freeway option has been built between major destinations since your three-year-old map was published (a good reason to travel with the most up-to-date maps available and study them before each drive, noting which exits you'll need and which major cities you'll be traveling toward). New superhighways have just opened between Dresden and Prague (the A17), and from Zagreb to Budapest (to the north) and Zagreb to Split (to the south). As soon as a long-enough section is completed, the roads are opened to the public. Only rarely are backcountry roads the only option (as with part of the trip between Prague and Kraków). These can be bumpy and slow, but they're almost always paved (or, at least, they once were).

Learn the universal road signs (see sidebar). Seat belts are required, and two beers under those belts are enough to land you in jail.

Tolls: Many countries charge drivers who use their roads. If you're driving on highways in the Czech Republic, buy a toll sticker *(dálniční známka)* at the border, a post office, or a gas station (100 Kč/10 days, 200 Kč/1 month). To drive on Hungary's three auto-bahns (M1, M3, and M7), you'll need a toll sticker *(autópálya matrica,* 1,900 Ft/10 days, 3,200 Ft/1 month, available at post offices and gas stations). In Slovenia and Croatia, you'll get a ticket as you enter the freeway, then pay when you get off, based on how far you've traveled. In Austria, you'll need a sticker to drive your rental car on freeways *(Vignette)*—€8 for one week or €22 for two months, sold at border crossings, big gas stations near borders, and rental car agencies. (Dipping into the country on regular roads requires no special payment.) No such tolls are charged in Poland, Slovakia, or Germany.

Metric: Get used to metric. A liter is about a quart, four to a gallon. A kilometer is six-tenths of a mile. I figure kilometers to miles by cutting them in half and adding back 10 percent of the original (120 km: 60 + 12 = 72 miles, 300 km: 150 + 30 = 180 miles).

Parking: Parking is a costly headache in big cities. You'll pay about $10–15 a day to park safely. Rental-car theft can be a big problem in cities, especially Prague. Ask at your hotel for advice. I

Driving: Distance and Time

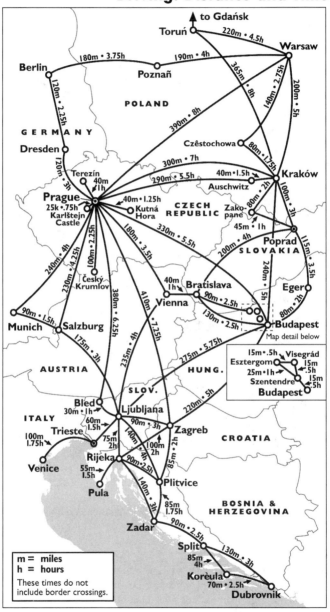

to Gdańsk

Toruń — 220m • 4.5h — Warsaw

Berlin — 180m • 3.75h — 190m • 4h — Poznañ

120m • 2.25h

365m • 8h

200m • 5h

POLAND

140m • 2.25h

GERMANY

390m • 8h

Dresden

Cżęstochowa — 80m • 1.75h

120m • 3h

Terezín 40m • 1h

300m • 7h

40m • 1.5h — Kraków

Prague — 290m • 5.5h — Auschwitz

25k • .75h

100m • 3h

Karlštejn Castle

40m • 1.25h — Kutná Hora

CZECH REPUBLIC

80m • 2h

Zako-pane

240m • 4h

4.25h

100m • 2.25h

180m • 3.5h

330m • 5.5h

45m • 1h

200m • 4h

Poprad

SLOVAKIA

115m • 3.5h

230m

Ceský Krumlov

380m • 6.25h

40m • 1h — Bratislava

240m • 5h

Eger

Vienna

410m • 7.25h

90m • 2.5h

80m • 2h

90m • 1.5h — Salzburg

Munich

175m • 3h

235m • 4h

130m • 2.5h — Budapest

Map detail below

AUSTRIA

275m • 5.75h

HUNG.

15m • .5h — Visegrád
Esztergom — 15m
25m • 1h — .5h
Szentendre — 15m
Budapest — .5h

SLOV.

Bled — 30m • 1h

220m • 5h

Ljubljana

ITALY

60m — 90m • 3h — Zagreb

Trieste — 1.5h

140m • 2h

100m — Venice — 75m — 2h

100m 1.75h

CROATIA

85m • 2h

Rijeka — 90m • 2.5h

55m 1.5h

Pula

140m • 3h — Plitvice

BOSNIA & HERZEGOVINA

85m 1.75h

Zadar — 90m • 2.5h

Split — 130m • 3h

85m 4h

Korèula — 70m • 2.5h

Dubrovnik

m = miles
h = hours
These times do not
include border crossings.

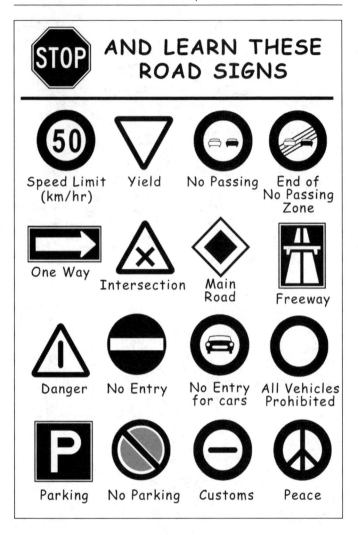

keep a pile of coins in my ashtray for parking meters, public phones, launderettes, and wishing wells.

Flying

Several new low-cost airlines have taken to the air in Eastern Europe over the last year. When connecting far-flung destinations in this wide-ranging guidebook, consider taking a plane—it may be less expensive than you'd think. As with other low-cost airlines, be aware of the limitations that come with these companies, such as minimal customer service, non-refundable tickets, and strict restrictions on the amount of baggage you're allowed to check without paying extra.

Europe by Air offers an innovative Flight Pass, charging $99 per leg (plus taxes and airport fees) for flights within Europe. They partner with various well-established airlines, providing good coverage for low prices (most useful for Croatia Airlines flights to and from the Dalmatian Coast; tickets can be purchased only in United States, www.europebyair.com, U.S. tel. 888/321-4737).

Sky Europe has hubs in Budapest, Kraków, Warsaw, Košice (Slovakia), and Bratislava, with flights to various destinations in both Eastern Europe (including Prague, Dubrovnik, and Split) and Western Europe (www.skyeurope.com).

Poland has a new budget airline: **Wizz Air** (hubs in Budapest, Warsaw, and Katowice—near Kraków; most flights to Western Europe rather than within Eastern Europe, www.wizzair.com).

In 2004, the more established discount company **easyJet** began flying from Berlin and London Stansted to Ljubljana, opening up the budget airline market to Slovenia (www.easyjet.com).

COMMUNICATING

Hurdling the Language Barrier

The language barrier in Eastern Europe is no bigger than in the West. In fact, I find that it's even easier to communicate in Hungary or Croatia than in Italy or Spain. Immediately after the Iron Curtain fell in 1989, English speakers were rare. But today, you'll find that most people in the tourist industry—and virtually all young people—speak excellent English.

Of course, not *everyone* speaks English. You'll run into the most substantial language barriers in situations when you need to deal with a lesser-educated clerk or service person (train stations and post office counters, maids, museum guards, bakers, and so on). Be reasonable in your expectations. Hungarian museum ticket-sellers are every bit as friendly and multilingual as they are in the United States. Luckily, it's relatively easy to get your point across in these places. I've often bought a train ticket simply by writing out the name of my destination (preferably with the local spelling—for example, "Praha" instead of "Prague"); the time I want to travel (using the 24-hour clock); and, if necessary, the date I want to leave (day first, then month as a Roman numeral, then year). Here's an example of what I'd show a ticket-seller at a train station: "Warszawa-17:30-15.VII.03."

Eastern Europeans, realizing that their language intimidates Americans, often invent easier nicknames for themselves—so Sarka goes by "Sara," András becomes "Andrew," and Jaroslav tells you, "Call me Jerry."

Most of the destinations in this book—the Czech Republic, Slovakia, Poland, Slovenia, and Croatia—speak Slavic languages. Czech, Slovak, Polish, Slovene, and Croatian are closely related to

Europe's Best Linguists

Why do Eastern Europeans speak English so well—especially since it wasn't commonly taught in schools before the last 15 years?

Residents of big, powerful Western countries, like Germany or France, might think that foreigners should learn their language. But Eastern Europeans are as practical as Westerners are stubborn. They realize that it's unreasonable to expect an American to learn Hungarian (with only 12 million speakers worldwide), Croatian (5 million), or Slovene (2 million). When only a few million people on the planet speak your language, it's essential to find a common language with the rest of the world—so they learn English early and well. In Croatia, for example, all schoolchildren start learning English in the third grade. (I've had surprisingly eloquent conversations with Croatian grade-schoolers.)

Many times, I've heard a German and a Hungarian conversing in English—a reminder that as Americans, we're lucky to speak the world's new lingua franca.

each other and to Russian, and are, to varying degrees, mutually intelligible (though many spellings change—for example, Czech *hrad,* or castle, becomes Croatian *grad*). Slavic languages have simple vocabularies but are highly inflected—that is, the meaning of a sentence depends on complicated endings that are tacked on to the ends of the words (as in Latin).

Slavic words are notorious for their seemingly unpronounceable, long strings of consonants. Slavic pronunciation can be tricky. In fact, when the first Christian missionaries, Cyril and Methodius, came to Eastern Europe a millennium ago, they invented a whole new alphabet to represent these strange Slavic sounds. The Cyrillic alphabet is still used today in the eastern Slavic countries (like Serbia and Russia). Fortunately, the destinations covered in this book all use the same Roman alphabet we do, but they add lots of different diacritics—little markings below and above letters—to represent a wide range of sounds (for example, *č, ą, ó, d, ł*). I explain each of these diacritics in this book's various country introductions.

Hungarian is another story altogether—it's completely unrelated to Slavic languages, German, or English. For more on the challenging Magyar tongue, see page 286.

German is the language in the gateway countries of Germany and Austria. As part of the same language family as English (other members include Dutch, Swedish, and Norwegian), German will sound noticeably more familiar to American ears than the Slavic languages.

Throughout Eastern Europe, German can be a handy second language (especially in Croatia, which attracts hordes of German tourists). And a few words of Italian can come in handy in Slovenia and Croatia. Aside from the English pleasantries, there's one word that people throughout Eastern Europe will understand: *Servus* (SEHR-voos)—the old-fashioned international greeting from the days of the Austro-Hungarian Empire. If you draw a blank on how to say hello in the local language, just offer a cheery, *"Servus!"*

Learn the key phrases and travel with a phrase book—consider *Rick Steves' German Phrase Book* for Germany and Austria, and Lonely Planet's good *Eastern Europe Phrasebook,* which covers the rest of the destinations in this book.

Don't be afraid to interact with locals. Eastern Europeans can seem brusque at first—a holdover from the closed communist society—but often a simple smile is the only icebreaker you need to make a new friend. You'll find that doors open a little more quickly when you know a few words of the language. Give it your best shot. The locals will appreciate your efforts.

Telephones

Smart travelers learn the phone system and use it daily to reserve or reconfirm rooms, get tourist information, or phone home.

Phone Cards: Phone cards have mostly replaced coin-operated phones in Eastern Europe. Instead of putting coins in pay phones, today's Europeans buy cards with prepaid time. There are two types of phone cards:

1. Insertable phone cards that you stick into the slot of a public pay phone. Simply take the phone off the hook, insert the prepaid card, wait for a dial tone, and dial away. The price of the call (local or international) is automatically deducted while you talk. These are a good deal for calling within Europe, but can make calling home to the United States expensive (at least 50 cents per minute). Each European country has its own insertable phone card—so your Czech phone card is worthless in Poland.

2. International phone cards that can be used from virtually any phone. These are not inserted into the phone. Instead, you dial the toll-free number listed on the card, reaching an automated operator. When prompted, you dial in a code number, also written on the card. A voice tells you how much is left in your account. Then dial your number. Since you don't insert the card in the phone, you can use these to make inexpensive calls from most phones, including the one in your hotel room, avoiding pricey hotel rates. Calls to the United States generally cost 20–30 cents per minute. You can use the cards to make local and domestic long-distance calls as well. These cards are a great deal...if they're available. In 2004, I used cheap international phone cards in the Czech Republic and Hungary, but couldn't find them in Slovakia, Poland, Slovenia, or Croatia. Still, they're all the rage in Western Europe, and sure to catch on soon in the East. Look for fliers advertising long-distance rates, or ask about the cards at newsstands, exchange bureaus, souvenir shops, and mini-marts. Request an international telephone card, tell the vendor where you'll be making most calls ("to America"), and he'll select the brand with the best deal. Because cards are occasionally duds, avoid the high denominations.

Non–Phone Card Options: If you use coins to make your calls, have a bunch handy. Avoid using hotel-room phones for anything other than local calls and phone card calls.

Dialing Direct: You'll save money by dialing direct, rather than going through an operator. You just need to learn to break the codes. For a list of country codes and a handy European calling chart, see the appendix. Remember that European time is six/nine hours ahead of the East/West Coasts of the United States.

Generally, when calling long distance within Poland, Slovakia, Slovenia, Croatia, Germany, or Austria, first dial the area code (starting with 0), then dial the local number. For example, Kraków's area code is 012, and the number of one of my recommended Kraków hotels is 431-0010. To call the hotel within Kraków, dial 431-0010. To call it from Warsaw, dial 012/431-0010. When dialing internationally, dial the international access code (of the country you're calling from), the country code (of the country you're calling to), the area code (without the initial zero), and the local number. To call the Kraków hotel from home, dial 011 (the international access code for the U.S. and Canada), 48 (Poland's country code), 12 (Kraków's area code *without* the initial zero), and 431-0010. Note that when you make an international call to any of the countries listed above, you must drop the initial zero of the area code.

Hungary also uses area codes. You follow the above procedure when making international calls to the country (dropping the initial zero of the area code), but things change when calling long-distance within Hungary: You first dial 06, then the area code and number (see page 281 for details).

The Czech Republic has dropped area codes in favor of a direct-dial phone system—so you'll always dial the entire number, whether you're calling across the street or across the country. For example, to call a recommended Czech hotel in Prague, you'd dial the same number (tel. 257-311-150) whether you're calling from the Prague train station or from Český Krumlov. If dialing the Czech hotel from outside the country, start with the international access code (011 from U.S. or Canada; 00 from Europe), the Czech Republic's country code (420), and then the local number (257-311-150).

To call my office from anywhere in Eastern Europe, I dial 00 (Europe's international access code), 1 (U.S. country code), 425 (Edmonds' area code), and 771-8303.

Don't be surprised that in some countries, local phone numbers have different numbers of digits within the same city, or even the same hotel (e.g., a hotel can have a 6-digit phone number and an 8-digit fax number).

Calling Cards from American Companies: Calling cards offered by AT&T, MCI, and Sprint used to be a good value, until direct-dialing rates dropped and international calling cards appeared. Now it's much cheaper to dial direct using an insertable phone card or—better yet—an international calling card (see above).

Mobile Phones: Many travelers buy cheap mobile phones in Europe to make both local and international calls. (Typical American mobile phones don't work in Europe, and those that do have horrendous per-minute costs.) For about $75, you can get a phone with $20 worth of calls that will work in the country where you purchased it. (You can buy more time at newsstands and mobile phone shops.) For about $100, you can get a phone that will work in most countries once you pick up the necessary chip per country (about $25 each). If you're interested, stop by any European shop that sells mobile phones; you'll see prominent store window displays. Depending on your trip and budget, ask for a phone that works only in that country, or one that can be used throughout Europe. If you're on a tight budget, skip mobile phones and buy cheap international calling cards instead.

E-mail and Mail

E-mail: You'll find Internet cafés and connection points on nearly every street corner and at many hotels throughout this region. Most hotels have e-mail addresses and Web sites (listed in this book) and prefer to receive bookings online rather than by fax or phone.

Mail: Get stamps at the neighborhood post office, at news-stands inside fancy hotels, and at some mini-marts and card shops. While you can arrange for mail delivery to your hotel (allow 10–15 days for a letter to arrive), phoning and e-mailing are so easy that I've dispensed with mail stops altogether.

SLEEPING

Much of Eastern Europe simply doesn't have the quaint little family-run pensions and B&Bs that I like to list for other destinations. In this book, I've focused my listings on small hotels, and prefer options that are friendly, comfortable, professional-feeling, centrally-located, English-speaking, and family-run. Obviously, a place meeting every criterion is rare, and all of my recommendations fall short of perfection—sometimes miserably. But I've listed the best values for each price category, given the above criteria. I've also thrown in a few hostels, private rooms, and other cheap options for budget travelers.

Prices in Eastern Europe are generally low compared to the

Sleep Code

I've divided the rooms into three categories, based on the price for a standard double room with bath:

$$$ **Higher Priced**
$$ **Moderately Priced**
$ **Lower Priced**

To save space while giving more specific information for people with special concerns, I've described my recommended hotels with a standard code. Prices listed are per room, not per person. When a range of prices is listed for a room, the price fluctuates with room size or season. You can assume a hotel takes credit cards unless you see "cash only" in the listing.

S   =   Single room (or price for 1 person in a double).
D   =   Double or twin. Double beds are usually big enough for non-romantic couples.
T   =   Triple (often a double bed with a single bed moved in).
Q   =   Quad (an extra child's bed is usually cheaper).
b   =   Private bathroom with toilet and shower or tub.
s   =   Private shower or tub only (the toilet is down the hall).
NSE   =   Does not speak English. Used only when it's unlikely you'll encounter English-speaking staff. Unless you see this in the listing, assume that the staff speaks English.

According to this code, a couple staying at a "Db-2,700 Kč" hotel in Prague would pay a total of 2,700 Czech crowns (about $108) for a double room with a private bathroom. English is spoken, and credit cards are accepted.

West—except for beds. You can find some bargains, but when traveling in the sometimes-more-challenging East, it's worth paying a little more for comfort and a central location. (In some places, especially the Dalmatian Coast, good values are virtually nonexistent, so I've listed the best of the worst.) Plan on spending $75 to $120 per hotel double in big cities, and $45 to $75 in smaller towns.

While most hotels listed in this book cluster around $70 to $100 per double, they range from $10 bunks to $200-plus splurges (maximum plumbing and more). The cost is higher in big cities and heavily touristed areas, and lower off the beaten track. Three or four people can save money by requesting one big room. Traveling alone can be expensive: A single room is often only 20 percent cheaper than a double.

I usually list hotel prices in the local currency. But some hotels prefer to list prices in euros. In these cases, I've listed the prices they gave me. (Usually their rates will be converted to the local currency on the day that you check out, so you'll actually be charged in koruna, złoty, forints, or whatever—not that you'll even notice, if you use a credit card.) Unless I note otherwise, the cost of a room includes a buffet breakfast.

For environmental reasons, towels are often replaced in hotels only when you leave them on the floor. In cheaper places, they aren't replaced at all, so hang them up to dry and reuse. The cord that dangles over the tub or shower in big Croatian and Slovenian resort hotels is not a clothesline—you pull it if you've fallen and can't get up.

If asked whether they have non-smoking rooms, most hotels in Eastern Europe will say yes. When pressed, they'll sheepishly admit, "Well, *all* of our rooms are non-smoking"...meaning they air them out after a smoker has stayed there. I've described hotels as "non-smoking" only if they have specially designated rooms for this purpose. Be specific and assertive if you need a strictly non-smoking room.

Before accepting a room, confirm your understanding of the complete price. The only tip my recommended hotels would like is a friendly, easygoing guest. And, as always, I appreciate feedback on your hotel experiences.

Private Rooms

A cheap option in Eastern Europe (especially in expensive Croatia) is a room in a private home (*sobe* in Slovenia and Croatia; the German word *Zimmer* works there, too, and throughout Eastern Europe). These places are inexpensive, at least as comfortable as a cheap hotel, and a good way to get some local insight. The boss changes the sheets, so people staying several nights are most desirable—and stays of less than three nights are often charged a lot more (up to 30 percent). For more on Croatian *sobe,* see page 478.

Hostels

For $10 to $20 a night, you can stay at a youth hostel. While most hostels admit nonmembers for an extra fee, it's best to join the club and buy a youth hostel card before you go ($28 per year, sold at hostels in most U.S. cities or online at www.hihostels.com, U.S. tel. 202/783-6161). Travelers of any age are welcome as long as they don't mind dorm-style accommodations and lots of traveling friends. Cheap meals are sometimes available, and kitchen facilities are usually provided for do-it-yourselfers. Expect crowds in the summer, snoring, and lots of youth groups giggling and making rude noises while you try to sleep. Family rooms and doubles are often available on request, but it's basically boys' dorms and girls' dorms. Many hostels are locked up from about 10:00 until 17:00, and they often enforce a 23:00 curfew. Hosteling is ideal for those traveling single: Prices are per bed, not per room, and you'll have an instant circle of friends. More and more hostels are getting their business acts together, taking credit-card reservations over the phone and leaving sign-in forms on the door for each available room. If you're serious about traveling cheaply, get a card, carry your own sheets, and cook in the members' kitchens.

Making Reservations

It's possible to travel at any time of year without reservations (especially if you arrive early in the day), but given the high stakes, erratic accommodations values, and quality of the places I've found for this book, I'd trade off the flexibility that comes with a loose no-reservations itinerary and instead, book rooms in advance. You can do this by e-mail long in advance from home, or by calling a day or two in advance as you travel. (Your receptionist, fluent in the local language, will likely help you call your next hotel if you pay for the call.) Even if a hotel clerk says the hotel is fully booked, you can try calling between 9:00 and 10:00 on the day you plan to arrive. That's when the hotel clerk knows exactly who's checking out and which rooms will be available. I've listed long-distance instructions in hopes that you'll use the phone as a tool this way (see "Telephones," above and in the appendix). Most hotels listed are accustomed to English-only speakers. A hotel receptionist will trust you and hold a room until 16:00 without a deposit, though some will ask for a credit-card number. Honor (or cancel by phone) your reservations. Long distance is cheap and easy from public phone booths.

If you know exactly which dates you need and really want a particular place, reserve a room long before you leave home. To reserve from home, e-mail, call, or fax the hotel. E-mail is a steal, phone and fax costs are reasonable, and simple English is usually fine. To fax, use the form in the appendix (or find it online at www.ricksteves .com/reservation). A two-night stay in August would be "2 nights, 16/8/05 to 18/8/05" (Europeans write the date in this order—day/month/year—and hotel jargon counts your stay from your day of arrival through your day of departure).

If you e-mail or fax a reservation request and receive a response with rates stating that rooms are available, this is not a confirmation. You must confirm that the rates are fine and that you indeed want the room. You'll often receive a response requesting one night's deposit. A credit-card number and expiration date will usually work. If you use your credit card for the deposit, you can pay with your card or cash when you arrive; if you don't show up, you'll be billed for one night. Ask about the cancellation policy when you reserve;

sometimes you may have to cancel as much as two weeks ahead to avoid paying a penalty. Reconfirm your reservations several days in advance for safety.

EATING

You'll find that the local cafés, cuisine, beer, and wine are highlights of your adventure. This is affordable sightseeing for your palate. Eastern Europe offers good food for very little money—especially if you venture off the main tourist trail.

Slavic cuisine is heavy, hearty, and tasty. Expect lots of meat, potatoes, and cabbage. Still, there's more variety to be had in the East than you might expect. Tune in to the regional and national special-

ties and customs (see each country's introduction in this book for details).

Ethnic restaurants provide a welcome break from Slavic fare. Seek out vegetarian, Italian, Chinese, or other similar places. They're especially good in big cities like Budapest or Kraków (I've listed tasty options). Hungarian cuisine enjoys some spicy Turkish influence (think paprika), Slovenia and Croatia are as much Italian as they are Slavic (tasty pastas and pizzas), and Croatia also has excellent seafood.

When restaurant-hunting, choose a spot filled with locals, not the place with the big neon signs boasting, "We Speak English and Accept Credit Cards." Incredible deals abound in Eastern Europe, where locals can't afford more than $5 for a fine dinner. Venturing even a block or two off the main drag leads to local, higher-quality food for less than half the price of the tourist-oriented places. Most restaurants tack a menu onto their door for browsers and have an English menu inside. Only a rude waiter will rush you. Good service is relaxed (slow to an American).

When you're in the mood for something halfway between a restaurant and a picnic meal, look for take-out food stands, bakeries (with sandwiches and small pizzas to go), delis with stools or a table, department-store cafeterias, salad bars, or simple little eateries for fast and easy sit-down restaurant food.

The Czech Republic is beer country, with Europe's best and cheapest brew. Poland also has fine beer, but the national drink is *wódka*. Hungary, Slovenia, and Croatia are known for their wines. Each country has its own distinctive liqueur, most of them a variation on *slivovice* (SLEE-voh-veet-seh)—a plum brandy so highly valued that it's the de facto currency of the Carpathian Mountains (often used for bartering with farmers and other mountain folk).

Menus list drink size by the tenth of a liter, or deciliter (dl).

TRAVELING AS A TEMPORARY LOCAL

We travel all the way to Europe to enjoy differences—to become temporary locals. You'll experience frustrations. There are certain truths that we find God-given and self-evident, such as cold beer, ice in drinks, bottomless cups of coffee, and bigger being better. One of the benefits of travel is the eye-opening realization that there are logical, civil, and even better alternatives. A willingness to go local ensures that you'll enjoy a full dose of hospitality.

While updating this book, I heard over and over again that my readers are considerate and fun to have as guests. Thank you for traveling as temporary locals who are sensitive to the culture. It's fun to follow you in my travels.

Send Me a Postcard, Drop Me a Line

If you enjoy a successful trip with the help of this book and would like to share your discoveries, please fill out the survey at www.ricksteves .com/feedback or e-mail me at rick@ricksteves.com. I personally read and value all feedback.

Judging from the happy postcards I receive from travelers, it's safe to assume you'll enjoy a great, affordable vacation—with the finesse of an independent, experienced traveler.

Thanks, and happy travels!

BACK DOOR TRAVEL PHILOSOPHY
From *Rick Steves' Europe Through the Back Door*

Travel is intensified living—maximum thrills per minute, and one of the last great sources of legal adventure. Travel is freedom. It's recess, and we need it.

Experiencing the real Europe requires catching it by surprise, going casual..."Through the Back Door."

Affording travel is a matter of priorities. (Make do with the old car.) You can travel—simply, safely, and comfortably—anywhere in Europe for $100 a day, plus transportation costs. In many ways, spending more money only builds a thicker wall between you and what you came to see. Europe is a cultural carnival, and, time after time, you'll find that its best acts are free and the best seats are the cheap ones.

A tight budget forces you to travel close to the ground, meeting and communicating with the people, not relying on service with a purchased smile. Never sacrifice sleep, nutrition, safety, or cleanliness in the name of budget. Simply enjoy the local-style alternatives to expensive hotels and restaurants.

Extroverts have more fun. If your trip is low on magic moments, kick yourself and make things happen. If you don't enjoy a place, maybe you don't know enough about it. Seek the truth. Recognize tourist traps. Give a culture the benefit of your open mind. See things as different but not better or worse. Any culture has much to share.

Of course, travel, like the world, is a series of hills and valleys. Be fanatically positive and militantly optimistic. If something's not to your liking, change your liking. Travel is addictive. It can make you a happier American, as well as a citizen of the world. Our Earth is home to six billion equally important people. It's humbling to travel and find that people don't envy Americans. They like us, but with all due respect, they wouldn't trade passports.

Globe-trotting destroys ethnocentricity. It helps you understand and appreciate different cultures. Travel changes people. It broadens perspectives and teaches new ways to measure quality of life. Many travelers toss aside their hometown blinders. Their prized souvenirs are the strands of different cultures they decide to knit into their own characters. The world is a cultural yarn shop. And Back Door travelers are weaving the ultimate tapestry. Come on, join in!

CZECH REPUBLIC
(Česká Republika)

Wedged between Germany and Austria, the Czech Republic is one of the most comfortable and easy-to-explore countries of the former Warsaw Pact. The Czech Republic is geographically small. In a quick visit, you can enjoy a fine introduction while still packing in plenty of surprises.

Despite their difficult 20th-century experience, the Czechs have managed to preserve their history. In Czech towns and villages, you'll find a simple joy of life—a holdover from the days of the Renaissance. The deep spirituality of the Baroque era still shapes the national character. The magic of Prague, the beauty of Český Krumlov, and the lyrical quality of the countryside relieve the heaviness caused by the turmoil that passed through here. Get beyond Prague and explore the country's medieval towns. These rugged woods and hilltop castles will make you feel like you're walking through the garden of your childhood dreams.

> # How Big, How Many, How Much
> - The Czech Republic is 30,500 square miles (the size of Maine).
> - Population is 10 million (about 330 per square mile).
> - 25 Czech crowns (*koruna*, Kč) = about $1
> - Country code: 420

The Czech Republic is made up of three regions: Bohemia ("Čechy" in Czech), Moravia ("Morava" in Czech), and Silesia. Bohemia—which has nothing to do with beatnik bohemians—has long been the home of the Czechs. Bohemia is circled by a naturally fortifying ring of mountains and cut down the middle by the Vltava River, with Prague as its capital. The wine-growing region of Moravia (to the east) is more Slavic and more colorful. Only a tiny bit of Silesia (around the town of Opava) is part of the Czech Republic today. (The Hapsburgs lost the traditionally Czech Silesia to Prussia in 1740s, and 200 years later Germany in turn ceded it to Poland.)

Ninety-five percent of the Czech Republic's 10 million people are ethnic Czechs. While nearly half of the people are nominally Catholic, church attendance is very low.

Since 1989, when the Czechs won their independence from Soviet control, more Czechs have been traveling. People are working harder—but the average monthly wage is still only about $600. Facades have gotten face-lifts, roads have been patched up, and neighborhood grocery stores have been pushed out by supermarkets.

Most young Czechs are caught up in the new freedom. Everyone wants to travel—to the practical West to study law, or to the mystical East to learn Egyptian. They want to work for big bucks at a multinational investment bank, or for a meager salary in a Chechnya-based nonprofit organization. With so many material dreams suddenly within reach, few Czechs are having children. In the 1990s, the birth rate fell dramatically, but since 2001 it has been slowly rising again.

Yet even faced with a bright future, some locals maintain a healthy dose of pessimism and are reluctant to dive headlong into the Western rat race. Things still go a little slower here.

Children, adults, and grandparents delight in telling stories. In Czech fairy tales, there are no dwarfs and monsters. To experience the full absurdity and hilarity of Czech culture, you need a child's imagination and the understanding that the best fun comes from being able to laugh at yourself. Czech writers invented the robot, the pistol, and Black Light Theater (an absurd show of illusion, puppetry, mime, and modern dance).

The most beloved Czech literary figure is the title character of Jaroslav Hašek's *Good Soldier Švejk,* who frustrates the WWI

Austro-Hungarian army he serves in by cleverly playing dumb. Other well-known Czech writers include Václav Havel (a playwright who went on to become Czechoslovakia's first post-communist president; he authored many essays and plays, including *The Garden Party*); Milan Kundera (author of *The Unbearable Lightness of Being*, set during the "Prague Spring" uprising); Karel Čapek (novelist and playwright who created the robot in the play *R.U.R.*); and Jára Cimrman (playwright, teacher, inventor, polar explorer, and biologist—considered by some locals to be the greatest Czech). Most famous of all is the existentialist great Franz Kafka—a Prague Jew who wrote in German about people turning into giant cockroaches *(The Metamorphosis)* and urbanites being pursued and persecuted for crimes they know nothing about *(The Trial)*.

Ninety percent of the tourists who visit the Czech Republic see only Prague. But if you venture outside the capital, you'll enjoy traditional towns and villages, great prices, a friendly and gentle countryside dotted by nettles and wild poppies, and almost no Western tourists. Since the time of the Hapsburgs, fruit trees have lined the country roads for everyone to share. Take your pick.

Practicalities

Telephones: Dial 112 for emergencies, 158 for police. If an 0800 number doesn't work, replace the 0800 with 822. The basic Český Telecom card (150 Kč, 200 Kč, or 300 Kč) works well.

To make phone calls anywhere within the Czech Republic, dial the entire nine-digit number. To call the Czech Republic from another country, first dial the international access code (00 if calling from Europe or 011 from America or Canada), then 420 (the Czech Republic's country code), then the nine-digit number. To call out of the Czech Republic, dial 00, the country code of the country you're calling (see chart in appendix), the area code if the country's phone system uses area codes (note that sometimes the initial zero is dropped depending on the country), and the local number.

Money: ATMs are the best way to get Czech cash. Don't exchange too much; Czech money is tough to change in the West. There is no black market. Assume anyone trying to sell money on the streets is peddling obsolete (or Bulgarian) currency. Buy and sell easily at train stations (5 percent fees), banks, or hotels. Change bureaus advertise no commission and decent but deceptive rates. These rates are for selling dollars. Their rates for buying your dollars are worse. Hidden fees abound; ask exactly how many crowns you'll walk away with before you agree to the transaction.

Lost Credit Cards: American Express tel. 222-800-222, Visa and MasterCard tel. 272-771-111 (see also "Damage Control for Lost or Stolen Cards," page 18).

Red Tape: Anyone planning to bring a rental car into the

Czech Republic should check with their car-rental company first (see page 23). To drive on Czech highways, you'll need a toll sticker *(dálniční známka)*, sold at borders, post offices, and gas stations (100 Kč/10 days, 200 Kč/1 month).

Transportation: If you have a Eurailpass, note that it doesn't cover the Czech Republic; you'll need to buy train tickets or a Prague Excursion pass for your travels to and from Prague (see page 21).

Czech History

The Czechs have always been at a crossroads of Europe—between the Slavic and Germanic worlds, between Catholicism and Protestantism, and between the Cold War East and West. As if foreseeing all of this, the mythical founder of Prague—the beautiful princess Libuše—named her city "Praha" (meaning "threshold" in Czech). Despite these strong external influences, the Czechs have retained their distinct culture...and a dark, ironic sense of humor to keep them laughing through it all.

Middle Ages

Prague's castle put Bohemia on the map in the 9th century. In the 10th century, the region was incorporated into the German Holy Roman Empire. The 14th century was Prague's golden age, when Holy Roman Emperor Charles IV ruled from here (see below), and Prague was one of Europe's largest and most highly cultured cities.

Emperor Charles IV

The greatest Czech ruler (14th century) was actually the Holy Roman Emperor, back when Prague was bigger and more important than Vienna. Born to a German nobleman and a Czech princess, he was a dynamic man on the cusp of the Renaissance. He spoke five languages, counted Petrarch as a friend, imported French architects to make Prague a grand capital, founded the first university north of the Alps, and invigorated the Czech national spirit. (He popularized the legend of the good king Wenceslas to give his people a near mythical, King Arthur–type cultural standard-bearer.) Much of Prague's history and architecture (including the famous Charles Bridge and St. Vitus Cathedral) can be traced to this man's rule. Under Charles IV, the Czech people gained esteem among Europeans.

Bucking the Pope and Germany

Jan Hus was a local preacher and professor who got in trouble with the Vatican a hundred years before Martin Luther. Like Luther, he preached in the people's language, rather than Latin. To add insult to injury, he complained about Church corruption. Tried for heresy and burned in 1415, Hus became both a religious and a national hero. While each age has defined Hus to its liking, the way he challenged authority while staying true to himself has always inspired and rallied the Czech people.

Religious Wars

The reformist times of Jan Hus (around 1400, when Czechs rebelled against both German and Roman Catholic control) led to a period of religious wars, and ultimately the loss of autonomy to Vienna. Ruled by the Hapsburgs of Austria, Prague stagnated—except during the rule of King Rudolf II (1552–1612), a Holy Roman Emperor. With Rudolph living in Prague, the city again emerged as a cultural and intellectual center. Astronomers Johannes Kepler, Tycho de Brahe, and other scientists flourished, and much of the inspiration for Prague's great art can be attributed to the king's patronage.

The Thirty Years' War (1618–1648) began in Prague, when locals (Czech nobles wanting religious and political autonomy) tossed two Catholic/Hapsburg officials out the window of the Prague Castle. Often called "the first world war" because it engulfed so many nations, this three-decade-long conflict was particularly tough on Prague. During this period, its population dropped from 60,000 to 25,000. The result of this war was 300 years of Hapsburg rule from afar, as Prague became a backwater of Vienna.

Czech Nationalist Revival

The 19th century was a time of nationalism for people throughout Europe, including the Czechs, as the age of divine kings and ruling families came to a fitful end. The Czech spirit was stirred by the completion of Prague's St. Vitus Cathedral, the symphonies of Antonín Dvořák, and the operas of Bedřich Smetana performed in the new National Theater. With the end of World War I, the Hapsburgs were history, and in 1918, the independent country of Czechoslovakia was proclaimed, with Prague as its capital.

Troubled 20th Century

Independence lasted only until 1939, when the Nazis swept in. Prague escaped the bombs of World War II, but went directly from the Nazi frying pan into the communist fire. A local uprising freed the city from the Nazis on May 8, 1945, but the Russians "liberated" them on May 9.

For centuries, the Czechs were mostly rural folks, with German merchants running the cities. Prague's cultural make-up comes from a rich mix of Czech, German, and Jewish people—historically about evenly divided. But after World War II, only 5 percent of the Jewish population remained, and virtually all the Germans were deported.

The communist chapter (1948–1989) was grim. The "Prague Spring" uprising—initiated by a young generation of reform-minded communists in 1968—was crushed. The charismatic leader Alexander Dubček was exiled (and made a forest ranger in the backwoods), and the years following the unsuccessful revolt were particularly disheartening. In the late 1980s, the communists began constructing Prague's huge TV tower (now the city's tallest structure)—not only to broadcast Czech TV transmissions, but also to jam Western signals. The Metro, built around the same time, was intended for mass transit, but first and foremost, it was designed to be a giant fallout shelter for protection against capitalist bombs.

But the Soviet empire crumbled. Czechoslovakia regained its freedom in the student- and artist-powered 1989 "Velvet Revolution" (so-called because there were no casualties). In 1993, the Czech and Slovak republics agreed on the "Velvet Divorce" and became two separate countries (see page 122).

Today, while not without its problems, the Czech Republic is enjoying a growing economy and a strong democracy, and Prague has emerged as one of the most popular tourist destinations in Europe. In May 2004, the Czech Republic joined the European Union.

Czech Food

Czech food is heavy on pork and kraut, but more modern eateries are serving up pasta and salads.

After a sip of beer, ask for the *jídelní lístek* (menu). *Polévka* (soup) is the most essential part of a meal. The saying goes: "The soup fills you up, the dish plugs it up." Some of the thick soups for a cold day are *zelná* or *zelňačka* (cabbage), *čočková* (lentil), *fazolová* (bean), and *dršťková* (tripe—delicious if fresh, but at worst, chewy as gum). The lighter soups are *hovězí* or *slepičí vývar s nudlemi* (beef or chicken broth with noodles), *pórková* (leek), and *květáková* (cauliflower). *Pečivo* (bread) is either delivered with the soup, or you need to ask for it; it's always charged separately, depending on how many *rohlíky* (rolls) or slices of *chleba* (yeast bread) you eat.

Main dishes are divided into *hotová jídla* (quick, ready-to-serve standard dishes, in some places available only during lunch hours, 11:30–14:30) and the more specialized *jídla na objednávku* or *minutky* (plates prepared when you order). Even the supposedly quick *hotová jídla* will take longer than what you're used to back home.

A Czech restaurant is a social place where people come to relax. Tables are not private. You can ask to join someone and will most likely make some new friends. Instead of worrying about how much sightseeing you're missing during your two-hour lunch, appreciate the opportunity to learn more about Czech culture.

Czech Beer

Czechs are among the world's most enthusiastic beer *(pivo)* drinkers—adults drink about 80 gallons a year. The pub is a place to have fun, complain, discuss art and politics, talk hockey, and chat with locals and visitors alike. The *pivo* that was drunk in the country before the Industrial Revolution was much thicker, providing the main source of nourishment for the peasant folk. As a result, even today it doesn't matter whether you are in a *restaurace* (restaurant), a *hostinec* (pub), or a *hospoda* (bar)—a beer will land on your table upon the slightest hint to the waiter, and a new pint will automatically appear when the old glass is almost empty. (You must tell the waiter *not* to bring more.) Order beer from the tap (*točené* means "draft," *sudové pivo* means "keg beer"). A *pivo* is large (0.5 liter, or 17 oz); a *malé pivo* is small (0.3 liter, or 10 oz). Men invariably order the large size.

The Czechs invented lager in nearby Plzeň ("Pilsen" in German). This is the famous Pilsner Urquell, on tap in many local pubs. But be sure to venture beyond Pilsner Urquell. There are plenty of other good Czech beers, including Krušovice, Gambrinus, Staropramen, and Kozel. Budvar, from the town of Budějovice ("Budweis" in German), is popular with Anheuser-Busch's attorneys. (The Czech and the American breweries for years disputed the "Budweiser" brand name. The solution: The Czech Budweiser—actually owned by South Africans—is sold in Europe and Africa, while the American one is sold in the rest of the world.)

The big degree symbol on bottles does not indicate alcohol content. Twelve degrees is about 4.2 percent alcohol, 10 degrees is about 3.5 percent alcohol, and 11 and 15 degrees are dark beers.

Each establishment has only one kind of beer on tap; to try a particular brand, look for its sign outside. A typical pub serves only one brand of 10-degree beer, one brand of 12-degree beer, and one brand of dark beer. Czechs do not mix beer with anything, and do not hop from pub to pub (in one night, you must stay loyal to one woman and to one beer).

Pivo for lunch has me sightseeing for the rest of the day on Czech knees. *Na zdraví* is "to your health" in Czech. Later, they say *Nádraží* (which means "train station").

Hotová jídla (ready-to-serve dishes) come with set garnishes. The standard menu across the country includes *smažený řízek s bramborem* (fried pork fillet with potatoes), *svíčková na smetaně s knedlíkem* (beef tenderloin in cream sauce with dumplings), *vepřová s knedlíkem a se zelím* (pork with dumplings and cabbage), *pečená kachna s knedlíkem a se zelím* (roasted duck with dumplings and cabbage), *maďarský guláš s knedlíkem* (the Czech version of Hungarian goulash), and *pečené kuře s bramborem* (roasted chicken with potatoes). In this landlocked country, fish options are limited to *kapr* (carp) and *pstruh* (trout), prepared in a variety of ways and served with potatoes or fries. Vegetarians can go for the delicious *smažený sýr s bramborem* (fried cheese with potatoes) or default for *čočka s vejci* (lentils with fried egg). If you are spending the night out with friends, have a beer and feast on the huge *vepřové koleno s hořčicí a křenem* (pork knuckle with mustard and horseradish sauce) with *chleba* (yeast bread).

The range of the *jídla na objednávku* (meals prepared on order) depends on the chef. You choose your garnishes, which are charged separately.

Šopský salát, like a Greek salad, is usually the best salad option (a mix of tomatoes, cucumbers, peppers, onion, and feta cheese with vinegar and olive oil). The waiter will bring it with the main dish, unless you specify that you want it before.

For *moučník* (dessert), there is *palačinka* (crêpes served with fruit or jam), *lívance* (small pancakes with jam and curd), or *zmrzlinový pohár* (ice-cream sundae). Many restaurants will offer different sorts of *koláče* (pastries) and *štrůdl* (apple strudel), but it's much better to get these directly from a bakery.

No Czech meal is complete without a cup of strong *turecká káva* (Turkish coffee—finely ground coffee that only partly dissolves, leaving "mud" on the bottom, drunk without milk). Although espressos and instant coffees have made headway in the past few years, many Czechs regard them as a threat to their culture.

A good alternative to beer is *minerálka* (mineral water). These healthy waters have a high mineral content. They're naturally carbonated, because they come from the springs in the many Czech spas (Mattoni, the most common brand, is from Carlsbad). If you want plain water, ask for *voda bez bublinek* (water without bubbles).

In bars and restaurants, you can go wild with memorable liqueurs, most of which cost about a dollar a shot. Experiment. *Fernet,* a bitter drink made from many herbs, is the leading Czech apéritif. *Absinthe,* made from wormwood and herbs, is a watered-down version of the hallucinogenic drink that's illegal in the United States and much of Europe. It's famous as the muse of many artists (including Henri de Toulouse-Lautrec in Paris a century ago). *Becherovka,* made of 13 herbs and 38 percent alcohol, was used to settle upset medieval tummies and as an aphrodisiac. This velvety drink remains popular today. *Becherovka* and tonic mixed together is nicknamed *beton* ("concrete"). Drink three and you'll find out why. *Medovina,* literally "honey wine," is mead. *Slivovice* is distilled from the best Moravian plums.

You can stay in a pub as long as you want—no one will bring you an *účet* (bill) until you ask for it: *"Pane vrchní, zaplatím!"* ("Mr. Waiter, now I pay!").

Key Czech Phrases

English	Czech	Pronounced
Hello. (formal)	Dobrý den.	DOH-bree dehn
Hi. / Bye. (informal)	Ahoj.	AH-hoy
Do you speak English?	Mluvíte anglicky?	MLOO-vee-teh ANG-lits-kee
Yes. / No.	Ano. / Ne.	AH-no / neh
Please. / You're welcome. / Can I help you?	Prosím.	PROH-zeem
Thank you.	Děkuji.	DYACK-quee
I'm sorry. / Excuse me.	Promiňte.	PROH-meen-teh
Good.	Dobře.	DOHB-zhay
Goodbye.	Na shledanou.	nah SKLEH-dah-now
one / two	jeden / dva	YAY-dehn / dvah
three / four	tři / čtyři	tree / chuh-TEE-ree
five / six	pět / šest	pyeht / shehst
seven / eight	sedm / osm	SEH-dum / OH-sum
nine / ten	devět / deset	DEHV-yeht / DEH-seht
hundred	sto	stoh
thousand	tisíc	TYEE-seets
How much?	Kolik?	KOH-leek
local currency	koruna (Kč)	koh-ROO-nah
Where is...?	Kde je...?	gday yeh
...the toilet	...vécé	vayt-SAY
men	muži	MOO-zhee
women	ženy	ZHAY-nee
water / coffee	voda / káva	VOH-dah / KAH-vah
beer / wine	pivo / víno	PEE-voh / VEE-noh
Cheers!	Na zdraví!	nah zdrah-VEE
the bill	Účet	OO-cheht

Czech Language

Czech, a Slavic language closely related to its neighbors Polish and Slovak, has little resemblance to Western European languages. These days, English is "modern" and you'll find the language barrier minimal. Among older people, German is a common second language.

An acute accent *(á, é, í, ó, ú, ý)* means you linger on that vowel. The letter *c* always sounds like "ts" (as in "cats"). The little accent *(háček)* above the *č, š,* or *ž* makes it sound like "ch," "sh", or "zh" (as in "leisure"), respectively. A *háček* above ň makes it sound like "ny" (as in "canyon"), and over *ě* makes it sound like "ye." Czech has one sound that occurs in no other language: *ř* (as in "Dvořák"), which sounds like a cross between a rolled "r" and "zh."

PRAGUE
(Praha)

It's amazing what a decade and a half of freedom can do. Prague has always been historic. Now it's fun, too. No place in Europe has become so popular so quickly. And for good reason: Prague—the only Central European capital to escape the bombs of the last century's wars—is one of Europe's best-preserved cities. It's filled with sumptuous Art Nouveau facades, offers tons of cheap Mozart and Vivaldi, and brews the best beer in Europe. But even beyond its architecture and traditional culture, it's an explosion of pent-up entrepreneurial energy jumping for joy after 40 years of communist rule. Its low prices can cause you to jump for joy, too. Travel in Prague is like travel in Western Europe—15 years ago and for half the price.

Planning Your Time

Prague demands a minimum of two full days (with 3 nights, or 2 nights and a night train). From Munich, Berlin, and Vienna, it's about a six-hour train ride (you can also take a longer night train from Munich). From Budapest, Warsaw, or Kraków, it's a handy night train.

With two days in Prague, I'd spend a morning seeing the castle and a morning in the Jewish Quarter. Use your afternoons for loitering around the Old Town, Charles Bridge, and the Little Quarter, and split your nights between beer halls and live music. Keep in mind that Jewish sights close on Saturday.

ORIENTATION

Prague unnerves many travelers—it's behind the former Iron Curtain, and you've heard stories of rip-offs and sky-high hotel prices (both are a real problem, but avoidable if you're smart).

Prague

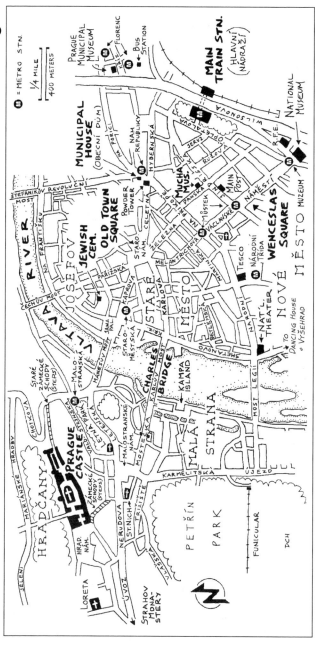

Prague Landmarks

English	Czech	Pronounced
Main Train Station	Hlavní Nádraží	hlav-nee nah-drah-zhee
Old Town	Staré Město	stah-reh myehs-toh
Old Town Square	Staroměstské Náměstí	star-roh-myehst-skeh nah-myehs-tee
New Town	Nové Město	noh-vay myehs-toh
Little Quarter	Malá Strana	mah-lah strah-nah
Jewish Quarter	Josefov	yoo-zehf-fohf
Castle Quarter	Hradčany	hrad-chah-nee
Charles Bridge	Karlův Most	kar-loov most
Wenceslas Square	Václavske Náměstí	vaht-slahf-skeh nah-myehs-tee
The River	Vltava	vul-tah-vah

Despite your fears, Prague is charming, safe, and ready to show you a good time. The language barrier is tiny. It seems every well-educated young person speaks English.

Locals call their town "Praha." It's big, with 1.2 million people, but focus on its relatively compact old center during a quick visit. As you wander, take advantage of brown street signs directing you to tourist landmarks.

The Vltava River divides the west side (castle and Little Quarter) from the east side (train station, Old Town, New Town, and most of the recommended hotels). Prague addresses come with references to a general zone. Praha 1 is in the old center on either side of the river. Praha 2 is in the new city, southeast of Wenceslas Square. Praha 3 and higher indicate a location farther from the center.

Tourist Information

TIs are at four key locations: **main train station** (roughly Easter–Oct Mon–Fri 9:00–19:00, Sat–Sun 9:00–16:00, but often closed; Nov–Easter Mon–Fri 9:00–18:00, Sat 9:00–15:00, closed Sun), **Old Town Square** (Easter–Oct Mon–Fri 9:00–19:00, Sat–Sun 9:00–18:00; Nov–Easter Mon–Fri 9:00–18:00, Sat–Sun 9:00–17:00, tel. 224-482-018), below **Wenceslas Square** at Na Příkopě 20 (Easter–Oct Mon–Fri 9:00–19:00, Sat–Sun 9:00–17:00; Nov–Easter Mon–Fri 9:00–18:00, Sat 9:00–15:00, closed Sun, tel. 224-226-087), and the castle side of **Charles Bridge** (Easter–Oct daily 10:00–18:00, closed Nov–Easter). For general tourist information in English, dial 12444 (Mon–Fri 8:00–19:00).

The TIs offer maps, phone cards, information on guided walks and bus tours, and bookings for concerts, hotel rooms, and rooms in private homes. There are several monthly events guides—all of them packed with ads—including *Prague Guide* (29 Kč), *Prague This Month* (free), and *Heart of Europe* (free, summer only).

The English-language weekly *Prague Post* newspaper is handy for entertainment listings and current events (sold cheap at newsstands). The Prague Information Service's useful Web site is www.pis.cz.

Arrival in Prague

Upon arrival, be sure to buy a city map, with trams and Metro lines marked and tiny sketches of the sights for ease in navigating (30–70 Kč, many different brands, sold at kiosks, exchange windows, and tobacco stands). It's a mistake to try doing Prague without a good map—you'll refer to it constantly.

By Train: Most travelers coming from and going to major international destinations—as well as trains to and from Český Krumlov and some other Czech towns—use the main station, Hlavní Nádraží. Other trains use the secondary station, Nádraží Holešovice. (For information on getting to Prague, see "Transportation Connections," page 104.)

Upon arrival, get money. The stations have ATMs (best rates) and exchange bureaus (rates are generally bad, but can vary—compare by asking at 2 windows what you'll get for $100, but keep in mind that many of the windows are run by the same company). Then buy your map and confirm your departure plans. Consider arranging a room or tour through the AVE travel agency (branches in both stations—see "Sleeping," page 91). Anyone arriving on an international train will be met at the tracks by room hustlers, trying to snare tourists for cheap rooms.

Main Station (Hlavní Nádraží): This station's low-ceilinged hall contains a fascinating mix of travelers, kiosks, gamblers, loitering teenagers, and older riffraff. The creepy station ambience is the work of communist architects, who expanded a classy building to make it just big, painting it the compulsory dreary gray with reddish trim. An ATM is near the subway entrance. The station's left-luggage counter is reportedly safer than the lockers. The Wasteels office can help you figure out train connections, and sells cheap phone cards and tickets for anywhere in Europe (no commission; Mon–Fri 9:00–17:00, Sat 9:00–16:00, closed Sun, tel. 224-641-954, www.wasteels.cz). The information office for Czech Railways (downstairs on the left) is less helpful, and the ticket windows downstairs don't give schedule information.

If you're killing time here (or you'd like a wistful glimpse of a more genteel age), go upstairs into the Art Nouveau hall. The station

Rip-Offs in Prague

Prague's new freedom comes with new scams. There's no particular risk of violent crime—but green, rich tourists do get taken by con artists. Simply be on guard, particularly at these times: when traveling on trains (thieves thrive on overnight trains), changing money (tellers with bad arithmetic and inexplicable pauses while counting back your change), dealing with taxis (see "Getting Around Prague," page 58), paying in restaurants (see "Eating," page 98), and in seedy neighborhoods (see below).

Anytime you pay for something, make a careful note of how much it costs, how much you're handing over, and how much you expect back. Count your change. Someone selling you a phone card marked 190 Kč might first tell you it's 790 Kč, hoping to pocket the difference. Call the bluff, and they'll pretend it never happened.

Plainclothes policemen "looking for counterfeit money" are con artists. Don't show them any cash or your wallet. If you're threatened with an inexplicable fine by a "policeman," conductor, or other official, you can walk away, scare him away by saying you'll need a receipt (which real officials are legally required to provide), or ask a passerby if the fine is legit. On the other hand, do not ignore the plainclothes inspectors on the Metro and trams who have shown you their badge.

was originally named for Emperor Franz Josef. Later, it was named for President Woodrow Wilson, because his promotion of self-determination led to the creation of the free state of Czechoslovakia in 1918. Under the communists (who weren't big fans of Wilson), it was renamed simply the "Main Station." Here, under an elegant dome, you can sip coffee, enjoy music from the 1920s, watch boy prostitutes looking for work, and see new arrivals spilling into the city.

From the main station, it's a 10-minute **walk** to Wenceslas Square (turn left out of the station and follow Washingtonova to the huge National Museum, and you're there). You could instead catch **tram** #9 or, at night, tram #55 or #58; to find the stop, walk into the park in front of the station (nicknamed "Sherwood Forest," filled with thieves and homeless people at night), take a right, and walk two minutes. Or take the **Metro** (inside station, look for the red M with 2 directions: Háje or Ládví; catch a train to the Muzeum stop, then transfer to the green line—direction Dejvická—and get off at either Můstek or Staroměstská; these stops straddle the Old Town).

The train station **cabbies** are a gang of no-neck mafia thugs who will wait all day to charge an arriving tourist five times the regular rate. To get an honest cabbie, I'd walk a few blocks (or ride the Metro one stop) and hail one off the street. A taxi should get you to your hotel for no more than 200 Kč (see "Getting Around Prague," page 58); to avoid the train station taxi stand, call AAA Taxi (tel. 233-113-311).

Pickpockets can be little children, or adults dressed as professionals or even as tourists. They target Western visitors. Many thieves drape jackets over their arms to disguise busy fingers. Thieves work the crowded and touristy places in teams. They use mobile phones to coordinate their bumps and grinds. Be careful if anyone creates a commotion at the door of a Metro or tram car (especially around the Národní and Vodičkova tram stops, or on the made-for-tourists trams #22 and #23)—it's a smokescreen for theft. Car theft is also a big problem in Prague (many Western European car-rental companies don't allow their rentals to cross the Czech border). Never leave anything valuable in your car—not even in broad daylight on a busy street. The sex clubs on Skořepka Steet, just south of Havelská Market, routinely rip off naive tourists and can be dangerous. They're filled mostly with Russian girls and German and Asian guys. Lately, this district has become the rage for British "stag" parties (happy to take cheap off-season flights to get to cheap beer and cheap girls). Be warned: Even on the street, aggressive girls can be all over gawkers.

This all sounds intimidating. But Prague is safe. It has its share of petty thieves and con artists, but very little violent crime. Don't be scared—just be alert.

Holešovice Station (Nádraží Holešovice): This station, slightly farther from the center, is suburban mellow. The main hall has all the services of the main station in a compact area. The friendly, little-frequented Internet café allows you to place cheap international calls through the Internet (7 Kč/min to the U.S., daily 8:00–19:30).

Outside the first glass doors, the ATM is on the left, the Czech Railways information office is on the right (daily 9:00–17:00), and the Metro is straight ahead (follow *Vstup*, which means "entrance"; take it 3 stops to the main station, 4 stops to the city-center Muzeum stop). Taxis and trams are outside to the right (allow 200 Kč for a cab to the center).

By Plane: Prague's new, tidy, low-key **Ruzyně Airport**—a delightful contrast to the old, hulking main train station—is 12 miles (about 30 min) west of the city center. The airport has ATM machines (avoid the change desks); desks promoting their transportation service (such as city transit and shuttle buses); kiosks selling city maps and phone cards; and a tourist service that has little printed material available. Airport info: tel. 220-113-314, operator tel. 220-111-111.

Getting to and from the airport is easy. You have several options:
- Dirt-cheap: Take bus #119 to the Dejvická Metro station, or #100 to the Zličín Metro station (20 min), then take the Metro

Prague's Four Towns

Until about 1800, the city was actually four distinct towns with four town squares separated by fortified walls.

Castle Quarter (Hradčany): Built regally on the hill, this was the home of the cathedral, monastery, castle, royal palace, and high nobility. Even today, you feel like clip-clopping through it in a fancy carriage. It has the high art and grand buildings, yet feels a bit sterile.

Little Quarter (Malá Strana): This Baroque town of fine homes and gardens was built by the aristocracy and merchant elite at the foot of the castle. The quarter burned in the 1500s and was rebuilt with the mansions of the generally domesticated European nobility, who moved in to be near the king. The tradition remains, as the successors of this power-brokering class—today's Parliament—now call this home.

Old Town (Staré Město): Charles Bridge connects the Little Quarter with the Old Town. A boom town in the 14th century, this has long been the busy commercial quarter—filled with merchants, guilds, and natural supporters of Jan Hus (folks who wanted a Czech stamp on their religion). Trace the walls of this town in the modern road plan (the Powder Tower is a remnant of a wall system that completed a fortified ring, half provided by the river). The marshy area closest to the bend—least inhabitable, and therefore allotted to the Jewish community—became the ghetto.

New Town (Nové Město): Nové Město rings the Old Town, cutting a swath from riverbank to riverbank, and is fortified with Prague's outer wall. In the 14th century, the king initiated the creation of this town, tripling the size of what would become Prague. Wenceslas Square was once the horse market of this busy, working-class district. When you cross the moat (Na Příkopě) that separates the Old and New Towns, you leave the tourists behind and enter the real, everyday town.

into the center (12 Kč, info desk in airport arrival hall).
- Cheap: Take the Čedaz minibus shuttle to Náměstí Republiky, across from Kotva department store (2/hr, pay 90 Kč directly to driver, info desk in arrival hall).
- Moderate: Take a Čedaz minibus directly to your hotel, with a couple of stops likely en route (360 Kč for a group of up to 4, tel. 220-114-296).
- Expensive: Catch a taxi. Cabbies wait at the curb directly in front of the arrival hall. Carefully confirm the complete price before getting in. It's a fixed rate of 600–700 Kč with no meter.

Helpful Hints

Internet Access: Internet cafés—which beg for business all along Karlova street, on the city side of the Charles Bridge—are commonplace. Consider Bohemia Bagel (see page 100).

Laundry: A full-service laundry near most of the recommended hotels is at Karolíny Světlé 10 (200 Kč/8-pound load, wash and dry in 2 hrs, Mon–Fri 7:30–19:00, closed Sat–Sun, 200 yards from Charles Bridge on Old Town side). Or surf the Internet while your undies tumble-dry at Korunní 14 (160 Kč/load wash and dry, Internet-2 Kč/min, daily 8:00–20:00, Praha 2, near Náměstí Míru Metro stop).

American Express: It's right on Wenceslas Square (foreign exchange daily 9:00–19:00; travel service Mon–Fri 9:00–18:00, Sat 9:00–12:00, closed Sun; Václavské Náměstí 56, Praha 1, tel. 222-211-136). AmEx also has offices on Celetná Street in the Old Town and on the Old Town Square.

Medical Help: A 24-hour pharmacy is at Palackého 5 (Praha 1, a block from Wenceslas Square, tel. 224-946-982). First aid and emergency medical service in the Czech Republic are free for everyone. For standard assistance, there are two state hospitals in the center: the General Hospital (open daily 24 hours, moderate wait time, U Nemocnice 2, Praha 2, use entry G, right above Karlovo Náměstí, tel. 224-962-564); and the Na Františku Hospital (go to the main entrance, Na Františku 1, on the embankment next to Hotel Intercontinental; for English assistance call Mr. Hacker between 8:00 and 14:00, tel. 222-801-278 or tel. 222-801-371, serious problems only). The reception staff may not speak English, but the doctors do.

For better-than-standard assistance in English (including dental service), consider the top-quality Hospital Na Homolce (less than 1,000 Kč for an appointment, from 8:00–16:00 call 252-922-146, after-hours emergency call 257-211-111, Roentgenova 2, Praha 5, bus #167 from Anděl Metro station).

The Canadian Medical Care Center is a small, private clinic with English-speaking Czech staff at Veleslavínská 1 in Praha 6 (tel. 235-360-133, after-hours emergency call 724-300-301, halfway between the city and the airport, 3,000 Kč for an appointment, 4,500 Kč for a home visit).

Local Help: Magic Praha is a tiny travel service run by hardworking Lída Šteflová. A charming Jill-of-all-trades who takes her clients' needs seriously, she's particularly helpful with accommodations and transfers throughout the Czech Republic, private tours, and side trips to historic towns. Lída, the best polka teacher in town, also arranges music evenings with the Prague Castle Orchestra—a fun-loving, mustachioed trio that plays a lively Czech mélange of Smetana, swing, old folk tunes, and

1920s cabaret songs (Národní 17, Praha 1, 5th floor, tel. & fax 224-230-914, tel. 224-232-755, mobile 604-207-225, www .magicpraha.cz, magicpraha@magicpraha.cz).

Athos Travel books rooms (see "Sleeping," page 91), rents cars, and has guides for hire (1–5 people-700 Kč/hr—see "Tours," page 60).

Best Views: Enjoy the "Golden City of a Hundred Spires" during the early evening, when the light is warm and the colors are rich. Good viewpoints include the terrace at the Strahov Monastery (above the castle), the top of St. Vitus Cathedral (at the castle), the top of either tower on Charles Bridge, the Old Town Square clock tower (elevator), the Restaurant u Prince terrace (see page 100), and the steps of the National Museum overlooking Wenceslas Square.

Getting Around Prague

You can walk nearly everywhere. But the Metro is slick, the trams fun, and the taxis quick and easy, once you're initiated. For details, pick up the handy transit guide at the TI.

Public Transportation: Affordable and excellent public transit is perhaps the best legacy of the communist era (locals ride all month for 275 Kč). The trams and Metro work on the same cheap tickets. Buy from machines (select ticket price, then insert coins), at kiosks, or at hotels. For convenience, buy all the tickets you think you'll need: 15-minute ticket with no transfer—8 Kč, 60-minute ticket with unlimited transfers—12 Kč, 24-hour ticket—70 Kč, three-day pass— 200 Kč. Estimate conservatively. Remember, Prague is a great walking town, so unless you're commuting from a hotel far outside the center, you will likely find that individual tickets work best. The cheapo 8-Kč tickets are not good on night trams or night buses. The Metro closes at midnight, and the nighttime tram routes (identified with white numbers on blue backgrounds at tram stops) run all night in 30-minute intervals. Metro and tram tips: Navigate by signs listing end stations, and when you come to your stop, push the yellow button if the doors don't automatically open.

City maps show the tram, bus, and Metro lines. The three-line Metro system is handy and simple. Although it seems that all Metro doors lead to the neighborhood of Výstup, that's simply the Czech word for "exit." Trams are also easy to use; track your route with your city map. They run every five to 10 minutes in the daytime (a schedule is posted at each stop). Be sure to validate your ticket on the tram, bus, or Metro by sticking it in the machine (which stamps a time on it). There's a complete route planner at www.dp-praha.cz. Inspectors routinely ambush ticketless riders (including tourists) and fine them 400 Kč on the spot.

Taxis: Prague's taxis—notorious for hyperactive meters—are

Prague Metro

being tamed. Still, many cabbies are crooks who consider taking one sucker for a ride a good day's work. While most hotel receptionists and guidebooks advise avoiding taxis, I find Prague is a great taxi town and use them routinely. With the local rate, they're cheap (read the rates on the door: drop charge—30 Kč; per-kilometer charge—22 Kč; and wait-time per-min charge—5 Kč). The key is to be sure the cabbie turns on the meter at the #1 tariff (look for the word *sazba*, meaning tariff, on the meter). Avoid cabs waiting at tourist attractions and train stations. Cabs labeled "AAA Taxi" and "City Taxi" are generally honest. I find that hailing a passing taxi generally gets me a fair price.

If a cabbie surprises you at the end with an astronomical fare, simply pay 200 Kč, which should cover you for a long ride anywhere in the center. Then go into your hotel. On the miniscule chance he follows you, the receptionist will take your side.

You're most likely to get a fair meter rate—which starts only when you take off—if you have a cab called from a hotel or restaurant (try AAA Taxi, tel. 233-113-311, or City Taxi, tel. 257-257-257; they're the most likely to have an English-speaking staff).

TOURS

Walking Tours—Prague Walks offers walking tours of the Old Town, the castle, the Jewish Quarter, and more (250–300 Kč, 90 min-3 hrs, tel. 261-214-603, mobile 723-262-980, www.praguewalks.com, pwalks@comp.cz). Consider their clever Good Morning Walk, which starts at 8:00 (April–Aug only), before the crowds hit. Several other companies offer good guided walks. For the latest, pick up the walking tour fliers at the TI.

Private Guides—Hiring your own personal guide can be an exceptional value in Prague, especially if you're traveling in a group. Guides meet you where you like and tailor the tour to your interests.

Šárka Pelantová, a wonderful young philosophy grad from a nearby town, runs "Personal Prague Guide" service. She expertly gets beyond the dates and famous buildings to provide insight into her culture, and is eager to build a walk around your interests (€13/hr, mobile 777-225-205, www.prague-guide.info, saraguide@volny.cz).

Katka Svobodová—a hardworking guide who knows her stuff and speaks excellent English—enjoys showing individuals and small groups around (400 Kč or €13 per hour, minimum 3 hrs, tel. 224-818-267, mobile 603-181-300, www.praguewalker.com, katerina @praguewalker.com).

Athos Travel's licensed guides can lead you on a general sightseeing tour or fit the walk to your interests: music, Art Nouveau, Jewish life, architecture, Franz Kafka, and more (1–5 people-700 Kč/hr, more than 5 people-800 Kč/hr, arrange tour at least 24 hrs in advance, tel. 241-440-571, info@athos.cz).

To get beyond Prague, call **Thomas Zahn,** who runs Pathways Guided Travel. Thomas, an American who married into the Czech Republic, specializes in helping Americans of Czech descent find their roots. He also organizes and leads creative, affordable (mostly 1-day and 2-day) excursions from Prague. Hiking, biking, horseback riding, or canoeing, you'll explore the unknown charms of the region with a small group and a committed guide. Explore Thomas' Web site for ways to connect with the rural Czech countryside and experience more than Prague on your visit (tel. 257-940-113, mobile 603-758-983, www.pathfinders.cz).

The **TI** also has plenty of private guides (for 3 hours: 1 person-1,200 Kč, 2 people-1,400 Kč, 3 people-1,600 Kč, 4 people-2,000 Kč, desk at Old Town Square TI, arrange and pay in person at least

Prague at a Glance

▲▲▲**Old Town Square** Colorful, magical main square of Old World Prague, with fanciful, medieval clock tower (listed below). **Hours:** Always open.

▲▲▲**Charles Bridge** Atmospheric, statue-lined bridge connecting the Old Town to the castle. **Hours:** Always open.

▲▲▲**St. Vitus Cathedral** The Czech Republic's most important church, featuring a climbable tower and a striking stained-glass window by Art Nouveau artist Alfons Mucha. **Hours:** April–Oct daily except Sunday morning, 9:00–17:00, Nov–March until 16:00.

▲▲▲**Jewish Quarter** The best Jewish sight in Europe, featuring various synagogues and an evocative cemetery. **Hours:** Sun–Fri 9:00–18:00, closed Sat.

▲▲**Prague Castle** Traditional seat of Czech rulers, with St. Vitus Cathedral (see above), Old Royal Palace, Basilica of St. George, shop-lined Golden Lane, and fun toy museum (see below). **Hours:** April–Oct daily 9:00–17:00, Nov–March daily 9:00–16:00. Castle grounds: Daily 5:00–24:00.

▲▲**Mucha Museum** Likeable collection of Art Nouveau works by Czech artist Alfons Mucha. **Hours:** Daily 10:00–18:00.

▲▲**Wenceslas Square** Lively boulevard at the heart of modern Prague. **Hours:** Always open.

▲**Old Town Hall Astronomical Clock** Intricate landmark clock attracting throngs of gawking tourists. **Hours:** Always viewable; clock strikes daily on the hour 8:00–21:00, until 20:00 in winter.

▲**Strahov Monastery and Library** Baroque center of learning with ornate reading rooms and old-fashioned science exhibits. **Hours:** Daily 9:00–12:00 & 13:00–17:00.

▲**Havelská Market** Bustling open-air market, perfect for gathering a picnic. **Hours:** Daily 9:00–18:00.

▲**Toy and Barbie Museum** Teddy bears through the centuries, plus a whole floor of Barbies. **Hours:** Daily 9:30–17:30.

▲**Museum of Communism** The rise and fall of the regime, from start to Velvet finish. **Hours:** Daily 9:00–21:00.

2 hrs in advance, tel. 224-482-562, guides@pis.cz). For a listing of private guides, see www.guide-prague.cz.

Tram Joyride—Trams #22 and #23 (following the same route) both make a fine joyride through town. Consider it a scenic lead-up to touring the castle. Catch it at the Náměstí Míru Metro station; roll through a bit of the New Town, the Old Town, and across the river, and hop out just above the castle (at Hotel Savoy, stop: Pohořelec); then hike down the hill into the castle area.

Bus Tours—Cheap big-bus orientation tours provide an efficient once-over-lightly look at Prague and a convenient way to see the castle. But in a city as walkable as Prague, bus tours should be used only in case of rain, laziness, or both. Several companies have kiosks on Na Příkopě. Premiant City Tours offers 20 different tours, including several overview tours of the city (250 Kč/1 hr, 380 Kč/2 hrs, 750 Kč/3.5 hrs), the Jewish Quarter (700 Kč, 2 hrs), Prague by night, Bohemian glass, Terezín Concentration Camp memorial, Karlštejn Castle, Český Krumlov (1,750 Kč, 10 hrs), and a river cruise. The tours feature live guides and depart from near the bottom of Wenceslas Square at Na Příkopě 23. Get tickets at an AVE travel agency, hotel, on the bus, or at Na Příkopě 23 (tel. 224-946-922, mobile 606-600-123, www.premiant.cz). Tour salespeople are notorious for telling you anything to sell a ticket. Some tours, especially those heading into the countryside, can be in as many as four different languages. Hiring a private guide can be a much better value.

SIGHTS

The King's Walk (Královská Cesta)

The King's Walk—the ancient way of coronation processions—is touristy, but a Prague highlight. Follow this self-guided walk—pedestrian-friendly and full of playful diversions—to connect nearly all of the essential Prague sites (except the Jewish Quarter).

The king would be crowned in St. Vitus Cathedral in the Prague Castle, walk through the Little Quarter to the Church of St. Nicholas, cross Charles Bridge, and finish at the Old Town Square. If he hurried, he'd be done in 20 minutes. Like the main drag in Venice between St. Mark's and the Rialto Bridge, this walk mesmerizes tourists. Use it as a spine, but venture off it.

While you could cover this route in the same direction as the king, he's long gone, and it's a new morning in Prague—so we'll go in the opposite direction. Here are Prague's essential sights in walking order, starting at Wenceslas Square (where modern independence was proclaimed), proceeding through the Old Town and across the bridge, and finishing at the castle.

▲▲**Wenceslas Square (Václavské Náměstí)**—More a broad boulevard than a square (until recently, trams rattled up and down its

The King's Walk

1. Wenceslas Square
2. Grand Hotel Evropa
3. Lucerna Gallery
4. Můstek
5. Havelská Market
6. Old Town Square
7. Karlova Street & Klementinum
8. Charles Bridge
9. Lennon Wall
10. Church of St. Nicholas (in Malá Strana)
11. Castle Square

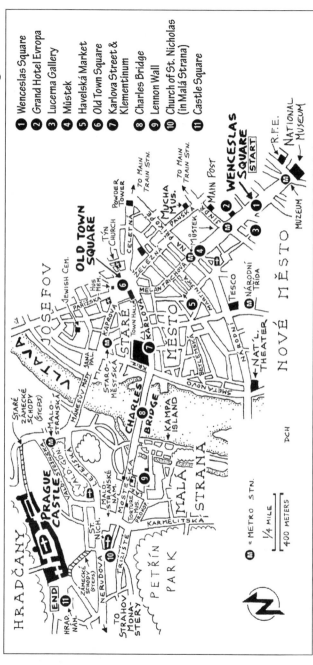

parklike median strip), this city landmark is named for King Wenceslas, who is featured in the equestrian statue that stands at the top of the boulevard. The area originated as a horse market when the New Town was founded by the order of Charles IV.

The square functions as a stage for modern Czech history: The creation of the Czechoslovak state was celebrated here in 1918; in 1968, the Soviets put down huge popular demonstrations here; and in 1989, more than 300,000 converged here to claim their freedom. Starting at the top (Metro: Muzeum), stroll down the square:

The **National Museum** (Národní Muzeum) stands grandly at the top. While the museum is dull, it enjoys a powerful view, and the interior is richly decorated in the Czech Revival neo-Renaissance style that heralded the 19th-century rebirth of the Czech nation (80 Kč, May–Sept daily 10:00–18:00, Oct–April daily 9:00–17:00, halls of Czech fossils and animals). A major renovation of the entire building is in the works.

Stand behind the statue, facing the museum (uphill). The light-colored patches in the columns show where Russian bullets hit during the crackdown in 1968. Lowly masons—defying their communist bosses, who wanted the damage to be forgotten—showed their Czech spirit by intentionally mismatching their patches.

The nearby Metro stop (Muzeum) is the crossing point of two Metro lines. From here, you could roll a ball straight down the boulevard, through the heart of Prague to Charles Bridge.

Look at the ugly **communist-era building** to the left of the National Museum. This place housed the rubber-stamp Parliament back when they voted with Moscow. A Social Realist statue showing workers triumphing still stands at its base. It's now home to Radio Free Europe. After communism fell, RFE lost its funding and could no longer afford its Munich headquarters. As gratitude for its broadcasts—which kept the people of Eastern Europe in touch with real news—the current Czech government now rents the building to RFE for one crown a year. (As RFE energetically beams its American message deep into Islam from here, it has been threatened recently by Al-Qaeda, and a move is underway to relocate it to an easier-to-defend locale.)

St. Wenceslas (Václav), commemorated by the statue, is the "good king" of Christmas carol fame. He was the wise and benevolent 10th-century duke of Bohemia. A rare example of a well-educated and literate ruler, he was credited by his people for Christianizing his nation and lifting up the culture. Wenceslas astutely allied the

Central Prague

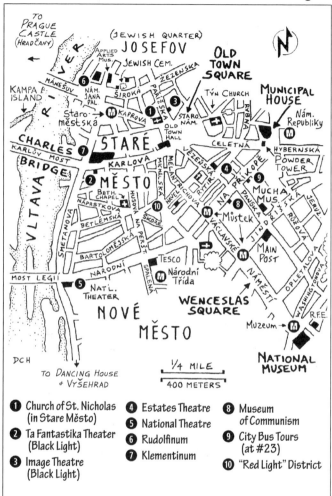

❶ Church of St. Nicholas (in Stare Město)	❹ Estates Theatre	❽ Museum of Communism
❷ Ta Fantastika Theater (Black Light)	❺ National Theatre	❾ City Bus Tours (at #23)
❸ Image Theatre (Black Light)	❻ Rudolfinum ❼ Klementinum	❿ "Red Light" District

Czechs with Saxony, rather than Bavaria, giving the Czechs a vote when the Holy Roman Emperor was selected (and therefore more political clout). After being murdered in 929, Wenceslas became a symbol of Czech nationalism and statehood—and remains an icon of Czech unity whenever the nation has to rally. Supposedly, when the Czechs face their darkest hour, Wenceslas will come riding out of Blaník Mountain (east of Prague) with an army of knights to rescue the nation. In 1620, when Austria stripped Czechs of their independence, many people went to Blaník Mountain to see whether it was opening. They did the same at other critical points in their history (in 1938, 1948, and 1968)—but Wenceslas never emerged. Although now safely part of NATO and the EU, some Czechs are reluctant to be optimistic: If Wenceslas hasn't come out yet, the worst times must still lie ahead....

Study the statue. Wenceslas—always sporting the Czech flag—is surrounded by the four other Czech patron saints. Notice the focus on books. A small nation without great military power, the Czech Republic chose national heroes who enriched the culture by thinking, rather than fighting. This statue is a popular meeting point. Locals say, "I'll see you under the horse's tail."

Thirty yards below the big horse is a small garden with a low-key **memorial** "to the victims of communism"—such as Jan Palach. In 1969, a group of patriots decided that an act of self-immolation would stoke the fires of independence. Jan Palach, a philosophy student who loved life but wanted it with freedom, set himself on fire for the cause of Czech independence and died a few yards from this memorial (on the steps of the National Museum). Czechs are keen on anniversaries. Huge demonstrations swept the city on the 20th anniversary of Palach's death. These led, 10 months later, to the overthrow of the Czech communist government.

This grand square is a gallery of modern **architectural styles**. As you wander downhill, notice the fun mix, all post-1850: Romantic neo-Gothic, neo-Renaissance, and neo-Baroque from the 19th century; Art Nouveau from 1900; ugly functionalism from the mid-20th century (the "form follows function" and "ornamentation is a crime" answer to Art Nouveau); Stalin Gothic from the 1950s "communist epoch" (a good example is the Jalta building—halfway downhill on the right); and glass-and-steel buildings of the 1970s.

Walk a couple blocks downhill through the real people of Prague (not tourists) to **Grand Hotel Evropa,** with its hard-to-miss, dazzling, Art Nouveau exterior and plush café interior.

In November of 1989, this huge square was filled with more than 300,000 ecstatic Czechs believing freedom was at hand. Assembled on the balcony of the building opposite Grand Hotel Evropa (look for *KNIHY BOOKS* sign) was a priest, a rock star (famous for his unconventional style, which constantly unnerved the regime), Alexander Dubček (hero of the 1968 revolt), and Václav Havel (the charismatic playwright, newly released from prison, and every freedom-loving Czech's Mandela). Through a sound system provided by the rock star, Havel's voice boomed over the gathered masses, announcing the resignation of the politburo and saying the Republic of Czechoslovakia's freedom was imminent. Picture that cold November evening, with thousands of Czechs jingling their key-chains in solidarity, chanting at the government, "It's time to go now!" (To quell this revolt, government tanks could have given it the Tiananmen Square treatment—which spilled lots of patriotic blood in China just 6 months earlier. Locals believe Gorbachev must have made a phone call recommending that blood not be shed over this.)

Havel, who became the nation's first post-communist president, ended his second (and, constitutionally, last) five-year term early in 2003. While he's still admired by Czechs, his popularity took a hit when he got married for the second time—to an actress 17 years his junior.

Immediately opposite Grand Hotel Evropa is the **Lucerna Gallery** (use entry marked *Divadlo Rokoko* and walk straight in). This is a grand mall from the 1930s with shops, theaters, a ballroom in the basement, and the fine Lucerna café upstairs. You'll see a sculpture—called *Wenceslas Riding an Upside-Down Horse*—hanging like a swing from a glass dome. Created in 1992 (3 years after freedom), it captured the topsy-turvy first days of free enterprise, and the scandal-ridden transition to privatization in a land with a weak legal system. Interestingly, the building (which also includes luxury apartments and offices) was built—and, until recently, owned—by the Havel family. Inside, you'll find a Ticketpro box office (with all available tickets, daily 9:30–18:00), a lavish 1930s Prague cinema (which shows artsy films in Czech with English subtitles or vice versa, 110 Kč), and the popular Lucerna Music Bar in the basement (nightly disco themes from the '70s, '80s, and '90s, 100 Kč, Tue–Sat from 21:00—see page 90).

If you're in the mood for a mellow hippie teahouse, consider a break at Dobrá Čajovna ("Good Teahouse") near the bottom of the square (#14; see page 104). Or, if you'd like an old-time wine bar, pop into the plain **Šenk Vrbovec** (nearby at #10); it comes with a whiff of the communist days, embracing the faintest bits of genteel culture in that age when refinement was sacrificed for the good of the working class. They serve traditional drinks, Czech keg wine, Moravian wines (listed on blackboard outside), *becherovka* (the 13-herb liqueur), and—only in autumn—*burčák* (young wine—grape juice halfway to wine).

The bottom of Wenceslas Square is called **Můstek**, which means "Bridge"; a bridge used to cross a moat here, allowing entrance into the Old Town (you can still see the original Old Town entrance down in the Metro station). Continuing straight, crossing that imaginary old bridge and moat, you enter the charm of Prague's Old Town. (Or, if you turn right at the bridge, you can stroll along the former moat on Na Příkopě, now a spacious pedestrian mall lined with stylish shops; for more on Na Příkopě and the nearby Municipal House, see pages 84 and 86, respectively.)

Heading straight from Můstek toward the Old Town Square, you'll find the...

▲**Havelská Market**—Central Prague's best open-air flower and produce market scene is a couple of blocks toward the Old Town

Square from the bottom of Wenceslas Square (daily 9:00–18:00). Laid out in the 13th century for the German trading community, it still keeps hungry locals and vagabonds fed cheaply. Since many of those who produce their goods personally have a stall here, you'll be often dealing with the actual farmer or craftsperson. This is ideal for a healthy snack; merchants are happy to sell single pieces of fruit or vegetables, and you'll find a washing fountain and plenty of inviting benches midway down the street.

▲▲▲**Old Town Square (Staroměstské Náměstí)**—The focal point for most visits, this has been a market square since the 11th century. It became the nucleus of a town (Staré Město) in the 13th century, when its Town Hall was built. Today, the old-time market stalls have been replaced by cafés, touristy horse buggies, and souvenir hawkers.

The **Jan Hus Memorial**, erected in 1915 (500 years after the Czech reformer's martyrdom by fire), marks the center of the square and symbolizes the long struggle for Czech freedom (see "Hus and Luther" sidebar on page 70). Walk around the memorial. Jan Hus stands tall between two groups of people: victorious Hussite patriots, and Protestants defeated by the Hapsburgs. One of the patriots holds a cup—in the medieval Church, only priests could drink the wine at Communion. Since the Hussites fought for the right to take both the wine and the bread, the cup is their symbol. Behind Hus, a mother with her children represents the ultimate rebirth of the Czech nation. Hus was excommunicated and burned in Germany a century before the age of Martin Luther.

Do a quick **spin tour** in the center of the square to get a look at architectural styles: Gothic, Renaissance, Baroque, rococo, and Art Nouveau.

Spin clockwise, starting with the green domes of the Baroque Church of St. Nicholas. Originally Catholic, now Hussite, it's a popular venue for concerts. (There's another green-domed Church of St. Nicholas—also popular for concerts—by the same architect across the Charles Bridge in the Little Quarter.) The Jewish Quarter (Josefov) is a few blocks behind the church, down the uniquely tree-lined Paris street (Pařížská). Paris street, an eclectic cancan of mostly Art Nouveau facades, leads to a bluff that once sported a 100-foot-tall stone Stalin. Demolished in 1962 after Khrushchev exposed Stalin's crimes, it was recently replaced by a giant ticking metronome.

Spin to the right past the Hus Memorial and the fine yellow Art Nouveau building. The large rococo palace on the right is part of the National Gallery—the temporary exhibits here tend to be the best in town. Notice the Gothic Týn Church (described below), with its fanciful spires flanking a solid gold effigy of the Virgin Mary. Lining the uphill side of the square is an interesting row of pastel houses with Gothic, Renaissance, and Baroque facades. The pointed, 250-foot-tall spire marks the 14th-century Old Town Hall, famous for its astronomical clock (described below).

In front of the Town Hall, **27 white inlaid crosses** mark the spot where 27 Protestant nobles, merchants, and intellectuals were beheaded in 1621 after rebelling against the Catholic Hapsburgs. The execution ended Czech independence for 300 years—and, for locals, it's still one of the grimmest chapters in their history. Until recently, Czechs walked around this sacred spot, avoiding stepping on it, and many would even stop to pay their respects. But today, the sacred soil is home to a hot-dog stand, and few notice the crosses in the pavement. Locals lament this transition: As the commercialized Old Town loses the power to evoke history, people trample over their own past here.

Týn Church—The towering Týn (teen) Church facing the Old Town Square was rebuilt fancier than the original—but enjoy it. For 200 years after Hus' death, this was Prague's leading Hussite church. The lane leading to the church from the Old Town Square has a public WC and the most convenient box office in town (see Týnska Galerie listing under "Entertainment," page 88).

▲Old Town Hall Astronomical Clock—Ignore the ridiculous human sales racks, and join the gang for the striking of the hour (daily 8:00–21:00, until 20:00 in winter) on the 15th-century Town Hall clock. As you wait, see if you can figure out how the clock works.

With revolving disks, celestial symbols, and sweeping hands, this clock keeps several versions of time. Two outer rings show the hour: Bohemian time (Gothic numbers, counts from sunset—find the zero, next to 23...supposedly the time of tonight's sunset) and modern time (24 Roman numerals, XII at the top being noon, XII at the bottom being midnight). Five hundred years ago, everything revolved around the earth (the fixed middle background).

To indicate the times of sunrise and sunset, arcing lines and moving spheres combine with the big hand (a sweeping golden sun) and the little hand (the moon showing various stages). Look for the orbits of the sun and moon as they rise through day (the blue zone) and night (the black zone).

If this seems complex to us, it must have been a marvel 500 years ago. Heavily damaged during World War II, a lot of what you see today is a reconstruction.

The circle below (added in the 19th century) shows the zodiac,

Hus and Luther

The word *catholic* means "universal." The Roman Catholic Church—in many ways the administrative ghost of the Roman Empire—is the only organization to survive from ancient times. For more than a thousand years, it enforced its notion that the Vatican was the sole interpreter of God's word on earth, and the only legitimate way to be a Christian was as a Roman Catholic. Jan Hus (c. 1369–1415) lived and preached 100 years before Martin Luther. Both were college professors, as well as priests. Both drew huge public crowds as they preached in their university chapels. Both promoted a local religious autonomy. And both helped establish their national languages. (Hus gave the Czechs their unique accents to enable the letters to fit the sounds.) Both got in big trouble. While Hus was burned, Luther survived. Living after Gutenberg, Luther was able to spread his message more cheaply and effectively, thanks to the new printing press. Since Luther was high-profile and German, killing him would have caused major political complications. While Hus may have loosened Rome's grip on Christianity, Luther orchestrated the Reformation that finally broke it. Today, both are revered as national heroes, as well as religious reformers.

scenes from the seasons of a rural peasant's life, and a ring of saints' names—one for each day of the year, with a marker showing today's special saint.

Four statues flanking the clock represent 15th-century Prague's four biggest worries: invasion (a Turkish conqueror, his hedonism symbolized by a mandolin), death (a skeleton), greed (a miserly moneylender, who used to have "Jewish" features until after World War II), and vanity (enjoying the mirror). Another interpretation: Earthly pleasures brought on by vanity, greed, and hedonism are fleeting, because we are all mortal.

At the top of the hour (don't blink—the show is pretty quick): First, Death tips his hourglass and pulls the cord, ringing the bell; then the windows open, and the 12 apostles parade by, acknowledging the gang of onlookers; then the rooster crows; and then the hour is rung. The hour is often off because of daylight saving time (completely senseless to 15th-century clock-makers). At  the top of the next hour, stand under the tower—protected by a line of banner-wielding, powdered-wigged concert salespeople—and watch the tourists.

Old Town Hall Tower, Hall, and Chapel—The main TI, left of the astronomical clock, contains a guides' desk and these two options: zipping up the only tower in town that has an elevator (40 Kč, fine views), or taking a 45-minute tour of the Gothic chapel and Town Hall, which includes a close-up of the 12 apostles and clock mechanism (50 Kč, 2/hr). A gallery inside the Town Hall features some of Prague's best temporary exhibits (especially photography—check in the office for schedule).

Next to the Old Town Hall, notice the elaborate Renaissance window on the house with the pink facade—the railings and the golden inscription *(Praga Caput Regni)* form Prague's most beautiful window.

Karlova Street—This street winds through medieval Prague from the Old Town Square to the Charles Bridge (it zigzags...just follow the crowds). This is a commercial gauntlet, and it's here that the touristy feeding-frenzy of Prague is most ugly. Street signs keep you on track, and *Karlův most* signs point to the bridge. Obviously, you'll find great people-watching on this drag, but few good values.

The exception is the colorful pub **U Tygra**, where you can rest your feet over a cheap Pilsner beer and watch locals (venture off 20 steps to the left, along Husova street). Bohumil Hrabal, the best modern Czech writer (best known for *Closely Watched Trains*), heard many of his famous stories from the regulars *(štamgast)* right here.

▲▲▲Charles Bridge (Karlův Most)—This much-loved bridge, commissioned by Charles IV in 1357, offers one of the most pleasant and entertaining 500-yard strolls in Europe. Until 1850, it was Prague's only bridge crossing the river. The bridge tower—once a tollbooth—is considered one of the finest Gothic gates anywhere. Climb it for a fine view...but nothing else (40 Kč, daily 10:00–19:00, as late as 22:00 in summer).

Be on the Charles Bridge when the sun is low for the best light, people-watching, and photo opportunities. Before the tacky commercialism and the camera-toting mobs get you down, remember the vacant gloom of this place before 1989. Think of the crowds of Charles Bridge as a celebration of freedom. (Better yet, arrive before 9:00 in the morning to have the place to yourself.)

The bridge is famous for its statues, but half of those you see today are replicas—the originals are in city museums and out of the polluted air. Two of the statues are worth a comment. First, the crucifix (facing the castle, near the start on the right) is the spot where convicts would pause to pray on their way to execution on the Old Town Square. Farther on (midstream, on right), the statue of John of Nepomuk—a Baroque saint of the Czech people—draws a crowd (look for

the guy with the 5 golden stars around his head and the shiny dog). Back in the 14th century, John of Nepomuk was the priest to whom the queen confessed all her sins. The king wanted to know her secrets, but Father John dutifully refused to tell. He was tortured, eventually killed, and tossed off the bridge. When he hit the water, five stars appeared. The shiny plaque at the base of the statue depicts the heave-ho. Devout Catholics—from Mexico and Moravia alike—touch it for a wish to come true. You only get one chance in life for this wish, so think carefully before you touch. Notice the date on the inscription: This oldest statue on the bridge was unveiled in 1683, on the supposed 300th anniversary of the martyr's death.

From the end of the bridge (TI in tower on castle side), the street leads two blocks to the Little Quarter Square at the base of the huge Church of St. Nicholas. But before you head up there, consider a detour to...

Kampa Island and Lennon Wall—One hundred yards before the castle end of the Charles Bridge, stairs on the left lead down to the main square of Kampa Island (mostly created from the rubble of the Little Quarter, which was destroyed in an 1540 fire). The island features relaxing pubs, a breezy park, a new art gallery, and river access.

From the main square, Hroznová lane (on the right) leads to a bridge. To the left of the bridge, notice the high-water marks from the flood of August 2002. The water mill is one of many that once lined the canal here.

Fifty yards beyond the bridge is the **Lennon Wall** (Lennonova zeď)—the only chance in Prague to legally try your graffiti art. While the ideas of Lenin hung like a water-soaked trench coat upon the Czech people, the ideas of John Lennon gave many locals hope and a vision. When Lennon was killed in 1980, a memorial wall filled with graffiti spontaneously appeared. Night after night, the police would paint over the "All You Need Is Love" and "Imagine" graffiti. And day after day, it would reappear. Until independence came in 1989, travelers, freedom-lovers, and local hippies gathered here. Silly as it might seem, it's remembered as a place that gave hope to locals craving freedom. Even today, while the tension and danger associated with this wall is gone, the message stays fresh.

▲▲**Little Quarter (Malá Strana)**—This is the most characteristic, fun-to-wander old section of town. It's one of four medieval towns (along with Hradčany, Staré Město, and Nové Město) that united in the late 1700s to make modern Prague (see "Prague's Four Towns," page 56). It centers on the Little Quarter Square

(Malostranské Náměstí), with the huge Church of St. Nicholas standing in the middle. For a short, vivid detour near the church, see the...

Torture Museum—This gimmicky moneymaker is similar to other European torture museums, but is nevertheless interesting, showing models of 60 gruesome medieval tortures, with well-written English descriptions (120 Kč, daily 10:00–22:00, just below Church of St. Nicholas at Mostecká 21, tel. 224-215-581).

Church of St. Nicholas (Kostel Sv. Mikuláše)—When the Jesuits came, they found the perfect piece of real estate for their church and its associated school—the Little Quarter Square. The Church of St. Nicholas (built 1703–1760 in the middle of the square) is the best example of High Baroque in town. It's giddy with curves and illusions. The altar features a lavish, gold-plated Nicholas flanked by the two top Jesuits: St. Ignatius Loyola and St. Francis Xavier.

Climb up the gallery through the staircase in the right transept to look at a collection of large canvases by Karel Škréta, the greatest Czech Baroque painter. Notice that at first glance, the canvases are utterly dark. But as sunbeams shine through the window, various parts of the painting brighten up. The painting is not two-dimensional; like a looking-glass, it's a play of light and darkness. This painting technique reflects a central Baroque belief: The world is full of darkness, and the only hope that makes it come alive comes from God.

For a good look at the city and the church's 250-foot dome, climb the tower for 30 Kč; the entrance is outside the right transept (church entry-50 Kč, daily 9:00–17:00, opens 30 min earlier for prayer; tower open April–Oct daily 10:00–18:00, closed off-season). The church is a concert venue in evenings; 400-Kč tickets are generally on sale at the door.

From here, hike 10 minutes uphill to the castle (and 5 min more to the Strahov Monastery).

Prague's Castle Area

Prague's castle—by some measures, the biggest on earth—is worth a half day of sightseeing. There are various ways to reach the castle and surrounding sights.

Getting to Prague Castle: Take **tram** #22 or #23, both of which go from the National Theater (Národní Divadlo) or Malostranská to the castle. You have two options: Get off at the stop Královský Letohrádek for the castle (see below); or stay on farther to Pohořelec to visit the Strahov Monastery (go uphill and through the gate toward the twin spires), and then hike down to the castle—this route is described under "Strahov Monastery and Library," below.

If you get off the tram at Královský Letohrádek, you'll see the **Royal Summer Palace** (Belvedér) across the street. This love gift—a Czech Taj Mahal—from Emperor Ferdinand I, who really did love

Prague's Castle Area

1. Castle Square & Plague Monument
2. Castle Gate
3. Museum of Military History
4. National Gallery
5. Tickets & Information
6. St. Vitus Cathedral
7. Old Royal Palace
8. St. George's Basilica
9. Golden Lane
10. Toy & Barbie Museum
11. Royal Gardens
12. Steps to Terraced Gardens
13. Café Espresso Kajetánka
14. Maly Buddha Tea House
15. U Hrocha Pub
16. To U.S. Embassy
17. To Loreta Church & Strahov Monastery/Library

his Queen Anne—is the finest Renaissance building in town. Notice that the reliefs, in good Renaissance style, are based on classical, rather than Christian, stories. The one depicted here is Virgil's *Aeneas*. The fountain in front of the palace features the most elaborate bronzework in the country. (If you stick your head under the bottom of the fountain, you'll find out why it's called the "Singing Fountain.") From here, walk through the Royal Gardens (with fine views of the cathedral) to the gate, which leads you over the moat and into the castle grounds. Once the private grounds and residence (you'll see the building) of the communist presidents, these Royal Gardens were opened to the public with the coming of freedom under Václav Havel.

Hikers can follow the main cobbled road from Charles Bridge through the Little Quarter (the nearest subway stop is Malostranská). From the big church, hike uphill along Nerudova Street (described below). After about 10 minutes, a steep lane on the right leads to the castle. (If you continue straight, Nerudova becomes Úvoz and climbs to the Strahov Monastery and Library.)

▲**Strahov Monastery and Library (Strahovský Klášter Premonstrátů a Strahovská Knihovna)**—Twin Baroque domes high above the castle mark the Strahov Monastery (a 15-min hike uphill from Little Quarter, or 5-min walk from castle). If coming by tram, take tram #22 or #23 (from the National Theater or Malostranská Metro station) to the Pohořelec stop, visit the monastery (go uphill 200 yards and through the gate into the monastery grounds), and then hike down to the castle.

The monastery had a booming economy of its own in its heyday (with vineyards and the biggest beer hall in town—still open). Its main church (dedicated to the Ascension of St. Mary) is an originally Romanesque structure decorated by the monks in textbook Baroque (usually closed, but look through the window inside the front door to see its interior).

The adjacent **library** offers a peek at how enlightened thinkers in the 18th century influenced learning (60 Kč, daily 9:00–12:00 & 13:00–17:00). Cases in the library gift shop show off illuminated manuscripts, some in old Czech. Two rooms are filled with 17th-century books under elaborately painted ceilings. Because the Czechs were a rural people with almost no high culture at this time, there were few books in the Czech language. The theme of the first and bigger hall is philosophy, with the history of man's pursuit of knowledge painted on its ceiling. The other hall focuses on theology. Notice the gilded locked case containing the *libri prohibiti* (prohibited books) at the end of the room. Only the abbot had the key, and you had to have his blessing to read these books—by Nicolas Copernicus and Jan Hus, even including the French encyclopedia. As the Age of Enlightenment began to take hold in Europe at the end of 18th century, monasteries still controlled the books. The hallway connecting these two library rooms was filled with cases illustrating the new practical approach to natural sciences. Find the baby dodo bird (which became extinct in the 17th century).

Just downhill from the monastery and through the gate, the views from the **monastery garden** are among the best in Prague. From the Panorama restaurant or the public perch below the tables, you can see the St. Vitus Cathedral (the centerpiece of the castle complex), the green dome of the Church of St. Nicholas (marking the center of the Little Quarter, or Malá Strana), the two dark towers fortifying the Charles Bridge, and the fanciful black spires of the Týn Church (marking the Old Town Square). On the horizon, the modern **Žižkov TV and radio tower** (conveniently marking the liveliest nightlife zone in town—see "Entertainment," page 88) is meant to attract extraterrestrials to Prague.

Loreta Church (a.k.a. Loreta Shrine)—This church (between the castle and the Strahov Monastery) has been a hit with pilgrims for centuries, thanks to its dazzling bell tower, peaceful yet plush cloister, sparkling treasury, and much venerated "holy house" (90 Kč, Tue–Sun 9:00–12:15 & 13:00–16:30, closed Mon).

The central **Santa Casa** (holy house) was considered by some pilgrims to be part of Mary's home in Nazareth. Because many pilgrims returning from the Holy Land docked at the Italian port of Loreto, it's called the Loreta Shrine. The Santa Casa is the "little Bethlehem" of Prague. It has long been the departure point for Czech pilgrims setting out on the long, arduous journey to Europe's most important pilgrimage site, Santiago de Compostela, in northwest Spain.

The small Baroque church behind the Santa Casa is one of the most beautiful in Prague. The frescoes on the ceilings of the ambits illustrate a prayer to St. Mary. The Santa Casa itself, with only a few 15th-century frescoes and an old statue of Mary, might seem like a bit of a letdown, but consider that you're entering the holiest spot in the country for generations of believers. Upstairs, the highlight is a room full of jeweled worship aids in the treasury (well-described in English). Behind vault doors, you'll squint at a monstrance (Communion wafer holder) from 1699 with over 6,000 diamonds. Enjoy the short carillon concert at the top of the hour; from the lawn in front of the main entrance, you can see the racks of bells being clanged.

On the opposite side of the square is the **Černín palace,** the largest Baroque palace in town. It once belonged to one of the most cosmopolitan Czech families, and so, in 1918, it was turned into the Ministry of Foreign Affairs.

Walking down the street from the Loreta Square, you'll reach...

Castle Square (Hradčanské Náměstí)—The big square facing the castle feels like the castle's entry, but it's actually the central square of the Castle Quarter. Enjoy the awesome city view and the two entertaining string quartets that play regularly at the gate. (If the Prague Castle Orchestra is playing, say hello to friendly, mustachioed Josef and consider getting the group's terrific CD.) A tranquil café called Espresso Kajetánka (see page 101) hides a few steps down, immediately to the right as you face the castle. From here, stairs lead into the Little Quarter.

Castle Square was a kind of medieval Pennsylvania Avenue— the king, the most powerful noblemen, and the archbishop lived here. Look uphill from the gate. The Renaissance **Schwarzenberg Palace** (on the left, with the big rectangles scratched on the wall, now under renovation) was where the Rožmberks "humbly" stayed when they were in town from their Český Krumlov estates. The Schwarzenberg family (marvel at their coat of arms, made of human bones, in the ossuary in Kutná Hora) inherited the Krumlov estates and aristocratic prominence in Bohemia, and stayed in the palace until 20th century.

The archbishop still lives in the yellow rococo **palace** across the square (with the 3 white goose necks in the red field—the coat of arms of Prague archbishops).

Through the portal on the left-hand side of the palace, a lane leads to the **Sternberg Palace** (Šternberský Palác), filled with the National Gallery's skippable collection of European paintings—mostly minor works by Albrecht Dürer, Peter Paul Rubens, Rembrandt, and El Greco (100 Kč, Tue–Sun 10:00–18:00, closed Mon).

The Baroque sculpture in the middle of the square is a **plague column**, erected as a token of gratitude to the saints who saved the population from the epidemic, and an integral part of the main square of any Hapsburg town.

Survey the castle from this square—the tip of a 1,500-foot-long series of courtyards, churches, and palaces.

▲▲**Prague Castle (Pražský Hrad)**—For more than a thousand years, Czech leaders have ruled from the Prague Castle. It's huge and confusing—with plenty of sights not worth seeing. Keep things simple, rather than worry about rumors that you should spend all day here with long lists of museums to see. Five stops matter and are all explained here: St. Vitus Cathedral, Old Royal Palace, Basilica of St. George, the Golden Lane, and the toy museum.

Huge throngs of tourists turn the castle grounds into a sea of people during peak times; late afternoon is least crowded. The guard changes on the hour (5:00–23:00), with the most ceremony at noon. Walk under the fighting giants, under an arch, and into the second courtyard. The modern green awning with the golden winged cat (just past the ticket office) marks the offices of the Czech president.

Hours: Castle sights open April–Oct daily 9:00–17:00, Nov–March daily 9:00–16:00, last entry 15 min before closing; grounds open daily 5:00–24:00. Tel. 224-373-368 or 224-372-434.

Tickets: You can choose from three ticket routes. Route A costs 350 Kč and includes everything: the cathedral sights (apse, crypt, and tower—just looking around the front part of the cathedral is free), Old Royal Palace, Basilica of St. George, Powder Tower, Golden Lane (during peak sightseeing hours—it's free in the morning and evening), and an exhibition on the castle's building history. Route B (220 Kč) includes the cathedral sights and Old Royal Palace. Route C (50 Kč) gets you into the Golden Lane only, and Route D (50 Kč) into the Basilica of St. George only. For the thorough visit described below, opt for Route A. If you want to save time and money, buy Route D—tour the Basilica of St. George, wander the grounds, and explore the front half of the cathedral and peek into the tomb of Prince Wenceslas (this part of cathedral is free).

Tours: Hour-long tours in English depart from the main ticket office about three times a day, but cover only the cathedral and Old Royal Palace (80 Kč; reserve a week in advance if you want a private guide-400 Kč for up to 5 people, then 80 Kč per additional person, tel. 224-373-368). If you rent the worthwhile **audioguide** (200 Kč/2 hrs, 250 Kč/3 hrs), you won't be able to exit the castle area from the bottom, since you need to backtrack uphill to return the audioguide where you got it.

▲▲▲**St. Vitus Cathedral (Katedrála Sv. Vita)**—This Roman Catholic cathedral symbolizes the Czech spirit—it contains the tombs and relics of the most important local saints and kings, including the first three Hapsburg kings.

To **avoid crowds**, be at the entrance at 9:00, when the doors open. For 10 minutes, you'll have the sacred space for yourself (after about 9:15, tour guides shouting over each other turn the church into a hawkers' square). Otherwise, come here in the afternoon, when the church is still relatively full, but most tour groups are gone.

Before entering, check out the **facade**. What's up with the guys in suits carved into the facade below the big round window? They're the architects and builders who finished the church. Started in 1344, construction was stalled by wars and plagues. But, fueled by the 19th-century rise of Czech nationalism, Prague's top church was finished in 1929 for the 1,000th anniversary of the death of St. Wenceslas. While it looks all Gothic, it's actually two distinct halves: modern neo-Gothic and the original 14th-century Gothic. For 400 years, a temporary wall sealed off the unfinished cathedral.

Go inside (pickpocket alert) and find the third **stained-glass window** on the left. This masterful 1931 Art Nouveau window is by Czech artist Alfons Mucha (if you like this, you'll love the Mucha Museum in the New Town—see page 86). Notice Mucha's stirring nationalism: Methodius and Cyril are top and center (leaders in Slavic-style Christianity). Cyril is baptizing the mythic, lanky, long-haired Czech man. In the center is a kneeling boy and a prophesizing elder—that's young St. Wenceslas and his grandmother, St. Ludmila. In addition to being specific figures, these characters are also symbolic: The old woman, with closed eyes, stands for the past and the memory, while the young boy, with a penetrating stare, represents the hope and future of a nation. Notice how master designer Mucha draws your attention to these two figures through the use of colors—the dark blue on the outside gradually turns into green, then yellow, and finally the gold of the woman and the crimson of the boy in the center. In Mucha's color language, blue stands for the past, gold for the mythic, and red for the future. Along with all the meaning, Mucha's art is simply a joy to look at.

Show your ticket and circulate around the **apse**. You'll pass a carved wood relief of Prague in 1620 depicting the victorious Hapsburg armies entering the castle after the Battle of White Mountain, while the Protestant king Frederic escapes over the Charles Bridge (before it had any statues). The second part of this Counter-Reformation wood relief, on the other side from the altar, captures the "barbaric" Protestant nobles destroying the Catholic icons in the cathedral after the Prague defeat.

A fancy, roped-off chapel (right transept) houses the **tomb of Prince Wenceslas,** surrounded by precious 14th-century murals showing scenes from his life, and a locked door leading to the crown jewels. The Czech kings used to be coronated right here in front of the coffin, draped in red.

You can climb 287 steps up the **spire** for one of the best views of the whole city (included in Route A or B ticket, or pay 20 Kč at the cathedral ticket window, April–Oct daily except Sun morning, 9:00–17:00, last entry 16:15, closes at 16:00 in winter).

Back Outside the Cathedral: Leaving the cathedral, turn left (past the public WC). The **obelisk** was erected in 1928—a single piece of granite celebrating the 10th anniversary of the establishment of Czechoslovakia. It was originally much taller, but broke in transit—an inauspicious start for a nation destined to last only 70 years. Up in the fat, green tower of the cathedral is the biggest Czech bell, nicknamed "Zikmund." In June 2002, it cracked—and two months later, the worst flood in recorded history hit the city. As members

of a nation sandwiched between great powers, Czechs are deeply superstitious. Often unable to influence the course of their own history, they helplessly look at events as we might look at the weather and other natural phenomena—trying to figure out what fate has in store for them next.

Find the 14th-century **mosaic** of the *Last Judgment* outside on the right transept. It was built Italian-style by King Charles IV, who was modern, cosmopolitan, and ahead of his time. Jesus oversees the action, as some go to heaven and some go to hell. The Czech king and queen kneel directly below Jesus and the six patron saints. On coronation day, they would walk under this arch, which would remind them (and their subjects) that even those holding great power are not above God's judgment. The royal crown and national jewels are kept in a chamber (see the grilled windows) above this entryway, which was the cathedral's main entry for centuries, while the church was incomplete.

Across the square and 20 yards to the right, a door leads to the...
Old Royal Palace (Starý Královský Palác)—This was the seat of the Bohemian princes starting in the 12th century. While extensively rebuilt, the **large hall** is late Gothic, designed as a multipurpose hall for the old nobility. It's big enough for jousts—even the staircase was designed to let a mounted soldier gallop in. It was filled with market stalls, giving nobles a chance to shop without actually going into town.

In the 1400s, the nobility met here to elect their king. This tradition survived until modern times, as the parliament crowded into this room until the late 1990s to elect the Czechoslovak (and later Czech) president. The last two elections happened in another, much more lavish hall in the castle. Look up at the flower-shaped, vaulted ceiling—far more elaborate than the simple cross ceiling in the cathedral.

On the right, enter the two small Renaissance rooms known as the "**Czech Office**." From these rooms, two governors used to oversee the Czech lands in the times when the Hapsburgs moved the capital to Vienna. In 1618, angry Czech Protestant nobles poured into these rooms and threw the two Catholic governors out of the window. This was the second of Prague's many defenestrations, and it sparked the Thirty Years' War. Look at the pictures illustrating the defenestration (a uniquely Czech solution to political discord, whereby offending politicians are literally tossed out of a window). The two governors landed—you could say, thankfully—in a pile of horse manure (there were royal stables under the window back then)...so, despite the height, they suffered only a broken arm. The Czech Estates Uprising lasted for two years and ended in the crushing defeat of the Czech army in the Battle of White Mountain, which marked the end of Czech freedom. Twenty-seven leaders of the uprising were executed, most of the old Czech nobility was dispossessed, and Protestants had to leave the country or convert to Catholicism.

Look down on the chapel from the end, and go out on the balcony for a fine Prague view. Is that Paris' Eiffel Tower in the distance? No, it's Petřín Tower, built for an exhibition in 1891 (200 feet tall, a quarter of the height of its Parisian big brother, built 2 years earlier). The spiral stairs on the left lead up to several rooms with painted coats of arms and no English explanations. The downstairs of the palace sometimes houses special exhibitions.

Across from the palace exit is the...

Basilica of St. George and Convent (Bazilika Sv. Jiří)—Step into the beautifully lit Basilica of St. George to see Prague's best-preserved Romanesque church. St. Wenceslas' mother, St. Ludmila, was reburied here in 973. The first Bohemian convent was established here near the palace.

Today, the **convent** next door houses the National Gallery's Collection of Old Masters (the best Czech paintings from Mannerism and Baroque periods, 100 Kč, Tue–Sun 10:00–18:00, closed Mon).

Continue walking downhill through the castle grounds. Turn left on the first street, which leads into the...

Golden Lane (Zlatá Ulička)—During the day, this street of old buildings, which originally housed goldsmiths, is jammed with tourists and lined with overpriced gift shops. Franz Kafka lived briefly at #22. There's a deli/bistro at the top and a convenient public

WC at the bottom. In the morning and at night, the tiny street is empty and romantic.

▲**Toy and Barbie Museum (Muzeum Hraček)**—At the bottom of the castle complex, just after leaving the Golden Lane, a long wooden staircase leads to two entertaining floors of old toys and dolls thoughtfully described in English. You'll see a century of teddy bears, 19th-century model train sets, and an incredible Barbie collection (the entire top floor). Find the buxom 1959 first edition, and you'll understand why these capitalistic sirens of material discontent weren't allowed here until 1989 (50 Kč, not included in any castle tickets, daily 9:30–17:30).

After Your Castle Visit: Tourists squirt slowly through a fortified door at the bottom end of the castle. From there, you can follow the steep lane directly back to the riverbank (and the Malostranská Metro station). Or you can take a hard right and stroll through the long, delightful park to the top of the castle, where you'll find two more options: a staircase leading down into the Little Quarter, or a cobbled street taking you to the historic Nerudova Street—described below. (Halfway through that long park is a viewpoint overlooking the terraced gardens; you can zigzag down through the gardens into the Little Quarter—120 Kč, April–Oct daily 10:00–18:00.)

Nerudova Street—The steep, cobbled street leading to the castle is named for Jan Neruda, a gifted 19th-century journalist (and somewhat less talented fiction writer). It's lined with old buildings still sporting the characteristic doorway signs that served as street addresses. In 1777, in order to collect taxes more effectively, Hapsburg Empress Maria Theresa decreed that numbers be used instead of these quaint house names. The surviving signs are carefully restored and protected by law. Signs (e.g., the lion, 3 violinists, house of the golden suns) represent the family name, the occupation, or the various passions of the people who once inhabited the houses. This neighborhood is filled with old noble palaces, now generally used as foreign embassies.

Prague's Jewish Quarter (Josefov)

Prague's Jewish Quarter neighborhood and its well-presented, profoundly moving museum tell the story of the Jews of this region. For me, this is the most interesting Jewish sight in Europe (and worth ▲▲▲).

As the Nazis decimated Jewish communities in the region, Prague's Jews were allowed to collect and archive their treasures in this "museum." While the archivists ultimately died in concentration camps, their work survives. Seven sights scattered over a three-block area make up the tourists' Jewish Quarter. Six of the sights, called "the Museum," are treated as one admission. Your ticket comes with a map locating the sights and listing admission

Prague's Jewish Quarter

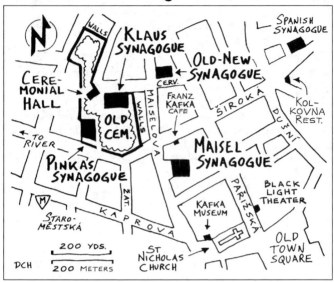

appointments—the times you'll be let in if it's very crowded. (Without crowds, ignore the times.) You'll notice plenty of security (stepped up since 9/11).

To visit all seven sights, you'll pay 500 Kč (300 Kč for the Museum and 200 Kč for the Old-New Synagogue; all sights open Sun–Fri 9:00–18:00, closed Sat—the Jewish Sabbath). There are occasional guided walks in English (40 Kč, 2.5 hrs, start at Maisel Synagogue, tel. 222-317-191). Most stops are described in English. The ticket lines at the cemetery and Pinkas Synagogue are longest. You'll likely save time if you buy your ticket at the Maisel Synagogue (the best place to start your visit, anyway).

Maisel Synagogue (Maiselova Synagóga)—This synagogue was built as a private place of worship for the Maisel family during the 16th-century golden age of Prague's Jews. Maisel was the financier of the Hapsburg king—and had lots of money. The synagogue's

interior is decorated neo-Gothic. In World War II, it served as a warehouse for the accumulated treasures of decimated Jewish communities that Hitler planned to use for his "Museum of the Extinct Jewish Race." The one-room exhibit (the upstairs "women's gallery" is closed for renovation) shows a thousand years of Jewish history in Bohemia and Moravia. Well-explained in English, the topics covered include the origin of the Star of David,

Jewish mysticism, discrimination, and the creation of Prague's ghetto. Notice the eastern wall, with the holy ark containing the scroll of the Torah. The central case shows the silver ornamental Torah crowns that capped the scroll.

Spanish Synagogue (Španělská Synagóga)—This 19th-century, ornate, Moorish-style synagogue continues the history of the Maisel Synagogue, covering the 18th, 19th, and tumultuous 20th centuries. The upstairs is particularly intriguing (with c. 1900 photos of Josefov). The Spanish Synagogue is now used for classical concerts, often featuring the music of Jewish composers, such as Felix Mendelssohn and Gustav Mahler (ticket desk just outside at the door). The building also contains the Jewish public library, the only one of its kind in Prague.

Pinkas Synagogue (Pinkasova Synagóga)—A site of Jewish worship for 400 years, today this is a poignant memorial to the victims of the Nazis. The walls are covered with the handwritten names of 77,297 Czech Jews who were sent from here to the gas chambers of Auschwitz and other camps. (You'll hear the somber reading of the names as you ponder this sad sight.) Hometowns are in gold, family names are in red, followed in black by the individual's first name, birthday, and last date known to be alive. Notice that families generally perished together. Extermination camps are listed on the east wall. Climb six steps into the women's gallery. The names in poor condition near the ceiling are from 1953. When the communists moved in, they closed the synagogue and erased everything. With freedom, in 1989, the Pinkas Synagogue was reopened and all the names rewritten. The Synagogue closed briefly in 2003, as flood damage meant the names needed to be rewritten once again.

Upstairs is the **Terezín Children's Art Exhibit,** displaying art drawn by Jewish children who were imprisoned at Terezín Concentration Camp, and later perished. Terezín is a powerful day trip from Prague, easily accessible by tour bus (see page 62) or local bus (1-hr trip, departs Prague's Florenc station).

Old Jewish Cemetery (Starý Židovský Hřbitov)—As you wander among 12,000 evocative tombstones, remember that from 1439 until 1787, this was the only burial ground allowed for the Jews of Prague. Because of limited space, the Jewish belief that the body should not be moved once buried, and the sheer number of graves, tombs were piled atop each other. With its many layers, the cemetery became a small plateau. And as things settled over time, the tombstones got crooked. The Jewish word for cemetery means "House of Life." Like Christians, Jews believe that death is the gateway into the next world. Pebbles on the tombstones are "flowers of the desert," reminiscent of the old days when a rock was placed upon the sand gravesite to keep the body covered. You'll likely see pebbles atop scraps of paper containing prayers.

Prague's Jewish Heritage

The Jewish people were dispersed by the Romans 2,000 years ago. Over the centuries, their culture survived in enclaves throughout the Western world: "The Torah was their sanctuary, which no army could destroy." Jews first came to Prague in the 10th century. The main intersection of Josefov (Maiselova and Široká streets) was the meeting point of two medieval trade routes.

When the pope declared that Jews and Christians should not live together, Jews had to wear yellow badges, and their quarter was walled in. It became a ghetto. In the 16th and 17th centuries, Prague had one of the biggest ghettos in Europe, with 11,000 inhabitants. Within its six gates, Prague's Jewish Quarter was a gaggle of 200 wooden buildings. It was said that "Jews nested, rather than dwelled."

The "outcasts" of Christianity relied mainly on profits from moneylending (forbidden to Christians) and community solidarity to survive. While their money protected them, it was often also a curse. Throughout Europe, when times got tough and Christian debts to the Jewish community mounted, entire Jewish communities were evicted or killed.

In the 1780s, Emperor Joseph II eased much of the discrimination against Jews. In 1848, the walls were torn down, and the neighborhood—named Josefov in honor of the emperor, who was less anti-Semitic than the norm—was incorporated as a district of Prague.

In 1897, ramshackle Josefov was razed and replaced with a new, modern town—the original 31 streets and 220 buildings became 10 streets and 83 buildings. This is what you'll see today: an attractive neighborhood of fine, mostly Art Nouveau buildings, with a few surviving historic Jewish buildings. By the 1930s, some 50,000 Jews lived in Prague. They were a hugely successful group, thanks largely to their ability to appreciate talent—a rare quality in the small Central European countries whose citizens, as the great Austrian novelist Robert Musil put it, "were equal in their unwillingness to let one another get ahead."

Of the 120,000 Jews living in the area in 1939, only 10,000 survived the Holocaust to see liberation in 1945. Today, only a couple of thousand Jews remain in Prague...but the legacy of their ancestors lives on.

Ceremonial Hall (Obřadní Síň)—Leaving the cemetery, you'll find a neo-Romanesque mortuary house built in 1911 for the purification of the dead (on left). It's filled with a worthwhile exhibition, described in English, on Jewish burial traditions. A series of crude but instructive paintings show how the "burial brotherhood" took care of the ill and buried the dead. As all are equal before God, the rich and poor alike were buried in embroidered linen shrouds similar to the one you'll see on display.

Klaus Synagogue (Klauzová Synagóga)—This 17th-century synagogue (also at the exit of the cemetery) is the final wing of the Museum, devoted to Jewish religious practices. On the ground floor, exhibits explain the festive Jewish calendar. The central case displays a Torah (the first 5 books of the Bible) and solid silver pointers—necessary, since the Torah is not to be touched. Upstairs is an exhibit on the rituals of Jewish life (circumcision, bar and bat mitzvah, weddings, kosher eating, and so on).

Old-New Synagogue (Staronová Synagóga)—For more than 700 years, this has been the most important synagogue and central building in Josefov. Standing like a bomb-hardened bunker, it feels like it has survived plenty of hard times. Stairs take you down to the street level of the 13th century and into the Gothic interior. Built in 1270, it's the oldest synagogue in Central Europe.

The lobby (where you show your ticket) has two fortified old lockers—where the most heavily taxed community in medieval Prague stored its money in anticipation of the taxman's arrival. As 13th-century Jews were not allowed to build, this was constructed by Christians. The builders were good at four-ribbed vaulting, but since that resulted in a cross, it wouldn't work for a synagogue. Instead, they made the ceiling using clumsy five-ribbed vaulting.

The interior is pure 1300s. The Shrine of the Ark in front is the focus of worship. The holiest place in the synagogue, it holds the sacred scrolls of the Torah. The old rabbi's chair to the right remains empty out of respect. The red banner is a copy of the one the Jewish community carried through town during medieval parades. Notice the yellow pointed hat, which the pope in 1215 ordered all Jewish men to wear. Twelve is a popular number (e.g., 12 windows) because it symbolizes the 12 tribes of Israel. The horizontal, slit-like windows are an 18th-century addition allowing women to view the men-only services (separate 200-Kč admission includes worthwhile 10-minute tour—ask about it, Sun–Thu 9:30–18:00, Fri 9:30–17:00, closed Sat).

More Sights in the Old Town and the New Town

▲**Na Příkopě**—Na Příkopě (meaning "The Moat") follows the line of the Old Town wall, leading from Wenceslas Square right to a former gate in that wall, the Powder Tower (Prašná Brána, not worth touring). City tour buses leave from along this street, which offers plenty of shopping temptations (see "Shopping," page 90). The neo-Renaissance Živnostenská Banka building on the corner of Nekázanka houses a modern bank in a classy, 19th-century ambience (enter and peek into the main hall upstairs).

▲**Museum of Communism**—The museum traces the story of communism in Prague: the origins, dream, reality, and nightmare; the cult of personality; and finally, the Velvet Revolution. Along the way, it gives a fascinating review of the Czech Republic's 40-year stint with Soviet economics. You'll find propaganda posters, busts of communist All-Stars (Marx, Lenin, Stalin), a photograph of the massive stone Stalin that overlooked Prague until 1962, and re-created slices of communist life—from a bland store counter to a typical classroom (with a poem on the chalkboard extolling the virtues of the tractor). Don't miss the 20-minute video showing how the Czech people chafed under the big red yoke from the 1950s through 1989—it plays continuously (180 Kč, daily 9:00-21:00, Na Příkopě 10, above a McDonald's and next to a casino—Lenin would turn over in his grave, tel. 224-212-966, www.museumofcommunism.com).

▲**Municipal House (Obecní Dům)**—The Municipal House is the "pearl of Czech Art Nouveau" (built 1905–1911, next to Powder Tower). It features Prague's largest concert hall, a great Art Nouveau café, and two other restaurants. Pop in and wander around the lobby of the concert hall. Walk through to the ticket office on the ground floor. Most days, there are guided tours through the Municipal House that show you all the halls worth seeing. Then choose your place for a meal or drink (see "Eating," page 98).

Standing in front of the Municipal House, you can survey four different styles of architecture. First, enjoy the pure Art Nouveau of the Municipal House itself. Featuring a goddess-like Praha presiding over a land of peace and high culture, the *Homage to Prague* mosaic on the building's striking facade stoked cultural pride and nationalist sentiment. Across the street, the classical fixer-upper from 1815 was the customs house (soon to be renovated). The stark national bank building (Česká Národní Banka) is textbook functionalism ("ornament is a crime") from the 1930s. And the big, black Powder Tower was the Gothic gate of the town wall, built to house the city's gunpowder. Crossing under it, you join the beaten path as Celetná Street leads to the Old Town Square.

▲▲**Mucha Museum (Muchovo Muzeum)**—This is one of Europe's most enjoyable little museums. I find the art of Alfons Mucha (MOO-kah, 1860–1939) insistently likeable. See the crucifixion scene he painted as an eight-year-old boy. Read how this popular Czech artist's posters, filled with Czech symbols and expressing his people's ideals and aspirations, were patriotic banners that aroused the national spirit. And check out the photographs of his models. With the help of this abundant supply of slinky models, Mucha was a founding father of the Art Nouveau movement. Prague isn't much on museums, but, if you're into Art Nouveau, this one is great. Run by Mucha's grandson, it's two blocks off Wenceslas Square and wonderfully displayed on one comfortable floor. Give it a once-over-lightly, just looking at the probing and haunting eyes of Mucha's models (120 Kč, daily 10:00–18:00, Panská 7, tel. 224-233-355, www.mucha.cz). While the exhibit is well-described in English, the 30-Kč English brochure on the art is a good supplement. The included 30-minute video is definitely worthwhile (English and Czech showings alternate, ask upon entry).

Bethlehem Chapel (Betlémská Kaple)—Emperor Charles IV founded the first university in Central Europe, and this was the university's chapel. Around the year 1400, priest and professor Jan Hus preached from the pulpit here (see "Hus and Luther" sidebar, page 70). While meant primarily for students and faculty, Hus' Masses were open to the public. Hus proposed that the congregation should be more involved in worship (e.g., actually drink the wine at Communion) and have better access to the word of God through services and scriptures written in the people's language, instead of Latin. Standing-room-only crowds of more than 3,000 were the norm when Hus preached. The stimulating, controversial ideas debated at the university spread throughout the city and, after Hus' death at the stake, sparked off the bloodiest civil war in Czech history. Each subsequent age has interpreted Hus to its liking: For the Protestants, Hus was the founder of the first Protestant church (though he was actually an ardent Catholic); for the revolutionaries, this critic of the power of the Church was a proponent of social equality; for the nationalists, the Czech preacher was the defender of the language; and for the communists, Hus was the first communist ideologue.

Today's chapel is a 1950s reconstruction of the original. Try the unbelievably bad acoustics inside—it demonstrates the sloppy work sponsored by the communists (tiny upstairs exhibit and big chapel with English info sheets available, 35 Kč, April–Oct daily 10:00–18:30; Nov–March Tue–Sun 10:00–17:30, closed Mon and during university functions; on Bethlehem Square—Betlémská Náměstí, tel. 224-248-595).

Klub Architektů, across from the entry, has an intriguing atmosphere and good food (see "Eating," page 99).

The Dancing House (Tančicí Dům)—Prague has some delightful modern architecture. If ever a building could get your toes tapping, it would be this one, nicknamed "Fred and Ginger" by American

architecture buffs. This metallic samba is the work of Frank Gehry (who designed the equally striking Guggenheim Museum in Bilbao, Spain, and Seattle's Experience Music Project). Eight-legged Ginger's wispy dress and Fred's metal mesh head are easy to spot (2 bridges down from Charles Bridge where Jiráskův bridge hits Nové Město, tram #17).

A pleasant, 10-minute, riverside walk from the Dancing House (towards the Charles Bridge) is the grand **National Theater** (Národní

Divadlo). Opened in 1883, this theater was the first truly Czech venue in Prague, and from the very start was nicknamed the "Cradle of Czech Culture." The productions are heavily subsidized—the state pours more money into this single theater than into all of Czech film production. It is the best place in town for opera or ballet.

Across the street from the theater is the formerly venerable haunt of Prague's intelligentsia, **Grand Café Slavia**, a Vienna-style coffeehouse fine for a meal or drink with a view of the river.

ENTERTAINMENT

Prague booms with live (and inexpensive) theater, classical, jazz, and pop entertainment. Everything's listed in several monthly cultural events programs (free at TI) and in the *Prague Post* newspaper.

You'll be tempted to gather fliers as you wander through the town. Don't. To really understand all your options (the street Mozarts are pushing only their concert), drop by the **Týnská Galerie** box office at Týn Church on the Old Town Square. The event schedule posted on their wall clearly shows what's playing today and tomorrow, including tourist concerts, Black Light Theater, and marionette shows, with photos of each venue and a map locating everything (daily 10:00–19:00, tel. 224-826-969).

Ticketpro at Rytířská 31 (between the Havelská Market and the Estates Theater) sells tickets for the serious concert venues and most music clubs (daily 8:00–12:00 & 12:30–16:30; also has a booth in the Tourist Center at Rytířská 12, daily 9:00–20:00).

Black Light Theater—A kind of mime/modern dance variety show, Black Light Theater has no language barrier and is, for many, more entertaining than a classical concert. Unique to Prague (though somewhat comparable to the Canadian Cirque du Soleil), Black Light Theater originated in the 1960s as a playful and mystifying theater of the absurd. The two main venues are **Ta Fantastika** (*Aspects of Alice* at 21:30, more poetic, more puppets, traditional, a little artistic nudity, 620 Kč, reserved seating, near Charles Bridge at Karlova 8, tel. 222-221-366, www.tafantastika.cz) and **Image Theatre** (more mime and absurd—"It's precisely the fact that we are all so different that unites us," shows at 18:00 and 20:00, 450 Kč, open seating—arrive early to grab a good spot, just off Old Town Square at Pařížská 4, tel. 222-314-448, www.imagetheatre.cz). Shows last about 90 minutes. Avoid the first four rows, which get you close enough to ruin the illusion. The other black light theaters advertising around town aren't as good.

Tourist Concerts—Each day, six or eight classical concerts designed for tourists fill delightful Old Town halls and churches with music of the crowd-pleasing sort: Vivaldi, Best of Mozart, Most Famous Arias, and works by local boy Antonín Dvořák. Concerts typically cost 400–1,000 Kč, start anywhere from 13:00 to 21:00, and last one hour. Common venues are two sites at the Little Quarter Square (at the Baroque Church of St. Nicholas and in the Prague Academy of Music in Liechtenstein Palace); in the Klementinum's Chapel of Mirrors; at the Old Town Square (in a different Church of St. Nicholas); and in the stunning Smetana Hall in the Municipal House (Obecní Dům). The artists vary from excellent to amateur.

To ensure quality, head for the Monday 17:00 concert at **St. Martin in the Wall** (Martinská street in the Old Town), where Prague's best professional musicians gather every week to tune in and chat with each other (400 Kč).

Serious Concerts—True music-lovers should consider the best symphonic venue, the **Rudolfinum** (the Prague Philharmonic, on Palachovo Náměstí, on the Old Town side of Mánes bridge). Concerts in the large Dvořák Hall or the small Suk Hall usually start at 19:30 (also afternoons on weekends). The ticket office is on the right side, under the stairs (250–1,000 Kč, open until few minutes before the show starts).

The **National Theatre** (Národní Divadlo, on the New Town side of Legií bridge)—with a must-see neo-Renaissance interior—is best for opera and ballet (shows from 19:00, 300–1,000 Kč, tel. 224-912-673, www.nationaltheatre.cz). The **Estates Theatre** (Stavovské Divadlo) is where Mozart premiered and personally directed many of his most beloved works. *Don Giovanni*, *The Marriage of Figaro*, and *The Magic Flute* are on the program a couple of times each month (shows from 20:00, 800–1,400 Kč, on square called Ovocný Trh, tel. 224-214-339, www.estatestheatre.cz). The ticket office for both of these theatres is in the little square (Ovocný Trh) behind the Estates Theatre.

The **State Opera** (Státní Opera) focuses on Verdi (tickets in the theatre, shows at 19:00 or 20:00, 400–1,200 Kč, on 5. Května—the busy street between the main train station and Wenceslas Square, tel. 224-227-693).

World-class musicians are in town during the **Prague Spring** (from May 12 to the beginning of June, www.festival.cz) and **Prague Autumn** (mid-Sept–mid-Oct, www.pragueautumn.cz) music festivals.

For any of these concerts, locals dress up, but many tourists wear casual clothes—as long as you don't show up in sneakers and ripped jeans, you'll be fine.

Music Clubs—Young locals keep Prague's many music clubs in business. Most clubs are neighborhood institutions with decades of tradition, generally holding only 100–200 people. Live rock and Bob

Dylan–style folk are what younger generations go for. A number of good jazz clubs attract a diverse audience, from 18 to 80. In the last decade, ethnic music has also become hugely popular: Gypsy bands, Moravian poets, African drummers, Cuban boleros, and Moroccan divas often sell out even the largest venues. You can buy tickets at the club, or, for most places, at the Ticketpro offices (see above).

The **Lucerna Music Bar** is popular for disco nights (music nightly from 21:00, around 100 Kč cover, at the bottom of Wenceslas Square, in the basement of Lucerna Gallery, Vodičkova 36, tel. 224-217-108). Friday and Saturdays are the "1980s Party," featuring the silly pop songs of the last years under communism. The scene is a big, noisy dance hall with a giant video screen. While young and trendy, it offers cheap prices, and even older tourists mix in easily. **Malostranská Beseda,** on the Little Town Square, was known in the communist era for playing host to underground rock bands, semi-legal bards, and daring jazzmen—a stark contrast to the regime-pampered pop-stars. Today, Beseda is the only club in the center with daily live performances, and the crowd tends to be a bit older than in the other clubs (shows from 20:30, about 150-Kč cover, Malostranské Náměstí 21, tel. 257-532-092).

Cruises—Prague isn't great for a boat tour. Still, the hour-long Vltava River cruises, which leave from near the castle end of Charles Bridge about hourly (100 Kč), are scenic and relaxing, though not informative. Consider renting a small rowboat or paddle boat on the island by the National Theater, so you can float between the swans at your own pace (about 60 Kč/hr, bring photo ID for deposit).

SHOPPING

Prague's entire Old Town seems designed to bring out the shopper in visitors. Shop your way from the Old Town Square up Celetná to the Powder Tower, then along Na Příkopě to the bottom of Wenceslas Square (Václavské Náměstí).

Celetná is lined with big stores selling all the traditional Czech goodies. Celetná Crystal, about midway down the street, sells the largest selection of affordable crystal. You can get the glass safely shipped home directly from the shop (for larger purchases, you can get a refund of the VAT tax; see "VAT Refunds for Shoppers," page 18).

Na Příkopě has a couple of good modern malls. The best is Slovansky Dům (Na Příkopě 22), where you wander deep past a 10-theater multiplex into a world of classy restaurants and designer shops surrounding a peaceful, parklike inner courtyard. Another modern mall is Černá Růže (Na Příkopě 12). Next door is Mosers, where you can climb upstairs to peruse its museum-like crystal showroom.

SLEEPING

Peak time is during the months of May, June, September, and October, and during Christmas and Easter holidays. July and August are not too bad. Expect crowds on weekends. I've listed peak-time prices. If you're traveling in July or August, you'll find slightly lower rates. Prices tend to go up even more on holidays. English is spoken everywhere. Reserve by phone or e-mail. Generally, you'll give your credit-card number to guarantee a room reservation.

As part of EU tax standardization, Czech taxes on accommodations and food went up 5 to 19 percent on January 1, 2005. The prices listed here are based on 2004 rates. Some hotels vow to keep their prices at the same level even after January 2005, while others plan to raise their rates.

Room-Booking Services

Prague is awash with fancy rooms on the push list; private, small-time operators with rooms to rent in their apartments; and roving agents eager to book you a bed and earn a commission. You can save about 30 percent by showing up in Prague without a reservation and finding accommodations upon arrival. If you're driving, you'll see booking agencies as you enter town. Generally, if you book here, your hosts can come and lead you to their place.

Athos Travel, run by Filip Antoš, will find the right room for you from among 140 properties (ranging from hostels to 5-star hotels), 90 percent of which are in the historical center. Or use their handy Web site, which allows you to search for a room based on various criteria (best to arrange in advance during peak season, can also help with last-minute booking off-season, tel. 241-440-571, fax 241-441-697, www.athos.cz, info@athos.cz).

AVE, at the main train station (Hlavní Nádraží), is a less personable but helpful booking service (daily 6:00–23:00, tel. 251-551-011, fax 251-555-156, www.avetravel.cz, ave@avetravel.cz). With the tracks at your back, walk down to the orange ceiling and past the "Meeting Point" (don't go downstairs)—their office is in the left corner by the exit to the rip-off taxis. AVE has several other offices—at Holešovice station, the airport, Wenceslas Square, and Old Town Square. Their display board shows discounted hotels. They have a slew of hotels and small pensions available ($80/2,000-Kč pension doubles in old center, $40/1,000-Kč doubles a Metro ride away). You can reserve by e-mail (using your credit card as a deposit) or just show up at the office and request a room. Many of AVE's rooms are not very convenient to the center; be clear on the location before you make your choice. They sell taxi vouchers for those who want the convenience of a ride from the station's taxi stand, though they cost double the fair rate.

Sleep Code

(25 Kč = about $1, €1 = $1.20, country code: 420)
S = Single, **D** = Double/Twin, **T** = Triple, **Q** = Quad,
b = bathroom, **s** = shower only. Unless otherwise noted, credit
cards are accepted and breakfast is included. Some hotels quote
prices in euros.

To help you sort easily through these listings, I've divided
the rooms into three categories based on the price for a standard
double room with bath:

$$$ **Higher Priced**—Most rooms 4,000 Kč (€133) or more.
$$ **Moderately Priced**—Most rooms between
3,000–4,000 Kč (€100–133).
$ **Lower Priced**—Most rooms 3,000 Kč (€100) or less.

For a more personal touch, contact Lída at **Magic Praha** for
help with accommodations (tel. & fax 224-230-914, tel. 224-
232-755, mobile 604-207-225, www.magicpraha.cz, magicpraha
@magicpraha.cz, see "Helpful Hints," page 57).

In the Old Town

You'll pay higher prices to stay in the Old Town, but for many travelers, the convenience is worth the expense. These places are all
within a 10-minute walk of the Old Town Square.

$$$ Hotel Central is a sentimental favorite—I stayed there in
the communist days. Like the rest of Prague, it's now changing with
the times: Its 69 rooms have recently been renovated, leaving it fresh
and bright. The place is well-run, and the location—three blocks
east of the Old Town Square—is excellent (Sb-3,800 Kč, Db-4,400
Kč, deluxe Db-4,600 Kč, Tb-4,900 Kč, 30–40 percent less
Nov–Feb, 5 percent discount for cash, ask for a "Rick Steves dis-
count" with your e-mail request in 2005, elevator, Rybná 8, Praha
1, Metro: Náměstí Republiky, tel. 224-812-041, fax 222-328-404,
central@orfea.cz).

$$$ Cloister Inn is well-located, with 75 modern rooms. The
exterior is more concrete than charm—the building used to be
shared by a convent and a secret-police prison—but inside, it's newly
redone and plenty comfortable (Sb-4,000 Kč, Db-4,200 Kč, Tb-
5,000 Kč, elevator, free Internet access and coffee, Konviktská 14,
Praha 1, tel. 224-211-020, fax 224-210-800, www.cloister-inn.com,
cloister@cloister-inn.com).

$$ Pension u Medvídků has 31 comfortably renovated rooms in
a big, rustic, medieval shell with dark wood furniture. Upstairs, you'll
find lots of beams to smack into (Sb-2,300 Kč, Db-3,500 Kč,

Prague Hotels

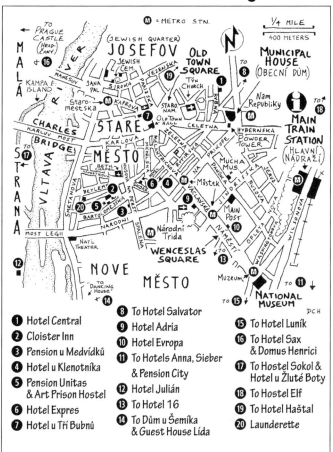

● Hotel Central
● Cloister Inn
● Pension u Medvídků
● Hotel u Klenotníka
● Pension Unitas
& Art Prison Hostel
● Hotel Expres
● Hotel u Tří Bubnů

● To Hotel Salvator
● Hotel Adria
● Hotel Evropa
● To Hotels Anna, Sieber
& Pension City
● Hotel Julián
● To Hotel 16
● To Dům u Šemíka
& Guest House Lída

● To Hotel Luník
● To Hotel Sax
& Domus Henrici
● To Hostel Sokol &
Hotel u Žluté Boty
● To Hostel Elf
● To Hotel Haštal
● Launderette

Tb-4,500 Kč, extra bed-500 Kč, "historical" rooms 10 percent more, apartment 20 percent more, prices flex with season, Internet access-70 Kč/hr, Na Perštýně 7, Praha 1, tel. 224-211-916, fax 224-220-930, www.umedvidku.cz, info@umedvidku.cz). The pension runs a popular beer-hall restaurant that has live music most Fridays and Saturdays until 23:00.

$$ Hotel u Klenotníka, with 11 modern, comfortable rooms in a plain building, is three blocks off the Old Town Square (Sb-2,500 Kč, Db-3,800 Kč, Tb-4,500 Kč, 10 percent off when booking direct with this book in 2005, Rytířská 3, Praha 1, tel. 224-211-699, fax 224-221-025, www.uklenotnika.cz, info@uklenotnika.cz).

$$ Hotel u Tří Bubnů ("Three Drums") is new, filling one of the oldest buildings in town, 50 yards toward the river from the Old Town

Square. Its 18 rooms are spacious, with high ceilings and wooden beams (Db-3,900 Kč, extra bed-1,000 Kč, U Radnice 8, tel. 224-214-855, fax 224-236-100, www.utribubnu.cz, utribubnu@volny.cz).

$$ Hotel Haštal, on a quiet, hidden square in the Old Town, is also new. Its 20 rooms combine the elegance of the Old World (this was a popular hotel in the 1920s) with the amenities of the 21st century (Sb-3,000 Kč, Db-3,600 Kč, Tb-4,200 Kč, Haštalská 16, tel. 222-314-335, info@hastal.com, www.hastal.com).

$ Pension Unitas rents 35 small, tidy, youth hostel–type rooms with plain, minimalist furnishings and no sinks (S-1,100 Kč, D-1,400 Kč, T-1,750 Kč, Q-2,000 Kč, T and Q are cramped with bunks in D-sized rooms, easy reservations without a deposit, non-smoking, quiet hours 22:00–7:00, Bartolomějská 9, Praha 1, tel. 224-221-802, fax 224-217-555, www.unitas.cz, unitas@unitas.cz). They run a fine little youth hostel in the former prison downstairs (see "Youth Hostels," page 97).

$ Hotel Expres rents 29 simple rooms and brings a continental breakfast to your room (S-1,000 Kč, Sb-2,600 Kč, D-1,400 Kč, Db-2,800 Kč, Tb-3,400 Kč, 5 percent discount for cash, elevator, Skořepka 5, Praha 1, tel. 224-211-801, fax 224-223-309, www.pragueexpreshotel.cz, info@pragueexpreshotel.cz). While a good value, this place is in a red light zone and comes with late-night music from nearby clubs on weekends.

$ Hotel Salvator rents 30 comfortable rooms on a quiet street above a fun South American restaurant (D-1,850 Kč, Db-2,850 Kč, Qb-3,850 Kč, extra bed-500 Kč, elevator, Truhlářská 10, 3 min from Republic Square, Metro: Náměstí Republiky, tel. 222-312-234, fax 222-316-355, www.salvator.cz).

On Wenceslas Square

$$$ Hotel Adria, with a prime Wenceslas Square location, cool Art Nouveau facade, and 88 completely modern and business-class rooms, is your big-time, four-star, central splurge (Db-€220 but often discounted, air-con, elevator, minibars...the works, Václavské Náměstí 26, tel. 221-081-111, fax 221-081-300, www.adria.cz, accom@adria.cz).

$$$ Hotel Evropa is in a class by itself. This landmark place, famous for its wonderful 1903 Art Nouveau facade, is the centerpiece of Wenceslas Square. But someone pulled the plug on the hotel about 50 years ago, and it's a mess. It offers haunting beauty in all the public spaces, 92 dreary and ramshackle rooms, and a weary staff. They're waiting for a billion-crown investor to come along and rescue the place, but for now, they offer some of the cheapest rooms on Wenceslas Square (S-1,600 Kč, Sb-3,000 Kč, D-2,600 Kč, Db-4,000 Kč, T-3,100 Kč, Tb-5,000 Kč, some rooms have been very slightly refurbished, some remain in unrefurbished old style, they cost the same either way, every room is different, elevator, Václavské Náměstí 25, Praha 1, tel. 224-228-117, fax 224-224-544, www .evropahotel.cz, info@evropahotel.cz).

East of the Center, in Vinohrady

$$$ Hotel Sieber, with 20 rooms, is in an upscale residential neighborhood (near the former royal vineyards, or Vinohrady). It's a classy, four-star, business-class hotel that does a good job of being homey and welcoming (Sb-4,480 Kč, Db-4,800 Kč, extra bed-1,000 Kč, 20 percent discount Fri-Sun, elevator, air-con, 3-min walk to Metro: Jiřího z Poděbrad, or tram #11, Slezská 55, Praha 3, tel. 224-250-025, fax 224-250-027, www.sieber.cz, reservations@sieber.cz).

$$ Hotel Anna, with 24 bright, pastel, and classically charming rooms, is a bit closer in—10 minutes by foot east of Wenceslas Square (Sb-2,300 Kč, Db-3,100 Kč, Tb-3,900 Kč, 20 percent cheaper off-season, non-smoking rooms, elevator, Budečská 17, Praha 2, Metro: Náměstí Míru, tel. 222-513-111, fax 222-515-158, www.hotelanna.cz). The hotel runs a cheaper but similarly pleasant annex, the **Dependence,** two blocks away (Sb-1,860 Kč, Db-2,560 Kč, cheaper off-season, no elevator but all rooms on first floor, reception and breakfast at main hotel).

$ Hotel Luník, with 35 rooms, is a dignified but friendly, no-nonsense place out of the medieval, faux-rustic world in a normal, pleasant business district. It's two Metro stops from the main station (Metro: I.P. Pavlova) or a 10-minute walk from Wenceslas Square (Sb-2,050 Kč, Db-2,900 Kč, Tb-3,350 Kč, 20 percent cheaper Nov–March, 10 percent discount with this book in 2005 if claimed with reservation, elevator, some street noise, Londýnská 50, Praha 2, tel. 224-253-974, fax 224-253-986, www.hotel-lunik.cz, recepce@hotel-lunik.cz).

$ Hotel Pension City is tucked away in a typical Prague apartment house in a quiet, circa-1900s area near some of Vinohrady's best pubs and restaurants. Red carpets lead to enormous bathrooms and large rooms with nostalgic furnishings from the 1970s. Signs posted on the walls will tell you exactly where to step, where not to step, what is permitted, and what isn't (Sb-1,670 Kč, Db-2,320 Kč, Tb-2,610 Kč, 25 percent cheaper off-season, Belgická 10, Prague 2, Metro: Náměstí Míru, tel. 222-521-606, www.hotelcity.cz).

Away from the Center

Moving just outside the Old Town saves you money—and gets you away from the tourists and into some more workaday residential neighborhoods. These listings (great values compared to Old Town hotels) are all within a five- to 15-minute tram or Metro ride from the center.

$$ Hotel Julián, an oasis of professional, predictable decency in a quiet, untouristy neighborhood, is a five-minute taxi or tram ride from the action on the castle side of the river. Its 32 spacious, fresh, well-furnished rooms and big, homey public spaces hide behind a noble neoclassical facade. The staff is friendly and helpful (Sb-3,500 Kč, Db-3,800 Kč, Db suite-4,500 Kč, extra bed-900 Kč, family room, 13 percent less July–Aug, 5 percent discount off best quoted rate with this book in 2005, elevator, free tea and coffee in room, Internet access, parking lot, Elišky Peškové 11, Praha 5, tel. 257-311-150, reception tel. 257-311-145, fax 257-311-149, www.julian.cz, casjul@vol.cz). Free lockers and a shower are available for those needing to check out early, but stay until late (e.g., for an overnight train). Mike's Chauffeur Service, based here, is reliable and affordable (see page 105).

$$ **Hotel 16,** a stately little place with an intriguing Art Nouveau facade, high ceilings, and a clean, sleek interior, rents 14 fine rooms (Sb-2,500 Kč, Db-3,400 Kč, Db suite-3,900 Kč, Tb-4,600 Kč, 10 percent cheaper off-season, back/quiet rooms face the garden, front/noisier rooms face the street, air-con, elevator, 10-min walk south of Wenceslas Square, Metro: I.P. Pavlova, Kateřinská 16, Praha 2, tel. 224-920-636, fax 224-920-626, www.hotel16.cz, hotel16@hotel16.cz).

$ **Dům u Šemíka,** a friendly hotel named for a heroic mythical horse, is in a residential neighborhood just below Vyšehrad Castle, a 10-minute tram ride from the center (25 rooms, Sb-1,700 Kč, Db-2,100–2,650 Kč, apartment-2,800–4,850 Kč depending on size, extra bed-700 Kč; from the center, take tram #18 to Albertov, then walk 2 blocks uphill; or take tram #7 to Výtoň, go under rail bridge, and walk 3 blocks uphill to Vratislavova 36; Praha 2, tel. 224-920-736, fax 224-911-602, www.usemika.cz).

$ **Guest House Lída,** with 12 homey and spacious rooms, fills a big house in a quiet residential area a 30-minute walk or 15-minute tram ride from the center. Jan and Jiří Prouza, who run the place, are a wealth of information and know how to make people feel at home (small Db-1,440 Kč, Db-1,760 Kč, Tb-2,110 Kč, 10 percent cheaper Nov–March, cash only, family rooms, top-floor family suite with kitchenette, garage parking-200 Kč/day, Metro: Pražského Povstání; exit Metro and turn left on Lomnicka between the Metro station and big blue glass ČSOB building, follow Lomnicka for 500 yards, then turn left on Lopatecka, go uphill, and ring bell at Lopatecka #26, no sign outside; Praha 4, tel. & fax 261-214-766, lida@login.cz). The Prouza brothers also rent four apartments across the river, equally far away (Db-1,500 Kč, Tb-1,920 Kč, Qb-2,100 Kč).

Across the River, near the Castle

$$$ **Hotel Sax,** on a quiet corner a block below the Little Quarter action, will delight the artsy yuppie with its 22 rooms, fruity atrium, and modern, stylish decor (Sb-3,700 Kč, Db-4,400 Kč,

Db suite-5,100 Kč, extra bed-1,000 Kč, cheaper off-season, elevator, near Church of St. Nicholas, 1 block below Nerudova at Jánský Vršek 3, Praha 1, reserve long in advance, tel. 257-531-268, fax 257-534-101, www.sax.cz, hotel@sax.cz).

$$$ Residence Domus Henrici, just above Castle Square, is a quiet retreat that charges—and gets—top prices for its eight smartly appointed rooms, some of which include good views (Ds-5,100 Kč, Db-5,600–6,200 Kč depending on size, extra bed-900 Kč, less off-season, pleasant terrace, Loretánská 11, Praha 1, tel. 220-511-369, fax 220-511-502, www.domus-henrici.cz, henrici@hidden-places .com). This is a five-minute walk above the castle gate in a quiet, elegant area.

$$$ Hotel u Žluté Boty ("By the Yellow Boot") is the most charming small hotel in Prague, hiding on a small lane in the Little Quarter. Each of its seven rooms has a completely different feel: Some preserve the 16th-century wooden ceilings, some feel like mountain lodges, and others are a bit marred by an insensitive 1970s adaptation. The manager's husband is a distinguished artist whose paintings (for sale) embellish the dining room and halls. The only drawback of this hotel are its thin walls—you'll know exactly what your neighbors are arguing about (Sb-3,700 Kč, Db-4,200 Kč, Tb-4,900 Kč, 25 percent less off-season, Jánský Vršek 11, tel. 257-532-269, fax 257-534-134, www.zlutabota.cz, hotel@zlutabota.cz).

Youth Hostels

$ Hostel Sokol, plain and institutional, with 100 beds, is peacefully located just off the parklike Kampa Island in the Tryš House buildings (the seat of the Czech Sokol Organization). Big, WWI hospital–style rooms are lined with single beds and lockers (8–14 per room, 350 Kč per bed, D-900 Kč, cash only, no breakfast, easy to reserve by phone or e-mail without deposit, open 24/7, members' kitchen, Nosticova 2, Praha 1, tel. 257-007-397, fax 257-007-340, www.sokol-cos.cz, hostel@sokol-cos.cz). From the main train station, ride tram #9 to Újezd. From the Holešovice station, take tram #12 to Újezd.

$ Art Prison Hostel fills a former prison in the basement of Pension Unitas (see page 94). With tiny, high windows and no plumbing, the rooms are stark—but not as stark as when Václav Havel did time here (64 beds, S-1,000 Kč, D-1,100 Kč, dorm beds in 4- to 5-bed cells for 370 Kč, includes sheets and breakfast, easy reservations without deposit if arriving by 17:00, no curfew, non-smoking, shared, modern facilities, lockers, Bartolomějská 9, tel. 224-221-802, www.unitas.cz, unitas@unitas.cz).

$ Hostel Elf, a fun-loving, ramshackle place covered with noisy, self-inflicted graffiti, has cheap, basic beds, a helpful staff, and lots of creative services—kitchen, free luggage room, laundry, no lockout, free tea, cheap beer, a terrace, and lockers (dorm beds-260–340 Kč,

D-820 Kč, includes sheets and breakfast, on a train line a 10-min walk from main train station and Florenc bus station, Husitská 11, Praha 3, tel. 222-540-963, www.hostelelf.com, info@hostelelf.com).

EATING

A big part of Prague's charm is enjoyed wandering aimlessly through the winding old quarters, marveling at the architecture, watching the people, and sniffing out fun restaurants. You can eat well here for very little money. What you'd pay for a basic meal in Vienna or Munich will get you an elegant feast in Prague. Choose between traditional, dark Czech beer-hall ambience; elegant *Jugendstil,* early-20th-century atmosphere; ethnic; or hip and modern.

Watch out for scams. Many restaurants put more care into ripping off green tourists (and even locals) than in their cooking. Tourists are routinely served cheaper meals than what they ordered, given a menu with a "personalized" price list, charged extra for things they didn't get, or shortchanged. Avoid any menu without clear and explicit prices. Carefully examine your itemized bill and understand each line (a 10 percent service charge is sometimes added—in that case, there's no need to tip extra). Be careful of waiters padding the tab: Tax is always included in the price, so it shouldn't be tacked on later. Part with very large bills only if necessary, and deliberately count your change. Never let your credit card out of your sight, and check the numbers carefully. Make it a habit to get cash from an ATM to pay for your meals. Remember, there are two parallel worlds in Prague: the tourist town and the real city. Generally, if you walk two minutes away from the tourist flow, you'll find better value, ambience, and service.

In the Old Town
Art Nouveau Restaurants
The sumptuous Art Nouveau concert hall—**Municipal House** (Obecní Dům)—has three special restaurants: a café, a French restaurant, and a beer cellar (Náměstí Republiky 5). The dressy café, **Kavarna Obecni Dům,** is drenched in chandeliered, Art Nouveau elegance (light, pricey meals and drinks with great atmosphere and bad service, 250-Kč hot meal special daily, open daily 7:30–23:00, live piano or jazz trio 16:00–20:00, tel. 222-002-763). **Francouzska Restaurace,** the fine and formal French restaurant, is in the next wing (700- to 1,000-Kč meals, daily 12:00–16:00 & 18:00–23:00, tel. 222-002-777). **Plzeňská Restaurace,** downstairs, brags it's the most beautiful Art Nouveau pub in Europe (cheap meals, great atmosphere, daily 11:30–23:00, tel. 222-002-780).

Restaurant Mucha is touristy, with decent Czech food in a formal Art Nouveau dining room (300-Kč meals, daily 12:00–24:00, Melantrichova 5, tel. 224-225-045).

Cheap, Uniquely Czech Places near Old Town Square

Prices go way down when you get away from the tourist areas. At least once, eat in a restaurant with no English menu.

Pivnice u Zeleného Stromu ("At the Green Tree") is a new beer garden/cellar in an old building serving great beer and inexpensive traditional cuisine from a fun, imaginative menu. The courtyard is quiet, and the cellar is bright and fresh (good veggies, daily 11:00–23:00, next to Bethlehem Chapel at Betlémská Náměstí 6, tel. 222-220-228).

Klub Architektů is a modern student hangout with a medieval cellar serving cheap vegetarian meals, hearty salads, and a few "gourmet entrées" next to Bethlehem Chapel (Betlémská Náměstí 169, tel. 224-401-214).

U Medvídků, which started out as a brewery in 1466, has been a huge and popular beer hall since the 19th century. The food, beer, and service are fine, and the ambience is bright, noisy, and not too smoky (daily 11:30–23:00, a block toward Wenceslas Square from Bethlehem Square at Na Perštýně 7, tel. 224-211-916).

Plzeňská Restaurace u Dvou Koček ("By the Two Cats") is a typical Czech pub with cheap, no-nonsense, hearty Czech food and beer, and—once upon a time—a local crowd. Sandwiched between the two red light district streets, the restaurant's name is a bit ambiguous (200 Kč for 3 courses and beer, serving original Pilsner Urquell with accordion music nightly until 23:00, under an arcade, facing tiny square between Perlová and Skořepka Streets).

Restaurace Mlejnice is a fun little pub strewn with farm implements and happy eaters, tucked away just out of the tourist crush two blocks from the Old Town Square (order carefully and understand your itemized bill, daily 11:00–24:00, between Melantrichova and Železná at Kožná 14, reservations smart in evening, tel. 224-228-635).

Country Life Vegetarian Restaurant is a bright, easy, non-smoking cafeteria with a well-displayed buffet of salads and veggie hot dishes. It's midway between the Old Town Square and the bottom of Wenceslas Square. They are serious about their vegetarianism, serving only plant-based, unprocessed, and unrefined food (Mon–Thu 8:30–19:00, Fri 8:30–18:00, Sun 11:00–18:00, closed Sat, through courtyard at Melantrichova 15/Michalská 18, tel. 224-213-366).

Česká Kuchyně ("Czech Kitchen") is a blue-collar cafeteria serving steamy, old-Czech cuisine to a local clientele. There's no English inside, so—if you want apple charlotte, but not tripe soup—be sure to review the small English menu in the window outside before entering. Note the numbers of the dishes you'd like that correspond to the Czech menu you'll see inside. Pick up your tally sheet as you enter, grab a tray, point liberally to whatever you'd like, and keep the paper to pay as you exit. It's extremely cheap...unless you lose your paper (daily 9:00–20:00, across from Havelská Market at Havelská 23, tel. 224-235-574).

Bohemia Bagel is hardly authentic Czech—exasperated locals insist that bagels have nothing to do with Bohemia. Owned by an American, this trendy place caters mostly to youthful tourists, with good sandwiches (100–125 Kč), a little garden out back, and Internet access (1.50 Kč/min). It's close to the Old Town Square (daily 7:00–24:00, locations at Újezd 16, tel. 257-310-529, and Masná 2, tel. 224-812-560, www.bohemiabagel.cz).

Havelská Market, surrounded by colorful little eateries, offers piles of picnic fixings (see page 67).

Ethnic Restaurants for Local Yuppies near the Old Town Square

With the recent economic boom, young professional Czechs have money to eat out, and trendy little ethnic eateries are popping up everywhere. Within the space of a couple of blocks, you can eat your way around the world. Two blocks north of Old Town Square (up Dlouhá Street), wander along Rámová Street to Haštalská Square. You'll pass the **Ariana** (Afghan), **Orange Moon** (Thai/Indian), **Chez Marcel** (French), and **Dahab** (fancy or cheap Moroccan buffet, daily 12:00–24:00, Dlouhá 33, tel. 224-827-375).

Dining with an Old Town Square View

Restaurant u Prince Terrace, in the five-star U Prince Hotel, facing the astronomical clock, is designed for foreign tourists. A sleek elevator takes you to its rooftop, where every possible inch is used to serve good food (fish, Czech, and international) to its guests. The view is arguably the best in town—especially at sunset, when a reservation is smart. The menu is a fun and impressively affordable mix, with photos to make ordering easy (daily until 24:00, Staroměstské Náměstí 29, tel. 224-213-807).

Above the Castle

To locate the following restaurants, see the map on page 74.

Malý Buddha ("Little Buddha") serves delightful food—especially vegetarian—and takes its theme seriously. You'll step into a mellow, low-lit escape of bamboo and peace to be served by people with perfect complexions and almost no pulse. Ethnic eateries like this are trendy with young Czechs (Tue–Sun 13:00–22:30, closed Mon, non-smoking, from the castle hike up the hill nearly to the monastery, Úvoz 46, tel. 220-513-894).

U Hrocha ("By the Hippo"), a very local little pub packed with

Prague Restaurants

❶ Municipal House (3 restaurants)

❷ Restaurant Mucha

❸ Pivnice u Zeleneho Stromu Pub & Klub Architektu

❹ Beerhall u Medvídků

❺ Plzeňská Restaurace u Dvou Koček

❻ Restaurace Mlejnice

❼ Country Life Vegetarian Restaurant

❽ Czech Kitchen

❾ Bohemia Bagel (2 locations)

❿ Havelská Market

⓫ Ethnic eateries

⓬ Restaurant Zofin

⓭ To Rest. La Perle de Prague

⓮ Grand Café Slavia

⓯ Restaurant u Prince Terrace

⓰ Pub u Zlateho Tygra

⓱ Dobrá Čajovna Teahouse

beer-drinkers and smoke, serves simple, traditional meals—basically meat dishes with bread. Just below the castle near Little Quarter Square, it's actually the haunt of many members of Parliament—located just around the corner (daily 12:00–23:00, chalkboard lists daily meals in English, Thunovská 10).

Espresso Kajetánka, just off Castle Square, is a pricey café worth considering for the view and convenience (daily 10:00–20:00, on Ke Hradu, tel. 257-533-735).

In the Jewish Quarter

To locate these restaurants, see the map on page 82.

Kolkovna is a big, new, woody-yet-modern place catering to locals and serving a fun mix of Czech and international cuisine (ribs, salads, cheese plates, good beer, daily 11:00–24:00, across from Spanish Synagogue at V Kolkovně 8, tel. 224-819-701).

Franz Kafka Café is pleasant for a snack or drink (daily 10:00–21:00, a block from the cemetery, Široká 12).

Fine Dining near the River in the New Town

Restaurant Žofín is a Prague institution, taking you back to the era of waltzing elegance. Nicknamed for Franz Josef's mother, Sofia, it shares a circa-1880 palace with a famous ballroom on a small island south of Charles Bridge (mostly traditional, 3-course *menus* range from simple/310 Kč to gourmet/990 Kč, huge and reasonable wine list, plain garden tables or sumptuous reserve-in-advance indoor tables, Slovanský Island, reach island by bridge south of National Theater, tel. 224-934-548).

La Perle de Prague fills the seventh and eighth floors of Frank Gehry's wild and modern Dancing House building with Prague's high society and top-end visitors enjoying a fine river view and gourmet French cuisine. It's white-tablecloth dressy and offers terrace seating in good weather. While few tables are actually by the window, be sure to enjoy a pre-dinner drink or sip your last glass of wine upstairs, next to Fred Astaire's wire-mesh head, on the roof terrace (500-Kč business lunch, 900-Kč dinner *menu*, daily 12:00–14:00 & 19:00–22:30, reservations required to even get in the elevator, 15-min walk south of Charles Bridge, Tancící Dům, Rašínovo Nábřeží 80, tel. 221-984-160, www.laperle.cz).

Grand Café Slavia, across from the National Theater (facing the Legií Bridge on Národní Street), is a fixture in Prague, famous as a hangout for its literary elite. Today, it's a bit tired, with an Art Deco interior, lousy piano entertainment, and celebrity photos on the wall. But its cheap and fun menu, filled with interesting traditional dishes (meals, sweets, coffees, liqueurs—including absinthe for 55 Kč), make it a fun stop (daily 8:00–23:00, sit nearest the river). Notice the *Drinker of Absinthe* painting on the wall (and on the menu)—with the iconic Czech writer struggling with reality.

In the Little Quarter

Restaurace Rybářský Klub, on Kampa Island, is run by the Society of Czech Fishermen and serves the widest and tastiest selection of freshwater fish in Prague, at reasonable prices. Dine on fish cream soup, pike, trout, carp, or catfish under the imaginative artwork of local Malá Strana painter Kuba (3-course meal for around 300 Kč, daily 12:00–23:00, U Sovových Mlýnů 1, tel. 257-534-200).

Restaurace David, with two little 18th-century rooms hiding on a small cobblestone street opposite the American embassy, is the best place in town for an elegant meal. The exquisite cuisine—a mix of Czech and European styles, ranging from game to roasted duck and liver—is served in the most artistic of arrangements, and the waiters move around with the grace of the 19th century (most meals 600–1,000 Kč, reservations highly recommended, Tržiště 21, tel. 257-533-109).

In Vinohrady and Žižkov

Café Medúza ("Jellyfish"), an authentic, between-the-world-wars café with plush sofas and pictures of 1930s movie stars, draws a crowd of dreamy young Czechs enjoying coffee, cigarettes, cheap lunch specials, and dark Svijany beer (Mon–Fri 11:00–1:00, Sat–Sun 12:00–1:00, Belgická 17, Metro: Náměstí Míru, from Metro stop walk a bit down and look for Belgická on your left, tel. 222-515-107).

At **Hlučná Samota** ("Too Loud a Solitude"), the wooden floor and brick walls are dedicated to the great Czech writer Bohumil Hrabal. Though he never visited here, Hrabal would surely be delighted by some of the most beautiful waitresses in Prague, as well as the rich mix of Czech and Italian cuisine (including honey ducks, spinach salmon, and Prague's own Staropramen beer to wash it all down). An outdoor lunch—under the shade of linden trees on the quiet, circa-1900 Zagreb street—can easily stretch out into an all-afternoon affair (daily 11:00–23:00, Záhřebská 14, tel. 222-522-839, www.hlucnasamota.cz).

Restaurace U Sadu, on Škroupa square below the Žižkov TV Tower, is popular with young Czechs in the summer. An outdoor lunch on this quiet square under a futuristic monument must be one of the most atmospheric eating options in Prague. The restaurant up in the TV tower itself is expensive, but gives you Neil Armstrong's perspective on Prague.

Hospůdka nad Viktorkou, named for this neighborhood's soccer team, is around the corner on Bořivojova street. This quintessentially blue-collar Žižkov pub features occasional live performances by local bands, a warm glass terrace in the winter, and a little courtyard with a shady canopy of chestnut trees in the summer. Sipping a beer while chatting with locals in this purest of Prague institutions—you'll feel like you've really found the true Prague.

Drinks

Beer

For many, *pivo* (beer) is the top Czech tourist attraction. Two classic places to enjoy a Pilsner are **U Zlatého Tygra** ("By the Golden Tiger"), just south of Karlova on Husova (daily 15:00–23:00, often jam-packed) and **Hostinec u Pinkasů**, in the dead-end alley just off the bottom of Wenceslas Square. While you're sipping your brew, read the "Czech Beer" sidebar on page 46.

Tea

Many Czech people are bohemian philosophers at heart and prefer the mellow, smoke-free environs of a teahouse to the smoky, traditional beer hall. Young Czechs are much more interested in traveling to exotic destinations like Southeast Asia, Africa, or Peru than to Western Europe, so Oriental teahouses set their minds into vacation mode.

While there are teahouses all over town, a fine example in a handy locale is Prague's original one, established in 1991: **Dobrá Čajovna** ("Good Teahouse," Mon–Sat 10:00–21:30, Sun 14:00–21:30, near the base of Wenceslas Square, opposite McDonald's at Václavské Náměstí 14, www.cajovna.com). This teahouse, just a few steps off the bustle of the main square, takes you into a very peaceful world that elevates tea to an almost religious ritual. At the desk, you'll be given an English menu and a bell. Grab a seat and study the menu, which lovingly describes each tea. The menu lists a world of tea (very fresh, prices by the small pot), "accompaniments" (such as Exotic Miscellany), and light meals "for hungry tea-drinkers." When you're ready to order, ring your bell to beckon a tea monk—likely a member of the "Lovers of Tea Society."

TRANSPORTATION CONNECTIONS

Getting to Prague: Centrally located Prague is a logical gateway between Western and Eastern Europe. If you're coming from the West and using a Eurailpass, you must purchase tickets to cover the portion of the journey from the Czech border into Prague (buy at station before you board train for Prague). Or supplement your pass with a Prague Excursion pass, giving you passage from any Czech border station into Prague and back to any border station within seven days (first class-€50, second class-€40, youth second class-€30). EurAide, a travel agency with offices in Berlin (see page 596) and Munich, also sells these passes for a bit less from their American office (U.S. tel. 941/480-1555, fax 941/480-1522, www.euraide.de/ricksteves). From the East, Prague has convenient night-train connections with Budapest, Kraków, and Warsaw (see below).

For Czech train and bus schedules, see www.vlak-bus.cz. Train info tel. 221-111-122 (little English).

From Prague by train to: Český Krumlov (8/day, 1/day direct, 4 hrs, verify departing station), **Berlin** (5/day, 5 hrs), **Munich** (3/day with changes, 6 hrs; 1 direct night train), **Frankfurt** (4 direct/day, 6 hrs), **Vienna** (3/day, 5 hrs), **Budapest** (5 direct/day, 7 hrs), **Kraków** (1 direct night train/day, 8.5 hrs; otherwise transfer in Katowice, Wrocław, or Ostrava-Svinov, 8–11 hrs), **Warsaw** (2/day direct, including 1 night train, 9–12 hrs; or 1/day, 9 hrs, with transfer in Ostrava-Svinov).

By bus to: Český Krumlov (7/day, 3.5 hrs, from Florenc station; an easy, direct 3-hr bus leaves at about 9:00).

By car with a driver: Mike's Chauffeur Service is a reliable, family-run little company with fair and fixed rates around town and beyond. Friendly Mike's motto is, "We go the extra mile for you" (round-trip fares with waiting time included, guaranteed through 2005 with this book: Český Krumlov-3,500 Kč, Terezín-1,700 Kč, Karlštejn-1,500 Kč, up to 4 people, minibus also available, tel. 241-768-231, mobile 602-224-893, www.mike-chauffeur.cz, mike .chauffeur@cmail.cz). On the way to Krumlov, Mike will stop at no extra charge at Hluboká Castle or České Budějovice, where the original Bud beer is made. Mike offers a "Panoramic Transfer to Vienna" for 7,000 Kč (depart Prague at 8:00, arrive Český Krumlov at 10:00, stay up to 6 hrs, 1-hr scenic Czech riverside-and-village drive, then 2-hr Autobahn to your Vienna hotel, maximum 4 people). Mike also offers a similar "Panoramic Transfer to Budapest" for 10,000 Kč (2 hrs to Český Krumlov, then 1 hr scenic drive to Linz, followed by 5-6 hrs on the expressway to Budapest).

ČESKÝ KRUMLOV

Lassoed by its river and dominated by its castle, this enchanting town feels lost in a time warp. While Český Krumlov is the Czech Republic's answer to Germany's Rothenburg, it has yet to be turned into a medieval theme park. When you see its awe-inspiring castle, delightful Old Town of shops and cobbled lanes, characteristic little restaurants, and easy canoeing options, you'll understand why having fun is a slam dunk here.

Český Krumlov (CHESS-key KROOM-loff) means roughly "Czech bend in the river." Calling it "Český" for short sounds silly to Czech-speakers (since dozens of Czech town names begin with "Český"). "Krumlov" for short is okay.

Since Krumlov is the second-most-visited town (1.5 million visits annually) in the Czech Republic, there's enough tourism to make things colorful and easy—but not so much that it tramples the place's charm. This town of 15,000 attracts a young, bohemian crowd, drawn here for its simple beauty and cheap living.

Planning Your Time

Because the castle and theater can be visited only with a guide (and English tours are offered just a few times a day), serious sightseers should call the castle to reserve these tours first thing, and then build their day around these times. (Those who hate planning ahead on vacation can join a Czech tour anytime with an English information sheet.)

A paddle down the river to Zlatá Koruna is a highlight (4 hrs, see "Canoeing and Rafting the Vltava," page 114), and a hike up to the mountain Kleť takes you into the heart of Czech woods (5 hrs round-trip, see "Hiking," page 114). Other sights are quick visits and worthwhile only if you have a particular interest (Egon Schiele, puppets, torture, and so on). The town itself is a joy and the major attraction. Evenings are for atmospheric dining and drinking. Sights are generally open 10:00 to 17:00 and closed on Monday.

ORIENTATION

Český Krumlov is extremely easy to navigate. The snaking Vltava River, which makes a perfect S through the town, ropes the Old Town into a tight peninsula. Český Krumlov's one main street starts at the isthmus and heads through the peninsula, winding through town, continuing across a bridge, and snaking through Castle Town, the castle complex (a long series of courtyards), and the castle gardens high above. The main square, Náměstí Svornosti—with the TI, ATMs, banks (close at 17:00), and taxis—marks the center of the peninsula and dominates the Old Town. All recommended restaurants and hotels are within a few minutes' walk of the square. No sight in town is more than a five-minute stroll away.

Tourist Information

The eager-to-please TI on the main square recently won an award as the best TI in the Czech Republic (July–Aug daily 9:00–20:00, June and Sept daily 9:00–19:00, March–May and Oct daily 9:00–18:00, Nov–Feb daily 9:00–17:00, tel. 380-704-622, www.ckrumlov.cz). Pick up the free city map. The 129-Kč *City Guide* book explains everything in town and includes a fine town and castle map in the back. The TI can check train, bus, and flight schedules, and will change traveler's checks (fair rate). Ask about concerts, city walking tours in English, car rentals, and canoe trips on the river. The TI can book rooms, but it'll take a 10 percent deposit (actually a commission) that will be "deducted" from your (inflated) hotel bill. Save your host money and go direct.

Arrival in Český Krumlov

Taxis are cheap; don't hesitate to take one into the center from the train station (about 100 Kč) or bus station (around 60 Kč).

By Train: The train station is a 15-minute walk from town (turn right out of the station, then walk downhill onto a steep cobbled path leading to an overpass into the town center).

By Bus: The bus station is just three blocks away from the Old Town (from the bus station lot, drop down to main road and turn left, then turn right at Potraviny grocery store to reach the center).

Český Krumlov

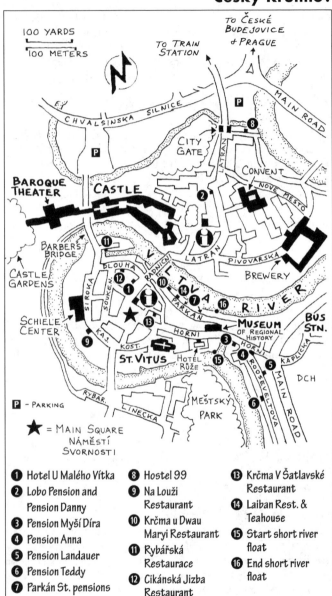

P – PARKING

★ = MAIN SQUARE
NÁMĚSTÍ
SVORNOSTI

1 Hotel U Malého Vítka
2 Lobo Pension and
  Pension Danny
3 Pension Myší Díra
4 Pension Anna
5 Pension Landauer
6 Pension Teddy
7 Parkán St. pensions

8 Hostel 99
9 Na Louži
  Restaurant
10 Krčma u Dwau
   Maryi Restaurant
11 Rybářská
   Restaurace
12 Cikánská Jizba
   Restaurant

13 Krčma V Šatlavské
   Restaurant
14 Laiban Rest. &
   Teahouse
15 Start short river
   float
16 End short river
   float

Helpful Hints

Internet Access: Fine Internet cafés and access points are all over town and in many of the accommodations. The TI on the main square has several fast, cheap, stand-up stations good for a quick visit.

Laundry: Pension Lobo runs a self-service launderette under the castle (daily, 100 Kč/load, Latrán 73).

Festivals: Locals drink oceans of beer and celebrate their medieval roots at big events such as the Celebration of the Rose (Slavnosti Růže), where blacksmiths mint ancient coins, jugglers swallow fire, mead flows generously, and pigs are roasted on open fires (June 18–19 in 2005). The summer also brings a top-notch jazz and alternative music festival to town, performed in pubs, cafés, and the castle gardens (Aug 20–21). During the St. Wenceslas celebrations, the square becomes a medieval market, and the streets come alive with theater and music (Sept 24–25). Reserve a hotel well ahead of time if you'll be in town for these dates.

TOURS

Walking Tours—The TI offers worthwhile, guided 90-minute historic town walking tours in English (July–Sept daily at 10:00 and noon, 225 Kč, just show up, meet in front of TI on main square, buy ticket from guide, minimum 2 people, self-guided audioguide also available—60 Kč/hr).

Also consider the one-hour brewing history tour, which takes you into the Eggenberg brewery (July–Sept daily at 12:00, 150 Kč, meet in front of the TI).

Private Guides—Jiří (George) Václavíček is a local teacher who enjoys showing visitors around during his off-hours (afternoons, evenings, and weekends). Jiří—a gentle and caring man who seems to fit mellow Český Krumlov perfectly—is a joy to share this town with. He's happy to work for as little as an hour (€10/hr, tel. 380-726-813, mobile 603-927-995, jiri.vaclavicek@seznam.cz). Another guide service provides private tours for 250 Kč per hour (you name the place and time, mobile 723-069-561).

SIGHTS

Old Town

Main Square (Náměstí Svornosti)—Lined by Renaissance and Baroque homes of burghers, the main square has a grand charm. There's continuity here. Lékárna, with the fine, red Baroque facade on the lower corner of the square, is still a pharmacy, as it has been since 1620. McDonald's tried three times to get a spot here, but was

Český Krumlov History

With the natural moat provided by the sharp bend in the Vltava, it's no wonder that this has been a choice spot for eons. Celtic tribes first settled here a century before Christ. Then came German tribes. The Slavic tribes arrived in the 9th century. The Rožmberks—Bohemia's top noble family—ran the city from 1302 to 1602. In many ways, the 16th century was the town's golden age, when Český Krumlov hosted an important Jesuit college. The Hapsburgs bought the region in 1602, ushering in a more Germanic period.

The rich mix of Gothic, Renaissance, and Baroque buildings is easy to underappreciate. As you wander, look up...notice the details in the stonework that survive. Step into shops, snoop into back lanes and tiny squares. Gothic buildings curve with the winding streets. Many precious Gothic and Renaissance frescoes were whitewashed in Baroque times (when the colorful trimmings of earlier times were way out of style). Today, these precious frescoes are being rediscovered and restored.

With its rich German heritage, it was easy for Hitler to claim that this region—the Sudetenland—was rightfully part of Germany. So, in 1938, in one of the bold and arrogant moves that led to World War II, he just took it. After the war, in a kind of Potsdam

turned away. The Town Hall flies the Czech flag and the town flag, which shows the rose symbol of the Rožmberk family, who ruled the town for 300 years.

Imagine the history this square has seen: In the 1620s, the rising tide of Lutheran Protestantism threatened Catholic Europe. As Krumlov was a seat of Jesuit power and learning, the intellectuals of the Roman church burned 5,000 books on this square. Later, when there was a bad harvest, locals blamed witches—and burned them. Every so often, terrible plagues rolled through the countryside. In a village nearby, all but two residents were killed by a plague.

But the plague stopped before devastating the people of Český Krumlov, and in 1715—as a thanks to God—they built the plague monument that marks the center of the square today. Much later, in 1938, Hitler stood right here before a backdrop of long Nazi banners to celebrate the annexation of the Sudetenland. And, in 1968, Russian tanks spun their angry treads on these same cobblestones to intimidate locals who were demanding freedom. Today, thankfully, this square is part of an unprecedented peace and prosperity for the Czech people.

Torture Museum—This is just a lame haunted house: dark, with sound effects, cheap modern models, and prints showing off the cruel and unusual punishments of medieval times (80 Kč, daily 9:00–20:00, English descriptions, facing the main square).

Treaty–approved ethnic cleansing, three million Germans in Czech lands were sent west to Germany. Emptied of its German citizenry, Český Krumlov turned into a ghost town inhabited mostly by robbers and Gypsies. Picture Gypsy squatters with their fires in the stately noble homes that line the town's main square.

In 1945, Americans liberated the town. But, in the post-WWII world as planned by Stalin and FDR, the border of the Soviet and American spheres of influence fell just about here. While the communist government established order, the period from 1945 to 1989 was a smelly time capsule. The town was infamously polluted—its now pristine river was foamy from the paper mill just upstream. The hills around the town were marred with blocks of prefabricated concrete. But the people who moved in never fully identified with town—in Europe, a place without ancestors is without roots that give it life. The bleak years of communism here paradoxically provided a cocoon to preserve the town. There was no money, so little changed, apart from a build-up of grime. But today, with its new prosperity, Český Krumlov is emerging as a fairytale town. In fact, movie producers consider it ideal for films. *The Adventures of Pinocchio,* starring Jonathan Taylor Thomas, was filmed right here.

Barber's Bridge (Lazebnicky Most)—This wooden bridge, decorated with 19th-century statues, separates the Castle Town and Old Town. On the center stands a statue of St. John of Nepomuk, the same guy as on the Charles Bridge. Among other responsibilities, he is the protector against floods. In the great floods of August 2002, the angry river submerged the bridge and swept away the banisters...but the bridge survived.

Church of St. Vitus—Český Krumlov's main church was built as a bastion of Catholicism in the 15th century, when the Roman Catholic Church was fighting the Hussites. The Baroque 17th-century high altar, showing St. Vitus and the Virgin Mary, is capped with St. Wenceslas. He is the patron saint of the Czech people, and long considered their ambassador in heaven. The canopy now in the back—featuring a Rožmberk atop a horse—was once at the high altar. Too egotistical for Jesuits, it was moved to the rear of the nave (daily 10:00–19:00, Sunday Mass at 9:30).

Museum of Regional History—Located in the town center, this small museum gives you a quick look at regional costumes, tools, and traditions. Ask for the simple English translation, which also includes a lengthy history of Krumlov. Start on the second floor, where you'll see old paintings, a glimpse of noble life in Krumlov, and a ceramic model of town as it was in 1800. The first floor comes with fine folk costumes and domestic art and a Bronze Age exhibit. The postcards in the hallway offer a fun look at Český Krumlov in the old days. Inside, you will also find the census from 1850, when 75 percent of the town's inhabitants were German. In 1945, the percentage was about the same—until most were expelled (50 Kč, daily 10:00–18:00, Horní 152).

Hotel Růže—Located across the street from the Museum of Regional History, this former Jesuit college hides a beautiful Renaissance courtyard. Pop inside to see a couple of bronze busts. The one on the right, dedicated by the Czech freedom fighters, commemorates the first Czechoslovak president, Tomáš Garrigue Masaryk (held office 1918–1934). The bust on the left recalls Masaryk's successor, Edvard Beneš (held office 1934–1948).

Egon Schiele Art Center—This classy contemporary art gallery has top-notch temporary exhibits, generally featuring 20th-century Czech artists, and a top-floor permanent collection celebrating the Viennese artist Egon Schiele (pronounced "Sheila," like the woman's name), who once spent a few weeks here during a secret love affair. A friend of Gustav Klimt and an important figure in the Secessionist movement in Vienna, Schiele lived a short life, from 1890 to 1918. His cutting-edge lifestyle and harsh and graphic nudes didn't always fit the conservative, small-town style of Český Krumlov, but townsfolk are happy to charge you to see some of his edgy art today (180 Kč, daily 10:00–18:00, Široká 70, tel. 380-704-011).

Krumlov Castle (Krumlovský Zámek)

No Czech town is complete without a castle—and now that the nobles are gone, their mansions are open to us common folk. The castle complex, worth ▲▲, includes bear pits, the castle itself, a rare Baroque theater, and groomed gardens.

Round Tower (Zámecká Věž)—The strikingly colorful round tower marks the place of the first castle, built here to guard the medieval river crossing. With its 16th-century Renaissance paint job colorfully restored, it looks exotic, featuring a fancy astrological decor, terra-cotta symbols of the zodiac, and a fine arcade. Climb its 162 steps for a great view (30 Kč, daily 9:00–18:00, last entry 17:30).

Bear Pits—At the site of the castle drawbridge, the bear pits hold a family of brown European bears, as it has since the Rožmberks started this tradition in the 16th century. Bears implied a long and noble family lineage.

Castle—The immense castle is a series of courtyards with shops, contemporary art galleries, and tourist services. To see the inside, you're required to choose between Tour I (Gothic and Renaissance objects—of most general interest) and Tour II (19th-century castle life, Baroque art, and tapestries). No pictures are allowed in the castle.

Most tours are in Czech, and English tours come with an extra cost and a longer wait. (Visit the richly decorated Renaissance courtyard—the third one—while you're killing time). The information on the English tour, mostly given by students working a summer job, comes straight from an English information sheet you can pick up yourself at the ticket office. If you're pressed for time or would rather go at your own pace, ask for the sheet and join a Czech-language tour. If you decide to take the English tour, chat up the guides as you go to divert them from their typical spiel.

Once inside, you'll get a glimpse of the places where the Rožmberks, Eggenbergs, and Schwarzenbergs dined, studied, worked, prayed, entertained, and slept. Imagine being an aristocratic guest here, riding the dukes' assembly line of fine living: You would promenade through a long series of elegant spaces and dine in the sumptuous dining hall before enjoying a concert in the Hall of Mirrors, which leads directly to the theater. After the play, you'd go out into the château garden for a fireworks finale (Tour I-150 Kč, Tour II-140 Kč, each tour 1 hr, 8–45 people per group, June–Aug Tue–Sun 9:00–12:00 & 13:00–18:00, spring and fall until 17:00, closed Mon and Nov–March, tel. 380-704-721).

▲▲**Baroque Theater (Zámecké Divadlo)**—Europe once had several hundred fine Baroque theaters. Using candles for light and fireworks for special-effects, most burned down. Today, only two survive in good shape and are open to tourists: One at Stockholm's Drottningholm Palace, and one here at this castle. Along with a look at the precious theater itself and a video of it in action, you'll see lots of surviving theater gear: a dozen or so painted sets, hundreds of costumes, and original special-effects and sound-making machinery. Scenes could be changed in 10 seconds. (Fireworks blinded the audience, and, when the smoke cleared, it was a new scene.) Unfortunately, the number of visitors is strictly regulated, and there are only three English tours a day—often sold out in advance. Call 380-704-721 to establish English-language tour times and reserve a space; getting a ticket is generally a frustrating experience (170 Kč, 45-min tours daily May–Oct only, departures at 10:00, 11:00, 13:00, 14:00, 15:00, and 16:00).

Castle Gardens—This 2,300-foot-long garden crowns the castle complex. It was laid out in the 17th century, when the noble family would light it with 22,000 oil lamps, torches, and candles for special occasions. The lower part is geometrical and symmetrical—French style. The upper is rougher—English style (free, daily 8:00–19:00, April and Oct until 17:00, closed in winter).

The Church of the Annunciation of St. Mary—In 1350, the town began building this church and its attached convent. Today, you can walk under the Gothic vaults and peek into Baroque chapels where monks once meditated (30 Kč).

ACTIVITIES

▲▲▲**Canoeing and Rafting the Vltava**—Český Krumlov lies in the middle of a popular boating valley. Make time to paddle around the town or through Bohemian forests and villages of the nearby countryside.

The easy half-hour experience is to float around the city's peninsula, starting and ending at opposite sides of the tiny isthmus. (Heck, you can do it twice.) Longer trips involve a minibus transfer. If you're starting upriver from Krumlov (Rožmberk direction), you'll go faster, with more white water—but the river parallels a road, so it's a little less idyllic. Going downstream from Krumlov (direction České Budějovice), you'll have more pastoral scenery and less excitement. You can choose among destinations that take one to eight hours of floating and paddling (lots of work involved, even though you're going downstream). At a set time and place, the minibus will meet you. You'll encounter plenty of inviting pubs and cafés for breaks along the way. Plan on getting wet. There's a little white water, but the river is so shallow that if you tip, you simply stand up and climb back in. (When that happens, pull the canoe out to the bank to empty it, since you'll never manage to pour the water out while still in the river.)

Choose from a kayak, canoe (fastest, less work, more likely to tip), or inflatable raft (harder rowing, slower, but very stable). Rates vary from 300 Kč for the 30-minute canoe or raft trip around the town; to 700 Kč for a three-hour, 15-km (9-mile) float; to 1,000 Kč for a 35-km (22-mile), all-day trip. Prices are per boat (2–6 people) and include a map and transportation to or from the start and end points. Several companies offer this lively activity. Perhaps the handiest are Půjčovna Lodí Maleček Boat Rental (open long hours daily April–Oct, closed Nov–March; they also run the recommended Pension Myší Díra—see "Sleeping," below, Rooseveltova 28, tel. 337-712-508, lode@malecek .cz) and the slightly less expensive Cestovní Agentura Vltava (April–Oct daily 9:00–18:00, closed Nov–March, in the Pension Vltava at Kájovská 62, tel. 380-711-988, www.ckvltava.cz). Vltava also rents mountain bikes for 320 Kč per day.

Slupenec Horseback Riding Club—Head about a mile out of town for horseback rides and lessons (Tue–Sun 10:00–18:00, closed Mon, 1 hour outdoors or in the ring-250 Kč, all-day ride-1,800 Kč, helmets provided, René Srncová, Slupenec 1, tel. 380-711-052, www .jk-slupenec.cz).

Hiking—Start at the trailhead by the bear pits below the castle. Red-and-white trail markers will take you on an easy six-mile hike around the neighboring slopes and villages. The green-and-yellow stripes mark a five-mile hiking trail up the Kleť mountain—with a 1,800-foot altitude gain. At the top, you'll find the oldest observation tower in the country (now a leading center in discovering new planets). On clear days, you can see the Alps (observatory tours July–Aug, Tue–Sun every hour 10:30–15:30, 30 Kč, www.hvezdarna.klet.cz).

SLEEPING

Krumlov is filled with small, good, family-run pensions offering doubles with baths for 1,000–1,500 Kč and hostel beds for 300 Kč. Summer weekends and festivals are busiest and most expensive (for dates, see "Festivals," on page 109); reserve ahead when possible. Hotels speak some English and accept credit cards; pensions rarely do either. While you can find a room upon arrival here, it's better to book at least a few days ahead if you want to stay in the heart of town.

In the Old Center

$$$ **Hotel u Malého Vítka** is right in the old center and consists of a tangle of Gothic vaults and staircases connecting comfy, woodsy rooms. As some standard doubles are much bigger than others, and all are the same price, it's worth requesting a larger standard room. The deluxe rooms—unless you're dying for a whirlpool tub—aren't worth the higher cost (standard Db-1,450 Kč, bigger deluxe Db-2,400 Kč, Radniční 27, tel. & fax 380-711-925, www.vitekhotel.cz, vitekhotel@email.cz).

Under the Castle

A quiet, cobbled pedestrian street (Latrán) runs below the castle just over the bridge from the Old Town. It's a 10-minute walk downhill from the train station. Lined with characteristic shops, the street has a couple of fine little family-run, eight-room pensions.

$ **Lobo Pension** fills a modern, efficient concrete building with fresh, spacious rooms (Sb-700 Kč, Db-1,000 Kč, Tb-1,400 Kč, includes parking, Latrán 73, tel. & fax 380-713-153, www.pensionlobo.cz).

$ **Pension Danny** is a little funkier, with homier rooms and a tangled floor plan above a restaurant (Db-850 Kč, apartment Db-1,000 Kč, breakfast in room, Latrán 72, tel. 380-712-710, www.pensiondanny.cz).

Between the Bus Station and Old Town

$$ **Pension Myší Díra** ("Mouse Hole") hides eight sleek, spacious, bright, and woody Bohemian-contemporary rooms overlooking the Vltava River, just outside the Old Town. The reception, which closes at 20:00, runs a tourist service and rents river boats (standard Db-1,000–1,700 Kč depending on season, bigger deluxe Db with river view-1,200–2,000 Kč, Fri–Sat most expensive, breakfast in your room, 28 Rooseveltova Street, tel. 337-712-853, fax 380-711-900,

---

Sleep Code

(25 Kč = about $1, country code: 420)
S = Single, **D** = Double/Twin, **T** = Triple, **Q** = Quad,
b = bathroom, **s** = shower only. Unless otherwise noted, credit
cards are accepted, and prices include breakfast.

To help you sort easily through these listings, I've divided
the rooms into three categories based on the price for a standard
double room with bath:

$$$ **Higher Priced**—Most rooms 1,300 Kč or more.
$$ **Moderately Priced**—Most rooms between 1,000–1,300 Kč.
$ **Lower Priced**—Most rooms 1,000 Kč or less.

---

www.ceskykrumlov-info.cz, pension@ceskykrumlov-info.cz).

$$ *Pensions on Rooseveltova:* Rooseveltova street, midway
between the bus station and the Old Town (a 4-minute walk from
either), is lined with fine little eight-room places, each with easy free
parking. **Pension Anna** is well-run, with cozy rooms and a restful little
garden (Db-1,200 Kč, apartment Db at 1,500 Kč is a great deal, Tb-
1,800 Kč, apartment Qb-2,100 Kč, Rooseveltova 41, tel. & fax 380-
711-692, pension.anna@quick.cz). **Pension Landauer**, with small and
simple but comfortable rooms, is a fair value (Sb-500 Kč, Db-1,000
Kč, cash only, Rooseveltova 32, tel. & fax 380-711-790). **Little
Pension Teddy** has several riverview rooms sharing a common balcony
(Db-1,200 Kč, Tb-1,700 Kč, cash only, Rooseveltova 38, tel. 380-711-
595, info@teddy.cz).

$ *Pensions on Parkán:* Parkán street, which runs along the river
below the square, has a row of pensions with one or two rooms
each. These places have a family feel and charge around 1,000 Kč
for two people: **Ubytování Novotný** (Parkán 106, tel. 380-716-575,
ubytovani.novotny@tiscali .cz), **U Vltavy** (Parkán 107, tel. 380-716-
396, mobile 603-338-008), **Miroslava Janotová** (Parkán 115, tel.
380-714-805), and **Sladová Hana** (Parkán 125, tel. 602-363-049).
For more rooms, check www.ckrumlov.cz.

$ **Hostel 99,** one of several hostels in the Old Town, is closest to
the train station and has a pleasant, mellow feel. Its fine picnic-table
terrace looks out on the Old Town, and the gentle sound of the river
gurgles outside your window. It caters to its guests, offering free inner
tubes for river floats, bike rentals, and a free keg of beer each
Wednesday. The adjacent Hospoda 99 restaurant serves good, cheap
soups, salads, and meals (55 beds in 6- to 10-bed rooms, 300 Kč, D-
700 Kč, T-900 Kč, use the lockers, no curfew or lockout, a 10-min
downhill walk from train station or two bus stops to Spicak, Vezni 99,
tel. & fax 380-712-812, www.hostel99.com, hostel99@hotmail.com).

EATING

Na Louži seems to be everyone's favorite little Czech bistro, with 40 seats in one 1930s-style room decorated with funky old advertisements. They serve inexpensive, tasty Czech cuisine and the hometown Eggenberg beer. If you've always wanted to play the piano for an appreciative Czech crowd in a colorful little tavern...do it here (Kájovská 66, tel. 337-711-280).

Krčma u Dwau Maryi ("Tavern of the Two Marys") is a characteristic old place with idyllic riverside picnic tables serving old Czech cuisine and drinks (daily 11:00–23:00, Parkán 104, tel. 337-717-228). The fascinating menu explains the history of the house and makes a good case that the food of the poor medieval Bohemians was tasty and varied. Buck up for buckwheat, millet, greasy meat, or the poor-man's porridge.

Cikánská Jizba is a Gypsy tavern filling one den-like, barrel-vaulted room. Krumlov has a big Gypsy history, and even today, 1,000 live on the edge of town. While this little, 40-seat restaurant won't win any cuisine awards, the characteristic Gypsy food is served under a mystic-feeling Gothic vault, and you never know what festive and musical activities will erupt (2 blocks toward castle from main square at Dlouhá 31, tel. 380-717-585).

Krčma V Šatlavské is an old prison gone cozy, with an open fire, big wooden tables under a rustic old medieval vault, and tables outdoors on the pedestrian lane. It's great for a late drink or game cooked on an open spit. *Medovina* is the hot honey wine (daily 12:00–24:00, on Šatlavská, follow lane leading uphill from TI on main square, tel. 608-973-797).

Laiban is the modern vegetarian answer to the carnivorous Middle Ages. Sit back in comfy straw chairs or head out onto the river terrace, and lighten up your pork-loaded diet with soy goulash or Mútábúr soup (daily 11:00–23:00, Parkán 105). The Krumlov Buddha dwells in the attached tea room (Tajemná Čajovna).

Rybářská Restaurace ("Fisherman's Restaurant") doesn't look particularly inviting from outside, but don't get discouraged. This is *the* place in town to taste freshwater fish you've never heard of (and never will again). Try eel, perch, shad-fish, carp, trout, and more (daily 11:00–22:00, on the island by the mill wheel).

TRANSPORTATION CONNECTIONS

Check both train and bus schedules at the TI or www.vlad-bus.cz. To get to Prague, take the bus—it's faster, cheaper, and easier than by train.

From Český Krumlov by train to: Prague (7/day, change usually required, 4 hrs), **Vienna** (4/day, 6 hrs), **Budapest** (4/day with at least one change, 11 hrs). Virtually all train rides to/from Český Krumlov require a transfer in České Budějovice.

By bus to: Prague (140 Kč, 7/day, 3.5 hrs, 2 departures a day—11:35 and 16:45—can be reserved and paid for at TI or simply buy tickets from driver), **Vienna** (the Travellers' Hostel offers a direct bus service to Vienna three times weekly in summer: Mon, Wed, and Fri at 14:00; 900 Kč, 4 hrs, tel. 380-711-345, www.travellers.cz). The Český Krumlov bus station, a five-minute walk out of town, is just a big parking lot with numbered stalls for various buses.

By private car: If money is no object, hiring a private car can be efficient, especially to Budapest (the TI has referrals).

SLOVAKIA
(Slovensko)

Slovakia is the West Virginia of Central Europe—poor, relatively undeveloped, but spectacularly beautiful in its own rustic way. Sitting quietly in the center of Central Europe, wedged between stronger and more prosperous nations (the Czech Republic, Hungary, and Poland), Slovakia was brutally disfigured by the communists, then overshadowed by the Czechs.

But make no mistake: Even though their nation is just over a decade old, Slovaks have their own distinct nation, language, and capital. The more time you spend here, the clearer it becomes: Slovaks are not Czechs. Now independent, the Slovaks are striving to define their own nation and pull their country up to Western standards.

For most of their histories, the Czechs and the Slovaks had little in common aside from geographic proximity and linguistic similarity. While the Czechs have generally looked to the Germans for cultural direction, Slovakia spent centuries as part of Hungary. The two peoples converged when they both became part of the same Hapsburg Empire, and melded together officially only in the 20th century, with the creation of Czechoslovakia. This union of the Czechs and the Slovaks came at the hands of a charismatic, visionary politician named Tomáš Masaryk, who was himself half Czech and

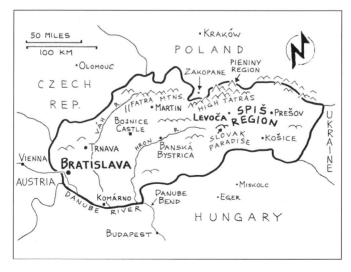

How Big, How Many, How Much

- Slovakia is 18,840 square miles (the combined size of New Hampshire and Vermont).
- Population is 5.4 million (10 percent Hungarian and—unofficially—about 10 percent Gypsy).
- 30 Slovak koruna (Sk) = about $1
- Country code: 421

half Slovak. Masaryk's tenuous union was useful for its time, but artificial and ultimately destined to dissolve. And dissolve it did—peacefully—in 1993's so-called Velvet Divorce (see sidebar on page 122).

Slovakia is far more ethnically diverse than the Czech Republic. Among Slovakia's large minority groups are Hungarians (about 10 percent of the population), many of whom still cling to the century-old glory days when this was called Upper Hungary and ruled from Budapest. Another large group—very loosely estimated at 10 percent of the population—are the Gypsies (see page 136). Rounding out the cultural cocktail are Czechs, Ruthenians (Carpathian Mountain peasants of Ukrainian origin), and a smattering of Germans.

While the Czechs take pride in a marked agnosticism, the Slovaks tend to be more devout Catholics—more like their *other* neighbors, the Poles. In fact, there are many commonalities between the Poles and the Slovaks—including their strong agricultural (rather than industrial) heritage before communism, and many linguistic similarities—leading to the conclusion that Slovaks are every bit as much like Poles as they are like Czechs.

The northeastern half of Slovakia features the beautiful rolling hills and spiky, jagged peaks of the Carpathian Mountains, while the southwestern half is quite flat—a continuation of the Hungarian Plain. Traditionally an agricultural region, Slovakia was heavily industrialized by the Soviets. Rusting factories now stand where fertile farmlands once were. Gradually, the Slovaks are rebuilding their ailing economy, often with the help of Western investors.

Why is there so little coverage of Slovakia in this book? Frankly, with so many other knockout destinations in Eastern Europe, Slovakia barely makes the "best of" cut. First-timers in a hurry will probably want to skip the country. But for some, Slovakia provides an opportunity to enjoy some fine natural beauty and ponder a European country that's poor and developing—yet still safe and friendly.

Slovakia vs. the Czech Republic

Slovakia, compared to the Czech Republic, is...
- less Germanic, more Slavic and Hungarian
- less agnostic, more Catholic (like the Poles)
- less urban, more agricultural
- less hilly, more dramatically mountainous
- less wealthy, with much higher unemployment
- less homogenous, more ethnically diverse (with Slovaks, Czechs, Hungarians, Gypsies, Ruthenians)
- less cultured and refined, more rough-and-tumble and salt-of-the-earth

Practicalities

Telephones: Insertable telephone cards, sold at newsstands and kiosks everywhere, get you access to the modern public phones.

When calling locally, dial the number without the area code. To make a long-distance call within the country, start with the area code (which begins with 0). To call a Slovak number from abroad, dial the international access number (00 if calling from Europe, 011 from the United States or Canada), followed by 421 (Slovakia's country code), then the area code (without the initial 0) and the number. To call out of Slovakia, dial 00, the country code of the country you're calling (see chart in appendix), the area code if applicable (you may need to drop initial zero), and the local number.

Slovak History

Even though it is more recently associated with the Czech Republic, Slovakia was for centuries ruled from Budapest and known as Upper Hungary. When the Ottoman Turks occupied most of Hungary, the Hungarians moved their capital to Bratislava. But even throughout the long era of Hungarian domination, most people living in Slovakia were Slavs. Today, there are large Hungarian, Gypsy, and Romanian minorities.

Czechoslovakia was formed at the end of World War I, when the Austro-Hungarian Empire was splitting into pieces. During this flurry of new nation-building, a small country of 10 million Czechs or five million Slovaks was unlikely to survive. These two Slavic peoples decided it was best to unite, allowing them to balance the many Germans and Hungarians that lived in the same region. The union was logical enough—especially in the eyes of Tomáš Masaryk, Czechoslovakia's first president (and a buddy of Woodrow Wilson's from Princeton). Masaryk was from the border of the two regions and spoke a dialect that mixed elements of Czech and Slovak. Czechoslovakia was born.

It's Not You, It's Me: The Velvet Divorce

In the autumn of 1989, hundreds of thousands of Czechs and Slovaks streamed into Prague to demonstrate on Wenceslas Square. Their "Velvet Revolution" succeeded, and Czechoslovakia's communist regime peacefully excused itself.

The Czechs and Slovaks were forced to redefine their roles in the post-communist world. Ever since they had joined with the Czechs in 1918, the Slovaks felt like second-class citizens within their own nation. Prague was unmistakably the political, economic, and cultural capital of Czechoslovakia. And the Czechs, for their part, resented the financial burden of their poorer neighbors to the east. With their new freedom, the Czechs found themselves with a 10 percent unemployment rate...compared to 20 or 30 percent unemployment in the Slovak lands. In this new world of flux, long-standing tensions came to a head.

The dissolution of Czechoslovakia began over a hyphen, as the Slovaks wanted to rename the country Czecho-Slovakia. Ideally, this symbolic move would come with a redistribution of powers: two capitals, two UN reps, but one national bank and a single currency. The Slovaks were also less enthusiastic about abandoning the communist society altogether, since the Soviet regime had fundamentally changed their agricultural-based economy to a heavily industrialized one that depended on a socialist element for survival.

The Czechs and the Slovaks were constantly reminded that they were countrymen in name only. In a prelude to World War II, these two peoples were again split along the cultural fault that always divided them: Today's Czech Republic was absorbed into Germany, while much of the Slovak land went to Nazi-friendly Hungary.

During the communist era, the regime decided to convert the Slovak economy from a low-key agricultural model to a base of heavy industry. But the industry was centrally planned for communist purposes, not organically developed—so it made sense only as a cog in the communist machine. Many of Slovakia's factories built heavy arms, making the country the biggest producer of tanks in the world. Slovakia became one of the ugliest and most polluted corners of the Eastern Bloc. The Slovak environment—and economy—are still recovering.

When the wave of uprisings spread across Eastern Europe in 1989, Czechoslovakia peacefully achieved its own freedom with the Velvet Revolution. But then the Slovaks wanted their own nation, capital, and parliament. On January 1, 1993, Czechoslovakia amicably split into two nations: the Czech and Slovak Republics (see sidebar). While this has proved beneficial for the Czechs, many Slovaks—now over their initial excitement—will tell you that the split was probably a mistake.

The Czechs rebuffed the Slovaks' requests—the Slovaks were just being silly, and should just keep quiet and enjoy the ample coattails the Czechs were providing. The first post-communist president of Czechoslovakia, the Czech Václav Havel, made matters worse when he took a rare trip to the Slovak half of his country in 1990. In a fit of terrible judgment, Havel promised he'd close the ugly, polluting Soviet factories in Slovakia...neglecting the fact that many Slovaks still depended on these factories for survival. Havel left in disgrace and visited the Slovak lands only twice more in the next two and a half years.

In June 1992, the Slovak nationalist candidate, Vladimír Mečiar, fared surprisingly well in the elections—proving that the Slovaks were serious about secession. At the ballot box, the Slovaks decisively sent the message: "We want to separate!" The Czechs said, incredulously, "Really?" Then, "Okay!"

Though public opinion in both halves of the country opposed separation (the people never actually voted on the split), the politicians soon agreed on the terms. The Velvet Divorce was official on January 1, 1993, and the Slovaks finally had their own capital (Bratislava), currency (Slovak *koruna*), and head of state (Mečiar). The Slovaks let loose a yelp of excitement, the Czechs emitted a sigh of relief...and geography teachers everywhere swore silently.

After the so-called Velvet Divorce, the first president of Slovakia was a former boxer named Vladimír Mečiar, whose authoritarian rule was not much better than the communists'. Mečiar was frequently accused of corruption (including pulling issues off the ballot when they seemed to be going against him), and people suspect he was involved in the kidnapping, torture, and humiliation of one of his political opponent's sons in 1995. He was also notorious for making offensive statements about his country's substantial Hungarian and Gypsy minorities. Mečiar drew criticism from neighboring Eastern and Western European nations, as well as the United States. He was finally defeated at the polls in 2000, but—like a bad penny—he keeps turning up, nearly winning elections in 2002 and 2004.

Though Mečiar remains a factor in the political landscape, support for him seems to be dwindling, and Slovakia's political situation is improving. Slovakia joined the Czech Republic, Poland, Hungary, and Slovenia in becoming EU members in May 2004—a monumental step forward. Still, the Slovaks are slow to embrace these changes. In the EU parliamentary elections held a few months after their joining, Slovakia had the lowest voter turnout of the 25 EU nations. While many cynics argue that Slovaks earned their EU membership only on the coattails of their onetime countrymen, the

Key Slovak Phrases

English	Slovak	Pronounced
Hello. (formal)	Dobrý deň.	DOH-bree dyehn
Hi. / Bye. (informal)	Ahoj.	AH-hoy
Do you speak English?	Hovoríte po anglicky?	hoh-VOH-ree-teh poh ANG-lits-kee
Yes. / No.	Áno. / Nie.	AH-no / nyeh
Please. / You're welcome. / Can I help you?	Prosím.	PROH-seem
Thank you.	Ďakujem.	DYAH-koo-yehm
I'm sorry. / Excuse me.	Prepáčte.	preh-PAHCH-teh
Good.	Dobro.	DOH-broh
Goodbye.	Do videnia.	doh vih-DAY-neeah
one / two	jeden / dva	YAY-dehn / dvah
three / four	tri / štyri	tree / SHTEE-ree
five / six	päť / šesť	peht / shehst
seven / eight	sedem / osem	SEH-dyehm / OH-sehm
nine / ten	deväť / desať	DYEH-veht / DYEH-saht
hundred	sto	stoh
thousand	tisíc	TYEE-seets
How much?	Koľko?	KOHL-koh
local currency	koruna (Sk)	koh-ROO-nah
Where is...?	Kde je...?	gday yeh
...the toilet	...záchod	ZAH-khohd
men	muži	MOO-zhee
women	ženy	ZHAY-nee
water / coffee	voda / káva	VOH-dah / KAH-vah
beer / wine	pivo / víno	PEE-voh / VEE-noh
Cheers!	Na zdravie!	nah ZDRAH-vyeh
the bill	účet	OO-cheht

Czechs, others point to Slovakia's increasingly strong economy. Although Slovakia is among the poorest EU countries, things are looking up—low costs and an unbeatable location have attracted many foreign automakers to build plants here, leading *The New York Times* to dub Slovakia "the European Detroit." While their path has not always been smooth, Slovaks are looking to the future with optimism about their role in a united Europe.

Slovak Food

Slovak cuisine is similar to Czech cuisine—with lots of starches and gravy, and plenty of pork, cabbage, and potatoes (see "Czech Food," page 45). If there's anything distinctive about Slovak food, it's the slight Hungarian influences—Slovaks use more paprika than their Czech cousins. Slovakia also has a strong tradition of grilling pickled meats. Also keep an eye out for Slovakia's national dish, *bryndzové halušky* (small potato dumplings with sheep's cheese and bits of bacon). Like the Czechs, the Slovaks produce fine beer *(pivo)*. One good brand is Zlatý Bažant ("Golden Pheasant").

Slovak Language

Many people assume Slovak is virtually the same as Czech. To be sure, there are similarities. But they're hardly identical.

Slovak is handy as a sort of a lingua franca of Slavic tongues. Czechs can understand Poles, but not Slovenes; Poles can understand Croatians, but not Czechs. But Slovak speakers generally find they can understand—and be understood in—any of these languages.

Slovak's similarity to Czech was exaggerated during the 75 years that they shared a country. Soccer games would be broadcast with two commentators—one spoke Czech, and the other spoke Slovak. Anyone growing up in this era grew comfortable using the languages interchangeably. But today's preteens—who have grown up speaking exclusively Czech or Slovak—find they have trouble understanding each other.

BRATISLAVA
and the SPIŠ REGION

There are two schools of thought on Slovakia. Some people love the country for its stark natural beauty and because it's an exciting cultural detour off the prettified tourist mainstream. Slovakia gives more adventurous travelers the opportunity to feel the pulse of a nation that's still struggling to transition into democracy—and yet is still stable and safe enough to be comfortable. These people enjoy hiking along Slovakia's glorious mountain trails, driving through its impoverished villages, interacting with its kind and simple people, and pondering the blemish that communism has left on its pastoral landscape.

Other people can't wait to leave Slovakia, turned off by its drab industrial skeletons, relative poverty, and dearth of must-see sights compared to the rest of Eastern Europe. Most first-timers blitzing pretty-as-a-postcard Eastern Europe wish they'd spend more time elsewhere...and should.

What is clear is that Slovakia is not your standard European country. With lots of pleasant surprises, Slovakia is worth a peek for hardy travelers in that first category. The country's capital, Bratislava, is perfectly situated at the western tip of the country, right on the train line between Budapest and Vienna. Meanwhile, up in the north—not far from the Polish border—is the most beautiful part of this mountainous country: the rolling hills of the Spiš Region and jagged peaks of the High Tatras.

For more in-depth information about Slovakia, pick up a copy of *Spectacular Slovakia*, an excellent annual magazine produced by the English-language newspaper in Bratislava (www.spectacularslovakia.sk).

Planning Your Time in Slovakia
Don't mistake Slovakia's convenient location for sightseeing worthiness. A couple of hours (as a layover on the Budapest–Vienna train) is plenty for Bratislava. The Spiš Region is a handy place to break up the

long drive between Kraków and Hungary, but it's a complicated detour if you're connecting those places by public transportation (since the train line actually veers far to the east, through Košice, and bus access is measly and frustrating). If relying on public transportation from Kraków to Hungary, I'd sleep through Slovakia on the night train.

Bratislava

For centuries, Bratislava—known as "Pressburg" to its German inhabitants—was a complex and beautiful city, with deep roots in many different cultures: Slovak, German/Austrian, Hungarian, Jewish, Romanian, and Roma (Gypsy). The Hungarians used the city—which they called "Poszony"—as their capital during the century and a half that Buda and Pest were occupied by Turkish invaders. Later, Bratislava was one of Hapsburg Empress Maria Theresa's favorite cities. Everyone from Hans Christian Andersen to Casanova sang the wonders of this city on the Danube. When Czechoslovakia was formed at the end of World War I, the city shed its German and Hungarian names, proudly taking the new Slavic name "Bratislava."

In the 20th century, Bratislava became the textbook example of a historic city whose multilayered charm and delicate cultural fabric were destroyed and shrouded in gray by the communist regime. The communists were more proud of their ultramodern suspension bridge, Most SNP, than of the historic Jewish quarter they razed to make way for it. Now the bridge and its highway slice through the center of the Old Town, and the heavy traffic rattles the stained-glass windows of St. Martin's Cathedral as it rumbles past.

But today's Bratislava is gradually coming back to life—more slowly, perhaps, and less confidently than Prague or Kraków. The city is blessed with a charming enough, increasingly rejuvenated Old Town and a priceless location on the Danube (and the tourist circuit) smack-dab between Budapest and Vienna. The outdoor cafés hum with life on a summer day, and the youthful city is looking to the future. Though it is unlikely that the Slovak capital will ever become the "next Prague," in the coming years, travelers are sure to rediscover its charms and put it squarely back on the list of worthwhile visits.

Planning Your Time
If you're passing through anyway, and have time to kill, Bratislava just barely merits a sightseeing sprint. The city is worth only a few hours—making it a rewarding stretch-your-legs stopover on a day going between two other European capitals, Budapest and Vienna. (Though frankly, I'd rather skip Bratislava altogether to spend more time in those other two capitals.)

I've listed no hotels in Bratislava. There's hardly any reason to spend the night here, and beds are better (and often cheaper) in nearby Vienna and Budapest.

ORIENTATION

(area code: 02)
Bratislava, with nearly half a million residents, is Slovakia's capital and biggest city. It has a small, colorful Old Town (Staré Mesto) surrounded by the ugly communist/functionalist sprawl of the new town and suburbs. Don't be distracted by the outskirts, and stay focused on what matters: the Old Town and castle.

Bratislava's grim Stalinist vibe isn't all bad. It offers an opportunity for a cultural scavenger hunt deep into the guts of apartment-block neighborhoods, where the average Jans of the "Evil Empire"—from here to Beijing—eked out their lives. Across the river from the Old Town, the suburb called Petržalka is gloomy and harrowing, in a *1984*-comes-to-life sort of way.

Beware: Bratislavans in the tourist zone sometimes try to short-change and otherwise rip off their city's visitors as brazenly as their Prague cousins do. Check your bill and count your change carefully.

Tourist Information
The TI, called the Bratislava Culture and Information Center, has two branches. There's a small window in the **train station** (Mon–Fri 8:00–18:00, closed Sat–Sun), and the **main branch** is across the square from the back of the town hall on Primaciálne Námestie (June–Sept Mon–Fri 8:30–19:00, Sat–Sun 10:00–17:00; Oct–May Mon–Fri 8:30–18:00, Sat 9:00–14:00, closed Sun; Klobučnícka 2, tel. 02/5443-3715, http://bkis.bratislava.sk). Pick up the free map and browse their strange assortment of brochures; they can also help you find a room for 50 Sk.

The main TI shares an office with the Bratislava **tour guide association** (tel. 02/5443-4059, bkis@bratislava.sk). They offer a one-hour Old Town walking tour in English every day at 14:00 (400 Sk, 2 people minimum). You can also hire your own local guide, but (strangely) it costs twice as much as hiring a guide in Prague or Kraków (1,000 Sk/hr).

Arrival in Bratislava
Bratislava's main train station, called Bratislava Hlavná Stanica, is about a half mile north of the Old Town. As you emerge from the tracks, an ATM and the TI are to your left, and the luggage check desk is to your right (look for *úschovňa batožín*; there are no lockers, and the check desk usually closes for 30-min lunch and dinner

Bratislava

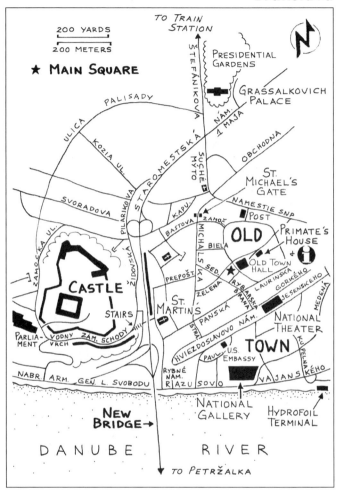

breaks; try to confirm that they'll be there when you get back if you'll be rushing to catch a train).

It's an easy 15-minute walk to the center. If you want to shave a few minutes off the trip, you can go part of the way by **tram** (from main hall, with tracks at your back, look for signs to *električky* on left; take escalator down, buy a "basic ticket" from the machine, and hop on tram #1).

To **walk**, leave through the front door and head past the buses to the busy street. Take the overpass across the street, and continue straight on Štefánikova. After about 10 minutes, you'll pass the nicely manicured presidential gardens on your left, then the Grassalkovich Palace, Slovakia's "White House." Continue straight, then bear right through the busy intersection, and head for the green onion dome. This is St. Michael's Gate, at the start of the Old Town.

SIGHTS

On a short visit, it's enough to simply wander the Old Town, enjoy a drink at an outdoor café, and soak in Slovakia. If you need more diversion than that, you can hike up to the castle. More low-impact sightseeing options include a pair of dusty, sleepy museums in the heart of the Old Town (described below).

Old Town Wander—Bratislava's mostly traffic-free Old Town is peppered with cute, colorful Baroque buildings. Once dreary, this area is slowly coming back to life. From the sta-

tion, you'll come through the onion-domed **St. Michael's Gate** (Michalská Brána), the last remaining tower of the city wall. From here, stroll down Michalská Street, lined with lively, colorful cafés (with relaxing outdoor tables in the summer). As you wander the Old Town, keep an eye out for **whimsical statues**—like the nosy admiral watching over the bench in the Main Square. The most famous—a guy dubbed Čumil ("the Peeper"), grinning at passersby from a manhole—is a block down, at the intersection of Panská and Rybárska. Others to look for are a sneaky paparazzo and a jovial chap doffing his top hat (named Schöner Náci).

Two blocks down, the name of this main drag changes to Ventúrska, and the café scene continues. When the street jogs right, turn left, along Zelená, and head for the Main Square—the bustling centerpiece of Old World Bratislava.

At the top of the **Main Square** (Hlavné Námestie) is the **Old Town Hall** (Stará Radnica). This place, constantly added on to over the centuries, is a mish-mash of architectural styles. It houses a ho-hum **town history museum**, with a climbable tower and a torture museum in the basement (50 Sk, Tue–Fri 10:00–17:00, Sat–Sun 11:00–18:00, closed Mon).

On the other side of the Old Town Hall is Bratislava's most interesting museum, the **Primate's House** (Primaciálny Palác, 40 Sk, Tue–Fri 10:00–17:00, Sat–Sun 11:00–18:00, closed Mon). This grand mansion, gradually expanded and glorified over several centuries by a series of archbishops who lived here, features fancy apartments, a Mirror Hall for concerts and meetings, a striking marble chapel, and a series of six English tapestries. While Bratislavans are very proud of this place, it simply doesn't rank with similar sights in Vienna or Budapest.

Backtrack to the Main Square. If you leave this square at the bottom (on Rybárska Brána), you'll reach the long, skinny square called **Hviezdoslavovo Námestie**—another part of Bratislava that has undergone much-needed rejuvenation recently, with sharp landscaping and cobbles upon cobbles of lazy cafés. At the east end of the square is the impressive, silver-topped Slovak National Theater (Slovenské Národné Divadlo), a reminder that Bratislava has long had a strong theatrical tradition.

From here, it's just a block to the Danube—passing the Slovak National Gallery, for those fascinated by Slovak art (big green building)—and a good look at the communists' pride and joy, the **New Bridge** (Nový Most, a.k.a. Most SNP). As with many Soviet-era landmarks around Eastern Europe, the locals aren't crazy about this structure—not only for the questionable starship *Enterprise* design, but also because of the oppressive regime it represents.

If you follow the Danube towards the bridge, before long you'll spot big **St. Martin's Cathedral** (Dóm Sv. Martina) on the right. This historic church isn't looking too good these days—and the highway thundering a few feet in front of its door (courtesy of the Soviets) doesn't help matters. If it were any closer, the off-ramp would go through the nave. Sad as it is now, the cathedral has been party to some pretty important history. Remember that while Buda and Pest were occupied by Turks for 150 years, Bratislava was the capital of Hungary. Many Hungarian kings and queens were coronated in this church. A replica of the Hungarian crown still tops the steeple.

If you walk under the highway, then start climbing the stairs marked *Zámocké Schody*, you'll wind up at...

Bratislava Castle (Bratislavský Hrad)—This imposing fortress, nicknamed the "upside-down table," is the city's most prominent landmark. The castle saw its finest days when Hapsburg Empress Maria Theresa took a liking to Bratislava in the 18th century, and decided she wanted to have a nice place to hold court here. But MT's castle burned to the ground in an 1811 fire, and it was left as a ruin for a century and a half—not reconstructed until 1953. The communist rebuild—especially inside the courtyard, which feels like a prison exercise yard—is drab and uninviting. The castle houses a few dull museums (history, musical instruments) and the chance to toss a coin down an

incredibly deep well (280 feet before you hear the plop—the same distance as to the Danube; find entrance at far left corner as you enter main courtyard). But the best reason to visit the castle is for the views—especially of the New Bridge and the endless communist apartment blocks of the Petržalka suburb across the river. By the way, the huge pointy monument back towards the train station is Slavín, where more than 6,800 Soviet soldiers who fought to liberate Bratislava from the Nazis are buried. A nearby church had to take down its steeple so as not to draw attention from the huge Soviet soldier on top of the monument.

TRANSPORTATION CONNECTIONS

From Bratislava by train to: Vienna (about hrly, 1 hr), **Budapest** (4/day direct, 2.25–4 hrs), **Prague** (3/day direct, 4.25–5.5 hrs).

You can also connect to both Vienna and Budapest by **boat** (see page 351).

The Spiš Region

The most beautiful part of Slovakia is the mountainous north-central region, comprising the jagged High Tatras and the Spiš region. The dramatic Carpathian Mountains slice through Central Europe here, dividing the Poles and Czechs in the north from the Hungarians and Yugoslavs in the south. With these Carpathian peaks as a backdrop, this region offers fine high-mountain scenery, easy river-rafting trips with a fun-loving guide through a breathtaking gorge, a classic, Old World walled town with one of Europe's finest Gothic altarpieces, a glimpse at Slovakia's complicated ethnic mix, and treacherous but legendary hiking trails in a place so pretty, they call it "paradise."

Planning Your Time

If you're driving south from Kraków, this region is right on the way to Eger in northern Hungary (and a workable detour en route to Budapest). It's trickier by public transportation; you'll have to approach it from Bratislava (not possible by train between Kraków and Eger/Budapest)—not worth the trip unless you're truly dedicated.

Getting Around the Spiš Region

I'd strongly suggest skipping this region if you don't have a car (take the night train between Poland and Hungary). If you do rely on public transportation, note that buses run between Levoča and Bratislava (often faster to train to Poprad, then bus to Levoča). For schedules, see www.cp.sk.

The Spiš Region

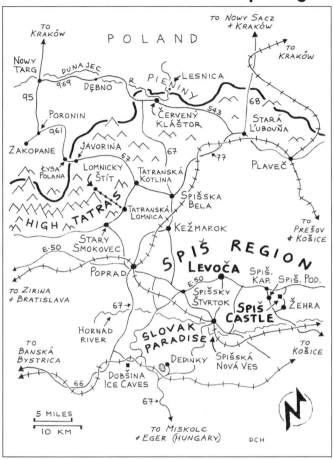

Levoča

It's not a stretch to call Levoča (LEH-voh-chah) Slovakia's finest small town—with a mostly intact medieval wall, a main square ringed by striking Renaissance facades, and one of the greatest Gothic altarpieces in all of Europe.

Levoča boomed in the Middle Ages, when trade between Hungary and Poland brought abundant merchant traffic through its gates. In the 15th century, the town's centerpiece was built: St. James Church. A local woodcarver named Master Pavol packed the church with one of the most impressive collections of altarpieces in the world—including the pièce de résistance, an exquisite 60-foot-high altar.

History of the Spiš Region

The Spiš (pronounced "speesh") region is one of the most historic and scenic corners of Slovakia. The region was named by the Hungarians, who controlled this area in the Middle Ages (the Hungarian word *szép* means "beauty"). After the Tartars swept through the region in the 13th century, decimating the local population, the Hungarians invited Saxons (from the region of Germany around Dresden) to come and resettle the land. Ore was discovered, and Spiš became a prosperous mining region, with 24 bustling, richly decorated Saxon towns (including Levoča). The region became a showcase of Gothic and, later, Renaissance architecture.

For centuries, the region was populated by a colorful mix of Saxons, Jews, and Slovaks. But after World War II, people of German heritage were brutally forced out of Czechoslovakia—including descendents of those Saxon settlers who arrived here centuries before. Spiš was abandoned, and many towns were repopulated by Slovaks, while others were settled by Roma (Gypsies).

Today's Spiš, while still suffering from economic ills, is emerging as a popular tourist destination (www.spis.sk).

In later years, Levoča fought and lost a PR war with the neighboring town of Spišská Nová Ves (8 miles south)—which was awarded a rail line in the 19th century and became a transportation hub for the region. S.N.V.'s loss was Levoča's gain, allowing Levoča to remain a wonderfully well-preserved Old World village of 10,000, rather than a glum, modern regional capital four times as large. If all of this makes Levoča feel off the beaten track, so much the better.

ORIENTATION

(area code: 053)

Levoča is small—you can walk from one end of the walled burg to the other in 15 minutes—and all roads lead to Námestie Majstra Pavla, the town's main square (named for the important woodcarver).

The **TI**, like most everything else of interest, is on the main square (tel. 053/451-3763, www.levoca.sk). You can hire your own **local guide** for just 500 Sk per hour. This is a cheap way to maximize your sightseeing time...and get to know a local (TI can help you arrange).

SIGHTS AND ACTIVITIES

▲**Church of St. James (Chrám Sv. Jakuba)**—This huge Gothic church, dominating Levoča's main square, contains 11 ornately decorated altars—including the tallest wooden altarpiece in the world.

The church dates from the 14th century. In the late 15th century, neighboring VIPs visited here. The greatest Hungarian king, Mátyás Corvinus, came in 1474 (for more on Corvinus, see sidebar on page 308). Two decades later, representatives of Poland's powerful Jagiellonian dynasty visited. These important visits remind us that Slovakia has long been at a crossroads of Eastern Europe.

In the early 16th century, the great sculptor Master Pavol left his mark on the church. Master Pavol's unique, almost cartoonish style features figures with too-big heads, strangely weepy eyes, and honest-to-goodness personalities. Pavol's masterpiece is the church's single most impressive sight: the 60-foot-tall **main altar**, carved out of linden wood and bathed in gold paint. The large central figures represent Mary and the Baby Jesus, flanked by St. James (the church's namesake, on left) and St. John the Evangelist (on right). The four panels surrounding these figures depict scenes from James' and John's lives and deaths. Beneath them is a depiction of the Last Supper. Unusual in Gothic art, each apostle has his own individual features (based on the local merchants who financed the work). With this and his other carvings, Master Pavol was knocking on the door of the Renaissance.

The nave is lined with several other altarpieces—some by Mastor Pavol, some by others. At the front of the right nave (right-hand corner), look for the altar depicting the **Passion of Christ**, carved for the 1474 visit of Hungarian King Mátyás Corvinus. Jesus looks like Mátyás, Mary resembles his Italian wife, and the altar was supposed to bring the couple good luck in having a child.

To the left as you view the main altar, notice the interesting medieval **frescoes** on the wall (splotchy from a bad 19th-century renovation job). The frescoes on the left depict the life of St. Dorothy. On the right are two strips. The upper strip shows a couple performing good deeds (feeding the hungry, visiting prisoners, and burying the dead). In the lower strip, they sit on animals representing the mortal sins.

As you leave, at the back of the left nave, look for Master Pavol's statue of **Mary**. As the Counter-Reformation swept Europe in the 16th century, locals feared for the fate of these sculptures from the iconoclasts (Catholics who destroyed religious symbols to unclutter their communion with God). They hid statues—including this one—in the Town Hall. Two centuries later, the long-forgotten statues were miraculously discovered, and brought back to the church....for you to enjoy.

The "Gypsy Question"

Eastern Europe is home to a silent population—mostly in Romania, Bulgaria, the Hungarian countryside, and this part of Slovakia—of millions of dark-skinned people who speak an Indian dialect and live according to their own rules. Whether roaming the countryside in caravans, squatting in dilapidated apartment blocks, conning tourists in big cities, or attempting to integrate with their white neighbors, these people are a world apart.

The better-known term for Europe's overlooked culture, "Gypsy," is increasingly considered derogatory. It isn't just politically incorrect—it's geographically mistaken, too...a holdover from the time when these people were thought to have come from Egypt. While the term isn't overtly offensive to most, it has taken on a neg-ative connotation (as with the ethnic slur, "I've been gypped!"). The situation is far worse in Slovakia, where the most widely used term for these people is *Cigany*—a term very closely related to the word for "liar." Today, among people in the know, the most widely accepted term for these people is "Roma" (though for ease of understanding, I've used the more familiar "Gypsy" elsewhere in this book).

The Roma most likely originated in today's India. (About two-thirds of today's European Roma speak a language called Romany—only written down in the last 20 years—which is related to contemporary Indian languages.) The Roma migrated into Europe through the Ottoman Empire (today's Turkey), arriving in the Balkan Peninsula in the 1300s. Under the Ottomans, the Roma weren't allowed into towns, but were still treated relatively well and were exempt from taxes. Traditionally, Roma earned their livelihood as entertainers (fortune telling, music and dancing, horse shows, dancing bears); as thieves; and as metalworkers (which is why they tended to concentrate in mining areas, like Slovakia and Kosovo).

Roma were initially not allowed to enter Austrian territory, but as the Hapsburgs recaptured lands once controlled by the Ottomans (like Slovakia and Hungary), they allowed the Roma to stay. In the 18th and 19th centuries—as "Gypsy music" funneled into the the-aters of Vienna and Budapest—a romantic image of Europe's Roma emerged. Though half a million Roma were butchered in Hitler's concentration camps, a large population continues to thrive here.

Cost, Tours, Hours: The cost is 50 Sk, and you can visit only at appointed times. The specific times are posted on the door of the church office, across the street from the church entrance (on the north side of the church, facing the top of the square). You'll be accompanied by a guide, but you don't have to listen to her spiel (usually Slovak only—but ask for English). Use the above informa-tion to appreciate the church, or find the talking box in the back of the nave and insert a coin for English. The church is open July–Aug Tue–Sat 9:00–17:00, Sun 13:00–17:00, Mon 11:00–17:00 (tours

Today's Roma are Europe's forgotten population—estimates range from 6 to 12 million. Unemployment among the Roma hovers around 70 percent. While only 3 percent of the Hungarian population is Roma, nearly two out of every three male prison inmates is a Roma.

Roma are subject to a pervasive bigotry otherwise unknown in today's Europe. Slovak news anchors—hardly fair or balanced—pointedly scapegoat the "liars" for problems. A small town in the Czech Republic tried to build a wall between its wealthy neighborhood and the Roma ghetto—until the European Parliament forced them to stop. Schools are sometimes carefully segregated, with signs reading, "Whites Only."

It's easy for us to criticize Eastern Europeans for their seemingly closed-minded attitudes. But to be fair, the Roma's poor reputation is at least partly deserved. Many Roma do turn to thievery for survival. It's downright foolish not to be suspicious if a Roma approaches you on the street. And the Roma population puts an enormous strain on the already overtaxed social welfare networks in these countries.

Still, the situation is tragic. Attempts at cooperation are often unsuccessful. The Roma—who, by their very nature, are nomadic and independent—generally aren't inclined to settle down and integrate. Roma who do find jobs and send their kids to school are shunned both by their fellow Roma, and by the white Europeans they're trying to integrate with. The communists attempted to force integration, sometimes splitting apartment buildings between Roma and Slavs. The Slavs moved out as soon as the regime fell.

So far, the Roma haven't produced a Martin Luther King, Jr., to organize and mobilize themselves—and many experts think they likely never will. The greatest "crossover" success stores are musicians and artists, with no political aspirations. Despite the best efforts of many well-intentioned people, the so-called "Gypsy Question" in Eastern Europe still doesn't have a satisfactory answer.

I'm not making excuses for the Roma. I try to approach the situation as an anthropologist would—considering both sides, and not allowing the prejudices of those I talk to most to influence my view of an entire population. If a Roma person approaches you on the street, keep your hand on your bag—but also try to keep an open mind.

every 30 min); Sept–Oct and Easter–June Tue–Sat 8:30–16:00, Sun 13:00–16:00, Mon 11:30–16:00 (tours roughly hourly, though not always at the top of the hour); Nov–Easter Tue–Sat 8:30–16:00, closed Sun–Mon (tours roughly hourly). Tel. 053/451-2347, mobile 0907-521-673, www.chramsvjakuba.sk/index.html.

House of Master Pavol—The biggest downside of the Church of St. James is that you can only see the breathtaking altarpieces from a distance, so you can't get a sense of what made Pavol the Master. At this museum, replicas of the statues allow you to get up close and personal with Pavol's creations—looking them right in their big, weepy eyes (30 Sk, daily 9:00–17:00, tel. 053/451-2786).

Levoča Town Hall (Radnica v Levoči)—The huge, Renaissance-style building behind the Church of St. James used to be the town

hall; now it's a museum of the town and region's history and colorful folk cultures. You'll watch a movie in English before wandering though a grand, wood-carved meeting hall (with beautifully painted ceiling) and rooms of maps of historic Levoča and the Spiš region (30 Sk, no good English information except paltry 20-Sk brochure, daily 9:00–17:00, tel. 053/451-2786). When Central Europe's presidents came to Levoča in 1998, they met in this building. Someone decided there weren't enough bathrooms, so they started to put more in the passage that connects the main building and the belfry. When construction began, they discovered fine sgraffito wall decorations under the plaster. They were uncovered, restored...and now adorn the new bathrooms (not open to the public).

Mariánska Hora—This humble church, overlooking Levoča from a dramatic perch on a nearby hill, has been an important site for pilgrimages for centuries. Every year, on the first weekend of July, hundreds of thousands of Slovaks flock to the hill from the surrounding countryside—many walking as far as 30 miles to get here. In 1995, the Pope made a pilgrimage here, saying Mass in front of some 650,000 people.

Near Levoča

Spiš Castle (Spišský Hrad)—Just a few miles from Levoča lies one of the largest and most dramatic cas-

tles in Europe: Spiš Castle. The castle watches over the Spiš from high on a bluff, overlooking a desolate terrain. Though there have been castles on this strategic spot for as long as there have been people here, the current version was built during the 15th century. Since its destruction in 1781, the castle has remained as the evocative ruins you see today.

The interior is tourable, though anyone you ask will tell you it's pretty dull in there (60 Sk, May–Oct daily 9:00–19:00, closed Nov–April, tel. 053/454-1336, www.spisskyhrad.sk). Even if there's not much to see inside, castle views don't get much more impressive than those from the surrounding countryside.

Spiš Castle is the centerpiece of a cluster of interesting sights. The town just below the castle is **Spišské Podhradie** (literally, "Under the Spiš Castle"). On a ridge opposite Spiš Castle is **Spišská Kapitula**, the site of the Spiš region's cathedral, surrounded by a modest village and an imposing 14th-century wall (cathedral entry-40 Sk, May–Sept daily 9:00–16:30, Nov–April Tue–Fri 11:00–14:45, closed Sat-Mon). And tucked behind Spiš Castle is **Žehra**, a village with a simple, onion-domed church that contains some impressive 13th- to 15th-century wall paintings.

Getting There: From Levoča, take the main road (E50) east. After 7.5 miles, you'll see the first turnoff, which takes you scenically past Spišská Kapitula and through Spišské Podhradie (park near town and hike all the way up, or cut through town back to the main road and wind around to "back way" up—see below). To get to the castle more directly, stay on past this exit and go another two miles, where there'll be a turnoff to the right leading up to the parking lot behind the castle.

Slovak Paradise (Slovenský Raj)—Outdoors enthusiasts from all over Central Europe flock to this paradise, and for good reason—it offers some of the most dramatic and enjoyable hikes this side of the Plitvice Lakes (see page 520). The Slovak Paradise is known for its seemingly treacherous trails—one oft-photographed stretch features ladders laid at sharp uphill angles, spanning a gaping gorge. The faint of heart should steer clear of these more challenging hikes; in other parts of the park, you'll find trails suitable for any hiker (www.slovenskyraj.sk). Spišská Nová Ves is the handiest gateway, on the northeastern fringe of the park (and with a convenient train station).

River Rafting in the Pieniny—A few miles north of Levoča, at the border with Poland, is the Pieniny region (www.pieniny.sk). Here, the Dunajec River flows through the impressive Dunajec Gorge in the shadows of sheer limestone cliffs, with Poland on one bank and Slovakia on the other.

The best way to experience the Pieniny is on a boat cruise. You'll board a *plt'*—a strange, pontoon-type raft made up of five canoe-like skiffs lashed together and bridged with long benches—and ply the waters of the Dunajec River. Your fun-loving conductor is dressed in the traditional costume of the Góral folk who populate this region. The trip is generally smooth—no white water to speak of—and offers a lazy chance to enjoy the scenery.

Rafting trips go roughly from early May through late October, weather permitting (daily 8:30–17:00, until 15:00 Sept–Oct, about 250 Sk per person, last about 1 hr). The best stretch of river is the 5.5-mile-long, U-shaped canyon that begins near the town of **Červený Kláštor** (literally, "Red Cloister"—which those not wanting to raft can also visit), and ends at the town of **Lesnica**. Hop on at a raft landing—marked as *prístav plt'í* on signs and maps. When you reach Lesnica, catch the bus back to your starting point...or hike the three miles back to Červený Kláštor.

SLEEPING

All of the presidents of Central European countries converged on Levoča for a conference in 1998, and you'll see photos of many of them decorating the few proud hotels in town. All of these hotels are right on the main square, Námestie Majstra Pavla.

$$$ Hotel Satel is a plush, swanky, soulless place that caters to tour groups. Its 23 frou-frou rooms are all pastel pinks, spread around a beautifully restored inner courtyard (Sb-1,850 Sk, Db-2,400 Sk, breakfast-150 Sk, elevator to some rooms, Námestie Majstra Pavla 55, tel. 053/451-2943, fax 053/451-4486, www.satel-slovakia.sk, hotel.satel.levoca@satel-slovakia.sk).

$$ Arkada Hotel is a nondescript place popular with tours. Its 32 rooms don't have much style (May–Sept: Sb-1,200 Sk, Db-1,800 Sk, lavish suite-2,000 Sk; Oct–April: Sb-1,040 Sk, Db-1,580 Sk, suite-1,780 Sk; extra bed-400 Sk, breakfast-120 Sk, Námestie Majstra Pavla 26, tel. 053/451-2372, fax 053/451-2255, www .arkada.sk, arkada@stonline.sk).

$$ Hotel Barbakan is a well-located, traditional-feeling place with character near the top of the main square. Though its 15 rooms are dark, it's a decent option for the price (May–Sept: Sb-1,100 Sk, Db-1,500 Sk, Tb/Qb-1,700 Sk; Oct–April: Sb-1,000 Sk, Db-1,300 Sk, Tb/Qb-1,500 Sk; extra bed-250 Sk, breakfast-150 Sk, secure parking-150 Sk, lots of stairs with no elevator, Košická 15, tel. 053/451-4310, fax 053/451-3609, www.barbakan.sk, recepcia.hot @barbakan.sk).

$ Penzión pri Košickej Bráne, at the top of the square, has

Sleep Code

(30 Sk = about $1, country code: 421, area code: 053)
S = Single, **D** = Double/Twin, **T** = Triple, **Q** = Quad,
b = bathroom, **s** = shower only. Credit cards are accepted and English is spoken at each place (unless otherwise noted).

To help you sort easily through these listings, I've divided the rooms into three categories, based on the price for a standard double room with bath:

$$$ **Higher Priced**—Most rooms 2,000 Sk or more.
$$ **Moderately Priced**—Most rooms between 1,000–2,000 Sk.
$ **Lower Priced**—Most rooms 1,000 Sk or less.

eight basic, cheap, thin-walled rooms that could be cleaner (prices per room, regardless of number of people: 1-bed room-600 Sk, 2-bed room-700 Sk, 3-bed room-800 Sk, cash only, Košická 16, mobile 0905-475-053, ubytovanie@penzionlevoca.sk, NSE).

EATING

Hotel Satel and **Hotel Barbakan**, above, both have restaurants. But **Reštaurácia u 3 Apoštolov** ("Three Apostles"), also right on the square, is a cut above, serving tasty Slovak cuisine. The decor is nothing special, but the food is delicious and cheap: pungent garlic soup, excellent trout, and the tasty "Apostle Specialty"—sautéed beef and vegetables in a spicy sauce, wrapped in a potato pancake (main dishes around 150 Sk, long hours daily, Námestie Majstra Pavla 11, tel. 053/451-2302).

The High Tatras (Vysoké Tatry)

While not technically in the Spiš region, Slovakia's most breathtaking mountain range is nearby. The High Tatras mountain range is small but mighty—dramatic, 9,000-foot peaks spiking up from the plains, covering an area of only about 100 square miles. This is the northernmost leg of the Carpathians, which stretch dramatically across the heart of Eastern Europe, extending all the way to Romania. The Tatras boast long, tranquil valleys, emerald mountain lakes, roaring waterfalls, and high mountain flora and fauna—including chamois, marmots, roebucks, stags, boars, bears, otters, and eagles. These cut-glass peaks have quickly become legendary among in-the-know Back Door travelers for the remarkably inexpensive hiking and skiing opportunities they present.

The High Tatras make up the Polish-Slovak border. Without a car, the most accessible approach is from the Polish resort town of **Zakopane** (an easy bus or train connection from Kraków). But for more rugged beauty, head to the southern part of the range, in Slovakia.

The mid-sized city of **Poprad**—not in the mountains, but sitting quietly on a plain about 10 miles from the range—is the most convenient launch pad for venturing into Slovakia's High Tatras. Along the base of the High Tatras are various modest resort towns (including the biggest, Starý Smokovec). There's no shortage of scenic hikes all over the region (good maps and guidebooks available locally). The best no-sweat high-altitude option is to take the **cable car** from the resort village of Tatranská Lomnica up to the viewpoint at Lomnický Štít (8,640 feet; popular and crowded, so visit early).

By car, take road 537 along the base of the High Tatras to

connect the various towns. By public transportation, you'll commute by electric trains *(električky)* from Poprad into Starý
Smokovec. (There are also direct, one-hour buses from Levoča to
Starý Smokovec.) From Starý Smokovec, you can continue by electric train on to Tatranská Lomnica and other villages. Each town
has its share of simple resort-type hotels, but serious hikers enjoy
staying in the High Tatras' many *chaty* (mountain huts). For more
details on the High Tatras, visit www.tanap.sk or www.tatry.net.
Spectacular Slovakia magazine, mentioned on page 126, also has
good coverage of the High Tatras (www.spectacularslovakia.sk).

POLAND
(Polska)

Americans who think of Poland as run-down—full of rusting factories, smoggy cities, and gloomy natives—are speechless when they step into Kraków's vibrant main square, Gdańsk's lively ulica Długa, or Warsaw's colorful Old Town. While parts of the country are still cleaning up the industrial mess left by the Soviets, Poland also has some breathtaking medieval cities that show off its warm and welcoming people, dynamic history, and striding-into-the-future optimism.

The Poles are a proud people—as moved by their spectacular failures as by their successes. They place a lot of importance on honor, and you'll find fewer scams and con artists here than in other countries.

Despite the many "Polack jokes" you've heard (and maybe repeated), Poles are smart. You know many famous Polish intellectuals—you just don't know they're Polish. The "Dumb Polack"

How Big, How Many, How Much

- Poland is 120,700 square miles (about the size of New Mexico).
- Population is 39 million (about 320 people per square mile); 95 percent are Catholic, 75 percent are practicing.
- 1 złoty (zł, or PLN) = 100 groszy (gr) = about 28 cents; 3.5 zł = about $1
- Country code: 48

Hall of Fame includes Karol Wojtyła (Pope John Paul II), Mikołaj Kopernik (Nicolas Copernicus), composer Fryderyk Chopin, scientist Marie Curie (née Skłodowska), writer Teodor Józef Korzeniowski (better known as Joseph Conrad, author of *Heart of Darkness*), filmmaker Roman Polański *(The Pianist)*...and one of this book's co-authors.

In a way, there are two Polands: Lively, cosmopolitan urban centers, and hundreds of tiny farm villages in the countryside. City-dwellers often talk about the "simple people" of Poland—those descended from generations of farmers, working the same plots for centuries and living an uncomplicated, traditional lifestyle. This large contingent of old-fashioned, salt-of-the-earth folks—who like things the way they are—is a major reason why Poland was so hesitant to join the European Union (see page 150).

Poland is one of Europe's most devoutly Catholic countries. Catholicism defines these people, holding them together through times when they had little else. Squeezed between Protestant Germany (originally Prussia) and Orthodox Russia, Poland wasn't even a country for generations (1795–1918). Its Catholicism helped keep it alive. In the last century, while "under communism" (as that age is referred to), Poles found their religion a source of strength as well as rebellion—they could express dissent by going to church. Some of Poland's best sights are churches, usually filled with locals praying silently. While these church interiors are worth a visit, be especially careful to show the proper respect (maintain silence, keep a low profile, and snap pictures only discreetly).

Visitors are surprised at how Jewish the story of Poland is. Before World War II, 80 percent of the world's Jews lived in Poland. Warsaw was the world's second-largest Jewish city, after New York, with 380,000 Jews (out of a total population of 1.2 million). Poland was a magnet for Jews because of its relatively welcoming policies. Still, Jews were forbidden to own land; that's why they settled mostly in the cities. Before the war, along with its huge Jewish minority, the country had an exhilarating ethnic mix—including Germans, Russians, Ukrainians, and Lithuanians. A third of Poland spoke no Polish. But World War II (and a later Soviet policy of sending troublemaking Jews to Israel) ended that. Today, 97 percent of the country speaks Polish, and only a few thousand Polish Jews remain.

Poland is historically extremely pro-American. Of course, their big neighbors (Russia and Germany) have been their historic enemies. When Hitler invaded in 1939, the Poles' supposed European friends (France and Britain) let them down. America has always been regarded as the big ally from across the ocean. In 1989, when Poland finally won its freedom, many Poles only half-joked that they should apply to become the 51st state of the United States. Not surprisingly, when President George W. Bush took America to war in Iraq, Poland supported him.

On my first visit to Poland, I had a poor impression of Poles, who seemed brusque and often elbowed ahead of me in line. I've since learned that all it takes is a smile and a cheerful greeting—preferably in Polish—to break through the thick skin that helped these kind people survive the difficult communist times. With a friendly hello *(Dzień dobry!)*, you'll turn any grouch into a new friend.

Practicalities

Train Station Lingo: In larger towns with several stations, you'll usually use the one called Główny (meaning "Main"—except in Warsaw, where it's Centralna). Underneath the stations are often mazes of walkways—lined with market stalls—that lead to platforms *(peron)* and exits *(wyjście)*. Most stations have several platforms, each of which has two tracks *(tor)*. Departures are generally listed by the *peron,* so keep your eye on both tracks for your train. Arrivals are *przyjazdy,* and departures are *odjazdy.* Left-luggage counters or lockers are marked *przechowalnia bagażu. Kasy* are ticket windows. "Information" windows are more often than not staffed by monolingual grouches. Smile sweetly, write down your destination and time, and hang on to your patience. To get into town, follow signs for *wyjście do centrum* or *wyjście do miasta.*

Restroom Signage: To confuse tourists, the Poles have devised a secret way of marking their WCs. You'll see doors marked with *męska* (men) and *damska* (women)—but even more often, you'll simply see a triangle (for men) or a circle (for women). Likewise, a sign with a triangle, a circle, and an arrow is directing you to the closest WCs.

Pay to Pee: To irritate tourists, Polish bathrooms often charge a small fee. Sometimes you'll even be charged at a restaurant where you're paying to dine. Sadly, many American visitors let this minor inconvenience interfere with their enjoyment of the trip. My advice: You don't have to like it, but get used to it—it's a hassle, but it's cheap (usually 1–2 zł).

Telephones: Insertable telephone cards, sold at newsstands and kiosks everywhere, get you access to the modern public phones.

Cheap international phone cards for calling the United States are hard to find now, but are sure to catch on soon (see page 31 for details).

In an emergency, dial 112; to summon the police, call 997. Remember these prefixes: 0800 is toll-free, and 0700 is expensive (like phone sex). Many Poles use mobile phones (which come with 060 and 050 prefixes).

When calling locally, simply dial the seven-digit number. To call long distance within the country, start with the area code (which begins with 0). To call Poland from another country, dial the international access number (00 if you're calling from Europe, or 011 from the United States and Canada), followed by 48 (Poland's country code), then the area code (without the initial 0) and the seven-digit number. To call out of Poland, dial 00, the country code of the country you're calling (see chart in appendix), the area code if applicable (may need to drop initial zero), and the local number (see page 673 for details).

Polish History

Poland is flat. Take a look at a topographical map of Europe, and you can immediately see the Poles' historical dilemma: The path of least resistance from northern Europe to Russia is right through Poland. Over the years, many invaders—from Napoleon to Hitler—have taken advantage of Poland's strategic location. The country is nicknamed "God's playground" for the many wars that have rumbled through its territory. Poland has been invaded by Soviets, Germans, French, Austrians, Russians, Prussians, Swedes, Teutonic Knights, Tartars, Bohemians, Magyars—and, about 1,300 years ago, Poles.

Medieval Greatness

The first Poles were a tribe called the Polonians ("people of the plains"), a Slavic band that showed up in these parts in the 8th century. In 966, Mieszko I, Duke of the Polonian tribe, adopted Christianity and founded the Piast dynasty (which would last for over 400 years). Poland was born.

Poland struggled with two different invaders on the 13th century: the Tartars (Mongols who ravaged the south) and the Teutonic Knights (Germans who conquered the north—see page 268). But despite these challenges, Poland persevered. The last king of the Piast dynasty was also the greatest: Kazimierz the Great, who famously "found a Poland made of wood and left one made of brick

Polish Artists

Though Poland has produced world-class scientists, musicians, and writers, the country isn't known for its artists. Polish museums greet foreign visitors with fine artwork by unfamiliar names. If you're planning to visit any museums in Poland, there are two artists worth remembering: **Jan Matejko,** a 19th-century positivist who painted grand historical epics (see page 228); and one of his students, **Stanisław Wyspiański,** a painter and playwright who led the charge of the Młoda Polska movement ("Young Poland," the Polish answer to Art Nouveau—see page 170) in the early 1900s.

and stone"—bringing Poland (and its capital, Kraków) to international prominence (see page 168). The progressive Kazimierz also invited Europe's much-persecuted Jews to settle here, establishing Poland as a haven for the Jewish people—which it would remain until the Nazis arrived.

Kazimierz the Great died at the end of the 14th century without a male heir. His grand-niece, Jadwiga, became queen and married Lithuanian Prince Władysław Jagiełło, uniting their countries against a common enemy, the Teutonic Knights. Their marriage marked the beginning of the Jagiellonian dynasty and set the stage for Poland's golden age. With territory spanning from the Baltic Sea to the Black Sea, Poland flourished.

Foreign Kings and Partitions

When the Jagiellonians died out in 1572, political power shifted to the nobles. Poland became a nation governed by its wealthiest 10 percent—the *szlachta,* or nobility, who elected a series of foreign kings. Many of these kings made bad diplomatic decisions and squandered the country's resources. To make matters worse, the Polish parliament *(Sejm)* introduced the concept of *liberum veto,* whereby any measure could be vetoed by a single member of parliament. This policy—which effectively demanded unanimous approval for any law to be passed—paralyzed the *Sejm's* waning power.

By the late 18th century, Poland was floundering—and surrounded by three land-hungry empires (Russia, Prussia, and Austria). Over the course of less than 25 years, these countries divided Poland's territory among themselves in a series of three partitions. In 1795, "Poland" (nicknamed "the cake of kings"—to be sliced and eaten at will) disappeared from Europe's maps, not to return until 1918.

Even though Poland was gone, the Poles wouldn't go quietly. As the partitions were taking place, Polish soldier Tadeusz

Kościuszko (a hero of the American Revolution) returned home to lead an unsuccessful military resistance against the Russians. After another failed uprising against Russia in 1830, many of Poland's top artists and writers fled to Paris—including pianist Fryderyk Chopin and Romantic poet Adam Mickiewicz (whose statue adorns Kraków's main square and Warsaw's Royal Way). These Polish artists tried to preserve the nation's spirit with music and words; those who remained in Poland continued to fight with swords and fists. By the end of the 19th century, the image of the Pole as a tireless, romantic insurgent emerged.

At the end of World War I, Poland finally regained its independence—but the peace didn't last long.

Saddle on a Cow: World War II and Communism

On September 1, 1939, Hitler began World War II by attacking the Baltic port city of Gdańsk. With six million deaths in the next six years, Poland suffered the worst per-capita WWII losses of any nation. At the war's end, Poland's borders were shifted significantly westward—forcing the resettlement of millions of Germans, Poles, and Ukrainians, resulting in Poland's becoming one of Eastern Europe's most ethnically homogenous countries (97 percent Polish).

Poland was arguably hit harder by the Soviet regime than the other countries in this book. As conditions worsened in the 1970s, food shortages were the norm. Stores were marked by long lines stretching around the block. (Visitors to Poland in the 1970s and 1980s adhered to a simple philosophy: If you see a line, get in it...then figure out what it's for.) Poles were issued ration coupons for food staples, and cashiers clipped off a corner when a purchase was made...assuming, of course, the item was in stock. It often wasn't. One Pole, born in 1973, told me that his mother used to joke that he was one-third Polish, one-third salmon (a local product), and one-third mango juice (from Egypt, traded by the government for Polish cars).

Everything was out of order and out of stock. A working telephone booth was cause for celebration. Visitors to Poland came back with poignant anecdotes. On returning home, one traveler was asked if he learned any Polish. "Yes!" he said. "I know the word for 'elevator.'" In fact, the word he had learned meant "out of order." In the waning days of communism, an American businessman went to a Polish restaurant with an extensive menu. He chose carefully, only to be told the item wasn't available. So, he chose again, and discovered this, too, was unavailable. After going through this a few more times, he grew frustrated. "Do you have *anything*?" "Sorry, sir. Only *pierogi* and borscht."

The little absurdities of communist life—which today seem almost comical—made every day a struggle. For years, every elderly

The Heritage of Communism

While Poland has been free, democratic, and capitalist since 1989, even young adults carry lots of psychological baggage from living under communism. Although the young generally embrace the fast new affluence with enthusiasm, many older people tend to be nostalgic about that slower-paced time that came with more security. And even young professionals, with so much energy and hope now, don't condemn everything about that stretch of history. A friend who was 13 in 1989 recalled those days this way:

"My childhood is filled with happy memories. Under communism, life was family-oriented. Careers didn't matter. There was no way to get rich, no reason to rush, so we had time. People always had time.

"But there were also shortages—many things were 'in deficit.' I remember my mother and father had to 'organize' for special events...somehow find a good sausage and some Coca-Cola. Sometimes my uncle would bring us several toilet paper rolls, held together with a string—absolutely the best gift anyone could give.

"We had real chocolate only for Christmas. The rest of the year, for treats we got something called 'chocolate-like product'—it was sweet, dark, and smelled vaguely of chocolate. And we had oranges from Cuba for Christmas, too. Everybody was excited when the newspapers announced, 'The boat with the oranges from Cuba is just five days from Poland.' We waited with excitement all year for chocolate and those oranges. The smell of Christmas was so special. Now we have that smell every day. Still, my happiest Christmases were under communism."

woman in Poland had hair the same odd magenta color. There was only one color of dye available, so the choice was simple: Let your hair grow out (and look foolishly half red and half white), or line up and go red—literally.

During these difficult times, the Poles often rose up—staging major protests in 1956, 1968, 1970, and 1976. Stalin famously noted that introducing communism to the Poles was like putting a saddle on a cow. In 1980, Lech Wałęsa, an electrician at the shipyards in Gdańsk, became the leader of the Solidarity movement, the first workers' union in communist Eastern Europe. After an initial 18-day strike at the Gdańsk shipyards, the communist regime gave in, legalizing Solidarity (for more on Solidarity, see page 235).

But the union grew too powerful, and the communists felt their control slipping away. On Sunday, December 13, 1981, Poland's head of state, General Wojciech Jaruzelski, declared martial law in order to "forestall Soviet intervention." (Whether the Soviets actually would have intervened remains a hotly debated issue.) Tanks ominously rolled through the streets of Poland on that snowy December morning, and the Poles were terrified.

Martial law would last until 1983. Each Pole has his or her own chilling memories of this frightening time. One twentysomething Pole remembers turning on the TV that Sunday morning expecting to see his favorite kids' show, *Teleranek*. Instead, he saw Jaruzelski announcing the Poles' new reality. School would be canceled for two weeks, the Polish premier announced. At first, the young Pole was excited. But then he looked out the window, saw tanks in the snowy streets...and realized just how serious it was. To this day, he and his friends call that fateful event the "day without *Teleranek*."

During riots, the people would flock into churches—the only place they would be safe from the ZOMO, or riot police. But Solidarity struggled on, going underground and becoming a united movement of all demographics, 10 million members strong (more than a quarter of the population).

In July 1989, the ruling Communist Party agreed to hold open elections (reserving 65 percent of representatives for themselves). Their goal was to appease Solidarity, but the plan backfired: Communists didn't win a single seat. These elections helped spark the chain reaction across Eastern Europe that eventually brought down the Iron Curtain. Lech Wałęsa, a shipyard electrician from Gdańsk, became Poland's first post-communist president. (For more on Lech Wałęsa, see page 254.)

Poland in the 21st Century: The European Union

When 10 new countries joined the European Union in May 2004, Poland was the most ambivalent of the bunch. After centuries of being under other empires' authority, the Poles were hardly eager to relinquish some of their hard-fought autonomy to Brussels. Many Poles see the EU as an unstoppable monster, but believe that to survive in the modern Europe, their country had to join. They expect things to get worse (higher prices, a loss of traditional lifestyles) before they get better. Though their adjustment to the EU has been fitful, most Poles believe it will be good for the next generation.

While other countries were planning their fireworks displays to celebrate EU enlargement on May 1, 2004, Poland was seized by a strange sort of mass hysteria. The country buzzed with rumors of increased prices. When the news reported that sugar would be subject to a higher tax rate, there was a run on the stores, as the Poles bought up as much sugar as they could stockpile. The result? A shortage of sugar...and higher prices, even before May 1. (Smug Americans who laugh at these silly Poles should remember the days after September 11, 2001, when U.S. stores ran out of tarp, duct tape, and bottled water.)

Polish Jokes

Through the dreary communist times, The Poles managed to keep their sense of humor. A popular target of jokes was the riot police, or ZOMO. Here are just a few of the things Poles said about these unpopular cops:

- It's better to have a sister who's a whore than a brother in the ZOMO.
- ZOMO police are hired based on the 90-90 principle: They have to weigh at least 90 kilograms (200 pounds), and their I.Q. must be less than 90.
- ZOMO would be dispatched in teams of three: one who could read, one who could write, and a third to protect those other two smart guys.
- A ZOMO policeman was sitting on the curb, crying. Someone came up to him and asked what was wrong. "I lost my dog!" he said. "No matter," the person replied. "He's a smart police dog. I'm sure he can find his way back to the station." "Yes," the ZOMO said. "But without him, *I* can't!"

The communists gave their people no options at elections: If you voted, you voted for the regime. Poles liked to joke that in some ways, this made communists like God—who created Eve, then said to Adam, "Now choose a wife." The communists could run a pig as a candidate, and it would still win. A popular symbol of dissent became a pig painted with the words, "Vote Red."

There were even jokes about jokes. Under communism, Poles noted that there was a government-sponsored prize for the funniest political joke: 15 years in prison.

Poland is by far the most populous of the new EU members, with nearly 40 million people (about the same as Spain, or two-thirds the size of Germany). This makes Poland the fifth largest of the 25 EU member states—giving it serious political clout (which it wields on behalf of its fellow Slavic, Eastern European nations). In late 2003, several wealthier, established EU countries (such as Germany) grew nervous about footing the bill for investment in the new members. Traditionally, voting within the EU was based solely on population. But with new members on the horizon, Germany led the charge in trying to tweak the new EU constitution to guarantee itself more pull. Poland stood up to the Germans and stalled ratification talks for the constitution for several months. As the EU learns to live with its new Eastern European comrades, Poland looks poised to take the lead in looking out for the Slavs and keeping Germany honest.

Bar Mleczny (Milk Bar)

Eating at a *bar mleczny* is an essential Polish sightseeing experience. These super-cheap cafeterias, which you'll see all over the country, are an incredibly cheap way to get a meal...and, with the right attitude, a fun cultural experience.

In the communist era, the government subsidized the food at milk bars, allowing lowly workers to enjoy a meal out. The tradition continues, and today, Poland still foots the bill for most of your milk-bar meal. Prices are astoundingly low—my bill usually comes to about $2—and, while communist-era fare was gross, today's milk-bar cuisine is usually quite tasty.

Milk bars usually offer many of the traditional tastes listed in this section. Common items are delicious soups (like *żurek* and *barszcz*), a variety of cabbage-based salads, *kotlet* (fried pork chops), *pierogi* (like ravioli, with various fillings), and *naleśniki* (pancakes). You'll often see glasses of juice and (of course) milk, but most milk bars also stock bottles of water and Coke.

The service is aimed at locals—no English menu and a confusing ordering system. Every milk bar is a little different, but here's the general procedure: Head to the counter, wait to be acknowledged, and point to what you want. Handy vocabulary: *to* (sounds like "toe") means "that"; *i* (pronounced "ee") means "and."

My milk-bar dialogue usually goes like this:

Milk Bar Lady: *Proszę?* (which means "Can I help you, please?").

Me: *To* (while pointing)...*i to* (pointing again)...*i to* (pointing once more). It means, "That...and that...and that."

If the milk bar lady asks you any questions, you have three options: nod stupidly until she just gives you something; repeat one of the things she just said (assuming she's asked you to choose between two options, like meat or cheese in your *pierogi*); or hope that a kindly English-speaking person in line will leap to your rescue. If nothing else, ordering at a milk bar is an adventure in gestures. Smiling seems to slightly extend the patience of milk-bar staffers.

Once your tray is all loaded up, pay the cashier (and do a double-take when you realize how cheap your bill is), then find a table. After the meal, it's generally polite, if not expected, to bus your dishes (watch locals and imitate).

And no, you don't have to order milk.

Polish Food

Hearty and tasty, Polish food has a lot in common with Czech, German, and Hungarian cuisine—but here on the north slope of the Carpathian Mountains, the weather is colder, the fruits and vegetables more northern, and the cuisine slightly more similar to that of Russia or Scandinavia. This means more dill, sour cream, vodka, berries, and bread. Much of what Americans think of as Jewish food turns up on Polish menus (gefilte fish, potato pancakes, chicken soup, and so forth)—not because either group influenced the other, but because they lived in the same area for centuries under the same climatic and culinary influences.

The two most typical Polish soups are *żurek* and *barszcz*. *Żurek* is a light-colored soup made from a sourdough base, usually with a hard-boiled egg and pieces of *kiełbasa* (sausage) in it. *Barszcz* (borscht) generally means *barszcz czerwony* (red borscht), made with beets. *Barszcz ukraiński* (Ukrainian borscht) starts with beets and adds cabbage, beans, carrots, and other vegetables. (Confusingly, there is also *biały barszcz,* or white borscht—with no beets at all.) In summer, you can try *chłodnik,* a cold beet soup (think gazpacho).

Main dish specialties include *bigos* (a tasty sauerkraut stew cooked with meat, mushrooms, and whatever's in the pantry), usually inexpensive *pierogi* (ravioli-like dumplings with various fillings—minced meat, sauerkraut and mushroom, cheese, or fruit), and *kotlet schabowy* (fried pork chops). You can also try *gołąbki*—cabbage leaves stuffed with minced meat and rice in a tomato sauce. Like Hungarians, Poles consume more *kaczka* (duck) than Americans do. Fish is common: Look for *pstrąg* (trout), *karp* (carp, beware of bones), and *węgorz* (eel). Poles eat lots of potatoes, which are served with nearly every meal.

Poland has excellent pastries. A *piekarnia* is a bakery specializing in breads. But if you really want something special, look for a *cukiernia* (pastry shop). The classic Polish treat is *pączki,* glazed jelly doughnuts. They can have various fillings, but most typical is a wild-rose jam. *Szarlotka* is apple cake—sometimes made with chunks of apples (especially in season), sometimes with apple filling. *Sernik* is cheesecake, and *makowiec* is poppy-seed cake. *Winebreda* is an especially gooey Danish. *Babeczka* is like a cupcake filled with pudding. You may see *jabłko w cieście*—slices of apple cooked in dough, then glazed. *Napoleonka* is a French-style treat with layers of crispy wafers and custard.

The bagel-like rings you'll see on the street, *obwarzanki,* are fresh, tasty, and cheap. *Lody* (ice cream) is popular. The most beloved traditional candy is *ptasie mleczko* (birds' milk), which is like a semi-sour marshmallow covered with chocolate.

Thirsty? *Woda* is water, *woda mineralna* is bottled water (*gazowana* is with gas/carbonation, *niegazowana* is without), *kawa* is

Key Polish Phrases

English	Polish	Pronounced
Hello. (formal)	Dzień dobry.	jehn DOH-bree
Hi. / Bye. (informal)	Cześć.	cheshch
Do you speak English? (asked of a man)	Czy Pan mówi po angielsku?	chee pahn MOO-vee poh ahn-GYEHL-skoo
Do you speak English? (asked of a woman)	Czy Pani mówi po angielsku?	chee PAH-nee MOO-vee poh ahn-GYEHL-skoo
Yes. / No.	Tak. / Nie.	tahk / nyeh
Please. / You're welcome. / Can I help you?	Proszę.	PROH-sheh
Thank you.	Dziękuję.	jehn-KOO-yeh
I'm sorry. / Excuse me.	Przepraszam.	pzheh-PRAH-shahm
Good.	Dobrze.	DOHB-zheh
Goodbye.	Do widzenia.	doh veed-ZAY-nyah
one / two	jeden / dwa	YEH-dehn / dvah
three / four	trzy / cztery	tzhee / chuh-TEH-ree
five / six	pięć / sześć	pyench / sheshch
seven / eight	siedem / osiem	SYEH-dehm / OH-shehm
nine / ten	dziewięć / dziesięć	JEH-vyench / JEH-shench
hundred	sto	stoh
thousand	tysiąc	TEE-shanch
How much?	Ile?	EE-leh
local currency	złoty (zł)	ZWOH-tee
Where is...?	Gdzie jest...?	gdzeh yehst
...the toilet	...toaleta	toh-ah-LEH-tah
men	męska	MEHN-skah
women	damska	DAHM-skah
water / coffee	woda / kawa	VOH-dah / KAH-vah
beer / wine	piwo / wino	PEE-voh / VEE-noh
Cheers!	Na zdrowie!	nah ZDROH-vyeh
the bill	rachunek	rah-KHOO-nehk

coffee, *herbata* is tea, *sok* is juice, and *mleko* is milk. Żywiec and Okocim are the best-known brands of *piwo* (beer). *Wódka* (vodka) is a Polish staple—the name is actually derived from the Polish word for "water." *Wódka* comes in many varieties. Żubrówka, the most famous brand, comes with a blade of grass from the bison reserves in eastern Poland (look for the bottle with the bison). The bison "flavor" the grass...then the grass flavors the vodka. Poles often mix Żubrówka with apple juice. For "Cheers!" say, *"Na zdrowie!"* (think "nice driving").

Unusual drinks to try if you have the chance are *kwas* (a cold, fizzy, Ukrainian-style non-alcoholic beverage made from day-old rye bread) and *kompot* (a hot drink made from stewed berries). Poles are unusually fond of carrot juice (often cut with fruit juice); Kubuś is the most popular brand.

"Bon appétit" *is "Smacznego."* To pay, ask for the *rachunek* (rah-KHOO-nehk) or say, *"Płacę"* (PWOTS-eh, "I'll pay").

Polish Language

Polish is closely related to its neighboring Slavic languages (Slovak and Czech), with the biggest difference being that Polish has lots of fricatives (hissing sounds—"sh" and "ch"—often in close proximity). Consider the opening line of Poland's most famous tongue-twisting nursery rhyme: *W Szczebrzeszynie chrzaszcz brzmi w trzcinie* ("In Szczebrzeszyn, a beetle is heard in the reeds"—pronounced vuh shih-chehb-zheh-shee-nyeh khzhahshch bzh-mee vuh tzhuh-cheen-yeh...or something like that).

Polish intimidates Americans with long, difficult-to-pronounce words. But if you take your time and sound things out, you'll quickly develop an ear for it. First of all, the stress is always on the next-to-last syllable. The letter *c* always sounds like "ts" (as in "cats"). The letter combinations *ć, ci,* and *cz* all sound like "ch"; *ś, si,* and *sz* all sound like "sh"; and *ź, ż, zi,* and *rz* all sound like "zh" (as in "leisure"). The letter *ń* and the combination *ni* sound like "ny" (as in "canyon").

Some Polish vowels have a nasalized sound, like in French. If you see *ę* or *ą,* pronounce them as "en" or "an."

One of the trickiest changes to get used to: *w* sounds like "v," and *ł* sounds like "w." So, "Lech Wałęsa" isn't pronounced "lehk wah-LEH-sah," as Dan Rather used to say—but "lehkh vah-WEHN-sah."

As you're tracking down addresses, these words may help: *miasto* (town), *plac* (square), *rynek* (big market square), *ulica* (road), *aleja* (avenue), and *most* (bridge).

KRAKÓW

Kraków is the Boston of Poland: a beautiful, old-fashioned city buzzing with history, enjoyable sights, tourists, and college students. Even though the country's political capital moved from here to Warsaw 400 years ago, Kraków remains Poland's cultural and intellectual center. Of all the Eastern European cities laying claim to the boast "the next Prague," Kraków is for real. Now's the time to visit: just as the tourist infrastructure ramps up, but before it's swamped with crowds.

Kraków grew wealthy from trade in the late 10th and early 11th centuries. Traders who passed through were required to stop here for a few days and sell their wares at a reduced cost. Local merchants turned around and sold those goods with big price hikes...and Kraków thrived. In 1038, it became Poland's capital.

Tartars invaded in 1241, leaving the city in ruins. Krakovians took this opportunity to rebuild their streets in a near-perfect grid, a striking contrast to the narrow, mazelike lanes of most medieval towns. The destruction also paved the way for the spectacular Main Market Square—still Kraków's best attraction.

King Kazimierz the Great sparked Kraków's golden age in the 14th century (see page 168). In 1364, he established the university that still defines the city (and counts Copernicus and Pope John Paul II among its alumni).

But Kraków's power waned as Poland's political center shifted to Warsaw. In 1596, the capital officially moved north. At the end of the 18th century, three neighboring powers—Russia, Prussia, and Austria—partitioned Poland, annexing all of its territory and dividing it among themselves. Warsaw ended up as a satellite of oppressive Moscow, and Kraków became a poor provincial backwater of Vienna. But despite Kraków's reduced prominence, Austria's comparatively liberal climate helped turn the city into a haven for

Kraków

intellectuals and progressives (including a young revolutionary thinker from Russia named Vladimir Lenin).

Kraków emerged from World War II virtually unscathed. But when the communists took over, they decided to give intellectual (and potentially dissident) Kraków an injection of good Soviet values—in the form of heavy industry. They built Nowa Huta, an enormous steelworks on the city's outskirts, which doomed the city to decades of smog. Thankfully, Kraków is now much cleaner than it was 15 years ago.

Pope John Paul II was born (as Karol Wojtyła) in nearby Wadowice, and served as archbishop of Kraków before being called to Rome. Poland is devoutly Catholic; make sure to visit a few of Kraków's many churches. University life, small but thought-provoking museums, great restaurants, sprawling parks, and Jewish history round out the city's attractions.

Planning Your Time

Kraków—with its important side-trips—deserves at least two full days on the busiest itinerary. The city's sights are quickly exhausted, but more than any town in Europe, Kraków is made for aimless strolling.

Ideally, spend two full days in Kraków itself, plus a visit to Auschwitz (either as a side-trip on the third day, or en route to or from Kraków). In a pinch, spend one day sightseeing in Kraków, another at Auschwitz, and two evenings on the Main Market Square. The Square is pure magic.

Visiting Auschwitz requires the better part of a day. If you have more time, nearby Wieliczka Salt Mine makes another good day trip. And even Warsaw, 2.5 hours away by train, is possible to do in a day (see Warsaw chapter).

With two full days in and around Kraków, this is the maximum you could do:

Day 1: Take "Krakow's Royal Way Walk" to cover the city's core. Visit any Old Town museums that interest you (Wyspiański Museum, Gallery of 19th-Century Polish Art, Czartoryski Museum, Jagiellonian University Museum), and have lunch on or near the Main Market Square. Spend the afternoon at the castle (note that many sights close at 15:00). Savor the Square over dinner or a drink, or enjoy traditional Jewish music and cuisine in Kazimierz.

Day 2: Get an early start to see the concentration camp at Auschwitz. With a local driver or a good public transit connection, you could get back in time to visit the Wieliczka Salt Mine or Kazimierz.

ORIENTATION

(area code: 012)

Kraków (KROCK-oof, sometimes spelled "Cracow" in English), unlike Prague or Budapest, is mercifully flat and easy to navigate. While the urban sprawl is big (with about 800,000 people), the tourist's Kraków feels small. You could easily do your entire visit on foot. A greenbelt called the Planty rings the Old Town (Stare Miasto) where the walls and moat once stood; today, it's a great place for a stroll or jog. Most sights—except for the castle and the Kazimierz Jewish quarter—and almost all recommended hotels and restaurants are in the Old Town, inside the Planty. In the center of the Old Town lies the Main Market Square (Rynek Główny), with

Kraków Landmarks

English	Polish	Pronounced
Main train station	**Kraków Główny**	KROCK-oof GWOHV-nee
Park around the Old Town	**Planty**	PLAHN-tee
Old Town	**Stare Miasto**	STAH-reh mee-AH-stoh
Main Market Square	**Rynek Główny**	REE-nehk GWOHV-nee
Cloth Hall	**Sukiennice**	soo-kyeh-NEET-seh
Castle Hill	**Wawel**	VAH-vehl
Jewish Quarter	**Kazimierz**	kah-ZHEE-mehzh
Vistula River	**Wisła**	VEES-wah

the Cloth Hall in the middle and St. Mary's Church at the corner.

From the Main Market Square, if you walk 10 minutes to the south, you'll find the Wawel sights (castle and cathedral) and just beyond, the Vistula River. If you take a five-minute walk north of the Square, you'll reach some remnants of the city walls, and five minutes beyond that (veering northeast), the train station. Kazimierz, the old Jewish quarter, is 20 minutes by foot to the southeast.

Tourist Information

Kraków has one listless, state-run **TI** (May–Sept Mon–Fri 8:00–19:00, Sat–Sun 9:00–15:00; Oct–April Mon–Fri 8:00–16:00, closed Sat–Sun; in round, green-roofed kiosk between train station and Square in the Planty park at ulica Szpitalna 25, tel. 012/432-0110, www.krakow.pl). This is your best chance to pick up a pile of free information: Grab the one-page map, the thick Kraków Tourist Information booklet, the *Karnet* cultural events booklet, and a copy of *Kraków in Your Pocket* (see below). Because it's government-funded, this office is not allowed to actually sell anything, so all resources are free. This is both good (to get things for free that cost money elsewhere) and bad (they can tell you about the Kraków Tourist Card...but they can't sell it to you).

More central, in the Cloth Hall on the Square, is the privately run, decidedly for-profit **MCIT** (Małopolskie Centrum Informacji Turystycznej, fluid hours based on demand, but generally summer Mon–Fri 8:00–20:00, Sat–Sun 9:00–16:00; winter Mon–Fri 9:00–17:00, Sat 9:00–14:00, closed Sun; in middle of Cloth Hall facing St. Mary's Church at Rynek Główny 1–3, tel. 012/421-7706, www.mcit.pl). They offer minimal tourist information, sell maps and

Kraków Tourist Cards, book tours, arrange local transportation and car rentals, and have a room-finding service. Be warned that this place's advice is colored by a thirst for profits.

Kraków in Your Pocket: This excellent bimonthly magazine is packed with up-to-date, comprehensive hotel and restaurant reviews, as well as good sightseeing coverage. The cover price is 5 zł, but you can usually find it for free in hotel lobbies or at the government-run TI.

Kraków Tourist Card: The card covers public transportation in Kraków, admission to several city museums (Czartoryski, Cloth Hall Gallery), and moderate discounts to outlying sights (40 percent off Cracow Tours to Wieliczka Salt Mine or Auschwitz). Since public transportation is mostly unnecessary and museums are so cheap, this card doesn't make sense for most visitors (45 zł/2 days, 65 zł/3 days; available at MCIT office in Cloth Hall, Orbis and other travel agencies, and many hotels).

Arrival in Kraków

By Train: The Kraków Główny ("main") station is a 10-minute walk northeast of the Square. The station has two parts, connected by a covered walkway: the arrival hall and main terminal. Stairs lead from the tracks down to the long, skinny, low-ceilinged arrival hall, which is stark and functional, with only a handful of ticket windows and luggage lockers. A parallel tunnel under the tracks is a second-hand book market. The big old-fashioned main terminal, closer to the center, is more comfortable, with more ticket windows, lockers, WCs, and other amenities.

From the long, skinny arrival hall, follow signs to the center *(wyjście do centrum)*. At street level, turn left into a construction zone; depending on when you visit, you'll pass the old bus station (across the street on the right) and/or the construction site of a shopping mall and brand-new bus station (just beyond the old station); the main train terminal is ahead on the left. Foreigners will encounter people hustling rides to Auschwitz and cheap rooms.

Getting downtown: **Taxis** park in front of the main terminal; the fair metered rate to downtown is 10–15 zł. To make the 10-minute **walk** to the center and most recommended hotels, exit the station to the left and head towards the big post office. Negotiate your way around the construction of the Nowy Miasto (or New Town)—which may be finished when you're here—and find the pedestrian underpass beneath the busy ring road. Take the underpass, bearing right. When you emerge in the Planty park, you'll see the round TI kiosk on your left; the Main Market Square is a few blocks straight ahead.

By Car: Check with your hotel. The most central parking lot is on ulica Szczepańska, a block west of the Square (10:00–20:00 it's 7 zł/hr; 20:00–10:00 it's 4 zł/hr; 90 zł/24 hr).

By Plane: The small, modern **John Paul II Kraków-Balice Airport** is 10 miles west of the center. Buses #192 and #208 take you to the train station and the edge of the Old Town (3 zł, 40 min), or you can catch a cab (around 50 zł). Airport info: tel. 012/285-5120, www.lotniski-balice.pl.

Helpful Hints

Sightseeing Schedules: Most museums are closed Monday, and many are free one day a week (which tends to change from year to year). Hours at museums tend to change frequently; carefully confirm the opening times of sights at the TI.

Internet Access: Kraków's many Internet cafés—it seems there's one on every corner—charge around 1 zł for 15 min. **Internet Klub Garinet** is convenient (daily until 24:00, on the Royal Way just a block north of the Square at ulica Floriańska 10).

Post Office: In peak season, a small postal wagon sells stamps in the middle of the Square (opposite what was Poland's first post office—back when a Pony Express–type system delivered mail to Vienna within 40 hours). The main post office (Poczta Główna) is at the intersection of Starowiślna and the Westerplatte ring road, a few blocks east of the Square.

Laundry: Doing laundry in Kraków is frustrating. There's no good self-service launderette in the center (unless you're staying at a hostel). Your hotel can do your wash, but it's expensive. If you must have something laundered, a central option is **Betty Clean** (about 9 zł per shirt, 12 zł for pants, takes 24 hrs, pay 50 percent more for express 3-hr service, Mon–Fri 7:30–19:30, Sat 8:00–15:30, closed Sun, just outside the Planty at ulica Zwierzyniecka 6, tel. 012/423-0848).

Travel Agency: Orbis, at the top of the Square, books local guides and bus tours, changes money, and sells train tickets (May–Sept Mon–Fri 9:00–19:00, Sat 9:00–15:00, closed Sun, closes 1 hr earlier Oct–April, Rynek Główny 41, www.orbis.krakow.pl, tel. 012/422-5584). The agency posts a handy complete train schedule in their window. Buy your train tickets in this central location (no fee, English spoken) to avoid the trip to the station and the frustration of dealing with the surly monolingual grannies at the ticket windows.

Car Rental: Avis, Hertz, and the other big guys all have offices in Kraków. I like a local company called E-car, run by can-do Marcin Taboł. This low-key, easygoing place won't give you maps for every city in Poland, or a contract filled out in triplicate—but they're usually the cheapest deal in town, and they'll bring your car right to your hotel (tel. 022/650-1483, www.ecar.pl, marcin.tabol@ecar.pl).

Getting Around Kraków

Kraków's top sights and best hotels are easily accessible by foot. You'll only need wheels if you're going to the Kazimierz Jewish quarter or the Nowa Huta suburbs.

By Public Transit: Trams and buses zip around Kraków's urban sprawl. The same tickets are used for both, and can be purchased at kiosks (cheaper) or on board (for 0.50 zł more). There are three kinds of tickets: A *bilet jednoprzejazdowy* (basic single ticket, no transfers) costs 2.40 zł at a kiosk. Technically, if you're using this cheap ticket, you have to buy a separate ticket for your bag (or risk a fine). So, you might as well get a *bilet godzinny*—good for an hour, and allowing transfers and luggage (3 zł). Always validate your ticket when you board the bus or tram. There are also longer-term tickets for 24 hours (10 zł), 48 hours (18 zł), and 72 hours (24 zł); these must be validated the first time you use them, and can only be purchased at special MPK ticket booths (the handiest is in the Planty near the TI). The trams you're most likely to use are #4 to Nowa Huta, and #3, #13, and #24 to get to Kazimierz, the Jewish quarter.

By Taxi: Just as in other big Eastern European cities, only take cabs that are clearly marked with a company logo and telephone number. Kraków taxis start at 5 zł and charge around 2.50 zł per kilometer. Rides are very short and generally run less than 10 zł. You're more likely to get the fair metered rate by hailing a cab, rather than taking one waiting at tourist spots. To call a cab, try **Radio Taxi** (tel. 012/919, or toll-free 0800-500-919).

By Buggy: Romantic, horse-drawn buggies trot around Kraków from the Main Market Square. The going rate is 70 zł for a 30-minute tour, but prices are slushy; ask three drivers, and go with the cheapest offer.

By Golf Cart: OK, it's not quite so romantic. But several golf-cart companies based on the Square offer both taxi and tour service. You can pay by the car (e.g., 20 zł taxi service to Kazimierz, 50 zł for half-hour tour of Old Town, 80 zł for full-hour tour) or join a tour (15 zł per person for half-hour tour, 25 zł for full-hour tour). The tours can be live or tape-recorded (just dial English). These guys are pretty competitive; it pays to shop around.

By Bicycle: Wypożyczalnja Rowerów Rent-a-Bike, half a block off the Square, is run by easygoing Michał Bisping. Biking the Planty park and along the riverside promenades gives your trip a great extra dimension and gets you out of the touristy old town zone to see a slice of untouristy Kraków (4 zł/hr, 30 zł/day, April–Oct Mon–Sat 9:00–dusk, closed Sun and Nov–March, ulica Św. Anny 4).

TOURS

Bus Tours—Cracow Tours runs several bus-plus-walking itineraries, including a general city overview (110 zł, daily, 3 hrs), Auschwitz (120 zł, daily, 6 hrs), Wieliczka Salt Mine (120 zł, daily, 4 hrs), and other regional side-trips (40 percent discount with Kraków Tourist Card, book tours at Orbis travel agency or MCIT office, both on the Square).

Walking Tours—There are walking tours in English daily April through October (70 zł, doesn't include admissions, 4.5 hours; leaves at 10:00 from MCIT office on the Square, route includes Kraków Old Town, then break, then Kazimierz Jewish quarter). But three people can actually hire their own excellent local guide for less money (see below).

Local Guides—Kraków has several affordable guides. Marta Chmielowska is good and has a car (200 zł/half day, 250 zł with her car, full day just a little more, mobile 0603/668-008, martachm @op.pl). Anna Gega also does a fine job (200 zł/4 hrs, 350 zł/full day, tel. 012/411-2523, mobile 0604/151-293, leadertour@wp.pl). Local guides have a passion for all the legends and stories. If Marta and Anna are booked, the Orbis travel agency (see above) can find a guide for you.

SIGHTS

Krakow's Royal Way Walk

Most of Kraków's major sights are conveniently connected by this self-guided walking tour. This route is known as the "Royal Way," because the king used to follow this same path when he returned to Kraków after a journey. After the capital moved to Warsaw, most kings were still both coronated and buried in Wawel Cathedral at the far end of town—and they followed this same route for both occasions. You could sprint through this three-part walk in an hour (less than a mile altogether), but it's much more fun if you take it slow.

Royal Way Walk
Part 1: Barbican to Main Market Square

Begin the walk at the north end of the Old Town, at the barbican.

▲▲**Barbican (Barbakan), Florian Gate (Brama Floriańska), and City Walls**—Tartars invaded Kraków three times in the 13th century. After the first attack destroyed the city in 1241, Krakovians built this wall. The original rampart had 47 watchtowers and eight gates. The big, round defensive fort standing outside the wall is a barbican. Structures like this provided extra fortification to weak sections. Imagine in 1500, when this barbican stood outside the town

Kraków at a Glance

Be warned: Kraków's museum hours tend to be flexible. If you want to be sure to get into a certain place, confirm the hours in advance.

▲▲▲**Main Market Square** Stunning heart of Kraków and a people magnet any time of day. **Hours:** Always open.

▲▲**Barbican and City Walls** Formidable 13th-century fort and walls. **Hours:** Always viewable.

▲▲**Planty** Once a moat, now a scenic park encircling the city. **Hours:** Always open.

▲▲**Floriańska Street** Kraków's main shop-lined, touristic artery. **Hours:** Always open.

▲▲**St. Mary's Church** Landmark church with extraordinary wood-carved Gothic altarpiece. **Hours:** Mon–Sat 11:30–18:00, Sun 14:00–18:00.

▲▲**Cloth Hall** Fourteenth-century market hall with 21st-century souvenirs. **Hours:** Summer Mon–Fri 9:00–18:00, Sat–Sun 9:00–15:00, sometimes later; winter Mon–Fri 9:00–16:00, Sat–Sun 9:00–15:00.

▲▲**St. Francis' Basilica** Lovely Gothic church with some of Poland's best Art Nouveau. **Hours:** Open long hours daily.

▲▲**Czartoryski Museum** Varied collection, with European paintings (da Vinci and Rembrandt) and Polish armor, handicrafts, and decorative arts. **Hours:** Generally Tue–Sat 10:00–16:00, Sun 10:00–15:00, closed Mon, open later some evenings in summer, shorter hours Nov–May.

moat with a long bridge leading to the Florian Gate—the city's main entryway.

Before you step through the gate yourself, look to the left and right of the barbican to see the...

▲▲**Planty**—By the 19th century, Kraków's no-longer-necessary city wall had fallen into disrepair. Krakovians decided to tear down what remained, fill in the moat, and plant trees. Today, the Planty is a beautiful park that stretches for 2.5 miles around the entire perimeter of Kraków's Old Town.

Go through the gate into the Old Town.

▲▲**Jewish Cemeteries** Two touching burial sites—the New (post-1800) and Old (1552–1800)—in Kazimierz. **Hours:** New Cemetery: Sun–Fri 9:00–18:00, until 16:00 in winter, closed Sat; Old Cemetery: Sun–Fri 9:00–16:00, closed Sat.

▲▲**Wawel Castle Grounds** Historic hilltop with views, castle, cathedral, courtyard with chakra, and a passel of museums. **Hours:** Grounds always open.

▲**Wawel Cathedral** Poland's splendid national church, with tons of tombs, a crypt, and a climbable tower. **Hours:** Ticket sales for crypt and tower May–Sept Mon–Sat 9:00–17:15, Sun 12:15–17:15; Oct–April Mon–Sat 9:00–15:45, Sun 12:15–15:45.

▲**Gallery of 19th-Century Polish Art** Easy-to-appreciate works by Poland's finest painters, little known outside of the country. **Hours:** Generally Tue–Sat 10:00–16:00, Sun 10:00–15:00, closed Mon, open later some evenings in summer, shorter hours Nov–May.

▲**Wyspiański Museum** Art by the talented leader of the Młoda Polska Art Nouveau movement. **Hours:** Generally Tue–Sat 10:00–16:00, Sun 10:00–15:00, closed Mon, open later some evenings in summer, shorter hours Nov–May.

▲**Kazimierz Market Square (Plac Nowy)** The people's market, good for lunching with locals. **Hours:** Stalls open Tue–Sat 6:00–14:00, a few also open later and Sun 7:00–14:00.

▲**Polish Folk Museum** Traditional rural Polish life on display—an open-air museum moved inside. **Hours:** Mon 10:00–16:00, Wed–Fri 10:00–15:00, Sat–Sun 10:00–14:00, closed Tue.

▲▲**Floriańska Street (Ulica Floriańska)**—You're standing at the head of Kraków's historic (and now touristy) gamut. On the inside of the city wall, you'll see a makeshift **art gallery** (left and right), where starving students hawk the works they've painted at the Academy of Fine Arts (across the busy street from the barbican). Portraits, still lifes, landscapes, local scenes, nudes...this might just be Kraków's best collection of art. If you were to detour along the gallery (to the left as you face the gate), in a block you'd arrive at another fine collection—the eclectic Czartoryski Museum, home to a rare Leonardo da Vinci oil painting (see "Museums," below).

Walking down Floriańska Street, you can't miss the **McDonald's.** When renovating this building, they discovered a Gothic cellar—so they excavated it and added seating. Today, you can super-size your ambience by dining on a Big Mac and fries under a medieval McVault.

Cukiarnia Jama Michalika (farther down on left at #45)—a dark, atmospheric café popular with locals for its coffee and pastries—began in 1895 as a simple bakery in a claustrophobic back room. A brothel upstairs scared off respectable types, so the owner attracted students by creating a cabaret act called "The Green Balloon." To this day, the cabaret—political satire set to music—still runs (in Polish only). Around the turn of the 20th century, this was a hangout of the Młoda Polska (Young Poland) movement—the Polish answer to Art Nouveau (see page 170). The walls are papered with sketches from poor artists who couldn't pay their tabs. (Poke around inside, and see how many green balloons you can spot. Consider having a snack or meal here—see page 191 of "Eating").

Two blocks ahead on the left (at #3, 50 yards before the big church), you'll see **Jazz Club U Muniaka.** In the 1950s, Janusz Muniak was one of the first Polish jazzmen. Now he owns this place, and jams regularly here in a cool cellar surrounded by jazzy art (live music nightly at 21:30, 10- to 20-zł cover, cheap drinks after that, best bands Thu–Sat, www.umuniaka.krakow.pl). If you hang around the bar before the show, you might find yourself sitting next to Janusz himself, smoking his pipe...and getting ready to smoke on the saxophone.

Continue into the Main Market Square, where you'll run into...

▲▲**St. Mary's Church (Kościół Mariacki)**—A church has stood on this spot for 800 years. The original church was destroyed by the first Tartar invasion in 1241, but all subsequent versions—including the current one—have been built on the same foundation. You can look down the sides to see how the Square has risen about seven feet over the centuries.

How many church towers does St. Mary's have? Technically, the answer is one. The shorter tower belongs to the church; the taller one is a municipal watchtower, from which you'll hear a bugler playing the hourly *hejnał*. During that first Tartar invasion, so the story goes, a watchman in the tower saw the enemy approaching and sounded the alarm. Before he could finish the tune, an arrow pierced his throat—which is why even today, the *hejnał* stops *subito* partway through. Today's buglers are firemen first, musicians second. Two at a time, they work a 48-hour shift as "fire lookouts," sharing a tiny apartment and taking turns playing the *hejnał* on the hour, every hour (broadcast on national Polish radio at noon). In July and August, you can climb up and meet them (Wed and Sat).

The church's front door is open 14 hours a day and free to those who come to pray. Tourists use the door around the right side (4 zł, Mon–Sat 11:30–18:00, Sun 14:00–18:00). The rusty neck-stock (behind the tourists' left door) was used for public humiliation until the 1700s.

Inside, you're drawn to one of the most impressive medieval woodcarvings in existence—the exquisite, three-part Gothic **altarpiece** by German Veit Stoss (Wit Stwosz in Polish). Carved in 12 years and completed in 1489, it's packed with emotion rare in Gothic art. Stoss used oak for the structural parts and linden trunks for the figures. When the altar doors are closed, you see scenes from the lives of Mary and Jesus. The open altar depicts the Dormition (death) of the Virgin. The artist catches the apostles (11, without Judas) around Mary, reacting in the seconds after she collapses. Mary is depicted in three stages: dying, being escorted to heaven by Jesus, and (at the very top) being crowned in heaven (flanked by 2 Polish saints—Adalbert and Stanisław). The six scenes on the sides are: the Annunciation, birth of Jesus, visit by the Three Magi, Jesus' Resurrection, his Ascension, and Mary becoming the mother of the apostles at Pentecost. The altar is open daily between noon and 18:00. Try to be here by 11:45 for the ceremonial opening or at 18:00 for the closing.

There's more to St. Mary's than the altar. While you're admiring this church's art, notice the flowery neo-Gothic painting covering the choir walls. Stare up into the starry, starry blue ceiling. As you wander around, realize that the church was renovated a century ago by three Polish geniuses from two very different artistic generations: the venerable positivist Jan Matejko, and his students, Stanisław Wyspiański and Józef Mehoffer (we'll learn more about these two later on our walk). The huge silver bird under the organ loft in back is the crowned eagle—symbol of Poland.

▲▲▲**Main Market Square (Rynek Główny)**—Kraków's marvelous Main Market Square is one of Europe's most gasp-worthy public spaces. The Square bustles with street musicians, colorful flower stalls, cotton-candy vendors, loitering teenagers, businesspeople commuting by foot, gawking tourists, and the lusty coos of pigeons. This Square is where Kraków lives. On my last visit, local teens practiced break-dancing moves at one end of the Square while activist types protested Poland's EU membership at the other.

The Square was established in the 13th century, when the city had to be rebuilt after being flattened by the Tartars. At that time, the Square was the biggest in medieval Europe. It was illegal to sell anything on the street, so everything had to be sold here on the Main

The Greatest Kazimierz: Kazimierz the Great (1333–1370)

Out of the centuries of Polish kings, only one earned the nickname "great," and he's the only one worth remembering: Kazimierz the Great.

K. the G., who ruled Poland from Kraków in the 14th century, was one of those larger-than-life medieval kings who left his mark on all fronts—from war to diplomacy, art patronage to womanizing. His scribes bragged that Kazimierz found a Poland made of wood, and left one made of brick and stone. He put Kraków on the map as a major European capital. He founded many villages (some of which still bear his name) and replaced wooden structures with stone ones (such as Kraków's Cloth Hall). He also established the Kraków Academy (today's Jagiellonian University), the second-oldest university in Central Europe.

Most of all, Kazimierz is remembered as a progressive, tolerant king. In the 14th century, other nations were deporting—or even interning—their Jewish subjects, who were commonly scapegoated for anything that went wrong. But the enlightened and kindly Kazimierz actively encouraged Jews to come to Poland by granting them special privileges, often relating to banking and trade—establishing the country as a safe haven for Jews in Europe.

Kazimierz the Great was the last of Poland's long-lived Piast dynasty. Although he left no male heir—at least, no legitimate one—Kazimierz's advances set the stage for Poland's golden age. After his death, Poland united with Lithuania (against the common threat of the Teutonic Knights), the Jagiellonian dynasty was born, and Poland became one of Europe's mightiest medieval powers.

Market Square. It was divided into smaller markets, such as the butcher stalls, the ironworkers' tents, and the Cloth Hall (see below).

The statue in the middle of the Square is Romantic poet **Adam Mickiewicz** (1789–1855). His epic masterpiece, *Pan Tadeusz*, is still regarded as one of the greatest works in Polish, and Mickiewicz is considered the "Polish Shakespeare." A wistful, nostalgic tale of Polish-Lithuanian nobility, *Pan Tadeusz* stirred patriotism in a Poland that had been dismantled by surrounding empires.

Near the end of the Square, you'll see the tiny **Church of St. Adalbert,** the oldest church in Kraków (10th century). This Romanesque structure predates the Square. Like St. Mary's (described above), it seems to be at an angle because it's aligned east–west, as was the custom when it was built. (In other words, the churches aren't crooked—the Square is.)

As the Square buzzes around you, imagine this place before 1989. There were no outdoor cafés, no touristy souvenir stands, no salesmen hawking cotton candy. The communist government shut down all but a handful of the businesses (keeping open, for instance, the Cloth Hall, which was a tourist arcade with shops, much like today). They didn't want people to congregate here—they should be at home, resting, because "a rested worker is a productive worker." The buildings were covered with soot from the nearby Nowa Huta steelworks. (The communists denied the pollution, and when the student "Green Brigades" staged a demonstration in this Square to raise awareness in the 1970s, they were immediately arrested.)

Drinks are cheap here (most under $2); find a place where you like the view and the chairs, then sit and sip. Enjoy the folk band. Tip them, and you can photograph their traditional Kraków garb up close. (A big tip gets you "The Star-Spangled Banner.")

The huge yellow building right in the middle of the Square is the...

▲▲**Cloth Hall (Sukiennice)**—In the Middle Ages, this was where the cloth-sellers had their market stalls. In the 14th century, Kazimierz the Great turned the Cloth Hall into a permanent structure. In 1555, it burned down, and was replaced by the current structure. The letter *S* (above the entryway) stands for King Sigismund the Old, who commissioned this version of the hall. As Sigismund fancied everything Italian (including women—he married an Italian

princess), this structure is in the Italianate Renaissance style. We'll see more works by Sigismund's imported Italian architects at Wawel Castle.

The Cloth Hall is still a functioning market—mostly souvenirs, including wood carvings, chess sets, jewelry, painted boxes, and trinkets (summer Mon–Fri 9:00–18:00, Sat–Sun 9:00–15:00, sometimes later; winter Mon–Fri 9:00–16:00, Sat–Sun 9:00–15:00). Cloth Hall prices are slightly inflated, but still cheap by American standards. You're paying a little extra for the convenience and the atmosphere, but locals insist they buy gifts here, too. Upstairs in the Cloth Hall is the very good Gallery of 19th-Century Polish Art (see page 178). WCs are at each end.

Browse through the Cloth Hall passageway. As you emerge into the other half of the Square, the big tower on your left is the...

Town Hall Tower—This is all that remains of a Town Hall building from the 14th century—when Kraków was the powerful capital of Poland. After the 18th-century partitions of Poland, Kraków's prominence took a nosedive. By the 19th century, Kraków was Nowheresville. As the town's importance crumbled, so did its Town

Młoda Polska
(Young Poland)

Polish art in the late 19th century was ruled by positivism, a school with a very literal, straightforward focus on Polish history (Jan Matejko led the charge; see page 228). When the new generation of Kraków's artists came into their own in the early 1900s, they became convinced that the old school was exactly that. The students of Jan Matejko moved in a totally different direction, experimenting with more wistful, creative interpretations of Polish history. Instead of a focus on actual historic events, they returned to Romanticism, with a renewed appreciation of folklore and country culture. Polish peasant life was held up as idyllic and beautiful. This movement became known as Młoda Polska (Young Poland)—Art Nouveau with a Polish accent.

Stanisław Wyspiański (vees-PAYN-skee, 1869–1907) was the leader of the Młoda Polska movement. He produced beautiful artwork, from simple drawings to the stirring stained-glass images in Kraków's St. Francis' Basilica. The versatile Wyspiański was also an accomplished stage designer and writer. His patriotic play *The Wedding*—about the wedding of a big-city artist to a peasant girl— is regarded as one of Poland's finest dramas. The largest collection of Wyspiański's art is in the museum devoted to him in Kraków, but you'll also see examples in Warsaw's National Gallery.

Józef Mehoffer (may-HOH-fehr), Wyspiański's good friend and rival, was another great Młoda Polska artist. See his work in Kraków's St. Francis' Basilica and at the artist's former residence; and in Warsaw, at the National Museum.

Hall. Krakovians tore down everything but this tower, nearly 200 feet tall. It's climbable, with 117 steps, a museum on Kraków history, and good views down over the Square (5 zł, May–Oct daily 10:30–14:00 & 14:30–18:00, closed off-season).

There are plenty of diversions to keep you busy here on the Square (including some good restaurants; see "Eating," page 190). When you're ready to continue down the Royal Way, follow Part 2 of the walk (below).

Royal Way Walk
Part 2: Main Market Square to Wawel Castle

After the king passed through the grand Main Market Square, he'd continue on to his castle. We'll take a one-block detour from his route to introduce you to one of Kraków's best churches. Leave on the street in the middle of the bottom of the Square. Ulica Bracka leads one long block (and across the busy Franciszkańska street) directly to the side door of a big red-brick church. Go ye.

▲▲**St. Francis' Basilica (Bazylika Św. Franciszka)**—This beautiful Gothic church features some of Poland's best Art Nouveau in situ (in the setting for which it was intended). After an 1850 fire, it was redecorated by members of the Młoda Polska (Young Poland) movement—the Polish version of Art Nouveau. It features brilliant works by the two men at the forefront of this movement: Stanisław Wyspiański and Józef Mehoffer. These two talented and fiercely competitive Krakovians were friends who apprenticed together under Poland's greatest painter, Jan Matejko. The glorious decorations of this church are the result of this great rivalry run amok. (For more Wyspiański or Mehoffer, visit their museums—see "Museums," page 177.)

Highlights include:

1. Paintings and stained-glass windows by **Stanisław Wyspiański.** The windows over the high altar represent the Blessed Salomea (the church's foundress, buried in a side chapel) and St. Francis (the church's namesake). The window in the rear of the nave is *God the Father Let It Be*, Wyspiański's finest masterpiece. The colors beneath the Creator change from yellows and oranges (fire) to soothing blues (water), depending on the light. Wyspiański was supposedly inspired by Michelangelo's vision of God in the Sistine Chapel. Wyspiański also painted the delightful floral designs decorating the walls of the nave. (For more on the artist, see page 170.)

2. The chapel on the left side of the nave (as you face the altar) is the response to Wyspiański's work by **Józef Mehoffer,** who decorated the chapel with the Stations of the Cross.

3. The modern painting (with an orange background, midway up the nave on the right as you face the altar) depicts **Saint Maksymilian Kolbe,** the Catholic priest who traded his own life to save a fellow inmate at Auschwitz (see his story on page 202).

Stepping outside (through the door you entered), look left. The light-yellow building (100 yards away) is the archbishop's palace, Pope John Paul II's home-away-from-Rome for visits to his hometown. From the window (above the ornate stone entryway), he's addressed thousands of Krakovians filling this street and the nearby park.

Once outside the church, turn right, cross the little square, and turn right again down Grodzka at the light purple building. You're back on the Royal Way proper. After two blocks, on the right (at #45), you'll see a...

Milk Bar (Bar Mleczny)—These government-subsidized cafeterias are the locals' choice for a quick, cheap, filling, lowbrow lunch. Prices are deliriously cheap (soup costs less than a złoty), and the food isn't bad. For more on milk bars, see page 152.

Just ahead, the square on your right is...

Mary Magdalene Square (Plac Św. Marii Magdaleny)—In the Middle Ages, Kraków was known as "Small Rome" for its many churches. Today, there are 142 churches and monasteries within the city limits (32 in the Old Town alone), more per square mile than anywhere outside Rome. You can see several of them from this spot: The nearest, with the picturesque white facade and red dome, is the **Church of Saints Peter and Paul** (Kraków's first Baroque church). The next one down, with the twin towers, is the Romanesque **St. Andrew's.** According to legend, a spring inside this church provided water to citizens who holed up here during Tartar invasions in the 13th century. If you look farther down the street, you can see three more churches. And the courtyard you're standing next to used to be a church, too—it burned in 1855, and only its footprint survives.

Go through the square (admiring the sculpture on the column that won Kraków's distinguished "ugliest statue" award in 2002), and turn left down...

Kanonicza Street (Ulica Kanonicza)—With so many churches around here, the clergy had to live somewhere. Many lived on this well-preserved street. Continue left down Kanonicza. As you walk, look for the cardinal hats over three different doorways. Find the yellow house (#19) on the right near the end of the street. The top window over the doorway is where a priest named **Karol Wojtyła** lived for 10 years after World War II. Wojtyła was born in nearby Wadowice in 1920. His mother died when he was a teenager, and he moved with his dad to Kraków to study drama at Jagiellonian University, just a few blocks from here. The Nazis shut down the school during World War II, and Wojtyła had to work in a quarry. When the war ended, he resumed his studies—this time at the theology faculty. Wojtyła graduated in 1947, and by 1964, he had become Archbishop of Kraków. In 1967, he became the youngest cardinal ever in the Roman Catholic Church. Eleven years after that, he was elected pope. Though the aging, ever conservative Pope John Paul II has lost stature in worldwide public opinion in recent years, he remains close to Poles' hearts. They still remember those frightening days under communism, when he would reassure them with his calming refrain, *"Nie lękajcie się"*—"Have no fear."

Your Majesty's journey is almost finished. At the end of Kanonicza street, a ramp leads up to the most important piece of ground in all of Poland.

Royal Way Walk
Part 3: Wawel Hill

Wawel (VAH-vehl), a symbol of Polish royalty and independence, is sacred territory to every Polish person. A castle has stood here since the beginning of recorded history. Today, Wawel—awash in tourists—is the most visited sight in the country. Crowds and a ridiculously complex admissions system for the hill's many historic sights can be exasperating. Thankfully, for most non-Polish visitors, a stroll through the cathedral and around the castle grounds requires no tickets, and—with the help of the following self-guided commentary—is enough. The many museums on Wawel (described below) are mildly interesting, but can be skipped.

Walk up the long ramp to the castle entry. When Kraków was part of the Hapsburg Empire in the 19th century, the Austrians turned this castle complex into a fortress—destroying much of its delicate beauty. When Poland regained its independence after World War I, the castle was returned to its former glory. The bricks you see on your left as you climb the ramp bear the names of Poles from around the world who donated to the cause.

The jaunty equestrian statue ahead is **Tadeusz Kościuszko** (1746–1817)—whom you might remember from your American History classes. Kościuszko was a hero of the American Revolution and helped design West Point before returning to Poland to fight bravely but unsuccessfully against the Russians (during the partitions that would divide Poland's territory among 3 neighboring powers).

Hiking through the gate next to Kościuszko, you pass the ticket office (see "Tickets and Reservations," page 177) and, as you crest the hill, you'll see to your left...

▲**Wawel Cathedral**—Poland's national church is its Westminster Abbey. While the history buried here is pretty murky to most Americans, to Poles, this church is *the* national mausoleum. It holds the tombs of nearly all of Poland's most important rulers and greatest historical figures.

Exterior: Go around to the far side of the cathedral to take in its profile. This uniquely eclectic church is the product of centuries of haphazard additions...yet somehow, it works. It began as a simple, stripped-down Romanesque church in the 12th century. (The white base of the nearest tower is original; you can see a model of the complete, basic structure in the "Lost Wawel" exhibit described below.) Kazimierz  the Great and his predecessors gradually surrounded the cathedral with some 20 Gothic chapels, which were further modified over the centuries. To the right of the tall tower are two particularly interesting domed chapels. The gold one is the Renaissance Sigismund's Chapel, housing memorials to the Jagiellonian kings. The green one (which looks the same—but is a copy, built 150 years later) is home to the Swedish Waza dynasty. As time went on, more additions were grafted on, making this beautiful church a happy hodgepodge of styles.

Go back around and face the front entry for more architectonic silliness. You see Gothic chapels flanking the door, a Renaissance ceiling, lavish Baroque decoration over the door, and big bones (thought to come from extinct animals). Years ago, these were taken for the bones of giants and put here for protection. It's said that as long as they hang here, the cathedral will stand. The door is the original from the 14th century, with fine wrought-iron work. The *K* with the crown stands for Kazimierz the Great. The black marble frame is made of Kraków stone from nearby quarries.

For a quick peek at the interior, step inside. (If you want to visit the other interior sights described below—a crypt and a tower climb to a big bell—first buy a 8-zł ticket in the building across the street.)

Interior: The cathedral interior is slathered in Baroque memorials and tombs. The silver tomb under a canopy in the center is that of St. Stanisław (dating from the 15th century, and inspired by the one in St. Peter's at the Vatican). Circling around to the right (behind the main altar), you'll find the sarcophagus of St. Jadwiga, the 14th-century "Queen of Poland," who helped Christianize Lithuania, fought the Teutonic Knights, and was sainted by Pope John Paul II in 1997. All the flowers here prove she's popular with Poles today. Across from Jadwiga, the 16th-century Sigismund Chapel—with its silver altar—is considered by Poles to be the finest Renaissance chapel north of the Alps. Farther back on the left is The Great One—Kazimierz, of course (look for *Kazimierz Wielki*). Poke into the choir for a look at the high altar. For 200 years, the colorful chair on the right has been the seat of Kraków's archbishops, including Karol Wojtyła, who served here for 14 years before becoming pope. Near the main door (on the left as you face outside), peek into the Gothic chapel with its Russian Orthodox–style 15th-century frescoes.

For most visitors, that's everything worth seeing in the cathedral. But if you're a fan of big bells and the tombs of VIPs (Very Important Poles), you can see—with a ticket—the...

Bell, Crypt, and Tombs: Claustrophobic wooden stairs lead up to the 11-ton **Sigismund Bell** and pleasant views of the steeples and spires of Kraków. Then, descend into the little **crypt** (housing Adam Mickiewicz—the Romantic poet whose statue dominates the Square). Finally, when you're ready to leave (since you'll exit back out into the courtyard), head through the chapel in the back-right corner to find the door down to the **royal tombs**. The first room houses Poland's greatest war heroes: Kościuszko (of American Revolution fame), Jan Sobieski III (who successfully defended Vienna from the Turks; in the simple black coffin with the gold inscription "J III S"), Sikorski, Poniatowski, and so on. Then you'll wander through several rooms of second-tier Polish kings, queens, and their kids. Marshal Józef Piłsudski, the WWI hero who ruled Poland from 1926 to 1935, has the last grave (in the room on the right, just before you exit). His tomb was moved here so the soldiers who came to party on his grave wouldn't disturb the others.

Cost and Hours: While most of the cathedral is free, you'll need a ticket to climb down through the royal tombs or up the tower to see the bell (tickets sold across from entrance, 8 zł, May–Sept Mon–Sat 9:00–17:15, Sun 12:15–17:15; Oct–April Mon–Sat 9:00–15:45, Sun 12:15–15:45).

Cathedral Museum—This small museum, with various holy robes and replicas of what's buried with the kings, plus the Sigismund Bell's original clapper, is nearby (5 zł, Tue–Sun 10:00–15:00, closed Mon).

When you're finished in the cathedral, stroll around the...

▲▲Wawel Castle Grounds—This hill has seen lots of changes over the years. Kazimierz the Great turned a small fortress into a mighty Gothic castle in the 14th century. Today, you'll see the cathedral and a castle complex, but little remains of Kazimierz's grand fortress, which burned to the ground in 1499. In the grassy field across from the cathedral, you'll see the foundations of two Gothic churches that were destroyed when the Austrians took over Wawel in the 19th century and needed a parade ground for their troops.

Behind the cathedral, a grand green entryway leads into the palace **courtyard.** When Kazimierz's castle burned down, this courtyard was rebuilt in the Italian Renaissance style. The dark, ivy-covered side later served as the headquarters of the notorious Hans Frank, Nazi governor of German-occupied Poland. (He was tried and executed in Nürnberg after the war.) The entrances to most Wawel museums are here, and some believe that you'll find something even more special: chakra.

Adherents of the Hindu doctrine of **chakra** believe that a powerful energy field connects all living things. There are seven points on the surface of the earth where this chakra energy is most concentrated: Delhi, Delphi, Jerusalem, Mecca, Rome, Velehrad...and Wawel Hill—specifically over there in the corner (immediately to your left as you enter the courtyard). Look for peaceful people (here or elsewhere on the castle grounds) with their eyes closed. One thing's for sure: They're not thinking of Kazimierz the Great. The smudge marks on the wall are from people pressing up against this corner, trying to absorb some of the chakra's power. The Wawel administration seems creeped out by all this. They've done what they can to discourage this ritual, but believers still gravitate from far and wide to hug the wall. Give it a try...and let the Force be with you. (Just for fun, ask a Wawel tour guide about chakra, and watch him squirm—they're forbidden to talk about it.)

If you plan to visit some of the castle museums, now's the time (see "Wawel Castle Museums," below). But if you're looking for a scenic wrap-up to this royal ramble, leave the courtyard the way you came in, and keep going straight toward the opening in the wall. You'll be rewarded with a beautiful view over the Vistula River and Kraków's outskirts. Directly below you, along the riverbank, is a fire-belching monument to the **dragon** that was instrumental in the founding of Kraków...

Once upon a time, a prince named Krak founded a town on Wawel Hill. It was the perfect location—except for the fire-breathing dragon who lived in the caves under the hill and terrorized the town. Prince Krak had to feed the dragon all of the town's livestock to keep the monster from going after the townspeople. But clever Krak had a plan. He stuffed a sheep's skin with sulfur and left it outside the dragon's cave. The dragon swallowed it down, and before long, he developed a terrible case of heartburn. To put the fire out, the dragon started drinking water from the Vistula. He kept drinking and drinking until he finally exploded. The town was saved, and Kraków thrived.

Our walking tour is finished. If you want to head down to see the Vistula and the dragon close up, take a shortcut through the nearby **Dragon's Den** (Smocza Jama). It's just a 135-step spiral staircase and a few underground caverns—worthwhile only as a quick way to get from the top of Wawel down to the banks of the Vistula (3 zł, enter around corner from bookstore on courtyard overlooking the river, April–Oct daily 10:00–17:00, closed Nov–March).

Wawel Castle Museums—There are five museums and exhibits in Wawel Castle (not including the cathedral and Cathedral Museum). Each has its own admission, ranging from 5–15 zł (slightly cheaper off-season; complex hours for all museums, unless otherwise noted: April–Oct Sun 10:00–15:00, Mon 9:30–12:00, Tue and Fri 9:30–16:00, Wed–Thu and Sat 9:30–15:00; Nov–March Sun 10:00–15:00, Tue–Sat 9:30–15:00, closed Mon, tel. 012/422-5155, www.wawel.krakow.pl).

The **Royal State Rooms** (Komnaty Królewskie), while precious to Poles, are mediocre by European standards (enter through courtyard). The top-floor rooms are best, with original wooden ceilings, "leather tooled" walls, and precious 16th-century Brussels tapestries (140 of the original series of 300 survive). Wandering these halls (with their period furnishings), you get a feeling for the 16th- and 17th-century glory days of Poland, when it was a leading power in Eastern Europe. The Senate Room, with its throne and fine tapestries, is the climax.

The **Royal Private Apartments** (Prywatne Apartamenty Królewskie) are more of the same, and the only part of the complex that must be visited with a guided tour (enter through courtyard, April–Oct English-language tours Tue–Sun at 10:50, 12:00, and 13:10; Nov–March English-language tour Tue–Sun at 12:00; always closed Mon).

The **Crown Treasury and Armory** (Skarbiec i Zbrojownia) is a decent collection of swords, saddles, and shields; ornately decorated muskets and crossbows; and cannons in the basement (free on Mon April–Oct; closed Sun–Mon off-season).

The small **Oriental Art** (Sztuka Wschodu) exhibit displays swords, carpets, vases, and remarkable Turkish tents (upstairs, next to the Senate Room) used by the Ottomans during the 1683 Battle of Vienna. These are trophies of Jan Sobieski, the Polish king who led a pan-European army to victory in that battle (tickets sold at the door, enter through courtyard, don't miss entry on your way back downstairs from Royal State Rooms; closed Mon in season, closed Sun–Mon off-season).

The **Lost Wawel** (Wawel Zaginiony) exhibit traces the history of this hill and its various churches and castles. The one-way route leads through excavations of a 10th-century church, and exhibits include a model of the cathedral in its original Romanesque form (much simpler, before all the colorful, bulbous domes, chapels, and towers were added) and a replica of the entire castle complex in the 18th century (pre-Austrian razing). There is also a display of fascinating decorative tiles from 16th-century stoves that once heated the place, and some medieval artifacts (enter near snack bar across from side of cathedral, open Mon but closed Tue off-season).

Tickets and Reservations: Tickets are sold at several points around the Wawel grounds (most convenient at top of long entry ramp, shorter lines inside bookstore around corner from Dragon's Den). Tickets are limited for the Royal State Rooms, Crown Treasury and Armory, and Royal Private Apartments (which can be visited only with a tour). Boards show how many tickets for each of these are still available today. Tickets come with an assigned entry time (though you can usually sneak in before your scheduled time). In the summer, ticket lines can be long, and sights can sell out by midday. You can reserve tickets ahead for the tour of the Royal Private Apartments (no fee) and the Royal State Rooms and the Crown Armory and Treasury (15-zł reservation fee; tel. 012/422-1697). Frankly, the sights aren't worth all the fuss—if they're sold out, you're not missing much.

Museums

Kraków's **National Museum** (Muzeum Narodowe) is made up of a series of small but interesting museums scattered throughout the city. Oddly enough, the main branch (Gmach Główny) is the least worth visiting, with 20th-century Polish art and temporary exhibits (9 zł, more for special exhibits, aleja 3 Maja 1). I've listed the best of the National Museum's branches below, followed by the Jagiellonian University Museum.

Be warned: It seems to be the inexplicable policy of the National Museum to completely overhaul the opening hours of its various branches about every six months. All of the museums below (except the Jagiellonian University Museum) are generally open Tue–Sat 10:00–16:00, Sun 10:00–15:00, closed Mon. Some evenings—especially in summer—these museums may be open later (until 19:00); hours can be shorter November through May.

▲▲Czartoryski Museum (Muzeum Czartoryskich)—The best of the museums is this eclectic collection, the life's work of Romantic-era princess Izabela Czartoryska. Inspired by Poland's 1791 constitution (Europe's first), she began collecting bits of Polish history and culture. She fled with the collection to Paris after the 1830 insurrection, and, 45 years later, her grandson returned it to its present Kraków location. When he ran out of room, he bought part of the monastery across the street, joining the buildings with a fancy passageway. The Nazis took the collection to Germany, and although most of it has been returned, some pieces are still missing.

The museum features armor, handicrafts, decorative arts, and paintings. The first floor is dedicated mostly to artifacts of Polish history and decorative arts; the top floor is European art. There are only three surviving portraits of women by Leonardo da Vinci in the world; *Mona Lisa* in the Louvre is the most famous, but another one is in this very museum—*Lady with an Ermine.* In the painting, the mistress of Leonardo's patron sensually strokes an ermine (like a ferret). The patron's nickname was Ermelino—meaning, um, "ermine." Hmm...

You'll also see Rembrandt's *Landscape with the Good Samaritan.* The Nazis swiped a famous Rembrandt self-portrait, which was never recovered (9 zł, more for special exhibits, generally open Tue–Sat 10:00–16:00, Sun 10:00–15:00, closed Mon, open later some evenings in summer, shorter hours Nov–May, 2 blocks north of the Square at ulica Św. Jana 19, tel. 012/422-5566).

▲Gallery of 19th-Century Polish Art (Galeria Sztuki Polskiej XIX Wieku)—This place is surprisingly classy for a museum above a market hall. The enjoyable collection features some significant painters, such as Jan Matejko (see his painting of Tadeusz Kościuszko doffing his hat after his unlikely victory over the Russians at the battle at Racławice—for more on Matejko, see page 228). But other paintings are clearly just plain good, even if you haven't heard of the artists—such as Józef Chełmoński's energy-charged *Four-in-Hand* and misty *Cranes.* Don't miss Władysław Podkowiński's gripping *Frenzy,* with a pale, sensuous woman clutching an all-fired-up black stallion. The painting caused a frenzy indeed at its 1894 unveiling—leading the unbalanced artist to attack his creation with a knife (8 zł, good 35-zł English guidebook, all paintings labeled in English, generally open Tue–Sat 10:00–16:00, Sun 10:00–15:00, closed Mon, open later some evenings in summer, shorter hours Nov–May; upstairs in big, yellow Cloth Hall on Main Market Square—enter on east side, facing St. Mary's; tel. 012/422-1166).

▲Wyspiański Museum (Muzeum Wyspiańskiego)—If you enjoyed Stanisław Wyspiański's stained glass and wall paintings in St. Francis' Basilica, visit the museum that collects his work. Housed in a renovated mansion, this museum traces the personal history and artistic development of the Młoda Polska poster boy (7 zł, good English descriptions in most rooms, the dry 5-zł English audioguide basically repeats posted information, generally open Tue–Sat 10:00–16:00, Sun 10:00–15:00, closed Mon, open later some evenings in summer, shorter hours Nov–May, 1 block west of the Square at ulica Szczepańska 11, tel. 012/292-8183).

You'll begin by climbing the stairs to view some of Wyspiański's precocious childhood sketchbooks, then move on to see works from his youthful collaboration with his teacher Jan Matejko and his friend Józef Mehoffer as they renovated St. Mary's Church (with designs for beautiful stained-glass windows). One of the museum's highlights is the design for the dramatic, stained-glass *Apollo,* which hangs in the House of the Medical Society. Also on this floor are portraits and self-portraits; the costumes and plans for sets Wyspiański designed for his own plays; and copies of Wyspiański's printed works, which he also designed himself.

On your way up to the next floor, you'll see the designs for Wyspiański's masterpiece, *God the Father Let It Be,* from St. Francis' Basilica. Once upstairs, head for the model of the elaborate acropolis Wyspiański planned for the top of Wawel Hill, with a domed palace, an amphitheater, and a circus maximus. Filling another room are portraits of Wyspiański's family—including his daughter Helenka, just waking up, and his wife breast-feeding their son Staś, with Helenka circling around to get good views of both of them (appearing twice in the painting). You'll end with a display of Wyspiański's serene landscapes.

More National Museum Branches—You can also check out the museum of Wyspiański's friend and rival, the **Józef Mehoffer House** (Dom Józefa Mehoffera, 6 zł, ulica Krupnicza 26, tel. 012/421-1143), and the former residence of their mentor, the **Jan Matejko House** (Dom Jana Matejki, 6 zł, ulica Floriańska 41, tel. 012/422-5926). Both are open the same hours as the Wyspiański Museum.

Jagiellonian University Museum: Collegium Maius—Kraków had the second university in Central Europe (after Prague), boasting over the centuries such illustrious grads as Copernicus and Pope John Paul II. This city is still very much a university town, and Jagiellonian University proudly leads tours of its historic oldest building, the 15th-century Collegium Maius. Tour groups routinely duck into the building's Gothic courtyard for free. To visit the interior, you'll choose between two different guided tours. The shorter route includes the library, refectory, treasury, assembly hall, and an exhibit of Copernicus' original instruments (10 zł, free on Sat, 30 min, leaves every 20 min Mon–Sat 10:00–14:20, Thu until 17:20, only some in English, none Sun). The deluxe version adds some medieval sculptures, a Rubens, a Rembrandt, some old scientific instruments, and Chopin's piano (usually in English, 15 zł, 1 hr, Mon–Fri at 13:00, none Sat–Sun). It's always smart to call ahead to find out when the shorter tour is scheduled in English, and to reserve for either tour; the shorter tour is especially popular and books up long in advance, particularly on Saturdays, when it's free (tel. 012/663-1307 or 012/422-0549, extension 1307, 1 block west of the Square at ulica Jagiellońska 15, www.uj.edu.pl/muzeum).

Aside from the courtyard, the only part of the Colleguim Maius you can see without a tour is an interactive exhibit that allows you to tinker with replicas of old scientific tools (6 zł, Mon–Sat 10:00–14:00, closed Sun).

Kazimierz (Jewish Quarter)

The neighborhood of Kazimierz (kah-ZHEE-mezh), 20 minutes by foot southeast of Kraków's Old Town, is the historic heart of Kraków's once thriving Jewish community. After years of neglect, the district is today being rediscovered by locals and tourists alike. With a smattering of new restaurants and hotels, it's accessible to travelers, but still retains its local flavor.

Visitors expecting a polished, touristy scene like Prague's Jewish Quarter will be surprised...and maybe disappointed. This is basically a local-feeling neighborhood with a handful of Jewish cemeteries, synagogues, and restaurants, and often a few pensive Israeli tour groups wandering the streets. But for me, the lack of crowds makes it an even more evocative experience than the Prague alternative.

Orientation: Start your visit to Kazimierz on **ulica Szeroka,** which is more of a long, parking-lot square than a street, surrounded by Jewish restaurants, hotels, and synagogues. Check in at the **Jarden Bookshop** at the top of the square (daily 10:00–18:00, ulica Szeroka 2, tel. 012/421-7166, www.jarden.pl, jarden@jarden.pl). It serves as a tourist information center for the neighborhood, and sells a wide variety of books on Kazimierz and Jewish culture in the region (including a good 4.50-zł Kazimierz map and well-illustrated 18-zł *Jewish Kraków* guidebook). They also run several tours: Jewish Kazimierz overview (35 zł, 2 hrs, walking), Kazimierz and the WWII ghetto (45 zł, 3 hrs, walking, the best overview), *Schindler's List* sights (65 zł, 2 hrs, by car), and Auschwitz-Birkenau (95 zł, 6 hrs, by car). Call to reserve ahead, as tours are by appointment only. Tours will run if a minimum of three people sign up, but pairs or singles can join an already scheduled tour.

If you visit on Saturday, you'll find only the Old Synagogue museum open. For hotel and restaurant suggestions, see page 189 of "Sleeping" and page 193 of "Eating." Some recommended restaurants offer live traditional Jewish music nightly in summer.

Getting to Kazimierz: It's about a 20-minute **walk** from the Old Town. From the Square, walk down ulica Sienna (near St.

Kazimierz

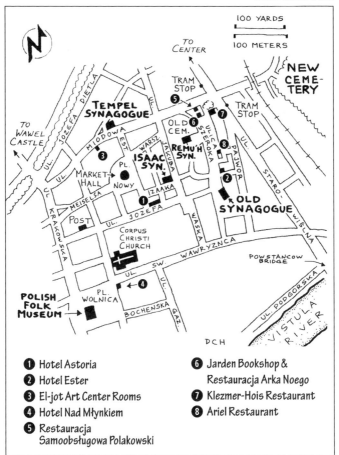

- ① Hotel Astoria
- ② Hotel Ester
- ③ El-jot Art Center Rooms
- ④ Hotel Nad Młynkiem
- ⑤ Restauracja Samoobsługowa Polakowski
- ⑥ Jarden Bookshop & Restauracja Arka Noego
- ⑦ Klezmer-Hois Restaurant
- ⑧ Ariel Restaurant

Mary's Church). At the fork, bear right through the Planty park. At the intersection with the busy Westerplatte ring road, you'll continue straight ahead (bear right at fork) down busy Starowiślna for 15 more minutes. To hop the **tram,** go to the stop on the left-hand side of ulica Sienna (at the intersection with Westerplatte, across the street from the Poczta Główna, or main post office). Catch tram #3, #13, or #24 and go two stops to Miodowa. Walking or by tram, at the intersection of Starowiślna and Miodowa, you'll see a small park across the street and to the right. To reach the heart of Kazimierz—ulica Szeroka—cut through this park. To get back into the Old Town, catch tram #3, #13, or #24 from the intersection of Starowiślna and Miodowa and go two stops back to the Poczta Główna stop.

Jews in Kraków

After King Kazimierz the Great encouraged Jews to come to Poland in the 14th century (see page 168), a large Jewish community settled in and around Kraków. According to legend, Kazimierz (the king) established Kazimierz (the village) for his favorite girlfriend—a Jewish woman named Ester—just southeast of the city walls. (If you have a 50-zł note, take a look at it: that's Kazimierz the Great on the front, and on the back is his capital, Cracovia, and the most important town he founded, Casmirus.)

It's a cute legend, but the village of Kazimierz didn't really become a Jewish enclave until much later. By the end of the 15th century, there were large Jewish populations in both Kazimierz and in Kraków. Kraków's Jewish community and the university students clashed, and when a destructive fire broke out in 1495, the Jews were blamed. The king at the time (not Kazimierz the Great) forced all of Kraków's Jews to move to Kazimierz.

Kazimierz was an autonomous community, with its own Town Hall, market square, and city walls (though many Jews still commuted into Kraków's Square to do business). The Christian (west) and Jewish (east) neighborhoods were also separated by a wall. But

▲▲**Jewish Cemeteries**—Kazimierz has two Jewish cemeteries, less touristy and equally powerful as the famous one in Prague. The more

notable of the two is the **New Cemetery** (Nowy Cmentarz), with graves of those who died after 1800 (free, Sun–Fri 9:00–18:00, until 16:00 in winter, closed Sat, tricky to find—go under railway bridge at east end of ulica Miodowa, jog left as you emerge, cemetery is to your right, enter through gate or door at #55). Nazis vandalized this cemetery—bulldozing it with their tanks—but many of the gravestones have since been returned to their original positions. Other headstones could not be replaced, and were used to create the moving mosaic wall and Holocaust monument (on the right as you enter).

The **Old Cemetery** (Stary Cmentarz), nearly as moving, was used from 1552 to 1800. It's smaller and has been renovated—so it actually feels newer. Like the New Cemetery, it features a wall made of pieces of shattered gravestones (5 zł, Sun–Fri 9:00–16:00, closed Sat, enter through Remu'h Synagogue at ulica Szeroka 40).

Synagogues—Two synagogues sit right on Kazimierz's main square, ulica Szeroka. The **Old Synagogue** (Stara Synagoga), the oldest surviving Jewish building in Poland, is now a three-room museum on local Jewish culture, with English descriptions (7 zł, free by 1800, the walls came down, Kazimierz became part of Kraków, and the Jewish community flourished.

By the start of World War II, 65,000 Jews lived in Kraków (mostly in Kazimierz)—making up more than a quarter of the city's population. Soon after the Nazis arrived, they forced Kraków's Jews into a walled ghetto at Podgórze, across the river. The Jews' cemeteries were defiled, and their buildings ransacked and destroyed. In 1942, the Nazis began transporting Kraków's Jews to death camps. Many others were worked to death in the Podgórze ghetto. Only a few thousand Kraków Jews survived the war.

Today's Kraków has only about a hundred Jewish residents. Kazimierz still has an empty feeling, but the neighborhood has enjoyed a renaissance of Jewish culture, following the popularity of *Schindler's List* (which was filmed partly in Kazimierz—look for handwritten letters from Steven Spielberg and the cast in local restaurants—such as Ariel—and hotels; these have more recently been joined by autographs from *The Pianist* director Roman Polański). While few Jews live here now, the spirit of the Jewish tradition lives on in the many synagogues, as well as in the soulful cemeteries.

on Mon, mid-April–mid-Oct Mon 10:00–14:00, Tue–Sun 10:00–17:00; mid-Oct–mid-April Mon 10:00–14:00, Wed–Thu and Sat–Sun 9:00–15:30, Fri 10:00–17:00, closed Tue, ulica Szeroka 24). **Remu'h Synagogue,** from 1553, is tiny and attached to the Old Cemetery (included in cemetery 5-zł entry fee, Sun–Fri 9:00–16:00, closed Sat, ulica Szeroka 40).

Isaac Synagogue (Synagoga Isaaka), a block west of ulica Szeroka, is the most accessible place to learn more about the Kazimierz Jewish community. This synagogue, the biggest in Kraków, was built in the 17th century. During a recent renovation, they discovered giant wall paintings of prayers (for people who couldn't afford to buy books). In a side room, the synagogue continually runs a 98-minute loop of six films (mostly silent, others in Hebrew, Polish, Yiddish, and English) showing the town before the Nazis came and then the forced transition to a ghetto. Two of the most important films (lasting a total of 7 min) run continuously in the main hall (7 zł, Sun–Fri 9:00–19:00, July–Aug until 20:00, closed Sat, closes at sundown on winter Fri—as early as 15:00 in Dec, ulica Kupa 18, tel. 012/430-5577).

Tempel Synagogue (Synagoga Templu), three blocks northwest of ulica Szeroka, has the grandest interior—big and dark, with elaborately decorated, gilded ceilings and balconies—and the most lived-in feel of the bunch (5 zł, Sun–Fri 9:00–16:00, closed Sat, corner of ulica Miodowa and ulica Podbrzezie).

▲**Kazimierz Market Square (Plac Nowy)**—Locals shop at plac Nowy's market stalls, a gritty, factory-workers-on-lunch-break contrast to Kraków's touristy Main Market Square (stalls open Tue–Sat 6:00–14:00, a few also open later and Sun 7:00–14:00). Consider dropping by here for some shopping (sorry, no souvenirs), people-watching, or a quick, cheap, and local lunch (see "Eating," page 190).

▲**Polish Folk Museum (Muzeum Etnograficzne)**—This clever and refreshingly good museum hides a few blocks west of the Jewish area of Kazimierz, in the former town hall. The square it's on, plac Wolnica, was Kazimierz's main market square, once almost as big as Kraków's. Inside the museum, you'll find models of traditional rural Polish homes, as well as musty replicas of the interiors (like an open-air folk museum—but inside). On the second floor are traditional Polish folk costumes, Christmas decorations, and even bagpipes. The top floor has some imaginatively carved beehives (6 zł, free on Sun, Mon 10:00–16:00, Wed–Fri 10:00–15:00, Sat–Sun 10:00–14:00, closed Tue, ulica Krakówska 46, tel. 012/430-6023).

Schindler's List Sights—Fans of Spielberg's Holocaust movie—and the compassionate Kraków businessman who did his creative best to save the lives of his Jewish workers—can see Oskar Schindler's actual factory, currently the Telpod electronics manufacturing plant (beyond Kazimierz, southeast of the Old Town, near Kraków-Zabłocie train station at ulica Lipowa 4; not much to see). Closer to the center, Schindler's apartment is a block from Wawel Castle at ulica Straszewskiego 7 (unmarked and not available for tours).

Near Kraków

▲▲**Wieliczka Salt Mine (Kopalnia Soli Wieliczka)**—This remarkable mine, 10 miles southeast of Kraków, has been producing salt since at least the 11th century. Under Kazimierz the Great, one-third of Poland's income came from these precious deposits. Wieliczka miners spent much of their lives underground, leaving for work before daybreak and returning after sundown, rarely emerging into daylight. To pass the time, 19th-century miners began to carve figures, chandeliers, and eventually even an elaborate chapel out of the salt.

From the lobby, your guide leads you 210 feet down a winding staircase to a spot where you begin a 1.5-mile generally downhill stroll past 20 of the mine's 2,000 chambers (with signs saying when they were dug), finishing 443 feet below the surface. When you're done, a lift beams you back up.

The tour shows how the miners lived and worked (using horses who spent their whole lives without ever seeing the light of day), takes you through some impressive underground caverns past subterranean lakes, and introduces you to some of the mine's many sculptures (including an army of salt elves and this region's favorite

son, Pope John Paul II). Your jaw will drop as you enter the enormous **Chapel of the Blessed Kinga,** carved over three decades in the early 20th century. Look for the salt-relief carving of the Last Supper.

While advertised as two hours, your tour finishes in a deep-down shopping zone 90 minutes after you started (they hope you'll hang out and shop). Note when the next elevator departs (just 3/hr), and you can be outta there on the next lift. Zip through the shopping zone in two minutes, or step over the rope and be immediately in line for the great escape (you'll be escorted 300 yards to the skinny industrial elevator, into which you'll be packed like mine workers).

Cost and Hours: Visits are by tour only (40 zł for a guided tour, 10 zł extra to use your camera). English tours are generally daily at 10:00 and 12:30 all year; June and Sept–Oct also at 15:00; July–Aug also at 11:30, 13:45, 15:00, and 17:00. If you miss the English-language tour (or decide to just show up and take whatever's going next), follow the fine 3-zł guidebook, which narrates the exact route the tours do and actually gives you more info than the tour guide (daily April–Oct 7:30–19:30, Nov–March 8:00–16:00, ulica Daniłowicza 10, tel. 012/278-7302, www.kopalnia.pl). Dress warmly—the mine is a constant 57 degrees Fahrenheit. When buying a ticket, you'll be asked if you want the mine museum. It adds an hour to the mine tour (and is discouraged by local guides: "1.5 miles more walking, colder, more of the same").

Getting to Wieliczka: The salt mine, 10 miles from Kraków, is best reached by minibus (2.50 zł, 4/hr or with demand). Buses leave from Kraków's train/bus station (look for *Wieliczka Soli* sign in window—confirm that it's actually going to the salt mine) and from the mine exit. Taking a taxi is fastest, and taking the train makes no sense.

▲**Nowa Huta**—Literally "New Steel Works," this factory was originally named for Lenin. When the communists took over Poland, they were nervous about Kraków's long tradition of progressives and intellectuals. To put the city in its place, they built a massive steelworks six miles east of the center (supposedly using plans stolen from a Pittsburgh plant). A walk through this planned worker town is a step back in time to the communist era. From its main square, Nowa Huta radiates numbered streets, and trolleys zip workers directly to the immense factory, which still produces steel.

For the best quick visit, take tram #4 from Kraków's old center (from Main Market Square, follow Szczepańska to the ring road outside the Planty park) or from Kraków's train station to Nowa Huta's main square, plac Centralny (about 30 min), and just wander.

Gape at the Stalinist architecture, and reflect on what it would be like to be one of the 200,000 Poles who live in Nowa Huta. (Actually, it may not be as bad as you imagine—these buildings look stark and gloomy outside, but they're packed with happy little apartments filled with color, light, and warmth.) Tram #4 continues a few minutes farther to the main gate of the factory (little to see other than the big sign, stern office headquarters, and smokestacks in the distance), and then it returns to Kraków.

The factory remains, but Krakovians had the last laugh: Nowa Huta, along with Lech Wałęsa's shipyard in Gdańsk, was one of the home bases of the Solidarity strikes that eventually brought down Poland's communist regime.

SLEEPING

Kraków's Old Town is filled with affordable hotels with similar prices and interchangeable rooms. This healthy competition has kept prices reasonable, even just a few steps off the Square. Rates are soft—hoteliers don't need much of an excuse to offer you 10 to 20 percent off, especially on weekends or in the off-season.

While you could stay away from the center, hotel values here are so good that there's not much need to sleep beyond the Planty. Most of my listings are inside (or within a block or two of) the old city walls.

To save a little more money and experience a more local alternative, consider the Kazimierz neighborhood—once Kraków's sister town, later the Jewish quarter, and now part of the city.

Old Town

$$$ **Hotel Maltański,** my favorite spot in Kraków, is in the beautifully renovated former royal stables, just outside the Planty and only two blocks from Wawel Castle. This fine hotel has an excellent location, friendly and helpful staff, and 17 rooms with all the classy little extras that add up to a pleasant experience (like a fluffy white bathrobe for every guest). It's a great-value splurge for its location and luxurious touches (Sb-350 zł, "business class" Sb-450 zł, Db-510 zł, 15 percent discount for readers of this book in 2005, off-season try to negotiate even better deal—up to 25 percent less, parking-30 zł/day, ulica Straszewskiego 14, tel. 012/431-0010, fax 012/431-0615, www.maltanski.com, hotel@maltanski.com). The Maltański also runs a six-room annex, **Hotel Pugetów**, with lower rates, plusher rooms, and a fun breakfast cellar. It's on the other side of town—actually slightly closer to the Square—but the neighborhood's a tad dingy (Sb-250 zł, Db-400 zł, Db suite-590 zł, 2-room Tb suite-500 zł, ulica Starowiślna 13-15, reception and contact at Hotel Maltański).

Sleep Code

(3.5 zł = about $1, €1 = about $1.20, country code: 48, area code: 012)
S = Single, **D** = Double/Twin, **T** = Triple, **Q** = Quad,
b = bathroom, **s** = shower only. Breakfast is included, credit
cards are accepted, and English is spoken at each place (unless
otherwise noted). Some hotels quote prices in euros.

To help you sort easily through these listings, I've divided
the rooms into three categories, based on the price for a standard
double room with bath:

$$$ Higher Priced—Most rooms 400 zł (€92) or more.
$$ Moderately Priced—Most rooms between 300–400 zł
(€69–92).
$ Lower Priced—Most rooms 300 zł (€69) or less.

$$$ Hotel Senacki is a professional-feeling, business-class place
renting 20 elegant rooms between Wawel Castle and the Main
Market Square (Sb-€105, Db-€120, deluxe Db-€155, extra bed-€25,
€10 cheaper Fri–Sun, 15 percent cheaper Nov–March, parking-80
zł/day, non-smoking rooms, elevator—but doesn't go to top floor,
ulica Grodzka 51, tel. 012/421-1161, fax 012/422-7934, www.senacki
.krakow.pl, recepcja@senacki.krakow.pl).

$$ Hotel Saski rents 60 high-ceilinged rooms a few steps from
the Square (10 of them with institutional-feeling bathrooms down
the hall). The frou-frou lobby—with its kitschy gift shops, uniformed
bellhop, and antique elevator—feels old-fashioned, but the hotel
somehow lacks soul. Still, it's an excellent value for the location (S-
210 zł, Sb-260 zł, D-220 zł, Db-330 zł, fancy superior Db-410–430
zł, T-265 zł, Ts-300 zł, Tb-385 zł, elevator, ulica Sławkowska 3, tel.
012/421-4222, fax 012/421-4830, www.hotelsaski.com.pl, info
@hotelsaski.com.pl).

$$ Hotel Wawel Tourist's classy marble lobby seems too fancy
for its prices, but its 49 rooms live up to the fuss—making it another
great value with a good location (Sb-230 zł, Db-330 zł, big "retro"
Db-370 zł, Tb-390 zł, Qb-380 zł, prices higher with air-con, eleva-
tor, ulica Poselska 22, tel. 012/424-1300, fax 012/424-1333, www
.wawel-tourist.pl, hotel@wawel-tourist.pl). They may have some
cheaper rooms with bathrooms down the hall, but these will likely be
renovated (and bathrooms added) soon.

$$ Hotel Pollera, in a grand, once plush old building, rents 42
fine rooms that are an especially good value off-season. The hotel is
popular with groups, despite its thin doors and echo-chamber hallways
(Sb-295 zł, Db-345 zł, Tb-420 zł, apartment-495 zł, extra bed-80 zł,

Kraków Hotels and Restaurants

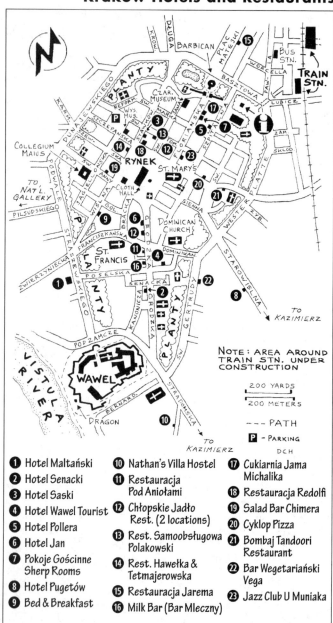

① Hotel Maltański

② Hotel Senacki

③ Hotel Saski

④ Hotel Wawel Tourist

⑤ Hotel Pollera

⑥ Hotel Jan

⑦ Pokoje Gościnne Sherp Rooms

⑧ Hotel Pugetów

⑨ Bed & Breakfast

⑩ Nathan's Villa Hostel

⑪ Restauracja Pod Aniołami

⑫ Chłopskie Jadło Rest. (2 locations)

⑬ Rest. Samoobsługowa Polakowski

⑭ Rest. Hawełka & Tetmajerowska

⑮ Restauracja Jarema

⑯ Milk Bar (Bar Mleczny)

⑰ Cukiarnia Jama Michalika

⑱ Restauracja Redolfi

⑲ Salad Bar Chimera

⑳ Cyklop Pizza

㉑ Bombaj Tandoori Restaurant

㉒ Bar Wegetariański Vega

㉓ Jazz Club U Muniaka

30 percent cheaper Nov–March, between station and Square, just inside Planty park at ulica Szpitalna 30, tel. 012/422-1044, fax 012/422-1389, www.pollera.com.pl, rezerwac@pollera.com.pl).

$$ Hotel Jan rents 40 rooms with contemporary decor a few feet from the Square. While a little boring and overpriced, it's central (Sb-236 zł, Db-353 zł, Tb-460 zł, a few newer rooms are more expensive, rooms on ground floor with a skylight and no window are 10 percent cheaper, all rates about 10 percent cheaper in winter, elevator, ulica Grodzka 11, tel. 012/430-1969, fax 012/430-1992, www .hotel-jan.com.pl, recepcja@hotel-jan.com.pl).

$ Bed & Breakfast offers 16 cheap, ramshackle rooms with a treehouse floor plan and mix-and-match furniture in a great location (S-85 zł, Sb-100 zł, D-155 zł, Db-180 zł, T-240 zł, Tb-270 zł, extra bed-50 zł, can pay with plastic only on weekdays, they'll do your laundry for 10 zł, ulica Wiślna 10, tel. & fax 012/421-9871, mobile 0604-199-902, www.noclegi.tk, wislna@wp.pl).

$ Pokoje Gościnne Sherp rents six simple but delightful little rooms (with no sinks and shared bathroom facilities) on the fourth floor of a building on Kraków's main tourist drag. Readers report some questionable business practices, but the price is right and the location is excellent (S-165 zł, D-240 zł, 10 percent cheaper without breakfast and off-season, ulica Floriańska 39, tel. 012/292-0266, tel. & fax 012/429-1778, www.sherp.com.pl, info@sherp.com.pl).

$ Nathan's Villa is Kraków's best hostel option, well-located halfway between Wawel Hill and Kazimierz, just south of the Planty park. It's a loose, easygoing, fun place with seven cleverly painted rooms and plenty of backpacker bonding. Their advertising promises advice on how to "get hammered"...if that's not your scene, sleep elsewhere (bunk in 4-bed room-60 zł, in 6-bed room-55 zł, in 8- or 10-bed room-50 zł, 10 zł less Oct–mid-April; includes breakfast, sheets, laundry facilities, and lockers; no curfew or lockout time, ulica Św. Agnieszki 1, tel. 012/422-3545, www.nathansvilla.com, krakow@nathansvilla.com).

$ *Very cheap private apartments:* You'll be met at the station by people renting cheap apartments, generally in the old center. From my experience, these folks are legit and offer great values for vagabonds who want a memorable local experience with comfort on a super-tight budget.

Kazimierz

Kazimierz has become a mecca for Jewish visitors to Eastern Europe. A decade ago, Kazimierz was crumbling, but today, the neighborhood is undergoing a wave of renovation. Sleep here to be close to Kraków's Jewish heart—or simply to experience a cheaper, less touristy, more local-feeling neighborhood outside the Old Town. The downside: You are a 20-minute walk from the fairytale medieval ambience of Kraków's old center. For locations, see map on page 181.

The following are the best hotel values in the neighborhood. Some of the klezmer music places listed in "Eating," below, also rent rooms—but they're generally an afterthought to the food and music, and not a good value.

$$ Hotel Astoria, a fine, new-feeling place renting 33 comfy rooms a couple of blocks from the center of Kazimierz, is popular with Israeli tour groups (Sb-295 zł, Db-375 zł, Db suite-430 zł, extra bed-70 zł, less on weekends and with an online reservation, underground parking-30 zł/day, air-con, non-smoking floor, elevator, ulica Józefa 24, tel. 012/432-5010, fax 012/432-5020, www .astoriahotel.pl, biuro@astoriahotel.pl).

$ Hotel Ester, fresh and modern, is a good value, with 32 rooms and friendly staff, perfectly located in the middle of the Kazimierz action (Sb-250 zł, Db-280 zł, Tb-320 zł, Qb-360 zł, prices 100 zł less Nov–Feb, air-con, non-smoking rooms, elevator, ulica Szeroka 20, tel. 012/429-1188, fax 012/429-1233, www.hotel -ester.krakow.pl, biuro@hotel-ester.krakow.pl).

$ El-jot Art Center rents 15 rooms, in addition to running a theater and an art gallery. It's a classy mix of old and new, with huge discounts (up to 25 percent) for booking rooms online or via e-mail (Sb-239 zł, Db-299 zł, Tb-379 zł, 2-room apartment-429 zł, prices 15 percent lower on weekends and Nov–March, ulica Miodowa 15, tel. & fax 012/421-3326, www.eljotartcenter.pl, recepcja@eljotartcenter.pl).

$ Hotel Nad Młynkiem, with four simple, fourth-floor rooms and no elevator, sits on a pretty, laid-back Kazimierz square over a funky café a few blocks from the Jewish sights. Since it's too small for groups, this place is more likely to have rooms when others are full (Sb-105 zł, Db-160 zł, Tb-240 zł, Qb-320 zł, all separate beds, cash only, free parking nearby, plac Wolnica 7, tel. 012/430-6100, calik.g@interia.pl, friendly Margaret SE).

EATING

Kraków is one of Eastern Europe's best dining towns, with surprising diversity, high quality, and low prices. Prices are reasonable even on the Square. And a half block away, they get even better. The city offers plenty of good Polish and Jewish cuisine, of course (see Poland introduction). But if you're tired of starchy Eastern European fare, this is also a great place to sample some international restaurants.

Polish Food in the Old Town

Restauracja Pod Aniołami ("Under Angels") offers a dressy, jazz-and-candles atmosphere outside on a covered patio, or inside in a romantic cellar with rough wood and medieval vaults. The cuisine is traditional Polish, with an emphasis on grilled foods and trout, and the service is top-notch (main dishes 20–40 zł, daily 13:00–24:00, reservations smart, ulica Grodzka 35, tel. 012/421-3999). If you want a fast, cheap, and tasty lunch, drop by their tiny sandwich bar for delightful open-faced sandwiches to take away or enjoy on their sidewalk tables (Mon–Fri 9:00–19:00, Sat 9:00–18:00, Sun 11:00–17:00).

Chłopskie Jadło ("Peasant Food") is part of a successful chain serving inexpensive, authentic Polish food (most main dishes 15–30 zł). The peasant theme begins with rustic bread that comes with farmer cheese and lard *(smalec)*. It's kitschy—touristy and fun, with "bed board" chairs—but the food is good, and it's packed with foreign visitors, Polish tourists, and locals. It's comparable to restaurants in the United States with cheesy down-home decor that promise "good country cookin'"...and deliver. Their two central locations are just off the Square: a smaller one north (ulica Św. Jana 3), and one with a farmyard patio and a sprawling, labyrinthine series of cellars south (ulica Grodzka 9).

Restauracja Samoobsługowa Polakowski is a homey little self-service cafeteria with a Polish-village interior—sort of a dressed-up milk bar. They serve fast, inexpensive, and tasty traditional meals a block off the Square, with delicious borscht and *gołąbki* (stuffed cabbage rolls) at a fraction of what you'd pay elsewhere (main dishes about 6 zł, point to what you want, daily 10:00–22:00, ulica Św. Tomasza 5, tel. 012/422-4822). There's another location in Kazimierz (see below).

Restauracja Jarema offers a tasty reminder that Kraków used to rule a large swath of Ukraine and Lithuania. They serve eastern Polish/Ukrainian cuisine, with savory borscht in a 19th-century aristocratic elegance. You'll feel like you're dining in an old mansion (main dishes 20–35 zł, daily from 12:00, generally live music from 19:00, reservations wise, across the street from barbican at plac Matejki 5, tel. 012/429-3669).

Cukiarnia Jama Michalika café—filled with green balloons—is legendary for its great homemade ice cream, *szarlotka* (apple cake), *kawa* (coffee), and early-1900s atmosphere (Sun–Thu 9:00–22:00, Fri–Sat until 23:00, a rare smoke-free interior, ulica Floriańska 45, tel. 012/422-1561). While most think of it as a café, this place is a restaurant with a full menu, too. Expect a grouchy greeting and a fee for the coat-check and bathrooms.

Dining on the Square

You'll find plenty of traditional, relatively expensive, tourist-oriented Polish food on the Square. While tourists go for the ye olde places, the most popular spots serve pizza to locals. Poles generally afford this zone on their meager incomes by just having a drink on the Square after eating at home.

Restauracja Redolfi comes with my favorite Square view, friendly service, great salads, international cuisine, and a wide selection of desserts. This place is fine for just a drink or for a full meal, and despite its prime location, it's not expensive (20-zł salads, main dishes around 30 zł, daily 9:00–24:00, Rynek Główny 38).

Restauracja Hawełka serves proudly traditional Polish cuisine, with good seats overlooking the Square's action (main dishes 20–40 zł, daily 11:00–23:00, near the corner of Szczepańska at Rynek Główny 34).

Tetmajerowska, with a plush dining room upstairs from Hawełka, serves up some of the finest cooking in town—game, Polish, and European—in an elegant Modernist (c. 1911) interior. The presentation is classy, the service formal, and the ambience as romantic as the piano is live. It's on the Square, but has no view (main dishes 30–60 zł, daily 13:30–23:00, reservations recommended, near the corner of Szczepańska at Rynek Główny 34, tel. 012/422-0631). You'll reach it by climbing a staircase lined with paintings by Młoda Polska also-rans.

Non-Polish Food

Salad Bar: **Bar Chimera,** just off the Square, is a cafeteria serving fast traditional meals to locals, either outside on their quiet courtyard, or inside in what seems like a fake Old World stage set (great salad buffet: small plate-7 zł, big plate-10 zł; 15-zł meals, fine for vegetarians, daily 9:00–23:00, near University at ulica Św. Anny 3). I'd skip their attached full-service restaurant (main dishes 25–30 zł).

Pizza: **Cyklop,** with 10 tables wrapped around the cook and his busy oven, has excellent wood-fired pizzas (1-person pizzas for about 15 zł, daily 11:30–22:00, near St. Mary's Church at Mikołajska 16, tel. 012/421-6603). But pizza places on the Square come with much better views and are popular with locals.

Indian: If you need a tandoori-and-naan fix, **Bombaj Tandoori** offers decent Indian fare two blocks off the Square (main dishes 10–30 zł, daily 12:00–23:00, ulica Mikołajska 11).

Vegetarian: For a healthy, cheap, fast meal, nothing beats **Bar Wegetariański Vega,** pleasantly mellow and packed with sophisticated university students (soups for 3 zł, main dishes 4–7 zł, salads about 2 zł per scoop, order at counter, then take food to table, daily 9:00–21:00, ulica Św. Gertrudy 7, tel. 012/422-3494).

Kazimierz

The entire district is bursting with lively cafés and bars—it's a happening night scene. See map on page 181.

Klezmer Concerts and Jewish Food: If you want fancy dining with a Jewish folk-music serenade, Kazimierz has it. Several restaurants on ulica Szeroka (Kazimierz's main square) offer klezmer concerts—traditional Jewish music from 19th-century Poland, generally with violin, string bass, clarinet, and accordion—nightly in the summer at 20:00 (unless otherwise noted). Each restaurant has a similar menu, with main dishes for around 20 zł; you'll pay an additional 20-zł cover charge per person just for the music. While it'd be nice to pop into each one to compare the music, it's customary to reserve ahead at a single place to dine. **Klezmer-Hois,** filling a venerable former Jewish ritual bathhouse, feels like you're dining in a rich grandparent's home (#6, music nightly year-round, tel. 012/411-1245, www.klezmer.pl). **Restauracja Arka Noego** ("Noah's Ark") has a good reputation for its music (15-zł cover, music nightly at 20:30 March–Oct, shares building with Jarden Bookshop at #2, tel. 012/429-1528). **Ariel** is an elegant restaurant that has gone downhill in recent years, and receives mixed reviews for its food (music in up to 4 different rooms, best upstairs in the larger dining hall, #18, tel. 012/421-7920).

Inexpensive Polish Food: **Restauracja Samoobsługowa Polakowski,** the cheap and tasty milk bar near the Square in central Kraków (see above), has another handy location in the heart of Kazimierz, with similar decor and menu (main dishes about 6 zł, point to what you want, daily 8:00–22:00, 100 yards from Szeroka at ulica Miodowa 39, tel. 012/421-2117). The **plac Nowy market** offers a fully authentic, blue-collar Polish experience—join the workers on their lunch break at the little food windows on Kazimierz's market square.

TRANSPORTATION CONNECTIONS

From Kraków by train to: Warsaw (hrly, 2.5 hrs), **Gdańsk** (2/day direct, 7 hrs; plus 1 direct night train, 10.75 hrs; more with transfer in Warsaw), **Toruń** (1/day direct, 7.75 hrs; better to transfer at Warsaw's Zachodnia station: 4/day, 5.75–6.5 hrs), **Prague** (1 direct night train/day, 8.5 hrs; otherwise transfer in Katowice, Wrocław, or Ostrava-Svinov, 8–11 hrs), **Berlin** (2/day direct, including 1 night train, 9.5–10.5 hrs; otherwise transfer in Warsaw, 9–11 hrs), **Budapest** (1 direct night train/day, 11 hrs; otherwise transfer in Katowice, Poland, or Břeclav, Czech Republic, 9-10 hrs), and **Vienna** (2/day direct, including 1 night train, 6.5–8.25 hrs).

Auschwitz-Birkenau

The unassuming regional capital of Oświęcim (ohsh-VEENCH-im) was the site of one of humanity's most unspeakably horrifying tragedies: the systematic murder of at least 1.1 million innocent people. From 1941 until 1945, Oświęcim was the site of Auschwitz, the biggest, most notorious concentration camp in the Nazi system. Today, Auschwitz is the most poignant memorial anywhere to the victims of the Holocaust.

A visit here is obligatory for Polish 14-year-olds; students usually come again during their last year of school as well. You'll also often see Israeli high school groups walking through the grounds waving their Star of David flags. Many people, including Germans, leave flowers and messages. One of the messages reads: "Nations who forget their own history are sentenced to live it again."

ORIENTATION

"Auschwitz" actually refers to a series of several camps in Poland—most importantly Auschwitz I, in the village of Oświęcim (50 miles west of Kraków, a 75-minute drive), and Auschwitz II (a.k.a. Birkenau, about 2 miles west of Oświęcim). Those visiting Auschwitz generally see both Auschwitz I and Birkenau.

Begin at Auschwitz I. The museum's main building has ticket booths, bookstores (consider the good 3-zł *Guide-Book*), exchange offices, WCs, and eateries. You'll also find maps of the camp (posted on the walls), a tour office (tours described below), and a theater that shows a powerful film (see below).

Cost, Hours, Information: Entrance to the camp is free, but donations are gladly accepted. The museum opens every day at 8:00, and closes June–Aug at 19:00, May and Sept at 18:00, April and Oct at 17:00, March and Nov–mid-Dec at 16:00, and mid-Dec–Feb at 15:00. Information: tel. 033/844-8107, www.auschwitz.org.pl.

Film: The 17-minute movie (too graphic for children) was shot by Ukrainian troops days after the Soviets liberated the camp. Upon your arrival, note the times the English-language version will run (2/day, always in English at 11:00, usually at 13:00, frequently at 15:00, and often at other times—schedule posted above cashier at the end of the hall of main building, buy your 3.50-zł ticket and come back for the showing).

Tours of Auschwitz: Round-trip tours from Kraków to Auschwitz take care of transportation for you (see "Tours," page 163). But with a tour, you pay triple and have to adhere to a strict schedule. The most rewarding way to visit is to go on your own, take one of the camp's organized tours, and then explore the grounds on your own.

Why Visit Auschwitz?

Why visit a notorious concentration camp on your vacation? Auschwitz-Birkenau is one of the most moving sights in Europe, and certainly the most important of all the Holocaust memorials. Seeing the camp can be difficult: Many visitors are overwhelmed by a combination of sadness and anger over the tragedy, as well as inspiration at the remarkable stories of survival. But Auschwitz survivors and victims' families want tourists to come here and experience the scale and the monstrosity of the place to be sure that the Holocaust is always remembered—so it never happens again.

Auschwitz isn't for everyone. But I've never met anyone who toured Auschwitz and regretted it. For many, it's a profoundly life-altering experience—and at the very least, it will forever affect the way you think about the Holocaust.

The Auschwitz Museum has a network of excellent guides who are serious and frank, and feel a strong sense of responsibility about sharing the story of the camp. To join a scheduled **English tour** of the camp, find the tour office (on right-hand side in main building, about halfway down hallway). There is a daily English-language tour of Auschwitz and Birkenau at 11:00 (26 zł, 3.5 hrs), which includes the film at the main museum and the bus between the two camps. There is usually another tour at 13:00, and, during busy times, there are often a lot more (likely at 15:00), depending on demand and the availability of an English-speaking guide.

You can also hire your own **private guide** for the basic 3.5-hour tour of the camp (192 zł), or for a longer six-hour "study tour" (224 zł). This guide service is an exceptional value and worthwhile if you have special interest in the camp. To hire a private guide, go to the cashiers at the end of the hall. Remember, you can also hire your own private guide in Kraków with a car (about 500 zł, 300 zł without a car).

Visiting without a guide (given the abundance of English descriptions, English-language tours to freeload on, and the self-guided tour of both camps described below) works just fine.

Getting to Auschwitz: Two different **bus** companies connect Kraków and Oświęcim; both leave from Kraków's bus station (10 zł, 1.5 hours): PKS Kraków (4/day, 3/day Sat–Sun) and PKS Oświęcim (14/day, tel. 012/430-4035). When you board the bus, tell the driver you want "Auschwitz Museum." Buses from Kraków first stop at the Oświęcim train station, then continue on to one of two stops near the museum: the main parking lot of Auschwitz I (in which case you can go right into the camp); or a low-profile bus stop on the edge of the camp grounds (you'll see a small *Muzeum Auschwitz* sign on

On the Way to Auschwitz: The Polish Countryside

You'll spend about an hour gazing out the window as you drive or ride the bus to Auschwitz. This may be your only real look at the Polish countryside. Ponder these thoughts about what you're passing: The small houses you see are traditionally inhabited by three generations at the same time. Nineteenth-century houses (the few that survive) often sport blue stripes. Back then, parents announced that their daughters were now eligible by getting out the blue paint. Once they saw these blue lines, village boys were welcome to come a-courtin'.

Big churches mark small villages. Tiny roadside memorials and crosses indicate places where fatal accidents occurred.

The farmers have small lots and are notorious for not being very productive. They dread the coming entry to the European Union, when a new economic toughness will sweep the land. But, for now, they remain Poland's sacred cows: producing little, paying almost no tax, and draining government resources.

Since most people don't own cars, bikes are common and public transit is excellent. There are lots of bus stops and minibuses that you can flag down anywhere for a 2-zł ride. The bad roads are a legacy of communist construction, exacerbated by heavy truck use and brutal winters.

Poland has well over 2,000 counties, or districts, each with its own coat of arms; you'll pass several along the way. The forests are state-owned, and locals enjoy the right to pick berries in the summer and mushrooms in the autumn. The mushrooms are dried and then boiled to make tasty soups in the winter.

the right just before the stop). From this bus stop, follow the sign down the road and into the parking lot; the main building is across the lot on your left.

You could ride the **train** to Oświęcim, but it's less comfortable than the bus (14/day, 1.25–1.75 hrs).

If you wind up at the **train station** (either by train or by bus), it's about a 25-minute walk to the camp (turn right out of station, go straight, then turn left at roundabout, camp is several blocks ahead on left). Or, from the Oświęcim station, you can reach the camp by catching a bus (#24, #25, #26, #27, #28, or #29, about 2 zł, 1–4/hr, 1–2/hr Sat–Sun) or taking a taxi (around 10 zł).

Several **minibuses** also depart from near Kraków's bus station, and head directly to the Auschwitz museum (8 zł, 1.5 hrs).

A **taxi** to Kraków runs about 200 zł one-way. But if you're splurging for a taxi, you might as well pay for a guide to drive you here, as well as show you around once you arrive (see "Tours," page 163).

Returning to Kraków: Buses back to Kraków do leave not from the camp parking lot itself (though some minibuses do). Instead, you'll catch the bus from the stop on the edge of the Auschwitz I grounds (described above). To reach this bus stop, leave the Auschwitz I building through the main entry and walk straight along the parking lot, then turn right on the road near the end of the lot. At the dead end, cross the street to the little bus stop. As this can be confusing and frustrating, figure out your return with the help of the information desk upon arrival in Auschwitz. Note that there's no public transportation back to Kraków from Birkenau, where most people end their tours; you'll have to take the shuttle bus back to Auschwitz I first.

Shuttle Bus from Auschwitz I to Birkenau: Buses shuttle visitors two miles between the camps nearly hourly (leaving Auschwitz I at the bottom of the hour and Birkenau at the top of the hour, confirm times posted at the bus stop outside the main building of each site, buy the 2-zł ticket on the bus). Taxis are also standing by (20 zł). Many visitors, rather than wait for the next bus, decide to walk between the camps—offering a much-needed chance for reflection.

Eating: There's a café and decent cafeteria at the main Auschwitz building (daily 8:00–19:00) and two places across the street (Art Burger is fast, Art Deco restaurant is slower but good).

Auschwitz I

Before World War II, this camp was a base for the Polish army. When Hitler occupied Poland, he took over these barracks and turned it into a concentration camp for his Polish political enemies. The location was ideal, with a nearby rail junction and rivers providing natural protective boundaries. In 1942, Auschwitz became a death camp for the extermination of European Jewry. By the time the camp was liberated in 1945, at least 1.1 million people had been murdered here—approximately 960,000 of them Jewish.

As you exit the entry building's back door and go towards the camp, you see the notorious gate with the cruel message, *"Arbeit Macht Frei"* ("Work sets you free"). Note that the B was welded on upside down by belligerent inmates. On their arrival, new prisoners were told the truth: The only way out of the camp was through the crematorium chimneys.

Just inside the gate and to the right, the camp orchestra (made up of prisoners) used to play marches; having the prisoners march made them easier to count.

Auschwitz I

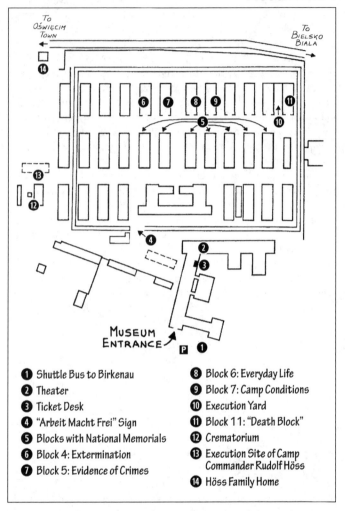

1 Shuttle Bus to Birkenau
2 Theater
3 Ticket Desk
4 "Arbeit Macht Frei" Sign
5 Blocks with National Memorials
6 Block 4: Extermination
7 Block 5: Evidence of Crimes
8 Block 6: Everyday Life
9 Block 7: Camp Conditions
10 Execution Yard
11 Block 11: "Death Block"
12 Crematorium
13 Execution Site of Camp Commander Rudolf Höss
14 Höss Family Home

The main road leads past the barracks. An average of 14,000 prisoners were kept at this camp at one time. (Birkenau could hold up to 100,000.) The first row of barracks contains the **National Memorials,** created by the home countries of the camps' victims. The most interesting are the **Suffering and Struggle of the Jews** exhibit (block 27) and the nearby **Gypsy** exhibit. Most of the other national memorials were created during the communist era, so they have a decidedly socialist spin; some have been updated (including Hungary, block 18, and the Czech and Slovak republics, block 16).

The most interesting part of the camp is the second row of

barracks, which holds the museum exhibitions. Blocks 4 and 5 focus on how Auschwitz prisoners were killed. Blocks 6, 7, and 11 explore the conditions for prisoners who survived here a little longer than most.

Block 4 features exhibits on extermination. In the first room is a map showing all of the countries Auschwitz prisoners were brought from—as far away as Norway and Greece. You'll also find an urn filled with ashes, a symbolic memorial to all of the camp's victims. In Room 2, a map shows that victims were transported here from all over Europe. To prevent a riot, the Nazis claimed at first that this was only a transition camp for resettlement in Eastern Europe. Room 3 displays the only photos that exist of victims inside the camp—taken by proud SS men.

Upstairs in Room 4 is a chilling model of a Birkenau crematorium. People entered on the left, then got undressed in the underground rooms (hanging their belongings on numbered hooks and encouraged to remember their numbers to retrieve their clothes later). They then moved into the "showers" and were killed by Zyklon-B gas. This efficient factory of murder took about 20 minutes to kill 20,000 people in four gas chambers. Elevators brought the bodies up to the crematorium. Members of the *Sonderkommand*—Jewish inmates who were kept isolated and forced by the Nazis to work here—removed the corpses' gold teeth and shaved off their hair (to be sold) before putting the bodies in the ovens. It wasn't unusual for a *Sonderkommand* worker to discover a wife, child, or parent among the dead. A few committed suicide by throwing themselves at electric fences; those who didn't were systematically executed by the Nazis after a two-month shift. Across from the model of the crematorium are canisters of Zyklon-B (hydrogen cyanide), the German-produced cleaning agent that is lethal in high doses. Across the hall in Room 5 is a wall of victims' hair—4,400 pounds of it—another source of camp income. Also displayed is cloth made of the hair, used to make Nazi uniforms.

Back downstairs in Room 6 is an exhibit on the plunder of victims' personal belongings. People being transported here were encouraged to bring luggage—and some victims had even paid in advance for houses in their new homeland. After they were killed, everything of value was sorted and stored in warehouses that prisoners named "Canada" (after a country they associated with great wealth). Although the Canada warehouses were destroyed, you can see a few of these items in the next building.

Block 5 focuses on material evidence of the crimes that took place here. It consists mostly of piles of the victims' goods, a tiny fraction of everything the Nazis stole. As you wander through the rooms, you'll see eyeglasses; fine Jewish prayer shawls; crutches and prosthetic limbs (the first people the Nazis ever exterminated were mentally and physically ill German citizens); a seemingly endless mountain of shoes; and suitcases with names of victims—many

Chilling Statistics:
The Holocaust in Poland

The majority of people murdered by the Nazis during the Holocaust were killed right here in Poland. For centuries, Poland was known for its tolerance of Jews, and right up until the beginning of World War II, Poland had Europe's largest concentration of Jews: 3,500,000. Throughout the Holocaust, the Nazis murdered 4,500,000 Jews in Poland (many of them brought in from other countries) at camps, including Auschwitz, and ghettos such as Warsaw's.

By the end of the war, only 300,000 Polish Jews had survived—less than one in 10 of the original population. Many of these survivors were granted "one-way passports" (read: deported) to Israel by the communist government in 1968 (following a big student demonstration with a strong Jewish presence). Today, only a few thousand Jews live in all of Poland.

As horrific as these statistics are, mere numbers on paper don't do justice to the scale of the atrocities committed here. A visit to Auschwitz-Birkenau hits you at a gut level, giving you a greater sense of the appalling inhumanity, suffering, and irreplaceable loss.

marked *Kind*, or "child." Visitors often wonder if the suitcase with the name "Frank" belonged to Anne, one of the Holocaust's most famous victims. After being discovered by the Nazis, the Frank family was transported here and split up, though it's unlikely the suitcase was theirs. Anne Frank and her sister Margot were sent to the Bergen-Belsen camp in northern Germany, where they died of typhus shortly before the war ended. Their father, Otto Frank, survived Auschwitz and was found barely alive by the Russians, who liberated the camp in January 1945.

Although the purpose of Auschwitz was to murder its inmates, not all of them were killed immediately. After an initial evaluation, some prisoners were registered and forced to work. (This did not mean they were chosen to live—but rather to die later.) In **Block 6,** you see elements of the everyday life of prisoners. The halls are lined with photographs of victims. Notice the dates of arrival *(przybył)* and death *(zmarł)*—those who were registered survived here an average of two to three months. (Flowers are poignant reminders that these victims are survived by loved ones.) Room 1 displays drawings of the arrival process—sketched by survivors of the camp. After the initial selection, those chosen to work were showered, shaved, and photographed. After a while, photographing each prisoner got to be too expensive, so prisoners were tattooed instead (see photographs): on the chest, on the arm, or—for children—on the leg. A display shows the symbols that prisoners had to wear to show their reason for internment—Jew, Gypsy, homosexual, political prisoner, and so on.

Room 4 shows the starvation that took place. The prisoners here when the camp was liberated were living skeletons (the healthier ones had been forced to march to Germany). Of the 7,500 prisoners who were liberated by the Soviets, 20 percent died soon after of disease and starvation. Look for the prisoners' daily ration (in the glass case): a pan of tea or coffee in the morning; thin vegetable soup in the afternoon; and a piece of bread (often made with sawdust or chestnuts) for dinner. This makes it clear that Auschwitz was never intended to be a "work camp," where people were kept alive, healthy, and efficient to do work. Rather, people were meant to die here—if not in the gas chambers, then through malnutrition and overwork (as Hitler put it, "extermination through work").

You can see scenes from the prisoner's workday (sketched by survivors after liberation) in Room 5. Prisoners worked as long as the sun shone—eight hours in winter, up to 12 hours in summer— mostly on farms or in factories. Room 6 is about Auschwitz's child inmates, 20 percent of the camp's victims. Blond, blue-eyed children—like the girl in the bottom row on the right—were either "Germanized" in special schools or, if younger, adopted by German families. Dr. Josef Mengele conducted experiments on children, especially twins and triplets, to try to figure out ways to increase fertility for German mothers.

Block 7 shows living and sanitary conditions at the camp— which you'll see in more detail later at Birkenau. Blocks 8–10 are vacant, but step into the **courtyard** between Blocks 10 and 11. The wall at the far end is where the Nazis shot several thousand political prisoners, leaders of camp resistance, and religious leaders. Notice that the windows are covered, so that nobody could witness the executions. Also take a close look at the memorial—the back of it is made of the same material designed by Nazis to catch the bullets without a ricochet. Inmates were shot at short range—about three feet. The pebbles represent prayers from Jewish visitors.

The most feared place among prisoners was the **"Death Block" (#11),** from which nobody ever left alive. In Room 5, you can see how prisoners lived in these barracks—three-level bunks, with three prisoners sleeping in each bed (they had to sleep on their sides so they could fit). Death here required a trial (the room in which sham trials were held—lasting about 2 minutes each—is on display). In Room 6, people undressed before they were executed. In the basement, you'll see several different types of cells. The Starvation Cell (#18) held prisoners selected to starve to death when a fellow prisoner escaped; Maksymilian Kolbe voluntarily spent two weeks here to save a man's life (see sidebar). In the Dark Cell (#20), which held up to 30, people had only a small window for ventilation—and if it

St. Maksymilian Kolbe

Among the many inspirational stories of Auschwitz is that of Maksymilian Kolbe, a priest interned here in 1941.

When a prisoner escaped, the Nazis punished remaining inmates by selecting 10 of them to put in the Starvation Cell until they died—based on the Nazi "doctrine of collective responsibility."

After the selection had been made, Kolbe offered to replace one of the men. The Nazis agreed. (The man Kolbe saved is said to have survived and raised a family after the war.)

All 10 of the men—including Kolbe—were put into Starvation Cell 18. Two weeks later, when the door was opened, only Kolbe had survived. The story spread throughout the camp, and Kolbe became a hero. To squelch the hope he had given the other inmates, Kolbe was executed by lethal injection. In 1982, Kolbe was canonized by the Catholic Church.

became covered with snow, the prisoners suffocated. At the end of the hall in Cell 21, you can see where a prisoner scratched a crucifix (left) and image of Jesus (right) on the wall. In the Standing Cells (#22), four people would be forced to stand together for hours at time (of course, the bricks went all the way to the ceiling then). Upstairs is an exhibit on resistance within the camp.

Before you leave Auschwitz, visit the **crematorium** (from Block 11, exit straight ahead and go past first row of barracks, then turn right and go straight on the road between the 2 rows of barracks; pass through the gap in the fence and look for the chimney on your left). People undressed outside, or just inside the door. Up to 700 people at a time could be gassed here. Inside the door, go into the big room on the right. Look for the vents in the ceiling—this is where the SS men dropped the Zyklon-B. Through the door is a replica of the furnace. This facility could burn 340 bodies a day—so it took two days to burn all of the bodies from one round of executions. The Nazis didn't like this inefficiency, so they built four more huge crematoria at Birkenau.

Shortly after the war, camp commander Rudolf Höss was tried, convicted, and sentenced to death for his work here. Survivors requested that he be executed at Auschwitz. In 1947, he was hanged. The site is preserved behind the crematorium (about a hundred yards from his home where his wife—who loved her years here—read stories to their children, very likely by the light of a human-skin lampshade).

Take your time with Auschwitz I. When you're ready, catch the 2-zł shuttle bus (or a 20-zł taxi) two miles to the second stage of the camp—Birkenau.

Auschwitz II—Birkenau

In 1941, when the original Auschwitz camp got to be too small for the capacity the Nazis envisioned, they began a second camp in some nearby farm fields. The original plan was for a camp that could hold 200,000 people, but at its peak, Birkenau (Brzezinka) held only about 100,000. They were still adding onto it when the camp was liberated in 1945.

Train tracks lead past the main building and into the camp. The first sight that greeted prisoners was the guard tower (familiar to  Americans from the stirring scenes in *Schindler's List*). Climb to the top of the entry building (also houses WCs and bookstore) for an overview of the massive camp. As you look over the camp, you'll see a vast field of chimneys and a few intact wooden and brick barracks. The train tracks lead straight back to the dividing platform, and then dead-end at the ruins of the crematorium and camp monument at the far side.

Some of the barracks were destroyed by Germans. Most were dismantled to be used for fuel and building materials shortly after the war. But the first row has been reconstructed (using components from the original structures). Visit the barracks on the right. The first building was the **latrine:** The front half of the building contained washrooms, and the back was a row of toilets. There was no running water; prisoners were in charge of keeping these clean. Because of the unsanitary conditions, the Nazis were afraid to come in here—so it was the heart of the black market and the inmates' resistance movement.

The fourth building was a **bunk** building. Each inmate had a personal number, a barrack number, and a bed number. Inside, you can see the beds (angled so that more could fit). An average of 400 prisoners—but up to 1,000—would be housed in each of these buildings. These wooden structures, designed as stables by a German company, came in prefab pieces that made them cheap and convenient (look for the horse-tying rings on the wall). Two chimneys connected by a brick duct provided a little heat. The bricks were smoothed by inmates who sat here to catch a bit of warmth.

Follow the train tracks toward the monument about a half mile away, at the back end of Birkenau. At the intersection of these tracks and the perpendicular gravel road (halfway to the monument) was the gravel **dividing platform.** A Nazi doctor would stand facing the

Auschwitz II—Birkenau

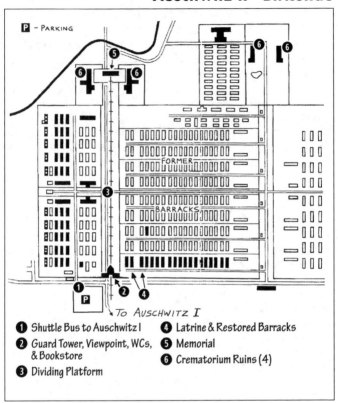

P — PARKING

FORMER

BARRACKS

To Auschwitz I

1. Shuttle Bus to Auschwitz I
2. Guard Tower, Viewpoint, WCs, & Bookstore
3. Dividing Platform
4. Latrine & Restored Barracks
5. Memorial
6. Crematorium Ruins (4)

guard tower and evaluate each prisoner. If he pointed to the right, the prisoner was sentenced to death, and trudged—unknowingly—to the gas chamber. If he pointed to the left, the person would be registered and live a little longer. It was here that families from all over Europe were torn apart forever.

On the left-hand side of the tracks are some **brick barracks.** Either now or on your way back, look inside one of them. The supervisors lived in the two smaller rooms near the door. Farther in, most barracks still have the wooden bunks that held about 700 people per building. Four or five people slept on each bunk, including the floor—reserved for new arrivals. There were chamber pots at either end of the building. After a Nazi doctor died of typhus, sanitation improved, and these barracks got running water.

As you walk along the camp's only road, which leads along the tracks to the crematorium, imagine the horror of this place—no grass, only mud, and all the barracks packed with people, with smoke blowing in from the busy crematoria. This was an even worse place to die than Auschwitz I.

The train tracks lead to the camp **memorial** and **crematorium.** Finish your visit with the memorial. At the end of the tracks, go 50 yards to the left and climb the three concrete steps to view the ruin. This one of four crematoria here at Birkenau, with a capacity to cremate more than 4,400 people per day. At the far-right end of the ruins, see the stairs where people entered the rooms to undress. People were given numbered lockers, conning them into thinking they were coming back. (Nazis didn't want a panic.) Then they piled into the "shower room"—the underground passage branching away from the memorial—and were killed. Their bodies were burned in the crematorium (on the left), giving off a scent of sweet almonds (the Zyklon-B). Beyond the remains of the crematorium is a hole—once a gray lake where tons of ashes were dumped. This efficient factory of death was destroyed by the Nazis as the Soviet army approached, leaving today's evocative ruins.

The Soviets arrived on January 27, 1945, and the nightmare of Auschwitz was over. The Polish parliament voted to turn these grounds into a museum, so that the world would understand, and never forget, the horror of what happened here. The **monument** at the back of the camp, built in 1967 (by the communist government in its heavy "Social Realist" style), represents gravestones and the chimney of a crematorium. The plaques, written in each of the languages spoken by camp victims (including English, far right), explain that the memorial is "a cry of despair and a warning to humanity."

WARSAW
(Warszawa)

Warsaw is Poland's capital and biggest city. It's huge, famous, and important...but not particularly pretty. Warsaw's outskirts look basically the way you'd expect: an endless sea of communist apartment blocks. The most appealing part of the city, the reconstructed Old Town, has lanes and squares as charming as any in Europe—an odd contrast to the concrete sprawl around it. And Warsaw's main urban drag, the Royal Way, is downright charming in a big-city sort of way. Even though it's not quaint or cute, Warsaw is fascinating. It's an open-air display of 20th-century history. As one proud Varsovian told me, "Warsaw is ugly because its history is so beautiful."

Warsaw (Warszawa, vah-SHAH-vah in Polish) was the capital of a once-mighty Polish empire, but the city saw more than its share of hardships during the last century. In the waning days of World War II, the Nazis systematically destroyed the city to avenge an uprising—literally working from block to block to demolish every building. At the war's end, Warsaw was devastated. An estimated 800,000 Varsovians were dead—nearly two-thirds of the city's prewar population. The city itself was more than 85 percent destroyed, and the Poles seriously considered building a brand-new capital from scratch elsewhere, rather than rebuild from the rubble.

But ultimately, a painstaking reconstruction did take place. Different sectors were rebuilt in different styles, creating today's Warsaw, a city of contrasts. Visitors encounter crumbling communist apartment blocks (*bloki* in Polish); cobbled medieval squares rebuilt in quaint fashion; and a new wave of post-communist, supermodern, glass-and-steel skyscrapers. Between the buildings, you'll find fragments of a complex, sometimes tragic, and often inspirational history. Parts of the city have an undeniable appeal (like the Old Town and Łazienki Park), but even Warsaw's "ugly" parts become beautiful when you know the history.

Planning Your Time

Although it's a major capital city, Warsaw doesn't compare to Budapest or Prague on the Richter scale of sightseeing thrills. And within Poland, Kraków and Gdańsk are more satisfying destinations. But a visit to the bustling and very urban capital is both convenient and essential for understanding modern Poland. Although it doesn't merit a time-consuming detour, it's well worth spending a few hours or a day for those passing through. If you're coming from Germany, consider connecting to Warsaw via an overnight train from Berlin, seeing the city, and then moving on to Kraków later that same day (hrly trains, 2.5 hrs).

With a few hours, gape at Stalin's towering Palace of Culture and Science, then wander through the Old Town. With a little more time, enjoy the city's beautiful Łazienki Park or seek out some museums and sights that interest you—whether it's Holocaust history, art galleries, Polish royalty, or Chopin.

ORIENTATION

(area code: 022)

Warsaw sprawls, with nearly two million residents. But virtually everything of interest to travelers is on the "Left Bank" (west) of the Vistula River. The city's main train station (Warszawa Centralna) is in the shadow of its biggest landmark: the can't-miss-it, skyscraping Palace of Culture and Science (Pałac Kultury i Nauki, a.k.a. "Stalin's Penis"). To the east of the station, parallel to the river, runs the "Royal Way" boulevard, connecting the sights in the north (Old Town and New Town) with the sights in the south (Łazienki Park, and beyond that, Wilanów Palace). Most major sights and recommended hotels and restaurants are along this spine.

Tourist Information

Warsaw's helpful, youthful, well-run TI has four offices: **Castle Square** in the Old Town (May–Sept daily 9:00–20:00, Oct–April daily 9:00–18:00, ulica Krakowskie Przedmieście 89), the **central train station** (May–Sept daily 8:00–20:00, Oct–April daily 8:00–18:00), the **western coach station** (May–Sept daily 9:00–18:00, Oct–April daily 8:00–17:00, aleja Jerozolimskie 144), and the **airport** (May–Sept daily 8:00–20:00, Oct–April daily 8:00–18:00). The general information number for all TIs is tel. 022/9431 (www.warsawtour.pl). All four branches offer several free, useful materials: a city map (with key phone numbers on the back), a well-produced booklet called *Warsaw: In Short*, and a series of brochures on sights and neighborhoods (Old Town, Royal Way, Jewish sights, and Chopin). Ask about the new Warsaw Tourist Card (35 zł/24 hrs, 65 zł/3 days). The TI also has a free room-booking service.

Warsaw

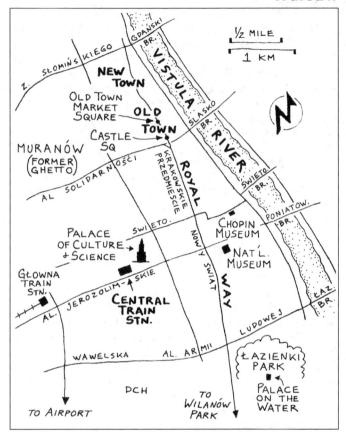

Tours of Warsaw: Mazurkas offers a pricey **bus tour** (plus some walking, 130 zł, 4.5 hrs, daily April–Oct, Sat–Sun only Nov–March; includes Old Town, Wilanów Palace, and other sights; picks up at various hotels around 9:00, tel. 022/629-1878, www .mazurkas.com.pl). A **tourist train** does a 30-minute circuit, leaving from in front of the Royal Castle (16 zł, daily May–Oct, not on Mon Nov–April).

Arrival in Warsaw

By Train: Most trains arrive at the big, dreary Warszawa Centralna station, a *Flying Nun* monstrosity next to the Palace of Culture and Science. As there's little to see around the station, most travelers head directly for the Royal Way and the Old Town.

You'll emerge from your platform *(peron)* into a confusing labyrinth of passageways. At this underground level, you'll find

Warsaw Landmarks

English	Polish	Pronounced
Warsaw	**Warszawa**	vah-SHAH-vah
Main Train Station	**Warszawa Centralna**	vah-SHAH-vah tsehn-TRAHL-nah
Palace of Culture and Science	**Pałac Kultury i Nauki (or simply "Pałac")**	PAH-wahts kool-TOO-ree ee nah-OO-kee
New Town	**Nowe Miasto**	NOH-vay mee-AH-stoh
Old Town	**Stare Miasto**	STAH-reh mee-AH-stoh
Old Town Market Square	**Rynek Starego Miasta**	REE-nehk stah-RAY-goh mee-AH-stah
Castle Square	**Plac Zamkowy**	plahts zahm-KOH-vee
Vistula River	**Wisła**	VEES-wah

lockers near *peron* 4—look for *przechowalnia bagażu*. It's best to emerge quickly into the **main arrival hall** (follow signs to *Hala Główna*) to get your bearings (and take your first gawk at the nearby Palace of Culture and Science). For **international tickets,** look for the *Kasy Międzynarodowe* office in the corner of the main hall (under the big, orange *Apteka Non Stop* sign). **Bus #175** takes you right to the Royal Way and Old Town in about 10 minutes (catch bus in front of LOT airlines office/Marriott Hotel across busy aleja Jerozolimskie from the station; exit to the south—near *peron* 1—and follow signs for *Al. Jerozolimskie*). Train info: tel. 022/9436.

By Car: Warsaw is a stressful city to drive and park in. Arrange parking with your hotel, and get around by foot or public transit. You must pay to park in the city Monday–Friday 8:00–18:00. Park your car (likely on a sidewalk), find the meter, and insert coins until the proper amount of time appears in the left-hand window (about 2.60 zł/hr). Press the green button, wait for your ticket, and put it on your dashboard. Sometimes public parking areas are monitored by "attendants"—unemployed creeps who kindly help you find a spot, then ask if you want them to "watch it" for you. Try to avoid parking where you see these crooks, but if you do, 1–2 zł is a small investment to prevent the car from being damaged.

By Plane: Warsaw's **Fryderyk Chopin International Airport** is about six miles southwest of the center. The airport is small and user-friendly (with English signs). You'll find a branch of the TI, plus lots of ATMs and exchange offices *(kantor)*. Bus #175 runs into the center (train station, Royal Way, and Old Town) from the bus stop just in front of the terminal (2.40 zł, 4–6/hr, less Sat–Sun, 30 min). A 20-minute taxi ride to the center shouldn't cost you more than 40 zł (though hucksters who approach you offering a ride may try to charge you more than twice that much—to get a fair deal, find a taxi marked with a company name and telephone number). The trip into town can take much longer during rush hour, because only one main thoroughfare connects the airport to the center. Airport info: tel. 022/650-4100.

Getting Around Warsaw

By Public Transit: You can use the same tickets on any of Warsaw's trams, city buses, or the Metro. A single ticket costs 2.40 zł *(bilet jednorazowy,* good for one trip, no transfers); a one-day ticket costs 7.20 zł *(bilet dobowy,* good until 24:00 on the day purchased); and a three-day ticket is 12 zł *(bilet trzydniowy).* Buy your ticket at a post office or kiosk (with a *RUCH* sign), and be sure to validate it as you board. You can also buy the basic one-ride tickets from your bus or tram driver for an extra 0.60 zł. Bus #100 runs a useful circular route to virtually all of the sights and neighborhoods of interest to tourists. Handy bus #175 connects the airport, train station, Royal Way, and Old Town.

By Taxi: As in most big Eastern European cities, it's wise to use only cabs that are clearly marked with a company logo and telephone number (or call your own: Locals like MPT Taxi, tel. 022/919). All official taxis have similar rates: a drop fee of 6 zł, then 2 zł per kilometer (more after 22:00 or in the suburbs). The drop fee may be higher if you catch the cab in front of a big, fancy hotel.

SIGHTS

Warsaw's Old Town (Stare Miasto)

In 1945, not a building remained standing in Warsaw's "Old" Town. Everything you see is rebuilt, mostly finished by 1956. This is the city's only must-see sight. Some find it artificial and phony, in a Disney World kind of way. For others, the painstaking postwar reconstruction just feels right, with its charming-enough Old World squares and lanes giving Kraków a run for its money. Before 1989, stifled by communist repression and choking on smog, the Old Town felt like an empty husk of its historic self. But now, the market stalls have returned, and the locals are out strolling.

These sights are listed in order from south to north, beginning at the Castle Square and ending at the entrance to the New Town. For an interesting route from the train station to the Old Town, see "Royal Way Stroll," page 217.

▲**Castle Square (Plac Zamkowy)**—This lively square is dominated by the big, pink Royal Castle, the historic heart of Warsaw's political power. After the second great Polish dynasty, the Jagiellonians, died off in 1572, the Republic of Nobles (about 10 percent of the population) elected various foreign kings to their throne. The guy on the 72-foot-tall **pillar** is Sigismund III, the first Polish king from the Swedish Waza family. In 1596, he moved the capital from Kraków to Warsaw. This made sense, because Warsaw was closer to the center of 16th-century Poland (which had expanded to the east), and because the city had been gaining political importance as the meeting point of the *Sejm,* or parliament of nobles, over the preceding 30 years. Along the right side of the castle, notice the two previous versions of this pillar lying on a lawn. The first one, from 1644, was falling apart and had to be replaced in 1887 by a new one made of granite. In 1944, a Nazi tank broke this second pillar—a symbolic piece of Poland's heritage—into the four pieces that you see here today. As Poland rebuilt, it put Sigismund III back on his pillar.

Across the square from the castle, you'll see the partially reconstructed defensive wall. This rampart once enclosed the entire Old Town. Situated at the crossroads of Central Europe, Warsaw—like all of Poland—has seen invasion from all sides.

Explore the café-lined lanes that branch downhill off Castle Square. Street signs (from the early 1950s) indicate the year that each street was originally built.

The first street leading off the square is **ulica Piwna** (literally, "Beer Street"), where you'll find **St. Martin's Church** (Kościół Św. Martina, on the left). Run by Franciscan nuns, this church has a simple, modern interior (free entry). Notice the partly destroyed crucifix—all that survived World War II. Farther down ulica Piwna (on right at #6), admire the carefully carved doorway of Restauracja Pod Gołębiami ("Under Doves")—dedicated to the memory of an old woman who fed birds amidst the Old Town rubble after World War II.

Back on the Castle Square, find the white **plaque** with the red stripes in the middle of the second block (by plac Zamkowy 15/19). It explains that 50 Poles were executed by Nazis on this spot on September 2, 1944. You'll see plaques like this all over the Old Town, each one commemorating victims or opponents of the Nazis. Notice the brick planter under the plaque; it's often filled with fresh flowers to remember the victims.

▲**Royal Castle (Zamek Królewski)**—After Warsaw became the capital in 1596, this massive building was used both as the king's residence and as the meeting place of the parliament *(Sejm).* There has been a castle here since the Mazovian dukes built a wooden version in the 14th century. It has shifted shape with the tenor of the times, being rebuilt and remodeled by many different kings. After it was destroyed in World War II, rebuilding began again in the 1950s and was not completed until the 1970s.

Warsaw at a Glance

▲▲**Old Town Market Square** Recreation of Warsaw's glory days, with lots of colorful architecture. **Hours:** Always open.

▲▲**Royal Way Stroll** Self-guided walk along the most interesting stretch of the Royal Way boulevard, starring statues, churches, and historic squares, with a viewpoint-tower finale. **Hours:** Always open.

▲▲**Palace of Culture and Science** Huge "Stalin Gothic" sky-scraper with a more impressive exterior than interior, housing theaters, multiplex cinema, observation deck, and more. **Hours:** Observation deck—June–Sept Mon–Thu 9:00–20:00, Sat–Sun until 24:00, Oct–May daily 9:00–18:00.

▲**Castle Square** Colorful spot with whiffs of old Warsaw—Royal Castle (below), monuments, and a chunk of the city wall, with cafés just off the square. **Hours:** Always open.

▲**Royal Castle** Warsaw's best palace, rebuilt after World War II, but stocked with original furnishings (hidden during the war). **Hours:** Various tour routes with different hours; generally open Tue–Sun 10:00–16:00 or 18:00, summer Mon 11:00–16:00 or 18:00, closed Mon in winter.

This is the most interesting to tour of Warsaw's many palaces—which isn't saying much. While the exterior is entirely reconstructed, many of the furnishings are original, having been hidden away before the city was destroyed. Each room is well-described in English.

The castle makes a great Polish history textbook. In fact, you'll likely see grade-school classes sitting cross-legged on the floors. Watching the teachers drilling eager young history buffs, you can only imagine what it's like to be a young Pole, with such a tumultuous recent history.

Touring the Castle: The castle has various parts, each with separate tickets. For a basic visit, you'll choose between two completely different tour routes: **Route I** (10 zł, year-round Tue–Sat 10:00–16:00; mid-April–Sept also open Mon 11:00–16:00) or **Route II** (18 zł, more expensive since it includes a tour with a Polish-speaking guide, mid-April–Sept Tue–Sat 10:00–18:00, Mon 11:00–18:00; Oct–mid-April Tue–Sat 10:00–16:00, closed Mon). On Sundays, admission is free, and there's a special **Sunday Route** that sometimes includes the "greatest

▲**Warsaw Historical Museum** Glimpse of the city before and after World War II, with excellent movie in English Tue–Sat at 12:00. **Hours:** Mid-March–mid-Sept Tue and Thu 12:00–19:00, Wed and Fri–Sun 11:00–16:30, closed Mon; mid-Sept–mid-March Tue and Thu 11:00–18:00, Wed and Fri 10:00–15:30, Sat–Sun 10:30–16:30, closed Mon.

▲**Piłsudski Square** Tomb of the Unknown Soldier, Saxon Garden, National Theater, and historic monuments. **Hours:** Always open.

▲**Łazienki Park** Lovely, sprawling green space with Chopin statue, peacocks, and neoclassical buildings. **Hours:** Always open.

▲**Ghetto Walking Tour** Pilgrimage from Ghetto Heroes Square along the Path of Remembrance to the infamous Nazi "transfer spot" where Jews were sent to death camps. **Hours:** Always open.

▲**National Museum** Collection of mostly Polish art, with unknown but worth-discovering works by Jan Matejko and the Młoda Polska crew. **Hours**: Tue–Sun 10:00–16:00, Thu until 18:00, closed Mon.

hits" of both routes (mid-April–Sept 11:00–18:00, Oct–mid-April 11:00–16:00). Route I—including the Senators' Chamber and Matejko Rooms (see below)—is more interesting and the better deal. The last entry for any route is one hour before closing. Be warned that opening times, tour routes, and castle layout frequently change depending on special events, temporary exhibitions, and the inexplicable whims of palace administrators.

There's also a **permanent exhibition** that includes decorative arts (17th–18th centuries), a porcelain gallery, a coin collection, some paintings (including a pair of Rembrandts), and various exhibits of interest only to Polish historians (9 zł, Tue–Sat 10:00–16:00, mid-April–Sept also open Mon 11:00–16:00, always closed Sun). Rounding out the attractions is a series of temporary exhibitions. The palace is at Plac Zamkowy 4 (tel. 022/657-2170, www.zamek-krolewski.art.pl). A public WC is on the courtyard just around the corner of the castle.

Route I Highlights: The grand **Senators' Chamber,** with the king's throne, is surrounded by coats of arms of the diverse kingdom's regions that existed back when Poland stretched from the Baltic to the Black Sea. In this room, Poland adopted the constitution of 1791. It was the first in Europe (soon after America's, and just months before France's). And, like the United States', it was very progressive, based on the ideals of the Enlightenment. But the final partitions followed in 1793 and 1795, Poland was divided between neighboring powers and disappeared from the map until 1918, and the constitution was never really put into action. The next room features paintings by **Jan Matejko** that capture the excitement surrounding the adoption of this ill-fated constitution (for more on Matejko, see page 228).

Route II Highlights: Climb the stairs and wander through the ornate rooms. In the **Throne Room,** note the crowned eagle, the symbol of Poland, decorating the banner behind the throne. The Soviets didn't allow anything royal or aristocratic, so postwar restorations came with crown-less eagles. Only after 1989 were the crowns replaced (in the case of this banner, sewn on). A few rooms later is the **Canaletto Room,** filled with canvases of late 18th-century Warsaw painted in exquisite detail by this talented artist. These paintings came in handy when the city needed to be rebuilt. (This Canaletto, also known for his panoramas of Dresden—see page 643—was the nephew of the artist with the same nickname, who was famous for painting Venice's canals.) Continue wandering through the sumptuous halls, saying hello to Ben Franklin (by the door in the Green Room) and gaping at the Marble Room (with portraits of Polish kings around the ceiling—find your favorite).

After you finish touring the castle and you're ready to resume exploring the Old Town, turn left at the end of the square onto...

St. John's Street (Świętojańska)—On the plaque under the street name sign, you can guess what the dates mean, even if you don't speak Polish: This building was constructed 1433–1478, destroyed in 1944, and rebuilt 1950–1953.

Partway down the street on the right, you'll come to the big brick...

Cathedral of St. John the Baptist (Katedra Św. Jana Chrzciciela)—This cathedral-basilica is the oldest (1339) and most important church in Warsaw. Poland's constitution was consecrated here on May 3, 1791. This church became the final battleground of the 1944 Warsaw Uprising—when a Nazi tank (appropriately named *Goliath*) literally drove into the church and intentionally exploded, massacring the rebels. You can still see part of that tank's tread hanging on the outside wall of the church (around the right side).

Despite its importance, the church's interior is pretty dull (free, closed 13:00–15:00). If you visit, look for the crucifix ornamented with real human hair (chapel left of high altar). The high altar holds a copy of the Black Madonna—proclaimed "everlasting queen of Poland" after a victory over the Swedes in 17th century. The original Black Madonna is in Częstochowa (125 miles south of Warsaw)—a mecca for Slavic Catholics, who visit in droves in hopes of a miracle.

Continue up the street and enter Warsaw's grand...

▲▲Old Town Market Square (Rynek Starego Miasta)—Seventy years ago, this was one of the most happening spots in Central Europe. Sixty years ago, it was rubble. And today, like a phoenix rising from the ashes, it reminds locals and tourists alike of the prewar glory of the Polish capital. Enjoy the colorful architecture.

Go to the **mermaid fountain** in the middle of the square. The mermaid is an important symbol in Warsaw—you'll see her everywhere. Legend has it that a mermaid lived in the Vistula River and protected the townspeople. While this siren supposedly serenaded

the town, Varsovians like her more for her strength (hence the sword). Each of the square's four sides is named for an prominent 18th-century Varsovian: Kołłątaj, Dekert, Barss, and Zakrzewski. These men served as "Presidents" of Warsaw (more or less the mayor), and Kołłątaj was also a framer of Poland's 1791 constitution. Take some time to explore the square. Find the jovial chap hanging out above a doorway (hint: He's at the mermaid's 4-o'clock and changes his clothes with the seasons). Notice that many of the buildings were built to intentionally lean out into the square—to simulate the old-age wear and tear of the original buildings.

On the Dekert (north) side of the square is the...

▲Warsaw Historical Museum (Muzeum Historyczne Warszawy)— This labyrinthine museum rambles through several buildings. With limited descriptions in English (and only a couple of paltry English brochures available for purchase), the museum is difficult to appreciate. The exhibits near the end—photos of the Old Town before and immediately after its WWII destruction—are best. The museum shows an excellent 15-minute film in English about wartime Warsaw that's worth the price of admission alone; unfortunately, it runs only Tuesday through Saturday at 12:00. The movie ends with, "They say that there are no miracles. Then what is this city on the Vistula?" Emotionally drained, you can only respond, "Amen." (5 zł, free entry but no movie on Sun, mid-March–mid-Sept Tue and Thu 12:00–19:00, Wed and Fri–Sun 11:00–16:30, closed Mon; mid-Sept–mid-March Tue and Thu 11:00–18:00, Wed and Fri 10:00–15:30, Sat–Sun 10:30–16:30, closed Mon; Rynek Starego Miasta 28/42, tel. 022/635-1625.)

Leave the square on Nowomiejska (at the mermaid's 2-o'clock, by the second-story niche sculpture of St. Anne). After a block, you'll reach the defensive gate of the **Barbican** (Barbakan). Cross through the gate and enter Warsaw's...

New Town (Nowe Miasto)—This 15th-century neighborhood is new in name only: It was the first part of Warsaw to spring up

The Warsaw Uprising

By the summer of 1944, it was becoming clear that the Nazis' days in Warsaw were numbered. The Red Army drew near, and by late July, Soviet tanks were beginning to gather just across the Vistula River from downtown Warsaw.

The Varsovians could have simply waited for the Soviets to cross the river and force the Nazis out. But they knew that Soviet "liberation" would also mean an end to Polish independence. The Polish Home Army (which numbered 400,000 and was the biggest underground army in military history) decided to take matters into its own hands. On August 1, 50,000 Polish resistance fighters launched a surprise attack on their Nazi oppressors. They poured out of the sewers and caught the Nazis off-guard, initially having great success.

But the Nazis regrouped quickly, and within a few days, they had retaken several areas of the city—murdering tens of thousands of innocent civilians as they went. By September 2, the Home Army was surrounded, and 2,000 soldiers fled through the sewers. Most drowned or were killed by Nazi bullets and bombs.

Just two months after it had started, the Warsaw Uprising ended, with the surrender of the Home Army. About 18,000 Polish uprisers were killed, along with nearly 200,000 innocent civilians. An infuriated Hitler ordered that the city be destroyed—which it was, systematically, block by block, until virtually nothing remained.

Through all of this, the Soviets sat across the river, watched, and waited. When the smoke cleared and the Nazis left, the Red Army marched in and claimed the pile of rubble that was once called Warsaw. After the war, General Dwight D. Eisenhower said that the scale of destruction here was the worst he'd ever seen.

Depending on whom you talk to, the desperate uprising of Warsaw was incredibly brave, stupid, or both. As for the Poles, they remain fiercely proud of their struggle for freedom.

outside of the city walls (and therefore newer than the Old Town). The New Town is a fun place to wander: Only slightly less charming than the Old Town, but with a more real-life feel, like people live and work here. It's also packed with affordable restaurants (see "Eating," page 232). Its centerpiece is the **New Town Square** (Rynek Nowego Miasta), watched over by the distinctive green dome of St. Kazimierz Church.

Scientists will want to pay homage at the museum dedicated to Warsaw native **Marie Skłodowska-Curie** (at her birthplace, ulica Freta 16). This Nobel Prize–winner was the world's first radiologist—discovering both radium and polonium (named for her native land) with her husband, Pierre Curie. Since she lived at a time when

Warsaw was controlled by oppressive Russia, she conducted her studies in France.

From New Town to Castle Square—You can backtrack the way you came, or, to get a look at Warsaw's back streets, consider this route from the big, round Barbican gate (where the New Town meets the Old): Go back through the Barbican and turn right, walking along the inside of the wall. You'll pass a courtyard on the left—a reminder that people actually live here inside the Old Town walls. Just beyond the garden on the right, look for the carpet-beating rack, used to clean area rugs (these are common fixtures in people's backyards). Go left into the square called Szeroki Dunaj ("Wide Danube") and look for another mermaid (hint: It's over the Thai restaurant). Continue through the square and turn right at Wąski Dunaj ("Narrow Danube"). After about 100 yards, you pass the city wall. Just to the right (outside the wall), you'll see the monument to the **Little Upriser** of 1944, an imp wearing a grown-up's helmet and too-big boots, and carrying a machine gun. Children—and especially Scouts (Harcerze)—played a key role in the resistance against the Nazis. Their job was mainly to carry messages and propaganda. They also marked walls with the symbol of the resistance: an anchor made up of a P atop a W (which stands for the Polish phrase for "Poland Fighting").

Warsaw's Royal Way (Szłak Królewski)

The Royal Way is the six-mile route that kings of Poland used to take from their main residence (at the Castle Square in the Old Town) to their summer residence (Wilanów Palace, south of the center). In the heart of the city, the Royal Way is made up of two busy boulevards: vibrant **Nowy Świat** (south), which offers a good look at urban Warsaw, and **Krakowskie Przedmieście** (north, ending at the Old Town), which is lined with historic landmarks and better for sightseeing.

Royal Way Stroll

This self-guided walk, rated ▲▲, takes 30 minutes and follows a straight line (with a small side-trip) down the last and best stretch of the Royal Way: from the Church of the Holy Cross (where the street becomes Krakowskie Przedmieście) to the Castle Square at the start of the Old Town. If you're walking from the train station to the Old Town, you could easily incorporate this stroll. Bus #175 from the train station to the Old Town also takes this route (get off at the Uniwersytet stop to start the walk).

The tour begins at the big statue of **Copernicus** in the middle of the street, in front of the Polish Academy of Science. Mikołaj Kopernik was born in Toruń and went to college in Kraków. The Nazis stole this statue and took it to Germany (which, like Poland,

Old Town and Royal Way

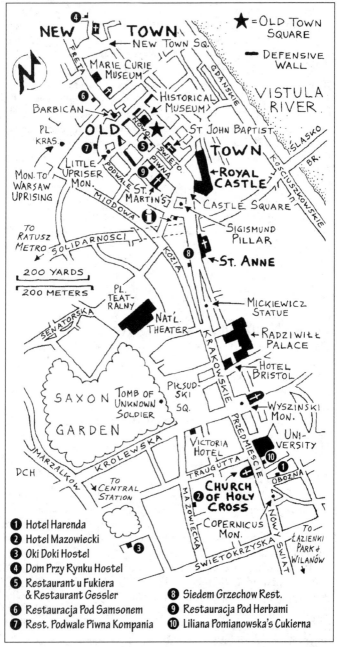

★ = OLD TOWN SQUARE

━ = DEFENSIVE WALL

Legend:

1. Hotel Harenda
2. Hotel Mazowiecki
3. Oki Doki Hostel
4. Dom Przy Rynku Hostel
5. Restaurant u Fukiera & Restaurant Gessler
6. Restauracja Pod Samsonem
7. Rest. Podwale Piwna Kompania
8. Siedem Grzechow Rest.
9. Restauracja Pod Herbami
10. Liliana Pomianowska's Cukierna

Map labels:

NEW TOWN
New Town Sq.
Marie Curie Museum
Historical Museum
Barbican
PL. KRAS
OLD
Little Upriser Mon.
Mon. to Warsaw Uprising
St. Martin's
Miodowa
To Ratusz Metro
Solidarnosci
200 YARDS
200 METERS
St John Baptist
TOWN
Royal Castle
Castle Square
Sigismund Pillar
St. Anne
Gdanskie
Vistula River
Slasko Br.
Kosciuszkowskie
Kozla
Pl. Teatralny
Nat'l Theater
Senatorska
Saxon Garden
Tomb of Unknown Soldier
Mickiewicz Statue
Radziwill Palace
Hotel Bristol
Pilsudski Sq.
Krakowskie
Wyszinski Mon.
University
Victoria Hotel
Krolewska
Marzalkow
DCH
To Central Station
Traugutta
Przedmiescie
Mazowiecka
Church of Holy Cross
Copernicus Mon.
Swietokrzyska
Obozna
Nowy Swiat
To Lazienki Park & Wilanow

claims Copernicus as its own). Now it's back where it belongs.

You'll pass many churches along this route, but the **Church of the Holy Cross** is unique (Kościół Św. Krzyża, across from Copernicus). Stepping inside, you feel it's more alive than other churches in Europe. Locals often drop in. Check out the bright gold chapel on the left. It's dedicated to a saint who Polish Catholics believe helps them with "desperate and hopeless cases." People praying here are likely dealing with some tough issues. The beads draped from the altarpieces help power their prayers, and the many little brass plaques are messages of thanks for prayers answered. The church's claim to fame? Composer Fryderyk Chopin's heart is in one of the pillars of the main nave. After two decades of exile in France, Chopin's final wish was to have his heart brought back to his native Poland. During the war, the heart was hidden away in the countryside to avoid being destroyed.

Just up and across the street from the Church of the Holy Cross are the gates to the main campus of **Warsaw University,** founded in 1816. This area is a lively student district with plenty of bookstores and cafés. A good, very local-style bakery is nearby (see "Uniquely Polish Treats on or near the Royal Way," page 233), as well as a milk bar (*bar mleczny,* at #20)—a subsidized government cafeteria filled with students and others in need of a bargain (see "*Bar Mleczny* (Milk Bar)" sidebar on page 152).

The 18th century was a time of great political decline for Poland, with a series of incompetent foreign kings mishandling crises and squandering funds. But ironically, it was also Warsaw's biggest economic boom time. Along this boulevard, aristocratic families of the period built **mansions**—destroyed during World War II and rebuilt since, some with curious flourishes. Just past the university on the right, look for the doorway supported by four bearded brutes admiring their overly defined abs. Over time, many of these families donated their mansions to the university.

The yellow church a block up from the university is the Church of the Nuns of the Visitation (Kościół Sióstr Wizytek). The monument in front of the church commemorates **Cardinal Stefan Wyszyński,** who was the Polish primate (head of the Polish Catholic Church) from 1948 to 1981. He took this post soon after the arrival of the communists, who opposed the Church, but also realized it would be dangerous to shut down the churches in such an ardently religious country. The Communist Party and the Catholic Church coexisted tensely in Poland, and when Wyszyński protested a Stalinist crackdown in 1953, he was arrested and imprisoned. Three years later, in a major victory for the Church, Wyszyński was released. He went on to become a great hero of the Polish people in their struggle against the regime.

Farther up, you'll see the elegant **Hotel Bristol,** Warsaw's classiest. Detour here to Piłsudski Square (a block away on the left, up the street opposite Hotel Bristol).

The historic **Piłsudski Square** (Plac Marszałka Józefa Piłsudskiego) has been important Warsaw real estate for years, constantly changing with the times. An Orthodox cathedral here was torn down in the 1920s, when anti-Russian passions ran high in newly independent Poland. During the Nazi occupation, it took the name "Adolf-Hitler-Platz." Under the communists, it was Zwycięstwa, meaning "Victory" (of the Soviets over Hitler's fascism). When martial law was imposed in 1981, the people of Warsaw silently protested by filling the square with a giant cross made of flowers. The huge plaque in the ground near the busy road commemorates two monumental communist-era Catholic events on this square: Pope John Paul II's first visit to his homeland on June 2, 1979; and the funeral on May 31, 1981, of Cardinal Stefan Wyszyński, whom we met across the street.

Find the sewer lid at the very center, and stand on it for this quick spin-tour orientation: Ahead are the Tomb of the Unknown Soldier and Saxon Garden; to the right is the old National Theater, eclipsed by a beautiful new shopping mall/parking garage; farther to the right is a statue of Piłsudski (which you passed to get here—see below); and to the right of that—past the big gray Polish Ministry of Defense building—is the Victoria Hotel, the ultimate plush, top-of-the-top hotel where all communist-era VIPs stayed.

Walk to the fragment of colonnade by the park that marks the **Tomb of the Unknown Soldier** (Grób Nieznanego Żołnierza). The colonnade was once part of a much larger palace built by the Saxon prince electors (Dresden's Augustus the Strong and his son), who became kings of Poland in the 18th century. After the palace was destroyed in World War II, this fragment was kept to memorialize Polish soldiers. The names of key battles are etched into the columns, urns contain dirt from major Polish battlefields, and the two guards are pretty stiff.

Just behind the Tomb is **Saxon Garden** (Ogród Saski), a pleasant park to stroll in, also built by the Saxon kings of Poland. Like most foreign kings, Augustus the Strong and his son cared little for their Polish territory, building gardens like these, instead of investing in more pressing needs. Poles say that foreign kings such as Augustus did nothing but "eat, drink, and loosen their belts" (it rhymes in Polish). According to Poles, these selfish absentee kings are the culprits for Poland's eventual decline.

Walk to the statue (on the side of the square where you first entered). In 1995, the square was again re-named—this time for **Józef Piłsudski,** the guy with the big walrus moustache. Piłsudski (1867–1935) forced out the Russian Bolsheviks from Poland in 1920 in the so-called Miracle on the Vistula. Piłsudski is credited with creating a once-again-independent Poland after over a century of foreign oppression, and he essentially ran Poland after World War I. Of course, under the communists, Piłsudski was swept under the rug, but today he's enjoying a renaissance as Poland's favorite proto-type anti-communist hero (his name adorns streets, squares, and bushy-mustachioed monuments all over the country). It's interest-ing to note that Piłsudski encouraged Britain and France to pre-emptively attack Hitler in 1933. He was ignored, and Poland was devastated a few years later. Perhaps that's why Poles were predis-posed to support America's preemptive war against Iraq.

Return to Hotel Bristol, turn left, and continue your Royal Way walk. Next door to the hotel, you'll see the huge **Radziwiłł Palace**—the Polish White House, with the offices of Poland's president. The Warsaw Pact was signed here in 1955, officially uniting the Soviet satellite states in a military alliance against NATO. The newest flag in the courtyard is Europe's (celebrating the May 1, 2004, entry of Poland into the EU).

Beyond Radziwiłł Palace, you'll reach a statue (on a pillar) of **Adam Mickiewicz,** Poland's national poet. Polish high school stu-dents have a big formal ball (like the prom) 100 days before gradua-tion. After the ball, if students come here and hop around the statue on one leg, it's supposed to bring them good luck on their finals. Mickiewicz, for his part, looks like he's suffering from a heart attack—perhaps in response to the impressively ugly National Theater and Opera a block in front of him.

For a scenic finale to your Royal Way stroll, climb the 150 steps of the view tower by **St. Anne's Church** (unpredictable hours). You'll be rewarded with a great view of the old town, river, and Warsaw's skyline, complete with Stalin's Penis (see "More Sights in Warsaw," page 226).

From St. Anne's Church, it's just another block—past inviting art galleries and restaurants (see "Eating," page 232)—to the Castle Square, the TI, and the start of the Old Town (to continue your walk all the way to the New Town, see "Warsaw's Old Town," page 210).

The Rest of the Royal Way

Nowy Świat—This is a charming, nearly traffic-free shopping boule-vard—nicknamed the "Champs-Elysées of Warsaw" by locals. This segment of the Royal Way stretches in the opposite direction from the walk described above, running south from the Copernicus monu-ment all the way to Łazienki Park (triple the distance from Copernicus north to the Old Town). Bus #503 runs along this route from the Old Town to the Chopin statue at Łazienki Park (see below).

On or near Nowy Świat, you'll find two venerable spots for memorable taste treats (both just a few blocks in front of the train station). On Nowy Świat (at #35) is the A. Blikle pastry shop.

The Rest of the Royal Way

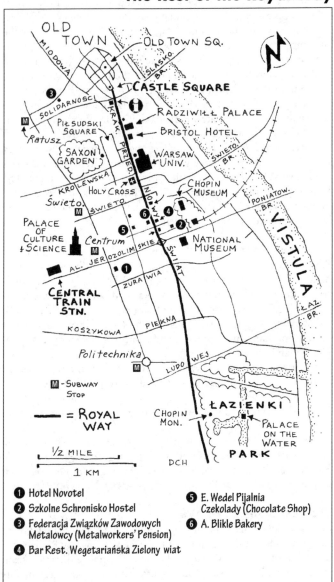

1. Hotel Novotel
2. Szkolne Schronisko Hostel
3. Federacja Związków Zawodowych Metalowcy (Metalworkers' Pension)
4. Bar Rest. Wegetariańska Zielony wiat
5. E. Wedel Pijalnia Czekolady (Chocolate Shop)
6. A. Blikle Bakery

Branching off Nowy Świat, ulica Chmielna (near the end, on the right) is an appealing pedestrian boutique street leading to Wedel's chocolate heaven. For more on both places, see "Uniquely Polish Treats on or near the Royal Way" (page 233).

Nowy Świat means "New World." The big, blocky building at the busy intersection of Nowy Świat and aleja Jerozolimskie (next door to the National Museum) used to be the headquarters of the Communist Party. A popular communist-era joke: What do you see when you turn your back on the Communist Party? A new world.

▲**Łazienki Park (Park Łazienkowski)**—This huge, idyllic park is where Varsovians go to play. The park is sprinkled with fun neoclassical buildings, peacocks, and young Poles in love. It was built by Poland's very last king (before the final partition), Stanisław August Poniatowski, to serve as his summer residence and provide a place for his citizens to relax.

On the edge of the park (along Belwederska) is a **monument to Fryderyk Chopin,** Poland's greatest composer. The monument, in a beautiful rose garden, is flanked by platforms, where free summer piano concerts are given weekly (generally Sun at 12:00 and 16:00). The statue (from 1926) shows Chopin sitting under a wind-

blown willow tree. While he spent his last 20 years and wrote most of his greatest music in France, his inspiration came from wind blowing through the willow trees of his native land, Poland. The Nazis melted the statue down for its metal. Today's copy was recast after World War II. Savor this spot; it's great in summer, with roses wildly in bloom, and in autumn, when the trees provide a golden backdrop for the black, romantic statue.

Venture to the center of the park, where (after a 10-min hike) you'll find King Poniatowski's striking **Palace on the Water** (Pałac na Wodzie)—literally built in the middle of a river. Nearby, you'll spot a clever amphitheater with seating on the riverbank and the stage on an island. Poniatowski was a real man of the Enlightenment, hosting weekly dinners here for artists and intellectuals (free entry to park, just south of the city center on the Royal Way, take buses #100, #116, #119, #180, #195, #318, #503, or #513 south from the center and get off at stop Bagatela by Belweder Palace). Maps at park entrances locate the Chopin monument, Palace on the Water, and other park attractions.

Jewish Sights

After centuries of living peacefully in Poland, Warsaw's Jews suffered terribly at the hands of the Nazis (see "Warsaw's Jews and the

Warsaw's Jews and the Ghetto Uprising

From the Middle Ages until World War II, Poland was a safe haven for Europe's Jews. When other kings were imprisoning and deporting Jews in the 14th century, the progressive king Kazimierz the Great welcomed Jews into Poland, even granting them special privileges (see page 168).

By the 1930s, there were more than 380,000 Jews in Warsaw—nearly a third of the population (and the largest concentration of Jews in the world). The Nazis arrived in 1939. Within a year, they had pushed all of Warsaw's Jews into one neighborhood and surrounded it with a wall, creating a miserably overcrowded ghetto (crammed full of half a million people, including many from nearby towns). Over the next year, the Nazis brought in more Jews from throughout Poland, and the number grew by a million.

By the summer of 1942, more than a quarter of the Jews in the ghetto had already died of disease, murder, or suicide. The Nazis started moving Warsaw's Jews (at the rate of 5,000 a day) into what they claimed were "resettlement camps." Most of these people were actually murdered at Treblinka or Auschwitz. After hundreds of thousands of Jews had been taken to concentration camps, the waning population—now about 60,000—began to get word from concentration camp escapees about what was actually going on there.

Ghetto Uprising" sidebar). You can visit several sights in Warsaw that commemorate those who were murdered—and those who fought back. Because of the ferocity of Nazi hatred, there is literally nothing left of the ghetto except the street plan and the heroic spirit of its former residents.

▲**Ghetto Walking Tour**—For a quick walking tour of the former ghetto site, begin at **Ghetto Heroes Square** (plac Bohaterow Getta). To get here from the Old Town, either hop a taxi (10 zł) or walk (go through Barbican gate 2 blocks into New Town, turn left on Świętojerska, and walk straight 10 min—passing new green-glass Supreme Court building—until you reach grassy park on Zamenhofa Street). The square is in the heart of what was the Jewish ghetto—now surrounded by bland Soviet-style apartment blocks. After the Uprising, the entire ghetto was reduced to dust by the Nazis—leaving the communists to rebuild to their own specifications. The district is called Muranów (literally, "Rebuilt") today.

The **monument** in the middle of the square commemorates those who fought and died "for the dignity and freedom of the Jewish Nation, for a free Poland, and for the liberation of humankind." The big park across the street is the future site of the Museum for the History of Polish Jews. It's been in the works for years, with its progress slowed by controversy over exactly what form

Spurred by this knowledge, Warsaw's surviving Jews staged a dramatic uprising.

On April 19, 1943, the Jews attacked Nazi strongholds and had some initial success—but within a month, the Nazis crushed the Ghetto Uprising. The ghetto's residents and structures were "liquidated." About 300 of Warsaw's Jews survived, thanks in part to a sort of "underground railroad" of courageous Varsovians.

The sights of Warsaw's Jewry are moving, but even more so if you know some of their stories. Many Americans have heard of **Władysław Szpilman,** a Jewish concert pianist who survived the war with the help of Jews, Poles, and even a Nazi officer. Szpilman's life story was turned into the highly acclaimed, Oscar-winning 2002 film *The Pianist,* which powerfully depicts events in Warsaw during World War II.

Less familiar to Americans—but equally affecting—is the story of Henryk Goldszmit, better known by his pen name, **Janusz Korczak.** Korczak wrote imaginative children's books that are still enormously popular among Poles. He also worked at an orphanage in the Warsaw ghetto. When his orphans were sent off to concentration camps, the Nazis offered the famous author a chance at freedom. Korczak turned them down, and chose to die at Treblinka with his children.

the museum will take (for the latest, see www.jewishmuseum.org.pl).

Facing the monument, head left (with the park on your left) up Zamenhofa—which, like many streets in this neighborhood, is named for a hero of the Ghetto Uprising. From the monument, you'll follow a series of three-foot-tall black stone monuments to Uprising heroes—the **Path of Remembrance.** Like Stations of the Cross, each recounts an event of the uprising. On April 19th (the day the Uprising began), huge crowds follow this path. In a block, at the corner of Miła, you'll find a **bunker** where organizers of the Uprising hid out (and where they committed suicide when the Nazis discovered them on May 8, 1943).

Continue following the black stone monuments up Zamenhofa, then turn left around the corner and cross busy Stawki street. A long block up Stawki and on the right, you'll see the **Umschlagplatz** monument—shaped like a cattle car. That's German for "transfer place," and it marks the spot where the Nazis brought Jewish families to prepare them to be loaded onto trains bound for Treblinka or Auschwitz (a harrowing scene vividly depicted in *The Pianist*). In the walls of the monument are inscribed the first names of some of the victims.

Jewish Historical Institute of Poland (Żydowski Instytut Historyczny)—For more in-depth information about Warsaw's Jewish community, including the Ghetto Uprising, visit this museum housed in the former Jewish Library building. The main floor displays well-described old photos. The 37-minute movie about life and death in the ghetto—played in English upon request—is graphic and powerful. Upstairs, you'll find more on Jewish art, culture, and temporary exhibits (10 zł, Mon–Wed and Fri 9:00–16:00, Thu 11:00–18:00, closed Sat–Sun, ulica Tłomackie 3/5, tel. 022/827-9221, www.jewishinstitute.org.pl).

The Peugeot building next door—appropriately and simply dubbed "the blue tower" by locals—is on the former site of Warsaw's biggest synagogue, destroyed by the Nazis as a victorious final kick.

More Sights in Warsaw

The following sights are all in central Warsaw, within a few blocks of the Royal Way. I've listed them from south to north.

▲▲**Palace of Culture and Science (Pałac Kultury i Nauki, or PKiN)**—This massive skyscraper, dating from the early 1950s, is Poland's tallest building (760 feet). It was a "gift" from Stalin that the people of Warsaw couldn't refuse. Varsovians call it "Stalin's Penis," using even cruder terminology than that. There were seven such "Stalin Gothic" erections in Moscow. Because it was to be "Soviet in substance, Polish in style," Soviet architects toured Poland to absorb the local culture before starting the project. Since the end of communism, the younger generation doesn't mind the structure so much—and some even admit to liking it. The clock was added in 1999 as part of the millennium celebrations.

Everything about the Pałac is big. It's designed to impress, to show off the strong, grand-scale Soviet aesthetic and architectural skill. The Pałac contains various theaters (the Culture), a museum of evolution (the Science), a congress hall, a multiplex (showing current movies), an observation deck (see below), and lots of office space (including UNICEF's Polish headquarters). With all of this Culture and Science under one Roof, it's a shame that none of it makes for worthwhile sightseeing—viewing the building from the outside is a quintessential Warsaw experience, but the interior is eminently skippable.

If you're killing time between trains, you could zip up to the observation deck (15 zł, more for special exhibitions, June–Sept Mon–Thu 9:00–20:00, Sat–Sun until 24:00, Oct–May daily 9:00–18:00, enter through main door on east side of Pałac—opposite from train station, tel. 022/656-6000, www.pkin.pl). Better yet, snap a photo from down below and save your money; the view's a letdown. You can hardly see the Old Town, and Warsaw's most prominent big building—the Pałac itself—is missing.

▲**National Museum (Muzeum Narodowe)**—This museum, while short on big-name pieces, interests art-lovers and offers a fine introduction to some talented Polish artists unknown outside their home country (11 zł, more for temporary exhibits, free on Sat, open Tue–Sun 10:00–16:00, Thu until 18:00, closed Mon, 1 block east of Nowy Świat at aleja Jerozolimskie 3, tel. 022/629-3093, www.mnw.art.pl).

Downstairs are exhibits of ancient art (from Egyptian and Greek to works by early Polish tribes), as well as room upon room of medieval altarpieces and crucifixes (including some of the most graphic I've seen). Upstairs are Polish paintings (and some Dutch and German). There's a whole room of Napoleon portraits. The Poles loved Napoleon, who bravely marched on Russia at a time when this part of Poland was occupied by the oppressive Russians (sadly, not for the last time).

While you won't recognize most names in here, focus on two areas:

First, find the **Jan Matejko** room, dominated by the enormous *Battle of Grunwald*. This epic painting commemorates the dramatic victory of a Polish-Lithuanian army against the Teutonic Knights, who had been terrorizing northern Poland for decades (for more on the Teutonic Knights, see page 268). In the center of the painting, the Teutonic Grand Master (in white) is about to become a shish kebab. In red, leading the fray, is the Lithuanian Duke Vytautas. And waaaay up on a hill (in the upper right-hand corner) is Władysław Jagiełło, the first king of the Jagiellonian dynasty...ensuring his bloodline will survive another 150 years. To the left of this huge canvas is a smaller, more intimate portrait by Matejko, depicting a popular Polish figure: the court jester Stańczyk, who's smarter than the king, but not allowed to say so. Other Matejko paintings include a pair depicting the tragic couple of the last Jagiellonian king and his wife, Barbara—whom he loved deeply, even though she couldn't bear him an heir. (In the next room, see the painful conclusion to their sad, sad tale: Barbara on her deathbed.)

Then take a look at the **Młoda Polska** ("Young Poland") collection, featuring paintings from Poland's version of Art Nouveau (see page 170). In addition to a room of beautiful works by movement headliner Stanisław Wyspiański, you'll see the hypnotically beautiful *Strange Garden* by Józef Mehoffer, as well as several works by Jacek Malczewski. Malczewski's paintings depict the goateed, close-cropped artist in a variety of different semi-surrealistic, Polish countryside contexts. There's also a room of canvases by the only prominent female Polish painter, Olga Boznańska—with a softer and more impressionistic touch than her male Młoda Polska counterparts.

Chopin Museum (Muzeum Fryderyka Chopina)—This modest museum in honor of Poland's most famous musician is housed in the beautifully reconstructed Ostrogski Castle, a few blocks off the

Jan Matejko
(1838-1893)

Jan Matejko (yawn mah-TAY-koh) is Poland's most important painter, period. In the late 19th century, the nation of Poland had been dissolved by foreign powers, and Polish artists struggled to make sense of their people's place in the world. Rabble-rousing Romanticism seemed to have failed (inspiring many brutally suppressed uprisings), so Polish artists turned their attention to educating the people about their history, with the goal of keeping the Polish traditions alive.

Matejko was at the forefront of this so-called positivist movement. He painted two types of works: huge, grand-scale epics depicting monumental events in Polish history; and small, intimate portraits of prominent Poles. Polish schoolchildren learn about history from books with paintings of virtually every single Polish king—all painted by the incredibly prolific Matejko.

Matejko is admired not for his technical mastery (he's an unexceptional painter), but for the emotion behind—and inspired by—his works. Matejko's paintings are utilitarian, straightforward, and dramatic, enough to stir the patriot in any Pole...precisely his goal. The intense focus on history by Matejko and other positivists is one big reason why today's Poles are still so in touch with their heritage.

You'll see Matejko's works in Warsaw's National Museum and Royal Castle, as well as in Kraków's Gallery of 19th-Century Polish Art (above the Cloth Hall). You can also visit his former residence in Kraków.

Royal Way (near the Copernicus monument). Everything of interest is upstairs: manuscripts, letters, and original handwritten compositions. You'll also see Chopin's last piano, which he used for composing during the final two years of his life (1848–1849). Nearby, flip through the guest book. Chopin's music is popular in Japan, and Japanese music-lovers flock here, almost as a pilgrimage. In the next room, find Chopin's bronze death mask and admire his distinctively Polish nose, shaped like an eagle's beak (5 zł, May–Sept Mon, Wed, and Fri 10:00–17:00, Thu 12:00–18:00, Sat–Sun 10:00–14:00, closed Tue; Oct–April Mon–Wed and Fri–Sat 10:00–14:00, Thu 12:00–18:00, closed Sun, 3 blocks east of Nowy Świat at ulica Okólnik 1, tel. 022/826-5935).

The top floor has a concert hall, open only for special concerts. If you're in town for one, go. There's nothing like hearing Chopin's music fill this fine mansion, passionately played by a teary-eyed Pole who really feels the music (call museum or check online for concert schedules, www.tifc.chopin.pl).

The **Ostrogski Castle**, which houses the museum, was destroyed down to the brick cellar in World War II. A plaque by the staircase around back notes that it was "voluntarily reconstructed" by the communists in 1970 "to celebrate the 25th anniversary of the People's Republic of Poland." In the courtyard behind is a statue of a golden duck *(złota kaczka)*, a mythical creature that supposedly lived in the castle's cellar. An often-repeated but strangely anticlimactic parable explains that this duck gave a cobbler's apprentice a huge amount of money, telling him that if he frittered it away by the end of the day, he'd win great rewards. The boy gave some to a beggar, which didn't fit the duck's idea of "frittering"—but the boy found happiness anyway.

Chopin's birth house is in Żelazowa Wola, 34 miles from Warsaw. It's tourable, but not worth the trek for anyone but the most rabid Chopin fan.

Warsaw Uprising Sights—The most convenient sight relating to the 1944 Warsaw Uprising is the **monument** at plac Krasińskich (intersection of ulica Długa and Miodowa, a few blocks northwest of the New Town). Larger-than-life soldiers and civilians race for the sewers in a desperate attempt to flee the Nazis. Just behind the monument is the rusting copper facade of Poland's Supreme Court.

Farther from the center, the brand-new **Warsaw Uprising Museum** (Muzeum Powstania Warszawskiego) opened on August 1, 2004—the 60th anniversary of the Uprising. Through film clips, photographs, and actual debris from the violence, the stark, modern museum tells the tragic and uplifting story of the brave Poles who fought for their freedom despite overwhelming odds (Thu 10:00–20:00, Fri–Sun 10:00–18:00, likely different hours in 2005, on the west edge of town at ulica Przyokopowa 28, bus #100, www.1944.pl).

SLEEPING

The budget hotel scene in central Warsaw is miserable. Most hotels are overpriced, with worn rooms and desk clerks doing their best to reinforce the communist-era stereotype of grouchy, incompetent service. Since this is a convention town, prices can go up during convention times and way down on weekends. With such poor hotel options, anyone should consider hosteling here—so I've listed several hostels, including some with single and double rooms.

$$$ Novotel, with 740 rooms, overlooks Poland's busiest intersection, across the street from the Palace of Culture and Science. Its prices plummet on weekends and in summer (Mon–Fri rack rates: Sb-€135, Db-€150; actual Mon–Fri rates usually closer to Sb-€110, Db-€120; Sat–Sun: Sb or Db-€78; sometimes even better deals in summer, elevator, ulica Nowogrodzka 24/26, tel. 022/621-0271, fax 022/625-0476, www.orbis.pl, nov.warszawa@orbis.pl).

Sleep Code

(3.5 zł = about $1, €1 = about $1.20, country code: 48, area code: 022)
S = Single, **D** = Double/Twin, **T** = Triple, **Q** = Quad,
b = bathroom, **s** = shower only. Unless otherwise noted, English
is spoken, breakfast is included, and credit cards are accepted.
Some places quote prices in euros.

To help you sort easily through these listings, I've divided
the rooms into three categories, based on the price for a standard
double room with bath:

$$$ Higher Priced—Most rooms 400 zł (€92) or more.
 $$ Moderately Priced—Most rooms between 250–400 zł (€58–92).
  $ Lower Priced—Most rooms 250 zł (€58) or less.

$$ Hotel Harenda rents out 43 rooms on the third floor of an
office building in the charming neighborhood where Nowy Świat
becomes Krakowskie Przedmieście, and the Royal Way really gets
interesting. The rooms are nothing special, but the location is excel-
lent, and this truly is one of central Warsaw's best values (mid-
Feb–June and Sept–Nov: Sb-320 zł, Db-360 zł; rest of year: Sb-290
zł, Db-320 zł; second night is free Fri–Sun, some rowdy street
noise—especially on weekends—so request quiet room, Krakowskie
Przedmieście 4/6, tel. & fax 022/826-0071, www.hotelharenda
.com.pl, hh@hotelharenda.com.pl).

$$ Hotel Mazowiecki is a family-run jewel on a drab urban
street between the Palace of Culture and Science and Nowy Świat.
Its 53 rooms are basic, but well-located for the price (S-150 zł, Sb-
200 zł, D-200 zł, Db-250 zł, 20 percent cheaper Fri–Sun, elevator,
ulica Mazowiecka 10, tel. & fax 022/827-2365, www.mazowiecki
.com.pl, rezerwacja@mazowiecki.com.pl).

$$ Hotel Gromada, a 320-room conference hotel, has a dreary
communist exterior, but the lobby and most rooms are nicely
renovated. There are three types of rooms: "tourist" (decent, but could
be spruced up); "standard" (nicely renovated and fresh); and "plus"
(similar to standard, but in a newer building—not worth the extra
expense). Though it has zero personality, the place offers a decent
value and a good location, between the Palace of Culture and Science
and Nowy Świat (tourist rooms: Sb-200 zł, Db-230 zł; standard
rooms: Sb-320, Db-350; plus rooms: Sb-420 zł, Db-450 zł; standard
and plus rooms about 25 percent cheaper Fri–Sat, non-smoking
rooms, elevator, plac Powstańców Warszawy 2, tel. 022/582-9900, fax
022/582-9527, www.hotels.gromada.pl, domchlopa@gromada.pl).

$ Boutique B&B is run by Jarek Chołodecki, who lived near
Chicago for many years. On returning to Warsaw, he converted

apartments in a conveniently located building into a quaint bed-and-breakfast with four rooms at good prices (standard Db-€55, junior suite-€75, big suite-€110, 15 percent cheaper Oct-March, elevator, ulica Smolna 14, tel. 022/829-4801, fax 022/829-4882, www .bedandbreakfast.pl, office@bedandbreakfast.pl).

$ The IYHF **Szkolne Schronisko** hostel is well-run, bright, and very clean. If you reserve ahead, this is the best deal on single and twin rooms in Warsaw. The downside: It's on the fifth floor, with no elevator (non-members welcome, all prices per person: dorm beds-36 zł, S-65 zł, twin D-60 zł, T-55 zł, Q-45 zł, plus 5 zł per person for sheets and 2 zł for towels, cash only, no breakfast but members' kitchen, closed 10:00–16:00, curfew at 23:00, e-mail or fax ahead to reserve S, D, and T rooms—there are only 2 of each, fine location across street from National Museum at ulica Smolna 30, tel. & fax 022/827-8952, www.ssmsmolna30.pl, ssmsmolna@poczta.onet.pl).

$ **Oki Doki Hostel** is a colorful, creative, easygoing, new place on a pleasant square a few blocks in front of the Palace of Culture and Science. Each of its 18 rooms was designed by a different artist with a special theme—Van Gogh, Celtic spirals, heads of state—and has a name instead of a number (S-115 zł, D-130 zł, Db-170 zł, T-185 zł; dorm bed in 4- to 6-bed room-50 zł; breakfast included, but not for dorm-dwellers, who pay 10 zł; free Internet access, kitchen, self-serve laundry with hang-dry-10 zł/load, plac Dąbrowskiego 3, tel. 022/826-5112, fax 022/826-8357, www.okidoki.pl, okidoki@okidoki.pl).

$ **Dom Przy Rynku Hostel** is a small, friendly, charming, 40-bed place with two goals: housing kids from dysfunctional families, and raising money for its work by renting out beds to tourists (when it's not housing children). Located in the peaceful New Town, the cozy rooms are decorated for grade-schoolers. Beds are rented in July and August, and on Friday and Saturday nights all year (35 zł per bed in 2- to 5-bed rooms, rooms segregated for boys and girls, bus #175 from station or airport to Franciszkańska stop, corner of Kościelna and Przyrynek streets at Rynek Nowego Miasta 4, tel. & fax 022/831-5033).

$ **Federacja Związków Zawodowych Metalowcy,** meaning "Federation of Trade Union Metalworkers," is a cheap, old, trade union–subsidized place with piles of stairs and 25 ramshackle rooms. This very communist-style time warp is a centrally located alternative to the hostel scene, in a neighborhood packed with apartment blocks a 10-minute walk from the Old Town (S-60–75 zł, D-114 zł, Db-161 zł, T-171 zł, Q-206 zł, Qs-219 zł, all doubles are twins, some with beds in different rooms, cash only, no breakfast, ulica Długa 29, tel. 022/831-4021, fax 022/635-3138, NSE).

EATING

In or near the Old Town

You'll pay triple to eat right on the Old Town Market Square, but some visitors figure it's worth the splurge (plan on 70–100 zł per main dish). I prefer to venture a few blocks to find a place with good food and much lower prices. Most restaurants say they're open until the "last guest," which usually means around 23:00 (sometimes later in summer). For locations, see the map on page 218.

On the Old Town Market Square: Locals agree that there are two good options. **U Fukiera** offers traditional Polish and pan-European meals in a sophisticated setting (daily 12:00–23:00, #27, tel. 022/831-1013). **Gessler** has two parts: traditional Polish dishes in an atmospheric cellar with dramatic brick vaults, or international cuisine in a swanky dining room (daily 10:00–23:00, #21, tel. 022/831-4427). In Gessler's lobby hang photos of famous patrons. It's the only place you'll see Hillary Rodham Clinton, George H. W. Bush, and Henry Kissinger side by side—and smiling. (A sly Fidel Castro watches over the three of them.)

At **Restauracja Pod Samsonem** ("Under Samson"), dine on affordable Polish-Jewish fare with well-dressed locals. The service is playfully opinionated, and the low prices make up for the fact that you have to pay to check your coat and use the bathroom (most main dishes 15–25 zł, daily 10:00–23:00, ulica Freta 3/5, tel. 022/831-1788).

Podwale Piwna Kompania is a lively, smoky, new-feeling place filled with locals. You'll enjoy the large plates of tasty food and the Czech beer-hall ambience (most main dishes 20–30 zł, daily 11:00–24:00, just outside Old Town walls near the Barbican at ulica Podwale 25, tel. 022/635-6314).

Siedem Grzechow ("Seven Sins") is an old-style Warsaw restaurant serving top-notch Polish and international cuisine in a 1930s lace, velvet, and burgundy ambience. The place fills a dressy cellar with locals and jazz (main dishes 30–60 zł, daily 11:00–23:00, a few blocks before the Old Town on the Royal Way at Krakowskie Przedmieście 45, tel. 022/826-4770).

Restauracja Pod Herbami ("Under the Coat of Arms") is a cozy, classy little place with good prices buried deep in the Old Town (main dishes 15–20 zł, daily 11:00–23:00, ulica Piwna 21-23, tel. 022/831-6447).

Quick and Tasty on Nowy Świat

These restaurants offer a break from heavy Polish food, close to the National Museum and train station on Nowy Świat.

Café Brama, part of a chain popular with local students, offers great sandwiches, salads, soups, and *pierogi* in a trendy atmosphere (sandwiches around 18 zł, salads around 20 zł, Mon–Fri 9:00–22:00,

Sat–Sun 10:00–22:00, Nowy Świat 60, actually just down Ordynacka street).

Bar Restauracja Wegetariańska Zielony Świat ("Green World") has good Asian-style vegetarian food (most dishes 20–30 zł, daily 10:30–21:30, enter through passageway at Nowy Świat 42 to reach ulica Gałczyńskiego 5/9, tel. 022/826-4677).

Sandwicz is a colorful glorified milk bar with Polish grub, a self-serve salad bar, and—of course—sandwiches (Mon–Fri 7:30–20:30, Sat–Sun 10:00–20:30, aleja Jerozolimskie 11/19).

Uniquely Polish Treats on or near the Royal Way

The first two places are on or close to the busy boulevard called Nowy Świat. The third is a few blocks north, near the big Copernicus monument and University at the start of my self-guided "Royal Way Stroll" (see page 217).

A. Blikle is Poland's most famous bakery, serving a wide variety of delicious pastries. This is where locals shop for cakes when they're having someone special over for coffee. The specialty: *pączki* (2 zł)—the quintessential Polish doughnut, filled with rose-flavored jam (Mon–Fri 9:00–19:00, Sat 9:00–18:00, Sun 10:30–17:00, Nowy Świat 35).

Chocoholics will venture to **E. Wedel Pijalnia Czekolady.** Emil Wedel made Poland's favorite chocolate, and today, his former residence houses this chocolate shop (Mon 10:00–17:00, Tue–Fri 9:00–20:00, Sat 9:00–16:00, closed Sun) and café (Mon–Sat 10:00–22:00, Sun 12:00–17:00, tel. 022/827-2916). This is the spot for delicious pastries and a *real* hot chocolate (that means a cup of melted chocolate, not just hot chocolate milk). Cadbury bought the company when Poland privatized after communism, but they kept the E. Wedel name, which is close to all Poles' hearts...and taste buds (between Palace of Culture and Science and Nowy Świat at ulica Szepitalna 1). *Czekolada do picia* is the basic drink (8 zł). The menu describes it as "true Wedel ecstasy for your mouth that will take you to a world of dreams and desires." Or, if you fancy pudding, try *pokusa*. Wedel's was *the* Christmas treat for locals under communism.

Liliana Pomianowska's Cukierna has tasty, fresh pastries, coffee, ice cream (summer only), and a local-student vibe (Mon–Fri 9:00–17:00, Sat 9:00–14:00, closed Sun, hiding down a passageway at Krakowskie Przedmieście 8).

TRANSPORTATION CONNECTIONS

Virtually all trains into and out of Warsaw go through the hideous, hulking Warszawa Centralna station (see "Arrival in Warsaw," page 208.) If you're heading to Gdańsk, note that the red-brick Gothic city of Toruń and the impressive Malbork Castle are on the way (though on separate train lines, so you can't do both en route; see Gdańsk and Pomerania chapter).

By train to: Kraków (hrly, 2.5 hrs), **Gdańsk** (hrly, 3.75 hrs), **Toruń** (5/day, 3 hrs direct; more with a transfer in Kutno), **Malbork** (hrly, 3.5 hrs), **Prague** (2/day direct, including 1 night train, 9–10 hrs; or 2/day, 9 hrs, with transfer in Ostrava-Svinov), **Berlin** (3/day direct, 5.75 hrs; plus 1 direct night train, 7.75 hrs), **Budapest** (2/day direct, including 1 night train, 10.5–11.5 hrs; or 1 each per day with transfer in Győr, Hungary, or Břeclav, Czech Republic, both 10 hrs), **Vienna** (2/day direct, including 1 night train, 7.75 or 9.5 hrs; or 1/day with transfer in Břeclav, Czech Republic, 7.75 hrs).

GDAŃSK
and POMERANIA

Gdańsk (guh-DANSK) is a true find on the Baltic coast of Poland, featuring breathtaking Old World architecture, quaintly creaky museums, and vivid, enthralling 20th-century history. It's the birthplace of the Solidarity movement that toppled Poland's communist regime. You might even see old Lech Wałęsa still wandering the streets.

Near Gdańsk, the faded elegance of the seafront spa resort Sopot merits a side-trip. The sandy Hel Peninsula is a popular spot in summer for sunbathing. Venture farther into the surrounding

region, Pomerania (Pomorze), and you'll find more northern Polish treats to enjoy. The biggest Gothic castle in Europe, Malbork, is yet another easy day trip, and fits well en route to or from Warsaw. And the Gothic town of Toruń—also between Warsaw and Gdańsk—is the birthplace of Copernicus, home to hundreds of red-brick buildings (and even more varieties of tasty gingerbread), and a favorite spot of every proud Pole.

Planning Your Time in the Region

This region merits at least two days to make the trip here worthwhile. Gdańsk has more than enough sightseeing for a full day, and a second day can be divided between your choice of day trips: Malbork Castle, Sopot, Gdynia, or the Hel Peninsula. En route to or from Warsaw, check out Toruń (or, if you haven't day-tripped there yet, Malbork).

With one full day for Gdańsk sightseeing, this is the best plan: Spend the morning following my self-guided "Royal Way Orientation Tour" to acquaint yourself with the stunning colors of ulica Długa—Gdańsk's showpiece main drag. Poke through the many nearby museums in the center. After lunch, trek to the shipyard where Solidarity was born, and learn about the inspirational story of Lech Wałęsa and the thousands of other brave Poles who defeated communism. For dinner, enjoy a seafood feast, then prowl the floodlit cobbles.

Gdańsk gets busy in late June, when school holidays begin. About half of the tourists to this part of Poland are Germans (some of them retracing their family roots). Scandinavian shoppers come across the Baltic Sea to take advantage of the low prices.

Gdańsk

Many Americans associate Gdańsk with the images of dreary ship-yards they saw on the nightly news in the 1980s. But it's surprisingly easy to look past the smoggy sprawl to the gem of an old town, with block after block of red-brick churches and narrow, colorful, ornately decorated Hanseatic burghers' mansions.

ORIENTATION

(area code: 058)

Gdańsk, with 460,000 residents, is part of a larger metropolitan area called the Tri-City (Trójmiasto, total population 750,000). But if you break it into chunks, Gdańsk feels small. The city has several surprisingly good museums and beautiful churches, but only two knockout sights: the colorful Hanseatic main drag, ulica Długa (also known as the "Royal Way"); and the shipyard at the north end of town where the Solidarity movement began (now home to a stirring monument and exceptional museum).

Tourists in Poland are used to looking to the Old Town (Stare Miasto) for sightseeing thrills. Gdańsk's Old Town has a handful of old brick buildings and faded, skinny, tall burghers' mansions—but the area is mostly drab and residential, and not worth much time. Focus your sights instead on the Main Town (Główne Miasto), home to most sights described in this chapter, with the Royal Way as its centerpiece.

You'll win no Polish friends calling the city by its more familiar German name, Danzig.

Tourist Information

Gdańsk's TI is in a red, high-gabled building across ulica Długa from the Town Hall. Pick up the free map and brochure, and browse through the other brochures and guidebooks (May–Sept daily 9:00–20:00, Oct–April Mon–Fri 9:00–17:00, closed Sat–Sun, ulica Długa 45, tel. 058/301-9151, pomerania.pttk-gdansk.pl, przewodnictwo@pttk-gdansk.pl).

Gdańsk

SOLIDARITY SHIPYARD

400 YARDS
400 METERS

GATE
SOLIDARITY MONUMENT

WATOWA
WAŁY PIAST
ŁAGIEWNIKI
LIBRARY
PODWALE GRODSKIE
RAJSKA
HEWELIUSZA
SOLARSKA
IGIEL.
OLEJARNA

OLD
ST. BRIDGET'S
TOWN
KARM
KORZENNA
ELŻ
PODBAŁTY
KATARZYNKI
STAROMIEJSKIE
GRO

TRAM STOP
TRAIN STN.
WAŁY
GARN
KOW.
PODWALE
PAŃSKA
STRAGA
SWIETO
JANSKA
NIARSKA

WARTAWA RIVER
MOTŁAWA RIVER

CENTRAL MARITIME MUSEUM
S.S. SOŁDEK

TARG DRZEWNY
WAŁY JAGIELLOŃSKIE
MAIN
KONA
ST. MARYS
SZEROKA
TOWN
SW. DUCHA
MARIACKA
THE CRANE

HUCISCO
ARMORY
LOT OFFICE
PIWNA
TOWN HALL
ARTUS COURT
GRANARY ISLAND
BOATS TO HEL

TRAM STOP
UPLAND GATE
GOLDEN GATE
POST
DŁUGA
DŁUGI TARG
STAGIEWNA

DCH
OGARNA
UPHAGEN HOUSE
NEPTUNE STATUE
GREEN GATE

TO NAT'L MUSEUM

Arrival in Gdańsk

By Train: Gdańsk has the prettiest train station (Gdańsk Główny) this side of Amsterdam—a frilly brick palace that immediately puts to rest your fears that this is an ugly industrial city. Trains to other parts of Poland and Europe use tracks 1–3; SKM trains—with connections to nearby Tri-City towns of Sopot and Gdynia—use the shorter tracks 3–5. Tickets and information are in the main building. For commuter SKM trains, buy tickets at the kiosks marked *SKM Bilety,* at the head of tracks 4–5.

The station is at the western edge of the less interesting Old Town, about a 15-minute walk from the colorful Main Town. An underpass (by the McDonald's) takes you beneath the busy road in

Gdańsk History

Visitors to Gdańsk are surprised at how "un-Polish" the city's history is. In this cultural melting pot of German, Dutch, and Flemish merchants (with a smattering of Italians and Scots), Poles were only one part of the picture until the city became exclusively Polish after World War II. And yet, in Gdańsk, cultural backgrounds traditionally took a back seat to the bottom line. Wealthy Gdańsk was always known for its economic pragmatism—no matter who was in charge, Gdańsk merchants made money. Jealous Poles from poorer towns called it *Gdańsk Chłańsk*—"Gdańsk the Greedy One."

Gdańsk is Poland's gateway to the waters of Europe—where its main river (Vistula) meets the Baltic Sea. The city was first mentioned in the 10th century, and was seized in 1308 by the Teutonic Knights (who called it "Danzig"; for more on the Teutonic Knights, see page 268). The Knights encouraged other Germans to come settle on the Baltic coast, and gradually turned Gdańsk into a wealthy city. In 1361, Gdańsk joined the Hanseatic League, a trade federation of mostly Germanic merchant towns that provided mutual security. By the 15th century, Gdańsk was a leading member of this mighty network, which virtually dominated trade in northern Europe (and also included Toruń, Kraków, Lübeck, Hamburg, Bremen, Bruges, Bergen, Tallinn, Novgorod, and nearly a hundred other cities). In 1454, the people of Gdańsk rose up against the Teutonic Knights, burning down their castle and forcing them out of the city. The Thirteen Years' War (1454–1466) raged between the Poles and the Teutonic Knights, and in 1457, the Polish king paid off Czech mercenaries to take the Teutonic Knights' main castle, Malbork. About half the money came from Gdańsk's 300 wealthiest noble families. In exchange, Gdańsk merchants were granted exclusive export rights—acting as a middleman for all trade passing through the city, and paying only a modest annual tribute to the Polish king.

The 16th and 17th centuries were Gdańsk's golden age. Now a part of the Polish kingdom, they had access to an enormous hinterland of natural resources to export (including spruce wood, whose

front of the station (first set of exits: tram stop; second exits: Old Town). To reach the heart of the Main Town, you have two options: **ride** the tram one stop to the LOT airlines office (Brama Wyżynna stop), just in front of the Main Town (buy ticket at *RUCH* kiosk, access tram stop via underpass in front of station, then board tram #8, #13, #14, or #63, going to the right with your back to the station); or **walk** 15 minutes (go through underpass, follow busy road to the right until you reach LOT airlines office, then head left towards all the brick towers).

By Plane: Gdańsk's small airport (recently named for Lech name comes from the Polish phrase *Z Prus*—"to Prussia"). The city was populated largely by Germanic and Dutch merchants, who enjoyed Gdańsk's privileged, semi-independent status. Wealthy burghers imported Dutch, Flemish, and Italian architects to give their homes an appropriately Hanseatic austerity. At a time of religious upheaval in the rest of Europe, Gdańsk became known for its tolerance—a place that opened its doors to all visitors (many Mennonites and Scottish religious refugees emigrated here). It was also a haven for great thinkers. Philosopher Arthur Schopenhauer lived in Gdańsk, as did Daniel Fahrenheit (who invented the mercury thermometer...even though they use Celsius here).

Gdańsk declined, along with the rest of Poland, in the late 18th century, and became a part of Prussia during the partitions. The people of Gdańsk—even those of Germanic heritage—had taken pride in their independence, and generally weren't enthusiastic about being ruled from Berlin. After World War I, Gdańsk once again became an independent city-state, the Free City of Danzig (with 400,000 Germans and only 15,000 Poles). The city, along with the so-called Polish Corridor connecting it to Polish lands, effectively cut off Germany from its northeastern territory. On September 1, 1939, Adolf Hitler started World War II when he invaded Gdańsk to bring it back into the German fold. Nearly 80 percent of the city was destroyed in the war.

After World War II, Gdańsk officially became part of Poland, and was painstakingly reconstructed (mostly replicating its 16th- and 17th-century golden age). In 1970, and again in 1980, the shipyard of Gdańsk witnessed strikes and demonstrations by the trade union Solidarity that would lead to the fall of European communism. Poland's great anti-communist hero and first post-communist president—Lech Wałęsa—is Gdańsk's most famous resident...and still lives here today.

After a recent history both tragic and uplifting, Gdańsk is looking to the future. The city's millennial celebration in 1997 came with a wave of renovation and refurbishment, which left the colorful gables of the atmospheric Hanseatic quarter gleaming.

Wałęsa) is about five miles west of the city center (tel. 058/348-1163, www.airport.gdansk.pl). Bus B connects the airport with downtown (2.50 zł, 30 min, buy ticket on board). A taxi into town will cost you about 50 zł.

Helpful Hints

Closed Day: In the off-season, most of Gdańsk's museums are closed Monday. In the busy summertime, some of these museums are open limited hours on Monday.

Opening Times: Gdańsk's museums are notorious for constantly tweaking their opening times, and for closing unexpectedly for special events. I've tried to list the correct hours, but be aware that it's virtually impossible to predict—confirm locally if you have your heart set on a particular place.

Post Office: It's handy as can be, right on ulica Długa (see "Royal Way Orientation Tour," below).

Local Help/Travel Agent: Gdynia-based Sports-Tourist (so named because they used to help the Polish Olympic team get visas during the communist days), run by friendly Mirek, is a reliable and helpful contact in the Tri-City area. They can book you a good local guide or driver, set you up with a rental car, book you a room at a big hotel for discounted rates, help with ferry and plane tickets (including the red tape for a day trip to Kaliningrad, Russia, by boat), or anything else you need (tel. 058/621-9164, fax 058/621-9921, www.sports-tourist.com.pl, info@sports-tourist.gdynia.pl).

Local Guides: There are no regularly scheduled bus or walking tours of Gdańsk, but hiring a private local guide for yourself is an exceptional value. I've worked with two young, bright, energetic guides: **Paweł Grochola** is smart as a whip and brings Gdańsk's history to life with humor (200 zł for up to 5 hrs, 250 zł for more than 5 hrs, mobile 0505/085-814, www.tourguide.gd.pl, office @tourguide.gd.pl); **Agnieszka Syroka** is bubbly and personable, and also does tours of Malbork Castle (300 zł/half day, mobile 0502/554-584, asyroka@interia.pl). If these two are busy, contact Sports-Tourist (listed above) for help finding a guide.

Getting Around Gdańsk

If you're staying at one of my recommended hotels, everything is within easy walking distance. Gdańsk has a fine network of buses and trams. Buy tickets at kiosks marked *RUCH*. Prices depend on the time limit on the ticket (about 1.50 zł/10 min, 2.50 zł/30 min, 4 zł/1 hr, 8 zł/24 hrs). The handiest stops for both buses and trams are in front of the main train station (Gdańsk Główny), and at the LOT airlines office (near the heart of the tourist zone, stop called Brama Wyżynna).

By Taxi: They cost 4.50 zł to start, then 2 zł per kilometer. Find a taxi stand, or call a cab (try Super Hallo Taxi, tel. 058/9191, or Super Neptun Taxi, toll-free tel. 0800-170-700).

TOURS

Royal Way Orientation Tour

Many Americans think there's nothing to Gdańsk besides old shipyards and industrial sprawl. But anyone who steps on to the city's main historic drag, ulica Długa, will agree that it's one of Eastern

Europe's most stunning sights. You're hardly the first to be impressed. In the 16th and 17th centuries, Gdańsk was Poland's wealthiest city, with beautiful architecture (much of it in the Flemish Mannerist style) rivaling that in the two historic capitals, Kraków and Warsaw. During this golden age, Polish kings would visit this city of well-to-do merchants on the Baltic coast, and they gawked along the same route taken by tourists today. The following self-guided walk, worth ▲▲▲, introduces you to the best of historic Gdańsk. Begin the walk at the west end of the Main Town, between the big white gate and the big brick gate (near the LOT airlines office, the busy road, and the Brama Wyżynna tram stop).

City Gates: Gdańsk thrived in the 15th, 16th, and 17th centuries as a leading city of the Hanseatic League trade federation in Poland's most strategic location—where the Vistula River meets the Baltic Sea. Medieval Gdańsk had an elaborate network of protection for the city, including several moats and gates—among them the big, white **Upland Gate** (Brama Wyżynna), the shorter, red-brick **Torture House** (Wieża Więzienna), and the taller, red-brick **Prison Tower** (Katownia). These were all connected back then, and visitors had to pass through all of them to enter the city. These buildings, with walls up to 15 feet thick, are being turned into a museum. But they keep discovering hidden passages, rooms, and other archaeological finds (such as spectacularly well-preserved 14th-century toilets)...so the plans keep getting delayed.

Now walk around the left side of the Torture House and Prison Tower. Look to your left to see a long brick building with four gables. This is the back of the 16th-century **Armory** (Zbrojownia), one of the best examples of Dutch Renaissance architecture in Europe. Though this part of the building looks like simple houses, it's a kind of urban camouflage to hide its real purpose from potential attackers—the flip-side, facing into the city, is more distinctive (you'll have a chance to see it in a minute). But there's at least one clue to what it's for: At the tops of the turrets are exploding cannonballs. The round, pointy-topped tower next door is the **Straw Tower.** Gunpowder was stored here, and the roof was straw—so, if it exploded, it wouldn't destroy the walls.

Continue around the brick buildings until you're face-to-face with the...

Golden Gate (Złota Brama): The other gates were defensive, but this one's purely ornamental. The four women up top represent virtues that the people of Gdańsk should exhibit towards outsiders: Peace, Freedom, Wealth, and Fame. The inscription, a psalm in medieval German, compares Gdańsk to Jerusalem: famous and important. In the middle is one of the coats of arms of Gdańsk—two crosses under a crown. You'll see this many times today. Earlier versions of the seal don't have the crown, which was added by a Polish king grateful that the people of Gdańsk loaned him money to defeat the Teutonic Knights.

Now go through the gate, entering...

Long Street (Ulica Długa): Take a look around. The women on top of this side of the gate represent virtues the people of Gdańsk should strive for: Wisdom, Piety, Justice, and Concord (if an arrow's broken, let's take it out of the quiver and fix it). The back of the armory we saw from the outside is just up the street to the right.

Begin to wander this intoxicating street. Gdańsk was always a relatively tolerant city, welcoming people who were persecuted in other parts of Europe—Jews, Scots, Dutch, Flemish, Italians, Germans, and more. Members of each group brought with them strands of their culture, which they wove into the tapestry of this city. The  colorful and eclectic homes along this street are one of the ways that cultures from throughout Europe left their mark on Gdańsk.

This lovely street was nothing but rubble at the end of World War II. The city was damaged when the Germans first invaded, sparking the war. But the worst devastation came when the Soviets arrived. This was the first traditionally German city that the Red Army reached on their march towards Berlin—and the soldiers were set loose to level the place in retaliation for all of the pain the Nazis had caused. (Soviets didn't destroy nearby Gdynia—which they considered Polish, not German.) Soviet officers turned a blind eye as their soldiers raped and brutalized residents. An entire order of nuns committed suicide by throwing themselves into the river. And upwards of 80 percent of this area was destroyed. It was only thanks to detailed drawings and photographs that they were so beautifully reconstructed, using mostly the original brick (though often only the exteriors have been rebuilt).

Like the homes lining Amsterdam's canals, these houses were taxed based on frontage—so, they were built skinny and deep (about 10 times as long as they are wide). The widest houses belonged to the super-elite. Different as they are from the outside, each house has the same general plan inside (with three parts, starting with the front and moving back). First was a fancy drawing room, to show off for visitors. Then came a narrow corridor to the back rooms—often along the side of an inner courtyard. Because the houses had only a few windows facing the outer street, this courtyard provided much-needed sunlight to the rest of the house. The residential quarters were in the back, where the people actually lived: bedroom, kitchen, office. To see the interior of one of these homes, pay a visit to the **Uphagen House** (#12, on the right, a block in front of the gate; described on page 245).

Across the street from Uphagen House are some of the most striking **facades** along all of ulica Długa. The big blue house with the three giant heads is from the 19th century, when eclecticism was hot—borrowing bits and pieces from various architectural eras. This was one of the few houses on the street that survived World War II.

A bit farther up on the right is the huge, blocky **post office**, which doesn't fit with the skinny facades lining the rest of the street (at least they painted it red). But step inside. With doves fluttering under a colorful glass atrium, the interior's a class act. (To mail postcards, take a number—category C—from the machine on the left.)

Across the street from the post office, notice the colorful **scenes** just overhead on the facade of the cocktail bar. These are slices of life from 17th-century Gdańsk: drinking, talking, buying, fighting, playing music. The ship is a *koga*, a typical symbol of Gdańsk.

A couple of doors down from the cocktail bar is **Neptun Cinema.** In the 1980s, this was the only movie theater in the city, and locals lined up all the way down the street to get in. Young adults remember coming with their grandparents to see a full day of cartoons. Now, like in the United States, the rising popularity of multiplexes threatens to close this place down.

Across the street from the theater are three important houses belonging to the very influential medieval **Ferber family**—which produced many burghers, mayors, and even a bishop. On the house with the little dog over the door (#29), look for the heads in the circles. These are Caesars of Rome. At the top of the building is Mr. Ferber's answer to the constant question, "Why build such an elaborate house?"—*PRO INVIDA,* "For the sake of envy."

Now you're just a hop, skip, and a jump from the **Main Town Hall** (Ratusz Głównego Miasta). This building houses an excellent museum with ornately decorated meeting rooms for the city council (see description on page 246).

Just beyond the Main Town Hall, Long Street widens and becomes...

Long Square (Długi Targ): The center-piece is one of Gdańsk's most important landmarks, the statue of **Neptune**—god of the sea. He's a fitting symbol for a city that dominates the maritime life of Poland. Behind him is the third fine museum on this tour, **Artus Court** (see page 247). This meeting hall for various Gdańsk brotherhoods comes with fine decorations and the most impressive stove you've ever seen.

As you continue down Long Square, notice the **balconies** extending out into the square, with access to cellars underneath. These were far more common along Long Street in Gdańsk's golden age, but were removed in the 19th century to make way for a new tram system. To get a feel for grand old Gdańsk, you'll have a chance later to wander down the balcony-lined Mariacka street, running parallel to this one (to the left) between the river and St. Mary's Church.

About a block after Neptune, the bright blue and green houses on the left make up the **Dutch House** (Dom Holenderski). The faces in the circles by the name of the house are famous Dutchmen. The house flies four flags: Polish, Dutch, Gdańsk, and European Union.

At the end of long square is the...

Green Gate (Zielona Brama): This huge gate was actually built as a residence for visiting kings...who usually preferred to stay back by Neptune instead (maybe because the river, just on the other side of this gate, stunk). It might not have been good enough for kings and queens, but it's plenty fine for a former president—Lech Wałęsa's office is upstairs (see the plaque, *Biuro Lecha Wałęsy*). Other parts of the building are used for temporary exhibitions.

Notice that these bricks are much smaller than the ones we've seen earlier on this walk. That's because those were locally made, but these are Dutch. Boats would come here empty, load up with goods, and take them back to Holland. For ballast, they brought bricks on the trip from Holland—which they left here, to be turned into this gate.

Now go through the gate, and turn left along the...

Riverfront Embankment: This is it—the source of Gdańsk's phenomenal medieval wealth. Actually, this isn't the Vistula, but a side channel called the Motława—still, you get the idea. This place was jam-packed in its heyday, the 14th century. It was so crowded with boats, you could hardly see the water, and boats had to pay a time-based tax for tying up to a post. Instead of an actual embankment (which was built later), there was a series of wooden piers to connect the boats directly to the gates of the city. Now it's a popular place to buy amber.

Across the river is **Granary Island** (Spichrze), where grain was stored until it could be taken away by ships. Before World War II, there were some 400 granaries here; now it's still ruins. Three granaries have been reconstructed on the next island up, and house exhibits for the Central Maritime Museum (see "Sights," below); another is Hotel Królewski (see "Sleeping," below).

Continue along the embankment until you see the five big, round stones on your left. These are the **five little ladies**—mysterious ancient sculptures of Prussian women. If you look closely, you can make out their features, especially the chubby one on the end. If you touch one, you'll come back to Gdańsk...or so the tour guides say.

The next huge red-brick fort houses the Archaeological Museum. The gate in the middle leads to **Mariacka Street**, a calm, atmospheric drag leading to St. Mary's Church (see page 248) and lined with old balconies, amber shops, and imaginative gargoyles (which locals call "pukers" when it rains).

Just up ahead on the embankment is Gdańsk's number one symbol, and our last stop...

The Crane (Żuraw): This monstrous 15th-century crane was used for loading ships, picking up small crafts for repairs, and uprighting masts...beginning a shipbuilding tradition that continued to the days of Lech Wałęsa. The crane mechanism was operated by several guys scrambling around in giant hamster wheels up top. Locals brag that this landmark is the oldest piece of technical equipment in Europe—even though it had to  be rebuilt after being destroyed in World War II. The crane houses part of the Central Maritime Museum (described on page 249, below).

Our orientation tour is over. Now get out there and enjoy Gdańsk...do it for Lech!

SIGHTS

Main Town (Główne Miasto)

The following sights are all in the Main Town, listed roughly in the order you'll see them on the Royal Way Orientation Tour. The first three sights are all part of the **Gdańsk Historical Museum,** and covered on the same discounted 12-zł combo-ticket.

▲▲**Uphagen House (Dom Uphagena)**—This wonderful place is your chance to get a glimpse into what's behind the colorful facades lining ulica Długa. Check out the model in the ticket office to see the three parts you'll visit: dolled-up visitors' rooms in front, a corridor along the courtyard, and private rooms in the back (6 zł, included in 12-zł combo-ticket with Main Town Hall and Artus Court, June–Sept Tue–Sat 10:00–18:00, Sun 11:00–18:00, Mon 10:00–15:00; Oct–May Tue–Sat 10:00–16:00, Sun 11:00–16:00, closed Mon; ulica Długa 12, tel. 058/301-2371).

You'll begin upstairs, in the salon—used to show off for guests. Most of this furniture is original (saved from WWII bombs by locals who hid it in the countryside). Then you'll pass into the dining room, with knee-high paintings of hunting and celebrations. Along the passage to the back, each room has a theme: butterflies in the smoking room, then flowers, then birds in the music room. Back in the private rooms, notice how much simpler the decor is (and how low the ceilings are). Back downstairs, you'll pass through the kitchen, the pantry, and a room with photos from the house before the war—used to reconstruct what you see today.

▲▲**Main Town Hall (Ratusz Głównego Miasta)**—Inside this landmark building, you'll find some remarkable decorations from Gdańsk's golden age (6 zł, included in 12-zł combo-ticket with Uphagen House and Artus Court, May–Sept Tue–Sat 10:00–18:00,

Sun 11:00–18:00, Mon 10:00–15:00; Oct–April Tue–Sun 10:00–16:00, closed Mon; ulica Długa 47, tel. 058/767-9100).

Head inside, to the main entry hall (with ticket and souvenir desk). Examine the photo showing Gdańsk at the end of World War II (you'll see more upstairs). The ornately carved wooden **door**, which you'll pass through in a minute, is also worth a close look. Above the door is the seal of Gdańsk (2 crosses under a crown) held, as it often is, by a pair of lions. These felines are stubborn and independent, just like Gdańsk. Close the door partway to look at the carvings of crops. Around the frame of the door are mermen, reminding us that these crops, like so many other resources of Poland, are transported on the Vistula and out through Gdańsk.

Go through the door into the **Red Hall,** where the Gdańsk city council met in the summertime. (The lavish fireplace—with another pair of lions holding the coat of arms of Gdańsk—was just for show.) City council members would sit in the seats around the room, debating city policy. The knee-level paintings depict the earth; the amazingly detailed inlaid wood just over the seats are animals; the paintings on the wall above represent people (more specifically, the 7 virtues that people—and especially the burghers meeting in this room—should have); and the ceiling is all about theology. Examine that ceiling. You'll see 25 paintings total, with themes about God as well as pagan religions—meant to inspire the decision-makers in this room to make good choices. The smaller ones around the edges are scenes from mythology and the Bible. The one in the middle (from 1607) shows God's relationship to Gdańsk. In the foreground, the citizens of Gdańsk go about their daily lives. Above, them high atop the arch, God's hand reaches down (from within clouds of Hebrew characters) and grasps the city's steeple. The rainbow arching above also symbolizes God's connection to Gdańsk; mirroring that is the Vistula River, which begins in the mountains of southern Poland (on the right), runs through the country, and exits at the sea in Gdańsk (on the left—where the rainbow ends).

Continue into the not-so-impressive **Winter Hall**, with

another fireplace and coat of arms held by lions. During World War II, a bomb actually came into this room—but didn't explode. It was a dud. (Maybe there's something to that connection-to-God thing, after all.)

Continue through the next room, into a room with before-and-after photos of **World War II damage**. At the foot of the destroyed crucifix is a book with a bullet hole in it. The twist of wood is all that's left of the main support for the spiral staircase (today reconstructed in the room where you entered). Ponder the tragedy of war...and the inspiring ability of a city to be reborn.

Upstairs are more exhibits, including a few examples of **Gdańsk-style furniture**. These pieces are characterized by three big, round feet in front, lots of ornamentation, and a virtually-impossible-to-find lock in front (often hidden behind a movable decoration). You'll also see a coin collection, from the days when Gdańsk had the elite privilege of minting its own coins.

▲▲**Artus Court (Dwór Artusa)**—In the Middle Ages, there were many businessmen's clubs in Gdańsk. For their meetings, the city provided this elaborately decorated hall, named for King Arthur (a medieval symbol for prestige and power). Halls like this one were once common in Baltic Europe, but only three survive, and Gdańsk's is by far the best (6 zł, included in 12-zł combo-ticket with Uphagen House and Main Town Hall, June–Sept Tue–Sat 10:00–18:00, Sun 11:00–18:00, Mon 10:00–15:00; Oct–May Tue–Sat 10:00–16:00, Sun 11:00–16:00, closed Mon; in tall, 3-arched building behind Neptune statue at ulica Długi Targ 43-44, tel. 058/767-9100).

In the first room, you'll see various cupboards lining the walls. Each organization that met here had a place to keep its important documents and office supplies. The big painting in the back depicts the Battle of Grunwald, where the Polish-Lithuanian army defeated the Teutonic Knights (see page 268).

To the right of that, you'll see a remarkable **stove,** decorated with 520 tiles featuring the faces of kings, queens, nobles, mayors, and burghers. Half of these people were Protestant, and half were Catholic, mixed together in no particular order—a reminder of the importance of religious tolerance. About 90 percent of these tiles are original, having survived WWII bombs. Of the missing tiles, three were recently discovered by a bargain-hunter wandering through a flea market in the southern part of the country—and returned to their rightful home.

Notice the huge paintings on the walls above—with 3-D animals emerging from flat frames. Hunting is a popular theme in local artwork. Like minting coins, hunting was a privilege usually reserved for royalty, but extended in special circumstances to special towns...like Gdańsk. If you look closely, it's obvious that these "paintings" are digitally-generated reproductions of the original ones (damaged in World War II).

The next room—actually in the next-door building—is a typical interior of the burghers' homes lining ulica Długa. As you exit to the back, you'll see a miniature reconstruction of the whole grand room, including paintings that have yet to be re-created. As you exit, you're just down the street from St. Mary's Church (below); to get back to the man drag, go back around the block, to the left.

▲St. Mary's Church (Kościół Mariacki)—Gdańsk has so many striking red-brick churches, it's hard to keep track of them. St. Mary's is the best one to visit, as it gives you a taste of the rest—only bigger. In fact, it's the biggest brick church in the world; it can fit up to 25,000 people. Built over 159 years in the 14th and 15th centuries, the church is an important symbol of Gdańsk. For many visitors, climbing the 408 steps up the church's 270-foot-tall tower is the quintessential Gdańsk experience. You'll be rewarded with sweeping views of the entire city (church entry-2 zł, tower climb-3 zł, tower climb includes church entry, so don't pay twice; Mon–Sat 9:00–17:30, Sun 13:00–17:30).

As you enter, notice all of the white, empty space—unusual in a Catholic country, where frilly Baroque churches are the norm. Gdańsk was a very tolerant city in the Middle Ages, attracting people who were suffering religious persecution from all over Europe (especially Mennonites). As the Protestant population grew, they needed a place to worship. St. Mary's, like most other Gdańsk churches, eventually became Protestant—leaving these churches with the blank walls you see today. (In fact, the colorful domed chapel outside behind St. Mary's was built in the late 17th century by the Polish king Jan Sobieski III because there were no remaining churches for Catholics. It's the only Baroque church in Gdańsk.)

Most Gothic stone churches are built in the basilica style—with a high nave in the middle, shorter naves on the side, and flying buttresses to support the weight (think of Paris' Notre-Dame). But that design doesn't work with brick. So, like all Gdańsk churches, St. Mary's is a "hall church"—with three naves the same height, and no exterior buttresses.

Also like other Gdańsk churches, St. Mary's gave refuge to the Polish people after martial law was declared by the communist government in 1981. If a riot broke out and violence seemed imminent, people would flock to churches for protection—the ZOMO riot police wouldn't follow them inside.

This church has some stories to tell. Head up the right nave and find the opulent family marker to the right of the main altar. Look for the falling baby. This is Constantine Ferber. As a precocious child, Constantine leaned out his window on ulica Długa to see the king's processional come through town. He slipped and fell, but landed in a salesman's barrel of fish. Constantine grew up to become the mayor of Gdańsk.

At the next post, look for the coat of arms with the three pigs' heads. This story relates to another member of the illustrious Ferber clan. An enemy army was laying siege to the town, and tried to starve them out. A clever Ferber decided to load the cannons with pigs' heads to show the enemy that they had plenty of food—it worked, and the enemy left.

Circle around, past the front of the beautifully carved main altar. Behind it is the biggest stained-glass window in Poland. On the far side of the altar is a colorful astronomical clock. Below is the calendar and the saint's day, and above are zodiac signs and the time (only 1 hand).

Most of the things you see in this church are originals. A few days before World War II broke out in Gdańsk, locals hid precious items in the countryside. But other items fell into the hands of the National Museum in Warsaw, which now refuses to give them back to the city of Gdańsk (saying they don't have the proper spaces to display them).

As you leave the church, duck into the chapel at the back right to see a replica of a *Final Judgment* painting by Hans Memling. The original, once on display here, now belongs to Gdańsk's branch of the National Museum (see below).

▲**Central Maritime Museum (Centralne Muzeum Morskie)**— This fine museum, spread out among several buildings on either side of the river, considers various aspects of the sea—which has defined the people of Gdańsk for centuries. There are four parts of the exhibit. Two of them are on the Main Town side of the river:

1. The Crane (Żuraw): The medieval crane of Gdańsk—the city's most important symbol—houses an exhibit on living in the city during its golden age (16th–18th centuries). You'll see models of Baltic buildings (including the crane you're inside) and traditional tools and costumes. For more on the crane, see page 245.

2. Boats of the World: The building next to the crane houses different kinds of boats from non-European cultures.

The other two parts of the museum are across the river on Ołowianka Island. You'll reach the island via the little ferry (4/hr during museum hours, 1.50 zł one-way, included in 12-zł ticket). This also gives fine views back on the crane. Once on the island, you'll visit the other two parts:

3. The Old Granaries (Spichlerze): These three rebuilt granaries make up the heart of the exhibit, tracing the history of Gdańsk—particularly as it relates to the sea—from prehistoric days to the present. A Venetian gondola greets you at the entry. Models of the town and region help put things into perspective. You'll see exhibits on underwater exploration, navigational aids, artifacts of the

Polish seafaring tradition, peek-a-boo cross-sections of multi-level ships, and models of the modern-day shipyard where Solidarity was born. This place is home to more miniature ships than you ever thought you'd see, and the Nautical Gallery upstairs features endless rooms with paintings of boats. The whole thing would probably be great...if you could speak Polish (paltry English loaner descriptions available in some rooms).

4. The Sołdek: Crawl through the holds and scramble across the deck of this decommissioned steamship—docked permanently across from the crane. Below decks, you'll see where they shoveled the coal, and wander through a maze of pipes, gears, valves, gauges, and ladders. You'll also see where the sailors lived, slept, and ate. You can even visit the bridge. The place would be much improved with a slicker exhibit and more English information—both of which are planned for the near future (ship sometimes closed Jan–Feb).

Cost, Hours, Location: The museum has a complicated pricing structure, as each component has its own admission fee (mostly 5 zł each); just buy the 12-zł ticket that covers everything, and you'll be set (though you'll have to buy another 3-zł ticket if you want to see the inner workings of the medieval crane up close). The complex is open June–Aug daily 10:00–18:00, Sept–May Tue–Sun 10:00–16:00, closed Mon (ulica Ołowianka 9-13, tel. 058/301-5311, ext. 36, www.cmm.pl). Throughout the museum, there's an irritating lack of English information. But a new guidebook is in the works, and hiring your own guide costs less than a Big Mac (see below).

Tour: If you have a serious fascination with all matters maritime, pay the unbelievably cheap price of 15 zł to get your own private English-speaking guide (smart to reserve ahead: tel. 058/301-5311, ask for ext. 36, if they speak only Polish, they'll figure it out and find an English-speaker). The tour can last two hours or more, so if you have only a passing interest, skip the guide and see the museum at your own pace.

St. Bridget's Church (Kościół Św. Brygidy)—This typical red-brick Gothic church has a special claim to fame, as the home church of Lech Wałęsa (and therefore Solidarity) during the tense days of the 1980s. While the Catholic Church was generally synonymous with dissent in the communist era, this church in particular—and its priest, Henryk Jankowski—was particularly aggressive in supporting Lech Wałęsa and Solidarity. Jankowski became a mouthpiece for Solidarity; Wałęsa named his youngest daughter Brygida in gratitude for the church's support.

The church features many Solidarity-era artifacts. Find the tomb of Jerzy Popiełuszko, a famously outspoken Warsaw priest who was kidnapped, beaten, and murdered by the secret police.

There's also a remarkable altar made entirely of amber—the ongoing megalomaniacal project of Wałęsa's former priest, Father Jankowski. But today, Jankowski is a highly controversial figure—often accused of explicit anti-Semitism, and a very vocal critic of Poland's joining the EU in 2004. Some locals claim his celebrity has gone to his head.

National Museum in Gdańsk (Muzeum Nardowe w Gdańsku)— This fine collection, housed in what was a 15th-century Franciscan monastery, features local works from the Gothic period; Flemish and Dutch art; fabrics and gold and silverware from the city's golden age; characteristic Gdańsk-style furniture; and lots more. Its highlight is Hans Memling's original *Last Judgment* triptych—though, if you're not a purist, you can skip the walk here and settle for seeing the replica in St. Mary's Church (8 zł, Tue–Fri 9:00–16:00, Sat–Sun 10:00–16:00, closed Mon, 5 blocks south of ulica Dluga at ulica Toruńska 1, www.muzeum.nardowe.gda.pl).

Gdańsk's Back Streets—Wander just a block or two from ulica Długa, and the brightly colored facades fade to gray. Perhaps nowhere else in Poland is the neglect and shoddy reconstruction of the communists more infuriating. But remember: Without the communist chapter, there wouldn't be the inspirational stories of Solidarity.

Solidarity (Solidarność) and the Gdańsk Shipyard (Stocznia Gdańska)

Exploring the shipyard that witnessed the beginning of the end of communism's stranglehold on Eastern Europe is Gdańsk's single best experience—easily worth ▲▲▲. Here in the industrial wasteland that Wałęsa called the "cradle of freedom," you'll learn the story of the brave Polish shipyard workers who, armed with little more than guts, took on and defeated an Evil Empire.

A visit to the Solidarity sights has two main parts: the memorial and gate out in front of the shipyard, and the excellent "Roads to Freedom" exhibit, housed in the meeting hall where the agreement to end the strike was signed. Allow 90 minutes to tour the grounds and learn the entire story.

Cost, Hours, Information: Visiting the memorial and the shipyard gate is free. The "Roads to Freedom" exhibit costs 5 zł (Tue–Sun 10:00–16:00, closed Mon, ulica Doki 1, tel. 058/769-2920, www.fcs.org.pl).

Getting to the Shipyard: The Solidarity monument and shipyard are at the north end of the Old Town, an easy 20-minute walk from the Main Town tourist action (no handy bus or tram). Walk northwest out of the Main Town, towards the big silver tower with the pink *Mercure* sign. Once you reach this tower, pass it on your left-hand side and walk up Łagiewniki. You'll go between two big brick churches, then pass the big, long, brick Biblioteka Gdańska library on your left. At the end of the library, turn right and head towards the tall crosses and big *STOCZNIA* sign.

Self-Guided Tour: After the communists took over Eastern Europe at the end of World War II, the oppressed people throughout the Soviet Bloc rose up in different ways. The most dramatic uprisings—Hungary's 1956 Uprising (see page 312), and Czechoslovakia's 1968 "Prague Spring" (see page 45)—were both brutally crushed under the treads of Soviet tanks. The formula for freedom that finally succeeded—and was lucky enough to coincide

with the *perestroika* and *glasnost* policies of Soviet premier Mikhail Gorbachev— was a patient, decade-long series of strikes spearheaded by Lech Wałęsa and his trade union, called Solidarność— "Solidarity." While some American politicians would like to claim responsibility for defeating communism, Wałęsa and his fellow workers were the ones fighting on the front lines. The following tour leads you through the place where the inspirational events of August 1980 took place, while explaining the story as it unfolded. Begin at the towering monument—with three anchor-adorned crosses— near the entrance gate to the shipyard.

Monument of the Fallen Shipyard Workers: The seeds of the August 1980 strikes were sown a decade before. Since becoming part of the Soviet Bloc, the Poles staged frequent strikes, protests, and uprisings to secure their rights, all of which were put down by the government. But the bloodiest of these took place in December 1970—a tragic event memorialized by this monument.

The strike was prompted by price hikes. The communist government set the prices for all products. As Poland endured drastic food shortages in the 1970s, the regime frequently announced what they called "regulation of prices"—increasing the cost of essential foodstuffs, while at the same time lowering prices of unimportant items (like elevators and TV sets). The regime was usually smart enough to raise prices on January 1—when the people were fat and happy after Christmas, and too hung over to complain. But on December 12, 1970, bolstered by an ego-stoking visit by West German Chancellor Willy Brandt, Polish premier Władysław Gomułka hiked up prices. The people of Poland—who cared more about the price of bread than relations with Germany—struck back.

A wave of strikes and sit-ins spread along the heavily industrialized north coast of Poland—most notably in Gdańsk, Gdynia, and Szczecin. Thousands of angry demonstrators poured through the gate of this shipyard, marched into town, and set fire to the

Communist Party Committee building. In an attempt to quell the riots, the government-run radio implored the people to go back to work. On the morning of December 17, they did. Workers showed up at shipyard gates across northern Poland—and were greeted by the army and police. Without provocation, the Polish army opened fire on the workers. While the official death toll for the massacre stands at 44, others say the true number is much higher.

This monument, with a trio of 140-foot-tall crosses, honors those lost to the regime that December. Go to the middle of the wall behind the crosses, to the monument of the worker wearing a flimsy plastic work helmet, attempting to shield himself from his government's bullets. Behind him is a list—pockmarked with symbolic bullet holes—of workers murdered on that day. *Lat* means "years"— many teenagers were among the dead. The quote at the top of the wall is from the first Polish Pope, John Paul II, who was elected eight years after this tragedy. Though the pope was obviously anti-communist, he had to carefully toe the communist line to keep the Church alive in his homeland. He was known for his clever way with words, and this very carefully phrased quote—which served as an inspiration to the Poles during their darkest hours—skewers the regime in a way subtle enough to still be tolerated: "Let thy spirit descend, and renew the face of the earth—*this* earth" (that is, specifically, Poland). Below that is the dedication: "They gave their lives so you can live decently."

Stretching to the left of this center wall are plaques representing labor unions from around Poland—and around the world (look for the Chinese characters)—expressing solidarity with these workers. To the right is an enormous Bible verse: "May the Lord give strength to his people. May the Lord bless his people with the gift of peace" (Psalms 29:11).

More than a decade after the strike, this monument was finally constructed. It marked the first time a communist regime ever allowed a monument built to honor its own victims. Inspired by the brave sacrifice of their true comrades, the shipyard workers rose up here in August of 1980, formulating the "21 Points" of a new union called Solidarity. These demands are listed in Polish on the panel at the far end of the right wall, marked *21 X TAK* ("21 times yes") *Solidarność*. For more on their story, continue to the gate and peer through into the birthplace of Eastern European freedom.

Gdańsk Shipyard (Stocznia Gdańska) Gate #2: When a Pole named Karol Wojtyła was elected pope in 1978—and visited his homeland in 1979—he inspired his 40 million countrymen to believe that impossible dreams can come true. Prices continued to go up, and the workers continued to rise up. It began with general strikes in response to an increase in meat prices in the southeastern city of Lublin on July 11, 1980. While quickly resolved, the Lublin

Lech Wałęsa

In 1980, the world was turned on its ear by a dynamic, walrus-mustachioed shipyard electrician. Within three years, this seemingly run-of-the-mill Pole had precipitated the collapse of communism, led a massive 10 million-member trade union with far-ranging political impact, was named *Time* magazine's Man of the Year, and won a Nobel Peace Prize.

Lech Wałęsa was born in Popowo, Poland, in 1943. After working as a car mechanic and serving two years in the army, he became an electrician at the Gdańsk Shipyard in 1967. Like many Poles, Wałęsa felt stifled by the communist government, and was infuriated that a system that was supposed to be for the workers clearly wasn't serving them.

When the shipyard massacre took place in December 1970, Wałęsa was at the forefront of the protests. He became marked as a dissident, and in 1976, he was fired. He hopped from job to job and was occasionally unemployed—a rock-bottom status reserved for only the most despicable protesters. But Wałęsa soldiered on, fighting for the creation of a trade union and building up quite a file with the secret police.

In August 1980, Wałęsa heard news of the beginnings of the Gdańsk strike, and made a beeline for the shipyard. In an act that has since become the stuff of legends, Wałęsa scaled the shipyard wall to get inside and participate in the strike. When Wałęsa arrived at the protest, the shipyard manager was addressing the crowd, telling them to get back to work. Wałęsa began heckling him, and eventually climbed up on stage to confront him. "Even though you fired me," Wałęsa said, "I'm still a shipyard worker at heart—and I have a right to speak!" His impassioned plea won over the crowd. The strike had found its leader.

Wałęsa went on to take a very public role in advancing the goals of the strike, becoming its spokesman and unofficial leader. He would address the nervous crowds of townspeople assembled at the gate, updating them on the progress of the negotiations and requesting their help. Thanks largely to Wałęsa's charisma and brilliant instincts, the people of Gdańsk and of Poland fell into line behind their striking workers—forging a movement that fully deserved the name Solidarity.

Wałęsa negotiated with the regime to hash out the August Agreements, becoming a rock star-type hero during the so-called 16

strikes were a sign to Poland that the dam was about to break.

A few weeks later in Gdańsk, Anna Walentynowicz—a crane operator and known dissident—was fired unceremoniously just short of her retirement. This sparked a strike in the Gdańsk Shipyard (then called the Lenin Shipyard) on August 14, 1980. An electrician named Lech Wałęsa had been fired as an agitator years before, and wasn't allowed into the shipyard. But on hearing news of the

Months of Hope...until martial law came crashing down in December 1981. Wałęsa was arrested and interned for 11 months in a country house. After being released, Wałęsa continued to struggle underground, becoming a symbol of anti-communist sentiment. Wałęsa won the Nobel Peace Prize in 1983—but the government wouldn't let him travel to Oslo to claim it, so his wife went in his place.

Finally, the dedication of Wałęsa and Solidarity paid off, and Polish communism dissolved—with Wałęsa rising from the ashes as the country's first post-communist president. But the skills that made Wałęsa a rousing success at leading an uprising did not translate to the president's office. Wałęsa proved to be a stubborn, headstrong president, frequently clashing with the parliament. He squabbled with his own party, declaring a "war at the top" of Solidarity and rotating higher-ups to prevent corruption and keep the party fresh. He also didn't choose his advisors well, enlisting several staffers who wound up immersed in scandal. His overconfidence was his Achilles' heel, and his governing style was not diplomatic enough—verging on authoritarian (the constitution has since been changed to limit the president's power). Unrefined and none too interested in scripted speeches, Wałęsa was a simple man, who preferred playing table tennis with his former driver to attending formal state functions. Wałęsa never had a formal education, but had sharp political instincts and unsurpassed charisma. In retrospect, most Poles agree that that's not enough to lead a country—especially during an impossibly complicated, fast-changing time, when even the most savvy politician would certainly have stumbled.

Wałęsa was defeated at the polls (by the Poles) in 1995, and when he ran again in 2000, he received a humiliating 1 percent of the vote. Since leaving office, Wałęsa has kept a lower profile, but still delivers speeches worldwide. Many poor Poles grumble that Lech, who started life simple like them, has forgotten the little people. But his fans point out that he gives much of his income to charity. And he still always wears a pin featuring the Black Madonna of Częstochowa—the symbol of Polish Catholicism—on his lapel.

Poles say there are at least two Lech Wałęsas: the young, working-class idealist Lech, at the forefront of the Solidarity strikes, who will always have a special place in their hearts; and the failed President Wałęsa, who got in over his head and—sadly—tarnished his legacy.

strike, Wałęsa went to the shipyard and climbed over the wall to get inside. The strike had a leader.

Imagine being one of the 16,000 workers who stayed here for 18 days during the strike—hungry, cold, sleeping on sheets of Styrofoam, inspired by the new Polish pope, excited about finally standing up to the regime...and terrified that you might be gunned down at any moment, like your friends who were massacred a decade before. Because you're afraid to leave the shipyard, your only way to communicate with the outside world is through this gate—your wife or brother shows up here and asks for you, and those inside spread the word until you come talk to them. Occasionally, a truck pulls up to the gate, and Lech Wałęsa stands on its cab and faces the thousands of people assembled here—giving them progress reports of the negotiations, and pleading for food. The people of Gdańsk respond, bringing armfuls of bread and other food, keeping the workers going. This truly is Solidarity.

Two items hung on the fence. One was a picture of the Polish Pope—which still hangs there today—reminding all involved to believe in their dreams and have faith in God. The other was a makeshift list of the strikers' 21 Points—demands scrawled in red paint and black pencil on pieces of plywood. The demands included the right to strike and form unions, the freeing of political prisoners, an increase in wages, and an end to Polack jokes.

For the rest of the story, continue through the gate and into the shipyard. Keep an eye out for graffiti depicting important symbols and events from Solidarity history.

Path Through the Shipyard and Symbolic Gateways: As you walk toward the "Pathways to Freedom" exhibit, you'll pass through two huge symbolic gateways. The first resembles the rusted hull of a

ship, representing the protest of the shipbuilders. Inside are two electronic strips: on the left, displaying communist slogans; on the right, the wisdom of Lech Wałęsa and Solidarity. The next gate—a futuristic, colorful tower—is a small-scale version of a 1,000-foot-tall monument planned by the prominent Soviet constructivist architect Vladimir Tatlin. This fanciful but unfulfilled design represents the misguided, failed optimism of the communist "utopia."

After the gateways, on the left, look for the two **wall fragments**. On the right is the shipyard wall that Lech Wałęsa famously scrambled over in August 1980 to join his comrades in the shipyard strikes. On the left, with the map of Europe, is a piece of another Wall—from Berlin—which fell less than a decade later. The message is simple: What began in this shipyard culminated in the fall of the Berlin Wall.

Now continue into the red-brick building.

"Roads to Freedom" Exhibit in BHP Conference Hall: Step inside and buy your ticket—which is designed to look like the communist ration coupons that all Poles had to carry and present before they could buy certain goods. Cashiers would stand with scissors at the ready, prepared to snip off a corner of your coupon after making the sale.

Continue into the first room, which shows a typical **Polish shop** (Spozyw) from the 1970s, at the worst of the food shortages. Great selection, eh? Often the only things in stock were vinegar and mustard. Milk and bread were generally available, but they were low quality—it wasn't unusual to find a cigarette butt in your loaf. The few blocks of cheese and other items in the case aren't real—they're props (marked *atrapy*—"fake"), so the shop wouldn't look completely empty. Sometimes they'd hang a few pitiful, phony salamis from the hooks—otherwise, people might think it was a tile shop. The only real meat in here was the flies on the flypaper. Shockingly, shoppers (mostly women) would sometimes have to wait in line literally all day long just to pick over these scant choices. In the corner, the phone booth is marked *Automat Nieczynny*—"Out of Order"—as virtually all phone booths were back then. Consider picking up a book or other souvenir at the excellent gift shop before moving into the next room.

The first part of the exhibit, called "**They Were the First**," explains the roots of the 1980 shipyard strikes. Then you move into the heart of the exhibit, **August 1980.** There are the original plywood boards featuring the 21 Points, which hung on the front gate we just saw.

The next room is **the Hall.** The statue of Lenin used to stand in the shipyard that was named for him. After 18 days of protests, it became clear to the communist government that Solidarity would not simply go away. On the afternoon of August 31, 1980, the Governmental Commission and the Inter-Factory Strike Committee (MKS) came together in this very room and signed the August Agreements, which legalized Solidarity—the first time any communist government permitted a workers' union. A video shows the giddy day. Lech Wałęsa—sitting at the big table, with his trademark walrus moustache—signed the agreement with the big red pen. Other union reps, sitting at smaller tables, tape-recorded the proceedings, and played them later at their own factories to prove the unthinkable had happened. While the government didn't take the agreements very seriously, the Poles did...and before long, 10 million of them—one in every four Poles—became members of Solidarity.

So began the **16 Months of Hope**—the theme of the next room. Newly legal, Solidarity continued to stage strikes and made its opposition known. Slick Solidarity posters and children's art convey the childlike enthusiasm with which the Poles seized their hard-won kernels of freedom. The poster with a baby in a Solidarity T-shirt—one year old, just like the union itself—captures the sense of hope. The grasp of the communist authorities on the Polish people began to slip. The rest of the Soviet Bloc looked on nervously, and the Warsaw Pact army assembled at the Polish border and glared at the uprisers. The threat of invasions hung heavy in the air.

In the next room, Solidarity's progress comes crashing down. On Sunday morning, December 13, 1981, the Polish head of state, General Wojciech Jaruzelski, appeared on national TV and announced the introduction of **martial law.** Solidarity was outlawed. Frightened Poles heard the announcement and looked out their windows to see Polish Army tanks rumbling though the snowy streets. Jaruzelski claimed that he imposed martial law to prevent the Soviets from invading (as they did in Budapest in 1956, and in Prague in 1968). Today, many historians question whether martial law was really necessary—though Jaruzelski remains remorseless. Martial law was a tragic, terrifying, and bleak time for the Polish people. But Solidarity moved underground and continued the fight for freedom. Notice that their martial-law-era propaganda was produced with far more primitive printing equipment than their earlier posters. As you leave the room, look for the clandestine print shop, and for the kitchen with Styrofoam pads on the floor—where those first strikers, who had no beds in the shipyard, were forced to sleep.

The exhibit concludes with **films** showing the ugly side of martial law. Chilling scenes show riots, demonstrations, and crackdowns by the ZOMO police. Sobering displays show the ZOMO riot gear. One old woman was literally stampeded by a pack of fleeing demonstrators.

But the ZOMO couldn't crush the human spirit. By the time the Pope visited his homeland again in 1983, martial law was lifted, and Solidarity—still technically illegal—gained momentum, gradually pecking away at the communists. With the moral support of the Pope and the entire Western world, the brave Poles were the first European country to throw off the shackles of communism when, in the spring of 1989, the "Round Table Talks" led to the opening up of elections. The government arrogantly called for parliamentary elections, reserving 65 percent of seats for themselves. The plan backfired, as virtually every contested seat went to Solidarity. The Polish success inspired people all over Eastern Europe, and by that winter, the Berlin Wall had crumbled and the Czechs and Slovaks had staged their Velvet Revolution. Lech Wałęsa—the shipyard electrician who started it all by jumping over a wall—became the first president of post-communist Poland. And a year later, in Poland's first true elections since World War II, 29 different parties won seats in the *Sejm* (Parliament). This celebration of democracy was brought to the Polish people by a brave electrician and the workers of Gdańsk.

Sights near Gdańsk

The Tri-City (Trójmiasto)—Gdańsk is the anchor of the three cities that make up the metropolitan region known as the Tri-City (Trójmiasto). The other two cities, while quite different, are each worth a visit.

Elegant **Sopot**, home to Europe's longest pleasure pier and dubbed the "Nice of the North," was a celebrated haunt of beautiful people during the 1920s and 1930s. The main drag, Monte Casino Heroes Street (ul. Bohaterów Monte Cassino)—a pedestrian promenade lined with 19th- and 20th-century mansions, and flanked by grand hotels and century-old casinos—ends at the Molo, the longest wooden pier in Europe (more than 1,600 feet long). Sopot is once again in vogue as a Baltic Coast destination, and boasts the best nightlife in the Tri-City.

Historic **Gdynia** has retained a more working-class vibe, still in touch with its salty, fishing-village roots. It feels much younger than Gdańsk, as it was built in the 1920s to be Poland's main harbor after Gdańsk became a free city. While not as attractive as Gdańsk or Sopot, Gdynia has an authentic feel and a fine waterfront promenade.

Getting There: To reach the other parts of the Tri-City from Gdańsk's main train station, you'll take the commuter SKM trains *(kolejka)*. These leave about every 10 minutes (less frequently after 19:30) from tracks 3–5 (see page 237). Figure on 3 zł to Sopot, 4 zł to Gdynia (buy at machines or *Bilety* kiosks, pay more to buy on board, validate by punching in yellow box at platform). Use the stops marked simply "Sopot" (only one word) and "Gdynia Główna" (the main station). For a more romantic approach, take the boat (see "Transportation Connections," page 264).

Oliwa Cathedral—The suburb of Oliwa, at the northern edge of Gdańsk, is home to this visually striking church. The quirky facade hides a surprisingly long and skinny nave. The ornately decorated 18th-century organ features angels who move and blow trumpets when the organ is played.

Getting There: Oliwa is about six miles northwest of central Gdańsk, on the way to Sopot and Gdynia. To get to Oliwa, take a commuter SKM train from Gdańsk's main station to the "Gdańsk Oliwa" stop and walk 10 minutes.

Hel Peninsula—Out on the edge of things, this slender peninsula juts 20 miles into the ocean, providing a sunny, sandy retreat from the big cities—even as its shelters them from Baltic winds. On hot summer days, Hel is a fine place to frolic on the beach with Poles. Among the towns lining Hel Peninsula is a fishing village also called Hel. The easiest way to go to Hel—aside from coveting thy neighbor's wife—is by boat (see "Transportation Connections," page 264). Trains from Gdańsk also reach Hel, and from Gdynia, you can take a train, bus, or minibus.

Westerplatte—World War II began on September 1, 1939, when Adolf Hitler sent the warship *Schleswig-Holstein* to attack this Polish munitions depot, which was guarding Gdańsk's harbor. Though it may interest World War II history buffs, there's little to see at this historic site aside from a modest museum and a towering monument. To get to Westerplatte, take bus #106 to the end (about 40 min). Even better, take a boat (see "Transportation Connections," page 264).

SLEEPING

Central Gdańsk has fine splurges and acceptable dives, with little in between. Travelers can pay a pretty penny for a plush place, settle for a private room in a hostel, or stay further from the Old Town. Prices virtually everywhere go up in the summer (at least July–Aug, often longer).

In the Main Town

$$$ **Kamienica Goldwasser**, renting seven apartments over a good restaurant, is worthwhile and very central, right on the river embankment next door to the crane. Each tastefully traditional apartment has two rooms, one overlooking the river and the other facing the back. The restaurant has a special room reserved every evening for its guests to congregate and socialize (Sb-390 zł, Db-490 zł, Tb-590 zł, Qb-690, all rates 100 zł less Oct–March, Długie Pobrzeże 22, tel. & fax 058/301-8878, www.goldwasser.pl, kamienica@goldwasser.pl).

$$$ **Hanza Hotel**, also on the riverfront, is new and fancy, with a fun, neo-Hanseatic exterior and classy, dark-wood interior. Their 60 rooms are comfortable and come with sky-high prices in the summer, but drop to tempting lows in the off-season (June–Aug: Sb-665 zł, Db-695 zł; Sept–Oct and May: Sb-565 zł, Db-595 zł; Nov–April: Sb-395 zł, Db-465 zł; request riverview room in summer, when it costs the same as non-view room; non-view rooms 100 zł cheaper Nov–April only, check for other discounts online, air-con, elevator, Tokarska 6, tel. 058/305-3427, fax 058/305-3386, www.hanza-hotel.com.pl, hotel@hanza-hotel.com.pl).

$$$ **Hotel Mercure Hevelius,** in a mighty silver tower dominating the Gdańsk skyline, doesn't look too inviting. But its 281 rooms are pleasant, well-located, and well-priced—an unusual combination in central Gdańsk (Sb-380 zł, Db-440 zł, cheaper Nov–March, big discounts Fri–Sat—as low as Sb/Db-250 zł, elevator, ulica Jana Heweliusza 22, reception tel. 058/321-0000, reservation tel. 058/321-0021, www.orbis.pl, mer.hevelius@orbis.pl).

$ **Pensjonat Dom Aktora**, on a drab street, comes with old rooms and difficult communication, but it's right in the Main Town (Sb-190 zł, twin Db-280 zł, small apartment-350 zł, bigger apartment-420 zł, even bigger apartment-520 zł, 20 percent cheaper

Sleep Code

(3.50 zł = about $1, €1 = about $1.20, country code: 48, area code: 012)
S = Single, **D** = Double/Twin, **T** = Triple, **Q** = Quad,
b = bathroom, **s** = shower only. Breakfast is included, credit cards
are accepted, and English is spoken at each place (unless
otherwise noted).

To help you sort easily through these listings, I've divided
the rooms into three categories, based on the price for a standard
double room with bath:

$$$ **Higher Priced**—Most rooms 400 zł (€92) or more.
$$ **Moderately Priced**—Most rooms between 300–400 zł (€69–92).
$ **Lower Priced**—Most rooms 300 zł (€69) or less.

Oct–May, ulica Straganiarska 55-56, tel. 058/301-6193, fax
058/301-5901, www.domaktora.pl, biuro@domaktora.pl).

$ **Przy Targu Rybnym** is an easygoing, low-key hostel at the
north end of the river embankment, just a three-minute walk from
the crane. With double and single rooms (bathroom down the hall),
it's an attractive option even for non-hostelers (1 or 2 people in 1-
bed room-120 zł, T-180 zł, bunk in 7-bed room-60 zł, bunk in
crowded basement slumbermill-40 zł, no breakfast, Internet, ulica
Grodzka 21, tel. 058/301-5627, www.gdanskhostel.com).

$ **Szkolne Schronisko Młodzieżowe** is Gdańsk's impossibly
cheap, institutional hostel. It's right near the Solidarity shipyard on
the north edge of the Old Town, in an old brick building that has
served as both a prison and a school. Its 96 beds are glorified cots,
but the place is clean and the price is right (S-30 zł, D-60 zł, per
person in 3- or 4- bed room-20 zł, in 5- to 10-bed room-18 zł, onetime 5-zł fee for sheets, closed 10:00–15:00, 24:00 curfew, upstairs at
ulica Wałowa 21, tel. & fax 058/301-2313, www.mokf.com.pl, biuro
@mokf.com.pl).

$ *Room-Booking Service:* The **Grand-Tourist** agency near the
station has a line on rooms in private homes and apartments in and
near the Main Town. Have them explain the location of the room
before you accept, and remember that the Main Town is closer to
the pretty tourist area than the Old Town (rooms: S-60 zł, D-
90–100 zł; apartments: Db-180 zł, Tb-230 zł, for up to 6 people-
295 zł; office open July–Aug daily 8:00–20:00, Sept–June Mon–Fri
10:00–18:00, Sat 10:00–14:00, closed Sun; at Old Town end of passage to train station, below the Holiday Inn and across from the
Empik Megastore at ulica Podwale Grodzkie 8, tel. 058/301-2634,
fax 058/301-6301, www.grand-tourist.pl, kwatery@gt.com.pl).

Across the River

$$ Hotel Królewski is Gdańsk's best value: a new, classy, well-priced hotel in a renovated red-brick granary with stylish rooms. It's near the granaries of the Maritime Museum and across the river from the crane—an easy 1.50-zł ferry ride (during museum opening hours) or 15-minute walk along and over the river from the Main Town action (Sb-260–290 zł, Db-310–340 zł, fancier Db "plus"-350–390 zł, higher prices are for May–Sept, ulica Ołowianka 1, tel. 058/326-1111, fax 058/326-1110, www.hotelkrolewski.pl, office @hotelkrolewski.pl).

$ Dom Muzyka is a great deal, with 87 simple, modern rooms a 10-minute walk from the Main Town. The catch: It's hiding in the back of the big Academy of Music building, virtually impossible to find in a nondescript residential neighborhood. Still, the prices are worth the hunt (Sb-150 zł, Db-200 zł, deluxe Db-230 zł, apartment-320 zł, extra bed-60 zł, cheaper Oct–April, ulica Łąkowa 1/2, tel. 058/326-0600, fax 058/326-0601, www.dom-muzyka.pl, biuro @dom-muzyka.pl). From the Green Gate in the Main Town, cross the two bridges, then take the first right (on Łąkowa). Walk to the end of the block; just before the busy road, go through the gate of the big, yellow-brick building on the right. Once through the gate, the hotel is around the back of the yellow building, the farthest door down (unmarked). If you get lost, just ask people, "Hotel?"

EATING

Gdańsk has some fine Baltic seafood. Herring *(śledź)* is popular here, as is cod *(dorsz)*. Locals also brag that their salmon *(łosoś)* is better than Norway's. For a stiff drink, sample *Goldwasser* (better known in the United States as Goldschlager); this strong liqueur, flecked with gold, was supposedly invented here in Gdańsk.

The following options are all in the Main Town, within three blocks of ulica Długa. The first three places are cheaper; the last two are splurges.

Bar Mleczny Neptun is your best milk-bar option in the Main Town, with tasty Polish food and low prices (a good meal, including a drink, runs around 10 zł). The items on the counter are for display; rather than take what's there, point to what you want and they'll dish it up fresh (Mon–Fri 7:00–18:00, until 19:00 in summer, Sat 9:00–18:00, open Sun only in summer 9:00–18:00, ulica Długa 33-34, tel. 058/301-4988). For more on milk bars, see page 152.

Bar pod Rybą ("Under the Fish") is nirvana for fans of baked potatoes—that's all they serve, piled high with a wide variety of tasty fillings and sauces. It's hearty, quick, and very central (10–15 zł, daily 11:00–19:00, until 22:00 in summer, Długi Targ 35-38, tel. 058/305-1307).

Gdańsk Hotels and Restaurants

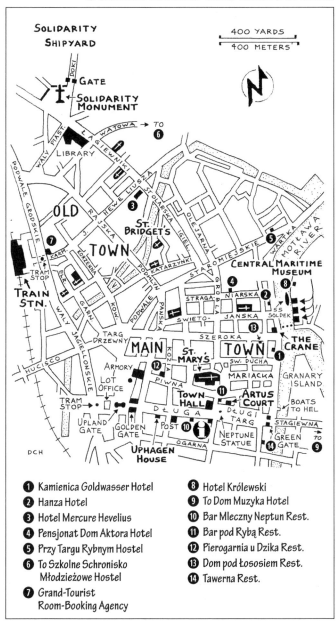

1. Kamienica Goldwasser Hotel
2. Hanza Hotel
3. Hotel Mercure Hevelius
4. Pensjonat Dom Aktora Hotel
5. Przy Targu Rybnym Hostel
6. To Szkolne Schronisko Młodzieżowe Hostel
7. Grand-Tourist Room-Booking Agency
8. Hotel Królewski
9. To Dom Muzyka Hotel
10. Bar Mleczny Neptun Rest.
11. Bar pod Rybą Rest.
12. Pierogarnia u Dzika Rest.
13. Dom pod Łososiem Rest.
14. Tawerna Rest.

Pierogarnia u Dzika ("By the Boar"), with contemporary decor enhanced with all manner of stuffed and skinned boar, is the Heinz of *pierogi* (Polish ravioli)—offering 57 varieties (10–15 zł, bigger dishes-20–30 zł, daily 10:00–22:00, ulica Piwna 59-60, tel. 058/305-2676).

Dom pod Łososiem ("House under the Salmon") will make you feel like a rich burgher's family invited you over for dinner. This elegant restaurant—where waiters wax their moustaches and wear tails—has reportedly been serving guests for over 400 years (and, somewhere in there, invented *Goldwasser*). If you're looking for relatively expensive but good food and over-the-top formality, this is the place (most main dishes 50–80 zł, ulica Szeroka 52-54, tel. 058/301-7652).

Tawerna, a venerable old place just off the end of Długi Targ, is every local's recommendation for good fish (with some Polish and French cuisine). The prices are high and it's packed with tourists, but the quality is undeniable (main dishes 50–70 zł, seafood splurges to 100 zł, daily 11:00–23:00, reservations smart, ulica Powroźnicza 19–20, tel. 058/301-4114).

TRANSPORTATION CONNECTIONS

Trains

Gdańsk is well-connected to the Tri-City via the commuter SKM trains (see "Sights near Gdańsk," page 259). It's also got frequent connections to Warsaw, and handy night trains to Berlin and Kraków.

From Gdańsk by train to: Hel (town on Hel Peninsula, 3/day direct, 2.25–3.25 hrs, more with transfer in Gdynia), **Malbork** (at least hrly, 1 hr), **Toruń** (4/day direct, 3 hrs; more with a transfer in Bydgoszcz or Ilawa, at least hrly, 3–4 hrs), **Warsaw** (nearly hrly, 4 hrs), **Kraków** (3/day direct, 7 hrs; plus 1 night train, 10 hrs; more with transfer in Warsaw), **Berlin** (4/day, 8.25–9.25 hrs, transfer in Szczecin, Poznań, or Frankfurt an der Oder; plus 1 direct night train, 10 hrs).

Boats

Zegluga Gdańska offers several boat trips, leaving from the riverfront near the Green Gate, just upriver from the crane (tel. 058/301-4926, www.zegluga.pl). You can visit Westerplatte (where World War II started) via fast 50-minute hydrofoil (35 zł round-trip, 6/day in each direction, less off-season). Other convenient boats: Leaving Gdańsk at 9:30, stopping at Sopot at 10:30, Gdynia at 11:10, and Hel at 12:40 (return boat leaves Hel at 16:30); leaving Gdańsk at 14:45, stopping at Westerplatte at 15:10, and Sopot at 15:55.

Pomerania

Malbork Castle

Malbork Castle is soaked in history. The biggest brick castle in the world, the largest castle of the Gothic period, and one of Europe's most picturesque fortresses, it sits smugly on a marshy plain at the edge of the town of Malbork, 35 miles southeast of Gdańsk. This was the headquarters of the notorious Teutonic Knights, a Germanic band of ex-Crusaders who dominated northern Poland in the Middle Ages.

When the Teutonic Knights were invited to Polish lands to convert neighboring pagans in the 13th century, they found the perfect site for their new capital here, on the bank of the Nogat River. Construction began in 1274. After the Teutonic Knights conquered Gdańsk in 1308, the order moved its official headquarters from Venice to Malbork. The Teutonic Knights remained here for nearly 150 years. They called the castle Marienburg, the "Castle

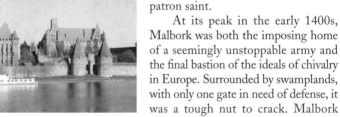

of Mary," in honor of the order's patron saint.

At its peak in the early 1400s, Malbork was both the imposing home of a seemingly unstoppable army and the final bastion of the ideals of chivalry in Europe. Surrounded by swamplands, with only one gate in need of defense, it was a tough nut to crack. Malbork Castle was never taken by force in the Middle Ages, though it had to withstand siege by the Poles during the Thirteen Years' War (1454–1466). Finally, in 1457, the Polish king gained control of Malbork by buying off Czech mercenaries guarding the castle (who had been hired by the Teutonic Knights, once mercenaries themselves). Malbork became a Polish royal residence for 300 years. But when Poland was partitioned in the late 18th century, this region went back into German (Prussian) hands. The castle became a barracks, windows were sealed up, delicate vaulting was damaged, bricks were quarried for new buildings, and Malbork deteriorated. In the late 19th century, Romantic German artist and poets rediscovered the place. An architect named Konrad Steinbrecht devoted 40 years of his life to Malbork, painstakingly restoring the palace to its medieval splendor. A half century later, the Nazis used the castle to house POWs, and about half of it was destroyed by the Soviet army, who saw it as a symbol of longstanding German domination. If you look closely, you can still see the original and reconstructed parts.

Gdańsk Day Trips

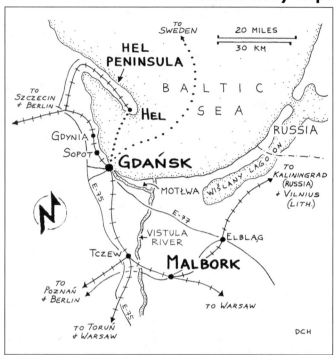

Today, Malbork has been restored to its Teutonic glory, and ranks among the most visit-worthy sights in Poland.

Cost, Hours, Information: May–Sept-22 zł; Oct–April-19 zł. Open May–mid-Sept Tue–Sun 9:00–19:00, late Sept and late April Tue–Sun 9:00–17:00, Oct–mid-April Tue–Sun 10:00–15:00, always closed Mon, ticket office generally opens 30 min before castle, www.zamek.malbork.pl.

Tours of Malbork: You are required to enter the castle with a three-hour tour. (It sounds like an intimidating commitment—but thoroughly seeing the place actually takes about that long; besides, you can split off whenever you like.) In summer (May–Sept), you'll wait until enough English-speakers gather, which generally takes no longer than an hour; pass the time by wandering the grounds. Off-season, it's trickier; English tours depend on guides and demand. You may have to wait longer, or you might have to just go with a Polish tour. You can try calling ahead the day before to see if and when any English tours are scheduled (tel. 055/647-0978). I'd recommend investing in a local guide to see the palace exactly as you like (see "Local Guides," page 240).

No matter which tour you take, it's generally accepted to split off from the group to explore the place on your own. You can use my self-guided tour (below).

Best Views: The views of massive Malbork are stunning—especially at sunset, when the red brick glows. Be sure to walk out across the bridge over the Nogat River. The most scenic part of the castle is probably the twin-turreted, riverside Bridge Gate, which used to be connected by a bridge to the opposite bank.

Sound-and-Light Show: Every night at dusk, mid-May through mid-October, there's a sound-and-light show in the castle courtyard.

Getting to Malbork: Frequent **trains** link both Gdańsk and Warsaw to the town of Malbork. The Malbork station has a baggage-check office (*przechowalnia bagażu,* by ticket windows); if it's closed, be insistent, and someone should eventually help you. From the station, it's a 15-minute walk to the castle. Taxis charge an exorbitant 20 zł; try to share the cab (and fare) with other travelers headed to the castle *(zamek).* To walk, leave the station to the right and cross the busy road; the castle is more or less dead ahead, through the center of town (you can see the highest, square tower already from the busy road; beware that there are some pointy-topped towers, once part of the complex, that are not very close to the castle).

Malbork Castle Self-Guided Tour

These are the highlights. This tour corresponds more or less to the route most Malbork guides take, but every guide is a little different, exhibits tend to move around, and entrances can be unexpectedly closed. Use a map to navigate and jump around as needed.

Entrance Gate: Stand in front of the gate to one of Europe's most intimidating fortresses—home to the Grand Master, monks, and knights of the Teutonic Order. Across from the gate is the **Lower Castle**, which was an infirmary and hospital for injured knights and retirees. The end closest to you is the Chapel of St. Lawrence; farther away, the former farm buildings have been converted into hotel rooms and restaurants (see "Sleeping," page 274).

Go through the first gate. Above the door to the second gate is a sculpture of St. Mary with the Baby Jesus...accompanied by a shield and helmet. The two messages to visitors: This castle is protected by Mary, and the Teutonic Knights are here to convert pagans by force, if necessary (or, as it turned out, even if not necessary). Imagine the gate behind you closing. You look up to see wooden chutes where archers are preparing to rain arrows down on you. Your last thought: Maybe we should have left the Teutonic Knights alone, after all.

Before being pierced by arrows, read the castle's history into its walls: The foundation is made of huge stones, which aren't abundant in these marshy lands—they were brought from Sweden. But most of

The Teutonic Knights

The Order of the Teutonic Knights began in the Holy Land in 1191, during the Third Crusade. Officially called the "Order of the Hospital of the Blessed Virgin Mary of the German House of Jerusalem," these German monks and knights took vows of poverty, chastity, and obedience; cared for injured knights; and built hospitals in the Holy Land. When the Crusades ended in the 12th century, the order found itself out of a job and went back to Europe. They set up shop in Venice and reorganized as a chivalric order of Christian mercenaries—pagan-killers for hire.

The Teutonic Knights were hired for a gig in northern Poland in 1226. Duke Konrad of Mazovia wanted to subdue a tribe of pagans, called the Prussians, who had been attacking his lands (confusingly, these were pagan Slavs—*not* the same as the later goose-stepping Prussians who lived in what would become eastern Germany). Claiming to be missionaries (and wearing white cloaks decorated with black crosses), the Teutonic Knights spent 60 years "saving" the pagan Prussians by brutally massacring them and turning them into serfs.

Like houseguests who didn't know when to leave, the Teutonic Knights decided they enjoyed northern Poland—and stuck around. The Knights made themselves at home, building one of Europe's biggest and most imposing fortresses: Malbork. Because they were fanatical Christians, they won the support of the pope and the Holy Roman Emperor. When the Teutonic Knights seized large parts of northern Poland in 1308, including Gdańsk—cutting off Polish access to the Baltic Sea—the Polish royals began to realize their mistake. The Teutonic Knights invited more Germans to come join them, building their numbers and tightening their grasp on the region. They grew rich from Hanseatic trade, specializing in amber, grain, and timber. The Knights conquered Estonia and Latvia, and began to threaten the Poles' pagan neighbor to the east, Lithuania. By the late 14th century, the Teutonic Knights were enjoying a golden age at the expense of the Prussians, Poles, and Lithuanians.

At about this time, Poland's long-lived Piast dynasty died out. Inspired by a mutual desire to fight back against the Teutonic

---

the castle, like so many other buildings in northern Poland, was built with handmade red brick. Throughout the castle, the darker-colored, rougher brick is original, and the lighter-colored, smoother brick was used for restoration (in the 19th century, and again after WWII).

Venture through two more enclosed spaces, watching for the holes in the wall (for more guards and soldiers). The Teutonic Knights connected nearby lakes to create a system of canals, forming a moat around the castle that could be crossed only by this drawbridge. Ponder the fact that you have to go through five separate, well-defended gates to reach the...

Knights, the Poles and the Lithuanians decided to join their king-doms. In 1386, the Polish Princess Jadwiga married Lithuanian Prince Władysław Jagiełło (who converted to Christianity for the occasion), uniting Poland and Lithuania and kick-starting a grand new dynasty, the Jagiellonians.

Just as every American knows the date July 4, 1776, every Pole knows the date July 15, 1410—the Battle of Grunwald. Władysław Jagiełło led a ragtag army of some 40,000 soldiers—Lithuanians, Poles, other Slavs, and even speedy Tartar horsemen—against 27,000 Teutonic Knights. At the end of the day, half of the Teutonic Knights were dead, and the other half had been captured. Poland and Lithuania were victorious. Though the Teutonic Knights remained in Poland—extending their Germanic cultural influence on the region well into the 20th century—their political power waned, they pulled out of Lithuania, and they once again allowed free trade on the Vistula. A generation later, the Thirteen Years' War (1454–1466) finally put an end to the Teutonic Knights' domination of northern Poland.

The Knights' influence on Poland persists today—even beyond the striking red-brick churches and castles scattered around the northern part of the country. The Polish novelist Henryk Sienkiewicz's *The Teutonic Knights* is a cultural benchmark and a favorite work of many Poles. The 19th-century Romantics who fanned the flames of Polish patriotism turned the Teutonic Knights into a symbol of Germanic oppression. Even today, Poles—and all Slavs—remember the Teutonic Knights as murderous invaders. For the Germans' part, the Teutonic Knights remain a footnote in their history books—as brave Christian soldiers who enlightened the east-ern boundaries of their lands. While every Pole knows the story of the Battle of Grunwald, most Germans—who call it the "Battle of Tannenburg"—are barely familiar with its significance. And yet, the age-old tensions between Germans and Slavs simmer just below the surface. When Adolf Hitler invaded Poland on September 1, 1939—reasserting German domination over northern Poland, and sparking World War II—he called it "Operation Tannenburg."

Middle Castle (Zamek Średni): This part of Malbork, built at an uphill incline to make it even more imposing, was designed to impress. Knights and monks lived here. Any person entering the castle had to first wash up at one of the very carefully guarded wells—a clean body led to a clean soul.

To your left is the east wing, where guests would sleep. Today, this wing houses various museum exhibits, including the astonishing **Amber Collection** (ground floor). Displayed chrono-logically to show how amber influenced this territory and its people over time, this display will make jewelry shoppers salivate. (Even as someone with zero interest in amber, I enjoyed it.) You'll see rough amber, with inclusions (bugs stuck in the amber, à la *Jurassic Park*) and imprints of tree bark. Some ancient amber artifacts were found in graves, put there by people who thought it would help the deceased enter a better world. Some of the finely decorated jewelry boxes and chests of amber have ivory, silver, or shell inlays (better for contrast than gold). The small, portable religious shrines and altars could be used for travel, allowing people to remain reverent on the road and still pack light. You'll see a take-along cabinet with tiny drawers belonging to the last Polish king; an amazing, bigger altar with biblical scenes; and a small replica of the six-foot-tall amber and silver cross presented to Pope John Paul II. Along with everyday objects (such as cutlery, candlesticks, and chess sets), there are impractically ornate brooches and far-out necklaces, including some resembling Hawaiian leis. Upstairs from the Amber Collection is a good **Armory.** Find the suits of armor from the Hussars (Polish horseback knights who had wings on their armor, which created a terrifying sound when galloping). Also in this building is an exhibit on the **architectural transformations** of Malbork over the centuries.

To the right (west) as you enter the main courtyard is the complex of the Great Refectory (closer to the entrance) and the Grand Master's Palace (the taller, squarer building at the far end of the wing). Go through the gate into the small courtyard. Before you head into the palace, find your way down the steep stairs into the **boiler room,** where a super-heated stove provided a kind of medieval central heating for the palace rooms (once inside the upstairs area, look for the plates in the floor to see where the heat came through).

The **Grand Refectory** (dining hall), damaged in World War II, is under renovation and generally closed to visitors. With remarkable palm vaulting and grand frescoes, this dining hall hosted feasts for up to 400 people to celebrate a military victory or to impress a visiting king.

Now head into the **Grand Master's Palace.** This was one of the grandest royal residences in medieval Europe, used in later times by Polish kings and German Kaisers. First, you'll see the **private rooms of the Grand Master**, with show-off decor (including some 15th-century original frescoes of wine leaves and grapes). The Grand Master even had his own chapel, dedicated to St. Catherine. Though the Teutonic Order dictated that the monks sleep in dormitories, the Grand Master made an exception for himself—and you'll see his private bedroom (with rough original frescoes of 4 female martyrs). Upstairs, you'll pass through **vestibules,** where visitors would wait to see the Grand Master. In the second vestibule, notice the troughs on the ground—anyone wanting an audience with the Grand Master had to wash both his

All About Amber

Poland's Baltic seaside is known as the Amber Coast. You'll see amber in the exhibit at Malbork, as well as in shop windows in Gdańsk (and throughout the country). This petrified pine tree sap originated here on the north coast of Poland 40 million years ago. It comes in as many different colors as Eskimos have words for snow: 300 distinct shades, from yellowish-white to yellowish-brown. (I didn't believe it either, until I toured Malbork's collection.) While the most transparent amber is generally more popular, it all costs the same—the color and transparency is a matter of personal preference.

Amber has been popular since long before there were souvenir stands. Archaeologists have found graves of Roman citizens (and their coins) who were buried with crosses made of amber. Almost 75 percent of the world's amber is mined in northern Poland, and it sometimes simply washes up on the beaches. Some of the elaborate amber sculptures displayed at Malbork are created by joining pieces of amber with "amber glue"—made of melted-down amber mixed with an adhesive agent.

In addition to being good for the economy, some Poles believe amber is good for their health. A traditional cure for arthritis pain is to pour strong vodka over amber, let it set, and then rub it on sore joints.

hands and his feet. Musicians entertained waiting guests from the balcony up above. Next is the elegant **Summer Refectory,** where the G.M. dined. With big stained-glass windows, and all of the delicate vaulting supported by a single pillar in the middle, this room clearly was not designed for defense. (In fact, Polish attacks on the palace in the Middle Ages were focused on this room, and once a cannonball just barely missed the pillar. Later, the ceiling collapsed during World War II.) As you continue into the **Winter Refectory,** notice fewer windows (better insulation) and the little manhole-like openings in the floor—where the "central heating" came into the room. Examine the faded frescoes of Grand Masters. You'll end up in the mostly reconstructed King's Chamber (where Polish kings spent their time in the post-Teutonic era) before heading back outside.

At the end of the main courtyard are **statues** of four of the Grand Masters of the Teutonic Knights. Though this was a religious order, these powerful guys look more like kings than monks. From right to left, shake hands with Hermann von Salza (who was Grand Master when the Teutonic Knights came to Poland); Siegfried von Feuchtwangen (the first Grand Master who actually lived at Malbork, and who conquered Gdańsk for the

Knights—oops, can't shake his hand, which was supposedly chopped off by Soviet troops who took Malbork at the end of World War II); Winrich von Kniprode (who oversaw Malbork's golden age, and turned it into a castle fit for a king); and Albrecht Hohenzollern (the last Grand Master before the Poles took over Malbork).

Now continue up over the **drawbridge.** As you cross, notice the extensive system of fortifications and moats protecting the inner part of the castle. Notice the cracks in the walls—a increasing threat to the ever-settling castle set on this marshy, unstable terrain. The passage is lined with holes (for guards to view who was entering), with chutes up above (to pour scalding water or pitch on unwanted visitors). It's not quite straight—so, a cannon fired here would hit the side wall of the passage, rather than entering the High Castle. Which is what you're doing now.

High Castle (Zamek Wysoki): This is the heart of the castle, and its oldest section. As much a monastery as a fortress, the High Castle was off limits to all but 60 monks of the Teutonic Order and their servants. (The knights stayed in the Middle Castle.) Here you'll find the monks' dormitories, chapels, church, and refectory.

In the middle of the High Castle courtyard is a **well.** At the top is a sculpture of a pelican. Because this noble bird is known to kill itself to feed its young (notice that it's piercing its own chest with its beak), it was often used in the Middle Ages as a symbol for the self-sacrifice of Jesus.

Around the courtyard on the ground floor, you'll see entrances to a prison/torture-chamber and a collection of medieval stained-glass windows, and a photograph in the corridor of the WWII destruction of Malbork. Beyond that is an exhibit about the **destruction and reconstruction** of the castle, with several photographs and an elaborate 1933 model of Malbork (looking a little different from today's version). Also in this exhibit are some pieces of mosaic belonging to an enormous, 26-foot-tall statue of Mary. This stood in a niche on the outer wall of Malbork's main church, facing the outside. Encrusted with small, colorful pieces of glass, the statue glittered in the sunlight—demonstrating that the Teutonic Knights were, indeed, protected by Mary. The statue fell into disrepair during the Prussian occupation, then was restored in the late 19th century—only to be damaged again in World War II. Today, the niche remains empty. Back out in the courtyard, near where you entered, you'll wind up at the **kitchen,** with displays that bring the medieval atmosphere to life. The monks who lived here ate three meals a day, along with lots of beer (made here) and wine (imported from France, Italy, and Hungary). A cellar under the kitchen was used as a primitive refrigerator—big chunks of ice were cut from the frozen river in winter, stored in the basement, and used to keep food cool in summer. Behind the table, see the big dumbwaiter—connecting this kitchen with the refectory upstairs. Step into the giant stove and look up the biggest chimney in the castle. In the next room, the bakery, is a demonstration of how medieval money was made. The Teutonic Knights minted their own coins—and you can buy your very own replica today.

Now head upstairs. Once at the top of the stairs, the first door to the left leads to the most important room of the High Castle, the **Chapter Room.** Monks gathered here after Mass to pray, confess their sins, and sing (imagine the voices of 60 monks bouncing around these acoustics). Monks from around the countryside came here for meetings—each with a seal and a name over his seat (for example, a hospitaler, who cared for the sick). The big chair belonged to the Grand Master. While monks are usually thought to pursue simple lives, the elegant vaulting in this room is anything but plain. The 14th-century frescoes (restored in the 19th century) depict Grand Masters. Facing the Grand Master's seat, the three rows of frescoes on the left wall depict poverty (wheat); chastity (white flour—no women under 60 were allowed to work in the High Castle...but one Grand Master supposedly bent the rules, and brought in two 30-year-olds); and obedience (hands tied). The Teutonic Knights' fourth vow—not pictured here—was to fight and kill pagans. An entrance to climb up to the tower is nearby (though a more convenient door is sometimes open one floor up, at the end of this tour). Also near the Chapter House is the **Church of St. Mary,** which was destroyed in World War II and sat for decades with no roof. After so much neglect, it's finally being renovated...slowly. (We'll circle back to this church—and its beautifully decorated entryway—later.)

For now, leave the Chapter House and walk straight, imagining the monk-filled corridors of Teutonic times. In the first door on the right is the **Treasury,** with a display of coins and of amber (which helped make the Teutonic Knights rich). Notice the very safe safe—with two doors and three independent keyholes. As you pass through the rooms of the tax collector and the house administrator, notice the small beds—for small medieval people.

Continue around the cloister. At the end of the corridor, look for the little devil at the bottom of the vaulting (on the right). He's pulling his beard and crossing his legs—pointing you down the long corridor to the **Gdanisko Tower**...housing the toilet, of course. Follow his directions to the medieval WCs, in a tower set apart from the main part of the castle. The toilets dropped straight down into the moat; the bins were for cabbage leaves, used by the Knights as TP. This tower could also serve as a final measure of defense. The passage connecting it to the main castle was partly made of wood, and could be burned down—signaling for help and turning the tower into an impenetrable keep. Food was stored above...just in case.

Head back to the main part of the High Castle and continue around the cloister. The door halfway down leads to the **church exhibition**, with pictures of various eras of Malbork Castle, as well as some fragments of St. Mary's Church, including the remains of a crucifix.

Nearby is the **Golden Gate** marking the entrance to St. Mary's Church. Ringed with exquisite carvings from the Old Testament, and symbolic messages about how monks of the Teutonic Order should live their lives, it's a marvelous example of late-13th-century art. On the left, find the five wise virgins who filled their lamps with oil, conserved it wisely, and are headed to Heaven. On the right, the five foolish virgins who overslept and used up all their oil are damned, much to their dismay. The church itself is still pretty glum, though ongoing renovations should restore it to its medieval splendor.

Take the narrow spiral staircase upstairs to the **Refectory**. Across from the door is the grate where the dumbwaiter comes up from the kitchen (which we saw below). In the big room with seven pillars, the monks ate in silence. Over the fireplace is a relief depicting the Teutonic Knights fighting the Prussians. Next is the room used for entertainment after the meal (musicians played from the balcony up above, which was covered with frescoes). Another relief over the fireplace shows the Knights killing pagans.

Your Malbork tour ends here. A nearby door (sometimes locked) leads to the stairs up to the top of the tower. When finished, you can head back the way you came. En route, you can walk around **terraces** lining the inner moat, between the castle walls (stairs lead down off of the drawbridge back to the Middle Castle). It's hardly a must-see, but pleasant enough, with the Grand Master's garden, a cemetery for monks, and the remains of the small St. Anne's Chapel (with Grand Master tombs).

SLEEPING

$$ Hotel Zamek is housed in Malbork's Lower Castle, a red-brick building that was once a hospital, just across from the main part of the fortress. The 42 rooms are dark, old-feeling, and a little creepy, but the prices are surprisingly affordable...especially for being next door to Europe's grandest Gothic castle (Sb-210–270 zł, Db-250–320 zł, Tb-330–500 zł, higher prices are for mid-May–Oct, elevator, ulica Starościńska 14, tel. & fax 055/272-3367). This is an especially smart option in the summer, when days are long and a sound-and-light show plays after dark.

Toruń

Toruń is a pretty, lazy, Gothic town conveniently located about halfway between Warsaw and Gdańsk. It's worth a couple of hours to stroll the wide pedestrian boulevards, ogle the huge red-brick buildings, and savor the flavor of one of Poland's most enjoyable mid-sized cities. With about 210,000 residents and 30,000 students (at Copernicus University), Toruń is a thriving burg.

Locals brag that Toruń is a "mini-Kraków." The squares are not nearly so grand, and the sights not as plentiful or as impressive, but the street life is arguably better—at once more bustling (with in-love-with-life, promenading locals who greet each other like they're long-lost friends) and more laid-back (fewer tourists and aggressive salesmen).

Toruń has two claims to fame: it's the proud birthplace of the astronomer Copernicus (Mikołaj Kopernik), and home to a dizzying variety of gingerbread treats *(piernikowa nuta).*

ORIENTATION

Everything in Toruń worth seeing is in the Old Town, climbing up a gentle hill from the Vistula River. From the station (Toruń Główny, lockers available), take the underpass beneath track 4 (following signs for *wyjście do miasta*—"exit to the town"), and catch bus #22 or #27 into the center (a little over a mile, get off at first stop after long bridge, called Plac Rapackiego). A taxi into town should cost no more than 10 zł.

Tourist Information
The TI is on the main square, behind the Town Hall. Pick up the free map, and get information about hotels in town and city tours (Tue–Fri 9:00–18:00, Mon and Sat 9:00–16:00, closed Sun except May–Aug, when it's open 9:00–13:00, Rynek Staromiejski 25, tel. 056/621-0931, www.it.torun.pl).

Walking Tour of Toruń
From the Plac Rapackiego bus stop, head into the town (through the passageways under the colorful buildings). Within a block, you're at the bustling **Old Town Market Square** (Rynek Staromiejski), surrounded by huge brick buildings and lively locals. The big building in the center is the **Old Town Hall** (Ratusz Staromiejski), with a boring museum and a climbable tower.

The guy playing his violin in front of the Town Hall is a **rafter**—one of the medieval lumberjacks who lashed tree trunks together and floated them down the Vistula to Gdańsk. This particular rafter came to Toruń when the town was infested with frogs. He wooed them with his violin and marched them out of town. (Hmm...sounds like a certain visitor to another medieval Hanseatic city, Bremen....)

The bigger statue, at the other end of the Town Hall, is of favorite son **Mikołaj Kopernik**. There's some dispute about Copernicus' origins; he was born in Toruń, all right, but at a time when it was a predominantly German town. So, is he Polish or German? You can visit his birth house, now a museum to the astronomer, in a marvelously decorated brick building a block away (head down Żeglarska, lined with gingerbread shops, and take the first right—on Kopernika, of course—to #15–17).

Pick up some of Toruń's trademark **gingerbread** at one of the shops on the square, or down ulica Żeglarska. You can get it topped with any kind of jam or chocolate—take your pick.

Then join the human stream down the appropriately named **ulica Szeroka** ("Wide Street"), an enjoyable pedestrian promenade through the heart of town. At Przedzamcze, you leave the Old Town and enter the New Town (chartered only about 30 years later—both in the 13th century). While these areas are both collectively known today as the unified "Old Town," they were quite different in the Middle Ages—each with its own market square, and separated by a wall.

For a detour, follow that wall to the right, down Przedzamcze, to reach the **ruins** of the castle built by the Teutonic Knights who were so influential in northern Poland in the Middle Ages (see page 268). The castle was destroyed in the 15th century by the locals—who, aside from a heap of bricks, left only the tower that housed the Teutonic toilets.

Beyond the castle ruins is the **Vistula** riverbank. The road that runs along the river here is called Bulwar Filadelfijski—for Toruń's sister city in Pennsylvania. (Likewise, Philly residents may be familiar with the "Torun Circle" in their city.)

SLEEPING

There are plenty of great options; Toruń has a surprising abundance of central, good-value places. The TI has a brochure listing the options, and can help you find a room for no extra charge.

$ Hotel Karczma "Spichrz" is a fresh, atmospheric hotel in a renovated old granary. Its 19 rooms and public spaces are a fun meld of old and new—with huge wooden beams around every corner, and the odor of the restaurant's wood-fired grill wafting through the halls. It's a little kitschy, but it's comfortable, central, and well-priced (Sb-190 zł, Db-250 zł, elevator, a block off the main drag towards the river at ulica Mostowa 1, tel. 056/657-1140, fax 056/657-1144, www.spichrz.pl, hotel@spichrz.pl).

TRANSPORTATION CONNECTIONS

Toruń is a handy stopover on the way between Warsaw and Gdańsk. Unfortunately, it's on a different train line than Malbork—so visiting both Toruń and the mighty Teutonic castle in the same day is surprisingly time-consuming, and not worth the bother. Consider visiting one on the way from Warsaw to Gdańsk, and the other on the way back (or day-trip to Malbork from Gdańsk).

From Toruń by train to: Warsaw (5/day direct, 3 hrs; more with a transfer in Kutno), **Gdańsk** (4/day direct, 3 hrs; more with a transfer in Bydgoszcz or Ilawa, at least hrly, 3–4 hrs).

HUNGARY
(Magyarország)

Hungary is an island of Asian-descended Magyars in a sea of Slavs. Even though the Hungarians have thoroughly integrated with their Slavic and German neighbors in the millennium since they arrived, there's still something about the place that's distinctly Magyar (MUD-jar). Visiting Hungary is like looking at the rest of Eastern Europe in a mirror: Everything's a little different—in terms of history, language, culture, customs, and cuisine—but it's hard to put your finger on exactly how.

Just a century ago, Hungary controlled half of one of Europe's grandest empires. Today, perhaps clinging to their former greatness, Hungarians remain old-fashioned and nostalgic. With their dusty museums and bushy moustaches, they love to remember the good old days. Buildings all over the country are marked with proud plaques boasting *MŰEMLEK* ("historical monument").

Thanks to this focus on tradition, the Hungarians you'll encounter are generally polite, formal, and professional. Hungarians have class. Everything here is done with a proud flourish. You get the impression that people in the service industry wear their uniforms as a badge of honor, rather than a burden. When a waiter comes to your table in a restaurant, he'll say, *"Tessék parancsolni"*—literally, "Please command, sir." The standard greeting, *"Jó napot kívánok,"* means "I wish you a good day." And when your train or

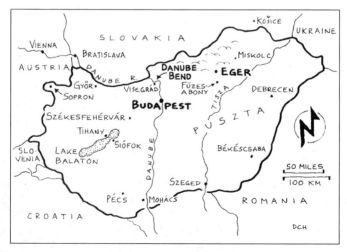

How Big, How Many, How Much

- Hungary is 35,653 square miles (the size of Indiana).
- Population is 10 million (about 280 people per square mile, 90 percent Hungarian).
- 200 forints (Ft, or HUF) = about $1
- Country code: 36

---

bus makes a stop, you won't be alerted by a mindless, blaring beep or hoot, but instead, peppy music. (You'll be humming these contagious little ditties all day.)

Hungarians are just as orderly and tidy as Germans...in their own sometimes unexpected ways. Yes, Hungary has as much litter, graffiti, and crumbling buildings as any other Eastern European country, but you'll find great reason within the chaos. My favorite town name in Hungary: Hatvan. This means "Sixty" in Hungarian...and it's exactly 60 kilometers from Budapest. You can't argue with that kind of logic.

This tradition of left-brained thinking hasn't produced many great Hungarian painters or poets. But it has made tremendous contributions to the field of science, technology, business, and industry. Hungarians of note include Edward Teller (instrumental in creating the A-bomb), John von Neumann (a pioneer of computer science), Andy Grove (who, as András Grof, immigrated to the United States and founded Intel), and George Soros (who fled to the United States under communism, became a billionaire through shrewd investment, and is loved by the Left and loathed by the Right as a major contributor to liberal causes). Perhaps the most famous Hungarian "scientist" created something you probably have in a box in your basement: Ernő Rubik, and his famous cube. Hungary's enjoyment of a good mind-bending puzzle is also evident in their fascination with chess, which you'll see played in cafés, parks, and baths.

Like their Austrian neighbors, Hungarians know how to enjoy the good life. Favorite activities include splashing and soaking in their many thermal baths (see sidebar on page 280). Hungarians are also reviving an elegant, Vienna-style café culture that was dismantled by the communists. Classical music is revered, perhaps as nowhere else outside Austria. Aside from scientists and businessmen, the best-known Hungarians are composers: Béla Bartók, Zoltan Kodály (who developed the famous solfege sight-singing method taught in music schools worldwide), and Franz Liszt (actually German, but of Hungarian ancestry).

As you can guess from the many grandiose structures built in Budapest in the late 1800s, Hungarians are also romantic. Over-the-top, melodramatic Latin American soap operas are popular here (dubbed into Hungarian, of course). When the European Union

Taking the Waters

Hungary's Carpathian Basin is a thin crust on top of a lot of hot water. The Romans named their settlement at present-day Budapest "Aquincum"—meaning "abundant waters"—and took advantage of those waters by building many baths. Centuries later, the occupying Turks revived the custom. Today, locals brag that if you poke a hole in the ground anywhere in Hungary, you'll find a hot-water spring. Judging from Budapest, they may be right: The city has 123 natural springs and some two dozen thermal baths *(fürdő)*. While these spas have traditionally served a medicinal purpose for the elderly, today Hungary is trying a new angle on its hot water: fun. Adventure water parks are springing up all over the country. (The preventative-health component is an added bonus.)

While American tourists often feel squeamish at the thought of bathing with Speedo-clad, pot-bellied Hungarians, "taking the waters" is a must during your stay in Hungary. Visiting a bath is invariably confusing, with monolingual staff, a confusing payment and locker-rental procedure, and overly complicated menus of massages and other treatments. But if you just go into it with an easygoing attitude and a sense of humor, I promise you'll have a blast. I've carefully described the procedure at the best (and most accessible) thermal-bath options in Budapest (see page 331) and in Eger (page 372). And no, you don't have to go naked.

expanded on May 1, 2004, the biggest celebrations anywhere were here in Hungary—where people love an excuse to party.

While one in every four Hungarians lives in Budapest, the countryside plays an important role in Hungary's economy—this has always been a highly agricultural region. You'll pass fields of wheat and corn, but the grains are secondary to Hungarians' (and tourists') true love: the wine. After Hungarian winemaking standards plummeted under the communists, many vintner families are now reclaiming their land, returning to their precise traditional methods, and making their wines worth being proud of once more.

In Hungary, a person's family name is listed first, and the given name is last—just as in many other Eastern cultures (think of Kim Jong Il). The composer known as Franz Liszt in German is Liszt Ferenc in his homeland. To help reduce confusion, many Hungarian business cards list the last name in capital letters.

Somehow, Hungary (particularly Budapest)—at the crossroads of Europe—has managed to become cosmopolitan while remaining perfectly Hungarian. In the countryside, where less mixing has occurred, Magyar culture and occasional Central Asian facial features are more evident. But in the cities, the Hungarians—like Hungary itself—are a cross-section of Central European cultures: Magyars, Germans, Czechs, Poles, Serbs, Jews, Turks, Romanians, Gypsies, and many others. In fact, a recent scientific study found that Hungarians are the most ethnically diverse nationality on the planet. Still, no matter how many generations removed they are from Magyar stock, there's something different about a Hungarian—and not just the language. Look a Hungarian in the eye, and you'll see a glimmer of the marauding Magyar, stomping in from the Central Asian plains a thousand years ago.

Practicalities

Telephones: Hungary's telephone system is uniquely confusing. You must dial different codes whether you're calling locally, long distance within the country, or internationally to Hungary.

To dial a number **in the same city,** simply dial direct, with no area code.

To dial **long-distance within Hungary,** you have to add the prefix 06, followed by the area code (e.g., Budapest's area code is 1, so you dial 06-1, then the rest of the number).

To make an **international call to Hungary,** start with the international access code (00 if calling from Europe, 011 from the United States or Canada), then Hungary's country code (36), then the area code (but not the 06) and number.

To make an **international call from Hungary,** dial 00, the country code of the country you're calling (see chart in appendix), the area code if applicable (may need to drop initial zero), and the local number.

Hungarian phone numbers beginning with 0680 are toll-free; those beginning with 0620, 0630, or 0670 are mobile phones; and 0681 or 0690 are expensive toll lines. To call these numbers from within Hungary, simply dial direct. To dial them from outside Hungary, you need to drop the 06 at the beginning. So to call the Hungarian mobile phone number 0620/926-0557 from the United States, you dial 011 (the U.S. international access code), then 20 (omitting the 06), then 926-0557.

Telephone cards, which you insert into pay phones, are sold locally at tobacco shops and newsstands. Cheap international telephone cards (which aren't insertable but can be used from virtually any phone—see page 31) are just catching on in Hungary. The ones you'll see sold in Budapest aren't as inexpensive as those in Western European countries (such as Austria), but rates are sure to drop as more choices become available. Ah, capitalism.

Hungarian History

Hungary has a colorful and illustrious history. In terms of political influence in Eastern Europe's past, the Hungarians rank with the Germans and the Russians. So, in a way, Hungarian history is Slovak, Czech, Polish, Croatian, and Slovenian history, too.

Welcome to Europe

The Magyars, led by the mighty Árpád, thundered into the Carpathian Basin from the steppes of Russia in A.D. 896. They were a rough-and-tumble nomadic people from Central Asia who didn't like to settle down in one place. They'd camp out in today's Hungary in the winters, and in the summers, they'd go on raids throughout Europe—terrorizing the Continent from Constantinople (modern-day Istanbul) to the Spanish Pyrénées. For half a century, they ranked with the Vikings as the most feared people in Europe. But the Hungarians were finally defeated by a German and Czech army at the Battle of Augsburg in 955. If they were to survive, the nomadic Magyars had to settle down. King Géza baptized his son, István (who was Árpád's great-great-grandson), and married him to a Bavarian princess at an early age.

Magyars Tamed

On Christmas Day in the year 1000, King István (Stephen) was crowned by the pope, and Hungary became a legitimate Christian nation (see page 310). The domestication of the nomadic Magyars was difficult—but Hungary eventually emerged as a major Central European power. The kingdom reached its peak in the late 15th century, when the enlightened King Mátyás Corvinus fostered the arts and sparked a mini-Renaissance (see page 308).

Turkish Invasion

Soon after the reign of good king Mátyás, the Turks came slicing their way through the Balkan Peninsula towards Central Europe. In 1526, they entered Hungary. By 1541, they took Buda. During the Turkish occupation, the Magyars moved the capital of the little that remained of their land—"rump Hungary"—to Bratislava (which they called "Pozsony"). During this era, the Ottomans built many of the baths that you'll still find throughout Hungary—and spiced up the food with paprika.

Crippled by the Turks and lacking power and options, Hungary came under control of the Austrian Hapsburg Empire, which finally wrested Buda from the Turks in 1686. The Hapsburgs repopulated Buda and Pest with Germans, while Magyars reclaimed the countryside.

The Hapsburgs

The Hungarians resisted Hapsburg rule, and three Magyars in particular are still noted for their rebellion against Vienna: Ferenc Rákóczi, who led Hungarians in the War of Independence (1703–1711); Lajos Kossuth, who was at the forefront of the 1848 Revolution; and Kossuth's contemporary, Count István Széchenyi, who fought the Hapsburgs with money—building structures like the iconic Chain Bridge (the first permanent link between Buda and Pest). Countless streets, squares, and buildings throughout the country are named for these three Hungarian patriots.

But centuries of alliance with the Hapsburgs eventually paid off. After the 1848 Revolution in Hungary and an important military loss to the Prussians, Austria realized that it couldn't control its rebellious Slavic holdings all by itself. With the Compromise of 1867, Austria granted Budapest the authority over the eastern half of their lands, creating the so-called Dual Monarchy of the Austro-Hungarian Empire (at the expense of the Slavs).

Hungary enjoyed a golden age and Budapest boomed, governing large parts of today's Slovakia, Croatia, and Transylvania (northwest Romania). Composers Franz Liszt (more German than Magyar) and Béla Bartók incorporated the folk and Gypsy songs of the Hungarian and Transylvanian countryside into their music.

The Crisis of Trianon

After Hungary came up on the losing end of World War I, the Treaty of Trianon (named for the palace on the grounds of Versailles where it was signed) reassigned two-thirds of its former territory and half of its population to Romania, Czechoslovakia, Slovenia, Croatia, and Serbia. Towns along the new borders were literally divided down the center, and many Hungarians found themselves unable to cross over to visit relatives or commute to a job that was in the same country the day before. This sent hundreds of thousands of Hungarian refugees—now "foreigners" in their own towns—into Budapest, sparking an enormous boom time in the capital.

Even today, the Treaty of Trianon is regarded as one of the greatest tragedies of Hungarian history. Many Hungarians claim that these lands still belong to the Magyars, and more than two million ethnic Hungarians live outside Hungary (mostly in Romania). The sizeable Magyar minorities in these countries have often been mistreated—particularly since World War II in Romania (under Ceauçescu), Yugoslavia (under Milošević), and Slovakia (under Mečiar). You'll still see maps, posters, and bumper stickers with the distinctive shape of a much larger, pre-WWI Hungary...patriotically displayed by Magyars who feel as strongly about Trianon as if it happened yesterday. When the European Union expanded in 2004, some Hungarians saw it as a happy ending in the big-picture sense—they were once again united with Slovakia, part of the territory they had lost.

Communism...with a Pinch of Paprika

After World War II, the Soviets moved into Hungary, installing Mátyás Rákosi as head of state. In 1956, Hungary staged an uprising, led by Communist Party reformer Imre Nagy (see page 312). Moscow sent in troops, 25,000 Hungarians were killed, and 250,000 fled to Austria. János Kádár was installed to run a harder-line government, and though he cooperated with Moscow, he gradually allowed the people of Hungary more freedom than citizens of neighboring countries had.

Life here was better and more colorful than elsewhere in the Soviet bloc—a system dubbed "goulash communism." With little fanfare, the Hungarian parliament—always skeptical of the Soviets—peacefully voted to end the communist regime in February of 1989. Later that year, Hungary was the first Eastern Bloc nation to open its borders to the West, a major advance in the fall of communist regimes across Eastern Europe.

Hungarian Food

Hungary is known in Eastern Europe for its spicy food—one of the many elements introduced by the Ottoman invaders. Hungarian cuisine is as rich and complex as Polish food is simple. Everything is heavily seasoned: with paprika, tomatoes, and peppers of every shape, color, size, and flavor.

The quintessential ingredient in Hungarian cuisine is paprika. Red shakers of paprika join the salt and pepper on tables. There are more than 40 varieties, with two main types: hot and sweet. Anything cooked *paprikás* (PAH-pree-kash) will be a little spicy. In the fall of 2004, Hungary endured a paprika crisis. The spice was banned because some warehouse supplies were contaminated with aflatoxin, a poisonous substance caused by fungus. Because aflatoxin doesn't grow in the Hungarian climate, imported paprika from the tropics was blamed.

Hungarians dine at a *vendéglő* or *étterem* (restaurant). They gather with friends at a *kávéház* (café, literally, "coffeehouse"), which sometimes has light food, too. And for dessert, it's a *cukrászda* (pastry shop—*cukr* means "sugar").

Hungary is known for its delicious soups *(levesek)*. Try *bableves* (bean soup), *zöldségleves* (vegetable soup—*zöldség*, literally, "greenery," i.e., vegetables), *gombaleves* (mushroom soup—*gomba* means "mushroom"), *halászlé* (fish broth with paprika), or *gulyás leves* (shepherd's soup—clear, spicy broth with meat and potatoes). *Gulyás leves* is the origin of the German term "Gulasch," from which English gets the word "goulash." (To Americans, "goulash" means a thick stew—but here in Hungary, it'll get you a thin broth with chunks of meat and vegetables.)

Aside from the obligatory *gulyás*, make a point of trying another unusual Hungarian soup: cold fruit soup *(hideg gyümölcs leves)*. This cream-based treat—eaten, like other soups, before the meal, even though it tastes more like a dessert—is usually made with *meggy* (sour cherries), but you'll also see versions with *alma* (apples) or *körte* (pears).

Hungarians adore all kinds of meat *(hús)*. *Csirke* is chicken, *borjú* is veal, *kacsa* is duck, *liba* is goose, *libamáj* is goose liver (which shows up more often than you'd think), *sertés* is pork, *sonka* is ham, *kolbász* is sausage, *szelet* is schnitzel (*Bécsi szelet* means Wiener schnitzel)—and the list goes on. Fat is used quite a bit in cooking, making Hungarian cuisine very rich and filling. Meat goes well with *káposzta* (cabbage), which may be *töltött* (stuffed) with the meat.

Vegetarians have a tricky time in Hungary, with many restaurants able to offer only a plate of deep-fried vegetables. They haven't quite figured out how to do a good, healthy, leafy salad; a traditional restaurant will generally offer only marinated cucumbers or peppers, or something with cabbage—using lettuce only as a garnish.

In Hungary, you sometimes pay for *köretek* (starches) separately from the meat course, which can be confusing for foreigners. You'll be asked to choose between *galuska* (noodles, traditional and recommended), *burgonya* (potatoes), *krumpli* (French fries), *krokett* (like Tater Tots), or *rizs* (rice). *Kenyér* (bread) often comes with the meal.

Pastries are a big deal here. Hungary's streets are lined with *cukrászda* (pastry shops). You have many options; simply point to what you want, and chow down. Try the *Dobos torta* (a layered chocolate and caramel cream cake), *somlói galuska* (a dumpling with vanilla, nuts, and chocolate), anything with *gesztenye* (chestnuts), and *rétes* (strudel with various fillings, including *túrós*, curds). On dessert menus at restaurants, you'll also see *palacsinta* (pancakes), usually served *diós* (with walnuts), *mákos* (with poppy seeds), or *gündel* (with nuts, chocolate, cream, and raisins). And many *cukrászda* also serve *fagylalt* (ice cream, *fagyi* for short), sold by the *gomboc* (ball).

To drink: *Sör* means "beer," and *bor* means "wine" (*vörös* is red and *fehér* is white). For more on Hungarian wines, see page 374. *Kávé* and *tea* (pronounced TEY-ah) are coffee and tea, and *víz* (water) comes as *szódavíz* (soda water, sometimes just carbonated tap water) or *ásványvíz* (spring water, more expensive).

If you're drinking with some new Magyar friends, impress them with the standard toast: *Egészségedre* (EH-gehs-sheh-geh-dreh; "to your health"). But don't clink your glasses with theirs. They still remember the 1848 Revolution against the Hapsburgs, which ended with the Hapsburg execution of 13 great Hungarian leaders. The Hapsburgs clinked their beer mugs to the victory. To this very day, clinking mugs is, for many Hungarians, just bad style.

When your waiter brings your food, he'll likely say, *"Jó étvá-gyat!"* (Bon appétit!). When you're ready for the bill, you can simply say, *"Fizetek"* (I'll pay).

Hungarian Language

Hungarians have an endearing habit of using the English word "hello" for both "hi" and "bye," just like the Italians use *"ciao."* You'll often overhear a Hungarian end a telephone conversation with a cheery "Hello!" While the language is overwhelming for tourists, one easy word is *"Szia"* (SEE-yah), which actually does mean hello or goodbye.

Even though Hungary is surrounded by Slavs, Hungarian is not at all related to Slavic languages. In fact, Hungarian isn't related to any European language (except for very distant relatives Finnish and Estonian). It isn't even an Indo-European language—which means that English is more closely related to Hindi, Russian, and French than it is to Hungarian. Not only do Americans struggle with Hungarian—but the Magyars' German- and Slavic-speaking neighbors do, too.

Hungarian is agglutinative, which means that you start with a simple root word and then start tacking on suffixes to create meaning—sometimes resulting in a pileup of extra sounds at the end of a very long word. The emphasis always goes on the first syllable, and the following syllables are droned downhill in a kind of a monotone—giving the language a distinctive cadence that Hungary's Slavic neighbors love to tease about.

But to be fair, Hungarian is easier to pronounce than some Slavic tongues. It's straightforward, once you remember a few key rules. The trickiest: *s* alone is pronounced "sh," while *sz* is pronounced simply "s." This explains why you'll hear in-the-know travelers pronouncing Budapest as "BOO-dah-pesht." You might catch the *busz* up to Castle Hill—pronounced just like we say "bus." And "Franz Liszt" is easier to pronounce than it looks: It sounds just like "list."

The letter *c* and the combination *cz* are both pronounced "ts" (as in "cats"). The combination *zs* is pronounced "zh" (like "measure"). The letters *j* and *ly* are interchangeable, and both are pronounced as "y."

Hungarian has a set of unusual palatal sounds that don't quite have a counterpart in English. To make these sounds, gently press the thick part of your tongue to the roof or your mouth (instead of using the tip of your tongue behind your teeth, as we do in English): *gy* sounds more or less like "dg" in "ledger"; *ny* sounds kind of like the "ny" in "canyon"; and *cs* sounds like "ch."

As for vowels: The letter *a* almost sounds like o (aw); but with an accent *(á)*, it brightens up to the more standard "ah." As with Czech, an accent *(á, é, í, ó, ú)* indicates that you linger on that vowel

Key Hungarian Phrases

English	Hungarian	Pronounced
Hello. (formal)	Jó napot kívánok.	yoh NAH-pot KEE-vah-nohk
Hi. / Bye. (informal)	Szia.	SEE-yah
Do you speak English?	Beszél angolul?	BEH-sehl AHN-goh-lool
Yes. / No.	Igen. / Nem.	EE-gehn / nehm
Please.	Kérem.	KAY-rehm
You're welcome.	Szívesen.	SEE-veh-shehn
Can I help you?	Tessék.	TEHSH-shehk
Thank you.	Köszönöm.	KUR-sur-nurm
I'm sorry. / Excuse me.	Bocsánat.	BOH-chah-nawt
Good.	Jól.	yohl
Goodbye.	Viszontlátásra.	VEE-sohnt-lah-tahsh-rah
one / two	egy / kettő	edj / KEH-tur
three / four	három / négy	HAH-rohm / nedj
five / six	öt / hat	urt / hawt
seven / eight	hét / nyolc	heht / NEE-ohlts
nine / ten	kilenc / tíz	KEE-lehnts / teez
hundred	száz	sahz
thousand	ezer	EH-zehr
How much?	Mennyi?	MEHN-yee
local currency	forint (Ft)	FOH-reent
Where is...?	Hol van...?	hohl vawn
...the toilet	...a toalet	aw TOH-ah-leht
men	férfi	FEHR-fee
women	női	NUR-ee
water / coffee	víz / kávé	veez / KAH-veh
beer / wine	sör / bor	shewr / bohr
Cheers!	Egészségedre!	EH-gehs-sheh-geh-dreh
the bill (literally, "I'll pay")	fizetek	FEE-zeh-tehk

(but not necessarily that you stress that syllable). Like German, Hungarian has umlauts *(ö, ü)*, meaning you purse your lips when you say that vowel. A long umlaut *(ő, ű)* is the same sound, but you hold it a little longer.

Okay, maybe it's not *so* simple. But you'll get the hang of it.

As you're tracking down addresses, these definitions will help: *tér* (square), *utca* (road), *út* (boulevard), *fürdő* (bath), and *híd* (bridge). Words ending in *k* are often plural.

BUDAPEST

Budapest is the capital of Eastern Europe. It's a city of nuance and paradox—cosmopolitan, complicated, and challenging for the first-timer to get a handle on. Novices are sometimes overwhelmed by Budapest—but seasoned travelers enjoy this grand city more with each return visit. Though Prague and Kraków have more romance (and crowds), travelers in the know find Budapest to be Eastern Europe's most fascinating and rewarding destination.

Budapest is hot—literally. The city sits on a skinny layer of earth above thermal springs, which power its many baths. Even the word *Pest* comes from a Slavic word for "oven." Two thousand years ago, the Romans had a settlement, Aquincum, on the north edge of today's Budapest. Several centuries later, in A.D. 896, the Magyars arrived from the steppes of Russia and took over the Carpathian Basin (roughly today's Hungary). In the 16th century, the Ottoman Turks invaded—occupying the region for 145 years. When the Turks were forced out, Buda and Pest were in ruins—so the Hapsburgs repopulated them, giving the cities a more Austrian style.

The Great Compromise of 1867 granted Hungary an equal stake in the Austro-Hungarian Empire. Six years later, the cities of Buda, Pest, and Óbuda united to form the capital city of Budapest, which governed a huge chunk of Eastern Europe. For the next few decades, Hungarian culture enjoyed a golden age, and Budapest was a boom-town. The expansion reached its peak with a flurry of construction sur-rounding the year 1896—Hungary's 1,000th birthday (see page 327).

During the Soviet era, Hungary's milder "goulash" communism meant that Budapest, though still oppressive, was a place where other Eastern Europeans felt they could let loose. Twenty years ago, a stroll down Váci utca was the closest Czechs and Poles could get to a day pass to the West—including a chance to taste a Big Mac at the first McDonald's behind the Iron Curtain.

Budapest was built as the head of a much larger empire than it currently governs. Like Vienna, the city today feels a bit too grandiose for the capital of a relatively small country. But Budapest remains the heart and soul of Eastern Europe. It's a rich cultural stew made up of Hungarians, Germans, Slavs, and Jews, with a dash of Turkish paprika—simmered for centuries in a thermal bath. Each group has left its mark, but through it all, something has remained that is distinctly...Budapest.

Planning Your Time

Budapest demands at least three nights and two full days.

Day 1: Begin at the square called Vörösmarty tér (stop by TI and decide on today's and tomorrow evening's entertainment), consider coffee at Gerbeaud, and stroll down Váci utca (see page 315). At the end of the street, explore the Great Market Hall, a fine place for a characteristic lunch. Take tram #2 to the Chain Bridge, stroll over the bridge, and ride the funicular to Castle Hill. Following my self-guided walk (page 302), visit Matthias Church, Fisherman's Bastion, and the museums of your choice (the Commerce and Catering Museum is best). Speedy sightseers can zip out to Statue Park. After dinner, take a twilight sightseeing cruise, go to a concert (folk music nightly at 20:00) or the opera, or stroll the Danube embankments and bridges.

Day 2: Start at the Great Synagogue (opens at 10:00). Then walk past the square called Deák tér to reach St. István's Basilica at the base of Andrássy út (boulevard). From there, work your way up Andrássy út. Depending on your interests, you can stop at (in this order): the Postal Museum, the Opera House (duck in to see the lobby, or return later for a full-blown tour at 15:00 or 16:00), Franz Liszt Square (lots of lunch options), lively Oktogon square, and the House of Terror museum (least crowded early and late, allow 90 min to visit). To skip ahead (or backtrack quickly), hop on the M1 Metro line, which runs beneath the boulevard from start to finish. At the end of Andrássy út, explore Heroes' Square and the City Park. Reward yourself with a nice long soak in the Széchenyi Baths (secure lockers, rental suits, open until 19:00 in summer, last entry 18:00, get there by 17:00 to have enough time). The ritzy Gundel Restaurant is across from the baths. For the evening, consider the same options as for Day 1. To fit in Statue Park on Day 2, start with the statues in the morning, then do the Andrássy ramble (skipping the Synagogue and Opera tour to make it all fit).

You'll have no trouble filling a third day—it gives you more time to fit in Statue Park and more museums. After many years, I still discover new joys each time I return.

Eger is the most enjoyable day trip (2 hrs by train each way, even better if you spend the night—see Eger chapter). Szentendre, on the Danube Bend, is closer but very touristy (doable in a half day

Budapest

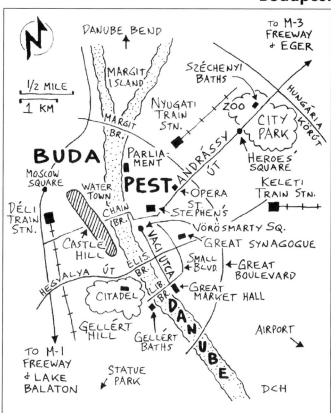

or even just in the late afternoon/evening). With a car (or a driver, cheaper than you'd think—see "Drivers," page 298), you could spend a day seeing the entire Danube Bend—Szentendre, Visegrád, and Esztergom—ideally on the way to Vienna or Bratislava (see Danube Bend chapter).

ORIENTATION

Budapest is big—with more than two million people, it's twice the size of Prague. The city is split down the center by the Danube River. On the west side of the Danube is hilly **Buda,** dominated by Castle Hill (packed with tourists by day, dead at night); the pleasant Víziváros ("Water Town"; VEE-zee-vah-rohsh) neighborhood is between the castle and the river.

On the east is flat **Pest** (pesht), the commercial heart of the city, which bustles day and night. The red-domed, riverside Parliament, visible from any point along the Danube, marks the northern edge of the tourists' Pest. A few blocks to the south, the Váci utca pedestrian drag runs parallel to the Danube, ending in the south at the steps of the Great Market Hall. From downtown, Andrássy út (and the yellow M1 Metro line beneath it) runs from the center of Pest (Deák Square) out past the Opera House to the Oktogon, House of Terror museum, Heroes' Square, City Park, and Széchenyi Baths.

Buda and Pest are connected by a series of very different **bridges.** From north to south, there's the relatively dull Margaret Bridge (Margit híd, crosses Margaret Island), the famous Chain Bridge (Széchenyi lánchíd), the white and modern Elisabeth Bridge (Erzsébet híd), and the green Liberty Bridge (Szabadság híd). The bridges are fun to cross by foot, but it's faster to go under the river (on the M2 line) or on a bus (#16 over the Chain Bridge and #8 across the Elisabeth Bridge are both handy).

Pest is surrounded by a series of **ring roads** *(körút)*. The innermost ring road—called the Kiskörút, or "Small Boulevard"—surrounds central Pest. The outer ring road—Nagykörút, or "Great Boulevard"— is about halfway between the river and City Park. The ring roads change names every few blocks, but they are always called *körút*. Arterial **boulevards** called *út* (such as Andrássy út) stretch from central Pest into the suburbs, like spokes on a wheel. Almost everything a tourist wants to see in Pest is either inside the innermost ring—in the **Belváros** ("Inner City")—or along one of these main boulevards (and therefore well-covered by public transit). Buda is also surrounded by a ring road, and the busy Hegyalja út rumbles through the middle of the tourists' Buda (between Castle and Gellért hills).

Budapest uses a **district** system (like Paris and Vienna), and addresses often start with the district number (as a Roman numeral). Districts are called *kerület*. Castle Hill is district I. Notice that the district number does not necessarily indicate how central a location is: Districts II and III are to the north of Buda, where few tourists go, while the very heart of Pest is district V.

Tourist Information

Budapest has five TIs. Four of them are run by the City of Budapest (www.budapestinfo.hu): **Castle Hill,** across from Matthias Church (mid-June–mid-Oct daily 9:00–20:00; mid-Oct–mid-March Mon–Fri 10:00–19:00, Sat-Sun 10:00–16:00; mid-March–mid-June daily 10:00–19:00; Szentháromság tér, tel. 1/488-0453); **Franz Liszt Square,** a block south of the Oktogon on Andrássy út (mid-June–mid-Sept daily 9:00–19:00; off-season Mon–Fri 10:00–18:00, Sat 10:00–16:00, closed Sun; Liszt Ferenc tér 11, tel. 1/322-4098); **Nyugati Train Station** (March–Oct daily 9:00–19:00; Nov–Feb Mon–Fri 9:00–18:00, Sat–Sun 9:00–15:00; tel. 1/302-8580); and at the **airport.**

Budapest Landmarks

English	Hungarian	Pronounced
Square	Tér	tehr (said pulling cheeks back)
Street	Utca	OOT-zah
Bath	Fürdő	FEWR-dur
(Buda) Castle	(Budai) vár	BOO-die vahr
Castle Hill	Várhegy	VAHR-hayj
Chain Bridge	Széchenyi lánchíd	SAY-chehn-yee LAHNTS-heed
Liberty Bridge (green, a.k.a. Franz Josef Bridge)	Szabadság híd	SAW-bawd-shahg heed
Elisabeth Bridge (white, modern)	Erzsébet híd	EHR-zheh-bayt heed
Margaret Bridge (crosses Margaret Island)	Margit híd	MAWR-geet heed
Danube River	Duna	DOO-naw
Eastern Rail Station	Keleti pályaudvar	KEH-leh-tee PAH-yuh-uhd-vahr
Western Rail Station	Nyugati pályaudvar	NYOO-gaw-tee PAH-yuh-uhd-vahr
Southern Rail Station	Déli pályaudvar	DAY-lee PAH-yuh-uhd-vahr
Suburban Train System	HÉV	hayv
City Park	Városliget	VAH-rohsh-lee-geht
Pest's main pedestrian street	Váci utca	VAH-tsee OOT-zah
Main square in Pest	Vörösmarty tér	VOO-roosh-mar-tee tehr
Grand boulevard	Andrássy út	AHN-drah-shee oot

The fifth TI, run by the Hungarian National Tourist Office (called TourInform), also provides information about other Hungarian destinations. This office, which generally seems uninterested in your questions compared to the city-run TIs, is just off **Deák tér** (daily 8:00–20:00, Sütő utca 2, tel. 1/318-8718, www.hungarytourism.hu).

At all of the TIs, you can collect a pile of free brochures (on sights, bus tours, and more). Most important: the free, good city map; the *Budapest Panorama* events guide; and the information-packed *Budapest Guide* booklet. TIs are handy places to buy your Budapest Card.

Budapest Card: The card, which is steadily increasing in cost, can be a good value for busy sightseers. Costing about $13 a day, it's a great tool, covering public transportation and entry to virtually all of Budapest's museums, plus discounts to other attractions, including boat tours and the Gellért Baths. With the Budapest Card, you have the freedom to hop the Metro for one stop to save 10 minutes of walking, or drop into that semi-interesting sight for a quick visit. Budapest has lots of quickie museums (rather than ones that merit a long visit). The card costs 4,900 Ft for 48 hours, or 5,700 Ft for 72 hours (includes handy 100-page booklet with maps, updated hours, and brief museum descriptions). You can buy the card all over Budapest—at TIs, travel agencies, major Metro stations, sights, and many hotels. Be sure to sign and date your card before you use it.

Arrival in Budapest

Budapest has three major train stations (*pályaudvar,* abbreviated *pu.*); the two most important are in Pest: **Keleti (Eastern) Station,** which handles most international trains and some domestic trains (such as those that connect to Eger), and the **Nyugati (Western) Station,** which has some international trains—especially those heading to the east—and many trains to the Danube Bend. Located in Buda, the **Déli (Southern) Station** (Déli pu.) has mostly domestic trains, including those to Lake Balaton.

The taxi stands in front of each train station are suspect—unless you want to get ripped off, it's better to call for one (see "Getting Around Budapest—By Taxi," page 300).

By Train at the Keleti (Eastern) Station: The Keleti Station (Keleti pu.) is just south of City Park, east of central Pest. On arrival, go to the front of the long tracks 6–9 to reach the exits and services. Near the head of the tracks cluster several travel agencies with "Tourist Information" signs; none is official, but all have a few helpful fliers, and most can sell you a Budapest Card. Along track 6, you'll find a baggage-check desk, an ATM (at K&H Bank), and international information and ticket windows (hiding down a hallway, look for *nemzetközi pénztár;* lockers nearby).

If you go out the front door, you'll stumble over a cluster of suspicious-looking taxis (call instead). The big staircase at the front of the tracks leads down to domestic ticket windows and WCs. To reach the Metro, go straight at the bottom of the stairs, then proceed straight through the open-air courtyard to the big "M" sign (M2 line, see "Getting Around Budapest—by Metro," below).

By Train at the Nyugati (Western) Station: The Nyugati Station (Nyugati pu.) is the most central of Budapest's stations, on the northeast edge of downtown Pest. Most international arrivals use tracks 1–5, which are set back from the main entrance. With these tracks at your back, exit straight ahead into a parking lot with

Sightseeing Modules

Budapest is a sprawling city, with sights scattered over a huge area. But if you organize your sightseeing efficiently and dive into the easy-to-master public transportation system, Budapest gets small. Break the city into manageable chunks, and digest them one at a time:

Buda
1. Castle Hill (Royal Palace, Matthias Church, and various museums)
2. Gellért Hill (Gellért Baths, Citadella, and Cave Church)

Pest
1. Central Pest, a.k.a. Belváros (north to south: Parliament and Kossuth Square, Vörösmarty Square, Váci utca, Danube embankment and cruises, Great Synagogue, and Great Market Hall)
2. Andrássy út (from center to outskirts: St. István's Basilica, Opera House, Oktogon, House of Terror, Heroes' Square, City Park, and Széchenyi Baths)

Near Budapest
1. Óbuda (Vasarely Museum, Imre Varga Collection, and Aquincum Roman ruins)
2. Statue Park
3. Danube Bend (begins just north of Óbuda: Szentendre, Visegrád, and Esztergom; see Danube Bend chapter)

taxis and buses, or use the stairs just inside the doors to reach an underpass and the Metro (M3 line, see "Getting Around Budapest—by Metro," below). If you're homesick, leave through the door that leads to the taxis and go immediately to the right to discover the huge, American-style **Westend Citycenter** mall (complete with a T.G.I. Friday's, daily 8:00–23:00).

To reach an official TI and ticket windows, follow tracks 10–13 to the station's main entrance. The TI is by the head of track 10 (March–Oct daily 9:00–19:00, Nov–Feb Mon–Fri 9:00–18:00, Sat–Sun 9:00–15:00). The TI can call you an honest taxi to avoid the crooked cabbies parked out front. Ticket windows are through an easy-to-miss door, across the tracks by platform 13 (marked *cassa* and *információ;* once you enter the ticket hall, international windows are in a second room at the far end—look for *nemzetközi*).

From the front of tracks 10–13, exit straight ahead and you'll be on Teréz körút, the very busy Great Boulevard ring road. (Váci utca, at the center of Pest, is dead ahead, about 20 minutes away by foot). In front of the building is another taxi stand and access to handy trams #4 and #6 (zipping all the way around Pest's great ring); to the right you'll find stairs leading to an underpass (use it to avoid crossing this busy intersection, or to reach the Metro's M3 line); and to the left you'll see the classiest Art Nouveau McDonald's on the planet. (Seriously. Take a look inside.)

By Car: A car is unnecessary at best and a headache at worst. Unless you're heading to an out-of-town sight (like Statue Park), park the car at your hotel and take public transportation. Public parking costs 120–400 Ft per hour (pay in advance at machine and put ticket on dashboard—watch locals and imitate; free parking Mon–Fri after 18:00, Sat after 12:00, and all day Sun—but you'll have to pay even on weekends in heavily touristed zones). A guarded parking lot is safer, but more expensive (figure 3,000–4,000 Ft per day, ask your hotel or look for the blue *P*s on maps).

By Plane: Ferihegy Airport is 15 miles east of Budapest. Hungarian Airlines uses Terminal A, and others use Terminal B. The general airport info line is tel. 1/296-9696 (departure info tel. 1/296-7000; www.bud.hu). The best inexpensive way downtown from the airport is by **minibus** (about 2,200 Ft per person to any hotel in the city center, 15 percent discount with Budapest Card—buy at airport TI, desk at arrival lobby, call 1/296-8555 to arrange a pickup). A **taxi** is a better deal for two or more people. A typical cab will charge about 5,000 Ft, but it's cheaper if you call Taxi 2000 (guaranteed no-meter rate of 3,000 Ft to Pest or 3,500 Ft to Buda, tel. 1/2000-000). The cheapest option is to take the BKV Plusz Reptér **bus** to the Kőbánya-Kispest M3 Metro station, and then take the Metro into town; allow about an hour total for the trip to the center.

Helpful Hints

Safety: Budapest feels—and is—safe, especially for a city of its size. While people routinely try to rip me off in Prague, I've never had a single problem in Budapest. Still, many of my readers report falling victim to scams and con artists in Budapest. As in any big city, it's especially important to beware of pickpockets in crowded and touristy places, particularly on the Metro and in trams. Wear a money belt and keep a close eye on your valuables.

Keep your wits about you and refuse to be bullied or distracted. Any deal that seems too good to be true—such as "discounted taxi vouchers" from the boat dock to your hotel—probably is. If you're a male in a touristy area and a gorgeous local girl (*konzumlany,* or "consumption girl") takes a liking to you, avoid her. The only foreplay going on here will climax in your grand rip-off. Another common scam involves a man stopping you on the street to "change money." A policeman arrests him—and you—and needs to see your wallet to find out if he's a con artist. They are a team and you are being robbed. And, as in many big cities, the famous shell games on the streets have everybody winning...until you give it a try.

Budapest's biggest crooks? Unscrupulous cabbies (see "Getting Around Budapest—By Taxi," page 300). I've said it before, I'll say it again: Locals *always* call for a cab, rather than hail one on the street or at a taxi stand.

Blue Monday: Virtually all of Budapest's museums are closed on Mondays. But never fear. You can still take advantage of these sights and activities: Both major baths, Statue Park, Great Synagogue, Matthias Church on Castle Hill, St. István's Basilica, Parliament tour, Opera House tour, City Park (and Zoo), Great Market Hall, Danube cruises, concerts, and bus and walking tours.

Internet Access: You'll find the easiest access (and highest prices) along the touristy north end of the Váci utca pedestrian drag in Pest. They all seem to charge about 800 Ft per hour. In Buda's Víziváros neighborhood, try the Soho Coffee Company (on Fő utca—see page 350).

Post Offices: These are marked with a smart green *poszta* logo (usually open Mon–Fri 8:00–18:00, Sat 8:00–12:00, closed Sun).

Banking: Banks are generally open Mon–Thu 8:00–15:00, Fri 8:00–13:00, closed Sat–Sun.

Laundry: Options are scarce. The most central is **Patyolat** at the corner of Vármegye utca and Városház utca (just up from Váci utca). The laundry ladies will monitor your use of the "self-service" facilities (allow 2,500 Ft to wash and dry a load, Mon–Fri 7:00–19:00, closed Sat–Sun). For full service, try your hotel or go to **Laundry Házimosoda,** centrally located in Pest between the Danube and Váci utca (figure 600 Ft per shirt, 950 Ft for pants, pick up after 17:00 the following day, Mon–Fri 7:30–19:00, Sat 9:00–13:00, closed Sun, Galamb utca 9).

English Newspaper: For an English-speaking expatriate take on the city, including listings of movies in English, pick up a copy of the weekly *Budapest Sun* (359 Ft, sold at newsstands).

Local Guidebook: András Török's *Budapest: A Critical Guide* is the best book by a local writer (available in English at most souvenir stands).

Bookstores: **Red Bus Bookstore**, run by the hostel of the same name, has shelves of used books in English, and they buy books, too (Mon–Fri 11:00–18:00, Sat 10:00–14:00, closed Sun, Semmelweis utca 14, tel. 1/337-7453). If all of this complicated history and culture piques your interest, **Central European University Bookshop** has the best selection anywhere of scholarly books about this region (all in English, Mon–Fri 9:00–18:00, closed Sat–Sun, Nádor utca 9, tel. 1/327-3096).

This university is predominantly funded by George Soros, a Hungarian who emigrated to the United States, only to become a billionaire and high-profile donor to Democratic causes.

Travel Agencies: Carlson Wagonlit Travel is 40 yards north of Pest's Vörösmarty tér and handy for rail and air needs (625-Ft service charge for train tickets, Mon–Fri 9:00–12:30 & 13:30–17:00, closed Sat–Sun, Dorottya utca 3, tel. 1/483-3380, www.carlsonwagonlit.hu). **Vista Travel Center**, at the base of Andrássy út, is a sprawling, user-friendly travel service with cheap flights, all the train ticket and reservation services, guidebooks, hotels, tours, and so on. Step in and grab a number from the receptionist (Mon–Fri 9:00–18:30, Sat 9:00–14:30, closed Sun, Andrássy út 1, tel. 1/429-9999). The central **MÁV** (National Hungarian Railways) train office, a block past the Opera House at the corner of Andrássy and Nagymező, is useful for any train ticket business you may have (Mon–Fri 9:00–18:00, until 17:00 Oct–March, closed Sat–Sun, www.mav.hu/eng).

Drivers: Friendly, English-speaking **Gábor Balázs** can drive you around the city or into the surrounding countryside (3,500 Ft/hr, 3-hr minimum in city, 4-hr minimum in countryside—good for a Danube Bend excursion, mobile 0620/936-4317, balazs.gabor@chello.hu). **József Király** runs a 10-car company with good, generally English-speaking drivers (€17/hr, more for larger cars and vans, mobile 0630/949-1253, artoli@axelero.hu).

Best Views: Budapest is a city of marvelous vistas. Some of the best are from the Citadella (high on Gellért Hill), the promenade in front of Buda Castle, the embankments or many bridges spanning the Danube (especially the Chain Bridge), and tour boats on the Danube—lovely at night. For a sky-high view down on Budapest, try the tethered **Budapest Eye** (Budapest Kilátó) balloon ride at the Westend Citycenter mall (next to Nyugati Station; 2,000 Ft for 15-min ride, daily 10:00–22:00 in summer, 12:00–20:00 in winter, in good weather only).

Getting Around Budapest

Budapest is huge. Connecting your sightseeing by foot is tedious and unnecessary; use the excellent public transportation system instead. The same tickets work for the Metro, trams, and buses (buy them at kiosks, Metro ticket windows, or machines; the new machines are slick and easy, but the old orange ones are trickier: Put in the appropriate amount of money—see below—then press button).

Your options are:

- Single ticket (*vonaljegy*, for a ride of up to an hour with no transfers) for 145 Ft
- Short single Metro ride (*metroszakaszjegy*, 3 stops or fewer on the Metro) for 105 Ft

- Transfer ticket (*átszállójegy*—allowing up to 90 minutes, including 1 transfer) for 250 Ft
- Unlimited travelcards (1,150 Ft/1 day, 2,300 Ft/3 days, 2,600 Ft/7 days)—but if you're here more than a day and plan to sightsee, you might as well get a Budapest Card instead (see "Tourist Information," above).

Always validate your ticket as you enter the bus, tram, or Metro station (stick it in the little elbow-high box). A transfer ticket must be validated a second time (at the other end of the ticket) when you transfer. The stern-looking guys with red armbands waiting as you exit the Metro want to see your validated ticket or signed and dated Budapest Card. Cheaters get fined 2,000 Ft, and you'll be surprised how often you're checked (some locals claim they target tourists). All public transit runs until 23:00. A useful route-planning Web site is www.bkv.hu.

By Metro: Riding Budapest's Metro, you really feel like you're down in the efficient guts of the city. It's every bit as convenient and slick as Paris', Vienna's, or Berlin's—but it has more character than those stodgy systems.

There are three lines:

- **M1 (yellow)**—The first Metro line on the Continent, this shallow line runs under Andrássy út from the center to City Park.
- **M2 (red)**—Built during the communist days, it's 115 feet deep, doubles as a bomb shelter, and comes with a tornado ventilation system—notice the gale. The only line going under the Danube to Buda, M2 connects the Déli station, Moszkva tér (where you catch the *vár* bus to the top of Castle Hill), Batthyány tér (where you catch the HÉV train to Óbuda or Szentendre), and the Keleti station.
- **M3 (blue)**—This line makes a broad, boomerang-shaped swoop north to south.

The three lines cross only once: at the **Deák tér** stop (sometimes signed as "Deák Ferenc tér") in the heart of Pest, where Andrássy út begins. Most M2 and M3 Metro stations are at intersections of ring roads and other major arterials. You'll usually exit the Metro into a confusing underpass. These are packed with kiosks, fast-food stands, and makeshift markets—but orange directional signs help you find the right exit.

The Metro stops themselves are usually very well marked, with a list of upcoming stops on the wall behind the tracks. The red digital clocks tell you how long it's been since the last train left; you'll rarely wait more than five or six minutes for the next.

You'll ride very long, steep, fast-moving escalators to access the M2 and M3 lines. Hang on tight, enjoy the breeze as trains below shoot through the tunnels...and don't make yourself dizzy by trying to read the Burger King ads.

By Tram: Budapest's trams are handy and frequent, taking you virtually anywhere the Metro doesn't. Here are some trams you might use:

Trams #2 and #2A: Run along Pest's Danube embankment.

Tram #19: Runs along Buda's Danube embankment, stopping at Gellért Hotel, the bottom of the Castle Hill funicular (Adam Clark tér), several recommended Víziváros hotels, and Batthyány tér (end of the line, M2 Metro station and HÉV trains to Óbuda and Szentendre).

Trams #4 and #6: Zip around Pest's Great Boulevard ring road (Nagykörút), connecting the Nyugati Station and Oktogon with Buda's Moszkva tér (M2 Metro station).

Trams #47 and #49: Connect the Gellért Baths in Buda with Pest's Small Boulevard ring road (Kiskörút), with stops at the Great Market Hall, the National Museum, the Great Synagogue, and Deák tér (end of the line).

By Bus: The tram and Metro network can get you nearly anywhere, so you're less likely to take a bus. One exception is getting to the top of Castle Hill—accessible only by the *várbusz* ("castle bus," from Moszkva tér—see page 302). Bus #16 is handy (Deák tér, Roosevelt tér, crosses Chain Bridge, Adam Clark tér, and up to Dísz tér atop Castle Hill near the Royal Palace).

By Taxi: Budapest's public transportation is good enough that you probably won't need to take many taxis. If you do, you may run into a dishonest driver. Locals always call a cab from a reputable company (Taxi 2000, tel. 1/2000-000; or Főtaxi, tel. 1/222-2222, toll-free 0680/222-222).

Cabbies are not allowed to charge more than a drop rate of 300 Ft, and then 240 Ft per kilometer (more expensive 22:00–6:00)—though the more reputable companies charge less. Prices are per ride, not per passenger. A 10 percent tip is expected.

Many cabs you'd hail on the streets are there only to prey on rich, green tourists. Avoid hotel taxis, unmarked taxis, and cabs waiting at tourist spots and train stations. If you do wave down a cab on the street, choose one that's marked with a company logo and telephone number. Ask for a rough estimate before you get in—if it doesn't sound reasonable, walk away. If you wind up being dramatically overcharged for a ride, simply pay what you think is fair and go inside. If the driver follows you (unlikely), your hotel receptionist will defend you.

TOURS

Bus Tours—Several companies run bus tours that glide past all the big sights (not hop-on, hop-off). A basic three-hour bus tour will run you about 6,000 Ft per person, and the different companies are essentially the same; pick up fliers at the TI or in your hotel lobby.

These companies also run a wide variety of other tours, including dinner boat cruises and trips to the Danube Bend. Perhaps the best quickie is **Budatours'** two-hour swing through town, with headphone commentary and one photo stop off the bus (4,300 Ft, covered bus leaves at 10:30 and 13:30 year-round, open-top bus in summer at 10:30 and 13:30, peak season hrly 9:30–17:30, departs from Andrássy út 3, near M1: Bajcsy-Zsilinszky).

Walking Tours—The youthful **Absolute Walking Tours**—run by an American, Ben Friday—offers an overview tour (4,000 Ft, June–Sept daily at 9:30 and 13:30, Oct–May daily at 10:30, Sat–Sun only in Jan, 3–4 hrs). Their inventive "Hammer and Sickle" tour includes a visit to Statue Park (5,000 Ft, departs 10:30, 4/week, 3 hrs). Their pub crawl sometimes continues late into the night (5,000 Ft, departs 20:00, 4/week, at least 3 hrs). All tours depart from Deák tér (tel. 1/266-8777, www.absolutetours.com). Travelers with this book get a 500-Ft discount in 2005, as does anyone under 26.

Private Guides—Budapest has plenty of enthusiastic, hardworking young guides who speak fine English and enjoy showing off their exciting city. Considering the reasonable fees and efficient use of your time, hiring your own personal expert is an excellent value. I have two favorites: **Peter Polczman** charges €70 for a four- or five-hour tour and €100 for a full day (mobile 0620/926-0557, polczman @freestart.hu or peter.polczman@guideclub.net). **Andrea Makkay** leads four-hour tours (20,000 Ft by foot, or 24,000 Ft by car) and seven-hour tours (35,000 Ft by foot, or 42,000 Ft by car, mobile 0620/9629-363, tel. 28/440-696, amakkay@axelero.hu, arrange details by e-mail). Both Peter and Andrea are good within town and for side-tripping up the Danube Bend.

Danube Boat Tours—Cruising the Danube, while touristy, is fun and convenient. The most established company, Legenda, runs boats day and night. By day, the one-hour cruise costs 3,600 Ft (2,750 Ft with Budapest Card) and includes an optional one-hour walking tour around Margaret Island, Budapest's playground (6/day July–Aug, 4/day May–June and Sept, 2/day mid-March–April, 1/day Oct, 1/day Fri–Sat only Nov–mid-Dec, no cruises mid-Dec–Feb).

By night, the one-hour cruise (with no Margaret Island option) costs 4,200 Ft (3,250 Ft with Budapest Card, 3/day May–Sept, 1/day mid-March–April and Oct–mid-Dec, no cruises mid-Dec–Feb).

Both cruises include two drinks and headphone commentary. TV monitors show the interior of the great buildings as you float by. The Legenda dock is in front of the Marriott on the Pest embankment (find pedestrian access under tram tracks just downriver from Vigadó tér, tel. 1/317-2203, www.legenda.hu).

SIGHTS

Buda

Castle Hill (Várhegy)

Buda's main sights are all on Castle Hill. While many visitors expect this high-profile district to be time-consuming, for most it's enough to simply stroll through in a couple of hours. The major landmarks are the huge, green-domed Royal Palace at the south end of the hill (housing 3 ho-hum museums) and the frilly-spired Matthias Church near the north end. In between are tourist-filled pedestrian streets and historic buildings. Several interesting but non-essential museums are also scattered around the hill. I've listed the sights in order from south to north, and linked them together on a self-guided tour.

Getting to Castle Hill: The Metro and trams won't take you to the top of Castle Hill. You can hike, taxi, ride the funicular (see below), or catch bus #16 from either side of the Chain Bridge (departs from Deák, Roosevelt, and Adam Clark squares). A special **castle bus** *(várbusz)* does a loop from Moszkva tér (Moscow Square) north of the castle (M2: Moszkva tér, bus stops just uphill from Metro station, look for small bus with the words *vár* or *Dísz tér* and a little picture of a castle). Castle Hill buses are specially designed to be light, as the hill is honeycombed with limestone caves. You'll notice the hill is a gated community with carefully regulated traffic.

The **funicular** *(sikló)*, lifting visitors from the Chain Bridge to the top of Castle Hill, is a Budapest landmark. Built in 1870 to provide cheap transportation to Castle Hill workers, today it's a pricey little tourist trip. Read the fun first-person history you'll see in glass cases at the top station (600 Ft up, 500 Ft down, not covered by Budapest Card, daily 7:30–22:00, departs every 5 min, closed for maintenance every other Mon).

From the funicular, enjoy the views of the Danube and go a few yards to the big bird at the top of the stairs overlooking the immense palace. You can survey the scene from here, or wander to the equestrian statue and circle through and around the huge building.

The Turul—This mythical bird of Magyar folk tales watches over the palace. The *turul* led the Hungarian migrations in the 9th century. He dropped his sword in the Carpathian Basin, indicating that this was to be the permanent home of the Magyar people. During a surge of nationalism in the 1920s, a movement named after this bird helped revive traditional Hungarian culture. *Turul* birds also top the towers of the green Liberty Bridge, just downriver.

Royal Palace (Királyi Palota)—The imposing palace on Castle Hill is a dull contemporary construction, barely hinting at the colorful story of this hill since the day that the legendary *turul* dropped his sword.

Originally, the main city of Hungary wasn't Buda or Pest, but Esztergom (just up the river; see Danube Bend chapter). In the

Buda Center Sights

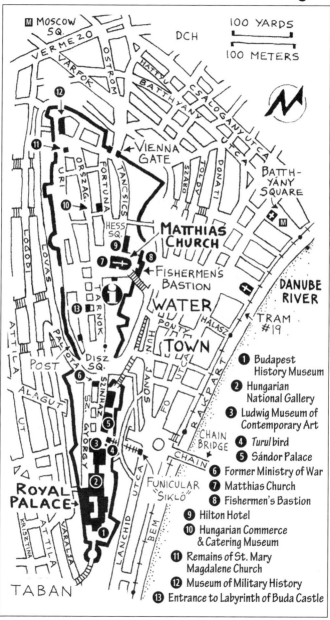

100 YARDS

100 METERS

❶ Budapest History Museum
❷ Hungarian National Gallery
❸ Ludwig Museum of Contemporary Art
❹ Turul bird
❺ Sándor Palace
❻ Former Ministry of War
❼ Matthias Church
❽ Fishermen's Bastion
❾ Hilton Hotel
❿ Hungarian Commerce & Catering Museum
⑪ Remains of St. Mary Magdalene Church
⑫ Museum of Military History
⑬ Entrance to Labyrinth of Buda Castle

Budapest at a Glance

▲▲▲**Baths** Budapest's steamy soaking scene—the city's best attraction. **Hours:** Széchenyi Baths in Pest, popular with locals—May–Sept daily 6:00–19:00, Oct–April Mon–Fri 6:00–19:00, Sat–Sun 6:00–17:00; touristy Gellért Baths in Buda—May–Sept daily 6:00–19:00, thermal bath only until 17:00 Sat–Sun, Oct–April Mon–Fri 6:00–19:00, Sat–Sun 6:00–17:00.

▲▲**Matthias Church** Landmark neo-Gothic church in Buda with revered 16th-century statue of Mary and Jesus. **Hours:** Mon–Sat 9:00–17:00, Sun 13:00–17:00, sometimes closed Sat after 13:00.

▲▲**Váci utca** Hopping pedestrian boulevard and tourist magnet in Pest with the East's first McDonald's. **Hours:** Always open.

▲▲**Great Market Hall** Colorful Old World mall in Pest with produce, cheap eateries, souvenirs, and great people-watching. **Hours:** Mon 6:00–17:00, Tue–Fri 6:00–18:00, Sat 6:00–14:00, closed Sun.

▲▲**House of Terror** Harrowing remembrance of Nazis and communist secret police in former headquarters/torture site in Pest. **Hours:** Tue–Fri 10:00–18:00, Sat–Sun 10:00–19:30, closed Mon.

▲▲**Heroes' Square** Mammoth tribute in Pest to Hungary's historic figures, fringed by a couple of art museums and Countryrama 3-D movie. **Hours:** Square always open, sights closed Mon.

▲▲**City Park** Pest's backyard, with Art Nouveau zoo, Transylvanian castle, amusement park, and Széchenyi Baths. **Hours:** Park always open.

▲▲**Statue Park** Larger-than-life communist big shots all collected in one park, on the outskirts of town. **Hours:** Daily 10:00–sunset.

▲**Fishermen's Bastion** Neo-Romanesque rampart in Buda with fabulous Parliament views across the Danube. **Hours:** Rampart always open; bastion climb daily 9:00–22:00.

13th century, Tartars swept through Eastern Europe, destroying much of Hungary. King Béla IV decided to rebuild a walled Buda here, a more protected location in the interior of the country. The city has dominated the region ever since, gradually becoming the Hungarian capital. Béla IV was smart enough to divide his new town of Buda in half between two feuding factions: the native Hungarians and the Germans, who came here to trade. They each had their own turf and church (we'll see both farther along the hill).

▲**Hungarian Commerce and Catering Museum** Intriguing time-tunnel look at 19th-century businesses. **Hours:** Wed–Fri 10:00–17:00, Sat–Sun 10:00–18:00, closed Mon–Tue.

▲**Vörösmarty tér** Lively people-watching square in Pest with venerable Gerbeaud café. **Hours:** Always open.

▲**Hungarian Parliament** Vast, riverside neo-Gothic government center in Pest. **Hours:** Tours usually daily at 10:00, 12:00, 14:00, and 18:00.

▲**Great Synagogue** The world's second largest after New York's, with museum and garden memorial in Pest. **Hours:** April–Oct Mon–Thu 10:00–17:00, Fri and Sun 10:00–14:00; Nov–March Mon–Thu 10:00–15:00, Fri and Sun 10:00–14:00; always closed Sat and Jewish holidays, often closed mid-Dec–mid-Jan.

▲**Holocaust Memorial Center** Excellent new center honoring Hungarian victims of the Holocaust. **Hours:** Tue–Sun 10:00–18:00, closed Mon.

▲**Danube Embankment** Pest's best stretch for a riverside stroll. **Hours:** Always open.

▲**Chain Bridge** Landmark lion-gated beauty connecting Pest and Buda. **Hours:** Always open.

▲**Postal Museum** Funky tribute to old postal service objects in elegant old Pest mansion. **Hours:** Tue–Sun 10:00–18:00, closed Mon.

▲**Hungarian State Opera House** Neo-Renaissance splendor and affordable opera in Pest. **Hours:** Lobby/box office open Mon–Sat 11:00–19:00, Sun 16:00–19:00; English tours nearly daily at 15:00 and 16:00; performances nearly nightly.

▲**Imre Varga Collection** Evocative sculpture collection capturing communist times, in Óbuda. **Hours:** Tue–Sun 10:00–18:00, closed Mon; artist visits at 10:00 Sat.

The first Hungarian dynasty (the Árpáds) died out in 1301, and a new French line—the Anjous (or Angevins)—took over Buda and the rest of Hungary. They replaced Béla IV's modest castle with a luxurious palace that expanded over the years until the early 15th century, when it was one of Europe's biggest. The 15th-century King Mátyás Corvinus made the palace even more extravagant, putting Buda—and Hungary—on the map.

Just a few decades later, the invading Ottoman Turks occupied

Buda and turned the elegant palace into a garrison. When the Hapsburgs laid siege to the hill for 77 days in 1686, gunpowder stored in the cellar exploded, destroying the palace. The Hapsburgs took the hill, but Buda was deserted and in ruins. The town was resettled by Austrians, who built a new Baroque palace, hoping that the Hapsburg monarch would move in—but none ever did (preferring to live up the river in Vienna, or occasionally in Prague). The useless palace became a garrison, then a university, and later the viceroy's residence. It was damaged again during the 1848 Revolution, but was repaired and continued to grow right along with Budapest's prominence.

As World War II drew to a close, Buda became the front line between the Nazis and the approaching Soviets, who laid siege to the hill for six months. The palace was again destroyed.

Most Budapesters (and historians) don't much care for the current tame, and historically inaccurate, post-WWII reconstruction of the palace. It's a loose rebuilding of previous versions, lacking the style and sense of history that this important site deserves. The most prominent feature of today's palace—the green dome—didn't even exist in earlier versions.

The palace has several museums. Visit one now (listed below), or head to Matthias Church from here (Castle Hill self-guided tour continues below).

Castle Museums—The palace houses three worthwhile (but not must-see) museums. The history museum is my favorite; both art museums rank low on a European scale. The first two listed below are off of the big enclosed courtyard (make your way into the courtyard on the other side of the dome; once you're there, face the dome: the Budapest History Museum is behind you, and the National Gallery is at 2 o'clock). The third is just north of the courtyard, across from the fancy fountain monument to Mátyás Corvinus.

The **Budapest History Museum** (Budapesti Történeti Múzeum), a good but stodgy museum crying out for a makeover, celebrates the earlier grandeur of Castle Hill. If Budapest really intrigues you, this is a fine place to learn about its history. You'll start at the top floor and work down. Along the way, you'll see artifacts of Budapest's prehistoric residents and a good collection of 14th-century sculptures, many of them with strong Magyar features—notice that they look Central Asian, like Mongolians. The highlight is the "Budapest in the Modern Times" exhibit, tracing the last two rocky centuries of the city, with a focus on the gradual movement towards merging Buda and Pest. The basement illustrates just how much this hill has changed over the centuries—and how tame today's version is in comparison. You'll wander through a maze of old palace parts, including the remains of an original

Gothic chapel, a knights' hall, and marble remnants (reliefs and fountains) of Mátyás Corvinus' lavish Renaissance palace (800 Ft, covered by Budapest Card, good English descriptions posted, others are borrowable, mid-May–mid-Sept daily 10:00–18:00; March–mid-May and mid-Sept–Oct Wed–Mon 10:00–18:00, closed Tue; Nov–Feb Wed–Mon 10:00–16:00, closed Tue; tel. 1/225-7815).

The huge **Hungarian National Gallery** (Magyar Nemzeti Galéria) has an excellent collection of 15th-century winged altars, plus halls and halls of paintings and sculptures by Hungarian artists you've never heard of—for good reason (free, charge for special exhibitions, March–Nov Tue–Sun 10:00–18:00, closed Mon; Dec–Feb Tue–Sun 10:00–16:00, closed Mon, tel. 1/375-8584).

The **Ludwig Museum of Contemporary Art** (Kortárs Művészeti Múzeum) features mostly Hungarian artists, with a few lesser works by the likes of Picasso and American Pop Artists Warhol and Lichtenstein. Almost everything is on the top floor, displayed around a grand atrium (600 Ft, covered by Budapest Card, Tue–Sun 10:00–18:00, Thu until 20:00, closed Mon, tel. 1/375-9175, www.ludwigmuseum.hu).

From the Funicular and Royal Palace to Matthias Church: To connect the palace to Matthias Church, the closest major sight, follow this self-guided walk:

From the *turul* bird and the top of the funicular (with your back to the Royal Palace), walk along the non-river side of the big white building, **Sándor Palace.** This mansion underwent a very costly renovation under the previous Hungarian prime minister, who hoped to make it his residence. But in 2002, the same year it was finished, he lost his bid for reelection. The spunky new PM refused to move in. By way of compromise, the president now lives here.

As you continue along the side of Sándor Palace, you'll notice the remains of a medieval monastery and church in the field to your left. Beyond that, past the flagpoles, is the ongoing excavation of the medieval Jewish quarter—more reminders that most of what you see on today's Castle Hill has been destroyed and rebuilt many times over.

After Sándor Palace, you'll pass the yellow National Dance Theater, where Beethoven once performed. Beyond that on the left is the still-damaged building that used to house the **Ministry of War.** Most of the bullet holes are from World War II; others were left by the Soviets who occupied this hill in response to the 1956 Uprising. The building is a political hot potato—prime real estate, but nobody can decide what to do with it. (Note that 50 yards beyond the Ministry of War is a bus stop for bus #16, offering a quick return to the Pest side of the Chain Bridge.)

Mátyás Corvinus: The Last Hungarian King

The Árpád dynasty—descendants of the original Magyar tribes—died out in 1301. For more than 600 years, Hungary would be ruled by foreigners...with one exception.

In the middle of the 15th century, Hungary had bad luck hanging on to its foreign kings: Two of them died unexpectedly within seven years. Meanwhile, military general János Hunyadi was enjoying great success on the battlefield against the Turks. When the five-year-old Ladislas V was elected king, Hunyadi was appointed regent and essentially ruled the country. Hunyadi defeated the Turks in the 1456 Battle of Belgrade—temporarily preventing them from entering Hungary—but he died of the plague soon after.

When Ladislas died in 1458 at the tender age of 16, Hunyadi's son, Mátyás (Matthias), rode his father's coattails to victory among the Hungarian nobility—becoming the first Hungarian-descended king in more than 150 years. Mátyás Hunyadi took the nickname Corvinus (Latin for "raven," which appears on his coat of arms). Progressive and well-educated, Mátyás Corvinus (r. 1458–1490) was the quintessential Renaissance king—a benefactor of the poor and a true humanist. He patronized the arts and built palaces legendary for their beauty. He dressed up as a commoner and ventured

Cross the street and continue uphill through "Parade Square" (Dísz tér) and up **Tárnok utca.** This area often disappoints visitors. After being destroyed by Turks, it was rebuilt in sensible Baroque, lacking the romantic time-capsule charm of a medieval old town (like perfectly preserved Prague or Kraków). But if you poke your head into some courtyards, you'll almost always see some original Gothic arches and other medieval features.

Continue along the street; after two blocks, past the TI (on your right), you'll see a warty plague column marking the main square of old Buda. It faces...

▲▲**Matthias Church (Mátyás Templom)**—One of Budapest's landmarks, Matthias Church has been destroyed and rebuilt several times in the 800 years since it was founded by King Béla IV.

The prominent church has a sumptuous gilded interior with a Gothic nucleus. The frilly, flamboyant steeple and other fanciful elements were added for the 1896 celebrations. Inside it's wallpapered with motifs reminiscent of various stages in local history since 896: Turkish rule, Magyar folk designs, and the Renaissance era—all under Gothic arches. Notice the 500-year-old Hungarian battalion banners, left here after the Mass that celebrated János Hunyadi's 1456 victory over the Turks. The stained glass is 160 into the streets to see firsthand how the nobles of his realm treated his people.

Mátyás was a strong, savvy leader. He created Central Europe's first standing army—30,000 mercenaries known as the Black Army. No longer reliant on the nobility for military support, Good King Mátyás was able to drain power from the nobles and make taxation of his subjects more equitable—earning him the nickname the "people's king."

King Mátyás was also a shrewd military tactician. Realizing that squabbling with the Turks would squander his resources, he made peace with the Ottoman sultan to stabilize Hungary's southern border. Then he swept north, invading Moravia, Bohemia, and even Austria. By 1485, Mátyás moved into his new palace in Vienna, and Hungary was enjoying a golden age.

Five years later, Mátyás died mysteriously at the age of 47, and his empire disintegrated. It is said that when Mátyás died, justice died with him. To this day, Hungarians consider him the greatest of all kings, and they sing of his siege of Vienna in their national anthem. They're proud that for a few decades in the middle of half a millennium of foreign oppression, they had a truly Hungarian king—and a great one at that.

years old; during World War II, it was removed and hidden to avoid destruction.

The **Loreto Chapel** (rear of nave, left of stairs) holds the church's prize possession. Peer through the black iron grill to see

the 1515 statue of Mary and Jesus. Anticipating Turkish plundering, locals walled over this precious statue. The occupying Turks used the church as their primary mosque—oblivious to the statue plastered over in the niche. Then, a century and a half later, during the siege of Buda in 1686, gunpowder stored in the castle up the street detonated, and the wall crumbled. Mary's triumphant face showed through, freaking out the Turks. According to legend, this was the only part of town taken from the Turks without a fight. Ever since, the church has officially been the Church of Our Lady. But it's more commonly referred to as Matthias Church, for the popular Renaissance king who got married here...twice (550 Ft, covered by Budapest Card, 12-stop audioguide-220 Ft, Mon–Sat 9:00–17:00, Sun 13:00–17:00, sometimes closed Sat after

13:00 for weddings, Szentháromság tér 2, tel. 1/355-5657, www.matyas-templom.hu).

The upstairs gallery holds the **Museum of Ecclesiastical Art** (Egyházművészeti Gyűjteménye, same ticket and hours as church). The original Hungarian crown is under the Parliament's dome, and a hassle to visit (see page 319), but a replica is up here, and worth a peek.

Toward the Danube from Matthias Church is the...

▲**Fishermen's Bastion (Halászbástya)**—This neo-Romanesque fantasy rampart offers beautiful views over the Danube to Pest. In the Middle Ages, the fish market was just below here (in today's Víziváros, or "Water Town"), so this part of the rampart actually *was* guarded by fishermen. The current structure, though, is completely artificial—one more example of Budapest sprucing itself up for 1896 (see page 327). Its seven towers represent the seven Magyar tribes. The cone-headed arcades are reminiscent of tents the nomadic Magyars called home before they moved west to Europe.

Survey Pest across the Danube from this viewpoint. The two domes are the Parliament and St. István's Basilica—both 96 meters high, built in...you guessed it...1896. The Chain Bridge cuts Pest in two: The left half is administrative, with government ministries, embassies, banks, and so on; the right half (stretching to the modern, white Elisabeth Bridge) is the commercial center of Pest, with the best riverside promenade (do this tonight).

Paying to climb up the bastion makes little sense (300 Ft, not covered by Budapest Card, daily 9:00–22:00, probably free Oct–mid-March and after 22:00). Enjoy virtually the same view through the windows (left of café) for free. The café offers a scenic break if you don't mind the tour groups.

Statue of St. István (Stephen)—Hungary's first Christian king sits atop his horse in the courtyard between the church and the bastion. He tamed the nomadic and pagan Magyars, established strict laws and the concept of private property, and made his people Christian. The reliefs show the pope crowning St. István (EESHT-vahn) in the year 1000, bringing Hungary into Christendom. This meant the rest of Europe was now inclined to help Hungary against the Turks and to bully Slavs. Without this pivotal event, locals believe that the Magyar nation would have been lost. A passionate evangelist—more for the survival of his Magyar nation than for the salvation of his people—István beheaded those who wouldn't convert. To make his point perfectly clear, he quartered his reluctant uncle and sent him on four separate, simultaneous tours of the country to show Hungarians that Christianity was a smart choice. Gruesome as he was, István was sainted within 30 years of his death.

To continue your exploration of Buda, take a self-guided walk along...

North Castle Hill—The following stroll takes you through Buda north of Matthias Church. As this was the site of the Nazi military headquarters, it was heavily bombed towards the end of World War II. (During a 6-week siege, 30 percent of the city was destroyed.)

Leave the courtyard beside the church and turn right—passing the 1713 Holy Trinity plague column on your left—so that you're walking along the front of the glassy modern **Hilton Hotel.** To minimize the controversy of building upon so much history, architects thoughtfully incorporated the medieval ruins into its modern design. Built in 1976, the Hilton was the first plush Western hotel in town. Before 1989, it was a gleaming center of capitalism, offering a cushy refuge for Western travelers and a stark contrast to what was, at the time, a very gloomy city. Halfway down the hotel's facade, you'll see fragments of a 13th-century wall, with a monument to the Renaissance King Mátyás Corvinus.

After the wall, continue along the second half of the Hilton Hotel facade. Turn right into the gift-shop entry, and then go right again inside the second glass door. Stairs on the left lead down to a reconstructed 13th-century Dominican cloister; at the far end of the cloister are more stairs, to the Faust Wine Cellar (daily 16:00–23:00), a friendly place with fine wine by the glass. For an even better look at what was here back then, go back up the stairs and turn left. As you enter the lounge, look out the back windows to see fragments of the 13th-century Dominican church incorporated into the structure of the hotel. If you stood here eight centuries ago, you'd be looking straight down the church's nave. You can even see tomb markers in the ground.

Back out on the street, cross the little park and duck into the entryway of the **Fortuna Passage.** Along the passageway to the courtyard, you can see the original Gothic arches of the house that once stood here. In the Middle Ages, every homeowner had the right to sell wine without paying taxes—but only in the passage of his own home. He'd set up a table here, and his neighbors would come by to taste the latest vintage. These passageways evolved into very social places, like the corner pub.

Leaving the Fortuna, turn left down Fortuna utca, where after a block you'll find the excellent little...

▲Hungarian Commerce and Catering Museum (Magyar Kereskedelmi és Vendéglátóipari Múzeum)—Far more interesting than it sounds, this museum—filling two ground-floor wings of an old building—takes a nostalgic look at workaday 19th-century Pest commerce. With the help of good English descriptions, you'll enjoy a peek into the fancy hotels, restaurants, and coffeehouses of the day. There's even a section on the 1896 festivities, including

Hungarian Revolutions

Foreign powers who have oppressed the Hungarians have found them tough to keep under control. Two revolutions in particular stand out. In each case, the Hungarians initially encountered bloodshed and more oppression, but ultimately brought about positive change. The dates these revolutions began remain national holidays.

Lajos Kossuth and the 1848 Revolution

Of the many Hungarian uprisings against Hapsburg rule (1526–1918), the 1848 Revolution was the most dramatic. In 1848, a wave of nationalism spread across Europe. The spirit of change caught on in Hungary, where lawyer and parliamentarian Lajos Kossuth led an uprising sparked on March 15. Though the Austrians were initially overwhelmed by the revolt, they eventually brought in Russian troops to regain control. For a few years, the Hapsburgs cracked down on their Hungarian subjects—but within 20 years, they ceded half the authority of their empire to Budapest, creating the Dual Monarchy.

Imre Nagy and the 1956 Uprising

The Hungarian politician Imre Nagy (EEM-ray nodge, 1896–1958)

---

kitschy souvenirs. The second half (across the driveway, opposite the entrance) is the "Made in Hungary 1900–1950" exhibit with fun ads, toys, and fashions. The attendants are enthusiastic grannies who seem old enough to remember all this history firsthand. If you're lucky, one of them will speak English well enough to take you by the hand and explain it all to you (300 Ft, covered by Budapest Card, audioguide-600 Ft, Wed–Fri 10:00–17:00, Sat–Sun 10:00–18:00, closed Mon–Tue, Fortuna utca 4, Budapest I, tel. 1/375-6249).

At the end of Fortuna utca, you'll come to the...

Remains of St. Mary Magdalene Church—Remember that medieval Buda consisted of two segregated towns. Matthias Church was for Germans. But this half of the town was Hungarian, and these are the remains of the Hungarian church. Later, it became known as the Kapisztrán Templom, named after a hero of the Battle of Belgrade in 1456, an early success in the struggle to keep the Turks out of Europe. (King Mátyás' father, János Hunyadi, was another hero of that battle.) The pope was so tickled by the victory that he decreed that all church bells should toll at noon in memory of the battle—and, technically, they still do. Californians will recognize the Kapisztrán's Spanish name—San Juan de Capistrano. This church was destroyed by bombs in World War II, though no worse than Matthias Church. But, since this part of town was depopulated after the war, there was no longer a need for a second was a lifelong communist. In the 1930s, he allegedly worked for the Soviet secret police. In the late 1940s, he quickly moved up the hierarchy of Hungary's communist government, becoming prime minister in 1953. But in the Moscow shuffle following Stalin's death, Nagy was quickly demoted.

When violence broke out in Budapest on October 23, 1956, Nagy reemerged as the leader of the reform movement. For a few short days, it seemed as though Hungary's communism would moderate—until Soviet tanks rumbled into Budapest, brutally put down the uprising, and occupied the city. By the time the Red Army left, 25,000 protesters were dead, and 250,000 Hungarians had fled to Austria. Nagy was arrested, given a sham trail, and executed in 1958. He was buried disgracefully, face-down in an unmarked grave, and his name was taboo in Hungary for 30 years.

Though the uprising met a tragic end, within a few years Hungary's harshness did soften, and the milder, so-called "goulash communism" emerged. As the Eastern Bloc thawed in 1989, Nagy became a hero. His body was discovered and given a proper reburial in July of that exciting year—heralding the quickly approaching end of the communist era.

church. The remains of the church were torn down, the steeple was rebuilt as a memorial, and a carillon was added—so that every day at noon, the bells can still toll.

Across the square from the church is a monument to San Juan de Capistrano. Walking around the big building, you come to a viewpoint overlooking modern Buda, and on the green hill beyond that, you find the Beverly Hills of Budapest—where the local rich and famous live. To the right, near the flagpole, is the entry to the...

Museum of Military History (Hadtörténeti Múzeum)—This fine museum explains in painstaking detail the history of various Hungarian military actions, with a special emphasis on the 1848 Revolution against the Hapsburgs. With enough old uniforms and flags to keep an army-surplus store in stock for a decade, this place will interest only military and history buffs (400 Ft, covered by Budapest Card, April–Sept Tue–Sun 10:00–18:00, closed Mon; Oct–March Tue–Sun 10:00–16:00, closed Mon; closed first half of Jan, Tóth Árpád sétány 40, Budapest I, tel. 1/356-9522).

Our guided stroll is finished. Under your feet lies one more sightseeing attraction:

Labyrinth of Buda Castle (Budavári Labirintus)—There are miles of caves burrowed under Castle Hill, carved out by water, expanded by the Turks, and used by locals during the siege of Buda at the end of World War II. If you've done everything else in town, you can explore these caverns and see a conceptual exhibit that traces human history (1,200 Ft, 25 percent discount with Budapest Card, daily 9:30–19:30, last entry 19:00, entrance between Royal Palace and Matthias Church at Úri utca 9, Budapest I, tel. 1/212-0207). After 18:00, they turn the lights out and give everyone gas lanterns. The exhibit loses something in the dark, but it's nicely spooky and a fun chance to startle amorous Hungarian teens—or be startled by mischievous ones.

Gellért Hill (Gellérthegy)

The hill rising from the Danube banks just downriver from the castle is Gellért Hill. When King István converted Hungary to Christianity in the year 1000, some of his relatives had other ideas. Bishop Gellért, a monk from Venice, came here to tutor István's son. But rebellious Magyars put the bishop in a barrel, drove long nails in from the outside, and rolled him down this hill...tenderizing him to death. Gellért became the patron saint of Budapest and gave his name to the hill that killed him.

Gellért Hill's only real attraction is the **baths** at Gellért Hotel (see page 333 of "Budapest's Baths"). The hill is a fine place to commune with nature on a hike or jog.

Monument Hike—The north slope of Gellért Hill is good for a low-impact hike. You'll see many interesting monuments, most notably the memorial to Bishop Gellért himself (can't miss it on the left as you cross the Elisabeth Bridge on Hegyalja út). A bit farther up, seek out a newer monument to the world's great philosophers—Eastern, Western, and in between, from Gandhi to Plato to Jesus. Nearby is a scenic overlook with a king and a queen holding hands on either side of the Danube.

Citadella—This strategic, hill-capping fortress was built by the Hapsburgs after the 1848 Revolution to keep an eye on their Hungarian subjects. There's not much to do up here (no museum or exhibits, just a hotel), but it's a good destination for an uphill hike, and provides excellent views over all of Budapest.

The hill is crowned by the **Liberation Monument,** featuring a woman holding aloft a palm branch. The locals call it "the lady with the big fish" or "the great bottle opener." She originally held a plane propeller, since the monument was designed to commemorate Admiral Horthy's son, who had died in a plane crash. But when the communists moved in, they decided to make it a monument to their own "liberation" of Hungary instead. The heroic Soviet soldier—who once inspired the workers with a huge red star from the base of the monument—is now in Statue Park (see page 336).

Cave Church (Sziklatemplom)—Hidden in the hillside on the south end of the hill (across the street from Gellért Hotel) is

Budapest's atmospheric cave church—literally burrowed into the rock face. The communists bricked up this church when they came to power, but now it's open for visitors once again (free entry, but closed to sightseers during frequent services).

Pest

Central Pest (Belváros), Along Váci utca

▲**Vörösmarty tér**—The prominent square called Vörösmarty tér (VOO-roosh-mar-tee tehr), at the north end of the Váci utca pedestrian boulevard, is named for a 19th-century Romantic poet (see his statue in the center) who stirred nationalistic spirit with his writing. It's a good place to get oriented in Pest. Find the landmark **Gerbeaud** pastry shop at the north end of the square. Between the World Wars, the well-to-do ladies of Budapest would meet here after shopping their way up Váci utca. Today it's still *the* meeting point in Budapest (described under "Cafés and Pastry Shops," page 349).

As you face the Gerbeaud, the street to your left leads to the Danube embankment (ideal for a scenic stroll), and the street to your right leads past Erzsébet tér (once Pest's market square) to Andrássy út, lined with sights, restaurants, and hotels (see "Andrássy út and City Parks," below). If you were to jog left around the Gerbeaud and then go straight, you'd reach the Parliament in about 10 minutes (see "More Sights in Central Pest," page 319).

The yellow Metro stop in the middle of the square is the entrance to the shallow *Földalatti,* or "underground"—the first subway on the Continent (built for the millennial celebration in 1896). Today, it still carries passengers to Andrássy út sights (it runs under that street all the way to City Park).

Three hundred years ago, Vörösmarty tér was a rough-and-tumble, often flooded quarter just outside the Pest city walls. People came here to enjoy brutal, staged fights between bloodhounds and bears (like cockfights, only bigger and angrier, with more fur and teeth). The Turkish invaders had finally been forced out of Pest, and the city was nearly deserted. After a series of battles for Hungarian independence, the Hapsburgs moved into ruined Pest in the 1710s. They populated the city with Austrians. (While there was a small Hungarian minority, most Magyars lived in the country.) The Austrians of Pest began rebuilding the city, virtually from scratch—so most of the buildings you'll see are no older than 300 years.

For more of the story, stroll down the street across the square from Gerbeaud: Váci utca.

▲▲**Váci utca**—This pedestrian boulevard—Budapest's shopping and tourism artery—was dreamland for Eastern Europeans back in the 1980s. It was here that they fantasized about what it might be like to be free, while drooling over Nikes, Reeboks, and Big Macs

Pest Center Sights

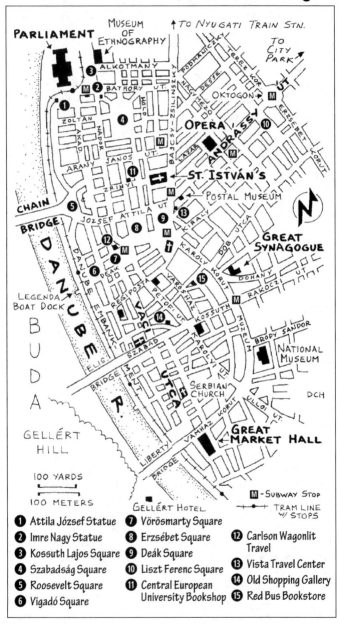

① Attila József Statue
② Imre Nagy Statue
③ Kossuth Lajos Square
④ Szabadság Square
⑤ Roosevelt Square
⑥ Vigadó Square
⑦ Vörösmarty Square
⑧ Erzsébet Square
⑨ Deák Square
⑩ Liszt Ferenc Square
⑪ Central European University Bookshop
⑫ Carlson Wagonlit Travel
⑬ Vista Travel Center
⑭ Old Shopping Gallery
⑮ Red Bus Bookstore

before any of these Western evils were introduced elsewhere in the Warsaw Pact region.

Many tourists are mesmerized by this people-friendly stretch of souvenir stands, Internet cafés, and upscale boutiques—thinking wrongly that this is the "real" Budapest. But a ramble along Váci utca (VAH-tsee OOT-zah) does have stories to tell, and you're sure to stroll here at some point during your visit. The following self-guided walk will help you uncover artifacts of authentic Pest between the postcard racks.

"Váci utca" means "street to Vác"—a town 25 miles to the north. This has long been the street where the elite of Pest would go shopping, then strut their stuff for their neighbors on an evening promenade (*korzó* in Hungarian). Today, the tourists do the strutting here—and the Hungarians go to suburban shopping malls.

As you walk, be sure to look up. Along this street and throughout Pest, spectacular facades begin on the second floor, above a plain entryway (in the 1970s, ground-floor shop windows were made uniformly dull by the communist government). Pan up to see some of Pest's best architecture. These were the townhouses of the aristocracy whose mansions dotted the countryside.

At the end of the first block, next to the Tatuum store on the right, a **plaque** notes that Pest's medieval town wall was torn down in 1789. The no-longer-needed wall had been gradually crumbling for centuries, and as residents rebuilt from the Turkish occupation, it was just getting in the way.

On the next block, find the quirky **Modernist facade** at #8 on the left (over the Clinique shop). Compare this one to the building marked *Douglas* (#11A, across the street a few doors up). The first is more traditional Modernism, but the second is a great example of the **Secession** style. Modernist architecture was rebellious: It rejected what came before—which is why it still looks weird to us today. But the Secession did one better and rejected Modernism.

At the end of the block, the unassuming **McDonald's** (on the right, down Régiposta utca) was a landmark in Eastern Europe—the first McDonald's behind the Iron Curtain. Budapest has always been a little more rebellious, independent, and cosmopolitan than its Eastern European neighbors, who flocked here during the communist era. Long lines for a burger famously went down the street—but it wasn't "fast food," it was "West food." Today McDonald's actually feels sophisticated and cutting-edge—definitely not a cheap place for locals, but popular nevertheless.

Continuing your stroll, you'll notice that some of the **facades** are plain (like the one above the tobacco shop on the right, just after the street leading to McDonald's). Many of these used to be more ornate, like the others, but they were destroyed by WWII bombs and rebuilt boring.

At the halfway point on your Váci utca stroll (midway between the square and Great Market Hall), an underpass takes you below busy Szabad street (Szabad sajtó út). While you're down there, enjoy photos of Budapest (with English descriptions) from the turn of the 20th century, when the city was booming.

The last stretch of Váci utca dead-ends at the huge market hall. This used to be a strongly Serbian neighborhood. (Around the next corner to the left, on Szerb utca, there's still a **Serbian Orthodox church**—heavy with incense and packed with icons.) Traditionally, Hungary's territory included most of Slovakia and large parts of Romania, Croatia, and Serbia—and people from all of those places (along with Jews and Gypsies) flocked to Buda and Pest. And yet, most of the locals in this cosmopolitan city still speak Hungarian. Through centuries of foreign invasions and visitors, Budapest remains Magyar. (Remember that after the Turks left, Budapest was mostly Austrian. The Austrians didn't go anywhere...they became Hungarian, assimilated into the local culture.)

At the end of Váci utca, you'll come to the...

▲▲Great Market Hall (Nagyvásárcsarnok)—This market hall (along with 4 others) was built—you know it—around the year 1896. The cavernous interior features three levels. The ground floor has produce stands, bakeries, butcher stalls, heaps of paprika, goose liver, and sausages. Upstairs are fun, super-cheap, stand-up, Hungarian-style fast-food joints and six-stool pubs, along with a great selection of traditional souvenirs (you're welcome to haggle). Downstairs, it's pungent with tanks of still-healthy carp, catfish, and perch, and piles of pickles.

The market was kept open during communism. Margaret Thatcher came to visit in 1989 (find the photo midway down the main aisle on right). She expected atrocious conditions compared to English markets, but was pleasantly surprised to find this place up to snuff. This was, after all, "goulash communism" (Hungary's pragmatic mix, which allowed a little private enterprise to keep  people going). On the steps of this building, she delivered a historic speech about open society, heralding the impending arrival of the market economy.

The market hall is ideal for lunch, picnic shopping, and people-watching (Mon 6:00–17:00, Tue–Fri 6:00–18:00, Sat 6:00–14:00, closed Sun, Fővám körút 1–3, Budapest IX, M3: Kálvin tér). See "Eating," page 345, for ideas.

From the market, walk to the river. You'll pass (on the left) the University of Economics, which was called Karl Marx University 15 years ago. The bridge leads straight to Gellért Hotel with its famous hot-springs bath at the foot of Gellért Hill (see "Budapest's Baths," page 331). Trams #2 and #2A run from here along the Danube directly back to central Pest, the Chain Bridge, and the Parliament.

More Sights in Central Pest

▲**Hungarian Parliament (Országház)**—The Parliament building, like so much of Budapest, was built around the city's millennial celebration in 1896. Its elegant neo-Gothic design and riverside location were inspired by its counterpart in London. This enormous building—with literally miles of stairs—was appropriate for a time when Budapest ruled much of Eastern Europe. But today it's just plain too big—the legislature only occupies an eighth of the building. Architecture snobs shake their heads and wonder why this frilly Gothic monstrosity is topped with a Renaissance dome. (To make matters worse, there used to be a huge red communist star on top of the tallest spire.) But I think it's beautiful.

The best views of the building are from across the Danube—especially in the late afternoon sunlight. Tours of the Parliament's

opulent interior include the elegant main entryway, a legislative chamber, and the Hungarian crown, under the ornate dome (2,070 Ft, English tours usually daily at 10:00, 12:00, 14:00, and 18:00, but can change so confirm in advance; follow signs around to entry *X*, find the line for individual tickets, join the disorganized queue, and make it clear to the guard that you want an *individual* ticket; eventually you'll be allowed to enter the door marked *X*, pay cashier, and return to the mob to wait for your tour; Kossuth tér 1–3, Budapest V, M2: Kossuth tér, tel. 1/441-4904, www.mkogy.hu).

Kossuth Tér—The square behind the Parliament building has several interesting monuments. Just behind the Parliament is a grassy park with statues of various important Hungarians. A newer monument features a Hungarian flag with a hole cut out of the middle. This commemorates the 1956 Uprising, when protesters removed the socialist-style seal the Soviets had added to their flag.

Also near the Parliament are two other monuments worth a visit. Close to the water, by the tram tracks on the end of the Parliament facing the Chain Bridge, look for a statue of **Attila József,** a popular modern poet who committed suicide at age 32. Straight back from the river, on Vértanúk tere, a statue of the pensive **Imre Nagy,** hero of the 1956 Uprising, stands on a bridge (see page 312).

At the top end of Kossuth tér is the...

Museum of Ethnography (Néprajzi Múzeum)—This museum, housed in one of Budapest's grandest venues, feels deserted. Its fine exhibit on Hungarian folk culture (mostly from the late 19th century) only takes up a small corner of the cavernous building. This permanent exhibit, with surprisingly good English explanations, shows off costumes, tools, wagons, boats, beehives, furniture, and ceramics of the many peoples who lived in pre-WWI Hungary (which also included much of today's Slovakia and Romania). The museum also has a collection of artifacts from other European and world cultures, which it cleverly assembles into good temporary exhibits (free, charge for special exhibitions, Tue–Sun 10:00–18:00, closed Mon, Kossuth tér 12, Budapest V, M2: Kossuth tér, tel. 1/473-2400).

Hungarian National Museum (Magyar Nemzeti Múzeum)—One of Budapest's biggest museums features all manner of Hungarian historic bric-a-brac, from the Paleolithic age to a more recent infestation of dinosaurs (the communists). The first floor focuses on the Carpathian Basin in the pre-Magyar days, with ancient artifacts and Roman remains. The basement features a lapidarium, with medieval tombstones and more Roman ruins. On the second floor, 20 rooms take you on a very fast overview trip from the arrival of the Magyars in 896 up to the 1989 revolution. Unless you've got a pretty good handle on Hungarian history, the exhibits are difficult to appreciate (with only a few big-picture English explanations). Perhaps the most interesting part comes at the very end, with an exhibit on the communist era, featuring both pro- and anti-Party propaganda. The exhibit ends with video footage of the 1989 end of communism— demonstrations, monumental parliament votes, and a final farewell to the last Soviet troops leaving Hungarian soil. Another uprising— the 1848 Revolution against Hapsburg rule—was declared from the steps of this impressive neoclassical building (free, charge for special exhibitions, Tue–Sun 10:00–18:00, closed Mon, last entry 30 min before closing, near Great Market Hall at Múzeum körút 14-16, Budapest VIII, tel. 1/338-2122, www.hnm.hu).

▲**Courtyards and Galleries**—If you only experience what's on the street in Budapest, you'll miss a big part of the story. Pest is filled with once-grand, now crumbling facades, and behind most of them, you'll find cozy courtyards where residents carry out much of their lives. These courtyards, shared among neighbors and ringed by a common balcony, stay cool through the summer. Poking into some of these courtyards (which are generally open to the public, offering a handy shortcut through city blocks) is an essential Back Door experience for understanding the inner life of the city.

Pest's streets also hide some impressive galleries—once used for elegant shopping, now faded and ignored. The most spectacular— with delicate woodwork and a breathtaking stained-glass dome—is dead-center in Pest, along the busy Lajos Kossuth út, a few blocks up from the big, white Elisabeth Bridge (enter at Lajos Kossuth út 11; can also enter the other end, around the corner at Petőfi Sándor utca 2). If you're passing by (it's near the recommended local-style

Millennium Underground of 1896

Built to get the masses of visitors conveniently out to Heroes' Square, this fun and extremely handy little Metro line follows Andrássy út from Vörösmarty Square (Pest's main square) to City Park. Just 20 steps below street level, it's so shallow that you must follow the signs on the street (listing end points) to gauge the right direction, because there's no underpass for switching platforms. The first underground on the Continent (London's is older), it originally had horse-drawn cars. Trains depart every couple of minutes. Recently renovated, the M1 line retains its 1896 atmosphere, along with fun B&W photos of the age.

Jégbüfé café and the Leo Panzió—see "Eating" and "Sleeping," below), it's certainly worth a look.

Andrássy út and City Park

Connecting central Pest to City Park, Andrássy út is Budapest's main boulevard, lined with shops, theaters, cafés, and locals living well. Budapesters claim it's like the Champs-Elysées and Broadway rolled into one. While that's a stretch, it is a good place to stroll and get a feel for today's urban Pest. The best part to wander is between the boulevard's beginning at Deák tér and the Oktogon.

The following sights are listed in order, from Deák tér (in central Pest) to City Park. The M1 line runs every couple of minutes just under the street—so if you get tired of walking it's easy to skip several blocks ahead (stops marked by yellow *Földalatti* signs; see sidebar).

St. István's Basilica (Szent István Bazilika)—Step into Budapest's largest Catholic church and you'll see not Jesus, but St. István (Stephen), Hungary's first Christian king, glowing above the high altar in the otherwise vast and gloomy interior. (See the "Statue of St. István" listing on page 310 for more on this important Hungarian.) The church is only about 100 years old—like most Budapest landmarks, it was built around 1896. Its primary claim to

fame is that it's the resting place of the "holy right hand" of St. István. The sacred fist is in a jeweled box in the chapel to the left of the main altar (follow signs for *Szent Jobb Kápolna*). Pop in a 100-Ft coin for two minutes of light. Although it looks like a major landmark and it's packed with tour groups, the rest of the church isn't that compelling (free, Mon–Fri 9:00–17:00, Sat 9:00–13:00, Sun 13:00–17:00, Szent István tér, Budapest V, M1: Bajcsy-Zsilinszky út or M3: Arany János utca).

The church also has a measly treasury and

Count Andrássy and Sissy

You'll see the names Andrássy and Sissy (or Elisabeth) a lot in Budapest. A key player in the 1848 Revolution, **Count Julius Andrássy** ultimately helped forge the Dual Monarchy of the Austro-Hungarian Empire. He served as the Hungarian prime minister and Austro-Hungarian foreign minister (1871–1879), eventually being forced to step down after his unpopular campaign to appropriate Bosnia and Herzegovina (and consequently boost the Slav population).

Sissy was **Empress Elisabeth,** the Princess Diana of the early 20th-century Hapsburgs (see page 555). Her pet project was advancing the cause of Hungarian autonomy within the empire. While she was married to Emperor Franz Josef, she spent seven years in Budapest—enjoying horseback riding, the local cuisine, and the company of the charming and good-looking Count Andrássy. Her third daughter—believed to be the count's—was known as the Little Hungarian Princess.

panoramic **observation deck,** with a decent view that gives a sense of the sprawl of Pest (600 Ft, 20 percent discount with Budapest Card, elevator to midlevel, then 137 stairs or smaller elevator, plus a few stairs to top of tower, April–May daily 10:00–16:30, June–Aug daily 9:30–18:00, Sept–Oct 10:00–17:30, closed Nov–March).

▲**Postal Museum (Postamúzeum)**—This quirky museum has a delightful collection of old post boxes, telephones, and paraphernalia that was cutting-edge a century ago. The elegant old merchant's mansion—with big glass chandeliers and creaky parquet floors, lived in until 1938—is as interesting as the museum's collection (100 Ft, covered by Budapest Card, Tue–Sun 10:00–18:00, closed Mon, take advantage of the loaner English-language sheets, just up the street from St. István's Basilica at Andrássy út 3, Budapest VI, M1: Bajcsy-Zsilinszky út, look for easy-to-miss sign and ring bell to get upstairs, tel. 1/269-6838).

▲**Hungarian State Opera House (Magyar Állami Operaház)**—The neo-Renaissance home of the Hungarian State Opera features performances at bargain prices almost daily (see "Budapest Music Scene," page 337). Even if you don't see an opera here, you can slip in the front door and check out the sumptuous entryway when the box office is open (Mon–Sat 11:00–19:00, Sun 16:00–19:00, Andrássy út 22, Budapest VI, M1: Opera).

For a more in-depth visit, take one of the excellent **tours** in English (nearly daily at 15:00 and 16:00, reservations not necessary, but it's smart to call ahead and confirm schedule; 2,200 Ft, 10 percent discount with Budapest Card, buy in opera shop—around to the right as you face main entrance, shop open Mon–Fri

Andrássy út

¼ MILE
500 METERS

SZÉCHENYI BATHS

ZOO

MUSEUM OF FINE ARTS

CITY
VAJDAHUNYAD CASTLE

PARK

PALACE OF ART

HUNG   KORUT

KAROLY

SOK

DURER SOR

AJTOSI

HEROES SQUARE

DOZSA GYORGY

BAJZA

BENCZUR

IGETI FASOR

VAROS

FELSO

KODÁLY KÖRÖND

HOUSE OF TERROR

NYUGATI TRAIN STN

WESTEND SHOPPING CENTER

VOROSMARTY UT

ARAD

PUPPET THEATER

LISZT MUSEUM

OKTOGON

SZENT ISTVAN

TEREZ   KORUT

ERZSEBET KORUT

JOKAI

NAGY   MEZO

HAJOS

OPERA

M – SUBWAY STOP

LISZT SQ.

REVAY

ZA

PAULAY

KIRALY

ST. STEPHEN'S

POSTAL MUSEUM

DANUBE

CHAIN BRIDGE

JOZSEF   ATTILA

DEÁK SQUARE

VÖRÖSMARTY SQUARE

DCH

① K+K Hotel Opera
② Cotton House
③ Hotel Ambra
④ Hotel Medosz

⑤ Hotel Délibáb
⑥ Bohémtanya Pub
⑦ Best Hostel
⑧ Liszt Sq. Eateries
⑨ Articsóka Rest.

⑩ Restaurant Művészinas & Duran Szendvics Sandwich Shop
⑪ Gundel Restaurant
⑫ Művész Kávéház Café
⑬ MÁV Office (train tickets)

10:30–13:00 & 13:30–17:00, Sat–Sun 13:30–17:00, open later during performances, tel. 1/332-8197).

Franz Liszt Square (Liszt Ferenc tér)—This leafy, trendy square on the right (south) side of Andrássy út is surrounded by hip, over-priced cafés and restaurants. This is *the* scene for Budapest's yuppies. At the far end of the square is the Music Academy also named for Liszt—a German composer with a Hungarian name, who loved his family's Magyar heritage (though he didn't speak Hungarian) and spent his last five years in Budapest.

Oktogon—During the communist era, this square—at the intersection of Andrássy út and the Great Ring Road *(Nagykörút)*—was called "November 7 tér" in honor of the Bolshevik Revolution. (Andrássy út was renamed "Sztálin út"; later, after Stalin fell out of fashion, it was simply "People's Republic Boulevard.") Today kids have nicknamed it "American tér" for the fast-food joints littering the square and streets nearby. From this square, Andrássy út gradually becomes the dull diplomatic quarter—less colorful, with tame, embassy-lined streets and stately mansions. From the center of Andrássy út, you can see the column of Heroes' Square at the end of the boulevard.

▲▲House of Terror (Terror Háza)—The former headquarters of the darkest sides of two different regimes—the Arrowcross (Nazi-occupied Hungary's version of the Gestapo) and the ÁVO/ÁVH (communist Hungary's secret police)—is now, fittingly, an excellent museum of that time of terror.

Hungary initially allied with Hitler to retain a degree of self-determination, to try and regain their huge territorial losses after World War I, and to avoid having to ship Jews to concentration camps. But in March 1944, the country was taken over by the Nazi-affiliated Arrowcross. The Arrowcross immediately set to work exterminating Budapest's Jews; by May, trains were already heading for Auschwitz. As the end of the war neared, Arrowcross members resorted to more desperate measures, lining Jews up along the Danube and shooting them into the river. To save bullets, they'd sometimes tie several victims together, shoot one of them, and throw him into the freezing Danube—dragging the others in with him. They executed hundreds in the basement of this building. When the communists moved into Hungary, they took over the same building as headquarters for their secret police (the ÁVO, later renamed ÁVH). To keep dissent to a minimum, the secret police terrorized, tried, deported, or executed anyone suspected of being an enemy of the state.

An overhang casts the shadow of the word "TERROR" onto the building. The museum's atrium features a Soviet tank and a huge wall covered with portraits of the victims of this building. The modern, stylish, high-tech exhibit (starting on the top floor and spiraling down) is designed for Hungarians, but the English audioguide (1,000 Ft extra) and free handouts offer tourists the same powerful experience.

The museum has many memorable exhibits—including rooms featuring gulag life, social realist art and propaganda, a labyrinth of pork-fat bricks reminding old-timers of the harsh conditions of the 1950s (lard on bread for dinner), and religion (joining the Church was a way to express rebellion). This is a powerful experience, particularly for elderly Hungarians who knew many of the victims and perpetrators and have personal memories of the terrors that came with Hungary's "double occupation."

The last section begins with a three-minute video of a guard explaining the execution process, which plays as you descend by elevator into the prison basement. In the early 1950s, this basement was the scene of torture; in 1956, it became a clubhouse of sorts for the local communist youth club. It was renovated circa 1955. During the 1956 Uprising, 250,000 fled to Austria and the West during the two weeks of chaos before the USSR pulled a Tiananmen Square–style crackdown (see page 312). The Hall of Tears remembers 25,000 who died in '56. The last two rooms—with the only color video clips—show the festive and exhilarating days in 1991 when the Soviets departed, making way for freedom. Scenes include the reburial of local hero, Imre Nagy; the Pope's visit; and walls of "victimizers"—local members and supporters of the Arrowcross and ÁVO, many of whom are still living, and who were never brought to justice.

The museum does an admirable job of conveying its story. But some locals believe that it's confusing and a little misleading to combine information on these two regimes (who hated each other, and came from opposite ends of the political spectrum) in the same building.

Cost, Hours, Location: 1,200 Ft, 20 percent discount with Budapest Card (that's 960 Ft), cash only, café, bookshop, Tue–Fri 10:00–18:00, Sat–Sun 10:00–19:30, closed Mon, Andrássy út 60, Budapest VI, M1: Vörösmarty utca, tel. 1/374-2600, www.terrorhaza.hu.

Audioguide: The 1,000-Ft English audioguide is good but almost too thorough, and can be difficult to hear over the din of the Hungarian soundtracks in each room. You can't fast-forward through the very dense and sometimes long-winded commentary. As an alternative, note that each room is stocked with good, free English fliers.

Crowd-Beating Tips: To prevent the museum from getting too crowded, the staff carefully monitors how many people they let in at one time—so you may be in for a wait. The lines are longest midday, especially when school is in session (it's a popular field-trip destination). Go early or late.

▲▲**Heroes' Square (Hősök tere)**—Like much of Budapest, this *Who's Who in Hungarian History* at the end of Andrássy út was built to celebrate the city's thousandth birthday in 1896 (M1: Hősök tere). More than just the hottest place in town for skateboarding, this is the site of several museums and the gateway to City Park (filled with diversions for sightseers).

Step right up to the **Millennium Monument** to meet the world's most historic Hungarians (who look to me like their language sounds). The granddaddy of all Magyars, Árpád, stands proudly at the bottom of the pillar, peering down Andrássy út. The 118-foot-tall pillar supports the archangel Gabriel as he offers the crown to St. István (he accepted it and Christianized the Magyars). In front of the pillar is the Hungarian War Memorial (fenced in now to keep skateboarders from enjoying its perfect slope). Behind the pillar, colonnades feature Hungarian VIPs. Look for names you recognize: István, Béla IV, Mátyás Corvinus. But hey...where are the Hapsburgs? At the time of the monument's construction, Budapest was part of the Austrian Empire, and Hapsburgs stood in the right-hand colonnade. When Hungary regained its independence in  World War I, the people tore down the sculpture of the unpopular Franz Josef. (The less hated Maria Theresa was left alone...but ultimately destroyed by a WWII bomb.) After World War II, the Hapsburgs were replaced by Hungarians. In fact, the last two heroes—Ferenc Rákóczi and Lajos Kossuth—were revolutionaries who fought against Austria. The sculptures on the top corners of the two colonnades represent, in order from left to right, Work and Welfare, War, Peace, and the Importance of Packing Light.

As you face Árpád, the **Museum of Fine Arts** (Szépművészeti Múzeum), which has an especially good Spanish collection, is to your left (free, charge for special exhibitions, Tue–Sun 10:00–17:30, closed Mon, tel. 1/469-7100). The **Palace of Art** (Műcsarnok), used for temporary contemporary art exhibits, is to your right (600 Ft, covered by Budapest Card, Tue–Wed and Fri–Sun 10:00–18:00, Thu 12:00–20:00, closed Mon, tel. 1/460-7000). In the basement of the Palace of Art, you'll find a fun but overpriced 20-minute **Countryrama 3-D movie** about Hungary (1,000 Ft, 50 percent discount with Budapest Card, shown every 30 min on the half hour; mid-March–Sept Tue–Sun 10:30–17:30, closed Mon; Oct–mid-March Fri–Sun 10:30–17:00, closed Mon–Thu; tel. 1/460-7014, www.countryrama.hu). While the 3-D is fuzzy, this tired video overview of the countryside is relaxing and affords a quick swing

Tonight We're Gonna Party Like It's 1896

Visitors to Budapest need only remember one date: 1896. For the millennial celebration of their ancestors' arrival in Europe, Hungarians threw a huge blowout party. In a thousand years, the Magyars had gone from being a nomadic Central Asian tribe that terrorized the Continent to sharing the throne of one of the most successful empires Europe had ever seen.

Much as the year 2000 saw a fit of new construction worldwide, Budapest used their millennial celebration as an excuse to build monuments and buildings appropriate for the capital of a huge empire, including:

- **Heroes' Square Millennium Monument**
- **Vajdahunyad Castle** (in City Park)
- The riverside **Parliament** building (96 meters tall, with 96 steps at the main entry)
- **St. István's Basilica** (also 96 meters tall)
- The M1 (yellow) Metro line, a.k.a. *Földalatti* ("Underground")—the first subway on the Continent
- The **Great Market Hall** (and 4 other market halls)
- **Andrássy út** and most of the fine buildings lining it
- The **State Opera House**
- A complete rebuilding of **Matthias Church** (on Castle Hill)
- The **Fishermen's Bastion** decorative terrace (by Matthias Church)
- The green **Liberty Bridge** (then called Franz Josef Bridge, in honor of the ruling Hapsburg emperor)

Ninety-six is the key number in Hungary—even the national anthem (when sung in the proper tempo) takes 96 seconds. But after all this fuss, it's too bad that the date was wrong: A commission—convened to establish the exact year of the Magyars' debut—determined it happened in 895. But city leaders knew they'd never make an 1895 deadline, and requested the finding be changed to 896.

through Hungary in a Travel Channel kind of way. Since majority rules for language, the movie is generally in English (and everyone else gets headphones).

If you leave Heroes' Square between the two colonnades behind the main pillar, you'll cross a bridge into...

▲▲**City Park (Városliget)**—This is the city's not-so-central Central Park. The park was the site of the overblown 1896 Millennium Exhibition, celebrating Hungary's 1,000th birthday...and it's still packed with huge party decorations: a zoo with quirky Art Nouveau buildings, a replica of a Transylvanian castle, a massive bath/swimming complex, walking paths, and an amusement park. The park is filled with unwinding locals. If the sightseeing grind gets you down, spend the afternoon taking a mini-vacation from your busy vacation, the way Budapesters do—stroll in the park and soak in the baths.

Orient yourself from the bridge behind Heroes' Square: The huge Vajdahunyad Castle is on your right (go straight and look for bridge to enter complex). Straight into the park and on the left are the big copper domes of the fun, relaxing Széchenyi Baths (see "Budapest's Baths," below). And the zoo is past the lake on the left. The fancy Gundel restaurant (see "Eating," page 348) is near the zoo.

Vajdahunyad Castle (Vajdahunyad Vára)—The huge complex is a replica of a famous castle in Transylvania (part of Hungary for centuries), surrounded by other styles of traditionally Hungarian architecture (textbook Romanesque, Gothic, Renaissance, and Baroque). Some find it artificial in a Walt Disney World sort of way; others think it's pretty cool. You can enter the castle complex for free to poke around the grounds. (After crossing the bridge behind Heroes' Square, turn right.)

As you enter the complex through the castle facade, you'll see a replica of a 13th-century **Benedictine chapel** on the left—Budapest's most popular spot for weekend weddings in the summer. Farther ahead on the right, you'll see an ornate Baroque mansion—which houses, of all things, the **Museum of Hungarian Agriculture** (Magyar Mezőgazdasági Múzeum, free, charge for special exhibitions; March–Oct Tue–Fri and Sun 10:00–17:00, Sat 10:00–18:00, closed Mon; Nov–Feb Tue–Fri 10:00–16:00, Sat–Sun 10:00–17:00, closed Mon; last entry 30 min before closing). The museum brags that it's Europe's biggest agriculture museum...but the lavish interior is more interesting than the exhibits.

Across the street from the museum entry, you'll see a monument to **Anonymous;** specifically, the Anonymous who penned the first Hungarian history in the Middle Ages.

Zoo (Állatkert)—Aside from animals, the zoo also has redeeming sightseeing value: Many of its structures—including the entry gate and the elephant house—are playful bits of turn-of-the-20th-century Art Nouveau. Just inside the gate, look for the *Információ* kiosk to the left and grab the handy *A Walk in the Zoo* brochure. To reach the Art Nouveau elephant house, turn right inside the entry, then right again at the fork, and look for the white-and-turquoise tower. The zoo is a perfect example of a sight that's not really worth the price of entry, but makes for a fun 15-minute walk-through with the Budapest Card (1,400 Ft, covered by Budapest Card, May–Aug daily 9:00–19:00, April and Sept daily until 18:00, March and Oct daily until 17:00, Nov–Feb daily until 16:00, Állatkerti körút 6–12, Budapest XIV, tel. 1/364-0109, www.zoobudapest.com).

Jewish Budapest

As the former co-capital of an empire that included millions of Jews, Budapest always had a high concentration of Jewish residents. Before World War II, 5 percent of Hungary's population and 25 percent of Budapest's was Jewish (the city was dubbed "Judapest" by their snide Viennese neighbors up the river). Hungary lost nearly 600,000 Jews to the Holocaust, at the hands of the brutal Nazi puppet government called the Arrowcross. (For more about the Holocaust in Hungary, see the "House of Terror" listing on page 324.) Today, only half of one percent of Hungarians are Jewish—and most of them are in Budapest. In recent years, since the thawing of communism, Hungarian Jews have been taking a renewed interest in their heritage.

The first sight listed here is very central, close to Pest's Deák tér; the other is just outside central Pest, a Metro ride plus a five-minute walk away.

▲**Great Synagogue (Zsinagóga)**—This impressively restored synagogue is the second biggest in the world, after New York City's.

While several traditional synagogues are nearby (this is Pest's Jewish quarter), the Great Synagogue is reformed, and—with its nave,

pulpit, and pipe organ flanking the high altar—it looks like a church with the symbols switched. It was built in the 1850s, when Jews wanted to feel more integrated into the community. The balconies were originally for women, but today men and women sit anywhere and together. The Moorish-flavored decor is a reminder of how Jewish culture flourished in Iberia. After World War II, the synagogue was refurbished with financial support from Tony Curtis, an American actor of Hungarian-Jewish origin (his daughter Jamie Lee continues to support these causes today).

Your synagogue ticket also includes the **Jewish Museum** (Zsidó Múzeum, in the same building; entry for both-1,000 Ft, probably not covered by Budapest Card, April–Oct Mon–Thu 10:00–17:00, Fri and Sun 10:00–14:00; Nov–March Mon–Thu 10:00–15:00, Fri and Sun 10:00–14:00; always closed Sat and Jewish holidays, often closed mid-Dec–mid-Jan, last entry 30 min before closing, Dohány utca 2, Budapest VII, M1, M2, or M3: Deák tér, tel. 01/342-8949).

Behind the synagogue, the *Tree of Life* sculpture was built on the site of mass graves of those killed by the Nazis. The willow makes an upside-down menorah, each individual leaf lists the name of a victim, and pebbles represent prayers. You can visit the *Tree* even if you don't buy a ticket for the synagogue (enter through synagogue security gate and go straight ahead through doors and under arcade to the park behind the synagogue; if synagogue is closed, go around left side to view monument through a fence).

Aviv Travel leads **tours** of the synagogue and the Jewish quarter (basic 1-hr English tour covers synagogue, museum, and *Tree of Life*, 1,900 Ft, includes admission, Mon–Thu hourly on the half hour 10:30–15:30; Fri and Sun 10:30, 11:30, and 12:30 only; kiosk by synagogue entry, tel. 1/462-0477).

▲**Holocaust Memorial Center (Holokauszt Emlékközpont)**— This brand-new center is making great strides in honoring the nearly 600,000 Hungarian victims of the Nazis. The impressive modern complex (with a beautifully restored 1920s synagogue as its center-piece) is intended to serve as a museum of the Hungarian Holocaust, a monument to its victims, and a research and documentation center of Nazi atrocities. A black marble wall in the courtyard is etched with the names of victims, and an information center downstairs helps teary-eyed Hungarians locate the names of their relatives.

The center—which opened on April 16, 2004, the 60th anniversary of the ghettoization of Hungary—presents very good temporary exhibitions (the "Auschwitz Album," which may still be on display in 2005, features chilling photographs by a family of vic-tims). A permanent exhibit, which promises to detail the history of the Hungarian Holocaust, opens in the fall of 2005 (free, Tue–Sun 10:00–18:00, closed Mon, Páva utca 39, Budapest IX, M3: Ferenc körút, tel. 1/216-6557, www.hdke.hu). To reach the complex, take the M3 Metro line to Ferenc körút. Use the exit marked *Üllői út 45–51*, walk straight ahead three blocks, and look right.

The Danube (Duna)

The mighty river coursing through the heart of the city defines Budapest. For many visitors, a highlight is taking a touristy but beautiful boat cruise up and down the Danube—especially at night (see "Tours," above). Here are some other river-related activities to consider.

▲**Danube Embankment (Dunakorzó)**—Pest's breezy riverfront promenade (from Elisabeth Bridge to the Chain Bridge) is a fine place for a stroll. Start on Vigadó tér, two blocks towards the river from Vörösmarty tér, and head southward. Along the way, keep an eye out for the Little Princess statue leaning on the railing—one of Budapest's symbols, even though it's just over a decade old. When Prince Charles visited Budapest, he liked this statue so much that he had a replica made for himself. You'll pass a few souvenir stalls and big, fancy hotels (including Hyatt and InterContinental), and enjoy sweeping views of Buda, some of the international river-cruise ships, and the city's many bridges.

Roosevelt Square—If you walk to the Chain Bridge, you'll hit Roosevelt Square, fringed by impressive architecture. The blocky "Spinach House"—an ugly green communist office block—is infa-mous for its terrible design and craftsmanship, a glaring reminder of how wretched those times were for most. The fine Art Nouveau Grasham Palace faces the bridge. Originally the local headquarters of an English insurance company, it's now a new Four Seasons hotel. (From here, the riverside tram #2 or #2A, which stops near the modern InterContinental hotel, zips you three stops to the Great Market Hall, or bus #16 will take you up Castle Hill.)

▲**Chain Bridge (Széchenyi Lánchíd)**—One of the world's great bridges connects Pest's Roosevelt tér and Buda's Adam Clark tér. This historic, iconic bridge, guarded by lions (symbolizing power), is Budapest's most enjoyable and convenient bridge to cross on foot.

(This is especially handy for commuting to the top of Castle Hill, since both bus #16 and the funicular to the top begin from the Buda end of the bridge.)

Until the mid-19th century, only pontoon barges spanned the Danube between Buda and Pest. In the winter, the pontoons had to be pulled in, leaving locals to rely on ferries (in good weather) or a frozen river. People often walked across the frozen Danube, only to get stuck on the other side during a thaw, with nothing to do but wait for another cold snap.

Count István Széchenyi was stranded for a week trying to get to his father's funeral. After missing it, Széchenyi decided to commission Budapest's first permanent bridge. The Chain Bridge was built by Scotsman Adam Clark between 1842 and 1849, and it immediately became an important symbol of Budapest. Széchenyi—a man of the Enlightenment—charged both commoners and nobles a toll for crossing his bridge, making it a symbol of equality in those tense times. Like all of the city's bridges, the Chain Bridge was destroyed by Nazis at the end of World War II, but was quickly rebuilt.

Margaret Island (Margitsziget)—Budapesters come to play in this huge, leafy park, a wonderful spot for strolling and people-watching (accessible from Margaret Bridge—trams #4 and #6 stop at the gateway to the island). The island is also home to some of Budapest's many baths.

Budapest's Baths

Splashing and relaxing in Budapest's thermal baths is the city's only ▲▲▲ activity. Though it might sound intimidating, bathing with the Magyars is far more accessible than you'd think. Overcome your jitters, follow my instructions, and dive in...or miss out on *the* quintessential Budapest experience. (For more on Hungary's thermal baths, see "Taking the Waters" on page 280.)

Budapest's two dozen baths *(fürdő)* were taken over by the communist government, and they're all still owned by the city. The two baths listed here are the best known, most representative, and most convenient for first-timers—one for locals, the other elegant and touristy. Both are equally good and should be a high priority during your visit. The uninitiated need not fear the baths—it's basically a series of warm swimming pools. While Budapest has some mostly nude, segregated Turkish baths, the following two baths are generally mixed, with men and women clothed and together most of the time. (Men are *férfi* and women are *női*.) For more information, see www.spasbudapest.com.

▲▲▲**Széchenyi Baths (Széchenyi Fürdő)**—To soak with the locals, head for this bath complex—the big, yellow, copper-domed building in the middle of City Park. Széchenyi Baths (SAY-chehn-yee) is the most local-feeling and fun of Budapest's many bath experiences. Relax and enjoy some Hungarian good living. Magyars of all shapes and sizes stuff themselves into tiny swimsuits and strut their stuff. Housewives float blissfully in the warm water. Intellectuals and Speedo-clad elder statesmen stand in chest-high water around chessboards and ponder their next moves. This is Budapest at its best.

Cost: The sliding entry-fee scale covers thermal baths, the swimming pool, sauna, and a changing cabin (2,000 Ft if you arrive before 15:00, 1,800 Ft if you arrive by 16:00, 1,500 Ft if you arrive by 17:00, 1,200 Ft if you arrive after 17:00; you also get money back later if your stay is short—explained below; no discount with Budapest Card). If you want a locker instead of a private changing cabin, you'll save 300 Ft. There's also a wide array of massages and other special treatments—find the English menu in the lobby (make an appointment as you enter). You can rent a swimsuit, towel, or robe (500 Ft each with deposit).

Hours and Location: May–Sept daily 6:00–19:00; Oct–April Mon–Fri 6:00–19:00, Sat–Sun 6:00–17:00; last entry 1 hour before closing, Állatkerti körút 11, Budapest XIV, M1: Széchenyi fürdő. The huge bath complex has three entries. The busiest one is the grand main entry, facing south (roughly towards Vajdahunyad Castle). During peak times, you may have to wait to enter these locker rooms. But you'll usually be able to walk right in if you use the entry on the other side of the complex (facing the Zoo). The third entry, to the right as you face the Zoo entry (near the Metro stops), is smaller (and therefore, again, comes with longer lines), but has windows with nice views into the complex.

Procedure: Pay the cashier, and you'll be given a receipt and an electronic chit. Again, men are *férfi* and women are *női*—but if you've paid for a private cabin, you'll be ushered into the same changing area, where everyone gets their own cabin. If you've paid for a locker, the locker rooms are gender-segregated.

As you enter the changing area, pass your electronic chit over the turnstile, and an attendant will show you to a changing cabin and give you a key or a little metal disc, either of which goes around your wrist. (This is where you can rent a swimsuit or towel if you need one. If using the entrance facing the zoo, you'll have to go downstairs before you head to the cabins. Do this before you change, as you'll need money.) After you change, lock your belongings in your cabin and hang on to your key or little metal disc—an attendant will double-lock the cabin with his or her own key. While leaving things in these cabins is at your own risk, I've found them to be safe. Still, you have the option of leaving valuables in a locker for a small fee (ask at desk). Many locals bring plastic shopping bags with the essentials: towels, leisure reading, and sunscreen.

Follow the crowds to a series of indoor pools (quite hot—most around 40 degrees Celsius, or 104 Fahrenheit—and some with green water, supposedly caused by the many healthy minerals). Beyond the pools you'll find your way outside, where the action is.

There are three outdoor pools. Orient yourself with your back to the main building: The pool to the right is for fun (cooler water—

30 degrees Celsius, or 86 Fahrenheit, warmer in winter, lots of jets and bubbles, lively and often crowded current pool); the pool on the left is for relaxation (warmer water—38 degrees Celsius, or 100 Fahrenheit, mellow atmosphere, chess); and the main pool in the center is all business (the coolest water, doing laps, swimming cap required). Stairs to saunas are below the doors to the inside pools. You get extra credit for joining the gang in a chess match.

On your way out, drop your electronic chit in the slot. A receipt will print out, indicating how much of a refund you get *(Visszatérités: Jár [amount] Ft)*. Present this and your original receipt at the cashier on your way out to claim your "time-proportional repayment." Then continue your sightseeing...soggy, but relaxed.

▲▲▲**Gellért Baths (Gellért Fürdő)**—Budapest's classic bath experience is at Gellért Hotel. You'll pay more, won't have as much fun, and won't run into nearly as many locals—this is definitely a more upscale, touristy scene. But if you want a soothing, luxurious bath experience in an elegant setting, this is the place.

Cost: 2,700 Ft includes changing cabin, 2,200 Ft includes locker, cheaper after 15:00, 10 percent discount with Budapest Card. A "visitor ticket" to see—but not use—the baths costs 500 Ft. Towel rental costs 500 Ft with a 4,000-Ft deposit, and swimsuit rental is also available (tell them you want to rent these when you buy your ticket).

Hours and Location: May–Sept daily 6:00–19:00, thermal bath only until 17:00 on Sat–Sun; Oct–April Mon–Fri 6:00–19:00,

Sat–Sun 6:00–17:00; last entry 1 hr before closing. It's on the Buda side of the green Liberty Bridge (trams #47 and #49 from Deák tér in Pest, or tram #19 along the Buda embankment from Víziváros below the castle). The entrance to the baths is under the white dome opposite the bridge (Kelenhegyi út 4–6, Budapest XI, tel. 1/466-6166).

Procedure: Choose from the dizzying array of options at the ticket window (from mud baths to foot massages—1,000–3,000 Ft), pay, and glide through the swanky lobby. Look for the swimming pool on your right about halfway down the main hall, and you'll find the stairs leading down to a maze of corridors that take you to the changing rooms (left for *férfi*—men—and right for *nöi*—women). If you paid to rent a towel or swimsuit, get it from the attendant on your way.

Once you've changed, you have three options: Outside is a big **wave pool** and several smaller pools (closed Oct–April). Inside is a cool-water **swimming pool** (swimming cap required—free loaners available) and a crowded hot-water pool. Off of that pool are doors to the gender-segregated, clothing-optional massage rooms and **thermal baths,** with pools at 36 and 38 degrees Celsius (97 and 100 Fahrenheit), as well as cold plunge pools and eucalyptus-scented steam rooms.

When you're finished, return your towel and swimsuit to get the slip to reclaim your deposit money (at cashier as you leave). If you were at the bath for less than four hours, you'll also get money back when you leave (take plastic card to cashier).

Away from Central Budapest

Óbuda

Budapest was originally three cities: Buda, Pest, and Óbuda. Óbuda (or "Old Buda") is the oldest of the three—the first known residents of the region (Celts) settled here, and today it's still littered with ruins from the next occupants (Romans). Despite all the history, the district is disappointing, worth a look only for those interested in Roman ruins or 20th-century Hungarian painting and sculpture. To reach Óbuda, go to Batthyány tér in Buda (M2 Metro line) and catch the HÉV suburban train north to the Árpád híd stop. The Vasarely Museum is 50 yards from the station. The town square is 100 yards beyond that, and 200 yards later (turn left at the ladies with the umbrellas), you'll find the Imre Varga Collection.

Vasarely Museum—This museum features two floors of eye-popping, colorful paintings by the founder of Op Art, Victor Vasarely. The exhibition follows his artistic evolution from his youth as a graphic designer to the playful optical illusions he was most famous for. If this art gets you pondering Rubik's cube, it may come as no surprise that Ernő Rubik was a professor of mathematics right here in Budapest. Vasarely, and the movement he pioneered (heavy on optical illusions), helped inspire the trippy styles of the 1960s (400 Ft, covered by Budapest Card, Tue–Sun 10:00–17:30, closed Mon, Szentlélek tér 6, Budapest III, HÉV north to Árpád híd stop, tel. 1/388-7551). This museum is immediately on the right as you leave the Árpád híd HÉV station.

Óbuda Main Square (Fő Tér)—If you keep going past the Vasarely Museum and turn right, you enter Óbuda's cute Main Square. The big, yellow building was the Óbuda Town Hall when this was its own city. Today it's still the office of the district mayor. To the right of the Town Hall, you'll see a whimsical, much photographed statue of women with umbrellas. Replicas of this sculpture, by local artist Imre Varga, decorate the gardens of wealthy summer homes on Lake Balaton. Varga created many of Budapest's distinctive monuments. His museum is just down the street (at the umbrella ladies, turn left).

▲**Imre Varga Collection (Varga Imre Kiállítóház)**—Imre Varga worked from the 1950s through the 1990s. His statues, while occasionally religious, mostly commented on life during communist times, when there were three types of artists: banned, tolerated, and supported. Varga was tolerated. Themes include forced marches and mass graves. One headless statue comes with medallions nailed into his chest. (These medallions were Varga's own, from his pre-communist military service. Anyone with such medallions was persecuted by communists in the 1950s...so Varga disposed of his this way.) Varga actually drops by each Saturday morning at 10:00 to chat with visitors. He speaks English, and, while now in his 80s, he enjoys explaining his art. Don't miss the garden, where you'll see three prostitutes illustrating "the passing of time" (250 Ft, covered by Budapest Card, Tue–Sun 10:00–18:00, closed Mon, Laktanya utca 7, Budapest III, tel. 1/250-0274).

Aquincum Museum—Long before Magyars laid eyes on the Danube, Óbuda was the Roman city of Aquincum. Here you can explore the remains of the 2,000-year-old Roman town and amphitheater. The museum is proud of its centerpiece, a water organ (700 Ft, covered by Budapest Card, May–Sept Tue–Sun 9:00–18:00, closed Mon; Oct and latter half of April Tue–Sun 9:00–17:00, closed Mon; closed Nov–mid-April, Szentendrei út 139, Budapest III, HÉV north to Aquincum stop, tel. 1/250-1650). From the HÉV stop, cross the busy road and turn to the right. Go through the railway underpass, and you'll see the ruins ahead and on the left as you emerge.

Statue Park (Szoborpark)

When regimes fall, so do their monuments. Just think of all those statues of Stalin and Lenin—or Saddam Hussein—crashing to the ground. Throughout Eastern Europe, people couldn't wait to get rid of these reminders of their oppressors. But some clever entrepreneur hoarded Budapest's, and now has collected them in a park just southwest of the city—where tourists flock to get a taste of the communist era. Though it can be time-consuming to visit, this collection is worth ▲▲—or ▲▲▲ for those fascinated by the Red old days.

Under the communists, creativity was discouraged. Art was acceptable only if it furthered the goals of the state. The only sanctioned art in communist Europe was **Social Realism.** Aside from a few important figureheads, individuals didn't matter. Everyone was a cog in the machine—strong, stoic, doing their job well and proudly for the good of the people. Individual characteristics and distinguishing features were unimportant; people are represented as machines serving their nation.

At Statue Park, you'll see the Communist All-Stars (Marx, Engels, and Lenin—in his favorite "hailing a cab" pose). They couldn't save the biggest "star" of all, Stalin—he was destroyed in the 1956 Uprising (but you can see a chunk of him in the Budapest History Museum on Castle Hill). Statue Park also features other socialist symbols (the stoic soldier, the faceless worker, and the tireless and heroic mother). The gift shop is a fun parade of communist kitsch; consider picking up the good English guidebook, the CD of *Communism's Greatest Hits,* and maybe a model of a Trabant.

Cost, Hours, Location: 600 Ft, covered by Budapest Card, daily 10:00–sunset, six miles southwest of center at the corner of Balatoni út and Szabadka út, Budapest XXII, tel. 1/424-7500, www.szoborpark.hu.

Getting There: The park runs a direct bus from Deák tér in downtown Budapest (where all three Metro lines converge, bus stop well-marked with Statue Park logo, year-round daily at 11:00, March–Oct also at 15:00, July–Aug also at 10:00 and 16:00; round-trip takes 105 min total, including a 40-min visit to the park, 2,450 Ft round-trip, 1,950 Ft with Budapest Card, price includes park entry). The trip by public transportation is too complicated: Take M3 line to Ferenciek tere, then red #7 bus to its end at Etele tér, then yellow Volán Bus from stall 7–8 in the direction Diosd-Erd (let the driver know your destination when you board); Statue Park is about 15 minutes into the trip—look for the red-brick entry and the statues on your right, and then signal for a stop.

ENTERTAINMENT

Budapest Music Scene

Budapest is a great place to catch a good—and inexpensive—concert. In fact, Viennese music lovers often make the three-hour trip here just to take in some fine, cheap opera in a luxurious setting. Options range from world-class opera in one of the world's great opera houses to light, touristy "Gypsy" folk concerts (with musicians and routines suspiciously similar to tomorrow's "Hungarian folk music" concerts). The tourist concerts are the simplest option—you'll see the fliers everywhere—but you owe it to yourself to do a little homework and find something more authentic. The monthly *Budapest Panorama* brochure makes it easier (free, available at the TI)—listing performances with dates, venues, performers, and contact information for getting tickets. Or check schedules online (try www.wherebudapest.com). The Megnyitotta Uj Irodajat box office lists everything on its walls and is a good clearinghouse for tickets and info (across from opera at Andrássy út 15, Mon–Fri 10:00–18:00, closed Sat–Sun, tel. 1/267-1267).

A Night at the Opera—Consider taking in an opera by one of the best companies in Europe, in one of Europe's loveliest opera houses, for bargain prices. The Hungarian State Opera performs almost nightly, both at the main Opera House (Andrássy út 22, Budapest VI, M1: Opera, see page 322) and in the Erkel Színház (not nearly as impressive, near the Keleti Train Station at Köztársaság tér 30, Budapest VIII, tel. 1/333-0540). Be careful to get a performance in the Opera House—not the Erkel Színház. Ticket prices range from 800 to 6,500 Ft, but the best music deal in Europe may be the 300-Ft, obstructed-view tickets (easy to get, as they rarely run out). If you chose to buy one of these opera-tickets-for-a-buck, you'll have a seat, and won't be able to see the stage—but you'll hear every note, along with the big spenders. If a full evening of opera is too much for you, you can leave early or come late (but buy ticket ahead of time, as box office closes when performance starts). To get tickets, call, fax, or visit the box office at the main Opera House, or order online (box office open and phone answered Mon–Sat 11:00–19:00, Sun 16:00–19:00, box office tel. 1/353-0170 or 1/472-0447, fax 1/311-9017, www.opera.hu). If you reserve by phone, fax, or online, pick up tickets at the Opera House two days before the performance (Andrássy út 22, Budapest VI, M1: Opera). You can pick up tickets 30 minutes before performance by request. There are generally some tickets available at the door.

Tourist Concerts—Concerts include Hungarian folk music and dancing by various interchangeable troupes (4,600–5,600 Ft, May–Oct almost daily at 20:00), classical "greatest hits" by the impressively named Danube Symphony Orchestra (the best group,

6,400–8,100 Ft, 15 percent discount with Budapest Card for this concert only, May–Oct Sat at 20:00), and organ concerts in a Baroque church (3,600 Ft, June–Sept Fri and Sun at 20:00, May only Fri at 20:00). While highbrow classical music buffs will want a more serious concert, these shows are real crowd-pleasers.

These concerts are all run by **Duna Palota** (main office Zrínyi utca 5, call or visit for tickets daily 8:00–20:00, open later during concerts, shorter hours in winter, tel. 1/317-2754, http://ticket .info.hu).

American-Style Musicals—If you've ever wanted to hear "Music of the Night" in the Magyar tongue—as it was meant to be performed— here's your chance. Two pieces of American-style musical theater run permanently in Budapest, both in Hungarian with English subtitles: *Phantom of the Opera* (the only company in Central Europe, www.azoperahazfantomja.hu) and *Mozart!* (www.mozartbudapest.hu). Pick up details at the TI.

SLEEPING

Budapest has lots of good hotel values—it's cheaper to sleep centrally here than in most European capitals. Stick with my listings and you'll get a good deal. Most rates drop 10–25 percent in the off-season (generally Nov–March). The Formula 1 races (July 29–31 in 2005) send rates everywhere through the roof. If you're arriving on an international train, you may be approached by room-hawkers on board, offering accommodations in private homes and hotels. These places get mixed reviews; you're better off using my listings.

Pest

Staying in Pest is more convenient, but a little less romantic, than sleeping in Buda. Most sights worth seeing are in Pest, and this half of the city also has a much higher concentration of Metro and tram stops, making getting around a snap. Pest also feels more lively and local than touristy Buda. I've arranged my listings by neighborhood, clustered around the most important sightseeing sectors.

Near Váci utca

Sleeping on the very central and convenient Váci utca comes with overly inflated prices. But these three gems—just a block or two off Váci utca—offer some of the best values in Budapest.

$$ Kálvin-Ház, a long block up from the Great Market Hall, is a little farther from the Váci utca action than the others (which some people think is a good thing). It offers 28 big, well-maintained rooms with old-fashioned furnishings and squeaky parquet floors (Sb-€60, Db-€80, apartment-€100, extra bed-€20, 20 percent cheaper Nov–March, non-smoking rooms, Gönczy Pál utca 6,

---

Sleep Code

(€1 = $1.20, 200 Ft = about $1, country code: 36, area code: 1)
S = Single, **D** = Double/Twin, **T** = Triple, **Q** = Quad,
b = bathroom, **s** = shower only. Unless otherwise noted, breakfast is included and credit cards are accepted. Everyone speaks English, and most prices are quoted in euros.

To help you sort easily through these listings, I've divided the rooms into three categories, based on the price for a standard double room with bath:

    $$$ **Higher Priced**—Most rooms €100 (24,000 Ft) or more.
    $$ **Moderately Priced**—Most rooms between €70–100
                            (16,800–24,000 Ft).
    $ **Lower Priced**—Most rooms €70 (16,800 Ft) or less.

Budapest IX, M3: Kálvin tér, tel. 1/216-4365, fax 1/216-4161, www .kalvinhouse.hu, info@kalvinhouse.hu).

$$ Peregrinus Hotel, with a fine location, classy lobby, and 25 decent rooms, is run by the big ELTE university—so many of its guests are visiting professors and lecturers (Sb-17,500 Ft, Db-23,000 Ft, extra bed-5,000 Ft, 25 percent cheaper Nov–March, elevator, just off Váci utca at Szerb utca 3, Budapest V, 5-min walk to M3: Kálvin tér, or tram #47 or #49 to Fövám tér, tel. 1/266-4911, fax 1/266-4913, www.peregrinushotel.hu, peregrinushotel@elte.hu).

$$ Leo Panzió is a peaceful oasis with 14 modern rooms in a hulking building that's seen better days. The location is central, the antique elevator is wonderfully rickety, and the double-paned windows keep out most of the noise from the busy street below (Sb-€66, Db-€82, extra bed-€26, 15 percent cheaper Nov–March, air-con, Kossuth Lajos utca 2A, Budapest V, M3: Ferenciek tere, tel. 1/266-9041, tel. & fax 1/266-9042, www.leopanzio.hu, leo@leopanzio.hu).

Near Andrássy út

Andrássy Boulevard is handy, local-feeling, and endlessly entertaining. It's lined with appealing cafés, restaurants, theaters, and bars—and the living is good. The frequent Metro stations make getting around the city easy from here. None of these hotels is on Andrássy út, but they're all within a two-block walk away. For locations, see map on page 323.

$$$ K+K Hotel Opera is wonderfully located, beside the opera in the fun "Broadway Quarter." True to its name, it's a regal splurge, where wicker seems classy. It has helpful, professional service and 205 rooms. The high rack rates (Sb-€110, Db-€130) are pretty firm in the summer, but drop to wonderful lows in the winter (Sb/Db-€90 Nov–Feb; non-smoking floors, air-con, elevator, free Internet,

Pest Hotels and Restaurants

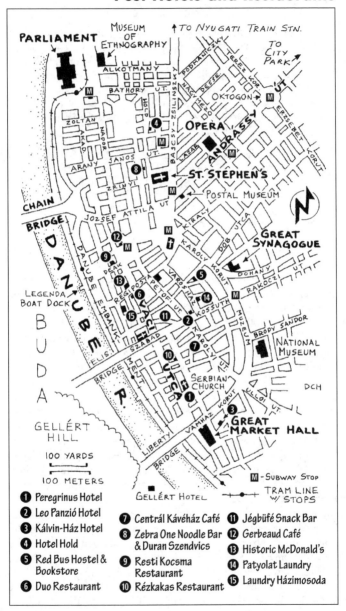

1. Peregrinus Hotel
2. Leo Panzió Hotel
3. Kálvin-Ház Hotel
4. Hotel Hold
5. Red Bus Hostel & Bookstore
6. Duo Restaurant
7. Centrál Kávéház Café
8. Zebra One Noodle Bar & Duran Szendvics
9. Resti Kocsma Restaurant
10. Rézkakas Restaurant
11. Jégbüfé Snack Bar
12. Gerbeaud Café
13. Historic McDonald's
14. Patyolat Laundry
15. Laundry Házimosoda

parking garage-€10/day, Révay utca 24, Budapest VI, M1: Opera, tel. 1/269-0222, fax 1/269-0230, www.kkhotels.com, kk.hotel.opera @kkhotel.hu).

$$ Hotel Ambra, centrally located two blocks from the Opera House, is bright and mod, with 16 spacious, well-decorated apartments and five rooms. Apartments give you double the size and a kitchenette for €10 more. It's a good value, but there's a catch: It's on a grimy, smelly, but safe street (rooms: Sb-€65, Db-€85; apartments: Sb-€75, Db-€95, Tb-€105, Qb-€120; 10 percent cheaper Oct–March, air-con, non-smoking rooms, elevator, garage-€9/day, Kisdiófa utca 13, Budapest VII, M1: Opera, tel. 1/321-1533, fax 1/321-1538, www .hotelambra.hu, ambrahotel@axelero.hu).

$ Hotel Medosz is cheap and dumpy, overlooking a seedy square. But the prices are low and the location is wonderfully central, around the corner from the Oktogon and the trendy Franz Liszt Square. Beyond the chilling concrete communist facade and gloomy lobby are 67 rooms—old and uninspired but perfectly adequate, comrade (Sb-€47, Db-€57, 15 percent cheaper Nov–March, elevator, Jókai tér 9, Budapest VI, M1: Oktogon, tel. 1/374-3000, fax 1/332-4316, www.medoszhotel.hu, info@medoszhotel.hu). When I asked if prices had gone up since last year, the tired, communist-era receptionist chuckled and said, "Nothing ever changes around here."

Elsewhere in Pest

These fine values are scattered around central Pest.

$$ Hotel Hold is in a peaceful business district between the Parliament and Váci utca, across from the interesting, old, beehive-lined facade of the National Bank building. The 28 rooms cluster around a quiet courtyard (Sb-€70, Db-€80, €10 less Oct–April, air-con, Hold utca 5, Budapest V, M3: Arany János utca, tel. 1/472-0480, fax 1/472-0484, www.hotelhold.hu, info@hotelhold.hu).

$$ Cotton House, close to the Nyugati Station, a few blocks from Andrássy út, is a fun, blast-from-the-past theme hotel. Its 13 retro rooms are fresh and comfy, with 1930s themes; each room is devoted to a different mobster (Al Capone) or old-time performer (Ella Fitzgerald). Some rooms are very plush—you can select from their Web site (Sb or Db-€80 with shower, €90 with bath, €100 for whirlpool tub, air-con, Jókai utca 26, Budapest V, M3: Nyugati pu., tel. 1/354-2600, fax 1/354-1341, www.cottonhouse.hu, cottonhouse @axelero.hu). In the basement is an elaborate jazz club, with a restaurant, "cigar room" with a wall of rentable humidor lockers, and oodles of atmosphere. In the summer, the ground floor becomes a hopping indoor-outdoor café with live music.

$$ Hotel Délibáb is spartan, but a great value, across the street from Heroes' Square. The 34 rooms are a little old and worn, but clean and comfy enough. Most face a busy street and come with some noise (Sb-€66, Db-€76, 15 percent cheaper Nov–March, free Internet access, parking-€10/day, Délibáb utca 35, Budapest VII, M1: Hősök tere, tel. 1/342-9301, fax 1/342-8153, www.hoteldelibab.hu, info@hoteldelibab.hu).

$ Mária and István, your chatty Hungarian aunt and uncle, are saving a room for you in their Old World apartment. For warmth and hospitality at youth-hostel prices, consider bunking in one of their two rooms, which share a bathroom (S-€18–22, D-€28-34, T-€36–42, price depends on size of room and length of stay—longer is cheaper, no breakfast, but guests' kitchen, cash only, elevator, Ferenc körút 39, Budapest IX, M3: Ferenc körút, tel. & fax 1/216-0768, www.mariaistvan.hu, mariaistvan@axelero.hu). Mária and István also rent two apartments farther from the center (Db-€44–54, Tb-€54–64, Qb-€60–72, family apartment, both near M3: Nagyvarad tér).

$ Red Bus Hostel is clean, well-run, and central—by most accounts, Budapest's best hostel deal. It's an old apartment with nine nicely renovated rooms. The place is popular, so it's smart to book ahead (S-6,500 Ft, D-7,500 Ft, T-10,500 Ft, dorm bed-2,900 Ft, Internet access, laundry service-1,200 Ft, no curfew, Semmelweis utca 14, Budapest V, M2: Astoria, tel. & fax 1/266-0136, www.redbusbudapest.hu, redbusbudapest@hotmail.com). They also have a second, less central location (Szövetség utca 35, tel. & fax 1/321-7100).

$ "Best Hostel" is not modest. Their brochure reads, "Staying at Best Hostel is a little bit like crashing at a friend's house on short notice." This super-casual, scruffy, trippy little commune is a ramshackle, transformed apartment. While it comes with lots of street noise, it's well-run and handy (some dorms mixed, some only women, bed in 6- to 9-bed room-3,000 Ft, in 4-bed room-3,600 Ft, D-8,400 Ft, discount with hostel membership, open to all, no curfew, 29 beds, lockers, not a party hostel, a block from Nyugati Station on the corner of Teréz körút and Podmaniczky utca, at Podmaniczky utca 27, doorbell #33, tel. 1/332-4934, www.besthostel.hu, bestyh@mail.datanet.hu). From the Keleti Station, take tram #73 to the eighth stop, Teréz körút.

Buda

Víziváros

The Víziváros neighborhood—literally, "Water Town"—is the lively part of Buda, squeezed between Castle Hill and the Danube, where fishermen and tanners used to live. Across the river from the Parliament building, it comes with fine views. Today, it's the most pleasant central area to stay on the Buda side of the Danube. It's expensive and a little less convenient than Pest, but also more charming.

The following hotels (except the last one) are between the Chain Bridge and Buda's busy Margit körút ring road. Batthyány tér, a few minutes' walk away, is a handy center with a Metro stop

(M2 line). For a good hangout with Internet access near these hotels, try Soho Coffee Company (see page 350).

$$$ art'otel impresses New York City sophisticates. Every detail of the 164-room art'otel—from the breakfast dishes to the carpets—was designed by American artist Donald Sultan. This big, stylish hotel (part of a German chain of upscale theme hotels) is a fun, classy splurge. The location on the Danube embankment, close to the Batthyány tér Metro stop, is another big plus (rack rates: Sb-€198, Db-€218, bigger "executive" rooms-€20 more, deluxe "art suites"-€100 more; rates drop as low as Sb-€114/Db-€134 during slow times, which are often Aug–Sept; you'll save lots—often Db-€120—by booking online; non-smoking rooms, elevator, free Internet access, Bem rakpart 16-19, Budapest I, tel. 1/487-9487, fax 1/487-9488, www.artotel.hu, budapest@artotel.hu).

$$$ Hotel Victoria, with 27 business-class rooms—each with a grand river view—is a fine value. This tall, narrow place (9 floors, 3 rooms on each) is run with pride (Sb-€97, Db-€102, extra bed-€41, 30 percent less Nov–March, non-smoking rooms, elevator, free sauna, Internet access, parking garage-€9/day or park free on street, Bem rakpart 11, Budapest I, tel. 1/457-8080, fax 1/457-8088, www.victoria.hu, victoria@victoria.hu).

$$$ Hotel Astra is quiet, old-fashioned, and well-maintained. Its 12 rooms—surrounding a peaceful courtyard—are woody, elegant, and spacious (Sb-€90, Db-€105, huge, sumptuous Sb or Db suite-€135, extra bed-€20, 10 percent less Nov–March, cash only, Vám utca 6, Budapest I, tel. 1/214-1906, fax 1/214-1907, www.hotelastra.hu, hotelastra@euroweb.hu).

$$$ Carlton Hotel, located where the Castle Hill funicular meets the Chain Bridge, has 95 small rooms in a great location for getting to either Buda or Pest (Sb-€90, Db-€105, extra bed-€21, prices 20 percent lower Nov–March, ask about lower prices on weekends, non-smoking rooms, elevator, Internet access, parking garage-€12/day, Apor Péter utca 3, Budapest I, tel. 1/224-0999, fax 1/224-0990, www.carltonhotel.hu, carltonhotel@axelero.hu).

$ Hotel Papillon is farther north—a 10-minute walk past Moszkva tér—in a forgettable residential area. It's a cheery little place with 20 pastel and homey rooms, a garden with a tiny pool, and great prices (Sb-€38, Db-€48, Tb-€58, 25 percent less Nov–March, tram #4 or #6 from Moszkva tér to Mechwart stop, Rózsahegy utca 3B, tel. 1/212-4750, www.hotelpapillon.hu, papillon2@axelero.hu).

Castle Hill

Romantics often like calling Castle Hill home. The next three hotels share Holy Trinity Square (Szentháromság tér) with Matthias Church. They couldn't be closer to the Castle Hill sights, but they're in a tourist zone—dead at night—and less convenient to Pest than other listings.

Buda Hotels and Restaurants

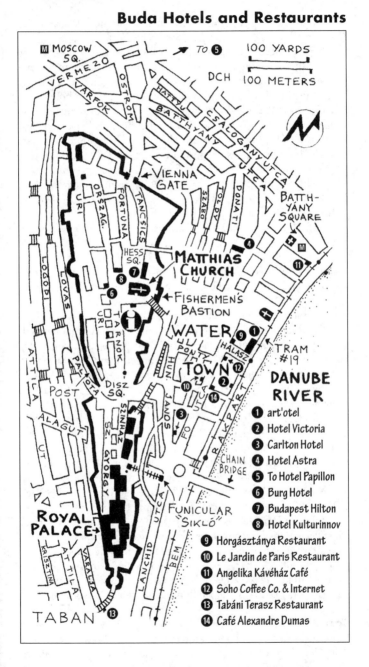

100 YARDS

100 METERS

- **1** art'otel
- **2** Hotel Victoria
- **3** Carlton Hotel
- **4** Hotel Astra
- **5** To Hotel Papillon
- **6** Burg Hotel
- **7** Budapest Hilton
- **8** Hotel Kulturinnov
- **9** Horgásztánya Restaurant
- **10** Le Jardin de Paris Restaurant
- **11** Angelika Kávéház Café
- **12** Soho Coffee Co. & Internet
- **13** Tabáni Terasz Restaurant
- **14** Café Alexandre Dumas

$$$ **Burg Hotel** is the best choice for those who want to stay on Castle Hill with a little more class than the Kulturinnov offers (see below). This 26-room place is simply efficient: concrete, spacious, and comfy, with a professional staff. You'll find more conveniently located hotels for less money elsewhere, but if you simply *must* stay in a modern hotel across the street from Matthias Church, this is it (Sb-€99, Db-€109, Db apartment-€129, extra bed-€39, 30 percent cheaper for 3-night stays, prices 15 percent cheaper Nov–March, non-smoking rooms, top-floor rooms are incredibly long, Szentháromság tér 7-8, Budapest I, tel. 1/212-0269, fax 1/212-3970, www.burghotelbudapest.com, hotel.burg@mail.datanet.hu).

$$$ **Budapest Hilton** is a 322-room landmark—the first big Western hotel in town, back in the gloomy days of communism. Today it remains the top of the top, offering a complete escape from Hungary and a chance to be surrounded by rich tourists from mostly Japan, Germany, and the United States (rack rates: Sb/Db-€220, drops to €180 if you book less than 3 days ahead, can be even cheaper in slow times—deals online, more for Danube-view rooms and suites, breakfast-€20, elevator, Hess András tér 1 on Castle Hill next to Matthias Church, tel. 1/889-6000, fax 1/889-6644, www.budapest.hilton.com, reservations.budapest@hilton.com).

$$ **Hotel Kulturinnov,** run by the Hungarian Culture Foundation, is in a big building that feels more like a museum than a hotel. The 16 rooms are basic, with old, frumpy furnishings, but it's still a great value for the location—or for anywhere in central Budapest (Sb-€64, Db-€80, Tb-€100, extra bed-€20, 25 percent less Nov–March, elevator, Szentháromság tér 6, Budapest I, tel. 1/355-0122, fax 1/375-1886, www.mka.hu, mka3hotel@dbassoc.hu).

EATING

Don't even bother trying to find a "local" restaurant in central Budapest. With the recent influx of tourists, and the resulting increase in prices, most Budapesters can't afford to eat out in the areas where you'll be spending your time. If you really want to eat local-style, head for the big shopping malls (like the Westend Citycenter near Nyugati Station, or Mammut near Moszkva tér). There, you can truly dine with the Budapesters...at T.G.I. Friday's and McDonald's, just like back home.

In lieu of actual "local" restaurants, I've unearthed a few good options with an at least partly local clientele—along with a few memorable, decidedly touristy places that are just plain fun. I've focused on eateries serving traditional Hungarian fare (see page 284), but also included some international and ethnic alternatives. Some Budapest restaurants endearingly suggest that they can make anything you want, even if it's not on the menu, so long as they've got the ingredients on hand. Don't leave town without sampling a *lángos,* a savory deep-fried doughnut spread with cheese, garlic, and sour cream (around 250 Ft).

Pest

Cheap and Moderate Places in Central Pest

Great Market Hall: At the far south end of Váci utca, you can eat a quick and cheap lunch on the upper floor of the Great Market Hall (Nagyvásárcsarnok). The **Fakanál Étterem** ("Wooden Spoon Cafeteria")—a glassed-in, sit-down cafeteria above the entrance—is good, with real tables and English on the blackboard (most main dishes 1,000–1,500 Ft, Mon–Fri 10:00–17:00, Sat 10:00–14:00, closed Sun, Fővám körút 1–3, Budapest IX, M3: Kálvin tér). But the stalls along the side of the building offer better prices with more choice and adventure. Grab a bar stool or you'll stand while you munch.

Centrál Kávéház, while famous as a grand, old-fashioned café, is also one of Budapest's best spots for a central, characteristic meal—with elegant turn-of-the-20th-century ambience to boot. The enticing menu offers traditional specials (especially the small but filling "Solo" plates, under 1,000 Ft), serious vegetarian offerings, sandwiches (600–1,000 Ft), elaborate salads (1,400–1,500 Ft), tempting desserts, and some fun history you should read (main plates 1,000–2,500 Ft, daily 8:00–24:00, Károlyi Mihály utca 9, Budapest V, tel. 1/266-4572).

Duran Szendvics, a cheery little eatery, is reminiscent of Scandinavian open-faced sandwich shops, where a dozen or so tempting little treats are displayed. Two sandwiches and a drink make a quick and healthy meal for about $2. Look at the window outside before ordering. This is your chance to try caviar cheaply (100 Ft per sandwich, they'll box things to go for a classy picnic, Mon–Fri 8:00–18:00, Sat 9:00–13:00, closed Sun; near Basilica, Postal Museum, and Deák tér Metro stop at the start of Andrássy út; Bajcsy-Zsilinszky utca 7, tel. 1/267-9624). There's a second location a few blocks in front of St. István's Basilica on Oktober 6 utca, near Zebra One (see below).

Bohémtanya ("Bohemian Pub") serves inexpensive, hearty Hungarian food in a humble restaurant actually frequented by some locals, huddled around their beers in a smoke-filled room (and neatly segregated from the tourists in the non-smoking room). The service can be stand-offish, the chef seems to have a thing for pigs' brains, and the food's pretty basic...but that's the point (most main dishes 1,000–1,500 Ft, daily 12:00–24:00, Paulai Ede utca 6, Budapest VI, tel. 1/267-3504). It's around the corner from Duran Szendvics (above), a block off Andrássy út and just up from Deák tér.

Zebra One Noodle Bar offers a refreshing break from all the

Pest's Best Dining Neighborhoods

When you ask locals about good places to eat on Váci utca, they just roll their eyes. Budapesters know that only rich tourists who don't know better would subject themselves to the exorbitant prices and relatively bad food and service along this very touristy pedestrian drag. But wander a few blocks off the tourist route, and you'll discover options with fair prices and better food.

If you want to do your own exploring beyond the specific eateries I've listed, here are a few neighborhoods to wander:

Franz Liszt Square (Liszt Ferenc tér), on the most interesting stretch of Andrássy út, has sprouted a stylish cluster of yuppie restaurants, many with outdoor seating (lively on a balmy summer evening). This is perhaps the most local dining neighborhood...for Budapesters who can afford it. Take the Metro to Oktogon and follow your nose (most main dishes hover around 2,000 Ft).

The **Danube Promenade,** the riverbank facing the castle, is lined with hotel restaurants and permanently moored restaurant boats. You'll find bad service, mediocre food, mostly tourists, and sky-high prices. But the atmosphere and people-watching are marvelous.

Ráday utca, stretching south from the Kálvin tér Metro stop (M3 line), has recently become a supremely hip place for young people to eat and hang out. With lots of trendy, inventive eateries and pubs, this is one of the hottest bits of central Budapest.

Veres Pálné utca, a low-key street hiding just two blocks up from Váci utca, is lined with colorful bars and restaurants more local-feeling than the norm.

meat, starch, and paprika. This flavorful, mod, pan-Asian restaurant—catering to businesspeople in the surrounding banking district—is the kind of place where it just feels right to use your chopsticks. Take advantage of their "business lunch" deal (available Mon–Fri 11:00–15:30), offering tasty soup and a generous entrée for 1,300 Ft (most main dishes 1,500–2,000 Ft, Mon–Sat 11:00–23:00, closed Sun, Oktober 6 utca #19, tel. 1/373-0092).

Resti Kocsma, with a communist-kitsch theme, is a time-warp trip to the days of Stalin. Live Gypsy music stirs the ambience (summer only), and even though the sign above the door eggs workers on with a "Let's cheer the First of May," the restaurant is often quiet and glum...with dreary communist food to match (most dishes 1,000–1,500 Ft, Sun–Thu 12:00–24:00, Fri–Sat 12:00–2:00 A.M., Deák Ferenc utca 2, Budapest V, tel. 1/226-6210). On Friday and Saturday nights, this place becomes a disco—and begins charging a 1,000-Ft cover—after 20:00.

If you absolutely *must* throw your money away on Váci utca, **Duo Restaurant** has acceptable Hungarian cuisine and good service in a classy setting with live Gypsy music (most main dishes 2,500–3,000 Ft, daily 12:00–23:00, music nightly 19:00–23:00, pricey wine list—the bottom-end Matraaljai Kékfránkos is fine, Váci utca 15–17, Budapest V, tel. 1/318-3814).

Worthwhile Splurges

Budapest is peppered with fancy splurge restaurants, pricey by tourist standards and impossibly expensive to locals (figure $10–20 per main dish). I recommend dining at at least one of these restaurants during your stay. But beware: Many of these restaurants feature nothing more than sub-par food and a packaged experience in the heart of the tourist zone. (One of the most prominent, Kárpátia, feels like eating in a lavishly decorated Byzantine church, with a Gypsy trio playing everything from traditional folk songs to adult contemporary hits. But the fact that you get a 15 percent discount with your Budapest Card should clue you in that it's 100 percent designed for tourists.) Instead, consider getting the most out of your splurge dollar at one of these fine choices.

Near City Park: **Gundel Restaurant** has been *the* dining spot for VIPs and celebrities since 1894. The place is an institution— President Bill Clinton ate here. The Pope didn't, but when his people called out for dinner, they called Gundel. The elegant main room is decorated with fine 19th-century Hungarian paintings. The furnishings come with an Art Deco flair. Reservations are wise— request near or far from the live Gypsy music. The food is traditional Hungarian (€20–30 main courses, music daily 18:30–24:00, in the park behind Heroes' Square at Állatkerti út 2, tel. 1/468-4040, www.gundel.hu). The dress code is formal. (While jackets are required, free loaners are available at the door if you travel like me. Ties and dresses are not required.)

Near the Opera House: **Articsóka** is hip, classy, romantic, and mellow, with its own theater in the back. This is where young Budapesters go to celebrate special occasions. You'll enjoy delicious Mediterranean cuisine, including vegetarian and pasta options...with a few Hungarian standbys on the menu, just in case (most dishes around 2,000 Ft, splurges up to 4,000 Ft, daily 12:00–24:00, a few blocks behind Opera at Zichy J. utca 17, Budapest VI, tel. 1/302-7757).

At Deák tér, near the bottom of Andrássy út: **Restaurant Művészinas** is fancy and central, serving traditional Hungarian and Mediterranean cuisine. Its 1920s and 1930s atmosphere is plush yet homey—like the candlelit living room of an artist who happens to be playing his favorite jazz on the phonograph (big-ticket main dishes 3,000–4,000 Ft, always several good vegetarian options, daily 12:00–24:00, 100 yards from Deák tér Metro stop, Bajcsy-Zsilinszky út 9, Budapest VI, tel. 1/268-1439).

Near Váci utca: **Rézkakas** (loosely translated as "Copper

Weathervane") is a genuinely classy, white-tablecloth place, with fine food to match. The high prices are justified, as this is a more sophisticated dining experience than the many slightly cheaper restaurants lining Váci utca a few blocks away (most dishes 3,000–5,000 Ft, daily 12:00–24:00, live music nightly from 19:00, reservations smart on weekends, Veres Pálné utca 3, tel. 1/318-0038).

Buda

These eateries are in or near the Víziváros ("Water Town") neighborhood, around the base of Castle Hill. You'll find plenty of touristy restaurants in the castle complex itself, but like the ones on Váci utca, those spots are overpriced. The following alternatives are just a quick downhill hike (or funicular ride) away. The first one is just beyond the south tip of Castle Hill (by the yellow church); the other three are in the heart of Víziváros, right between Castle Hill and the river. For specific locations, see page 344.

Tabáni Terasz is a newish place offering delicious, well-priced food (most main dishes 1,600–3,000 Ft) with several seating options: in a cozy, classy drawing-room interior; on a terrace out front; in the inner courtyard; or down below, in a beer hall (daily 10:00–24:00, Árpód utca 10).

Horgásztánya ("Fishermen's Pub") is a local spot for reliable, traditional Hungarian food—and a confused fisherman suspended from the ceiling. The staff can be quirky, but the restaurant is tasty and popular, with lots of fish on the menu (most main dishes around 1,500 Ft, daily 12:00–23:00, a block up from Danube at corner of Halász utca and Fő utca, Fő utca 27, Budapest I).

Le Jardin de Paris is small and peaceful, with an upscale clientele and live jazz nightly from 19:00 to 23:00. Depending on the weather, the music is either in the leafy garden (May–Sept) or in the charming dining room (Oct–April). Most main dishes run 2,500–3,000 Ft (daily 12:00–23:00, reservations smart, Fő utca 20, Budapest I, tel. 1/201-0047).

Café Alexandre Dumas, an airy, modern, glassy eatery on the ground floor of the French Institute, is a good option for Internet access and inexpensive salads and sandwiches (around 1,000 Ft) a block up from the Danube promenade (Mon–Fri 8:00–21:00, closed Sat–Sun, across the street from Jardin de Paris at Fő utca 17).

Cafés and Pastry Shops (*Kávéház* and *Cukrászda*)

Budapest once had a thriving café culture, like Vienna's. But realizing that these neighborhood living rooms were breeding grounds for dissidents, the communists closed the cafés or converted them into *esszpresszó*s (with uncomfortable stools instead of easy chairs) or *bisztro*s (stand-up fast-food joints with no chairs at all). Today Budapest's café scene is slowly coming back to life.

In Buda's Víziváros Neighborhood

Angelika Kávéház, in the heart of Víziváros, has coffee, pastries, and light food inside—or outside, with a riverside Parliament view. While the terrace is simply riverfront, the charmingly stale 1960s interior was a famous spot during communist days. It's changed little, and while it's hard to imagine this being posh...it was (main dishes 1,500–2,500 Ft, daily 9:00–24:00, Batthyány tér 7, tel. 1/212-3784).

Soho Coffee Company is a taste of Seattle with a Hungarian accent, combining good American-style lattes, cozy stay-awhile atmosphere, Internet access, and a jazz soundtrack (daily 8:00–21:00, Fő utca 25).

In Pest

On Vörösmarty Square: **Gerbeaud** (zher-BOW) isn't just a café—it's a landmark, the most famous restaurant in Budapest. Aside from coffee and pastries, you can also get a sandwich, salad, or other light meals. It's touristy, but central, historic, and great for people-watching (daily 9:00–21:00, on Vörösmarty tér).

Two blocks up from Váci utca: **Centrál Kávéház** is the Budapest café that best recaptures the turn-of-the-20th-century ambience, with elegant cakes and coffees, loaner newspapers, and a management that encourages loitering (daily 8:00–24:00, Károlyi Mihály utca 9, Budapest V, tel. 1/266-4572). This is also a great spot for a meal (see "Cheap and Moderate Places in Central Pest," above).

Near Ferenciek tere: **Jégbüfé** is where Pest urbanites get their quick, cheap, stand-at-a-counter fix of coffee and cakes. And for those feeling nostalgic for the communist days, little has changed here: First choose what you want at the counter, try to explain it to the cashier where you pay, then take your receipt back to the appropriate part of the counter (look up at the 4 signs: coffee, soft drinks, ice cream, cakes). Finally, trade your receipt for your goodie, go to the bar, and enjoy it standing up (daily 7:00–21:30, Ferenciek tere 10). Now...back to work.

Across from the Opera House: **Müvész Kávéház** is a classic coffeehouse with 19th-century elegance and a convenient location (daily 9:00–23:45, Andrássy út 29).

TRANSPORTATION CONNECTIONS

Budapest has three main stations (*pályaudvar,* or *pu.* for short): **Keleti** (Eastern, most international trains), **Nyugati** (Western, domestic and some international—especially eastbound), and **Déli** (Southern, mostly domestic trains and some international—especially southbound). Expect exceptions, and always confirm carefully which station your train leaves from. For general rail information in Hungary, call 1/461-5400; for information about international trains, call 1/461-5500.

By train to: Vienna (that's *Bécs* in Hungarian, 7/day direct, 3 hrs, from Keleti/Eastern; or hrly with a transfer in Bruck an der Leitha, Austria, from Keleti/Eastern, 3 hrs), **Bratislava** (that's *Pozsony* in Hungarian, hrly, direct, 2.5–3 hrs from either Keleti/Eastern or Nyugati/Western), **Prague** (5/day direct, including 1 night train, 7–9.5 hrs; most from Keleti/Eastern, some from Nyugati/Western), **Kraków** (1 direct night train/day from Keleti/Eastern with early arrival in Kraków, 11 hrs; otherwise transfer in Katowice, Poland, or Břeclav, Czech Republic, 9–10 hrs), **Ljubljana** (2/day direct, 8.5 hrs from Deli/Southern; no direct night train), **Munich** (1/day direct from Deli/Southern, 7.5 hrs; plus 1 direct night train/day from Keleti/Eastern, 10 hrs; otherwise transfer in Regensburg, Germany, or Vienna), **Berlin** (1/day direct, 12 hrs from Nyugati/Western; plus 1 direct night train/day, 14 hrs from Keleti/Eastern), **Zagreb** (2/day direct, 5 or 7 hrs) **Eger** (5/day direct, 2 hrs from Keleti/Eastern; or more from same station with transfer in Füzesabony), **Szentendre** (4–7/hr, 40 min on suburban HÉV train, leaves from Batthyány tér), **Visegrád** (trains arrive at Nagymaros, across the river—take shuttle boat to Visegrád; hrly, 1 hr from Nyugati/Western), and **Esztergom** (hrly, 1.5 hrs from Nyugati/Western). Note that Nagymaros (the Visegrád station) and Esztergom are on opposite sides of the river— and on different train lines.

By Boat: In the summer, Mahart runs daily high-speed hydro-foils up the Danube to Vienna. While this is not particularly scenic and slower than the train, it's a fun and romantic alternative. The boat leaves Budapest in April and September–October at 9:00 and arrives in Vienna at 15:20 (Vienna to Budapest: 9:00–14:30); May through August, the boat leaves Budapest at 8:00 and arrives in Vienna at 14:20 (Vienna to Budapest: 8:00–13:30). In August, a second boat does the same trip, leaving Budapest at 13:00 and arriving Vienna at 19:20 (Vienna to Budapest 13:00–18:30). The trip costs €75 one-way. On any of these boats, you can also stop in the Slovak capital, Bratislava. To confirm times and prices, and to buy tickets, contact Mahart (Budapest tel. 1/484-4013, www.mahartpassnave.hu).

The
DANUBE BEND
(Dunakanyar)

The Danube, which begins as a trickle in Germany's Black Forest, becomes the Mississippi River of Central Europe as it flows east through Vienna, then makes a sweeping right turn—called the Danube Bend—south towards Budapest, Belgrade, and the Black Sea. Three river towns, north of Budapest on the Danube Bend, offer a convenient day-trip getaway for urbanites who want to commune with nature.

Hungarians sunbathe and swim along the banks of the Danube, or hike in the rugged hills that rise up from the river. This is also one of Hungary's most historic stretches—for centuries, Hungarian kings ruled not from Buda or Pest, but from Visegrád and Esztergom.

Closest to Budapest is Szentendre, whose colorful, storybook-cute Baroque center is packed with tourists. The ruins of a mighty castle high on a hill watch over the town of Visegrád. Esztergom, birthplace of Hungary's first Christian king, has the country's biggest and most important church. All of this is within a one-hour drive of the capital, and also reachable (up to a point) by public transportation.

Planning Your Time

Szentendre is the easiest Danube Bend destination—just a quick suburban-train (HÉV) ride away, it can be done in a half day. Visegrád and Esztergom are more difficult to reach by public transportation; both require a substantial walk from the train or bus stop to the town's major sight.

Don't try to see all three towns in one day by public transportation—focus on one or two. Take a tour or rent a car to see all

The Danube Bend

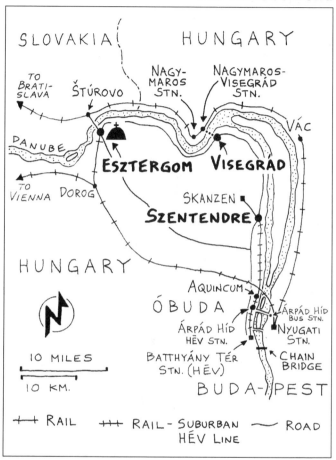

three (see "Helpful Hints" in Budapest chapter). With a car, do the Danube Bend this way: 9:00-Leave Budapest, 9:30-Arrive at Szentendre and see the town, 12:00-Leave Szentendre, 12:30-Lunch in Visegrád, 13:30-Tour Visegrád Royal Palace and Citadel, 15:30-Leave Visegrád, 16:00-Visit Esztergom Basilica, 17:00-Head back to Budapest. With extra time, or if you enjoy folk architecture, add a visit to the Hungarian Open-Air Museum ("Skanzen") near Szentendre.

If you're driving between Budapest and Vienna (or Bratislava), the Danube Bend towns are a fine way to break up the journey, but seeing all three en route makes for a very long day. Again, choose one or two.

Getting Around the Danube Bend

Going north from Budapest, the three towns line up along the same road on the west side of the Danube—Szentendre, Visegrád, Esztergom—each spaced about 15 miles apart.

By Car: It couldn't be easier. Get on road #11 going north out of Buda, and it'll take you through each of the three towns—the road bends with the Danube. As you approach Szentendre, watch for signs for *Centrum Szentendre* to branch off to the right, towards the old center and the river promenade.

Returning from Esztergom to Budapest, consider cutting the "bend." Road #10 is most direct, but can have heavy traffic on weekdays. The smaller road farther north (via Pilisszentkereszt) is slower and windier, but more scenic and less crowded.

By Boat: From early April to late October, Budapest-based Mahart runs boats and hydrofoils up the Danube Bend, some going all the way to Vienna. Confirm 2005 times and prices and buy tickets at Mahart in Budapest (dock near Vigadó tér in Pest, tel. 1/484-4000, www.mahartpassnave.hu). For details, see "Transportation Connections" at the end of the Budapest chapter (page 350).

Slower **"pleasure boats"** connect **Budapest to Szentendre and Visegrád** daily from early April to late October. Departure from Budapest is at 9:00, reaching Szentendre at 10:40 and Visegrád at 12:30; the return trip leaves Visegrád at 16:30 and Szentendre at 17:45, arriving back in Budapest at 19:00 (one-way Budapest–Szentendre-950 Ft, Budapest–Visegrád-1,050 Ft). From mid-May to mid-September, an express service runs from **Budapest to Szentendre** (only this direct boat uses Szentendre's convenient downtown dock; leaves Budapest at 10:30 and 14:00, leaves Szentendre at 12:20 and 17:00, trip takes 1.5 hrs upstream, 1 hr downstream, 1,400 Ft one-way).

If you want to get to Esztergom by boat, it can happen only from late May to late August, when there is daily service from **Budapest via Visegrád to Esztergom** (leaves Budapest 7:30, arrives Visegrád 10:50 and Esztergom 13:00; leaves Esztergom 16:00, arrives Visegrád 17:30 and Budapest 19:55). From early June to late August, another boat runs between **Esztergom and Visegrád** (leaves Esztergom 9:00, arrives Visegrád 10:25; returns from Visegrád 15:30, arrives Esztergom 17:30). One-way prices: Budapest–Visegrád-1,050 Ft, Budapest–Esztergom-1,200 Ft, Esztergom–Visegrád-700 Ft.

On summer weekends only, a high-speed **Budapest–Visegrád–Esztergom hydrofoil** leaves Budapest at 9:30, arriving in Visegrád at 10:30 and Esztergom at 11:00; the return trip leaves Esztergom at 16:15 and Visegrád at 16:45, arriving back in Budapest at 17:40 (runs Sat–Sun June–Aug, one-way to Visegrád-2,000 Ft, to Esztergom-2,300 Ft; round-trip to Visegrád-3,300 Ft, to Esztergom-3,800 Ft; doesn't stop in Szentendre).

By Train: The three towns are on three separate train lines. Szentendre is handy by train, while Esztergom and Visegrád are less convenient.

Szentendre is easy to reach by train; the HÉV, Budapest's suburban rail, zips you right there (catch train at Batthyány tér Metro station, 4–7/hr, 40 min each way, 374 Ft, 234 Ft with Budapest Card, buy tickets at windows marked *HÉV Jegypénztár*, sometimes requires change in Békásmegyer, last train returns from Szentendre around 23:00).

The nearest train station to **Visegrád** is actually across the river in Nagymaros (this station is called "Nagymaros-Visegrád"; don't get off at the station called simply "Nagymaros"). From the station, you'll walk five minutes to the river and take a ferry across to Visegrád (see "Arrival in Visegrád," page 359). Trains between Nagymaros-Visegrád and Budapest's Nyugati (Western) Station take an hour (hrly, 490 Ft).

To **Esztergom**, trains run hourly from Budapest's Nyugati Station (1.5 hrs, 490 Ft), but the Esztergom train station is 45 minutes' walk from the basilica.

By Bus: Buses are the best way to hop between the three towns. They're as quick as the train if coming from Budapest, but can be standing-room only. All buses to the Danube Bend leave from Budapest's Árpád híd bus station (by the M3 Metro station of the same name). There are two main routes. The river route (roughly hourly, more frequent during weekday rush hours) runs along the Danube through Szentendre (30 min) and Visegrád (80 min), then past Esztergom Basilica to the Esztergom bus station (120 min from Budapest). The inland route goes over the hills to Esztergom bus station via Piliscsaba (every 15–30 min, 80 min, last bus back leaves Esztergom 22:00). Buses make many stops en route, so you'll need to pay attention. One-way prices: Budapest–Szentendre-231 Ft, Szentendre–Visegrád-289 Ft, Visegrád–Esztergom Basilica-289 Ft.

By Tour from Budapest: If you want to see all three towns in one day, don't have a car, don't want to hassle with public transportation, and don't want to shell out for a private driver, a bus tour is the most convenient way to go. All of the companies are about the same (all three towns in 9–10 hrs, including Renaissance lunch feast in Visegrád and shopping stops, plus return on boat, for around 18,000 Ft); look for fliers at the TI or in your hotel's lobby.

Szentendre

The old town of Szentendre (SEHN-tehn-dreh, "St. Andrew" in English, pop. 23,000) rises gently from the Danube, a postcard-pretty village with a twisty Mediterranean street plan filled with

Austrian Baroque houses. Szentendre's old center rivals Budapest's
Castle Hill as the most touristy spot in Hungary. It promises a taste
of Hungarian village life without having to stray far from
Budapest...but it sometimes feels like too many people had this same
idea. This is where Budapesters bring their wives or girlfriends for
that special weekend lunch. The town has a long tradition as an
artists' colony, and it still has more than its share of museums and
galleries. The downside: streets clogged with tourists, ice-cream
stands, and tacky shops. But venture off the crowded main streets
and you'll soon have quiet back lanes under colorful Baroque steeples
all to yourself.

Tourist Information: The TI is along the tourist-clogged route
between the station and the main square (Mon–Fri 9:30–13:00 &
13:30–16:30, closed Sat–Sun, Dumtsa Jenő utca 22, just by the stream,
tel. 26/317-965, www.szentendre.hu, tourinform@szentendre.hu).

Arrival in Szentendre

The combined **train/HÉV and bus station** is at the southern edge of
town. To reach the center from the station, go through the pedestrian underpass at the head of the train tracks. This funnels you onto
the small Kossuth Lajos utca, which leads in 10 minutes to the main
square. (A handy map of town is posted by the head of the tracks.)
Some **boats** arrive right near the main square, but most come to a
pier about a 15-minute walk north of the center. After you get off
the boat, take the first path to your left; stay on this, and it'll lead
you straight ahead into town.

SIGHTS

▲**Main Square (Fő Tér)**—Szentendre's top sight is the town itself.
Start at the main square, Fő tér. Take a close look at that cross,
erected in 1763 to give thanks for surviving the plague. Notice the
Cyrillic lettering? After the Turks were forced out of Hungary, this
town was rebuilt primarily by Serbs who had fled those same Turks
down south. Look at the very narrow alleyways around the square.
Mediterranean towns often have walls close together to create shade
in the hot sun. Even though Hungary has a milder climate, old
habits die hard: The Serbs built the town in that style, anyway.
Various minor sights and museums line the lanes that branch off this
square.

Just up Alkotmány utca from the square, the tallest of
Szentendre's church spires belongs to the red-painted **Serbian
Orthodox cathedral,** with a fine iconostasis (partition with icons)
inside, and an icon collection in the attached museum (400 Ft,
Tue–Sun 10:00–18:00, closed Mon).

Leave the square on Görög utca and take your first right to find the **Margaret Kovács Museum** (Kovács Margit Múzeum), dedicated to a local artist (1902–1977) famous for whimsical, wide-eyed pottery sculptures based on Hungarian folktales and biblical themes (600 Ft, mid-March–Sept daily 10:00–18:00; Oct–mid-March Tue–Sun 9:00–16:00, closed Mon; Vastagh György utca 1).

Between the square and the TI, you'll find the "**Marzipan Museum**"—a candy and ice cream store whose upper floor displays marzipan models of the Hungarian Parliament, the *turul* bird, the Muppets, Michael Jackson, and much more. It's fun for kids, but skippable for adults (shop free, upper floor 350 Ft, May–Sept daily 9:00–19:00, Oct–April daily 10:00–18:00, Dumtsa Jenő utca 12, tel. 26/311-931).

Enjoy a stroll through town. Head off to the back streets (try the hill behind the square) and you'll be surprised at how quickly you find yourself alone with Szentendre.

▲**Hungarian Open-Air Folk Museum (Szabadtéri Néprajzi Múzeum, a.k.a. Skanzen)**—Three miles northwest of Szentendre is an open-air museum featuring examples of traditional Hungarian architecture from all over the country. As with similar museums all over Europe, these aren't replicas—each building was taken apart at its original location, transported piece by piece, and reassembled here. Five of 10 planned museum modules are now complete. The museum is huge and spread out, so a thorough visit could take several hours. The admission price includes a map in English, and the museum shop sells a more comprehensive English guidebook (600–700 Ft, April–Oct Tue–Sun 9:00–17:00, closed Mon and Nov–March, last entry 30 min before closing, Sztaravodai út, tel. 26/502-500, www.skanzen.hu).

Buses leave from the Szentendre station for Skanzen every 60–90 minutes (100 Ft, departs from platform 7, 12-min trip, no buses 12:00–14:00 on weekends). A **taxi** to the museum should cost no more than 2,000 Ft; the TI can call one for you.

SLEEPING

(200 Ft = about $1, country code: 36, area code: 26)
In recent years, the delightful little burg of Szentendre has become a bedroom community for nearby Budapest. I don't advise staying here if Budapest is your main interest—it takes too long to get into the city, and hotels in Budapest aren't expensive. But if you must stay here, these two places rent acceptable second-story rooms along the Danube embankment just north of the center.

Corner Panzió has five cozy, woody rooms. Prices rise in the summer, when they turn on the air-conditioning (Sb/Db: June–Sept 10,000 Ft, breakfast-1,000 Ft; Oct–May 8,000 Ft, breakfast-500 Ft; cash only, Duna korzó 4, tel. & fax 26/301-524, www.radoczy.hu).

Centrum Panzió has six pleasant enough rooms with a dark red color scheme (Sb-8,000 Ft, Db-10,000–12,000 Ft, includes breakfast, cash only, Bogdányi utca 15, at corner of Duna korzó, tel. & fax 26/302-500, www.hotels.hu/centrum_panzio, hotel.centrum @axelero.hu).

Visegrád

Visegrád (VEE-sheh-grahd, Slavic for "High Castle," pop. 1,400) is a small village next to the remains of two major-league castles: a hilltop citadel and a riverside palace.

At this strategic site overlooking the river, there has been—since Roman times—a citadel atop the steep hill. When Károly Róbert (Charles Robert), from the French Anjou dynasty, became Hungary's first non-Magyar king in 1323, he was so unpopular with the nobles in Buda that he had to set up court in Visegrád, where he built a new residential palace down closer to the Danube. Later, King Mátyás Corvinus—notorious for his penchant for Renaissance excess—ruled from Buda but made Visegrád his summer home, and turned the riverside palace into what some called a "paradise on earth." Mátyás knew how to party; during his time here those red marble fountains flowed with wine.

In memory of these grand times, **Hotel Visegrád** today runs a Renaissance-themed restaurant, with period cookware, food, costumed waitstaff, and live lute music—just the spot for Danube Bend tour groups (can't miss it, by the palace).

Today, both citadel and palace are but a shadow of their former selves. The citadel was left to crumble after the Hapsburg reoccupation of Hungary in 1686, while the palace was covered by a mudslide during the Turkish occupation, and is still being excavated. The citadel is more interesting, but difficult to reach by public transport. Non-drivers who don't want to make the steep hike to the citadel, and are in too much of a hurry to sort through the taxi and bus options up, should skip this town.

ORIENTATION

Visegrád is basically a wide spot in the riverside road, squeezed between the hills and the riverbank. At the main intersection of Visegrád (coming from Szentendre/Budapest), the cross road leads to the left through the heart of the village, then hairpins up the hills to the citadel. To the right is the dock for the ferry to Nagymaros (home to the closest train station, called Nagymaros-Visegrád—see "Arrival in Visegrád," below).

The town has two sights. The less interesting riverside Royal

The Visegrád Connection

The Royal Palace at Visegrád has been the site of two important meetings of Central European leaders. In 1335, as Hapsburg Austria was rising to the west, the kings of Hungary, Poland, and Bohemia converged on the Visegrád Palace to strategize against this new threat. The meeting wasn't successful; all of the countries involved ultimately lost territory to the Hapsburgs.

In February 1991, the Iron Curtain had fallen, and the East was looking to the future. The heads of state of these same countries—Hungary, Poland, and Czechoslovakia—once again came together in the Visegrád Palace, this time to compare notes about Westernization. To this day, these countries are still often referred to as the "Visegrád countries."

Palace is a 15-minute walk downriver (towards Szentendre/Budapest) from the village center. The hilltop citadel, high above the village, is the focal point of a larger recreation area best explored by car.

Tourist Information: The **Visegrád Tours** travel agency at the village crossroads is not an official TI, but does have transport schedules posted in the window, sells maps, and hands out a few free leaflets (April–Oct daily 8:00–17:30, Nov–March 10:00–16:00, Rév utca 15, tel. 26/398-160, www.visegradtours.hu).

Arrival in Visegrád

Train travelers arrive across the river at the Nagymaros-Visegrád station (don't get off at the station called simply "Nagymaros"—see "Getting Around the Danube Bend," above). Walk five minutes to the river and catch the ferry to Visegrád, which lands near the village's main crossroads (250 Ft, hrly, usually in sync with the train, last ferry 20:45). Visegrád's most convenient **bus stop** is at the main crossroads, but there's also a stop a little downstream, by the river boat dock. The **dock**, near the Royal Palace and Hotel Visegrád, is where boats from Budapest stop. To reach the village center from the dock, follow the paved riverside footpath 15 minutes upriver (towards Esztergom).

SIGHTS

▲**Visegrád Citadel (Fellegvár)**—The remains of Visegrád's hilltop citadel are fun to explore. Scramble across the ramparts, try your hand with a bow and arrow, or pose with a bird of prey perched on your arm. See fun wax sculptures enjoying a medieval feast—and demonstrating the collection of torture devices. Only a few exhibits have English labels, but borrow the free English audioguide. You can also sometimes find a small English book about the citadel (350 Ft). At the top, you have commanding views over the Danube Bend—which, of course, is exactly why they built it here (750 Ft, mid-March–Oct daily 9:00–17:00; Nov–mid-March Sat–Sun 9:30–15:30 in good weather only, usually closed Mon–Fri).

Around the citadel is a **recreational area** that includes three restaurants, a picnic area, a luge and toboggan run, a network of hiking paths, a Waldorf school, and a children's nature education center and campground. By the luge run and walkable from the citadel, the **Nagy-Villám restaurant** is elegant, with breathtaking views from the best tables (April–Oct daily 12:00–22:00, closed Nov–March, tel. 26/398-070). A bit farther away, the simpler **Mogyoróhegy restaurant** is in an early building by Organic architecture pioneer Imre Makovecz, who also designed the striking school gymnasium in Visegrád village—white and brown, with a row of 12 spikes on the roof (restaurant open mid-April–Sept daily 9:00–20:00, closed Oct–mid-April, tel. 26/398-237). For more on Makovecz, see page 375. Only drivers can reach the **picnic area** (called Telgárthy-rét), in a shady valley with paths and waterfalls.

Getting to Visegrád Citadel: To **drive** to the citadel, simply follow signs for *Fellegvár* down the village's main street and up into the hills. To get to the citadel from the town center without a car, you have three options:

1. **Hike.** Buy a map at the Visegrád Tours office and figure on 40 steep min from the village center.

2. Take the **taxi service** called "City Bus." The minivan trip up and back costs 2,000 Ft total, no matter how many people ride along (ask at Visegrád Tours or call 26/397-372).

3. Take the **public bus** (200 Ft, April–Sept only, 2/day, catch from bus stop on Danube side of main road at the crossroads at 12:28 and 15:28 or 1 min earlier at Royal Palace, reconfirm schedules in advance; this bus comes from Szentendre, where it departs at 11:45 and 14:45).

Royal Palace (Király Palota)—Under King Mátyás Corvinus, this
riverside ruin was one of Europe's most elaborate Renaissance palaces. During the Turkish occupation, it was deserted and eventually buried by a mudslide. For generations, the existence of the palace faded into legend, so its rediscovery in 1934 was a surprise. Today the partially excavated remains are tourable and interesting;
unfortunately, there's no English-language guidebook. Keep your eye out for the red marble fountain, which spouted wine for parties (500 Ft, Tue–Sun 9:00–16:30, closed Mon, tel. 26/398-026, www.visegrad.hu/muzeum).

Esztergom

Esztergom (EHS-tehr-gohm, pop. 29,000) is an unassuming town with a big Suzuki factory. You'd never guess it was the first capital of Hungary—until you see the towering 19th-century Esztergom Basilica, built on the site where István (Stephen) I, Hungary's first Christian king, was crowned in 1000 A.D.

Arrival in Esztergom

Esztergom's **boat dock** is more convenient to the basilica than are the bus or train stations (can't miss the basilica as you disembark—hike on up). If arriving by **bus** from Visegrád, get off by the basilica, not at the bus station. (Buses from Budapest via Piliscsaba do not pass the basilica.) To reach the basilica on foot from the **train station**, allow at least 45 minutes. Continue in the same direction as the train tracks, and when the street forks go straight along the residential Ady Endre utca. After a few minutes, you'll pass the bus station, from which it's 30 minutes farther to the basilica. Local buses run between the train station and the basilica roughly hourly. On Wednesdays and Fridays, an open-air market livens up the street between the bus station and the center.

If you happen to be on your way to Bratislava, there is also a handy train station across the river in **Štúrovo, Slovakia** (cross the border on foot as you cross the bridge).

SIGHTS

Esztergom Basilica

The basilica commemorates Hungary's entry into the fold of Western Christendom. It tops a hill a steep hike up from the center of town and the boat dock. The hill was once strongly fortified, and some ruins of its castle survive (housing a mediocre museum). The  neoclassical basilica, completed in 1869, was built on top of these remains. With a 330-foot-tall dome, this is the biggest church in Hungary. St. István was born in Esztergom, and on Christmas Day in the year 1000—shortly after marrying the daughter of the king of Bavaria and accepting Christianity—he was crowned here by the Pope (for more on St. István, see page 310).

Enter through the side door, which is on the left as you face the front of the basilica (free, daily 6:00–18:00). In the foyer, the stairway leading down to the right takes you to the crypt housing the remains of **Cardinal József Mindszenty,** revered for standing up to

Cardinal József Mindszenty
(1892–1975)

Mindszenty was a Catholic Church leader who spoke out aggressively against the communist government. In 1948, the communists arrested him and tortured him for 39 days. He was imprisoned in Budapest until the 1956 Uprising, when he was freed and took refuge in the U.S. Embassy. There he stayed for 15 years, unable to leave for fear of being captured. (Many Catholic Americans remember praying for Cardinal Mindszenty every day when they were kids.) In 1971, he agreed to step down from his position, then fled to Austria.

On his deathbed in 1975, Mindszenty said that he did not want his body returned to Hungary as long as there was a single Russian soldier still stationed there. As the Iron Curtain was falling in 1989, Mindszenty emerged as an important hero to post-communist Hungarians, who wanted to bring his remains back to his homeland. But Mindszenty's secretary, in accordance with the Cardinal's final wishes, literally locked himself to the coffin—refusing to let the body be transported as long as any Soviet soldier remained in Hungary. In May 1991, when only a few Russians were still in Hungary, Mindszenty's remains were finally brought to the crypt in the Esztergom Basilica.

the communist government (100 Ft, daily 9:00–16:30, last entry 15 min before closing). The stairway leading up goes to the church tower (200 Ft).

Enter the cavernous **nave**. There are plenty of fancy tour-guide stats about this church—for example, the altarpiece is the biggest single-canvas painting in the world. But mostly, the sheer size of the church is what impresses visitors.

As you face the altar, find the chapel on the left before the transept. This Renaissance **Bakócz Chapel** actually predates the basilica by 350 years. When the basilica was built, they broke the chapel into 1,600 pieces and rebuilt it, piece by piece, inside the new structure. The heads around the chapel's altar had been defaced by Turks, who believed that only God—not sculptors—can create man.

Consider visiting the **treasury,** to the right of the main altar (400 Ft, daily 9:00–16:30). Though the collection is standard ecclesiastical stuff, there are some interesting models inside the entry: a big one showing off the even more ambitious original plans for the basilica complex; smaller ones of the frames of the basilica's wooden nave and metal dome; and yet another showing what Esztergom looked like in the early 16th century (notice the more modest church that stood where this basilica is today).

When you're finished in the basilica, head around to the back for a thrilling **Danube overview**. That's Štúrovo, Slovakia, across the river. The bridge connecting them was destroyed in World War II and rebuilt only recently. Before its reconstruction, no bridges spanned the Danube between Budapest and Bratislava.

A cavernous restaurant catering to tour groups is built into the fortifications underneath the basilica (enter from bus parking lot). On Batthyány Lajos utca, a block into the residential neighborhood across the street, are two smaller restaurants with garden seating: the Szent Tamás-hegyi Kisvendeglő and the more expensive Csülök Csárda.

EGER

You've probably never heard of the enchanting Back Door town of Eger (EH-gehr). It's a midsized city (pop. 70,000) in northern Hungary, the seat of a bishop and home to a small teacher-training college. Hungarians think proudly of Eger as the town that, against all odds, successfully held off the Turkish advance into Europe in 1552. Eger is the mecca of Hungarian school field trips because of its stirring history. If the town is known internationally for anything, it's for the surrounding wine region (the best-known product is Bull's Blood, or Egri Bikavér).

But don't let its lack of popularity keep you away—in fact, that's part of Eger's charm. Rather than growing jaded from floods of American tourists, Egerites go about their daily routines amidst charming Baroque buildings, watched over by one of Hungary's most important castles. It all comes together to make Eger an ideal introduction to small-town Hungary.

Planning Your Time

Eger is worth a relaxing day on a trip between Kraków and Budapest (or as a side-trip from Budapest—possible in a day, but better as an overnight). The sights are few but fun, the ambience is great, and strolling is a must.

A perfect day in Eger begins with a browse through the colorful market and a low-key ramble on the castle ramparts. Then head to the Lyceum to visit the library and astronomy museum, and climb up to the thrillingly low-tech camera obscura. Take in the midday organ concert in the cathedral across the street from the Lyceum. In the afternoon, relax on the square or, better yet, at the spa. If you need more to do, consider an afternoon drive into the countryside (including visits to local vintners—get details at TI). Round out your day with a visit to Eger's touristy wine caves in the Sirens' Valley.

Eger

1. Panoráma Hotel
2. Imola Udvarház Rooms
3. Offi Ház Hotel
4. Szent János Hotel
5. Senator Ház Hotel & Rest.
6. Dobó Vendégház Rooms
7. HBH Bajor Sörház Rest.
8. Elefanto Pizza
9. Palacsintavár Rest.
10. Szantofer Vendéglő Restaurant
11. Dobós Cukrászda Pastries
12. Sárvári Cukrászda Pastries
13. Népműveszét Shop
14. Castle Entrance

ORIENTATION

(area code: 36)

Eger Castle sits at the top of the town, hovering over Dobó Square (Dobó István tér). This main square is divided in half by the Eger Creek, which bisects the town. Two blocks west of Dobó Square is the main pedestrian drag, Széchenyi utca, where you'll find the Lyceum and the cathedral. A few blocks due south from the castle (follow Eger Creek) are Eger's various spas and baths.

Tourist Information

Eger's on-the-ball, eager-to-please TI (TourInform) is the most efficient place to get any Eger question answered. They give out a free brochure and town map, as well as piles of other brochures about the city and region. They can't book rooms, but they can help you find one—or anything else you're looking for (mid-June–mid-Sept daily 9:00–20:00; off-season Mon–Fri 9:00–17:00, Sat 9:00–13:00, closed Sun, Bajcsy-Zsilinszky utca 9, tel. 36/517-715).

Arrival in Eger

By Train: Eger's tiny train station is a 20-minute walk south of the center. The closest **ATM** is at the Spar grocery store just up the street (turn left out of station, go straight about 2 blocks between seemingly abandoned warehouses, and look for red-and-white supermarket on your right). A taxi into the center will cost you around 1,000 Ft.

To catch the **bus** towards the center, go straight out of the station, and when the road you're on veers right, cross it to get to the bus stop on the busier road above it. Bus #11, #12, or #14 cuts about 10 minutes off the walk into town (160 Ft, buy ticket from driver, cheaper if you buy from kiosk, get off when you see the big, yellow cathedral). To **walk** all the way, leave the station straight ahead, turn right with the road, and then continue straight ahead (on Deák Ferenc utca) until you run into the cathedral. With your back to the cathedral entry, the main square is two blocks in front of you and to the left.

By Car: In this small town, most hotels will provide parking or help you find a lot. For a short visit, the most central lot is behind the department store on Dobó Square.

Getting Around Eger

Everything of interest in Eger is within walking distance, except maybe the Sirens' Valley wine caves—for these, catch a cab (starts at 220 Ft, then around 250 Ft/km; try City Taxi, tel. 36/555-555).

Eger Landmarks

English	Hungarian	Pronounced
Main Square ("Dobó Square")	**Dobó István tér**	DOH-boh EESHT-vahn tehr
(Eger) Castle	**(Egri) Vár**	(EHG-ree) vahr
Market Hall	**Csarnok**	CHAWR-nohk
Bull's Blood (local blend of red wines)	**Egri Bikavér**	EH-gree BEE-kah-vehr

Helpful Hints

Language Barrier: Having fewer American visitors means that Egerites are not as likely to speak English as in more mainstream Eastern European destinations. (Consider it part of the adventure.) Eger does get lots of German tourists, so if you speak any German, it may come in handy. Even if you don't share a language, most people from Eger are eager to find some way to communicate. The TI is happy to act as a go-between with a Hungarian-only sight or business.

Tours of Eger: A couple of hokey little **tourist trains** do circuits around Eger, leaving the main square every hour on the hour. The blue one is a bigger operation (400 Ft, 75 min, includes a trip to Sirens' Valley wine caves); the white one is smaller (just around town, 45 min). There are no organized town walking tours, but the TI can put you in touch with a **local guide.**

Internet Access: Broadway Café, hiding under the cathedral, has fast, cheap access (Mon–Sat 11:00–23:00, Sun 15:00–23:00; as you face the front of the cathedral, it's around the left side).

Shopping: For folk art, try the Népműveszét shop (Mon–Fri 9:30–18:00, Sat–Sun 9:30–17:00, Bajcsy-Zsilinszky utca 1).

Concerts: Daily from mid-May to mid-October, Hungary's second biggest organ booms out a 30-minute concert in the cathedral (400 Ft, Mon–Sat at 11:30, Sun at 12:45). Some Mondays in June and July, children perform a musical about Eger history on a stage in Dobó Square ("Little Stars of Eger," free, starts at 18:00, check with TI for schedule).

SIGHTS

▲▲Dobó Square (Dobó István tér)—Dobó Square is the heart of Eger. In most towns this beautiful, the main square is packed with postcard stalls and other tourist traps. Refreshingly, Eger's square seems mostly packed with Egerites. Ringed by breathtaking Baroque buildings, decorated with vivid sculptures depicting the city's noble

István Dobó and the Siege of Eger

In the 16th century, Turkish invaders swept into Hungary. They easily defeated a Hungarian army—in just two hours—at the notorious Battle of Mohács in 1526. After the victory, the Turks gradually worked their way up the Balkan Peninsula, threatening to overrun the entire Continent. When Buda and Pest fell to the Turks in 1541, all of Europe looked to Eger as the last line of defense. István Dobó and his second-in-command, István Mekcsey, were put in charge of Eger's forces. They prepared the castle (which still overlooks the square) for a siege and waited.

On September 11, 1552—after a summer spent conquering more than 30 other Hungarian fortresses on their march northward—40,000 Turks arrived in Eger. Only about 2,000 Egerites (soldiers, their wives, and their children) remained to protect their town. The Turks expected an easy victory, but the siege dragged on for 39 days. Eger's soldiers fought valiantly, and the women of Eger also joined the fray, pouring hot tar down on the Turks...everyone pitched in. A Hungarian officer named Gergely Bornemissza, sent to reinforce the people of Eger, startled the Turks with all manner of clever and deadly explosives. Finally, the Turks left in shame, Eger was saved, and Dobó was a national hero.

The unfortunate epilogue: The Turks came back in 1596 and, this time, succeeded in conquering an Eger Castle guarded by unmotivated mercenaries. The Turks sacked the town and controlled the region for close to a century.

In 1897, a castle archaeologist named Géza Gárdonyi moved from Budapest to Eger, and tales of the siege captured his imagination. Gárdonyi wrote a book about István Dobó and the 1552 Siege of Eger called *Egri Csillagok* (literally, "Stars of Eger," translated into English as *Eclipse of the Crescent Moon,* available at local bookstores and souvenir stands). The book—a favorite of many Hungarians—is taught in schools, keeping the legend of Eger's heroes alive today.

past, and watched over by Eger's historic castle, this square is one of the most pleasant spots in Hungary.

The statue in the middle is **István Dobó,** the square's namesake and Eger's greatest hero, who defended the city—and all of Hungary—from a Turkish invasion in 1552 (see his story in the sidebar). Next to Dobó is his co-commander, István Mekcsey. And right at their side is one of the brave women of Eger—depicted here throwing a pot down onto the attackers.

Use the square to orient yourself to the

town. Behind the statue of Dobó is a bridge over the stream that bisects the city, and on the other side of the bridge is the charming **Little Dobó Square,** home to the town's best hotels (see "Sleeping," page 376). As you cross the bridge towards Little Dobó Square, look to the left and you'll see the northernmost minaret in Europe—once part of a Turkish mosque (see below). Hovering above Little Dobó Square is Eger Castle (see below).

Now face in the opposite direction, with Dobó's statue at your back. On your right is a handy department store. On your left, dominating the square, is the beautiful pink Minorite Church. The

monument in front of you and on the left also commemorates the 1552 defense of Eger: one Egerite against two Turkish soldiers, reminding us of the townspeople's bravery despite the odds. Straight ahead, two blocks beyond the end of the square, runs Széchenyi utca, Eger's main pedestrian drag. At the left end of Széchenyi utca are the cathedral and Lyceum. To reach the TI, jog left at the end of the square, then right onto Bajcsy-Zsilinszky utca (TI one block ahead on right). To visit the Market Hall, leave Dobó Square to the right (on Zalár József utca, with department store on your right-hand side; you'll see Market Hall on left).

▲**Eger Castle (Egri Vár)**—This castle is Hungary's Alamo, where István Dobó defended Eger from the Turks in 1552. Today it's usually crawling with school-age kids on field trips from all over the country.

The great St. István—Hungary's first Christian king—built a church on this hill a thousand years ago. The church was destroyed by Tartars in the 13th century, and this fortress was built to repel another attack.

The castle grounds feature several small museums, including a history museum, picture gallery, dungeon, underground casements (tunnels through the castle walls), Heroes' Hall (with the grave of István Dobó), and temporary exhibits. None of the castle museums is particularly fascinating, but most merit a quick look. For those of us who didn't grow up hearing the legend of István Dobó, the whole complex is hard to appreciate. Most visitors find that the most rewarding plan is to stroll up, wander around the grounds, enjoy the view overlooking the town (find the minaret and other landmarks), maybe pay a visit to the waxworks (see below), and then head back down past a gaggle of colorful shops.

Cost and Hours: 300 Ft for grounds only; 800-Ft ticket gets you into any museum you want. The underground casements and Heroes' Hall are only accessible by one-hour tour (500 Ft extra, call ahead to ask if English tour is scheduled, tel. 36/312-744, ext. 111;

tours likely July–Aug, otherwise depends on guides' schedules). The castle grounds are open April–Aug daily 8:00–20:00, Sept until 19:00, March and Oct until 18:00, Nov–Feb until 17:00. The castle museums are open March–Oct Tue–Sun 9:00–17:00, Nov–Feb Tue–Sun 10:00–16:00, always closed Mon. General castle info: tel. 36/312-744, www.div.iif.hu.

Other Castle Sights: In addition to the castle museums, there are three privately run exhibits, each with its own hours and prices: the **archery** exhibit (100–200 Ft per arrow to use old-fashioned bows and crossbows); the **mint** (200 Ft, usually 9:00–15:30, unpredictable hours); and the **waxworks,** or "Panoptikum" (350 Ft, daily 9:00–18:00, less in winter). Of these, the waxworks is by far the best—it's the most enjoyable part of the whole castle complex. You'll see a handful of eerily realistic heroes and villains from the siege of Eger (including István Dobó himself, and the leader of the Turks sitting in his colorful tent). Notice the exaggerated Central Asian features of the Egerites—a reminder that the Magyars were more Asian than European. Sound effects add to the fun...think of it as a very low-tech, walk-through *Ottomans of the Caribbean*. You'll also have the chance to scramble through a segment of the casements that run inside the castle walls.

Getting to Eger Castle: To reach the castle from Dobó Square, go toward Senator Ház Hotel, then jog right around the hotel, turning right on Dobó István utca. Take this street a few blocks until it swings down to the right; the ramp up to the castle is to your left.

▲▲**Eger Cathedral**—Eger's 19th-century bishops peppered the city with beautiful buildings—including the second biggest church in Hungary (after Esztergom's—see Danube Bend chapter). With a quirky, sumptuous, Baroque-feeling interior, Eger's cathedral is well worth a visit.

Eger Cathedral was built in the 1830s by an Austrian archbishop who had previously served in Venice and thought Eger could use a little more class. The colonnaded neoclassical facade, painted a pretty Baroque yellow, boasts some fine Italian sculpture. As you walk up the main stairs, first you'll pass saints István and László—Hungary's first two Christian kings—and then the apostles Peter and Paul.

Enter the cathedral (free) and walk to the collection box partway down the nave. Then, facing the door, look up at the ornate **ceiling fresco:** On the left, it shows Hungarians in traditional dress, and on the right, the country's most important historical figures. At the bottom you see this cathedral, celestially connected with St. Peter's in Rome (at the top). This symbol of devotion to the Vatican was a brave statement when it was painted, in 1950. The communists were closing churches in other small Hungarian towns, but the Eger archbishop had enough clout to keep this one open.

Continue to the **transept.** A few years ago, the windows at either end were donated to the cathedral by a rich Austrian couple to commemorate the millennial anniversary of Hungary's conversion to Christianity—notice the dates 1000 (when King István was crowned by the Pope) and 2000.

As you leave, notice the enormous **organ**—Hungary's second largest—above the door. In the summer, try to catch one of the cathedral's daily half-hour organ concerts (400 Ft, Mon–Sat at 11:30 and Sun at 12:45, mid-May–mid-Oct only; cathedral is the big, can't-miss-it yellow building at Pyrker János tér 1, just off Széchenyi utca).

If you walk up Széchenyi utca from here, you'll see the fancy Archbishop's Palace on your left—still home to Eger's archbishop.

▲▲Lyceum (Líceum)—In the mid-18th century, Bishop Károly Eszterházy wanted a university in Eger, but Hapsburg Empress Maria Theresa refused to allow it. So, instead, Eszterházy built the most impressive teacher-training college on the planet. The elegant Lyceum still trains local teachers (enrollment: about 2,000). Since Eger is expensive by Hungarian standards, many families live in the surrounding countryside. The kids all come into Eger for school—and lots of teachers are needed.

Aside from training teachers, the Lyceum houses three small, offbeat, interesting museums (450 Ft for library, another 450 Ft for astronomical tower and camera obscura, April–Sept Tue–Sun 9:30–15:30, closed Mon; Oct–March Sat–Sun only 9:30–13:30, closed Mon–Fri; last entry 30 min before closing, Eszterházy tér 1, at south end of Széchenyi utca at intersection with Kossuth utca, enter through main door across from cathedral and buy tickets just inside and to the left; www.ektf.hu/eger/english).

First, visit the old-fashioned **library** (from main entry hall, head right and go up stairs partway down the hall on your right-hand side; at top of first flight of stairs, turn right into the hall and look for the library halfway down on the right; watch for easy-to-miss signs). The library houses 50,000 books (plus another 100,000 elsewhere in the building). Say hello to Dénes Szabó, who has spent the last 11 years cataloging these books—no easy task, since they're in over 100 languages (from Eskimo to Ethiopian) and are shelved according to size, rather than topic. If he's not away for a choral contest, Mr. Szabó will be happy to show you a copy of the library's pride and joy, a letter from Mozart. While the Lyceum now belongs to Eger, the library is still the property of the archbishop.

A few flights above (leave library to the right, go to end of hall to reach stairs) is the **Astronomical Tower,** with some dusty old stargazing instruments, as well as a meridian line in the floor (the dot of sunlight hits the line every day exactly at noon).

Yet a few more flights up is the Lyceum's treasured **camera obscura.** You'll enter a dark room around a big, bowl-like canvas, and the guide will fly you around the streets of Eger. Fun as it is today, this camera must have seemed like a miracle when it was built in 1776—before TV or movies. It's a bit of a huff to get up here (9 flights of stairs all together)—but the camera obscura and the view of Eger from the outdoor terrace are worth it.

▲**Market Hall (Csarnok)**—Wandering Eger's big indoor market will give you a taste of local life—and maybe some local food, too. It's packed with Egerites choosing the very best of the fresh produce. Tomatoes plus peppers of all colors and sizes are abundant—magic ingredients that give Hungarian food its kick (and that won't grow in colder Poland or the Czech Republic, with tamer cuisine). To reach the market, leave Dobó Square with the castle to your back; turn right on Zalár József utca, and you'll see the market on your left in two blocks at the intersection with Dr. Sándor utca (mid-April–mid-Oct Mon–Fri 6:00–18:00, Sat–Sun 6:00–10:00; mid-Oct–mid-April Mon–Fri 6:00–17:00, Sat 6:00–13:00, closed Sun).

Minaret—Once part of a mosque, this slender, 130-foot-tall minaret represents the century of Turkish rule that left its mark on Eger and all of Hungary. The little cross at the top symbolizes the eventual Christian victory over Hungary's Turkish invaders. You can climb the minaret's 97 steps for fine views of Eger—but it's not for those scared of heights or tight spaces (200 Ft, April–Oct daily 10:00–18:00, closed Nov–March; if it's locked, ask for the key at nearby Hotel Minaret).

Minorite Church—The church that stands over Dobó Square is often said to be the most beautiful Baroque church in Hungary—even if it could use some touch-up work. It's exquisitely photogenic outside, but the shabby interior is less interesting, aside from the hand-carved pews, each of which is a little different.

Other Museums—Two small museums lie between Little Dobó Square and the entrance to the castle; neither is worth a visit, unless you have a special interest in the subject matter. The **Palóc Folklore Museum** is a measly little place with a handful of traditional tools, textiles, ceramics, costumes, and pieces of furniture (140 Ft, no English whatsoever, April–Oct Tue–Sun 9:00–17:00, closed Mon and Nov–March, Dobó utca 12). The **Historical Exhibition of Weapons** is just that, featuring centuries of Eger armaments: clubs, rifles, and everything in between (400 Ft, Tue–Sun 9:00–17:00, closed Mon, 450-Ft booklet labels weapons in English, 1,600-Ft English book gives more info, Dobó utca 9).

EXPERIENCES

Aqua Eger

Swimming and water sports are as important to Egerites as good wine. They're proud that many of Hungary's Olympic medalists in aquatic events have come from this county.

To test the waters of this part of Eger, you can join the locals lounging and laughing around in the city bath (see "Taking the Waters" on page 280). Or you can take a more serious approach—doing laps (and appreciating the unique architecture) at the city swimming pool.

▲Thermal Bath Complex (Eger Thermálfürdő)—For a refreshing break from the sightseeing grind, consider a splash in the spa. This is a fine opportunity to try a Hungarian bath: modern enough to feel accessible (opened just recently), but frequented mostly by locals. While Budapest has many great baths (see page 331), you may want to take a dip in low-key Eger and save your Budapest time for big-city sights.

You'll enter and be given a little barcode to swipe across the turnstile scanner. Trade this in for a key to a locker. Change, stow your stuff in a locker, put the key around your wrist, then join the fun. The heart of the complex is the new, green-domed, indoor-outdoor "adventure bath." Its cascades, jets, bubbles, geysers, and powerful current pool will make you feel like a kid again. For some warmer water, follow your nose to the old-fashioned sulfur pool—where Egerites sit peacefully, ignore the slight stink, and (supposedly) feel their arthritis ebb away. There's also a big outdoor lap pool (closed off-season).

Note that you can't rent a swimsuit or a towel; bring both with you, along with shower sandals for the locker room (if you've got them).

Cost, Hours, Location: 800 Ft, adventure bath included Oct–April but 500 Ft extra May–Sept; kids get their own adventure bath (500 Ft). Open May–Sept Mon–Fri 6:00–19:30, Sat–Sun 8:00–19:00; Oct–April daily 9:00–18:30. It's at Petőfi tér 2 (tel. 36/314-142, www.egertermal.hu). From Dobó Square, follow the stream four blocks south (signs for *Strand*), past the big, unusual swimming pool building (described below). Continue following the stream into the park; you'll see the main entrance to the bath on your left over a bridge.

Turkish Bath—This traditional place, next door to the city bath, is open to the public only on weekends (700 Ft, Sat 14:00–18:00, Sun 8:00–18:00, Fürdő utca 1–3, tel. 36/413-356).

Bitskey Aladár Pool—This striking new swimming pool—built at great expense to Eger taxpayers, stirring up controversy—was designed

by Imre Makovecz, the father of Hungary's trendy Organic style of architecture. You don't need to be an architecture student to know that the pool is something special. It's worth the five-minute walk from Dobó Square just to take a look...oh, and you can swim in it, too (690 Ft, Mon, Wed, and Fri 6:00–21:00, Tue and Thu 6:00–22:00, Sat

8:00–20:00, Sun 8:00–18:00, follow Eger Creek south from Dobó Square to Frank Tivadar utca, tel. 36/511-810). Like the city bath, this place does not rent out swimsuits—B.Y.O.S.S.

Eger Wine

Eger is at the heart of one of Hungary's best-known wine regions, internationally famous for its **Bull's Blood** (Egri Bikavér). You'll likely hear various stories as to how Bull's Blood got its name during the Turkish siege of Eger. My favorite version: The Turks were amazed at the ferocity displayed by the Egerites, and wondered what they were drinking that boiled their blood and stained their beards so red...it must be some pretty potent stuff. Local merchants, knowing that the Turks were Muslim and couldn't drink alcohol, told them it was bull's blood. The merchants made a buck, and the name stuck.

Creative as these stories are, they're all bunk—the term dates only from 1851. Egri Bikavér is a blend—everyone has their own recipe—so you generally won't find it at small producers. Cabernet Sauvignon, Merlot, Kékfránkos, and Kékoportó are the most commonly used grapes.

Try Egri Bikavér, but then move quickly on to the more special and characteristic Hungarian wines, such as Leányka ("Little Girl"), Kékfránkos ("Blue Frankish"), Furmint, Hárslevélű, and Kéknyelű. You also might have heard of Tokaji Aszú wine (a sweet white made from a grape of Hungarian origin, also grown in the Alsace region of France—where it's known as *tokay*). Tokaj is a town (not too far from Eger), and Aszú is the method for producing the wine (involving paste made from "noble rot" grapes).

Sirens' Valley (Szépasszony-völgy)—When the Turkish invaders first occupied Eger, residents moved into the valley next door, living in caves dug into the hillside. Eventually the Turks were driven out, the Egerites moved back to town, and the caves became wine cellars. (Most Eger families who can afford it have at least a modest vineyard in the countryside.) There are more than 300 such caves in the valley to the southwest of Eger, several of which are open for visitors.

The best selection of these caves (about 50) is in the Sirens' Valley (sometimes also translated as "Valley of the Beautiful Women," or, on local directional signs, the less poetic "Nice Woman Valley"). It's a fun scene—locals showing off their latest vintage, with picnic tables and tipsy tourists spilling out into the street. Most caves offer something to eat with the wine, and you'll also see lots of non-cave, full-service restaurants. Some of the caves are fancy and finished, staffed by multilingual waiters in period costume. Others feel like a dank basement, with grandpa leaning on his moped out front. (The really local places—where the decor is cement, bottles don't have labels, and food consists of potato chips and buttered Wonder

Hungary's Organic Architecture

In recent years, a uniquely Hungarian style of architecture has caught on—Organic—developed and championed by Imre Makovecz. After being blackballed by the communists for his nationalistic politics, Makovecz was denied access to building materials, so he taught himself to make impressive structures with nothing more than sticks and rocks.

Now that the regime is dead and Makovecz is Hungary's premier architect, he still keeps things simple. He believes that a building should be a product of its environment, rather than a cookie-cutter copy. Organic buildings use indigenous materials (especially wood) and take on untraditional forms—often inspired by animals or plants—that blend in with the landscape. Organic buildings look like they're rising up out of the ground, rather than plopped down on top of it. You generally won't find this back-to-nature style in big cities like Budapest; Makovecz prefers to work in small communities such as Eger (see photo on page 373), instead of working for corporations.

Organic architecture has caught on throughout Hungary, becoming *the* post-communist style. Even big supermarket chains are now imitating Makovecz. If you see a building with white walls and a big, overhanging roof (resembling a big mushroom)...that's Organic.

Bread—can be the most fun.) Hopping from cave to musky cave can make for an enjoyable evening, but be sure to wander around a bit to see the options before you dive in (cellars generally open 10:00–22:00 in summer, best June–Aug after 19:00; it's much quieter off-season, when only a handful of cellars remain open, with shorter hours).

Getting to the Sirens' Valley: The valley is a 25-minute walk southwest of Eger. Figure around 1,000 Ft for a **taxi** between your hotel and the caves. To **walk,** leave the pedestrian zone on the street next to the cathedral (Törvényház utca), with the cathedral on your right-hand side. Take the first left just after the back end of the cathedral (onto Trinitárius utca), go one long block, then take the first right (onto Király utca). At the fork, bear to the left. You'll stay straight on this road—crossing busy Koháry István utca—for several blocks, through some nondescript residential areas (on Szépasszony-völgy utca). When you crest the hill and emerge from the houses, you'll see the caves (and tour buses) below you on the left—go left (downhill) at the fork to get there. First you'll come to a stretch of touristy non-cave restaurants; keep going past these, and eventually you'll see a big loop of caves on your left.

SLEEPING

Eger is a good overnight stop, and a couple of quaint, well-located hotels in particular—Senator Ház and Offi Ház—are well worth booking in advance. The TI can help you find a room; if you're stumped, the area behind the castle has a sprinkling of guesthouses *(vendégház)*. A tax of 300 Ft per person will be added to your bill (not included in the prices listed here).

$$$ **Panoráma Hotel** is a good big-hotel option, still close to Dobó Square. You'll miss the quaintness of some of the other listings—its 38 rooms are all business—but you get free access to its "Unicornis Thermarium" spa facility (small Sb-12,500 Ft, large Sb-16,500 Ft, Db-19,500 Ft, Tb-23,500 Ft, 10 percent cheaper Nov–March, apartments also available, non-smoking rooms, elevator, free parking, Dr. Hibay K. utca 2, tel. 36/412-886, fax 36/410-136, www.hotels.hu/panorama_hotel, hoteleger@panoramahotels.hu).

$$$ **Imola Udvarház** rents six spacious apartments—with kitchen, living room, bedroom, and bathroom—all decorated modern Scandinavian (read: Ikea). They're pricey, but roomy and well-maintained, with a great location near the castle entrance (prices per night no matter how many people: April–Oct 22,000 Ft, Nov–March 16,500 Ft, prices soft during slow times; 1,500 Ft per person for breakfast in restaurant, or use your kitchen to make your own breakfast; enter through restaurant courtyard at Dózsa György tér 4, tel. & fax 36/516-180, www.imolanet.hu, udvarhaz@imolanet.hu).

$$ **Senator Ház Hotel** is my favorite spot in Eger, and one of the best small, family-run hotels in all of Eastern Europe. Though the 11 rooms are a bit worn, it's cozy and well-run by András Cseh, with oodles of character and a picture-perfect location just under the castle on Little Dobó Square (Sb-13,000 Ft, Db-17,800 Ft, extra bed-4,600 Ft, 15-30 percent cheaper Nov–April, Dobó István tér 11, tel. & fax 36/320-466, www.hotels.hu/senatorhaz, senator @enternet.hu). The Cseh family also runs **Pátria Vendégház**—two doubles and four apartments with the same rates, new, woody decor, and a little less character around a courtyard in a nearby building.

$$ **Offi Ház Hotel** shares Little Dobó Square with Senator Ház. Its five rooms are classy and romantic (Sb-15,500 Ft, Db-17,500 Ft, Db suite-20,500 Ft, Tb suite-23,500 Ft, extra bed-4,000 Ft, 10 percent cheaper Jan–April, 25 percent cheaper Oct–Dec, non-smoking, Dobó István tér 5, tel. & fax 36/311-005, www.offihaz.hu, offihaz@axelero.hu).

$$ **Szent János Hotel,** less charming and more businesslike than the Senator Ház and Offi Ház, offers a decent but less atmospheric location, 10 straight-laced rooms, and a slightly better value (Sb-€50 Db-€68, extra bed-€22, 25 percent cheaper Nov–March, non-smoking rooms, McDonald's walk-up window across the street can

---

Sleep Code

(€1 = about $1.20, 200 Ft = about $1, country code: 36, area code: 36)
S = Single, **D** = Double/Twin, **T** = Triple, **Q** = Quad,
b = bathroom, **s** = shower only, **NSE** = does not speak English.
Unless otherwise noted, English is spoken, breakfast is included,
and credit cards are accepted.

To help you sort easily through these listings, I've divided
the rooms into three categories, based on the price for a standard
double room with bath:

 $$$ **Higher Priced**—Most rooms 19,000 Ft (€80) or more.
 $$ **Moderately Priced**—Most rooms between
          12,000–19,000 Ft (€50–80).
 $ **Lower Priced**—Most rooms 12,000 Ft (€50) or less.

---

be noisy at night—especially weekends—so request a quiet back
room, a long block off Dobó Square at Szent János utca 3, tel. 36/510-
350, fax 36/517-101, www.hotelszentjanos.hu, hotelszentjanos
@hotelszentjanos.hu).

$ Dobó Vendégház, run by friendly Mariann Kleszo, has seven
basic but colorful rooms just off Dobó Square. Mariann speaks nothing but Hungarian, but gets simple reservation e-mails and faxes
translated by a friend (Sb-€30, Db-€40, Tb-€45, Qb-€55, cash only,
Dobó utca 19, tel. 36/421-407, fax 36/516-612, www.hotels.hu
/dobo_vendeghaz, csillagd@axelero.hu).

EATING

Bajor Sörház (a.k.a. **HBH** for the brand of beer on tap) is favored
by tourists and locals alike for its excellent Hungarian cuisine.
Everything's good here; I especially like their spicy *gulyás leves* soup
(that's *real* Hungarian goulash—see page 284). They also feature
some Bavarian specialties...but with a Hungarian accent (most main
dishes 1,000–1,500 Ft, daily 11:30–22:00, right at the bottom of
Dobó Square at Bajcsy-Zsilinszky utca 19, tel. 36/515-516).

The recommended hotels **Senator Ház** and **Offi Ház** both
have restaurants at the top end of Dobó Square. These places have
fine food and picturesque outdoor seating that shares Little Dobó
Square with a gazebo featuring cheesy live music in summer. This is
the place to see and be seen in Eger (see "Sleeping," above).

Elefanto, above the Market Hall, offers good, inexpensive
pizzas (mostly 600–900 Ft) and a pleasant ambience. In warm
weather, enjoy the covered terrace seating (daily 12:00–24:00,
Katona István tér 2, tel. 36/412-452).

Palacsintavár ("Pancake Castle"), near the castle entrance, isn't your hometown IHOP. This place serves up inventive crêpe-wrapped main courses, popular with local students (most main dishes 1,000–1,200 Ft, open long hours daily, Dobó utca 9).

Szantofer Vendéglő serves mostly traditional Hungarian food at local prices to both Egerites and tourists. The decent, fill-the-tank food is presented with an artistic flourish—some plates fly miniature Hungarian flags. Steer clear of the few ethnic offerings (like chicken tikka), and you'll do fine (most main dishes under 1,100 Ft, daily 11:30–22:00, Bródy Sándor utca 3, tel. 36/517-298). The creatively translated menu is good for a laugh while you're choosing your food.

Dessert: You'll see *cukrászda* (pastry shops) lining the streets. For deluxe, super-decadent pastries of every kind imaginable—most for under $2—drop by **Dobós Cukrászda** (daily 9:00–21:00, point to what you want inside and they'll bring it out to your table, Széchenyi utca 6, tel. 36/413-335). For a more local scene, find the tiny **Sárvári Cukrászda,** behind the Lyceum. Their pastries are good, but Egerites line up here after a big Sunday lunch for their homemade gelato (100 Ft/scoop, Mon–Fri 7:00–18:00, Sat–Sun 10:00–18:00, Kossuth utca 1, between Jókai utca and Fellner utca).

TRANSPORTATION CONNECTIONS

From Eger by train: The only major destination you'll get to directly from Eger's train station is **Budapest** (5/day direct to Budapest's Keleti Station, 2 hrs; more with a transfer in Füzesabony—see below). For most other destinations, you'll connect through Budapest. For destinations to the north—like Kraków—you'll save time by transferring in **Füzesabony** (13/day, 50 min), a nearby smaller village that happens to be on the Budapest–Kraków line. The very rustic Füzesabony station does not have lockers, but—oddly enough—does have a modest museum of local artifacts. If arriving on an international night train (i.e., from Kraków), note that there is no ATM at the station; venture two blocks into town to find one (bear to the left), or wait until Eger.

SLOVENIA
(Slovenija)

Tiny, overlooked Slovenia is one of Europe's most unexpectedly charming destinations. At the intersection of the Slavic, German, and Italian worlds, Slovenia is an exciting mix of the best of each culture. Though it's just a quick trip away from the tourist throngs in Venice, Munich, Salzburg, and Vienna, Slovenia has stayed off the tourist track, a handy detour for in-the-know Back Door travelers.

Today, it seems strange to think that Slovenia was ever part of Yugoslavia. Both in the personality of its people and in its landscape, Slovenia feels more like Austria. Slovenes are more industrious, organized, and punctual than their fellow former Yugoslavs...yet still friendly, relaxed, and Mediterranean. Locals like the balance. Visitors expecting minefields and rusting Yugo factories are pleasantly surprised to find Slovenia's rolling countryside dotted instead with quaint alpine villages and the spires of miniature Baroque churches, with breathtaking, snow-capped peaks in the distance.

Only half as big as Switzerland, but remarkably diverse for its size, Slovenia can be easily appreciated on a brief visit of even just a day or two. Travelers can hike on Alpine trails in the morning and explore some of the world's best karstic caves in the afternoon, before relaxing with a seafood dinner on the Adriatic (along the nation's 29 miles of coastline).

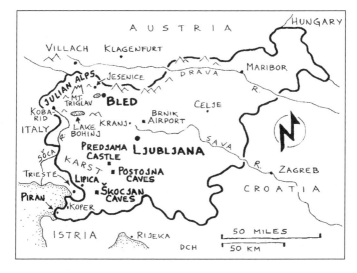

How Big, How Many, How Much

- Slovenia is 7,800 square miles (smaller than New Hampshire, or about the same size as Israel).
- Population is 2 million (about 255 people per square mile).
- 200 tolars (SIT) = about $1
- Country code: 386

Slovenia enjoys a powerhouse economy—the healthiest in Eastern Europe. Of the 10 new nations that joined the European Union in 2004, Slovenia was the only one rich enough to be a net donor (with a higher per-capita income than the average), and the only one already qualified to join the euro currency zone (even so, it won't begin using the euro until 2007). Thanks to its long-standing ties to the West and can-do spirit, Slovenia already feels more Western than any other destination in this book.

The country has a funny way of making people fall in love with it. Many of today's American visitors are soldiers who participated in the conflict in nearby Bosnia and have good memories of their vacations here. Now they're bringing their families back with them. They're not the only ones. One of your co-authors has decided that Slovenia is his hands-down favorite European country.

The Slovene language is as mellow as the people. While Slovenes use Serb and German curses in abundance, the worst they can say in their native tongue is, "May you be kicked by a horse." For "Darn it!" they say, "Three hundred hairy bears!"

Coming from such a small country, locals are proud of the few things that are distinctly Slovenian, such as the roofed hayrack. Foreigners think that Slovenes' fascination with these hayracks is strange...until they visit, and see them absolutely everywhere (especially in the northwest). Because of the frequent rainfall, the hayracks are covered by a roof that allows the hay to dry thoroughly. The most traditional kind is the *toplar,* consisting of two hayracks connected by one big roof. It looks like a skinny barn with open, fenced sides. Hay hangs on the sides to dry; firewood,

carts, tractors, and other farm implements sit on the ground inside; and dried hay is stored in the loft up above. These wooden *toplarji* are firetraps, and a stray bolt of lighting can burn one down in a flash. In recent years, more farmers are moving to single hayracks *(enojni);* these are still roofed, but look less quaint, with posts made of concrete, rather than wood. You'll find postcards and miniature wooden models of both kinds of hayracks (a fun souvenir).

Another good (and uniquely Slovenian) memento is a creatively decorated front panel from a beehive *(panjske končnice)*. Slovenia has a strong beekeeping tradition, and beekeepers once believed that painting the fronts of the hives made it easier for bees to find their way home. Replicas of these panels are available at gift shops all over the country. (For more on beekeeping, see page 433.)

To really stretch your tolar, try one of Slovenia's more than 200 farmhouse B&Bs, called "tourist farms" *(turistične kmetije)*. Use the B&B as a home base to explore the entire country—remember, the farthest reaches of Slovenia are only a day trip away. You can get a comfortable, hotelesque double with private bathroom—plus a traditional Slovenian dinner and a hearty breakfast—for as little as $40. Request a listing from the Slovenian Tourist Board (see page 9), or visit www.slovenia-tourism.si/touristfarms.

Slovenia is destined to become one of Eastern Europe's top destinations in the next few years. Now is the time to visit, while the locals are still friendly, the prices are still reasonable, and the lanes and trails are yours alone.

Practicalities

Telephones: Chip cards, sold at newsstands and kiosks everywhere, get you access to the modern public phones.

When calling locally, dial the seven-digit number. To make a long-distance call within the country, start with the area code (which begins with 0). To call a Slovenian number from abroad, dial the international access number (00 if calling from Europe, 011 from the United States or Canada) followed by 386 (Slovenia's country code), then the area code (without the initial 0) and the seven-digit number. To call out of Slovenia, dial 00, the country code of the country you're calling (see chart in appendix), the area code if applicable (may need to drop initial zero), and the local number.

Slovenian phone numbers beginning with 080 are toll-free; 090 and 089 denote expensive toll lines. Mobile phone numbers usually begin with 031, 041, 051, 040, or 070.

Slovenian History

Slovenia has a long and not very interesting history as part of various larger empires. Charlemagne's Franks conquered the tiny land in the 8th century, and, ever since, Slovenia has been a backwater of the German world—as a holding of the Germanic Holy Roman Empire and, later, the Hapsburg Empire. Slovenia often seems as much German as Slavic. But even as the capital, Ljubljana, was populated by Austrians (called "Laibach" by its German-speaking residents), the Slovenian language and cultural traditions survived in the countryside.

Ljubljana rose to international prominence for half a decade (1809–1813) when Napoleon named it the capital of his "Illyrian

Slo-what?-ia

"The only thing I know about Slovakia is what I learned firsthand from your foreign minister, who came to Texas."
—George W. Bush, to a Slovak journalist
(Bush had actually met with Dr. Janez Drnovšek,
then Slovenia's prime minister)

Maybe it's understandable that many Americans confuse Slovenia with Slovakia. Both are small, mountainous countries that not too long ago were parts of bigger, better known, now defunct nations. But anyone who has visited Slovenia and Slovakia will set you straight—they feel worlds apart.

Slovenia, wedged between the Alps and the Adriatic, is a tidy, prosperous country with a strong economy that led the pack of nations who joined the European Union in 2004. Until 1991, Slovenia was one of the six republics that made up Yugoslavia. Historically, Slovenia has had very strong ties with Germanic culture—so it feels German.

Slovakia, two countries away—to the northeast—is slightly bigger. Much of its territory is covered by the Carpathian Mountains, most notably the dramatic, jagged peaks of the High Tatras. In 1993, the Czechs and Slovaks peacefully chose to go their separate ways, so the nation of Czechoslovakia dissolved into the Czech Republic and the Slovak Republic (a.k.a. Slovakia). Slovakia is at the bottom of the heap of new EU members, with a weak economy and high poverty levels. Slovakia was part of Hungary until the end of World War I, and feels Hungarian (especially the southern half of the country, where many Hungarians still live).

To make things even more confusing, there's also **Slavonia.** This is the thick, inland "panhandle" that makes up the northeast half of Croatia, along Slovenia's southeast border. Much of the warfare in Croatia's 1991–1995 war took place in Slavonia (including Vukovar; see Understanding Yugoslavia chapter).

I won't tell on you if you mix them up. But if you want to feel smarter than the president, do a little homework and get it right.

Provinces," stretching from Austria's Tirol to Croatia's Dalmatian Coast. During this time, the long-suppressed Slovene language was used for the first time in schools and the government. Inspired by the patriotic poetry of France Prešeren, nationalism surged.

The most interesting chapter in Slovenian history happened in the last century. Some of World War I's fiercest fighting occurred at the Soča (Isonzo) Front in northwest Slovenia, witnessed by young Ernest Hemingway, who drove an ambulance. After the war, from 1918 to 1991, Slovenia was Yugoslavia's smallest, northernmost, and most affluent republic. Concerned about Slobodan Milošević's politics, Slovenia seceded in 1991. Because more than 90 percent of the people here are ethnic Slovenes, the break with Yugoslavia was simple and virtually uncontested. Its war for independence lasted just 10 days and claimed only 66 lives (For more details, see the Understanding Yugoslavia chapter, page 663).

After centuries of looking to the West, Slovenia became the first of the former Yugoslav republics to join the European Union in May 2004. The Slovenes are practical about this move, realizing it's essential for their survival as a tiny nation in a modern world. But there are trade-offs, and "Euro-skeptics" are down on EU bureaucracy. As borders disappear, Slovenes are experiencing more crime. Local farming is threatened by EU standards. There are no more cheap bananas (because the brown ones must be trashed), and "you can't sell a cucumber with more than a three-degree curve." Slovenian businesses are having difficulty competing with big German and Western firms. Before EU membership, only Slovenes could own Slovenian land. Now foreigners are buying property, driving up real estate prices.

Still, the Slovenes have kept their sense of humor about the change. The port city of Trieste, which used to be a Yugoslav/Slovenian city, was claimed by Italy after World War II—a move that still strikes many Slovenes as unfair. The day after Slovenia joined the EU, graffiti in the streets of Ljubljana bragged, "We got Trieste back!"

Slovenian Food

Slovenian cuisine has enjoyed influence from a wide variety of sources. Like Croatian food, it features some pan-Balkan elements. The red-bell-pepper condiment *ajvar* is popular here. For fast food, you'll find *burek, čevapčići, pljeskavica,* and *ražnjići* (see "Croatian Food," page 453). Italian influence is notable in Slovenia, with a pizza or pasta restaurant on seemingly every corner. Hungarian food simmers in the northeast corner of the country (where many Magyars reside).

But most of all, Slovenian food has a distinctly German vibe—sausages, schnitzels, strudels, and sauerkraut are common here, as well as *repa* (turnip prepared like sauerkraut). Slovenes brag that their cuisine melds the best of Italian and German cooking.

Traditional Slovenian dishes are prepared with groats—kind of a grainy mush made with buckwheat, barley, or corn. Buckwheat is often on Slovenian menus, because the country's climate is ideal for growing it. You'll also see plenty of *štruklji* (dumplings), which can be stuffed with cheese, meat, or vegetables. Among the hearty soups in Slovenia is *jota*—a staple for Karst peasants, made from *repa*, beans, and vegetables.

The cuisine of Slovenia's Karst (the arid limestone plain south of

Ljubljana) is notable. The small farms and wineries of this region have been inspired by Italy's "Slow Food" movement (www.slowfood.com), and believe that cuisine is meant to be gradually appreciated, not rushed—making the Karst a destination for gourmet tours. Karstic cuisine is similar to France's nouvelle cuisine—several courses in small portions, with a focus on unusual combinations and preparations—but with an Italian flair. The Karst's tasty air-dried ham *(pršut),* available throughout the country, is worth seeking out. Istria (the peninsula just to the south of the Karst, in southern Slovenia and Croatia) produces truffles that, locals boast, are as good as Piedmont's, but much cheaper.

Slovenian food, with all of its influences—Italian, Austrian, Balkan, Hungarian, and Karstic—comes together in Ljubljana. The capital city also has a cosmopolitan diversity of options, from Mexican to Chinese to Moroccan.

Voda is water, and *kava* is coffee. Radenska, in the bottle with the three little hearts, is Slovenia's best-known brand of mineral water—good enough that the word *Radenska* is synonymous with bottled water all over Slovenia and throughout the former Yugoslavia. Adventurous teetotalers should forego the Coke and sample Cockta (a Slovenian soft drink like a cola, but with a slight cherry, smoky aftertaste).

To toast, say, *"Na ZDRAV-yeh!"*—if you can't remember it, think of "Nice driving!" The premier Slovenian brand of *pivo* (beer) is Union (OO-nee-ohn). Slovenia also produces some fine *vino* (wine). The Celts first grew wine in Slovenia; the Romans improved the process and spread it throughout the country. Slovenia has three primary wine regions. Podravje, in the northeast, is dominated by Laški and Renski Riesling and other top-quality wines. Posavje, in the southeast, produces both white and red wines, but is famous for the light, russet-colored Cviček wine. Primorska, in the southwest, has a Mediterranean climate and produces mostly reds, including Teran, made from *refošk* grapes.

Slovenia's most popular desserts are *potica* (filled nut roll) and *prekmurska gibanica* (pastry filled with poppy seeds, walnuts, apple, and cheese). Bled is known for its *kremna rezina,* a vanilla custard and cream cake. Locals claim that Ljubljana has the finest gelato outside of Italy—which, after all, is just 90 minutes away by car.

Slovenian Language

Slovene is surprisingly different from languages spoken in the other former Yugoslav republics. While Serbian and Croatian are virtually identical, Slovene is another story. Of all Slavic languages, Slovene has changed the least over the centuries—it's still closest to the proto-Slavonic spoken over a millennium ago in the plains of present-day Ukraine.

Key Slovene Phrases

English	Slovene	Pronounced
Hello. (formal)	**Dober dan.**	DOH-behr dahn
Hi. / Bye. (informal)	**Živjo.**	ZHEEV-yoh
Do you speak English?	**Ali govorite angleško?**	AH-lee goh-VOH-ree-teh ahng-LEHSH-koh
yes / no	**ja / ne**	yah / neh
Please. / You're welcome.	**Prosim.**	PROH-seem
Can I help you?	**Izvolite?**	eez-VOH-lee-teh
Thank you.	**Hvala.**	HVAH-lah
I'm sorry. / Excuse me.	**Oprostite.**	oh-proh-STEE-teh
Good.	**Dobro.**	DOH-broh
Goodbye.	**Nasvidenje.**	nahs-VEE-dehn-yeh
one / two	**ena / dve**	EH-nah / dveh
three / four	**tri / štiri**	tree / SHTEE-ree
five / six	**pet / šest**	peht / shehst
seven / eight	**sedem / osem**	SEH-dehm / OH-sehm
nine / ten	**devet / deset**	deh-VEHT / deh-SEHT
hundred	**sto**	stoh
thousand	**tisoč**	TEE-sohch
How much?	**Koliko?**	KOH-lee-koh
local currency	**tolar (SIT)**	TOH-lar
Where is...?	**Kje je...?**	kyeh yeh
...the toilet	**...vece**	VEHT-seh
men	**moški**	MOHSH-kee
women	**ženski**	ZHEHN-skee
water / coffee	**voda / kava**	VOH-dah / KAH-vah
beer / wine	**pivo / vino**	PEE-voh / VEE-noh
Cheers!	**Na zdravje!**	nah ZDRAHV-yeh
the bill	**račun**	rah-CHOON

Most Slovenes know Serbo-Croatian because, a generation ago, everybody in Yugoslavia had to learn it (along with the Cyrillic alphabet used in Serbia). The tiny country of Slovenia borders Italy and Austria, with important historical and linguistic ties to both. For self-preservation, the Slovene population has always been forced to function in many different languages. All of these factors make Slovenes excellent linguists. Most young Slovenes speak effortless, flawless English—then admit that they've never set foot in the United States or Britain, but love watching American movies and TV shows (which are always subtitled, never dubbed).

Slovene is perhaps the easiest Eastern European language to pronounce. As with most Slavic languages, *c* is pronounced "ts" (like "cats"). The letter *j* is pronounced as "y"—making "Ljubljana" easier to say than it looks (lyoob-lyonna). In contrast to other Eastern European languages—which tend to have a wide array of confusing little doohickeys over the letters—Slovene only has one diacritical mark: the *strešica*, or "little roof." This makes *č* sound like "ch," *š* sound like "sh," and *ž* sound like "zh" (as in "measure").

The only trick: As in English, which syllable gets the emphasis is unpredictable. Slovenes use many of the same words as Croatians, but put the stress on an entirely different place. While Croatians call their favorite coastal city "doo-BROHV-neek," Slovenes say it "DOO-brohv-neek."

As you're tracking down addresses, these definitions will help: *trg* (square), *ulica* (road), and *most* (bridge).

LJUBLJANA

Slovenia's capital, Ljubljana (lyoob-lyonna)—with a lazy old town clustered around a castle-topped mountain—is often compared to Salzburg. It's an apt comparison—but only if you inject a healthy dose of breezy Adriatic culture, add a Slavic accent, and replace Mozart with local architect Jože Plečnik. Laid-back Ljubljana is the kind of place where crumbling buildings seem elegantly atmospheric, instead of shoddy.

Ljubljana feels much smaller than its population of 300,000 would indicate. Festivals fill the summer, and people enjoy a Sunday stroll any day of the week. Fashion boutiques and cafés jockey for control of the old town, and the leafy riverside promenade crawls with stylishly dressed students sipping *kava* and polishing their near-perfect English.

Centuries ago, Ljubljana was on the trade route connecting the Mediterranean (just 60 miles away) to the Black Sea (toss a bottle off the bridge here, and it can float to the Danube and, eventually, all the way to Russia). Legend has it that Jason and his Argonauts founded Ljubljana when they stopped here for the winter on their way home with the Golden Fleece. The town was Romanized (and called Emona) before being overrun by Huns—only to be resettled later by Slavs. In 1335, Ljubljana fell under the jurisdiction of the Hapsburg Emperors (who called it Laibach). After six centuries of Hapsburg rule, Ljubljana feels Austrian—especially the abundant Austrian Baroque and Viennese *Jugendstil* (Art Nouveau) architecture—but with a Mediterranean flair. Being the cultural midpoint between Germanic Vienna and Romantic Venice gives Ljubljana a special spice.

Napoleon put Ljubljana on the map when he made it the capital of his Illyrian Provinces (1809–1813). A half century later, the railway connecting Vienna to the Adriatic (Trieste) was built through town—and Ljubljana boomed.

Much of the city was destroyed by an earthquake in 1895. It was rebuilt in the Art Nouveau style so popular in Vienna, its capital at the time. A generation later, architect Jože Plečnik bathed the city in his distinctive, artsy-but-sensible, classical-meets-modern style.

Planning Your Time

Ljubljana deserves at least a full day. While there are few must-see sights, Ljubljana's biggest attraction is its ambience. You'll spend much of your time strolling the pleasant town center, exploring the many interesting squares and architectural gems, shopping the boutiques, and sipping coffee at sidewalk cafés along the river.

Begin your day on Prešeren Square, at the heart of the city. Then wander through the market across the river (best in the morning). If you're here on a Tuesday or Thursday, the Jože Plečnik House is a must. Otherwise, the next best museum in town is the Modern History Museum (which comes with a peaceful stroll through Tivoli Park). A visit to the castle is also worthwhile (reached by a good hike or an easy ride on the tourist train).

There are plenty of good day trips close to Ljubljana. With a second day, visit a cave system and nearby sights in the Karst region south of the city (see next chapter).

Ljubljana is dead and disappointing on Sundays. The city is also relatively quiet in August, when the students are on break and many locals head to beach resorts. They that say in August, even homeless people go to the coast.

ORIENTATION

Ljubljana—with narrow lanes, Old World-meets-modern sprawl, and cobbles upon cobbles of wonderful distractions—can be disorienting for a first-timer. But the charming central zone is compact, and with a little wandering, you'll quickly get the hang of it.

The Ljubljanica River, lined with cafés, restaurants, and a buzzing outdoor market, bisects the city. Most sights are either on or just a short walk from the river, which is crossed by several distinctive bridges, including Plečnik's prominent Triple Bridge. The center of Ljubljana is Prešeren Square, watched over by a big statue of Slovenia's national poet, France Prešeren.

I've organized the sights based on which side of the river they're on: the east (castle) side of the river, where Ljubljana began, with more medieval charm; and the west (Prešeren Square) side of the river, which has a more Baroque/Art Nouveau feel. At the northern edge of the tourist's Ljubljana is the train station; at the southern edge is the city's best sight, the Jože Plečnik House.

Ljubljana

1. Hotel Slon
2. Grand Hotel Union
3. To Union Hotel Garni
4. City Hotel Turist
5. Pension Gostilna Pri Mraku
6. To Hotel Park and Hostel Celica
7. Sokol Restaurant
8. Pizzeria Foculus
9. Ljubljanski Dvor Pizzeria
10. Tomato Café
11. Pri Sv. Florijan Restaurant
12. Gostilna As Rest. & Pub
13. Paninoteka Sandwiches
14. CHA Teahouse
15. To Nobel Burek and Olympia Burek Fast Food
16. Ursula Ice Cream & Emonska Klet Pizzeria
17. Chez Eric Restaurant
18. Zvezda Kavarna Ice Cream
19. Interesting Art Nouveau buildings

Ljubljana's Two Big Ps

The two most important names you'll hear in Ljubljana are easy to confuse:

Jože Plečnik (YOH-zheh PLAYCH-neek, 1872–1957) is the architect who shaped Ljubljana, designing virtually all of the city's most important landmarks. For more information, see page 402.

France Prešeren (FRAHN-tseh preh-SHAY-rehn, 1800–1849) is Slovenia's greatest poet and the namesake of Ljubljana's main square.

Mind your Ps, and your visit to Ljubljana becomes more meaningful.

Tourist Information

Ljubljana's helpful TI has an office at the **Triple Bridge** (across from Prešeren Square; June–Sept daily 8:00–21:00, Oct–May daily 8:00–19:00, Stritarjeva ulica, tel. 01/306-1215, www.ljubljana-tourism.si). Another TI is at the **train station** (June–Sept daily 8:00–22:00, Oct–May daily 10:00–19:00, Trg O.F. 6, tel. 01/433-9475). A third TI, at the top of the **market** at Krekov trg 10, also offers information about the rest of Slovenia, Internet access, and a ticket box office (June–Sept daily 8:00–21:00, Oct–May daily 8:00–19:00, tel. 01/306-4575).

At any TI, pick up a pile of free resources: the Tourist Guide, the *Ljubljana A to Z* directory, the monthly *Where to?* events guide, *Ljubljana Life* magazine (with restaurant reviews), the detailed one-page city map, and the bigger map with sight information. If you want to learn more about this city's quirky buildings, consider the excellent but expensive 8,000-SIT *Architectural Guide to Ljubljana*. The **Ljubljana City Card** includes access to public transportation and free entry or discounts at several city museums (3,000 SIT/3 days—skip it).

Arrival in Ljubljana

By Train: Ljubljana's modern, user-friendly train station (Železniška Postaja) is on the north edge of the city center. In the underground passage that connects the tracks *(tiri)*, you'll find a library branch with free **Internet access** (many terminals for members, 1 for free use by tourists, usually limited to 15 min, look for the @ sign). Emerging from the passage up to track 1a, turn right to find the Tir Bar (**bike rental**—see "Helpful Hints," below) and the Cybercity **Internet** joint. The yellow arrivals hall has a **TI** (see above), an **ATM** (by the ticket windows), and helpful English signage (station open daily 5:00–22:00). Arrivals are *prihodi* and departures are *odhodi*.

Taxis, often with unscrupulous cabbies, wait for you in front of

Ljubljana Landmarks

English	Slovene	Pronounced
Prešeren Square	**Prešernov trg**	preh-SHEHR-nohv turg
Ljubljana Castle	**Ljubljanski Grad**	lyoob-lyon-skee grahd
Triple Bridge	**Tromostovje**	troh-moh-STOHV-yeh
Dragon Bridge	**Zmajski Most**	ZMAY-skee mohst

the station. You're better off calling for one (see "Getting Around Ljubljana—By Taxi," below). It's a 10-minute **walk** to get to the city center: Leave the arrivals hall to the right and walk a long block along the busy Trg Osvobodilne Fronte (or "Trg O.F." for short). At the post office (yellow *pošta* sign), cross Trg O.F., head straight down Miklošičeva, and you'll reach Prešeren Square.

By Bus: Ljubljana's bus station (Autobusna Postaja) is a low-profile building in the middle of Trg O.F., right in front of the train station (see above).

By Car: Follow signs for *Center*. For longer visits, park in one of the many well-marked garages (about 400 SIT/hr) or lots (around 250 SIT/hr).

By Plane: Slovenia's only airport, Aerodrom Ljubljana (airport code: LJU), is at Brnik, 14 miles north of the city—conveniently located about halfway between Ljubljana and Bled. Almost every flight is operated by Adria, Slovenia's national airline (www.adria-airways.com), but recently, easyJet (www.easyjet.com) and Czech Airlines (www.csa.cz) have also entered the fray. At this tiny airport, check-in doesn't even start until 90 minutes before each flight (tel. 04/206-1000, www.lju-airport.si). An airport **bus** connects Brnik with Ljubljana's bus station (850 SIT, Mon–Fri hrly, Sat–Sun every 2 hrs, 50 min); a private **shuttle** does the same trip in half the time (1,000 SIT, every 2 hrs). Figure 6,000 SIT for a **taxi** to the airport.

Getting Around Ljubljana

By Bus: Virtually all of Ljubljana's sights are easily accessible by foot, so public transportation probably isn't necessary. But just in case, here's what you need to know: One trip on an LPP bus costs 300 SIT (pay exact change on bus, or buy a 190-SIT token—*žeton*—in advance at kiosk or bus station). An all-day ticket costs 900 SIT (sold only at bus station or LPP office).

By Taxi: Taxis start around 200 SIT, then cost 200 SIT per kilometer. There are some dishonest cabbies in Ljubljana (especially those hanging out at the train station and any tourist attractions), so it's smart to establish the complete price up front (including luggage and other "surcharges"). Even better, call for a cab—it's cheaper, anyway. There are 10 different companies, all essentially the same (dial any number between 01/9700 and 01/9709). Intersiti Taxi has a good reputation (tel. 01/9708).

By Bike: Ljubljana is a biker's delight, with lots of well-marked bike lanes. Tir Bar rents bikes at the train station (200 SIT/2 hrs, 700 SIT/day, low prices subsidized by mobile phone company Debitel, which puts ads on bikes, daily 6:00–22:00, by passageway to tracks). In an attempt to lessen car traffic in the center, the city provides bikes nearly free at five downtown depots. Handiest is the depot just off Prešeren Square at the Centromerkur department store (first 2 hrs free, 100 SIT/hr after that, 1,000-SIT deposit, daily 8:00–20:00).

Helpful Hints

Important Days: Many Ljubljana museums (except the castle) are closed on Mondays. On Tuesdays and Thursdays, make it a priority to visit the Jože Plečnik House (open only these 2 days 10:00–14:00).

Flea Market: Every Sunday from 8:00 to 13:00, a colorful flea market sprawls along the castle side of the Ljubljanica River (south of the TI)—ideal for bargain-hunting and people-watching.

Banking: Most banks are open Mon–Fri 9:00–12:00 & 14:00–17:00, Sat 9:00–12:00, closed Sun.

Internet Access: Cyber Café Xplorer has lots of fast terminals in a pleasant space (daily 10:00–22:00, across the river from the market at Petkovškovo nabrežje 23). Many hotel lobbies have Internet access for guests. Free terminals in the TIs allow you to check your e-mail (but only Hotmail and Yahoo). The Müller department store just up Čopova from Prešeren Square has three free terminals on the fourth floor (Mon–Fri 8:30–20:00, closed Sat–Sun).

Post Office: The main post office *(pošta)* is a block up Čopova from Prešeren Square, at the intersection with the busy Slovenska cesta (Mon–Fri 7:00–20:00, Sat 7:00–13:00, closed Sun).

Laundry: Self-service places, used mainly by students, are far from the center (get details at TI). Most hotels can do laundry, but it's expensive. Hostel Celica sometimes lets non-guests use their self-service laundry facilities; call first (Metelkova 9, tel. 01/430-1890).

Car Rental: Avis is friendly and central (about €60/day includes tax and insurance, Čufarjeva 2, tel. 01/583-3572).

Best Views: The best view in Ljubljana is from atop the Nebotičnik skyscraper, followed by the castle tower. On sunny, blue-sky days, the colorful architecture on Prešeren Square springs to life, and you'll burn through film quickly along the river promenade.

TOURS

In Ljubljana

Walking Tour—The TI organizes a two-hour guided town walk of Ljubljana in Slovene and English (1,500 SIT, June–Sept daily at 17:00, June and Sept also Fri–Sun at 11:00, July–Aug also daily at 11:00, Oct–May Sat–Sun only at 11:00, meets at Town Hall around corner from Triple Bridge TI).

Boat Tour—Consider seeing Ljubljana from the Ljubljanica River. Guided cruises leave a block from the Triple Bridge TI (away from the market) Mon–Fri at 17:30 and Sat–Sun at 11:30 from mid-May through Sept (1,500 SIT, 1 hr).

Local Guide—Having the help of a local guide for two hours for $35 has to be the best value in town. Ljubljana's hardworking guides lead tours on a wide variety of topics and can tailor their tour to your interests (figure 7,000 SIT/2 hrs, 25 percent more on Sun or for same-day booking, contact TI for details). **Marijan Krišković** is an excellent guide (7,000 SIT/2 hrs, mobile 031/815-509, kriskovic @yahoo.com).

From Ljubljana

Several small outfits lead mini-bus day-trip excursions from Ljubljana into the nearby countryside. These are worth considering simply for their efficient transportation. WildJump is one of many new companies that would love to take you sightseeing through Slovenia's mountains, caves, and lakes (most excursions cost about €40, leave at 8:00, return around 16:00, www.wildjump.com). These companies also offer more active adventure-travel options (river rafting, kayaking, horse riding, and more). Get details at the TI.

SIGHTS

Prešeren Square Spin-Tour

The heart of Ljubljana is lively Prešeren Square (Prešernov trg). The city's meeting point is the large **statue of France Prešeren,** Slovenia's greatest poet, whose work includes the Slovenian national anthem. Prešeren, an important catalyst of 19th-century Slovenian nationalism, is being inspired from overhead by the Muse. This statue provoked a scandal and outraged the bishop when it went up a

Ljubljana at a Glance

▲▲▲**Jože Plečnik House** Final digs of the famed hometown architect who built so much of Ljubljana. **Hours:** Tue and Thu 10:00–14:00.

▲▲**Riverside Market at Vodnikov Trg** Lively market area in the old town with produce, clothing, souvenirs—even wild boar salami. **Hours:** Best in the morning, especially Sat.

▲▲**Ljubljana Castle** Tower with stunning views and decent 3-D film. **Hours:** Grounds open daily until 22:00 in summer, 20:00 in winter; film plays on the half hour all day, May–Sept daily 9:00–21:00, Oct–April daily 10:00–18:00.

▲▲**Modern History Museum** Baroque mansion in Tivoli Park, with exhibit highlighting Slovenia's last 100 years. **Hours:** Tue–Sun 10:00–18:00, closed Mon.

▲▲**National and University Library** Plečnik's pièce de résistance, with an intriguing facade, piles of books, and a bright reading room. **Hours:** July–Aug Mon–Sat 8:00–14:00, Wed until 16:00, closed Sun; Sept–June Mon–Fri 8:00–20:00, Sat 8:00–14:00, closed Sun.

▲**Skyscraper** Art Deco high-rise with view café on top. **Hours:** Café hours unpredictable, often closed.

▲**Architectural Museum of Ljubljana** Castle with Plečnik exhibit on the edge of town. **Hours:** Mon–Fri 10:00–14:00, closed Sat–Sun.

---

hundred years ago—a naked woman sharing the square with a church! To ensure that nobody could be confused about the woman's intentions, she's conspicuously depicted with typical Muse accessories: a laurel branch and a cloak.

Stand at the base of the statue to get oriented. Notice the bridge crossing the Ljubljanica River. This is one of Ljubljana's most important landmarks, Jože Plečnik's **Triple Bridge** (Tromostovje). The bridge's Venetian vibe is intentional: Plečnik recognized that Ljubljana, midway between Venice and then-capital Vienna, is itself a bridge between the Italian and Germanic worlds. On the other side of the bridge is the TI, WCs, the market and cathedral (to the left), and the Town Hall (straight ahead).

Now turn 90 degrees to the right, and look down the first street after the riverbank. Find the pale woman in the picture frame on the second floor of the yellow house. This is **Julija,** the love of Prešeren's life. Tour guides spin romantic tales about how the couple met. But the truth is far less exciting: He was a teacher in her father's house when he was in his 30s and she was four. Later in life, she inspired him from afar—as she does now, from across the square—but they never got together. She may have inspired him, but when it came to marriage, she opted for wealth and status.

Ljubljana—especially the streets around this square—is an architecture-lover's paradise, starting with **Hauptmann House,** to the right of Julija. This was the only building in town that survived the devastating 1895 earthquake. A few years later, the owner renovated it, anyway, in the then-trendy Viennese Secession style you see today. All that remains of the original is the Baroque balcony above the entrance.

Just to the right of the Hauptmann House is a car-sized **model** of the city center—helpful for orientation. The street next to it (with the McDonald's) is **Čopova**, once the route of Ljubljana's Sunday promenade. A century ago, locals would put on their Sunday best and stroll from here to Tivoli Park, listening to musicians and dropping into cafés along the way. Today, busy Slovenska cesta and railroad tracks cross the route, making the promenade less inviting. But in the last decade, Ljubljana has been trying to recapture its golden age, and parts of the center are pedestrian-only on weekends once again. The new evening paseo thrives along the river between the Triple Bridge and Cobblers' Bridge.

Continue looking to the right, past the big, pink landmark Franciscan Church of St. Mary. The street to the right of the church, **Miklošičeva cesta,** connects Prešeren Square to the train station. When Ljubljana was rebuilding after the 1895 earthquake, local architects and designers envisioned this street as a showcase of its new, Vienna-inspired Art Nouveau image. Down the street and on the left is the prominent **Grand Hotel Union,** with a stately domed spire on the corner. When these buildings were designed, Prague was the cultural capital of the Slavic world. The new look of Ljubljana paid homage to "the golden city of a hundred spires" (and copied Prague's romantic image). There was actually a law for several years that corner buildings had to have these spires. Even the trees you'll see around town were part of the vision. When the architect Plečnik designed the Ljubljanica River embankments a generation later, he planted tall, pointy poplar trees and squat, rounded willows—imitating the spires and domes of Prague.

Across from the Grand Hotel Union (not visible from here, but worth a wander up the street) is a Secessionist building with classic red, blue, and white colors (for the Slovenian flag) next to the noisy, pink, zigzagged **Cooperative Bank.** The bank was designed by Ivan Vurnik, an ambitious Slovenian architect who wanted to invent a distinctive national style after World War I, when the Hapsburg Empire broke up and Eastern Europe's nations were proudly emerging for the first time. What he came up with is unusual, to be sure, but it didn't catch on—architecture highbrows say he borrowed too much from other styles.

On the near corner of Miklošičeva cesta, look for the distinctive glass awning of **Centromerkur**—the first big post-quake department store, today government-protected. Step inside to admire the interior, which is exactly the same as when it was built. The old-fashioned layout isn't convenient for modern shoppers—no elevator, tight aisles—but no matter how much anyone complains, the management isn't allowed to change anything.

Prešeren Square is the perfect springboard to explore the rest of Ljubljana. Now that you're oriented, visit some of the areas listed below.

East of the River, under the Castle

The castle side of the river is the city's most colorful and historic quarter, packed with Old World ambience.

▲▲**Stroll through Riverside Market at Vodnikov Trg**—In Ljubljana's thriving old town market, big-city Slovenes enjoy buying directly from the producer. The market, worth an amble anytime, is best on Saturday mornings, when the locals take their time wandering the stalls. In this tiny capital of a tiny country, you may even see the president searching for the perfect melon.

Begin your walk through the market at the Triple Bridge (and TI). The riverside **colonnade** was designed by (who else?) Jože Plečnik. This first stretch—nearest the Triple Bridge—is good for souvenirs. Farther in, the market is almost all local, and the colonnade is populated by butchers, fishermen, and lazy cafés. Peek down at the actual river and see how the architect wanted the town and river to connect. The lower arcade is a people zone, with easy access from the bridge, public WCs, inviting cafés, and a fish market. The restaurant just below, Ribca, serves fun fishy plates, beer, or coffee with great riverside seating (open only 7:00–14:00).

Walk along the colonnade with the river on your left. When you come to the first small market square on your right, notice the 10-foot-tall concrete **cone**. Plečnik wanted to make Ljubljana the "Athens of the North," and imagined a huge hilltop cone as the center of a national acropolis—a complex for government, museums, and culture. This ambitious plan never panned out, but part of Plečnik's Greek idea did: the marketplace, based on an ancient Greek *agora*.

At the top of this square, you'll find the 18th-century **cathedral** *(stolnica)* standing on the site of a 13th-century Romanesque church. The cathedral is dedicated to St. Nicholas, patron saint of the fishermen and boatmen who have long come to sell their catch at the market. Take a close look at the intricately decorated side door under the passageway. This remarkable door, created for the Pope's visit here in 1996, traces the history of Christianity and the history of Slovenia in one swoop. Rooted deeply in the fecund soil of their ancient and pagan history, the nation's linden tree of life sprouts with the story of the Slovenes: Crusaders, Turks, Pope John Paul II (at the top), the man who will become Slovenia's first saint (below the Pope), and lots more. Around back is a similar door, carved with images of the six 20th-century bishops of Ljubljana. The interior is stunning Italian Baroque.

The building at the end of this first market square is the seminary palace. In the basement is a **market hall,** with vendors selling cheeses, meats, dried fruits, and other goodies (Mon–Sat 7:00–14:00, Thu–Fri until 16:00, closed Sun). This place is worth a graze. Most merchants are happy to give you a free sample (point to what you want, and ask for a *probat*).

When you leave the market hall, continue downstream into the big **main market square,** packed with produce and clothing stands. (The colorful flower market hides behind the seminary palace/market hall.) Over time, shoppers develop friendships with their favorite producers. On busy days, you'll see a long line at one stand, while the other merchants stand bored. Your choice is simple: Get in line, or eat sub-par produce.

Look for the little **scales** in the wooden kiosks marked *Kontrola Tehtnica*—allowing buyers to immediately check whether the producer cheated them (not a common problem...but just in case). The Hapsburg days left locals with the old German saying, "Trust is good; control is better."

Near the middle of the market, you'll notice a big gap along the riverfront colonnade. This was to be the site of a huge, roofed **Butchers' Bridge** designed by Jože Plečnik, but the plans never materialized. Aware of Plečnik's newfound touristic currency, some local politicians have recently dusted off the old plans and proposed building the bridge after all these years. (If you look across the river, you'll see that the cornerstone was already put in place by an overzealous politician.) It's a controversial project, and anytime a new mayor is elected, the decision is reversed.

If you want a unique taste as you finish exploring the market, enter the colonnade near the very end and find the **Divjač'na Hubert** stand at #22, specializing in game. Ask charming Minka (it's her shop) for a *probat* (taste) of *div. prašič salama*—wild boar salami.

Just beyond the end of the market colonnade is the...

▲**Dragon Bridge (Zmajski Most)**—The dragon has been the symbol of Ljubljana for centuries, ever since Jason (of Argonauts and Golden Fleece fame) supposedly slew one in a nearby swamp. While the dragon is the star of this very photogenic Secessionist bridge, it was officially dedicated to Hapsburg Emperor Franz Josef. (Tapping into the emp's vanity got new projects funded—vital as the city rebuilt after its devastating earthquake of 1895.) But the Franz Josef name never stuck; those dragons are just too darn memorable.

▲▲**Town Square (Mestni Trg)**—This square is home to the **Town Hall** (Rotovž), highlighted by its clock tower and pillared loggia. Step inside the Renaissance courtyard to see artifacts and a map of late-17th-century Ljubljana. Studying this map, notice how the river, hill, and wall worked together to fortify the town. Courtyards like this (but humbler) are hidden through the city. As rent in these old places is cheap, many such courtyards host funky and characteristic little businesses. Be sure to get off the main drag and poke into Ljubljana's charming nooks and Back Door crannies.

In the square is the **Fountain of Three Carolinian Rivers**, inspired in style and theme by Rome's many fountains. The figures with vases represent this region's three main rivers: Sava, Ljubljanica, and Krka.

In the early 19th century, Ljubljana consisted mainly of this single street, running along the base of Castle Hill (plus a small "New Town" across the river). Stretching south from here are two other "squares"—Stari trg (Old Square) and Gornji trg (Upper Square)—that have long since grown together into one big, atmospheric promenade lined with quaint shops and cafés (perfect for a stroll). Virtually every house along this drag has a story to tell, of residents famous or infamous. As you walk, keep your eyes open for Ljubljana's mascot dragon—it's everywhere. At the end of the pedestrian zone (at Gornji trg), look uphill and notice the village charms of the oldest buildings in town.

▲▲**Ljubljana Castle (Ljubljanski Grad)**—The castle above town offers marvelous views of Ljubljana and the surrounding countryside. There has probably been a settlement on this site since prehistoric times, though the first castle here was Roman. The 12th-century version was gradually added on to over the centuries, until it fell into disrepair in the 17th century. Today's castle was rebuilt in the 1940s, renovated in the 1970s, and is still technically unfinished (subject to ongoing additions). The castle houses a restaurant, a gift shop, temporary exhibition halls, and a Gothic chapel with Baroque paintings of the coat of arms of St. George (Ljubljana's patron saint, the dragon-slayer). Above the restaurant are two wedding halls—Ljubljana's most popular places to get married.

It's free to enter the castle grounds (open daily until 22:00 in summer, 20:00 in winter, tel. 01/232-9994). Inside are two optional

activities you have to pay for (800 SIT covers both): the **castle tower**, with 92 steps leading to one of the best views in town; and a 20-minute **3-D film** about the history of Ljubljana (touted as a "virtual museum," but barely worth your time; plays on the half hour all day, May–Sept daily 9:00–21:00, Oct–April daily 10:00–18:00).

Tours of the castle in Slovene and English leave from the entry bridge daily June–September at 10:00 and 16:00 (1,100 SIT, tour lasts 60–90 min). The castle is also home to the Ljubljana Summer Festival, with **concerts** throughout the summer (tel. 01/426-4340, www.festival-lj.si).

Getting to the Castle: A sweat-free route to the top is via the **tourist train** that leaves at the top of each hour from Prešeren Square (600 SIT, June–mid-Sept daily 10:00–16:00). There are also two handy **trails** to the castle. The steeper-but-faster route begins near the Dragon Bridge (find Studentovska lane, just past the statue of Vodnik in the market). Slower but easier is Reber, just off Stari trg (Old Square), a few blocks south of the Town Hall (once on the trail, always bear left, then go right when you're just under the castle—follow signs). For years, Ljubljana politicians have been debating the construction of a funicular that would connect the market to the castle. Given the project's on-again, off-again history, it may be years more before work begins.

West of the River, beyond Prešeren Square

The Prešeren Square (west) side of the river is the heart of modern Ljubljana, and home to several prominent squares and fine museums. These sights are listed roughly in order from Prešeren Square, and can be linked to make an interesting walk.

If you leave Prešeren Square in the direction the poet is looking and bear to your left, by the picture of Julija, you'll walk a block to...

Congress Square (Kongresni Trg)—This grassy, tree-lined square is ringed by some of Ljubljana's most important buildings: the University headquarters, the Baroque Ursuline Church of the Holy Trinity, a classical mansion called the Kažina, and the Philharmonic Hall. At the top end of the square, by the entry to a pedestrian underpass, a Roman sarcophagus sits under a gilded statue of a **Roman citizen**, a replica of an artifact from 1,700 years ago, when this town was called Emona. The busy street above you has been the main trading route through town since ancient Roman times. This square hosts the big town events. Locals remember how, when President Clinton visited, tens of thousands packed the square. (When President Bush came, almost nobody showed up.)

Take the underpass beneath busy Slovenska street (the town's main traffic thoroughfare) to the...

▲**Square of the Republic (Trg Republike)**—This unusual square is essentially a parking lot ringed by an odd collection of buildings. While hardly quaint, the Square of the Republic gives you a good taste of a modern corner of Ljubljana. And it's historic—this is where Slovenia declared its independence in 1991.

The **twin office towers** (with the world's biggest digital watch) were designed by Plečnik's protégé, Edvard Ravnikar. As harrowing as these seem, imagine if they had followed the original plans—twice as tall as they are now, and connected by a bridge, representing the gateway to Ljubljana. These buildings were originally designed as the Slovenian parliament—but the ambitious plans were scaled back when Tito didn't approve (since it would have made Slovenia's parliament bigger than the Yugoslav parliament in Belgrade). Instead, the **Slovenian Parliament** is across the square, in the strangely low-profile office building with the sculpted entryway. The carvings are in the Social Realist style, celebrating the noble Slovenian people conforming to communist ideals for the good of the entire society. Completing the square are a huge conference center (Cankarjev Dom, the yellow building behind the skyscrapers), a shopping mall, and some intriguing public art.

Just a block north (on Trg Narodni Herojev, more interesting public art), you'll find the...

Slovenian Museum of Natural History (Prirodoslovni Muzej Slovenije)—Find your mummy downstairs and lots of stuffed reptiles, fish, and birds upstairs, along with a big exhibit on human fish (500 SIT, daily 10:00–18:00, Thu until 20:00, Muzejska 1, tel. 01/241-0940, www2.pms-lj.si).

Another block to the northwest, you'll find two decent but skippable art museums:

National Gallery (Narodna Galerija)—This museum has three parts: European artists, Slovenian artists, and temporary exhibits. Find the work of Ivana Kobilca, a late-19th-century Slovenian Impressionist. Don't miss her self-portrait in *Summer*. If you're going to Bled, you can get a sneak preview with Marko Pernhart's huge panorama of the Julian Alps (800 SIT, free on Sat after 14:00, open Tue–Sun 10:00–18:00, closed Mon, enter through big glass box between 2 older buildings at Prešernova 24, tel. 01/241-5434, www.ng-slo.si).

Museum of Modern Art (Moderna Galerija Ljubljana)—This has a ho-hum permanent collection of modern and contemporary Slovenian artists, as well as temporary exhibits by both Slovenes and international artists (1,000 SIT, Sept–June Tue–Sat 10:00–18:00, closed Mon; July–Aug Tue–Sat 12:00–20:00, closed Mon; Tomšičeva 14, tel. 061/241-6800).

Near the art museums, look for the...

Serbian Orthodox Church—The church was built in 1936, soon after the Slovenes joined a political union with the Serbs. Wealthy Slovenia attracted its poorer neighbors from the south—so it built this church for that community. It's decorated without a hint of the 20th century, mirroring a very conservative religion. You'll see Cyrillic script in this building, which feels closer to Moscow than to Rome.

Nearby is...

Tivoli Park (Park Tivoli)—This huge park, just west of the center, is where Slovenes relax on summer weekends. The easiest access is by underpass from Cankarjeva cesta (between the National Gallery and the Museum of Modern Art). As you emerge, the neoclassical pillars leading down the promenade clue you in that this part of the park was designed by Jože Plečnik. Aside from taking a leisurely stroll, the best thing to do in the park is visit the...

▲▲Modern History Museum (Muzej Novejše Zgodovine)—In a Baroque mansion in Tivoli Park, a well-done exhibit called "Slovenians in the 20th Century" traces the last hundred years of Slovenian history. Downstairs is a replica of a 1950s-era house, and upstairs are several rooms using models, dioramas, and light-and-sound effects to creatively tell the story of one of Europe's youngest nations. The most moving room has artifacts from the Slovenes' brave declaration of independence from a hostile Yugoslavia in 1991. (The well-organized Slovenes had only to weather a 10-day skirmish to gain their autonomy.) The free English brochure explains everything, but consider the thought-provoking 2,000-SIT essay collection *Over the Hill Is Just Like Here,* which all Slovenian schoolchildren study (entry-500 SIT, free first Sun of the month, open Tue–Sun 10:00–18:00, closed Mon, in Tivoli Park at Celovška cesta 23, tel. 01/232-3968).

The museum is a 20-minute walk from the center, best combined with a wander through Tivoli Park (fastest approach: As you emerge from Cankarjeva cesta underpass into park, turn right and go straight ahead for 5 min, continue straight up ramp, then turn left after tennis courts and look for the big pink mansion).

On your way back to the center, consider a trip to the top of the...

▲Skyscraper (Nebotičnik)—This 1933 Art Deco building was the first skyscraper in Slovenia, for a time the tallest building in Central Europe, and one of the earliest European buildings that was clearly influenced by American architecture (especially inside). The 12th-story observation deck—with Ljubljana's best view—had to close a few years back because it had become the most popular spot in the country for suicide attempts (Slovenia has one of Europe's highest suicide rates). Now it has been (ineffectively) retrofitted to try to prevent people from diving off.

Unfortunately, the observation deck—which is sometimes home to a breezy café—is usually closed to visitors. But if you're in

Jože Plečnik
(1872–1957)

There is probably no single architect who has shaped one city as Jože Plečnik (YOH-zheh PLAYCH-neek) shaped Ljubljana. Everywhere you go, you can see where he left his mark. While he may not yet register very high on the international Richter scale of important architects, the Slovenes' pride in this man's work is understandable.

Plečnik was born in Ljubljana and studied in Vienna under the Secessionist architect Otto Wagner. His first commissions, done around the turn of the 20th century in Vienna, were pretty standard Art Nouveau stuff. Then Tomáš Masaryk, president of the new nation of Czechoslovakia, decided that the dull Hapsburg design of Prague Castle could use a new look to go with its new independence. But he didn't want an Austrian architect; it had to be a Slav. In 1921, Masaryk chose Jože Plečnik, who sprinkled the castle grounds with his distinctive touches. By now, Plečnik had perfected his simple, eye-pleasing style, which mixes modern and classical influences, with lots of columns and pyramids—an architectural cousin of Art Deco.

By the time Plečnik finished in Prague, he had made a name for himself. His prime years were spent creating for the Kingdom of

the neighborhood, it's worth poking your head in the door to see if you can take the elevator up top (2 blocks from Prešeren Square at Štefanova ulica 1).

Jože Plečnik's Architecture

Like Antoni Gaudí in Barcelona, Ljubljana has a way of turning people who couldn't care less about architecture into huge Jože Plečnik fans. There's plenty to see. In addition to the top sights listed below, Plečnik designed the embankments along the Ljubljanica and Gradaščica Rivers in Trnovo; the rebuilt Roman wall along Mirje, south of the center; the Church of St. Francis, with its classicist bell-tower; St. Michael's Church on the Marsh; Orel Stadium; Žale Cemetery; and many more buildings throughout Slovenia.

▲▲▲**Jože Plečnik House (Plečnikova Zbirka)**—Ljubljana's favorite son lived here from 1921 until his death in 1957. Today, it's decorated exactly as it was the day he died, and contains much of Plečnik's equipment and plans. There are no cordons or barriers, so you are in direct contact with the world of the architect. Perhaps no other museum in Europe gives such an intimate portrait of an artist; you'll feel like Plečnik invited you over for dinner. This museum is a hit even with people who've never heard of its former resident. It's officially open only eight hours each week—Tuesday and Thursday from 10:00 to 14:00—but you can sometimes visit by appointment

Yugoslavia (before the ideology-driven era of Tito). Plečnik returned home to Ljubljana and set to work redesigning the city, both as an architect and as an urban planner. He lived in a simple house behind the Trnovo Church (now a tourable museum), and on his walk to work every day, he pondered ways to make the city even more livable. Wandering through town, notice how thoughtfully he incorporated people, nature, the Slovenian heritage, town vistas, and symbolism into his works. Many of his ideas became reality; even more did not. (It's fun to imagine what this city would look like if Plečnik always got his way.)

After his death in 1957, Plečnik was virtually forgotten by Slovenes and scholars alike. His many works in Ljubljana were taken for granted. But in 1986, an exposition about Plečnik at Paris' Pompidou Center jump-started interest in the architect, and within a few years, Plečnik was back in vogue. Today, scholars hail him as a genius who was ahead of his time...while locals and tourists simply enjoy the beauty of his brilliant works.

during regular weekday business hours (usually only for groups of 7 or more, but they'll often open for even a couple of people—call and ask; 600 SIT, from the center, it's a 15-min stroll south through the delightful Krakovo gardens to Karunova ulica 4, after the canal and behind the twin-spired church; tel. 01/280-1600, www.arhmuz.com).

▲▲**National and University Library (Narodna in Univerzitetna Knjižnica, or NUK)**—Just a block up from the river at Novi trg is Plečnik's masterpiece. The library, housing about 1.5 million books, is all about the transcendence of obstacles to attain knowledge. The facade has blocks of odd sizes and shapes, representing a complex numerological pattern that suggests barriers on the path to enlightenment. The sculpture on the river side is Moses—known for leading his people through 40 years of hardship to the Promised Land. On the right side of the building, find the horse-head doorknobs—

representing the winged horse Pegasus (grab hold, and he'll whisk you away to new levels of enlightenment). Step inside. The main staircase is dark and gloomy—modeled after an Egyptian tomb. But at the top, through the door marked *Velika Čitalnica*, is the bright, airy main reading room: the ultimate goal, a place of learning (free, July–Aug Mon–Sat 8:00–14:00, Wed until 16:00, closed Sun; Sept–June Mon–Fri 8:00–20:00, Sat 8:00–14:00, closed Sun; corner of Turjaška and Gosposka ulica). You can duck into the main stairwell without a problem, but you'll need a visitor's badge to get into the reading room. (Ask at the reception desk inside and to the right; depending on who's on duty, you'll either get a badge or be told it's impossible. In that case, if you're determined, just stick close to a student going inside. To get out, use your finger as a security card...it works.) In a freaky bit of bad luck, this was the only building in town bombed in World War II.

▲**French Revolution Square (Trg Francoske Revolucije)**—Many of Plečnik's finest works are on or near this square, just around the corner from NUK (the library described above). To reach this square from Prešeren Square, follow the river several blocks south (with the castle on your left), then cut up (right) two blocks at Salendrova.

Plečnik designed the **obelisk** in the middle of the square to commemorate Napoleon's short-lived decision to make Ljubljana the capital of his Illyrian Provinces. It's rare to find anything honoring Napoleon in Europe (outside of Paris), but he was good to Ljubljana. Under his rule, Slovenian culture flourished, schools were established, and roads and infrastructure were improved. Slovene was made the official language, and Ljubljana became the capital of a realm that stretched (for only 4 years, 1809–1813) from the Danube to Dubrovnik. The monument contains ashes of the unknown French soldiers who died in 1813, when the region went from French to Austrian control.

The Teutonic Knights of the Cross established the nearby **monastery** (Križanke, ivy-capped wall and gate, free entry) in 1230. The adaptation of these monastery buildings into the Ljubljana Summer Theatre was Plečnik's last major work (1950–1956).

At the river side of the square, the newly renovated **City History Museum** (Mestni Muzej Ljubljana) plans to collect many disparate collections from around town into one fresh and modern exhibit describing the town's history (scheduled to open in 2005, well-described in English, likely open Tue–Sun 10:00–18:00, closed Mon, Gosposka 15, www.mm-lj.si).

▲**Architectural Museum of Ljubljana (Arhitekturni Muzej Ljubljana)**—Plečnik fans can make a trek out to this interesting museum, located in Fužine Castle on the outskirts of Ljubljana. The permanent exhibit features parts of the 1986 Paris exhibition that made Plečnik famous all over again. Downstairs is a display of plans and photos from Plečnik's earlier works in Vienna and Prague, and upstairs, you'll find an exhibit on his works in Slovenia, including some detailed plans and models for ambitious projects he never completed (like the huge, cone-shaped parliament atop Castle Hill). It's worthwhile, but a bit of a hassle to reach. Only true fans should pay a visit

(500 SIT, Mon–Fri 10:00–14:00, closed Sat–Sun, Pot na Fužine 2, tel. 01/540-9798, www.arhmuz.com). Take bus #20 from Congress Square (direction: Fužine) to the end of the line (about 20 min).

SLEEPING

Ljubljana's biggest downside is its abysmal accommodations scene. Only a handful of places are within convenient walking distance of the center, and they're all shockingly overpriced. The most expensive places raise their prices even more during conventions (often Sept–Oct, and sometimes also June). While most Slovenes are unaccountably friendly, hotel desk clerks are the rare exception—indifferent and cranky. The city is aware of the problem, and is working on establishing a network of inexpensive private rooms (ask TI for details). For cheap beds, try the new Hostel Celica, near the train station in a unique building that's more museum than hostel (see below).

$$$ The Best Western **Hotel Slon** has 171 fine, modern rooms just a block off Prešeren Square on busy Slovenska cesta (request quieter back room). This site is legendary as the home of an elephant *(slon)* who visited Ljubljana with a circus in 1552 and drew a bigger crowd than the emperor (Sb-€86–106, Db-€117–157—twins and tubs cost the most, extra bed-€28, non-smoking rooms, air-con, elevator, Internet access, parking lot-€7/day, Slovenska cesta 34, tel. 01/470-1100, fax 01/251-7164, www.hotelslon.com, sales@hotelslon.com).

$$$ **Grand Hotel Union** is as much an Art Nouveau landmark as a hotel. You'll pay dearly for its Old World elegance, friendly staff, big pool, and perfect location, right on Prešeren Square. The 193 plush "Executive" rooms are in the main building (Sb-€136–145, Db-€177, prices 20 percent higher during conventions, can be 20 percent cheaper during slow times, non-smoking floors, elevator, Internet access, parking-€10/day, Miklošičeva cesta 1, tel. 01/308-1270, fax 01/308-1015, www.gh-union.si, hotel.union@gh-union.si). Its 133 "Business" rooms next door are a lesser value: more modern, soulless, and almost as expensive (Sb-€129–140, Db-€164, prices go up or down 20 percent if busy or slow, non-smoking floors, elevator, parking and Internet access at main hotel, Miklošičeva cesta 3, tel. 01/308-1170, fax 01/308-1914, www.gh-union.si, hotel.business @gh-union.si).

$$$ **Union Hotel Garni** was recently bought out by the Grand Hotel Union up the street (above), and will likely change its name in the near future. It has 74 modern, business-class rooms, well-situated between Prešeren Square and the train station (Sb-€107, Db-€140, more during conventions, 20 percent less July–Aug, non-smoking rooms, elevator, free Internet access, parking garage-€9/day, Miklošičeva cesta 9, tel. 01/308-4300, fax 01/230-1181, www.gh-grandunion.si, hotel.garni@gh-union.si).

Sleep Code

(€1 = about $1.20, 200 SIT = about $1, country code: 386, area code: 01)
S = Single, **D** = Double/Twin, **T** = Triple, **Q** = Quad, **b** = bathroom, **s** = shower only. Unless otherwise noted, credit cards are accepted, breakfast is included, and the modest tourist tax (154 SIT per person, per night) is not. Hotels generally quote prices in euros, rather than tolars. Everyone speaks English.

To help you easily sort through these listings, I've divided the rooms into three categories based on the price for a standard double room with bath:

$$$ **Higher Priced**—Most rooms €100 (24,000 SIT) or more.
  $$ **Moderately Priced**—Most rooms between €50–100 (12,000–24,000 SIT).
   $ **Lower Priced**—Most rooms €50 (12,000 SIT) or less.

$$$ City Hotel Turist, recently renovated, has 123 tight, cookie-cutter rooms and an indifferent staff, in a handy but urban-feeling neighborhood just a few blocks off Prešeren Square (Sb-€90, Db-€114–139, prices depend on room size and season, non-smoking rooms, elevator, Internet access, bike rental, Dalmatinova 15, tel. 01/234-9130, fax 01/234-9140, www.hotelturist.si, info @hotelturist.si).

$$ Gostilna Pri Mraku would be no great shakes in other cities—but it's Ljubljana's best value, with 30 comfortable if worn rooms, and a convenient location near French Revolution Square (Sb-13,000 SIT, Db-18,000–23,000 SIT, Tb-21,500 SIT, air-con costs 3,000 SIT extra, prices about 20 percent cheaper July–Aug, non-smoking floor, lots of stairs with no elevator, Rimska 4, tel. 01/421-9600, fax 01/421-9655, www.daj-dam.si, mrak@daj-dam.si).

$$ Hotel Park has 91 simple but fresh rooms at good prices. But it's poorly located in a sea of communist apartment blocks a 10-minute walk from Prešeren Square—and has an often-frustrating staff (D-€42, Db-€63, elevator, Tabor 9, tel. 01/433-1306, fax 01/433-0546, www.tabor.si, hotel.park@siol.net).

$ Hostel Celica, the lone bright spot in Ljubljana's dreary accommodations scene, rents the cheapest beds in town in an unforgettable setting. This innovative new hostel is funded by the city and run by a nonprofit student arts organization. This remarkable place, once an old military prison, has 20 cells *(celica)* converted into hostel rooms—each one unique, decorated by a different designer. (Guests are asked to leave the outer door open and the inner door—with bars—locked, so that visitors can look into the rooms.) There are more typical dorm rooms on the top-floor loft. The building also houses an art gallery, tourist information point, Internet access, self-serve laundry, restaurant, and shoes-off Oriental café. The neighborhood is a bit run-down, but safe (prices range from €20 per person in a "cell"—some for 2 people—to a spot in the 14-bed dorm for €15, Db–€40, Tb–€54, includes breakfast and sheets, non-smoking, a 10-min walk from Prešeren Square or the train station, Metelkova 9, tel. 01/430-1890, fax 01/231-9488, www.souhostel.com, info@souhostel.com).

EATING

Though plenty of heavy, meat-and-starch Slovenian food is available, Ljubljana also offers an abundance of pizza and other Italian fare (you're just 150 miles from Venice), as well as other international options (Moroccan, Chinese, even Mexican). The main drag through the old town is lined with inviting restaurants, with their tables spilling into the cobbled pedestrian street. For people-watching, I'd choose one of the many places with tables right on the riverside between the Triple Bridge and the Cobblers' Bridge. Prešeren Square thrives in the evenings, often with live bands leading a celebration of life and youth.

Traditional

Sokol, with brisk, traditionally clad waiters serving typical Slovenian food, is a good bet for local cuisine in a fun, woody atmosphere right in the center. It's deluged by tourists, so don't except top quality (main dishes 1,500 SIT, salads, veggie options, daily 12:00–23:00, on castle side of Triple Bridge at Ciril-Metodov trg 18, tel. 01/439-6855).

Pizzerias

Ljubljana has lots of great sit-down pizza places; expect to pay 1,000–1,500 SIT for an average-sized pie (wide variety of toppings).

Pizzeria Foculus, tucked in a boring alleyway a few blocks up from the river, has Ljubljana's best pizza and a good salad bar (Mon–Fri 10:00–24:00, Sat–Sun 12:00–24:00, Gregorčičeva 3, tel. 01/251-5643).

Ljubljanski Dvor enjoys the most convenient location and most scenic setting...even if the pizza isn't quite as good. This place has great indoor and outdoor seating overlooking the river just 50 yards from the Cobblers' Bridge (daily 12:00–23:00, Dvorni trg 1, tel. 01/251-6555). For cheap take-away, go around back to the walk-up window on Congress Square (400-SIT slices to go, picnic in the park or down on the river—plenty of welcoming benches).

Emonska Klet, a student favorite, is in a monastery cellar. With energetic music and fine pizzas under a medieval vault, it's a fun dining experience (salad bar, daily 11:00–22:00, go through

---

The Student Curse

In most European cities, it's a smart idea to seek out places where locals eat—and students are a sure sign of cheap, good grub. But in this university town, a student crowd is not necessarily a good omen. Ljubljana's university students can buy government coupons that subsidize 80 percent of their restaurant bill. When a restaurant starts accepting these coupons, locals take it as a sure sign that the place is going downhill. Even if the food is decent, the service is sure to get grouchier.

---

underpass at the top of Congress Square—it's hiding on your right as you emerge on the other side, Plečnikov trg 1, tel. 01/421-9300).

Fast and Cheap

Tomato offers colorful, inexpensive, and tasty meals in an old-fashioned Slovenian diner (good sandwiches and salads, most items about 1,000 SIT, Mon–Fri 7:00–22:00, Sat 7:00–16:00, closed Sun, near the top of Congress Square at Šubičeva ulica 1, tel. 01/252-7555).

Paninoteka serves 500-SIT grilled sandwiches, just over the Cobblers' Bridge from the castle (order at the display case, daily 8:00–23:00, fine outdoor seating, Jurčičev trg 3, tel. 01/425-0055).

Burek, the typical Balkan snack (see "Croatian Food," page 453), can be picked up at street stands around town. Most are open 24 hours and charge 400 SIT for a hearty portion. Try **Nobel Burek,** next to Miklošičeva cesta 30, or **Olympia Burek,** around the corner on Pražakova ulica.

Upscale

Gostilna As (literally, "Ace"), tucked into a courtyard just off Prešeren Square, offers fish-lovers the best splurge in town. It's a pricey and pretentious place (waiters recommend what's fresh, rather than what's on the menu), with dressy indoor and pleasant outdoor seating. Everything is freshly prepared each day and beautifully presented (mostly fish and Italian, pastas 2,000 SIT, meals 4,000–6,000 SIT, daily 12:00–24:00, Čopova ulica 5A, or enter courtyard with *As* sign near image of Julija, tel. 01/425-8822). **Gostilna As Pub** uses the same kitchen, but offers salads and simple meals outside (salads 1,600 SIT, pastas 2,000 SIT, daily until 23:00). This is a great leafy-courtyard scene, with live music and several other happening places nearby. They also have a much-loved gelato stand.

Around Levstikov Trg: Several fine restaurants cluster just underneath the castle around Levstikov trg and Gornji trg in the old town, away from the crowds. Take your pick. **Pri Sv. Florijan** is a dressy, upscale place serving modern French/Slovenian/Moroccan cuisine (figure 5,000 SIT per person, attractive indoor or good sidewalk seating, daily 12:00–23:00, Gornji trg 20, tel. 01/251-2214).

Restaurant **Chez Eric** is *the* place for French cuisine in town, with white-tablecloth-and-shiny-crystal formality (3-course lunches 2,000 SIT, dinner for around 6,000 SIT, elegant indoor and scenic outdoor seating, closed Sun, Mestni trg 3, tel. 01/251-2839).

Coffee, Tea, and Treats

Be sure to spend some time along the Ljubljanica River embankment, people-watching and sipping coffee. If coffee's not your cup of tea, go a block inland to the teahouse **CHA,** with a wide range of exotic flavors (Mon–Fri 9:00–23:00, Sat 9:00–15:00 & 18:00–23:00, closed Sun, on castle side of the river a few steps from Cobblers' Bridge at Stari trg 3, tel. 01/425-5213).

Zvezda Kavarna, an Old World place at the bottom of Congress Square, is the local favorite for cakes, pastries, and ice cream (long hours daily, a block up from Prešeren Square at Wolfova 14, tel. 01/421-9090).

Ice Cream: Ljubljana is known for its Italian gelato–style ice cream. Good options are the courtyard garden at **Gostilna As** (see above); **Ursula** (next to Tomato diner, at the corner of Slovenska cesta just above Congress Square); and **Zvezda Kavarna** (see above).

TRANSPORTATION CONNECTIONS

Note that in Slovene, Vienna is "Dunaj." There's no easy way to get to Dubrovnik, short of flying (long bus, no train).

From Ljubljana by train to: Lesce-Bled (roughly hrly, 1 hr), **Postojna** (roughly hrly, 1 hr), **Zagreb** (8/day, 2.5 hrs), **Vienna** (that's *Dunaj* in Slovene, 1/day direct, 6 hrs; otherwise 6/day, 7 hrs with transfer in Villach, Maribor, or Graz), **Venice** (2/day direct, 4 hrs), **Munich** (3/day direct, 7 hrs, including 1 night train; otherwise transfer in Salzburg), **Salzburg** (5/day direct, 5 hrs), **Budapest** (2/day direct, 9 hrs). Train info: tel. 01/291-3332, www.slo-zeleznice.si.

By bus to: Bled (hrly, 1.25 hrs, 1,400 SIT), **Divača** (close to Škocjan caves and Lipica, every 2 hrs, 1.5–2 hrs, 1,740 SIT), **Postojna** (at least hrly, 1 hr, 1,400 SIT), **Piran** (6/day, 2.5 hrs, 2,700 SIT). Bus info: tel. 090/4230 (toll number—about 160 SIT/min), www.ap-ljubljana.si. If you pick up the blue phone in the bus station, you'll be connected to a free information line.

The KARST and the COAST

In the Karst region, south of Ljubljana, you'll find some of the most impressive cave systems on the planet, a chance to see the famous Lipizzaner stallions for a fraction of what you'd pay in Vienna, and one of Europe's most dramatically situated castles—built into the face of a mountain. And picture-perfect Piran, Slovenia's diminutive answer to Venice, sparkles on its skinny coastline. A brand-new expressway connecting Ljubljana and the coast laces all these sights conveniently together.

The Karst

Slovenia's Karst region, about an hour by expressway south of Ljubljana, is fertile ground for a day trip (easier by car than by public transportation; non-drivers might consider taking a tour from Ljubljana—see page 393). The term "karst" is used worldwide to refer to an arid limestone plateau, but Slovenia's is the original. It comes from the Slovenian word "Kras"—a specific region near the Italian border.

Your top Karst priority is a cave visit. Since limestone is easily dissolved by water, karstic regions are punctuated by remarkable networks of caves and underground rivers. Choose between Slovenia's two best caves, Škocjan or Postojna—each with a handy side-trip nearby (to help you pick, see the sidebar on page 412).

In the neighborhood of Škocjan is Lipica, where the famous Lipizzaner stallions strut their stuff. Just up the road from Postojna is Predjama Castle, picturesquely burrowed into the side of a cliff.

The Karst Region

SLEEPING

Tourist Farm Hudičevec, halfway between Škocjan and Postojna, is as comfortable and private as a hotel. A roomy, spick-and-span double with a private bathroom—including a delicious Slovenian feast for dinner and farm-fresh eggs for breakfast—costs only €40 for two people (Db without dinner-€32, €4 more for 1- or 2-night stays, Razdrto 1, tel. 05/703-0300, fax 05/703-0320, www.hudicevec.com, hudicevec@siol.net, Simčič family).

Škocjan Caves and the Lipica Stud Farm

Škocjan Caves (Škocjanske Jame)

Škocjan (SHKOHTS-yahn)—with good formations and a vast canyon with a raging underground river—is arguably Slovenia's best cave system. You'll end up walking around two miles, going up and down more than 400 steps. While anyone in good shape can enjoy Škocjan, those who have trouble walking or tire easily are better off touring Postojna (see below).

Upon arrival, get a ticket for the next tour (they rarely fill up). You'll pass waiting time at a covered terrace with a tiny gift kiosk and a bar serving light meals and drinks. At tour time, your guide

Postojna vs. Škocjan: Which Caves to Visit?

To Postojna or to Škocjan?—that is the question. Each system is massive, cut into the limestone by rivers for over two million years. Stalagmites and stalactites—in a slow-motion love story—silently work their way towards each other until that last drip never drops. Colors are mixed in by whatever minerals the water seeps through (iron makes red, limestone makes white, and so on). Both caves were excavated and explored in the mid-19th century.

Slovenes debate long and hard about which cave system is better. The formations at Postojna are slightly more abundant, varied, and colorful, with stalagmites and stalactites as tall as 100 feet. Postojna is easier to reach by public transportation, and far less strenuous to visit than Škocjan—of the three-mile route, you'll walk only about a mile (the rest of the time, you're on a Disney World–type people-mover). But Postojna is also more expensive and much more touristy—you'll wade through tour buses and tacky souvenir stands on your way to the entrance. Most importantly, Postojna lacks Škocjan's spectacular, massive-cavern finale. Škocjan also comes with a fairly strenuous hike, leaving you feeling like you really did something adventurous. Finally, the choice of likely side-trip might help you decide: Near Postojna is the cliff-hanging Predjama Castle, while Škocjan is closer to the Lipica Stud Farm.

No matter which cave you visit, you'll find it chilly, but not really cold (a light sweater is fine). Both caves forbid photography (a laughable rule that nobody takes seriously).

(toting an industrial-strength flashlight) calls everyone together, and you march silently for 10 minutes to the cave entrance. There you split into language groups and enter the cave.

The first half of the experience is the "dry caves," with wondrous formations and what seem like large caverns. Then you get to the truly colossal "finale" cavern, with a mighty river crashing through the bottom. You feel like a bit player in a sci-fi thriller. It's a world where a thousand evil *Wizard of Oz* monkeys could comfortably fly their formations. You hike high above the river for about a mile, crossing a breathtaking (but stable-feeling) footbridge 150 feet above the torrent. Far below, the scant remains of century-old trails from the early days of tourism are evocative. The cave finally widens, sunlight pours in, and you emerge—like lost creatures seeking daylight—into a lush canyon. A steep, somewhat strenuous hike leads to a small funicular, which lifts you back to the ticket booth/café/shop.

Cost and Hours: The guided tour is mandatory and takes about two hours (2,000 SIT, tours almost hourly 10:00–17:00 June–Sept, fewer tours off-season with last tour at 15:00 or 15:30, call or pick up brochure to confirm schedule before making the trip, tel. 05/763-2840, www.park-skocjanske-jame.si).

Getting to Škocjan: By car, take the expressway south from Ljubljana about 90 minutes and get off at the Divača exit (also marked with brown signs for *Lipica* and *Škocjanske jame*) and follow signs for *Škocjanske jame*. (Before or after Škocjan, drivers can easily visit the Lipica Stud Farm, described below.) The caves have free and easy parking.

By public transportation, it's trickier. Take the train or bus to Divača (see Ljubljana's "Transportation Connections," page 409), which is about three miles from the caves. Either hike in or take a taxi from the Divača station (tel. 05/734-5428). A better but less predictable option is to take one of the buses from Ljubljana to Piran that goes along the older road (not all of them do; ask for details at bus station). This bus can drop you off closer to the caves (1 mile away—ask for "Škocjanske jame").

Lipica Stud Farm (Kobilarna Lipica)

The Lipica (LEE-peet-suh) Stud Farm, a short drive from the Škocjan Caves, was founded in 1580 to provide horses for the Hapsburg court in Vienna. Horse-loving Hapsburg Archduke Charles wanted to create the perfect animal: He imported Andalusian horses from his homeland of Spain, then mixed them with a local line to come up with an extremely intelligent and easily trainable breed. Charles' creation, the Lipizzaner stallions—known for their noble gait and Baroque shape—were made famous by Vienna's Spanish Riding School. Italian and Arabian bloodlines were later added to tweak various characteristics. These regal horses have changed shape with the tenor of the times: They were bred strong and stout during wars, frilly and slender in more cultured eras. But they're always born black, fade to gray, and turn a distinctive white in adulthood.

Until World War I, Lipica bred horses for Austria's needs. Now Austria breeds its own line, and these horses prance for Slovenia—a treasured part of its cultural heritage. Tour the stables to visit the magnificent animals (labeled with purebred bloodlines). Unlike in Vienna, tickets to see the horses perform here are cheap and easy to get. Visitors thrill to the Lipizzaners' clever routine—stutter-stepping sideways to the classical beat.

This excursion—offering an up-close horse encounter—is less polished (and cheaper) than the Lipizzaner experience in Vienna (see page 559). It's worth a visit only if you're a horse enthusiast, or if you have a car and it fits your schedule (for example, drivers visiting the Škocjan Caves, which are only a few minutes away).

By the way, the hills less than a mile away are in Italy. Aside from the horses, Lipica's big draw is its casino. Italians across the border are legally forbidden from gambling in their own town's casinos—for fear of addiction—so, they flock here to Slovenia to try their luck. Farther north, the Slovenian border town of Nova Gorica has Europe's biggest casino, packed with gamblers from the Italian side of town.

Visiting the Stud Farm: There are three activities at Lipica: **Touring** the farm for a look at the horses; watching a **performance** of the prancing stallions; and, on days when there's no performance, watching a **training session.** If you're coming all the way to Lipica, you might as well time it so that you can do both the tour and a performance (or a training session). Call ahead to confirm performance and tour times before you make the trip.

Cost: Stud farm tour only-€6, tour plus performance-€12, tour plus training session-€8. Tel. 05/739-1580, www.lipica.org.

Tours: April–June and Sept–Oct daily on the hour 10:00–17:00 except 12:00 (also at 9:00 Sat–Sun); July–Aug daily on the hour 9:00–18:00 except 12:00; off-season daily at 11:00, 13:00, 14:00, and 15:00 (plus 10:00 and 15:00 Sat–Sun in March).

Performances: May–Oct Tue, Fri, and Sun at 15:00, April Fri and Sun at 15:00, none Nov–March.

Training Sessions: April–Oct Wed and Thu at 12:00. Note that on days when there's a performance, you can tour the farm before (14:00) or after (15:40) the show; for a training session, the tour is before (11:00).

Getting to Lipica: Lipica Stud Farm is in Slovenia's southwest corner (a stone's throw from Trieste, Italy). By car, exit the freeway at Divača and follow brown signs to Lipica. (As you drive into the farm, you'll go through pastures where the stallions often roam.) It's a major hassle by public transportation. You can take the train or bus from Ljubljana to Divača (see "Getting to Škocjan," above)—but that's about five miles from Lipica, with no bus connections. You could take a taxi (about 3,000 SIT one-way from Divača station, tel. 05/734-5428) or try hitching a ride on a friendly tour bus.

Postojna Caves and Predjama Castle

Postojna Caves (Postojnska Jama)

Postojna (poh-STOY-nah) is the most accessible—and touristy—cave experience in the region. It's the biggest cave system in Slovenia (and, before borders shifted a few generations ago, it was the biggest in Italy...a fact that envious Italians still haven't forgotten).

Whether you arrive by car, tour bus, or on foot, you'll walk past a paved outdoor mall of shops, eateries, and handicraft vendors to the gaping hole in the mountain. Buy your ticket and board a train, which slings you deep into the mountain, whizzing past wonderful formations. (The ride alone is exhilarating.) Then you get out, assemble into language groups, and follow a guide on a well-lit, circular, paved path through more formations. You'll see 100-foot-tall stalagmites and stalactites, as well as translucent "curtains" of rock and ceilings dripping with skinny "spaghetti stalactites." You'll wind up peering at the strange "human fish" *(Proteus anguinus)*—sort of a long, skinny, flesh-colored salamander with fingers and toes. The world's biggest cave-dwelling animal, the human fish can survive up to seven years without eating (the live specimens you see here are never fed during the 4 months they're on display). Then you'll load back onto the train and return to the bright daylight.

Cost, Hours, Location: Your visit, which is by tour only, costs 3,500 SIT and lasts 90 minutes. Tours leave May–Sept daily at the top of each hour 9:00–18:00 (off-season daily at 10:00 and 14:00, also Nov–Feb Sat–Sun at 12:00, sometimes additional tours depending on month—especially Sat–Sun in Oct; call to get schedule or pick up brochure at any TI). From mid-May through August, try to show up 30 minutes early for the morning tours (popular with tour buses); otherwise, aim for 15 minutes ahead. The caves are just outside the town of Postojna, about an hour by expressway south of Ljubljana (Jamska cesta 30, tel. 05/700-0100, www.postojna-cave.com). The cave temperature is a steady 8 degrees Celsius (46 degrees Fahrenheit).

Getting to Postojna: By car, take the expressway south from Ljubljana and get off at the Postojna exit. Turn right after the toll-booth and follow the *jama/grotte/cave* signs through town until you see the tour buses. Drivers will pay 500 SIT to park 200 yards from the cave entry. The train from Ljubljana to Postojna arrives at a station 20 minutes by foot from the caves. The bus drops you just five minutes from the caves. If side-tripping from Ljubljana without a car, this is a case where a tour could be efficient and economic (see page 393).

Predjama Castle (Predjamski Grad)

Burrowed into the side of a mountain close to Postojna is dramatic Predjama Castle (prehd-YAH-mah), one of Europe's most scenic castles. Predjama is a hit with tourists for its striking setting, exciting exterior, and romantic legend (even if the inside is almost worthless).

What a wonderful site for a castle. Notice as you approach that you don't even see Predjama—crouching magnificently in its cave—until the last moment. The first castle here was actually a tiny 9th-century fortress embedded deep in the cave behind the present castle (you'll see its front wall as you explore the place). Over the centuries, different castles were built here, and they gradually moved out to the mouth of the cave. While the original was called "the castle in the cave," the current one is *pred jama*—"in front of the cave."

While enjoying the view, ponder this legend: In the 15th century, a nobleman named Erasmus killed the emperor's cousin in a duel. He was imprisoned under Ljubljana Castle, and spent years nursing a grudge. When he was finally released, he used his castle—buried deep inside the cave above this current version—as a home base for a series of Robin Hood–style raids on the local nobility and merchants. (Actually, Erasmus stole from the rich and kept for himself—but that was good enough to make him a hero to the peasants, who hated the nobles.)

Soldiers from Trieste were brought in to put an end to Erasmus' raids, laying siege to the castle for over a year. Back then, the only way into the castle was through the cave in the valley below—then up, through an extensive labyrinth of caves, to the top. While the soldiers down below froze and starved, Erasmus' men sneaked out through the caves to bring in supplies. (They liked to drop their leftovers on the soldiers below to taunt them, letting them know that the siege wasn't working.)

Eventually, the soldiers came up with a plan. They waited for Erasmus to visit the latrine—which, by design, had to be on the thin-walled outer edge of the castle—and then, on seeing a signal by a secret agent, blew Erasmus off his throne with a cannonball. Today, Erasmus is supposedly buried under the huge linden tree in the parking lot.

As the legend of Erasmus faded, the function of the castle changed. By the 16th century, Predjama had become a castle for hunting more than for defense. After driving all the way here, it seems a shame not to visit the interior—but it's truly skippable. The management (which also runs the nearby Postojna Caves) is very strict about keeping the interior 16th-century in style, so there's virtually nothing inside except 20th-century fakes of 16th-century furniture, plus a few forgettable paintings and cheesy folk displays. English descriptions are sparse, and the free English history flier is not much help. But for most, the views of the place alone are worth the drive.

Cost, Hours, Location: 1,000 SIT, June–Sept daily 9:00–19:00, May daily 9:00–18:00, March–April and Oct daily 10:00–17:00, Nov–Feb Mon–Fri 10:00–16:00, Sat–Sun 10:00–17:00. Predjama Castle is on a twisty rural road 5.5 miles beyond Postojna Caves (tel. 05/751-6015).

Cave Tours: If you're already visiting the caves at Postojna or Škocjan, a visit to the caves under this castle is unnecessary (900

SIT, 45 min, May–Sept daily at 11:00, 13:00, 15:00, and 17:00).

Getting to Predjama: By car, just continue on the winding road past Postojna, following signs for *Predjama* and *Predjamski Grad* (coming back, follow signs to *Postojna*). By public transportation, it's difficult. There is one bus per day from Postojna to Predjama, and another to Bukovje (just over a half mile from Predjama)—but you'll be stranded at Predjama, with no return bus. A taxi is easier, but pricey—expect around 5,000 SIT round-trip from Postojna, including one-hour waiting time (mobile 040/217-169). Consider hitching a ride at Postojna on a friendly Predjama-bound tour bus or tourist's car, as most visitors do both sights.

Piran:
The Slovenian Adriatic

Along this stretch of the Adriatic, Croatia's Istria Peninsula—just a few hours from Ljubljana—gets all the press. Seedy, touristy, but fun Croatian resort towns such as Rovinj or Poreč deserve a visit. But don't overlook Slovenia's own 29 miles of Adriatic coastline. As with

other attractions in Slovenia, it's friendlier, quainter, and tidier than the alternatives in other countries.

There is only a handful of towns on the Slovenian coast: big, industrial Koper; lived-in and crumbling Izola; and the swanky but soulless resort of Portorož. But the Back Door gem of the Slovenian Adriatic is Piran. Most Adriatic towns are all tourists and concrete, but Piran has kept itself charming and in remarkably good repair while holding the tourist sprawl at bay. In peak season, it's overrun with Italian vacationers and can feel a bit greedy at first. But as you get to know it, Piran becomes one of the most pleasant Adriatic towns from here to Dubrovnik.

Planning Your Time

Piran is a popular base for exploring the caves, horses, and castles of the nearby interior (described earlier in this chapter). You can see everything in Piran (including a pop into the Maritime Museum and a hike up the bell tower) in a quick hour-long walk—then just bask in the town's ambience. Enjoy a gelato or a *kava* on the sleek, marbled Tartini Square, surrounded by neoclassical buildings and watched over by the bell tower. Wander its piers and catch the glow of Piran at sunset.

Piran History

Piran (or "Pirano" in *Italiano*) is home to a long-standing Italian community (about 1,500 today)—so it's legally bilingual, with signs in two languages. As with most towns on the Adriatic, it has a Venetian flavor. Piran wisely signed on with Venice as part of its trading empire in 933. Because of its valuable salt industry and strong trade, it managed some autonomy in later centuries. In the 15th century, after plagues killed most of Piran's population, local Italians let Slavs fleeing the Turks repopulate the town. As the Turkish threat grew, the town's impressive walls were built. Too much rain ruined its salt basins, but in the 19th century, the Austrian Hapsburg rulers rebuilt the salt industry. With that came a new economic boom, and Piran grew in importance once again. After World War I, this part of the Hapsburg Empire was assigned to Italy, but fascism never set well with the locals. After World War II, the region was made neutral, then became part of Yugoslavia in 1956. And in 1991, with the creation of Slovenia, the Slovenes of Piran were finally independent.

ORIENTATION

(area code: 05)

Piran (pee-RAHN) is small; everything is within a few minutes' walk. Crowded onto the tip of its peninsula, the town can't grow. Its population—7,500 a century ago—has dropped to about 4,200 today, as many young people find more opportunity in bigger cities.

Piran clusters around its boat-speckled harbor and main show-piece square, Tartini Square (Tartinijev trg). Up the hill behind Tartini Square is the landmark bell tower of the Cathedral of St. George. A few blocks towards the end of the peninsula from Tartini Square is the heart of the old town, May 1 Square (Trg 1 Maja).

From Tartini Square and the nearby marina, a concrete prome-nade—lined with rocks to break the storm waves, and with expensive tourist restaurants—stretches along the town's waterfront, inviting you to stroll.

The **TI** is on Tartini Square facing the marina (daily June–Aug 9:00–13:30 & 15:00–21:00, Sept–May 10:00–17:00, at #2, tel. 05/673-0220, www.portoroz.si). For **Internet access**, get online at the Val Youth Hostel (see "Sleeping," below).

Arrival in Piran: During peak times, parking is a headache. While you can drive inside the town to drop things at your hotel, most visitors end up parking at the harborside lot, a 10-minute walk up the coast (€8/day). Buses drop visitors right on Tartini Square.

Piran

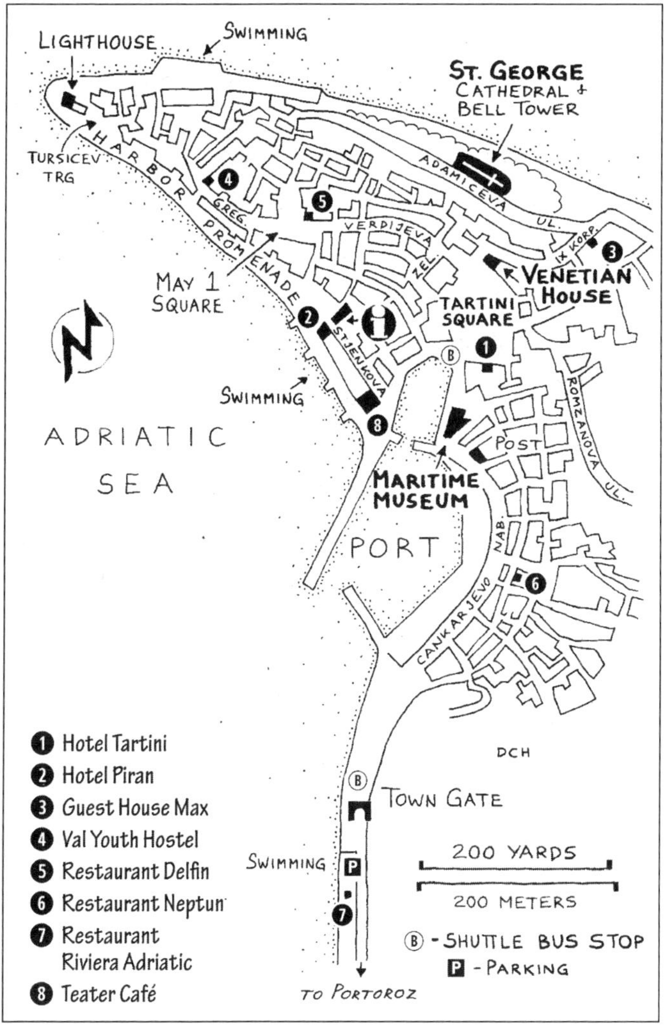

LIGHTHOUSE
SWIMMING
ST. GEORGE
CATHEDRAL &
BELL TOWER
TURSICEV TRG
HARBOR
GREG.
PROMENADE
ADAMICEVA
UL.
VERDIJEVA
ZEL
IX KORP.
VENETIAN HOUSE
MAY 1 SQUARE
TARTINI SQUARE
STJENKOVA
SWIMMING
ADRIATIC SEA
POST
ROMZANOVA UL.
MARITIME MUSEUM
PORT
NAB.
CANKARJEVO
DCH
TOWN GATE
200 YARDS
200 METERS
SWIMMING
B - SHUTTLE BUS STOP
P - PARKING
TO PORTOROZ
1 Hotel Tartini
2 Hotel Piran
3 Guest House Max
4 Val Youth Hostel
5 Restaurant Delfin
6 Restaurant Neptun
7 Restaurant Riviera Adriatic
8 Teater Café

SIGHTS AND ACTIVITIES

▲Tartini Square (Tartinijev trg)—Tartini Square, with its polished marble, was once part of a protected harbor. In 1894, the harbor smelled so bad that they decided to fill it in. Today, rather than fishing boats, it's filled with kids on skateboards.

The statue honors Giuseppe Tartini (1692–1770), a famous composer and violinist once known throughout Europe. While the Church of St. Peter has overlooked this spot since 1272, its current facade is neoclassical, from the early 1800s. The neo-Renaissance Town Hall dates from the 1870s.

The fine, little, red palace in the corner (at #4) evokes Venice. This **"Venetian House"** (c. 1450) is the oldest preserved house on the square. Classic Venetian Gothic, it was built by a wealthy Venetian merchant and comes with a legend: The merchant fell in love with a simple local girl when visiting on business, became her "sugar daddy," and eventually built her this flat. When the townsfolk began to gossip about the relationship, he answered them with the relief you see today (with the Venetian lion): *Lassa pur dir...* (Let them talk).

May 1 Square (Trg 1 Maja)—This square marks the center of medieval Piran, where its main streets converged. Once the administrative center of town, today it's the domain of local kids and ringed by a few humble eateries. The stone rainwater cistern dominating the center of the square was built in 1775 after a severe drought. Rainwater was captured here with the help of drains from roofs, and channeled by hardworking statues into the system. The water was filtered through sand and stored in the well, clean and ready for townspeople to draw—or, later, pump—for drinking.

Cathedral and Bell Tower of St. George (Stolna Cerkev Sv. Jurija)—Piran is proud of its many churches, numbering more than 20. While none is of any real historic or artistic importance, the Cathedral of St. George—dating from the 14th century, and decorated Baroque by Venetian artists in the 17th century—is worth a look. It dominates the old town with its bell tower (campanile), a miniature version of the more famous one in Venice. The tower (with bells dating from the 15th century) welcomes tourists willing to pay 100 SIT to climb 146 rickety steps for the best view in town and a chance for some bell fun. Stand inside the biggest bell. Chant, find the resonant frequency, and ring the clapper ever so softly. Snap a portrait of you, your partner, and the rusty clapper. Brace yourself for *fortissimo* clangs on the quarter hour.

Sergej Mašera Maritime Museum (Pomorski Muzej Sergej Mašera)—The humble museum faces the harbor and the square, filling an elegant old building with meager but faintly endearing exhibits about the "Slovenian sailors" and this town's history (600 SIT, 100-SIT English booklet, poorly described in English, July–Aug Tue–Sun 9:00–12:00 & 18:00–21:00, closed Mon; Sept–June 9:00–12:00 & 15:00–18:00, closed Mon; Cankarjevo nabrežje 3, www.pommuz-pi.si).

Harborfront Stroll—Wandering along the harborfront is a delight. Almost no pesky mopeds or cars, and no American or Japanese tourists—just Slovenes and Italians. The people-watching is decidedly Slavic. Children sell shells on cardboard boxes. Husky sunbathers lay like large limpets on the rocks. Walk around the lighthouse at the tip of the town and around the corner, checking

out the cafés and fishy restaurants along the way.

Swimming—While there is no sandy beach, the water is warm and clean, and swimming is a major activity in Piran. There are two pebbly beaches (one just outside of town before the car park, and the other at the end of the harbor promenade past the lighthouse). From the town promenade, there are two designated swimming areas—both very slippery concrete embankments, with ladders and showers (one in front of Hotel Piran, the other around the corner from the lighthouse).

SLEEPING

$$$ *Big, Top-End Hotels:* Piran has two comparable hotels, each very central, big (with 80 rooms), expensive (Db-€85–120, price depends on view, air-con, and season), and unsmiling: **Hotel Tartini** faces the main square 50 yards from the waterfront (Tartinijev trg 15, tel. 05/671-1666, fax 05/671-1665, www.hotel-tartini-piran.com, info@hotel-tartini-piran.com). **Hotel Piran** is right on the water, with swimming and a concrete "beach" directly in front of it (Kidričevo nabrežje 4, tel. 05/676-2502, fax 05/676-2520, www.hoteli-piran.si, marketing@hoteli-piran.si).

$$ Guest House Max is a clean-yet-funky place just under the town's bell tower, where mellow and friendly Max welcomes travelers with six simple, mod, and comfy rooms. He speaks English and enjoys sharing his long afternoon siesta time with guests in his bar (Db-€60, fans, ulica 9. Korpusa 26, tel. 05/673-3436, www.maxpiran.com, info@maxpiran.com).

Sleep Code

(€1 = about $1.20, 200 SIT = about $1, country code: 386, area code: 05)
S = Single, **D** = Double/Twin, **T** = Triple, **Q** = Quad, **b** = bathroom, **s** = shower only. Unless otherwise noted, credit cards are accepted and breakfast is included. Everyone speaks English and quotes prices in euros.

To help you sort easily through these listings, I've divided the rooms into three categories based on the price for a standard double room with bath:

$$$ **Higher Priced**—Most rooms €85 or more.
  $$ **Moderately Priced**—Most rooms between €50–85.
    $ **Lower Priced**—Most rooms €50 or less.

$ Val Youth Hostel rents the cheapest beds in this otherwise expensive town. It's a friendly place, half a block off the waterfront (56 beds in 22 2-, 3-, or 4-bed rooms, €24 per person mid-May–mid-Sept, €20 per person off-season, includes breakfast and sheets, prices are the same regardless of room size, laundry, kitchen, Internet, 20 yards in from waterfront near tip of peninsula, Gregorčičeva 38A, tel. 05/673-2555, fax 05/673-2556, www.hostel-val.com, yhostel.val@siol.net).

EATING

Pricey tourist bars and restaurants face the sea (figure about €20 per person), while the laid-back, funky, and colorful local joints seem to seek shade from both the tourists and the sun in the back lanes. Get off the beaten track to find one of my recommended restaurants, and you'll enjoy a seafood-and-pasta feast for a third what you'd pay in Venice (just across the sea). If you can't resist dining at the touristy harborfront places, watch your bill and be deliberate with prices (e.g., notice that fish is sold by the gram, rather than the portion).

Restaurant Delfin serves good fish at a good price, as it's family-run and off the waterfront on the old town's May 1 Square (good indoor and outdoor seating, Kosovelova ulica 4, tel. 05/673-2448).

Restaurant Neptun is another fine place, just inland from the waterfront, with tasty food at fair prices (Župančičeva ulica 7, tel. 05/673-4111).

Restaurant Riviera Adriatic, overlooking a pebbly beach at the parking-lot end of town (a 10-min walk from the old center), serves good-value seafood with a wonderfully fishy ambience (Dantejeva ulica 8, tel. 041/673-846).

Drinks: **Teater Café** is the place for drinks with Adriatic views and a characteristic old interior. Catching the sunset here is a fine way to kick off your Piran evening (Stjenkova ulica 1).

TRANSPORTATION CONNECTIONS

The best way to connect Piran with Ljubljana is by **bus** (6/day, 2.5 hrs, 2,700 SIT). By **train**, the trip takes 90 minutes longer (train to Koper, then catch bus). By **car**, Piran is a straight shot—about 90 minutes—on the freeway from Ljubljana.

By boat to Venice: Piran is a fun and handy gateway for connecting Eastern Europe to Venice. A boat called the *Prince of Venice*—designed for day-trippers, but handy for one-way transport—sails from the nearby town of Izola four times each week in peak season (generally on weekends, fewer departures off-season, 2.5-hr trip; €32–50 one-way, depending on season; departs Izola at 8:00, or 7:30 on Mon; shuttle bus picks up at Piran's Tartini Square

1 hr before departure; boat returns from Venice on the same day at 17:00, arriving Izola at 19:30; book through Kompas Travel Agency in nearby Portorož: tel. 05/617-8000, portoroz@kompas.si). Once a week from April through October, Italian-run Venezia Lines does a similar trip, departing directly from Piran (€45 one-way, departs Piran at 8:45, arrives Venice at 11:00, boat returns same day 17:00–19:15, www.venezialines.com).

BLED
and the JULIAN ALPS

The Alps begin in France, tumble across Central Europe, and come to an end here, along Slovenia's northern border. These are the Julian Alps—named for Julius Caesar—where mountain culture has a Slavic flavor. The Slovenian mountainsides are laced with hiking paths, blanketed in a deep forest, and speckled with ski resorts and vacation chalets. Around every ridge is a peaceful Alpine village sprawled around a quaint Baroque steeple. In the center of it all is Mount Triglav, ol' "Three Heads"—Slovenia's symbol and tallest mountain.

Spend a day or two exploring the Julian Alps and Triglav National Park and relaxing in the region's tourism capital, the resort town of Bled. Hike up to Bled Castle for beautiful views, make a wish and ring the bell at the island church, and wander the dreamy path around the lake. To get up into the mountains, drive the 50 hairpin turns of the breathtaking Vršič Pass, then explore the Hemingway-haunted WWI sights of the Soča River Valley.

Planning Your Time in the Julian Alps

On a three-week trip through Eastern Europe, the Julian Alps deserve two days. With one day, spend it in and around Bled. With a second day and a car, drive the circular route up and over the stunning Vršič Pass, down the scenic and historic Soča River Valley, and back to Bled (or on to Ljubljana). Without a car, skip the second day—or, to relax, spend it doing nearby day trips: Bus to Radovljica to see the bee museum, hike to Vintgar Gorge, or (less convenient) visit the more rustic Lake Bohinj.

Getting Around the Julian Alps

By public transportation, you can easily get a good taste of the Julian Alps: Bled and nearby side-trips. But to really tackle the high-mountain scenery—the Vršič Pass and Soča Valley—you'll need a car.

By Bus: Bled is a good home base, with easy and frequent bus connections to day-trip destinations (Radovljica, the Vintgar Gorge, and Bohinj; specific bus connections explained under "Sights and Activities—Near Bled" and "Transportation Connections," below).

By Car: The region is ideal by car. The good *Autokarta Slovenija* map sold by the TI and other local shops is all you need for the country (1,400 SIT), though smaller-scale maps focusing on the Bled region and the whole of Triglav National Park are also available. Even if you're doing the rest of your trip by train, consider renting a car here in tiny, easy-to-navigate Slovenia to take advantage of its many enjoyable day trips. Hiring a local guide with a car can be a great value, making your time not only fun, but also informative. (See car rental tips and local guide information under "Helpful Hints," below.)

By Tour: To hit several far-flung day-trip destinations in one go, consider taking a tour from Bled (sold by various agencies, including Kompas Bled—see "Tourist Information," page 428). Destinations range from Ljubljana (see Ljubljana chapter) and the Karst region (see The Karst and the Coast chapter) to the Austrian or Italian Alps to Venice (yes, Venice—it's doable as a long day trip from here). An all-day Julian Alps trip to the Vršič Pass and Soča Valley runs about 6,600 SIT. This tour is handy, but two people can rent a car for the day for less (see "Helpful Hints," below) and do it at their own pace using the information in this chapter.

By "Old-Timer Train": This old-fashioned steam engine chugs from Bled past Lake Bohinj and on to Most na Soči (at the southern end of the Soča River Valley). It's essentially an expensive package tour by train instead of by bus, with a stop at a gorge and a riverboat ride on the Soča (12,500 SIT, leaves Bled Thu at 9:30 July–Sept, get details at Kompas Bled—see "Tourist Information," below).

Bled

Lake Bled—Slovenia's leading mountain resort—comes complete with a sweeping Alpine panorama, a fairytale island, a cliff-hanging medieval castle, a lakeside promenade, and the country's most sought-after desserts. While Bled has all the modern resort-town amenities, its most endearing qualities are its stunning setting, its natural romanticism, and its fun-loving wedding parties.

The first official mention of Bled was in the year 1004, when Holy Roman Emperor Henry II turned it over to the Bishops of Brixen. Bled proudly celebrated its millennium in 2004. You'll see the town's symbol everywhere: a peacock, or "bird of paradise," based on an artifact found under the castle.

Since the Hapsburg days, Lake Bled has been the place where

Slovenes have wowed visiting diplomats. Tito had one of his vacation homes here (today's Hotel Vila Bled), and more recent visitors have included Prince Charles and Madeleine Albright.

The lake's main town, also called Bled, has plenty of ways to enjoy a lazy afternoon. While the town itself is more functional than quaint, it offers handy access to the region and breathtaking views of the lake. Bled quiets down at night—no nightlife beyond a couple of pubs—giving hikers and other vacationers a chance to recharge.

Planning Your Time

On a speedy visit, you can get a good-enough taste of Bled in one day. Spend the morning strolling around the lake; along the way, hire a gondolier to take you out to visit the island. In the afternoon, hike up to the castle for great views, take a side-trip to Radovljica or Bohinj, hike to Vintgar Gorge, or linger along the lakeside with swans, the Alpine panorama, and a piece of cream cake. With more time, spread these activities over two days, relax more, or—better yet, if you have a car—use Bled as a springboard for a drive over the Vršič Pass to Ljubljana (or loop back to Bled).

ORIENTATION

(area code: 04)
The town of Bled is on the east end of 1.5-mile-long Lake Bled. The lakefront is lined with cafés and resort hotels. A 3.5-mile path leads around the lake.

The tourists' "center" of Bled is a cluster of big resort hotels, dominated by the giant red Hotel Park (dubbed the "red can" by locals). The busy street **Ljubljanska cesta** leads out of Bled town towards Ljubljana and most other destinations. Just up from the lakefront, across Ljubljanska cesta from Hotel Park, is the modern **commercial center** (Trgovski Center Bled), with a travel agency, Internet café, grocery store, ATM, and (on Thursday evenings) a traditional polka dance. If the commercial center feels like it belongs somewhere in North Africa, that's because it does. Nicknamed "Gadhafi," it was designed for a Libyan city, but the deal fell through—so the frugal Slovenes built it here instead. Just up the road from the commercial center, you'll find the **post office** and library (with more Internet access).

Bled's less-touristy old town is under the castle, surrounding the pointy spire of St. Martin's Church. There, you'll find the bus station, several good restaurants, a few hotels, and more locals than tourists.

The mountains poking above the ridge at the far end of the lake (in good weather) are the Julian Alps, including Mount Triglav. The big mountain behind the town of Bled is Stol (literally, "Chair"), part of the Karavanke range that makes up the Austrian border.

Bled Town

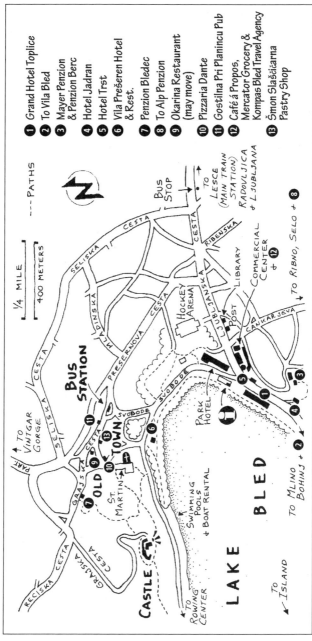

1. Grand Hotel Toplice
2. To Vila Bled
3. Mayer Penzion & Penzion Berc
4. Hotel Jadran
5. Hotel Trst
6. Vila Prešeren Hotel & Rest.
7. Penzion Bledec
8. To Alp Penzion
9. Okarina Restaurant (may move)
10. Pizzaria Dante
11. Gostilna Pri Planincu Pub
12. Café á Propos, Mercator Grocery & Kompas Bled Travel Agency
13. Šmon Slaščičarna Pastry Shop

Tourist Information

Bled's helpful TI is in the long, lakefront building across from the big, red Hotel Park (as you face the lake, the TI is hiding around front at the far left end, by the casino). Pick up the free information brochure, which has updated prices and schedules, along with the helpful Bled guide booklet (if they have it in stock). Get advice on local hikes and day trips. If you're doing any hiking, spring for a good regional map. The TI can't find you a room, but can give you a list of local accommodations (open unpredictable hours, but usually May–Sept Mon–Sat 8:00–19:00, Sun 11:00–17:00; July–Aug Mon–Sat until 21:00, Sun until 18:00; Oct–April Mon–Sat 9:00–18:00, Sun 12:00–16:00, Cesta Svobode 10, tel. 04/574-1122, www.bled.si).

Kompas Bled travel agency, in the commercial center, picks up where the TI leaves off. They exchange money, rent bikes, offer a room-booking service (including many cheap rooms in private homes—though most are away from the lake), and sell various tours around the region (Mon–Sat 8:00–19:00, Sun 8:00–12:00 & 16:00–19:00, June–Sept until 20:00, Ljubljanska cesta 4, tel. 04/574-1515, www.kompas-bled.si, info@kompas-bled.si).

Arrival in Bled

By Train: Two train stations have the name "Bled." You want the station called "Lesce-Bled." The "Bled Jezero" (literally, "Bled Lake") station isn't on the main line and only sees a few regional trains a day. So, if you're buying a train ticket to Bled, specify that you want to go to **Lesce** (lest-SEH)—not just "Bled." If the ticket agent types in "Bled," you'll be routed to the poorly connected Bled Jezero station.

The small Lesce-Bled station is in the village of Lesce, about 2.5 miles from Bled. The nearest ATM is upstairs in the shopping center (with your back to the station, it's across the street and to the left). A taxi to Bled should run around 2,000 SIT, or you can take the bus (at least hrly, 10 min, 300 SIT). If taking the train out of Lesce-Bled, simply buy your ticket from the conductor on the train.

By Bus: Bled's bus station is just up from the lake in the old town. To reach the lake, walk downhill on Cesta Svobode. To get to the commercial center, jog uphill and turn right on Prešernova cesta, which runs into Ljubljanska cesta just above the commercial center.

By Car: Traffic from the freeway comes into Bled on Ljubljanska cesta, which rumbles through the middle of town before swinging left at the lake. Ask your hotel about parking.

Helpful Hints

Banking: The handiest ATMs are SKB Banka (in upstairs of round building at commercial center) and Gorenjska Banka (at far end of Hotel Park).

Internet Access: Most of the bigger hotels have access for guests in the

Lake Bled Landmarks

English	Slovene	Pronounced
Lake Bled	**Blejsko Jezero**	BLAY-skoh YAY-zay-roh
The Island	**Otok**	OH-tohk
Bled Castle	**Blejski Grad**	BLAY-skee grahd

lobby. The public library has fast and reasonable Internet access with a one-hour minimum (1,000 SIT/hr, daily 14:00–19:00, just beyond the post office on Ljubljanska cesta). For a shorter session or longer hours, several other spots in town—such as Café à Propos in the commercial center—have access.

Post Office: Coming up from the lake, it's just beyond the commercial center at Ljubljanska cesta 4 (Mon–Fri 7:00–19:00, Sat until 12:00, closed Sun; July–Aug Mon–Fri until 20:00, Sat until 13:00, closed Sun, tel. 04/575-0200).

Laundry: Most hotels can do laundry for you, but it's expensive. The only self-service option is at the campground at the far end of the lake (950 SIT/load, April–Oct only). The more convenient Pension Bledec youth hostel does laundry for guests (2,000 SIT/load), and may also do it for non-guests off-season if you ask nicely (call first, tel. 04/574-5250).

Car Rental: The Julian Alps are ideal by car. The only locally owned outfit in Bled is InterGlobe (Mon–Fri 8:00–19:00, Sat 8:00–17:00, closed Sun, shorter hours off-season, downstairs along Ljubljanska cesta in commercial center, tel. 04/576-6310, www.interglobe.si). Several big chains rent cars in Bled (around €55–60/day); Avis is also in the commercial center (tel. 04/576-8700).

Local Guides: Tina Hiti and **Sašo Golub** are fine guides who enjoy sharing the town and region they love with American visitors. Hiring them can add immeasurably to your enjoyment and understanding of Bled (7,000 SIT/2 hrs; Tina: mobile 041/375-435, tinahiti@hotmail.com; Sašo: mobile 031/557-331, sasogolub @hotmail.com). Either one can drive you in their car on a long day tour for €100—not much more than the cost of renting your own car. I spent a great day with Tina and was thankful she was behind the wheel.

Getting Around Lake Bled (Literally)

By Bike: You can rent a mountain bike at the Kompas Bled travel agency, great for biking around the lake (700 SIT/hr, 1,500 SIT/half day, 2,200 SIT/ day, see "Tourist Information," above).

By Buggy: Buggies called *fijakers* are easily the most expensive—and romantic—way to get around the lake (5,000 SIT; also 5,000 SIT up to the castle, or 6,000 SIT includes waiting time and trip back down; along the lakefront between Hotel Park and the castle, mobile 041/516-688).

By Tourist Train: A touristy little train makes a circuit around the lake every 40 minutes in summer (600 SIT, daily 11:00–18:00, tel. 04/163-7211).

By Shuttle Bus: A handy tourist bus passes through Bled once daily in summer. It leaves the bus station at 10:00, stops at a few hotels (including Grand Hotel Toplice), then goes up to the castle and on to the Vintgar Gorge entrance (500 SIT, mid-June–Sept only, confirm schedule at TI or bus station).

By Taxi: Štefan Jerebic, who runs Štefan Tours, can take you to various destinations near Bled (2,000 SIT to Lesce-Bled train station, 2,500 SIT to Radovljica, 10,500 SIT to airport, mobile 041/633-772). You'll pay more than these rates if you let your hotel or a travel agency call a taxi for you.

By Boat: For information on boat rental, see "Boating," page 432. For details on the cute, characteristic *pletna* boats, see "Getting to the Island," page 431.

SIGHTS AND ACTIVITIES

Lake Bled

Bled doesn't have many "sights" (except the dull castle museum, described below). But there are plenty of rewarding and pleasant activities.

▲▲**The Island (Otok)**—Bled's little island—topped with a super-cute church—nudges the lake's quaintness level over the top. Since this is the only island in Slovenia, locals call it simply "the island" *(otok)*. While it's pretty to look at from afar, it's also fun to visit (for options, see below).

The island has long been a sacred site with a romantic twist. On summer Saturdays, a steady procession of brides and grooms cheered on by their entourages head for the island. Leading up from the island's dock to the Church of the Assumption on top are 98 steps. It's tradition for the groom to carry—or try to carry—his bride up these steps. About four out of five are successful (proving themselves "fit for marriage"). During the commu-nist era, the church was closed, and weddings were outlawed here. But the tradition reemerged—illegally—even before the regime ended, with a clandestine ceremony in 1989.

An 8th-century Slavic pagan temple dedicated to the goddess of love and fertility once stood here; the current Baroque version (with Venetian flair—the bell tower separate from the main church) is the fifth to occupy this spot. As you enter the church, look straight ahead to the fresco of Mary on the wall. She doesn't quite look like other Madonnas, because she has the face of Maria Theresa—the Hapsburg empress who controlled Slovenia when this fresco was done (see page 546). This kind of not-so-subtle propaganda was typical in those times.

During renovation in the 1970s, medieval graves were discovered around the church (you can see one through the Plexiglas under the bell rope). They also discovered Gothic frescoes on either side of the altar, including, above the door on the right, an unusual ecclesiastical theme: the bris (Jewish circumcision ritual) of Christ. Superstitious locals (and every tour guide in town) claim that if you ring the church bell, your dreams will come true. (Go ahead—ring it.)

A café and tourist stands are near the church at the top of the steps.

Getting to the Island: The most romantic route to the island is on one of the distinctive *pletna* boats. There are 22 *pletnas* on Lake Bled, and they all cost the same (€10 per person round-trip, includes 30-min wait time at the island, catch one at several spots around the lake, including just below Hotel Park, generally run from dawn until around 20:00 in summer, stop earlier off-season, none in winter, mobile 031/316-575). The *pletna* gondoliers all belong to the same union. They dump all of their earnings into one fund and divide it evenly among themselves. Still, competition is fierce...and gondo-

liers have been known to sink rival boats if someone doesn't report all of his earnings or if a new family tries to break into the cartel.

You can also **rent your own boat** to get to the island (see "Boating," below). It's even possible to **swim** to the island, especially from the far end of the lake (see "Swimming," below). But note that you're not allowed into the church in your swimsuit.

▲▲**Walk Around the Lake**—Strolling the 3.5 miles around the lake is fun, peaceful, and scenic. It takes about 1.5 hours—not counting stops to snap photos of the ever-changing view. On the way, you'll pass some great villas, mostly from the beginning of the 19th century, including the former residence of Marshal Tito— today, the Hotel Vila Bled (big, white villa with long staircase at southern end of lake, near village of Mlino—see "Tito's Vila Bled," below). For the more adventurous, there are also hiking paths up into the hills surrounding the lake (ask TI for details and maps; or hike to Vintgar Gorge, described under "Near Bled," below).

▲**Bled Castle (Blejski Grad)**—Bled's cliff-hanging castle, dating in one form or another from a thousand years ago, was the seat of the Austrian Bishops of Brixen. The castle offers a range of sightseeing opportunities: a small castle museum (with a couple of interesting video screens and good English descriptions), a small theater continuously showing a fun 20-minute movie about Bled, a tiny, frescoed chapel, a working replica of a printing press from Gutenberg's time (in the castle's oldest tower—from the 11th century, daily 10:00–13:00, closed Oct–March), a wine cellar (Klet, daily 10:00–13:00 & 16:00–19:00, closed Oct–March), a scenic rampart walk with an "herbal gallery" (gift shop of traditional-meets-modern herbal brandies, cosmetics, and perfumes), and a fancy restaurant. None of these attractions is worth the hike up, but the spectacular views are (castle and museum entry-1,000 SIT, May–Sept daily 8:00–20:00, Oct–April daily 9:00–17:00, tel. 04/578-0525). There's a fine little picnic spot in the castle courtyard, with fine tables and views.

Getting to the Castle: Most people **hike** up the steep hill (20 min). The handiest trails are behind big St. Martin's Church: Walk past the church with the lake at your back, and look left after the first set of houses for the *Grad* signs; or, for a longer but less steep route, continue on the street, bear uphill at the fork, and find the *Grad* sign just after the Pension Bledec hostel on the left. Once you're on this second trail, don't take the sharp-left uphill turn at the fork. Instead of hiking, you can take the 10:00 **bus** (see "Getting Around Bled," above), your **rental car**, a **taxi** (around 1,500 SIT), or, if you're wealthy and romantic, a **buggy** (5,000 SIT—see "Getting Around Lake Bled," above).

Tito's Vila Bled—Before World War II, this villa on Lake Bled was the summer residence for the Yugoslav royal family. When Tito ran Yugoslavia, he entertained international guests here (big shots from the communist and non-aligned world, from Indira Ghandi to Khrushchev to Kim Il Sung). Since 1984, it's been a classy hotel and restaurant, offering guests grand Lake Bled views and James Bond ambience. For some, this is a nostalgic opportunity to send e-mail from Tito's desk, sip tea in his lounge, and gawk at his Social Realist wall murals.

The villa is a 20-minute lakeside walk from the town of Bled at Cesta Svobode 26 (southern end of lake, near village of Mlino). Those hiking around the lake will pass the gate leading through Tito's garden to the restaurant, where they are welcome to drop in for a meal, the salad bar, or just a cup of coffee. Tito fans might want to splurge for an overnight here (Db-€180, tel. 04/579-1500, www.vila-bled.com).

Boating—Bled is the rowing center of Slovenia. Local officials even lengthened the lake a bit so it would perfectly fit the standard two-kilometer laps, with 100 meters more for the turn. Three world championships have been held here. The town has produced many Olympic medalists, winning gold in Sydney and silver in Athens. You'll notice that local crew guys are characters—with a tradition of wild and colorful haircuts. You'll likely see them running or rowing. This dedication to rowing adds to Bled's tranquility; no motorized boats are allowed on the lake.

If you want to get into the action, you'll find **rental rowboats** at the swimming pool under the castle (small 3-person boat: 2,000 SIT/1 hr, 3,000 SIT/2 hrs, 900 SIT/each additional hr; bigger 6-person boat: 2,300 SIT/1 hr, 4,000 SIT/2 hrs, 1,100 SIT/each additional hr), or at the campground on the far side of the lake (4-person boat-2,000 SIT/hr, closed in bad weather and off-season).

Swimming—Lake Bled has several suitable spots for a swim. The swimming pools under the castle are filled with lake water and routinely earn the "blue flag," meaning the water is top-quality (all day-1,000 SIT, afternoon only-700 SIT, closed Oct–May). Bled's two beaches are at the far end of the lake. Both are free; the one at the campground (southwest corner) has lots of tourists, and locals prefer the one at the rowing center (northwest corner). If you swim to the island, remember that you can't get into the church in your swimsuit.

Near Bled

The countryside around Bled offers several day trips that can be done easily without a car. The three listed here are the best (one village/museum experience, two hiking/back-to-nature options). They're more convenient than can't-miss, but each one is worthwhile on a longer visit, and all give a good taste of the Julian Alps.

▲**Radovljica**—The village of Radovljica (rah-DOH-vleet-suh) is larger than Bled, perched on a plateau above the Sava River. The **TI** is at the start of the old town, behind the bus station (go behind station and to the right to find small passageway next to Mercator supermarket). The town itself is so-so, though its old center pedestrian zone, Linhartov trg, makes for a pleasant stroll. But the town is home to a fascinating and offbeat beekeeping museum—which, with only a few rooms, still ranks as one of Europe's biggest.

Radovljica's **Apicultural Museum** (Čebelarski Muzej) celebrates Slovenia's long beekeeping heritage. Since the days before Europeans had sugar, Slovenia has been a big honey-producer. The Slovenian farmer Anton Janša is considered the father of modern beekeeping; he was Europe's first official teacher of beekeeping (in Hapsburg Vienna).

The first two rooms of the museum trace the history of beekeeping, from the time when bees were kept in hollowed-out trees to the present day. Notice the old-fashioned tools in the first room. When a new queen bee is born, the old queen takes half the hive's bees to a new location. Experienced beekeepers used the long, skinny instrument (a beehive stethoscope) to figure out when the swarm would fly the coop. Then, once the bees had moved to a nearby tree, the beekeeper used the big spoons to retrieve the queen—surrounded by an angry ball of her subjects—from her new home before she could get settled in. The beekeeper transported that furious gang into a manmade hive designed for easier, more sanitary collection of the honey. You can also see the tools beekeepers used to create smoke, which makes bees less aggressive. But even today, some of Slovenia's old-fashioned beekeepers simply light up a cigarette and blow smoke on any bees that get ornery.

The third room features the museum's highlight: whimsically painted beehive frontboards (called *panjske končnice*). Nineteenth-century farmers, believing these paintings would actually help the bees find their way home, developed a tradition of decorating their hives with religious, historical, and satirical folk themes (look for the devil sharpening a woman's tongue). The depiction of a hunter's funeral shows all the animals happy...except his dog. There's everything from portraits of Hapsburg emperors, to a "true crime" sequence of a man murdering his family as they sleep, to proto-"Lockhorns" cartoons, to 18th-century erotica (one with a woman showing some leg, and another with a flip-up peekaboo panel).

The life-size wooden statues were used to "guard" the beehives—and designed to look like the Slovenes' most feared enemies (Turkish and French soldiers).

You'll also find an interactive multimedia exhibit, a good video in English, temporary exhibitions, and—in the summer only—an actual, functioning beehive (try to find the queen). The gift shop is a good place for souvenirs, with hand-painted replicas of frontboards, honey brandy, candles, ornaments, and other bee products (museum entry-400 SIT, fine English descriptions, free sheet of English info, 400-SIT English-language guidebook is a nice souvenir, May–Oct Tue–Sun 10:00–13:00 & 15:00–18:00, closed Mon; Nov and March–April Wed and Sat only 10:00–12:00 & 15:00–17:00; Dec Sun only 10:00–12:00 & 15:00–17:00; closed Jan–Feb; Linhartov trg 1, tel. 04/532-0520).

Eating in Radovljica: Several Radovljica restaurants near the bee museum have view terraces overlooking the surrounding mountains and valleys. One of them, **Lectar,** offers hearty Slovenian fare in a characteristic setting with a user-friendly, super-traditional menu (3,000-SIT plates, daily 12:00–23:00, family-friendly, Linhartov trg 2, tel. 04/537-4800). The restaurant is also known for its heart-shaped cookies, decorated with messages of love.

Getting to Radovljica: Buses to Radovljica generally leave Bled every half hour (fewer on weekends, check schedules at hotel or station, 400 SIT, buy ticket from driver, trip takes about 15 min). To reach the old town square and the bee museum, leave the station going straight ahead, cross the bus parking lot and the next street, then turn left down the far street (following brown sign for *Staro Mesto*). In five minutes, you'll get to the pedestrianized Linhartov trg; at the end of the square, just before the church, you'll see the bee museum, which shares an old Baroque mansion with a music school (bee museum upstairs). Coming back to Bled, there are fewer buses; check the schedule when you arrive (at least 2/hr, but fewer Sat–Sun). **Drivers** leave Bled on Ljubljanska cesta, then turn right at the sign for Radovljica and go through the village of Lesce; the road dead-ends at Radovljica's pedestrian zone. A new **bike** path, which will scenically and peacefully connect Bled with Radovljica (about 4 miles), opens in 2005.

▲**Vintgar Gorge**—Just north of Bled, the river Radovna has carved this mile-long, picturesque gorge into the mountainside. Boardwalks and bridges put you right in the middle of the action of this "poor man's Plitvice." You'll cross over several scenic waterfalls and marvel at the clarity of the water. The easy hike is on a boardwalk trail with handrails (sometimes narrow and a bit slippery). At the end of the gorge, you'll find a restaurant, WCs, and a bridge with a gorgeous view. Go back the way you came, or take a prettier return to Bled (see "Scenic Hike Back to Bled," below). The gorge is easily reachable from Bled by bus or foot (see below), and is the best option for those who are itching for a hike and don't have a car (600 SIT, mid-April–late Oct daily 8:00–19:00 or until dusk, June–Aug until 20:00, closed late Oct–mid-April).

Getting to Vintgar Gorge: The gorge is 2.5 miles north of Bled. You can walk (1 hr) or bus (10-min ride plus 20-min walk, or 30-min ride on summer "tourist bus") to the gorge entrance. **Walkers** leave Bled on the road between the castle and St. Martin's Church and take the uphill (left) road at the fork. Soon after you pass the Pension Bledec hostel, turn right at the stop sign, then turn left at the bend in the road (following signs for *Podhom* and *Vintgar;* ignore the other *Vintgar* sign pointing back toward the way you came). At the fork just after the little bridge, go left for Podhom, then simply follow signs for *Vintgar.* You can also take a **local bus** to Podhom (10 min, almost hourly). You'll be dropped at a pedestrian underpass; go through it and follow the *Vintgar* signs for 20 minutes. In summer, a **tourist shuttle bus** takes you right to the gorge entrance in 30 minutes (see "Getting Around Lake Bled," above). **Drivers** follow signs to *Podhom,* then *Vintgar* (see walking instructions, above).

Scenic Hike Back to Bled: If you still have energy once you reach the end of the gorge, consider this longer hike back with panoramic views. Behind the restaurant, find the trail marked *Katarina Bled.* You'll go uphill for 25 fairly strenuous minutes (following the red-and-white circles and arrows) before cresting the hill and enjoying beautiful views over Bled town and the region. Continue straight down the road 15 minutes to the typical, narrow, old village of Zasip, then walk (about 30 min) or take the bus back to Bled.

Lake Bohinj—Pristine Alpine Lake Bohinj (BOH-heen), 16 miles southwest of Bled, enjoys a quieter scene and (some locals argue) even better vistas of Triglav and the surrounding mountains. This is a real back-to-nature experience, with just a few campgrounds and lodges. A visit to Bohinj has three parts: a village, a cable car, and a waterfall hike.

Coming from Bled, your first views of Bohinj will be from **Ribčev Laz** (loosely translated as "Good Fishin' Hole"), a little village at the southeast corner of the lake.  Here you'll find a TI, a smattering of hotels and ice-cream stands, a bus stop ("Bohinj Jezero"), and boat docks (with boats to other parts of the lake—for example, 45 min to "Bohinj Zlatorog" to catch the cable car to Vogel Mountain, below). Across from the docks is a fun concrete 3-D model of Triglav (compare to the real thing, hovering—in clear weather—across the lake). The town's church, St. John the Baptist, is one of the area's oldest, with a beautiful rustic exterior and a fresco-packed interior (if it's locked, borrow key from TI).

If you like mountain perches without the sweat, take the cable car up to **Vogel Mountain,** offering panoramic views of the Julian Alps (2,000 SIT round-trip, every 30 min, daily 8:00–18:00). While you're up there, visit the Alpine hut Merjasec ("Wild Boar"), offering tasty strudel and brandy. You can catch the lift from near the Zlatorog Hotel, at the southwest corner of Lake Bohinj (take bus or boat to Bohinj Zlatorog stop).

Hikers follow the moderate-to-strenuous uphill trail to see the **Savica Slap** (sah-VEET-seh) waterfall cascading into a remarkably pure pool of snowmelt. Hardy hikers find it worth the 553 stairs (400 SIT, daily from 8:00 until dusk in summer, round-trip about 2 hrs, trailhead at far end of lake). Getting to the trailhead is a hassle without a car. The public bus from Bled (and boats on the lake) get you only as far as the Bohinj Zlatorog stop, which is still a 45-minute walk from the trailhead. (In summer, a shuttle bus takes you right to the trailhead.)

Getting to Bohinj: From Bled, seven **buses** a day head for Bohinj, stopping at two different destinations: "Bohinj Jezero" (at the village of Ribčev Laz, 30 min, 790 SIT), then "Bohinj Zlatorog" (at base of cable car, 45-min walk from waterfall hike, 40 min, 910 SIT). **Boats** connect various points on the lake, including Ribčev Laz and Zlatorog. **Drivers** leave Bled south along the lakefront; once you reach the village of Mlino, you'll peel off from the lake and follow signs to *Bohinjska Bistrica* (a midsize town near Lake Bohinj).

From there, you'll cruise through Ribčev Laz and along the south side of the lake.

NIGHTLIFE

Bled is quiet after hours. If you're not a drinker or a dancer, you're down to mini golf...open late behind the commercial center.

Pubs—Locals in Bled enjoy three characteristic and fun bars, all within a few blocks of each other. Gostilna Pri Planincu, near the bus station in the old town, attracts a fun-loving local crowd (see "Eating," below). The Irish pub (a.k.a. simply "The Pub") is rollicking, with Guinness and both indoor and outdoor seating (below Hotel Jelovica, by the path leading from the lake to the bus station). And Bled Pub (a.k.a. "The Cocktail Bar"), just above the commercial center, is a trendy late-night spot. Try a "Smile," the local Corona-type lager. *Slivovka* is the local firewater—honey and blueberry are popular flavors.

Polka—Slovenia is the land of polka. Locals claim it was invented here. Each Thursday at the commercial center, there's a free polka evening featuring a local band (from around 20:00, outside on the lower terrace). While it's mostly locals, tourists are more than welcome. (You can spot the tourists—they're the ones who can't polka.) There's also a Slovenian folk evening once a week at a Bled hotel (ask at TI).

SLEEPING

Bled is packed with gradually decaying convention hotels from the communist era. A few have been halfheartedly renovated, but most are stale, outmoded, and overpriced. It's a strange, incestuous little circle—nearly three-quarters of the town's big hotels and restaurants are owned by the Sava company (which is in turn part of the Goodyear tire company). Only a handful of Bled accommodations are modern and a good value, and I've listed them here—along with a few older places that work in a pinch. Quaint little family-run pensions are rare, and they book up fast with Germans and Brits; reserve these places as far ahead as possible. I've listed the high-season prices (May–Oct). Off-season, the big hotels lower prices 10–15 percent. For cheaper beds, consider one of the many *sobe* (rooms in private homes) scattered around the lake (around €15–20 per person in peak season, often with a hefty 30 percent surcharge for stays shorter than 3 nights). Several agencies in town can help you find a *soba* (including Kompas Bled, listed under "Tourist Information," page 428)—but if you don't have a car, be sure the location is convenient before you accept.

$$$ **Grand Hotel Toplice** is Bled's best splurge, with 87 rooms, an elegant view lounge, posh service, all the amenities, and a long list of high-profile guests—from Madeleine Albright to

Sleep Code

(€1 = about $1.20, 200 SIT = about $1, country code: 386, area code: 04)
S = Single, **D** = Double/Twin, **T** = Triple, **Q** = Quad, **b** = bathroom, **s** = shower only. Unless otherwise noted, breakfast is included and credit cards are accepted. Everyone speaks English, and prices are quoted in euros. Bled levies a €0.80 tourist tax per person, per night (not included in below prices unless noted).

To help you sort easily through these listings, I've divided the rooms into three categories based on the price for a standard double room with bath:

$$$ **Higher Priced**—Most rooms €90 (21,600 SIT) or more.
$$ **Moderately Priced**—Most rooms between €60–€90 (14,400–21,600 SIT).
$ **Lower Priced**—Most rooms €60 (14,400 SIT) or less.

Jordan's King Hussein. Non-lakeview rooms in the back are cheaper, but overlook a noisy street—try to get one as high up as possible (non-view: Sb-€120, Db-€150; lakeview: Db-€200; suites mostly with lake views-€250, less off-season, elevator, Cesta Svobode 12, tel. 04/579-1000, fax 04/574-1841, www.hotel-toplice.com, info @hotel-toplice.com). The hotel's name—*toplice*—means "spa"; guests are free to use the hotel's natural-spring-fed indoor swimming pool (a chilly 22 degrees Celsius, or 72 degrees Fahrenheit).

$$ **Mayer Penzion,** perched on a bluff above Grand Hotel Toplice (a steep 5-min uphill walk from lake), is a family-run place with 13 great-value rooms, a friendly and professional staff, and an excellent restaurant. The summer books up fast with return clients, so reserve early (Sb-€40, Db-€60–75 depending on size and balcony, extra bed-€20, elevator, Želeška cesta 7, tel. 04/576-5740, fax 04/576-5741, www.mayer-sp.si, penzion@mayer-sp.si, Trseglav family). They also rent a cute little two-story Slovenian farm cottage next door (Db-€60, Tb-€80, Qb-€85).

$$ **Vila Prešeren,** named for Slovenia's national poet, is literally a few steps from the lake. Its eight rooms are small but well-maintained, furnished in classy Biedermeier, and wonderfully located. This is clearly your best bet for affordable lakeside elegance. Enjoy their buffet breakfast on the waterfront terrace (non-view: Sb-€52, Db-€72; lakeview: Sb-€68, Db-€88; cheaper off-season, lakeview apartment-€140–155, depending on size, non-smoking rooms, Kidričeva 1, tel. 04/578-0800, fax 04/578-0810, www.vila.preseren .s5.net, vila.preseren@siol.net).

Grand Hotel Toplice (listed above) runs two nearby annexes with worn rooms and much lower prices: $$ **Hotel Jadran,** on a hill behind the Toplice, has 45 rooms (save money and gain sleep by foregoing the lakeview rooms overlooking the noisy street; reception tel. 04/579-1365). **$$ Hotel Trst**'s 31 rooms are a little bigger (reception and breakfast at the Toplice). Both have the same prices and can be reserved through Grand Hotel Toplice (non-view: Sb-€55, Db-€70; lakeview: Sb-€70, Db-€90; Cesta Svobode 12, tel. 04/579-1000, fax 04/574-1841, www.hotel-toplice.com, info @hotel-toplice.com). At either place, ask for a room on the higher floors to avoid road noise (both have elevators).

$ Penzion Bledec is just below the castle at the top of the old town. While it's technically an IYHF hostel, each of the 13 rooms has its own bathroom, and some can be rented as doubles (though "doubles" are actually underutilized triples and quads, with separate beds pushed together—so they're not reservable July–Aug). The friendly staff is justifiably proud of the bargain they offer (bed in 3- to 7-bed dorm-€19, Db-€46, Tb-€60, prices lower Nov–April, members pay 10 percent less, includes sheets and breakfast, non-smoking rooms, great family rooms, Internet access, full-service laundry-2,000 SIT/load, Grajska 17, tel. 04/574-5250, fax 04/574-5251, www.mlino.si, bledec@mlino.si).

$ Penzion Berc, next door to Mayer Penzion (listed above) and run by a cousin, offers 11 cheaper, almost-as-nice rooms. Very quiet, with a characteristic lounge and breakfast room, it's equally good and worth reserving ahead (Sb-€27–30, Db-€50–54, 10 percent more for 1-night stays and off-season, includes tax, cash only, free loaner bikes, free Internet access, free self-serve laundry with hang-dry, Želeška cesta 15, tel. & fax 04/574-1838, www.berc-sp.si, penzion @berc-sp.si, Berc family). Their new, adjacent Hotel Berc—opening in the spring of 2005—rents 15 fancier rooms (Db-€60).

$ Alp Penzion, sitting in cornfields a 10-minute walk from the lake and just out of town, is the most tranquil and only farm-feeling option. Its 11 rooms are small and faded, but comfortable. The place is enthusiastically run by the Sršen family, who offer lots of fun activities: tennis court, summer barbecue grill, and sauna (Sb-€40, Db-€50–60, Tb-€80, 10 percent more for 1-night stays, family room, free loaner bikes, Cankarjeva cesta 20A, tel. 04/574-1614, fax 04/574-4590, www.alp-penzion.com, bled@alp-penzion.com).

EATING

Okarina, run by charming, well-traveled Leo Ličof, serves excellent Slovenian cuisine with an Indian twist. He has a respect for salads and vegetables and a passion for fish. The location and name might change in the future, but Leo's creative cooking, fine presentation, and atmosphere are worth seeking out (call ahead or ask locally for new location, Riklijeva 9, tel. 04/574-1458).

Bled Desserts

While you're in Bled, be sure to enjoy the town's specialty, a vanilla-custard-and-cream cake called *kremna rezina* (KRAYM-nah ray-ZEE-nah). It's often referred to by its German name, *kremšnita* (KRAYM-shnee-tah). This dish was first created right here in Bled, at the big, red Hotel Park. Slovenes travel from all over the country to sample this famous dessert.

Slightly less renowned—but just as tasty—is *grmuda* (gur-MOO-dah, literally, "bonfire"). This dessert was developed by Hotel Jelovice as a way to get rid of their day-old leftovers. They take yesterday's cake, add rum, milk, custard, and raisins, and top it off with whipped cream and chocolate syrup.

These desserts are typically enjoyed with a lake-and-mountains view—the best spots are the Panorama restaurant by Grand Hotel Toplice, the recommended Vila Prešeren restaurant, and the terrace across from the Hotel Park (figure around 800 SIT for cake and coffee at any of these places). For a more local (but non-lakeview) setting, consider Šmon Slaščičarna (only slightly cheaper; see "Dessert," page 441).

Mayer Penzion, just up the hill from the lakefront, has a dressy restaurant with good traditional cooking that's worth the short hike (2,000- to 3,000-SIT plates, indoor or outdoor seating, Tue–Sun 17:00–24:00, closed Mon, above Hotel Jadran at Želeška cesta 7, tel. 04/576-5740).

Pizzeria Dante is popular with local office workers for its good wood-fired pizzas, pastas, and salads (daily 12:00–23:00, marked only with low-profile *pizzeria* sign at Riklijeva cesta 13, tel. 04/576-8900). Its upstairs roof terrace is relaxing on a balmy evening.

Gostilna Pri Planincu is a homey, informal bar packed with fun-loving and sometimes rowdy locals. Behind the small, characteristic pub sprawls a large dining area. The big menu features good-enough Slovenian pub grub (1,500-SIT plates, huge portions, traditional daily specials, daily 9:00–23:00, Grajska cesta 8, tel. & fax 04/574-1613).

Vila Prešeren serves expensive food in a swanky dining room or on a scenic terrace right on the lake. For a romantic lakeside dinner, look no further (modern international cuisine with a focus on fish, main dishes 2,000–3,000 SIT, smart to reserve a lakeside table, daily 12:00–23:00, Kidričeva 1, tel. 04/578-0800).

Café à Propos, in the commercial center, features light sandwiches, fancy drinks and sweets, slow Internet access, and cocktails in the evening (daily 8:00–24:00, Ljubljanska cesta 4, tel. 04/574-4044).

The **Mercator** grocery store, also in the commercial center, has the makings for a bang-up picnic. They sell premade sandwiches, or will make you one to order (point to what you want). This is a great option for hikers and budget travelers (Mon–Sat 7:00–19:00, Sun 8:00–12:00).

Dessert: While tourists generally gulp down their cream cakes on a hotel restaurant's lakefront terrace, locals know the best desserts are at the **Šmon Slaščičarna** (a.k.a. the "Brown Bear," for the bear on the sign). It's nicely non-touristy, but with less atmosphere than the lakeside spots (daily 7:30–22:00, near bus station at Grajska cesta 3, tel. 04/574-1616).

TRANSPORTATION CONNECTIONS

The most convenient train connections to Bled leave from the Lesce-Bled station, about 2.5 miles away. Remember, when buying a train ticket to Lake Bled, make it clear that you want to go to the "Lesce-Bled" station. The "Bled Jezero" station is closer to the town of Bled, but it takes much longer to reach because it's served by only a handful of regional trains. No one in Bled sells train tickets; buy them on the train.

From Bled by train to: Ljubljana (11/day, 1 hr—but bus is better, since it departs conveniently from Bled town, not from train station outside of town), **Salzburg** (5/day, 4 hrs), **Munich** (3/day, 6 hrs), **Vienna** (that's *Dunaj* in Slovene, 5/day, 6 hrs, transfer in Villach, Austria), **Venice** (3/day with transfer in Ljubljana or Villach, 6 hrs), **Zagreb** (5/day, 3.5 hrs).

By bus to: Ljubljana (Mon–Fri 11/day, Sat–Sun 8/day, 80 min, 1,400 SIT), **Radovljica** (Mon–Fri at least 2/hr, Sat hrly, Sun almost hrly, 15 min, 400 SIT), **Lesce-Bled train station** (at least hrly, 10 min, 300 SIT), **Lake Bohinj** (7/day, 30 min to "Bohinj Jezero" stop, 40 min to "Bohinj Zlatorog" stop), **Podhom** (20-min hike away from Vintgar Gorge, Mon–Fri 9/day, none Sat, 1/day Sun, 15 min, 290 SIT). Confirm times at the helpful Bled bus station.

By plane: Brnik Airport is between Bled and Ljubljana. A taxi costs 10,500 SIT (set price up front—since it's outside of town, they don't use the meter). The bus connection from Bled to the airport is cheap (total cost: 1,200 SIT), but complicated: First, go to Kranj (Mon–Fri 12/day, Sat–Sun 8/day, 35 min), then transfer to a Brnik-bound bus (at least hrly, 20 min).

Triglav National Park
(Triglavski Narodni Park)

The countryside around Lake Bled has its own distinctive beauty: Alpine rivers with great fishing, rural rest stops, and charming mountain hamlets. But the best day in the Julian Alps is spent driving up and over the Vršič Pass (vur-SHEECH, open May–Oct), and back down via the Soča River Valley (SOH-chah). This day-long circular drive features some stunning high-altitude scenery (on challenging, twisty roads), as well as some offbeat WWI sights.

This drive is divided into two parts: the Vršič Pass and the Soča River Valley. You can start and finish in Bled, or start in Bled and end in Ljubljana. Give it a whole day. Not counting stops, figure an hour from Bled to the top of the pass, a half hour back down to the start of the Soča Valley, and an hour on to the town of Kobarid. From Kobarid, figure another two hours back to the expressway via Idrija, then an hour to Ljubljana or 90 minutes back to Bled. Returning via Nova Gorica (explained below) takes slightly longer.

Vršič Pass

This self-guided driving tour takes you up and over the highest mountain pass in Slovenia—with stunning scenery and a few quirky sights along the way. While it's not for stick-shift novices, all but the most timid drivers will agree the scenery is worth the many hairpin turns.

Begin in Bled. Take the freeway north towards Jesenice (follow green signs), enjoying views of **Mount Triglav** on the left as you drive. As you approach the industrial city of Jesenice (its iron- and steelworks now all closed)—within yodeling distance of Austria—keep your eye out for the Hrušica exit (also marked for Jesenice, Kranjska Gora, and the Italian border; it's after the gas station, just before the tunnel to Austria). When you exit, turn left towards Kranjska Gora (yellow sign) and the Italian border.

Slovenes brag that their country—"with 56 percent of the land covered in forest"—is one of Europe's greenest. As you drive towards Kranjska Gora, take in all this greenery...and the characteristic Slovenian hayracks (recognized as part of the local heritage and now preserved; see page 380).

The **Vrata Valley** (on the left) is the starting point for climbing Mount Triglav. On the right, keep an eye out for the statue of **Jakob Aljaž,** who actually bought Triglav back when such a thing was possible (he's pointing at his purchase). Ten minutes later, you'll cross a bridge and enjoy a great head-on view of **Špik Mountain.**

Entering Kranjska Gora, you'll see a turnoff to the left marked for *Vršič.* But winter sports fanatics may want to take a 15-minute detour to see the biggest ski jump in the world, a few miles ahead (stay straight through Kranjska Gora, then turn left at signs for **Planica,** the last stop before the Italian border). Every year, tens of thousands of sports fans flock here to watch the ski-jumping world

Mount Triglav

Mount Triglav (literally, "three heads") stands watch over the Julian Alps and all of Slovenia. Slovenes say that its three peaks are the guardians of the water, air, and earth. This mountain defines Slovenes, even adorning the nation's flag: Look for the national seal, with three peaks. The two squiggly lines under it represent the Adriatic.

From the town of Bled, you'll see Triglav peeking up over the ridge on a clear day. (You'll get an even better view from nearby Lake Bohinj.)

It's said that you're not a true Slovene until you've climbed Triglav. One native took these words very seriously, and climbed the mountain 853 times...in one year. Climbing to the summit—at 9,396 feet—is an attainable goal for any hiker in decent shape. If you're here for a while and want to become an honorary Slovene, befriend a local and ask if he or she will accompany you to the top.

If mountain climbing isn't your style, relax at an outdoor café with a piece of cream cake and a view of Triglav. It won't make you a Slovene...but it's close enough on a quick visit.

championships. This is where a local boy was the first human to fly over 100 meters (328 feet) on skis. Today's competitors routinely set new world records (currently 820 feet—that's 17 seconds in the air). From the ski jump, you're a few minutes' walk from Italy or Austria. This region—spanning three nations—lobbied unsuccessfully to host the 2006 Winter Olympics. (Things *"senza confini"*—Italian for "without borders"—are in tune with the European Union's vision for a Europe of regions, rather than nations.)

Back in Kranjska Gora, follow the signs for *Vršič* (often closed in winter, generally open May–Oct). Before long, you'll officially enter **Triglav National Park** and come to the first of this road's 50 hairpin turns—each one numbered and labeled with the altitude in meters. In addition to the ever-changing Alpine panorama, there are several worthwhile stops along the way, as well as frequent pullouts for photo stops. If the drive seems intimidating, remember that 50-seat tour buses routinely conquer this pass...if they can do it, so can you.

After switchback #8, park on the right and hike 100 yards up the stairs to the little **Russian chapel.** This road was built during World War I by 10,000 Russian POWs of the Austro-Hungarian Empire to supply the front lines of the Soča Front. The POWs lived and worked in terrible conditions, and several hundred died of illness and exposure. On March 8,

Northwest Slovenia

1916, an avalanche thundered down the mountains, killing hundreds of workers. This chapel was built where the final casualty was found. (Notice the group shot of those comrades on the wall inside the church.) Sign the little guest book and pay your respects to the men who built the road you're enjoying today.

After #22, at the pull-off for Erjavčeva Koča restaurant, you may see tour buses making a fuss about the mountain vista. They're looking for a ghostly face in the cliff wall, supposedly belonging to the mythical figure **Ajda.** This village girl was cursed by the townspeople after correctly predicting the death of the Golden Horn (Zlatorog), a magical, goat-like animal. Her tiny image (with a Picasso nose) is just above the treeline, a little to the right—try to get a local to point her out to you (you can see her best if you stand at the signpost near the road).

After #24, you reach the **summit** (5,285 feet). On the right, a long gravel chute gives hikers a thrilling glissade down. (It's easy to view hikers "skiing" down from the pullout just beyond #26.) On the 26 hairpin turns on the way down, keep an eye out for old WWI debris (this national park owes its fine roads to World War I). Just after the pass, the tunnel marked *1916* on the left used to be the original path of this road. After #28, you'll see abandoned checkpoints from when this was the border between Italy and the Austro-Hungarian Empire. At #48 is a statue of **Julius Kugy,** a Slovenian botanist who wrote books about Alpine flora. Nearing the end of the switchbacks, follow signs for *Bovec.* Crossing the Soča River, you begin the second half of this trip.

Soča River Valley

During World War I, the terrain between here and the Adriatic made up the Soča (Isonzo) Front. As you follow the Soča River south, down what's nicknamed the "Valley of the Cemeteries," the scenic mountainsides around you tell the tale of this terrible warfare. Imagine a young Ernest Hemingway driving his ambulance through these same hills.

The last Vršič switchback (#50) sends you into the village of Trenta. On the left, look for the **Triglav National Park Information**

Center (May–Oct daily 10:00–18:00, closed Nov–April, tel. 05/388-9330, www.tnp.si). The humble museum here provides a look (with English explanations) at the park's flora, fauna, traditional culture, and mountaineering history (900 SIT). A poetic 15-minute slide-show explains the wonders and fragility of the park (ask for English version as you enter).

About five miles after Trenta, in the town of Soča, visit the **Church of St. Joseph** (with red onion dome, hiding behind the big tree on the right, damaged in earthquakes of 1998 and 2004). During World War II, a local artist hiding out in the mountains filled this church with patriotic symbolism. The interior is bathed in Yugoslav red, white, and blue—a brave statement made when such nationalistic sentiments were dangerous. On the ceiling is St. Michael (clad in Yugoslav colors) with Yugoslavia's three WWII enemies at his feet: the eagle (Germany), the wolf (Italy), and the serpent (Japan). The tops of the walls along the nave are lined with saints—but these are Slavic, not Catholic. Finally, look carefully at the Stations of the Cross and find the faces of hated Yugoslav enemies: Hitler (fourth from altar on left) and Mussolini (first from altar on right). Behind the church is a typical local cemetery—with civilian and (on the hillside) military sections.

For a good example of the how rivers cut like God's bandsaw into the land, stop about two minutes past the church at Velika

The Soča (Isonzo) Front

The northwest corner of Slovenia—called Soča in Slovene, and Isonzo in Italian—saw some of World War I's fiercest fighting. While the Western Front gets more press, this eastern border between the Central Powers and the Allies was just as significant. In a series of 13 battles involving 16 different nationalities, 300,000 soldiers died, 700,000 were wounded, and 100,000 were declared MIA. In addition, tens of thousands of civilians died. Among the injured soldiers was a young Ernest Hemingway, who drove an ambulance for the Italian army. (Later in life, he would write the novel *A Farewell to Arms* about his experiences here.)

On April 26, 1915, Italy joined the Allies. A month later, they declared war on the Austro-Hungarian Empire (which included Slovenia). Italy invaded the Soča Valley, quickly taking the tiny town of Kobarid, which they planned to use as a home base for attacks deeper into Austrian territory. For the next 29 months, Italy launched 10 more offensives, all of them unsuccessful. This was difficult warfare—Italy had to attack uphill, waging war high in the mountains, in the harshest of conditions.

In October 1917, the Central Powers of Austria-Hungary and Germany retook Kobarid, launching a downhill attack of 600,000 soldiers. For the first time ever, the Austrian-German army used a new surprise-attack technique called *Blitzkrieg,* which was carried out by a German general named Erwin Rommel—against orders from a superior. (He was demoted for his insolence despite its success, but climbed the ranks again to become famous as Hitler's "Desert Fox" in North Africa.) The Central Powers caught the Italian forces off-guard, quickly breaking through three lines of defense. Within three days, the Italians were forced to retreat. The Austrians called it the "Miracle at Kobarid," but Italy felt differently—to this day, when an Italian finds himself in a mess, he says he had a *Caporetto* (the Italian name for Kobarid).

A year later, Italy came back—this time with the aid of British, French, and U.S. forces. The Allies were successful, and on November 4, 1918, Austria-Hungary conceded defeat. After more than a million casualties, the fighting at Soča was finally over.

Korita Soča, where you can venture out onto a bouncy **suspension bridge** over a gorge.

Roughly five miles after the town of Soča, you exit the National Park and come to a fork. The main route leads to the left, through Bovec. But first, take a two-mile detour to the right, where the WWI **Kluže Fort** keeps a close watch over the narrowest part of a valley leading to Italy (350 SIT, daily 10:00–19:00). In the 15th century, the Italians had a fort here to defend against the Turks. Half a millennium later, during World War I, it was used by Austrians to keep Italians out of their territory. Notice the ladder rungs fixed to the cliff face across the road from the fort—allowing soldiers to quickly get up to the mountaintop. Today, the fort hosts a peace festival every summer, where costumed Italian and Austro-Hungarian soldiers stop traffic for stern military checks, then perform a show and embrace each other.

Continue back through **Bovec.** This town, which saw some of the most vicious fighting of the Soča Front, was hit hard by a 2004 earthquake. Today, it's being rebuilt and remains the adventure-sports capital of the Soča River Valley, famous for its whitewater activities. For a good lunch stop in Bovec, try the busiest place in town, Letni Vrt Pizzeria, with pizzas, pastas, salads, and more (closed Tue, on main square, tel. 05/389-6383.)

Heading south along the river (with water somehow both perfectly clear and spectacularly turquoise), watch for happy kayakers. When you pass the intersection at Žaga, you're just over four miles from Italy.

Signs lead to the town of **Kobarid,** home to the world-class **Kobarid Museum** (Kobariški Muzej)—offering a haunting look at the tragedy of the Soča Front (800 SIT, good 600-SIT museum guide, 1,900-SIT *Soča Front* book, April–Sept Mon–Fri 9:00–18:00, Sat–Sun 9:00–19:00; Oct–March Mon–Fri 10:00–17:00, Sat–Sun 9:00–18:00; Gregorčičeva 10, www.kobariski-muzej.si, tel. 05/389-0000). This proud little place, with fine English descriptions, was voted Europe's best museum in 1993. The entry is lined with hastily made cement and barbed-wire gravestones, pictures of soldiers, and flags of all of the nationalities involved in the fighting. Maps show how Europe changed from 1914 to 1918. The rotating ground-floor exhibit features one country in particular (Italy in 2005). Upstairs are exhibits on the way these soldiers lived, the tragedies they encountered (with some horrific images of war injuries), the devastating effects of the war on local civilians, the strategies involved in the various battles (including a huge model of the successful Austrian-German *Blitzkrieg* attack), and the history of this region before and after World War I. Upon arrival, ask for an English playing of the 22-minute video on the history of the Front (plays on top floor). At the museum, WWI buffs can pick up free brochures on self-guided "walks of peace" through town; call ahead if you want a private guide (2,500 SIT/hr, tel. 05/389-0000).

The 55 miles between here and the Adriatic are dotted with more than a hundred cemeteries, reminders of the countless casualties of the Soča Front. One of the most dramatic is the **Italian Mausoleum** (Kostnica) overlooking Kobarid. The access road (across Kobarid's main square from the church, with a gate featuring a cross on one side and a star on the other) leads up Gradič Hill—

passing Stations of the Cross—to the
mausoleum. Built in 1938 around the
existing Church of St. Anthony, this
fascist-style octagonal pyramid holds
the remains of 7,014 Italian soldiers.
Names are listed alphabetically, along
with the names of mass graves for more
than 1,700 unknown soldiers *(militi
ignoti)*. Walk behind the church and

find the WWI battlements high on the mountain's rock face (with
your back to church, they're at 10 o'clock). Incredibly, the fighting
was done on these treacherous ridges; civilians in the valleys only
heard the distant battles. Inside the church, look above the door to
see a brave soldier standing over the body of a fallen comrade, fend-
ing off enemies with nothing but rocks. When Mussolini came to
dedicate the mausoleum, local revolutionaries plotted an assassination attempt that couldn't fail. But at the last minute, the trigger-
man had a change of heart, Mussolini had an uneventful trip, and
fascism continued to thrive in Italy.

Continue south along the Soča to **Tolmin**. Before you reach
Tolmin, decide your route back to Ljubljana or Bled: Hook south
along smoother roads via Nova Gorica, or take windier mountain
roads via Idrija. Either option brings you back to the expressway
south of Ljubljana.

The option you'll encounter first (turnoff to the right before
Tolmin) is the smoother, longer route southwest through Tuscan-
esque landscapes towards Nova Gorica (literally divided in half by
the Italian border) and eventually to the bustling Italian port of
Trieste, which was Slovenian before World War II. From Nova
Gorica or from Trieste, freeways lead back to Ljubljana and Bled.

I prefer the more rural second option: Continue through
Tolmin, then head southeast through the hills back towards
Ljubljana. Keep an eye out for the distinctive Slovenian hay-drying
racks—but notice that here, unlike in the northern part of the country, they don't have roofs (less rain). Along the way, you could stop
for a bite and some sightseeing at **Idrija** (EE-dree-yah), known to all
Slovenes for three things: its tourable mercury mine, fine delicate
lace, and tasty *žlikrofi* (like ravioli). Back at the freeway (at Logatec),
head north to Ljubljana or on to Bled. If you prefer a more direct,
non-expressway route back up to Bled—and don't mind skipping
Idrija—you can turn north in Želin (before Idrija) towards Skofja
Loka and Kranj.

CROATIA
(Hrvatska)

Croatia is known for two very different reasons: as a top fun-in-the-sun tourist destination, and as the site, only a decade ago, of one of the most violent European wars in a generation. Thankfully, today the bloodshed is in the past. Be aware of the war, but focus on Croatia's natural beauty—the dramatic Dalmatian coastline and the striking waterfalls of Plitvice Lakes National Park—and its underrated capital, Zagreb.

Croatia feels more Mediterranean than "Eastern European." Especially on the coast, it's sometimes difficult to distinguish this lively, chaotic place from Italy. Be prepared to fall victim to the Croatian Shrug—a simple gesture that conveys the message, "Don't know, don't care."

Ten years of war, no tourists, and economic troubles mean that Croatia's service standards and infrastructure still lag behind other parts of Eastern Europe. (Notice that Croatia is the only country in this book that is not yet a member of the European Union.) While

How Big, How Many, How Much

- Croatia is 21,800 square miles (the size of West Virginia, but with a boomerang shape).
- Population is 4.5 million (about 200 people per square mile, 90 percent Catholic—about half of them practicing—and 5 percent Serbian Orthodox).
- 1 kuna (kn, or HRK) = about 17 cents, and 6 kuna = about $1 (Interestingly, "kuna" is Croatian for "fox.")
- Country code: 385

prices are on par with Western Europe, you get less for your money, especially at coastal hotels.

But most visitors happily put up with Croatia's minor frustrations to take advantage of its spectacular scenery. Comparable to Mexico as a getaway retreat for Americans, Croatia is known among Europeans as a popular, inexpensive place for a sunny holiday.

Nude beaches are a big deal in Croatia, especially for vacationing Germans and Austrians. If you want to work on an all-around tan, seek out one of the beaches marked *FKK* (from the German *Freikörper Kultur*, or "free body culture"). First-timers get comfortable in a hurry, finding they're not the only pink novices on the rocks. But don't get too excited—these beaches are most beloved by people you'd rather see with their clothes on.

Croatian music, the mariachi music of Europe, graces German and Italian airwaves. The crooner Oliver Dragojević—singing soulful Mediterranean ballads with his gravelly, passionate voice—is the Croatian Tony Bennett.

Even a few years ago, the newly rebuilt streets of Dubrovnik were empty. But not anymore. Croatian resorts and beaches are quickly filling back up to pre-war levels. Visit soon, before the crowds return in full force.

Practicalities

Safety: Americans worry about the potential dangers of traveling in a country that was in the headlines for its bloody war just a decade ago. But as soon as visitors arrive, they're surprised by how peaceful and stable Croatia feels. Croatia's primary tourist region—the coast—was barely touched by the war (except Dubrovnik, which has been painstakingly restored). The inland is sprinkled with destroyed homes and churches—some standing gutted, skeletons of their original structures—but villages are gradually being refurbished.

If there's anything visitors need to be aware of, it's that much of the Croatian interior was once full of landmines. Almost all have been removed, and fields that may be dangerous are usually clearly marked. But as a precaution, stay on roads and paths, and don't go wandering through overgrown fields and deserted villages.

The biggest impact from the war has been on the people. Throughout the country, but especially in the war-torn interior, sadness and anger hang heavy in the air. Though the country is repairing itself admirably, the Croatians' souls will take the longest to heal.

For more on Croatia during and after the war, see the Understanding Yugoslavia chapter, page 663.

Stow Your Euros: Tourists are notorious for confusing euro bills with Croatian kuna bills (both modeled after the old German *Deutschmark,* and therefore similar). Make a point of deep-storing all euros while outside the euro zone, or you'll be paying about seven times more than you should to enjoy Croatia.

Telephones: Croatia's phone system uses area codes. To make a long-distance call within the country, start with the area code. To call Croatia from another country, first dial the international access code (00 if calling from Europe, 011 from United States or Canada), 385 (Croatia's country code), the area code (without the initial zero), and the local number. To call out of Croatia, dial 00, the country code of the country you're calling (see chart in appendix), the area code if applicable (may need to drop initial zero), and the local number.

Free Tourist Help by Phone: The "Croatian Angels" service gives free information over a toll-free line in English (tel. 062/999-999, mid-June–Sept daily 8:00–24:00).

Addresses: Addresses listed with a street name, followed by "b.b.," have no street number.

Croatian History

Croatia's history is complicated. For nearly a millennium, bits and pieces of what we today call "Croatia" were batted back and forth between foreign powers: Hungarians, Venetians, Turks, Hapsburgs, and—of course—Yugoslavs. Only in 1991 did Croatia (violently) regain its independence.

Early History

Croatia's first inhabitants were the Illyrians (ancestors of today's Albanians). Romans began to settle the Dalmatian Coast as early as 229 B.C., and Emperor Diocletian had his retirement palace in the coastal town of Split. The Slavic Croats—ancestors of today's Croatians—arrived in the 7th century, and in A.D. 925, the Dalmatian duke Tomislav united most of present-day Croatia.

Loss of Independence

By the early 12th century, the Croatian kings had died out and neighboring powers (Hungary, Venice, and Byzantium) threatened the Croats. For the sake of self-preservation, Croatia entered into an alliance with the Hungarians in 1102—and for the next 900 years, Croatia was ruled by foreign states. The Hungarians gradually took more and more power from the Croats, exerting control over the majority of inland Croatia. Meanwhile, the Venetian Republic conquered most of the coast and peppered the Croatian Adriatic with bell towers and statues of St. Mark. Through it all, the tiny Republic of Dubrovnik flourished—paying off whomever necessary to maintain its independence, and becoming one of Europe's most important shipbuilding and maritime powers.

The Ottoman Turks conquered most of inland Croatia in the 15th century, and challenged the Venetians—unsuccessfully—for control of the coastline. In the 17th century, the Turks were forced out and the Hapsburgs arrived, taking over inland Croatia. After Venice and Dubrovnik fell to Napoleon, the coast went to the Hapsburgs—beginning a long tradition of Austrians basking on Croatian beaches.

The Yugoslav Era

When the Austro-Hungarian Empire broke up at the end of World War I, Croats banded together with the Serbs and Slovenes in the union that would become Yugoslavia. But throughout the Yugoslav era, the Croats often felt they were treated as lesser partners under Serbia. (Many Croats objected to naming the country's official language "Serbo-Croatian"—why not "Croato-Serbian?")

For more details about this complicated union and its breakup, see the Understanding Yugoslavia chapter, page 663.

Independence Regained

Croatia became its own nation in 1991 after nine centuries of foreign domination. The Croatians seized their hard-earned freedom with a nationalist fervor that bordered on fascism. This was a heady and absurd time, which today's Croatians recall with disbelief, sadness...and maybe a tinge of nostalgia.

In the Croatia of the early 1990s, even the most bizarre notions seemed possible. Croatia's first post-Yugoslav president, the extreme nationalist Franjo Tuđman, proposed ludicrous directives for the new nation—such as privatizing all of the nation's resources and handing them over to 200 super-elite families (which, thankfully for everyone else, never came to pass). The government began calling the language "Croatian" rather than "Serbo-Croatian," creating new words from specifically Croat roots (see "Croatian Language," below). The Croats even briefly considered replacing the Roman alphabet with the 9th-century Glagolitic script to invoke Croat culture and further differentiate Croatian from Serbia's Cyrillic alphabet. Fortunately for tourists, this plan didn't take off.

After Tuđman's death in 1999, Croatia began the new

millennium with a more truly democratic leader, Stipe Mesić. The popular Mesić, who was once aligned with Tuđman, split when Tuđman's politics grew too extreme. Tuđman spent years tampering with the constitution to give himself more and more power, but when Mesić took over, he reversed those changes and handed more authority back to the parliament. After a fitful adjustment to independence, today's Croatia is on the right track.

Croatian Food

Like its people, the food in Croatia's different regions has been shaped by various influences—predominantly Italian, Turkish, and Hungarian. No single cuisine is distinctly Croatian. Choosing between strudel and baklava on the same menu, you're constantly reminded that this is a land where East meets West.

To the north (Zagreb) and east (Slavonia), the food has more of a Hungarian flavor—heavy on meat, and served with cabbage, noodles, or potatoes (see "Hungarian Food," page 284). If different types of Croatian food have one thing in common, it's lots and lots of meat.

The Ottoman Turks left their mark on inland Croatia (around Plitvice Lakes), where a popular fast food is *burek*—phyllo dough filled with meat, cheese, spinach, or apples. The more familiar *baklava* is phyllo dough layered with honey and nuts. Also look for *čevapčići* (minced meat in a pita wrap, like a kebab); *pljeskavica* (similar to *čevapčići*, except the meat is in the form of a hamburger-like patty, instead of cut up); and *ražnjići* (small pieces of steak on a skewer, like a shish kebab). While Balkan cuisine favors meat, a nice veggie complement is *duved*—a spicy mix of stewed vegetables, flavored with tomatoes and peppers. A popular condiment you'll enjoy throughout the Balkans is *ajvar,* made from red bell pepper and eggplant; it's like ketchup with a kick.

On the Dalmatian Coast, seafood is a specialty, and the Italian influence is obvious. Dalmatians say that a fish should swim three times: once in the sea, then in olive oil, and finally in wine—when you eat it. You can get all kinds of seafood along the coast: fish, scampi, mussels, calamari, you name it. On menus, prices for seafood dishes are listed by the kilogram (figure about a half kilo, or one pound, for a large portion). Consider *riblja juha*—fish soup.

If you're not a seafood eater, keep an eye out for pizza and pasta (try the gnocchi). Another Dalmatian specialty is *pašticada*—braised beef in a wine-and-herb sauce. Finally, Dalmatia is known for its mutton. Since the lambs graze on salty seaside herbs, the meat—often served on a spit—has a distinctive flavor.

Franjo Tuđman
(1922–1999)

Independent Croatia's first president was the complicated, controversial Franjo Tuđman (FRAHN-yoh TOOJ-mahn). Tuđman began his career fighting for Tito on the left, but later had a dramatic ideological swing to the far right. His anti-communist, highly nationalistic HDZ party was the driving force for Croatian statehood, making him the young nation's first hero. But even as he fought for independence from Yugoslavia, his own ruling style grew more and more authoritarian. As president, he expressed support for the Ustaše, who had ruled Croatia under the Nazis (and whom he considered to be the original Croatian "freedom fighters"). Croatia's currency, the kuna, seems harmless enough…but since it was first used during the Ustaše era, Tuđman raised some eyebrows when he reintroduced it.

Tuđman espoused some of the same single-minded attitudes about ethnic divisions as the ruthless Serbian leader Slobodan Milošević, with whom he had secret, under-the-table, Hitler-and-Stalin-esque negotiations for divvying up Bosnia. When Tuđman's successor moved into the president's office, he discovered a top-secret hotline to Milošević's desk. And even today, Croatian newspapers routinely uncover decade-old photos of secret summits between the two leaders in Vienna.

To ensure that he stayed in power, Tuđman played fast and loose with his new nation's laws. He was notorious for changing the

Throughout Croatia, salad is served with the main dish unless you request it be served beforehand.

There are many good local varieties of cheese made with sheep's or goat's milk. Pag, an island in the Kvarner Gulf near Rijeka, produces a famous, very salty, fairly dry sheep's milk cheese *(paški sir)*, which is said to carry the flavor of the sparse herbs that the sheep graze on.

For dessert, you'll find lots of good, homemade ice cream *(sladoled)*, especially on the Dalmatian Coast. Dalmatia's typical dessert is a very strong flan (crème caramel), which they call *rozata.*

Mineral water is *mineralna voda.* Jamnica is the main Croatian brand (its spokesperson is the similarly-named Croatian skiing sensation Janice Kostelić, who won three medals at the 2002 Winter Olympics in Salt Lake City). As in most Slavic countries, *voda* gets you water, *kava* gets you coffee, *pivo* gets you beer, and *vino* gets you wine. When toasting with some new Croatian friends, raise your glass with a hearty *"Živjeli!"* (ZHEE-vyeh-lee).

Croatia has good wine, but it's comparatively expensive. The sunny mountains north of Zagreb are covered with vineyards constitution as it suited him. By the late 1990s, when his popularity was slipping, Tuđman extended Croatian citizenship to anyone who lived in Croatia, or anyone of Croatian heritage—a ploy aimed at getting votes from Croats living in Bosnia, who were sure to line up with him on the far right.

Through it all, Tuđman kept a tight grip on the media, making it illegal to report anything that would disturb the public—even if true. When Croatians turned on their TV sets and saw the flag flapping in the breeze to the strains of the national anthem, they knew something was up...and switched to CNN to get the real story. In this oppressive environment, many bright, young Croatians fled the country, causing a "brain drain" that hampered the country's recovery after the war.

Tuđman died of cancer at the end of 1999. While it seems that history will judge him harshly, the opinion in today's Croatia is qualified. Most agree that Tuđman was an important and even admirable figure in the struggle for Croatian statehood, but he ultimately went too far and got too greedy. All over the country, streets, squares, and bridges have recently been named for this "hero" of Croatian nationalism (by local politicians belonging to his still-active party). But if he were still alive, Tuđman would be standing trial in The Hague next to Milošević.

producing white wine. In the south and along the coast, you'll find mostly reds—except in the Istrian peninsula to the far north, which corks up some whites, including *malvazija,* a very popular midrange wine. On the coast, Croatian red wines are served proudly and offer a velvety new frontier. Each Adriatic island produces its own wine. Along the coast, it's very common to drink wine mixed with mineral water.

To request a menu, say, *"Meni, molim"* (MEH-nee, MOH-leem; "Menu, please"). To get the attention of your waiter, say *"Konobar"* (KOH-noh-bahr; "Waiter"). When he brings your food, he'll likely say, *"Dobar tek!"* ("Bon appétit!"). When you're ready for the bill, ask for the *račun* (RAH-choon).

Croatian Language

Croatian was once known as "Serbo-Croatian," the official language of Yugoslavia. Despite what Croatians and Serbians tell you, the languages spoken in today's Croatia and Serbia are essentially the same—like the English spoken in New York versus New Orleans. The biggest difference is in the writing: Croatian uses our Roman

Key Croatian Phrases

English	Croatian	Pronounced
Hello. (formal)	**Dobar dan.**	DOH-bahr dahn
Ciao. (both "Hi" and "Bye"—informal)	**Bog.**	bohg
Do you speak English?	**Govorite li engleski?**	GOH-voh-ree-teh lee eng-LEHS-kee
yes / no	**da / ne**	dah / neh
Please. / You're welcome.	**Molim.**	MOH-leem
Can I help you?	**Izvolite?**	EEZ-voh-lee-teh
Thank you.	**Hvala.**	HVAH-lah
I'm sorry. / Excuse me.	**Oprostite.**	oh-PROH-stee-teh
Good.	**Dobro.**	DOH-broh
Goodbye.	**Do viđenija.**	doh-veed-JAY-neeah
one / two	**jedan / dva**	YEH-dahn / dvah
three / four	**tri / četiri**	tree / cheh-TEE-ree
five / six	**pet / šest**	peht / shehst
seven / eight	**sedam / osam**	SEH-dahm / OH-sahm
nine / ten	**devet / deset**	DEH-veht / DEH-seht
hundred	**sto**	stoh
thousand	**tisuća**	TEE-soo-chah
How much?	**Koliko?**	KOH-lee-koh
local currency	**kuna**	KOO-nah
Where is...?	**Gdje je...?**	guh-DYEH yeh
...the toilet	**...vece**	VEHT-seh
men	**muški**	MOOSH-kee
women	**ženski**	ZHEHN-skee
water / coffee	**voda / kava**	VOH-dah / KAH-vah
beer / wine	**pivo / vino**	PEE-voh / VEE-noh
Cheers!	**Živjeli!**	ZHEE-vyeh-lee
the bill	**račun**	RAH-choon

alphabet, while Serbian uses Cyrillic letters (which every young Yugoslav had to learn).

In recent years, a fit of hyper-nationalism has led Croatia to intentionally distance its vocabulary from Serbian. A decade ago, you'd catch a plane at the *Aerodrom*. Today, you'll catch that same flight at the *Zračna Luka*—a new coinage that combines the old Croatian words for "air" and "port." These new words, once created, are artificially injected into the lexicon. Croatians watching their favorite TV show will suddenly hear a character use a word they've never heard before...and think, "Oh, we have another new word."

Croatian is relatively easy to pronounce (and if you're just coming from Slovenia, you'll notice definite similarities). The accent is usually on the first syllable (and never on the last). As with other Slavic tongues, *c* is pronounced "ts" (as in "cats"). The letter *j* is pronounced as "y." The letters *č* and *ć* are slightly different, but they both sound more or less like "ch"; *š* sounds like "sh" and *ž* sounds like "zh" (as in "leisure"). One Croatian letter that you won't see in other languages is *đ*, which sounds like the "dj" sound in "jeans." In fact, this letter is often replaced with "dj" in English.

As you're tracking down addresses, these definitions will help: *trg* (square), *ulica* (road), and *most* (bridge).

The
DALMATIAN COAST

Sunny beaches, succulent seafood, and a taste of *la dolce vita*...in Eastern Europe? Croatia's Dalmatian Coast—the southern half of the country's coastline, stretching from Zadar to Dubrovnik—is Eastern Europe's Riviera. Many tourists were scared off after the recent war with Serbia (which damaged only Dubrovnik—completely repaired since). Now Croatia's resorts are aggressively advertising their once-again-discovered charms...and the tourists are back, in droves.

Dalmatia feels like Italy. Historically, it has more in common with Venice and Rome than Vienna or Budapest. People here speak Croatian with a lively Italian rhythm, and live the easygoing lifestyle that comes with it.

Dubrovnik is Croatia's top destination. With a picture-perfect Old Town and colorful history, it's like Venice without the canals. Big, bustling Split is the capital of the coast, boasting an in-love-with-life seaside promenade and a lived-in warren of twisting lanes sprouting out of a massive Roman palace. Right between them, the island town of Korčula may be the best village on the Croatian coast.

Getting Around the Dalmatian Coast

There are no trains along the Dalmatian Coast (the southernmost station is in Split, with only a few slow trains to Zagreb). You'll rely on ferries, buses, or a rental car.

By Boat: Ferries and speedy hydrofoils shuttle tourists between major cities and quiet island towns. Most of the ferries are run by Jadrolinija, which conveniently connects the three destinations in this chapter, plus a lot more. Advance reservations are not necessary for deck passengers; you can almost always find a seat on the deck or in the on-board café. To reserve a cabin or take a car, make the arrangements several weeks in advance (main office in

Rijeka: tel. 051/211-444, fax 051/211-485, www.jadrolinija.hr, passdept_e @jadrolinija.hr). I've listed the most useful boat schedules in the "Transportation Connections" section for each destination.

By Boat to Italy: Four different companies connect Croatia to Italy, across the Adriatic Sea, at least once daily in summer. Split is the main hub for these boats, but you can also go from other cities (usually Dubrovnik or Zadar; many international ferries also stop at smaller Dalmatian towns). Almost all boats go to Ancona, Italy. Most trips are overnight and last about 10 hours, but there is one super-fast catamaran that takes only four hours (by Aliscafi SNAV, see below). On the slower boats, figure about €40 per person for one-way deck passage (about 10–20 percent more in peak season, roughly July–Aug), plus more for on-board accommodation (around €10 per person for a *couchette* in a 4-berth compartment, €45 per person in 2-bed compartment with private shower and WC).

These are your options to get to Italy: **Jadrolinija** runs boats from Split to Ancona or from Zadar to Ancona, as well as from Dubrovnik to Bari (Croatian tel. 051/211-444, www.jadrolinija.hr). **Blue Line/SEM** offers sailings from the towns of Split, Stari Grad (on island of Hvar), and Vis to Ancona (www.bli-ferry.com, can book at SEM Marina travel agency in Split, tel. 021/338-292).

Aliscafi SNAV is the speedy catamaran connecting Split with Ancona in just four hours (daily mid-June–Sept, €60 one-way, or €75 in Aug; also links Zadar with Ancona, and Split plus various smaller islands—such as Brač, Hvar, and Vela Luka on Korčula—to Italian towns Giulianova and Pescara, Croatian tel. 021/322-252, Italian tel. 0814/285-555, www.snav.it). **Adriatica Navigazione** does Split to Ancona (can book at Jadroagent in Split, tel. 021/338-335, Italian tel. 041/781-611, www.adriatica.it).

By Bus: Buses run between Dubrovnik and Split nearly hourly (5 hrs). The island town of Korčula is off the main route, and sees only one direct bus from Dubrovnik each day (but it's no faster than the boat). Don't attempt the lengthy, complicated bus connection between Split and Korčula; take the boat instead.

By Car: Considering the long distances, cheap and frequent buses, fun boat options, and worthlessness of a car in Dubrovnik or Split, those simply lacing together the major sights are better off without a car. Drivers should be prepared for twisty seaside roads, wonderful views, and plenty of tempting stopovers. Notice that between Split and Dubrovnik, you'll actually pass through Bosnia-Herzegovina for a few miles (the borders are a breezy formality). As you approach any town, follow the signs to *Centar*. Get parking advice from your hotel, or look for the blue-and-white *P* signs.

By Plane: The Dalmatian Coast is time-consuming to reach overland from northern Croatia (e.g., Zagreb to Split takes at least 6 hrs by bus; to Dubrovnik, 11 hrs). The best sight between Zagreb and

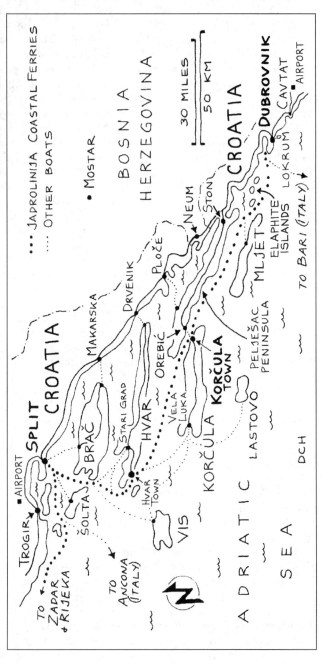

The Dalmatian Coast

the Dalmatian Coast is Plitvice Lakes National Park (see Zagreb and the Plitvice Lakes chapter)—but if you just want to make a beeline for the sea, skip the park and catch an inexpensive flight from Zagreb. Croatia Airlines flies from Zagreb to the small airports in Zadar, Split, and Dubrovnik (Croatian tel. 062/777-777, from outside Croatia call 385-1/487-2727, www.croatiaairlines.hr). American-based Europe by Air sells one-way tickets on Croatia Airlines for $99, though taxes and other fees bring the price closer to $160 (tickets can be purchased only in United States, www.europebyair.com, U.S. tel. 888/321-4737).

Helpful Hints

Siesta: Dalmatians eat their big meal at lunch, then take a traditional Mediterranean siesta. This means that many stores, museums, and churches close in the midafternoon. It can make for frustrating sightseeing—but you're on vacation. If you can't beat 'em, join 'em.

Seasonal Changes: Dalmatia's crowds fluctuate wildly by season. Some museums literally double their opening hours overnight when peak season hits. But here on the Adriatic, schedules are made to be broken, and opening times can change suddenly based on demand. The hours I've listed *should* be right...but if you have your heart set on a certain sight, confirm times with the TI on your arrival.

Dubrovnik

Dubrovnik is a living fairytale that shouldn't be missed. It feels like a small town today, but 500 years ago, Dubrovnik was a major maritime power, with the third biggest navy in the Mediterranean. Still jutting confidently into the sea and ringed by thick medieval walls, Dubrovnik deserves its nickname: the Pearl of the Adriatic. Within the ramparts, the traffic-free Old Town is a fun jumble of quiet, cobbled back lanes; tasty seafood restaurants; narrow, steep alleys; and kid-friendly squares. After all these centuries, the buildings still hint at old-time wealth, and the central promenade remains *the* place to see and be seen.

Dubrovnik, which feels Italian, actually began as a Roman colony. Although Croatian eventually became the official language, even today, people from Dubrovnik are teased by their Zagreb cousins for their Italian-influenced accent and vocabulary.

The city's charm is the sleepy result of its no-nonsense past. Busy merchants, the salt trade, and shipbuilding made Dubrovnik rich. But the city's most valued commodity was always its freedom— even today, you'll see the proud motto *Libertas* displayed all over town (see *"Libertas"* sidebar, next page).

Libertas

Libertas—liberty—has always been close to the heart of every Dubrovnik citizen. Dubrovnik was an independent republic for centuries, even as most of Croatia became Venetian and Hungarian. Dubrovnik believed so strongly in *libertas* that it was the first foreign state in 1776 to officially recognize an upstart, experimental republic called the United States of America.

In the Middle Ages, the city-state of Dubrovnik (then called Ragusa) had to buy its independence from whomever was strongest—Byzantium, Venice, Hungary, the Turks—sometimes paying off more than one at a time. Dubrovnik's ships flew whichever flags were necessary to stay free, earning the nickname "Town of Seven Flags." As time went on, Europe's major powers were glad to have a second major seafaring power in the Adriatic to balance the Venetian threat. A free Dubrovnik was more valuable than a pillaged, plundered Dubrovnik.

In 1808, Napoleon conquered the Adriatic and abolished the much-loved Republic. After Napoleon was defeated, the fate of the continent was decided at the Congress of Vienna. Anyone who wanted to participate had a seat at the table...but Dubrovnik's delegate was denied entry. The more powerful nations, no longer concerned about Venice and fed up after years of being sweet-talked by Dubrovnik, were afraid that he'd play old alliances off of each other to reestablish an independent Republic of Dubrovnik. Instead, the city became a part of the Hapsburg Empire, and entered a long period of decline.

Libertas still hasn't completely died in Dubrovnik. In the surreal days of the early 1990s, when Yugoslavia was reshuffling itself, a movement for the creation of a new Republic of Dubrovnik gained some momentum (led by a judge who, in earlier times, had convicted others for the same ideas). But today's locals are content to be part of an independent Republic of Croatia.

Dubrovnik flourished in the 15th and 16th centuries, but an earthquake destroyed nearly everything in 1667. Most of today's buildings in the Old Town are post-quake Baroque, although a few palaces, monasteries, and convents survive from Dubrovnik's earlier golden age.

Dubrovnik remained a big tourist draw through the Tito years, bringing in much-needed hard currency from Western visitors. Consequently, the city was never given the hard socialist patina of other Yugoslav cities (such as the nearby Montenegrin capital Podgorica, then known as "Titograd").

As Yugoslavia fell apart, the Croats fought for their independence. The 1991 war took its toll, and Dubrovnik was devastated (see "The Siege of Dubrovnik" sidebar, page 468). Imagine having youthful memories of good times romping in the surrounding hills replaced by heavily armed Serbs shooting down on your city. The only physical reminders of the war in today's Dubrovnik are lots of new, orange roof tiles...but locals who lived through the war will be forever hardened.

While the war killed tourism in the 1990s, today the crowds are back. The city's popularity has yet to match pre-war highs, but the economy is booming and Dubrovnik is thriving once again.

Planning Your Time

Dubrovnik's individual sights are pleasant, but nothing to jump ship for: several convents, a few works by famous painters, some mediocre museums, and Europe's oldest pharmacy. The attraction here is the city itself. While Dubrovnik could easily be seen in a day, a second day to unwind makes the long trip here more worthwhile.

Dubrovnik is most crowded during the Summer Festival, a month and a half of theater and musical performances held yearly from July 10 to Aug 25 (www.dubrovnik-festival.hr).

ORIENTATION

(area code: 020)

All of the sights worth seeing are in Dubrovnik's traffic-free, walled Old Town (Stari Grad) peninsula. The main pedestrian promenade through the middle of town is called Stradun (most locals don't use its official name, Placa); from this artery, the Old Town climbs uphill in both directions to the walls. The Old Town connects to the mainland through two gates (Pile Gate to the west and Ploče Gate to the east; there is also a stairway and passage to the mainland at the top of Boško Vićeva). The Old Port (Gradska Luka), with leisure boats to nearby destinations, is at the east end of town. While greater Dubrovnik has around 30,000 people, the local population within the Old Town is just 5,000 in the winter—and even less in summer, when many residents move out to let agencies rent their apartments to tourists (see "Sleeping," below).

Pile Square, a pincushion of tourist services, is located just beyond the west end of the Old Town, where the real world meets the fantasy of Dubrovnik. You'll find ATMs, a post office, the Atlas travel agency (books private rooms—see "Helpful Hints," below), the TI (with Internet access), the Croatia Airlines office, taxis, buses (heading to hotels on Lapad Peninsula), and the cheap Konzum grocery store.

Since there's only one affordable hotel in Dubrovnik's Old Town (Hotel Stari Grad—see "Sleeping," below), most visitors stay in big resorts a mile or two away. Most are on the lush Lapad

Greater Dubrovnik

TO KORČULA,
HVAR & SPLIT

TUĐMAN BRIDGE

½ MILE
1 KM

FERRY TERMINAL

BABIN KUK

IVA DULCICA

RIJEČKA

GRUŠKA OBALA

KARDINALA

STEP

POST

DALMATINSKA

PORT GRUŽ

BUS STN.

LAPAD BAY

ISPOD

OD BATALE

JADRANSKA CESTA

MASARYKOV

IVANSKA

IVA BANA JELAČIĆA

PUT REPUBLIKE

GORNJI KONO

ZAGREBAČKA

MOUNT SRĐ

LAPAD

HOSP.

VOJNOVIĆA

LIECHT.

PUT

ANTE STARČEVIĆA

TO AIRPORT

BONINOVO BAY

PILE

PLOČE

STRADUN

BUS STOP

OLD TOWN

TO LOKRUM & CAVTAT

① Hotel Bellevue
② Hotel Lero
③ Youth Hostel & Dubravka Vnučec Rooms
④ Hotel Kompas
⑤ Hotel Villa Wolff & Casa Bar/Rest.
⑥ Hotel Zagreb & Hotel Sumratin
⑦ Šetalište Kralja Zvonimira eateries

ADRIATIC SEA

DCH

Peninsula to the west (buses run frequently from just outside Pile Gate and take 10 min). North of Lapad Peninsula is Port Gruž, where ferries connect Dubrovnik to other Adriatic destinations.

Tourist Information

Dubrovnik's three TIs all have the same hours (May–Oct daily 8:00–20:00, Nov–April Mon–Sat 8:00–12:00 & 16:00–19:00, closed Sun, www.tzdubrovnik.hr). The main branch is on **Pile Square**, 100 yards up the street from Pile Gate (Dr. Ante Starčevića 7, tel. 020/427-591; Internet access in the same office—see "Helpful Hints," below). Another branch is inside the **Old Town** (about midway down the main drag, tel. 020/323-587), and the third is across the street from the Jadrolinija ferry dock at **Port Gruž** (Gruška obala, tel. 020/417-983). All are government-run and legally can't sell you anything—but they can answer questions and give you a copy of the free monthly information booklet *Dubrovnik Riviera,* which contains helpful maps, hotel and restaurant listings, bus and ferry schedules, current museum prices and hours, and more.

Dubrovnik Landmarks

English	Croatian	Pronounced
Old Town	**Stari Grad**	STAH-ree grahd
Old Port	**Stara Luka**	STAH-rah LOO-kah
Pile Gate	**Gradska Vrata Pile**	GRAHD-skah VRAH-tah PEE-leh
Ploče Gate	**Gradska Vrata Ploče**	GRAHD-skah VRAH-tah PLOH-cheh
Main Promenade	**Stradun** or **Placa**	STRAH-doon, PLAH-tsah
Adriatic Sea	**Jadran**	YAH-drahn

Arrival in Dubrovnik

By Boat: The big boats arrive at Port Gruž, two miles northwest of the Old Town. On the road in front of the ferry terminal, you'll find a bus stop (#1a, #1b, and #3 go to Old Town's Pile Gate; wait on side of street facing the water) and a taxi stand (figure 70 kn to the Old Town and most hotels). Across the street is the Jadrolinija office (with an ATM out front) and a TI. You can book a private room *(soba)* at Atlas Travel Agency (room-booking desk in boat terminal building) or at Gulliver Travel Agency (behind TI); you'll likely also be ambushed by locals wanting you to stay at their place (for more on the *sobe* option, see page 480).

By Bus: Dubrovnik's bus station (Autobusni Kolodvor) is 1.5 miles northwest of the Old Town, where Lapad Peninsula connects to the mainland (Put Republike 19). Out front, you'll find city bus stops (#1a, #1b, #3, #6, and #9 to Old Town's Pile Gate) and a taxi stand (around 50 kn to the Old Town and most hotels). Bus info: tel. 020/357-088.

By Plane: Dubrovnik's small airport (Zračna Luka) is in a place called Čilipi, 13 miles south of the city. A Croatia Airlines bus leaves from Dubrovnik's bus station 90 minutes before each regular flight, and meets each arriving flight at the airport (30 kn, 40 min). Airport info: tel. 020/773-377, www.airport-dubrovnik.hr. Figure 220 kn for a taxi or hotel shuttle between the airport and the center.

Helpful Hints

Slick Pavement: The Old Town, with its well-polished pavement stones and many slick stairs, is quite treacherous, especially after a rainstorm. Tread with care.

Internet Access: The best access is at the Mimosa Café, inside the main TI just outside the Pile Gate (5 kn/15 min, daily 8:00–23:30, Dr. Ante Starčevića 7). Internet signs advertise handy but more expensive terminals along the Old Town's main drag.

Travel Agency: Of the many travel agencies in town, **Atlas** has the most convenient locations and most helpful staff. They book rooms in private homes, sell seats on excursions, rent cars, and provide other travel-related services. Their handiest office is just outside the Pile Gate (Sv. Đurđa 1, June–Sept daily 8:00–20:00, until 19:00 and closed Sun off-season, tel. 020/442-574, www.atlas-croatia.com, atlas@atlas.hr). Their other offices are at the ferry-terminal building at Port Gruž, and by St. Blaise's Church in the Old Town (June–Sept Mon–Sat 8:00–21:00, Sun 8:00–13:00; Oct–May Mon–Sat 8:00–16:00, closed Sun, Lučarica 1, tel. 020/323-609).

Tours of Dubrovnik: Several local travel agencies (including Atlas, listed above) book seats on bus-plus-walking tours of Dubrovnik, as well as guided excursions throughout the region (about 140 kn for a 2.5-hr tour of the city).

Local Guide: Štefica Čurić is a good, young local guide (440 kn for a 2-hr private tour, tel. 020/450-133, dugacarapa@yahoo.com).

Best Views: Walking the wall at sunset is a treat; film disappears fast. A stroll east of the city walls offers nice views back on the Old Town (best light early in the day).

Getting Around Dubrovnik

Since most hotels are a mile or two out of town, you'll likely rely on the bus to connect to Dubrovnik's Old Town. Once there, everything is easily walkable. Get comfortable with the buses—they work great, and the system is quite easy.

By Bus: Libertas runs Dubrovnik's public buses, which go to all hotels west of the center from just outside the Old Town's Pile Gate (10 kn if you pay on bus, 8 kn if you buy ticket from your hotel or a kiosk—ask for *autobusna karta;* bus schedules and map in TI booklet). Each ticket is good for an hour. When you enter the bus, stamp your ticket or drop your payment (no change given) in the little box by the driver.

By Taxi: Taxis start at 25 kn, then cost 8 kn per kilometer. Figure 60 kn between the Old Town and most Lapad hotels. You call for a taxi based on the neighborhood you're in. Old Town's Pile Gate: tel. 020/424-343; Lapad (most hotels): tel. 020/435-715; bus station: tel. 020/357-044; ferry dock: tel. 020/418-112; Ploče (just east of Old Town): tel. 020/423-164.

SIGHTS

These sights are listed roughly in order from Pile Gate (at the west end of the Old Town), along Dubrovnik's main promenade, to Luža Square just inside Ploče Gate (at the east end of town).

▲▲▲**Walk the Walls (Gradske Zidine)**—Dubrovnik's single best attraction is strolling the scenic mile around the city walls. If you bring your map and pick out landmarks as you go, it's an ideal way to

get your bearings. Walking the walls also offers the best illustration of the damage Dubrovnik sustained during the recent war. It's easy to see that more than 70 percent of Dubrovnik's roofs were replaced after the bombings (notice the new, bright-orange tiles—and how some buildings salvaged the old tiles, but have bright 20th-century ones underneath).

There have been walls here almost as long as there's been a Dubrovnik. The fortifications were beefed up in the 15th century, when the Turks became a threat. Around the perimeter are several substantial forts, which protected residents both during the Republic of Dubrovnik's golden age and during the recent war with Serbia.

You can enter the walls at three points: just inside Pile Gate, near the Dominican Monastery north of Ploče Gate, and by the Maritime Museum south of the Old Port. The highest point is the Minčeta Tower, above the Pile Gate at the west end of town. The tower, while empty, rewards those who climb it with a fine view. If you climb here first from the Pile Gate and then proceed clockwise, it's mostly downhill all the way around. Speed demons with no cameras can walk the walls in less than an hour; strollers and shutterbugs should plan on two hours (30 kn to enter walls, 30-kn audioguide narrates a 1-hr circular tour of the walls, July–Aug daily 9:00–20:30, progressively shorter hours off-season until 9:00–15:00 in winter).

▲**Pile Gate (Gradska Vrata Pile)**—The west entrance to the Old Town is the Pile (PEE-leh) Gate. Just outside the gate is a leafy café terrace, and beyond that, the TI and bus stops to get to Lapad hotels. The huge, fortified peninsula just outside the city walls is the **Fort of St. Lawrence** (Tvrđava Lovrijenac), Dubrovnik's oldest fortress and one of the top venues for the Dubrovnik Summer Festival. Shakespeare plays are often performed here, occasionally starring Goran Višnjić, the Croatian actor who has become an American star on the TV show *ER*.

Within the Pile Gate, a metal sign shows where each Serbian bomb dropped on the Old Town. Passing through the gate, you find a lively little square surrounded by landmarks. To the left, a steep

The Siege of Dubrovnik

In June 1991, Croatia declared independence from Yugoslavia. Within weeks, the nations were at war (see the Understanding Yugoslavia chapter, page 663). Though warfare raged in the Croatian interior, nobody expected that it would reach Dubrovnik.

At 6:00 in the morning on October 1, 1991, Dubrovnik residents were stunned to see Yugoslav warships on the horizon. The ships shelled the hillsides above Dubrovnik to disable a strategic communications tower (which you can see today) and clear the way for land troops—who quickly surrounded the city. For the first time in generations, the city walls were used to protect its people from an invading army. A month later, the Serb-dominated Yugoslav National Army began bombing the Pearl of the Adriatic. Defenseless townspeople took shelter in their cellars, and sometimes even huddled together in the city wall's 15th-century forts.

Dubrovnik resisted the siege better than anyone expected. The Serbs were hoping that residents would flee the town, allowing the Yugoslav National Army to move in. But the people of Dubrovnik stayed. Many brave young locals lost their lives when they slung old hunting rifles over their shoulders and, under the cover of darkness, climbed the hills above Dubrovnik to meet the Serbs face-to-face.

After eight months of bombing, Dubrovnik was liberated by the

stairway leads up to the imposing Minčeta Tower (a good starting point for walking the walls—see above). Next to that is the small **Church of St. Savior** (Crkva Svetog Spasa). This votive church was built as a thanks to God after Dubrovnik made it through a 1520 earthquake. When the massive 1667 quake destroyed the city, this church was one of the only buildings left intact. And during the recent war, the church survived another close call when a shell exploded on the ground right in front of it (you can still see pockmarks from the shrapnel).

The big, round structure in the middle of the square is **Onofrio's Big Fountain** (Velika Onofrijea Fontana—named for its architect). In the Middle Ages, Dubrovnik had a complicated aqueduct system that brought water from the mountains seven miles away. The water ended up here, at the town's biggest fountain, before continuing through the city. This plentiful supply of water, large reserves of salt (a key source of Dubrovnik's wealth), and a massive granary made little, independent Dubrovnik very siege-resistant.

The big building on the left just beyond the small St. Savior church is the...

Franciscan Monastery Museum (Franjevački Samostan-Muzej)—

In the Middle Ages, Dubrovnik's monasteries flourished. While all you'll see here are a fine cloister and a one-room museum in the old

Croatian army, which attacked Serb positions from the north. Two-thirds of Dubrovnik had been damaged, but the failed siege was over.

Why was Dubrovnik—so far from the rest of the fighting—dragged into the conflict? The Serbs wanted to catch the city and the region off-guard, gaining a toehold on the southern Dalmatian Coast so they could push north to Split, Croatia's second city. They also hoped to ignite pro-Serb passions in the nearby Serb-dominated areas of Bosnia and Montenegro. But perhaps most of all, Yugoslavia wanted to hit Croatia where it hurt—its proudest, most historic, and most beautiful city, the tourist capital of a nation dependent on tourism.

The war initially devastated the tourist industry. Now, to the casual observer, Dubrovnik seems virtually back to normal. Aside from a few pockmarks and bright, new roof tiles, there are few reminders of what happened here just over a decade ago. If you're curious, drop by a souvenir shop and page through the *Dubrovnik at War* book, filled with photos showing the city desolate and in flames.

Though the city is physically back to normal, locals will tell you that people are different than before the war: still friendly, but wary...and a little less in love with life.

pharmacy, it's a delightful space. Enter through the gap between the small church and the big monastery (10 kn, daily 9:00–18:00, less off-season, Placa 2). Just inside the door, a century-old pharmacy still serves residents. (You'll see the monastery's original medieval pharmacy at the far end of the cloister.)

Explore the peaceful **cloister.** Examine the capitals at the tops of the 60 Romanesque-Gothic double pillars. Each one is different. Notice that some of the portals inside the courtyard are made with a lighter-colored stone; these had to be repaired after being damaged in the recent war.

In the far corner stands the medieval **pharmacy.** Part of the Franciscans' mission was to contribute to the good health of the citizens, so they opened this pharmacy in 1317. The monastery has had a pharmacy in continual operation ever since. On display are jars, pots, and other medieval pharmacists' tools. The sick would come to get their medicine at the little window (on left side), which limited contact with the pharmacist and reduced the risk of passing on disease. Around the room, you'll also find some relics, old manuscripts, and an interesting detailed painting of 16th-century Dubrovnik.

▲▲**Stradun Promenade (a.k.a. Placa)**—Dubrovnik's main pedestrian drag—officially called Placa, but better known as Stradun—is alive with locals and tourists alike. This is the heartbeat of the city: an

Dubrovnik's Old Town

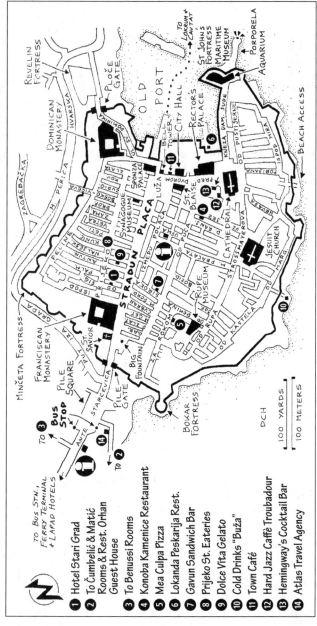

1 Hotel Stari Grad
2 To Čumbelić & Matić
   Rooms & Rest. Orhan
   Guest House
3 To Benussi Rooms
4 Konoba Kamenice Restaurant
5 Mea Culpa Pizza
6 Lokanda Peskarija Rest.
7 Gavun Sandwich Bar
8 Prijeko St. Eateries
9 Dolce Vita Gelato
10 Cold Drinks "Buža"
11 Town Café
12 Hard Jazz Caffè Troubadour
13 Hemingway's Cocktail Bar
14 Atlas Travel Agency

Old World shopping mall by day and sprawling cocktail party after dark, when everybody seems to be doing the traditional *korzo,* or evening stroll—flirting, ice-cream-licking, flaunting, and gawking. A coffee and some of Europe's best people-watching in a prime Stradun café is one of travel's great $3 bargains.

When Dubrovnik was just getting its start in the 7th century, this street was a canal. Romans fleeing from the invading Slavs lived on the island of Ragusa, and the Slavs settled on the shore. In the 11th century, the canal separating Ragusa from the mainland was filled in, the towns merged, and a unique Slavic-Roman culture and language blossomed. While originally much more higgledy-piggledy, this street was rebuilt in the current, more uniform style after the 1667 earthquake.

▲▲**Luža Square**—Dubrovnik's central square is just inside Ploče Gate at the east end of the Stradun. The centerpiece is **Orlando's Column** (Orlandov Stup). Columns like this were typical of towns in northern Germany. Dubrovnik erected the column in 1417, soon after it had shifted allegiances from the oppressive Venetians to the Hungarians. By putting a northern European symbol in the middle of its most prominent square, Dubrovnik decisively distanced itself from Venice. Anytime a decision was made by the Republic, the town crier came to Orlando's Column and announced the news. The step he stood on indicated the importance of his message—the higher up, the more important the news. It was also used as the pillory, where people were publicly punished. The thin line on the top step in front of Orlando is exactly as long as the statue's forearm. This mark was Dubrovnik's standard measurement—not for a foot, but for an "elbow" (no kidding).

Now stand in front of Orlando's Column and orient with the following spin-tour. Orlando is looking toward the **Sponza Palace** (Sponza-Povijesni Arhiv). This building, from 1522, is the finest surviving example of Dubrovnik's golden age in the 15th to 16th centuries; it's a combination of Renaissance (ground-floor arches) and Venetian Gothic (upstairs windows). Houses up and down the main promenade used to look like this...but after the 1667 earthquake, they were replaced with boring uniformity. This used to be the customs office *(dogana),* but now it's an exhaustive archive of the city's history, with temporary art exhibits and a war memorial. The poignant **Memorial Room of Dubrovnik Defenders** (in the back left corner) has photos of dozens of people from Dubrovnik who were killed fighting the Serbs in 1991. Note the photos of the bombed town high above (free, English descriptions, daily 8:00–14:00, often later).

To the right of Sponza Palace is the town's **Bell Tower** (Gradski Zvonik). The original dated from 1444, but it was rebuilt when it started to slide in the 1920s. The big clock may be an octopus—but it has only one hand. Below that, the circle shows the phase of the moon (the greener, the fuller the moon). At the bottom, the old-fashioned digital readout tells the hour (in Roman numerals) and the minutes (in 5-min increments). At the top of each hour (and again 3 minutes later), the time is clanged out on the bell up top by two bronze bell ringers: Maro and Baro. (If this seems like a copy of the very similar clock on St. Mark's Square in Venice, locals are quick to point out that this clock predates that one by several decades.) The clock still has to be wound every two days. Notice the little black hole between the moon phase and the "digital" readout: The clock-winder opens this window to get some light. During the recent war, the clock-winder's house was destroyed—with the keys inside. For days, the clock bell didn't run. But then, miraculously, the keys were discovered lying in the street. The excited Dubrovnik citizens came together in this square and cheered as the clock was wound and the bell chimed, signaling to the Serbs surrounding the city that they hadn't won yet.

The big building to the right of the Bell Tower is the **City Hall** (Vijećnica). Next to it is **Onofrio's Little Fountain** (Mala Onofrijea Fontana)—the little brother of the one at the other end of the Stradun (see above)—and the **Town Café** (Gradska Kavana), historically Dubrovnik's favorite spot for gossiping and people-watching. This is a great place for a scenic coffee break. They have prime seating here, overlooking the pedestrian square, or opposite, with views over the old port. The handy WC is just inside the door on the left (2 kn). Just down the street from the Town Café is the Rector's Palace, and then the cathedral (for more on each, see below).

Behind Orlando is **St. Blaise's Church** (Crkva Sv. Vlaha), dedicated to the patron saint of Dubrovnik. You'll see statues and paintings of St. Blaise all over town, always holding a model of the city in his left hand. According to legend, a millennium ago, St. Blaise came to a local priest in a dream and warned him that the up-and-coming Venetians would soon attack the city. The priest alerted the authorities, who prepared for war. Of course, the prediction came true. St. Blaise has been a Dubrovnik symbol—and locals have resented Venice—ever since.

▲**Rector's Palace (Knežev Dvor)**—In the Middle Ages, the Republic of Dubrovnik was ruled by a rector (similar to a Venetian doge), elected by the nobility. To prevent any one person from getting too powerful, the rector's term was limited to one month. Most rectors were in their 50s—near the end of the average lifespan, and less likely to shake things up. During his term, a rector lived upstairs in this palace. Today, it's open for visitors (20 kn, June–Sept daily 9:00–18:00, Oct–May daily 9:00–14:00, Pred Dvorom 3).

The exterior is decorated in the Gothic-Renaissance mix (with particularly finely carved capitals) that was so common in Dubrovnik before the 1667 earthquake. The Baroque interior houses some old jail cells (downstairs), and apartments (upstairs) that serve as a painting gallery. The only vaguely authentic room is the red room in the corner, decorated more or less as it was in 1500, when it was the rector's office. The exquisite *Baptism of Christ* painting, inspired by Italian painter Andrea Mantegna, is an early Renaissance work from the "Dubrovnik School" (see "Dominican Monastery Museum," below).

The courtyard is a venue for the Summer Festival, hosting music groups ranging from the local symphony to the Vienna Boys' Choir. In the courtyard is the only secular statue created during the centuries-long Republic. Dubrovnik republicans, mindful of the dangers of hero-worship, didn't believe that any one citizen should be singled out. They made only one exception—for Miho Pracat (a.k.a. Michaeli Prazatto), a rich citizen who willed a fleet of ships to the city. But notice that Pracat's statue is displayed in here, behind closed doors, not out in public.

▲▲**Cathedral (Katedrala)**—Dubrovnik's original 12th-century cathedral was funded largely by the English king Richard the Lionheart. On his way back from the Third Crusade, Richard was shipwrecked nearby. He promised God that if he survived, he'd build a church on the spot where he landed—which happened to be on the island of Lokrum, just offshore. At Dubrovnik's request, Richard agreed to build his token of thanks inside the city instead. It was the finest Romanesque church on the Adriatic...before it was destroyed by the 1667 earthquake. This version is 18th-century Roman Baroque.

Inside, you'll find an original Titian *(Assumption of the Virgin)*, a stark contemporary altar, and a quirky **treasury** *(riznica)* packed with 138 relics (church entry free, treasury entry-7 kn, Mon–Sat 9:00–20:00, Sun 11:00–17:30). Notice that there are three locks on the treasury door—the stuff in here was so valuable, three different VIPs (the rector, the bishop, and a local aristocrat) had to agree before it could be opened. On the table near the door are several of St. Blaise's body parts (pieces of his arm, skull, and leg—all encased in fancy silver). In the middle of the wall above the altar, look for the crucifix with a piece of the "true cross." On a dig in Jerusalem, St. Helen (Emperor Constantine's mother) discovered what she believed to be the cross that Jesus was crucified on. It was brought to Constantinople, and the Byzantine czars doled out pieces of it to Balkan kings. Note the folding three-paneled altar painting (underneath the cross). Dubrovnik ambassadors packed this on road trips (such as their annual trip to pay off the Turks) so they could worship wherever they traveled. On the right side of the room, the silver casket supposedly holds the actual swaddling clothes of the Baby Jesus. Dubrovnik bishops secretly passed these clothes down from generation to generation...until a nun got wind of it, and told the whole town. Pieces of the cloth were cut off to miraculously heal the sick, especially new mothers recovering from a difficult birth. No matter how often it was cut, the cloth always went back to its original form. But then someone tried to use it on the wife of a Bosnian king. Since she was Muslim, it couldn't help her, and it never worked again. Whether or not it's true, this legend hints at the prickly relationships between faiths here in the Balkans.

▲▲Dominican Monastery Museum (Dominikanski Samostan-Muzej)—You'll find many of Dubrovnik's art treasures—paintings, altarpieces and manuscripts—gathered around the peaceful Dominican Monastery cloister just north of Ploče Gate (10 kn, art buffs enjoy the 70-kn English book, June–Sept daily 9:00–18:00, off-season until 17:00).

One room contains paintings from the **"Dubrovnik School,"** the Republic's circa-1500 answer to the art boom in Florence and Venice. While the 1667 earthquake destroyed most of these paintings, about a dozen survive, and five of those are in this room. Don't miss the triptych by Nikola Božidarović, with St. Blaise holding a detailed model of 16th-century Dubrovnik; you'll see this image all over town.

The striking **church** is decorated with modern stained glass, a fine 13th-century pulpit that survived the earthquake (reminding visitors of the intellectual approach to scripture that characterized the Dominicans), and a precious 14th-century Paolo Veneziano crucifix hanging above the high altar. The most memorable piece of art in the church is the *Miracle of St. Dominic,* showing the founder of the order bringing a child back to life. It was painted in the Realist style (late 19th century) by Vlaho Bukovac.

▲Synagogue Museum (Sinagoga-Muzej)—When Jews were forced out of Spain in 1492, many of them passed through here en route to Turkey. Finding Dubrovnik to be a flourishing and relatively tolerant city, many stayed. Žudioska ulica (literally, "Jewish Street"), just inside Ploče Gate, became the ghetto in 1546. Today, the same street is home to the second-oldest synagogue in Europe (after Prague's). The top floor houses the synagogue itself (with the lattice windows through which Orthodox Jewish women would peer). Below that, a small museum with good English descriptions gives meaning to the various Torahs (including a 13th-century one from Spain) and other items—such as the written orders *(Naredba)* that Jews in Nazi-era Yugoslavia had to identify their shops as Jewish-owned and wear armbands. Of Croatia's 24,000 Jews, only 3,000 survived the Holocaust. Today, 45 Jews call Dubrovnik home, and a rabbi visits this synagogue five times a year from Zagreb (10 kn, May–Sept daily 10:00–20:00, shorter hours off-season).

Rupe Granary and Ethnographic Museum (Etnografski Muzej Rupe)—This huge, 16th-century building was Dubrovnik's biggest granary.

Rupe means "holes"—and it's worth the price of entry just to look down into these cavernous underground grain stores, designed to maintain the perfect temperature to preserve the seeds (63 degrees Fahrenheit). When the grain had to be dried, it was moved upstairs—which today houses a surprisingly well-presented Ethnographic Museum, with tools, jewelry, clothing, and other artifacts from Dubrovnik's colorful history (5 kn, borrow English-language info sheet, June–Oct daily 9:00–18:00, Nov–May Mon–Sat 9:00–14:00, closed Sun).

▲**Old Port (Stara Luka)**—The picturesque old port, carefully nes-tled behind St. John's Fort, faces away from what was Dubrovnik's biggest threat, the Venetians. The long seaside building across the bay on the left was the medieval quarantine house. In those days, all visitors were locked in here for 40 days before entering town. A bench-lined harborside walk leads around the fort to a breakwater, provid-ing a peaceful perch.

At the port, you can haggle with captains selling excursions (see "Activities," below).

▲**Maritime Museum (Pomorski Muzej)**—By the 15th century, when Venice's nautical dominance was on the wane, Dubrovnik emerged as a maritime power and the Mediterranean's leading ship-building center. The Dubrovnik-built "argosy" boat (from the word "Ragusa," an early name for the city) was the Cadillac of ships, fre-quently mentioned by Shakespeare. This small museum traces the history of Dubrovnik's most important industry with contracts, maps, and models—all well-described in English. Boaters will find the museum particularly interesting (15 kn, English booklet-5 kn, daily June–Aug 9:00–18:00, Sept–Oct 9:00–17:00, Nov–May 9:00–14:00, upstairs in St. John's Fort, at far, or south, end of Old Port).

Aquarium (Akvarij)—Dubrovnik's aquarium, housed in the cav-ernous St. John's Fort, is an old-school place, with 27 tanks on one floor giving you a close look at the local marine life (and a cool refuge from the midday heat). The English descriptions give your visit meaning (20 kn, kids-10 kn, mid-June–Aug daily 9:00–21:00, April–mid-June and Sept–Oct daily 9:00–19:00, Nov–March daily 9:00–13:00, ground floor of St. John's Fort).

ACTIVITIES

Swimming—If the weather's good and you've had enough of muse-ums, spend a sunny afternoon at the beach. There are no sandy beaches on the mainland near Dubrovnik, but there are lots of suitable pebbly options, plus several concrete perches with easy access steps. Your hotel can direct you to the nearest one (or has its own). The best public beaches are Banje (just outside Ploče Gate, east of Old Town), the beach in the middle of the Bay of Lapad (near Hotel Kompas), and the nude beach on Lokrum Island (see below).

Lokrum Island—This island, just offshore from the Old Town, provides a handy escape from the city. Unfortunately, during a 2004 storm, a cruise ship dragged its anchor nearby, ripping apart the cables that provided water and electricity to the island—effectively closing it down. But Lokrum should be up and running again in 2005. Boats run regularly from Dubrovnik's old port (30 kn round-trip, 5 kn for map, hrly 9:00–17:00, 2/hr in summer, none in winter).

Lokrum features a monastery-turned-Hapsburg-palace, a small botanical garden, an old military fort, hiking trails, a café, some rocky beaches, and a little lake called the "Dead Sea" (Mrtvo More) that's suitable for swimming. Since the 1970s, when Lokrum became the "Island of Love," it's been known for its nude sunbathing. If you'd like to subject skin that's never seen the sun to those burning rays (carefully), follow the *FKK* sign from the boat dock for about five minutes to the slabs of waterfront rock where naturalists feel right at home.

Other Excursions by Boat from the Old Port—The old port is where tenders drop their cruisers, and where local captains set up tiny booths to hawk touristy boat trips. It's fun to chat with them, page through their sun-faded photo albums, and see if they can sell you on a short cruise.

In addition to Lokrum Island (above), boats go regularly to **Cavtat,** a small, forgettable port town 12 miles away...but a fun excuse to take a boat somewhere. You'll sail for 45 minutes, and return when you like (60 kn round-trip).

The best day trip from Dubrovnik is to join an excursion to the three **Elaphite Islands,** including a "fish picnic" cooked up by the captain as you cruise. The trip visits all three islands, with short stops at each (220 kn with lunch, 160 kn without, prices often soft—feel free to bargain, several boats depart daily at around 11:00, return around 18:00). Each island has sleepy escape mansions of old Dubrovnik aristocracy, fishing ports, shady forests, and sandy beaches. You generally stay 45 minutes each on Koločep and Šipan, and three hours on the most interesting island, Lopud. To get to the Elaphite Islands without a tour (on a cheap ferry), you'll sail from Dubrovnik's less convenient Port Gruž (see "Arrival in Dubrovnik— By Boat," above).

NIGHTLIFE

In the Old Town

Dubrovnik's Old Town is one big romantic parade of relaxed and happy people out strolling. The main drag is brightly lit and packed with shops, cafés, and bars, all open late. This is a fun scene. And if you walk away from the crowds, out on the port, or even up on the city walls, you'll be alone with the magic of the Pearl of the Adriatic. Everything feels—and is—very safe after dark. Buses run late.

Bars—**Cold Drinks "Buža,"** clinging scenically to Dubrovnik's outer wall, is a fine place for a drink day or night (see listing on page 484). **Hard Jazz Caffè Troubadour** is cool, owned by a former member of the Dubrovnik Troubadours, Croatia's answer to the Beatles (or, perhaps more accurately, the Turtles). On balmy evenings, 50 comfy wicker chairs with tiny tables are set up theater-style in the dreamy courtyard facing the musicians. Step inside to see old 1970s photos of the band (30- to 40-kn drinks and light sandwiches, daily 9:00–24:00, live jazz nightly from about 22:00 or whenever the boss shows up, next to cathedral at Bunićeva poljana 2, tel. 020/323-476). **Hemingway's Cocktail Bar,** on a square near the cathedral, is an outdoor lounge with big, overstuffed chairs at a fine vantage point for people-watching (50-kn cocktails).

Folk Music—Spirited folk-music concerts are performed for tourists twice weekly in or just outside the Old Town (80 kn, usually at 21:30, details at TI).

On Lapad Bay

Lapad, the peninsula with several recommended hotels (see "Sleeping," below), offers a fine evening break. The Šetalište Kralja Zvonimira is an amazingly laid-back pedestrian lane where bars have hammocks, Internet terminals are scattered through a forested park, and a folksy Croatian family ambience holds its own against the better-funded force of international tourism. Stroll from near Hotel Zagreb to the bay, where you'll find my favorite splurge restaurant (Casa Bar and Restaurant—see page 484) and schmaltzy music nightly on the harborside terrace of Hotel Kompas. From Hotel Kompas, a romantic walk—softly lit at night—leads along the bay through the woods, with plenty of private little stone coves for lingering. If you're not staying here, Lapad is an easy bus ride (or a 60-kn taxi trip) from the Old Town.

SLEEPING

Unless you want to spend a fortune, you basically have two options in Dubrovnik: a big resort hotel (most of these are a bus ride from the Old Town), or a room in a private home *(soba)*. Considering the relatively poor value that hotels provide, I'd give the *sobe* a careful look. No matter where you stay, prices are much higher in July and August. Reserve ahead in these peak times, especially during the Summer Festival (July 10–Aug 25 every year).

Sleep Code

(€1 = about $1.20, 6 kn = about $1, country code: 385, area code: 020)
S = Single, **D** = Double/Twin, **T** = Triple, **Q** = Quad,
b = bathroom, **s** = shower only. Unless otherwise noted, English is
spoken, credit cards are accepted, breakfast is included, and the
modest tourist tax (7 kn/€1 per person, per night, lower off-season)
is not. All Dubrovnik hotels provide free guest parking. Because
they get so many European visitors, most hotels quote prices in
euros, then make the conversion to kunas when you arrive.

To help you sort easily through these listings, I've divided
the rooms into three categories based on the price for a standard
double room with bath:

$$$ **Higher Priced**—Most rooms 700 kn (€97) or more.
 $$ **Moderately Priced**—Most rooms between 400–700 kn (€55–97).
  $ **Lower Priced**—Most rooms 400 kn (€55) or less.

Sobe (Private Rooms): A Dubrovnik Specialty

One way to combat the high prices and inconvenient locations of
Dubrovnik's hotels is to stay in a *soba* (see "Dalmatian Accommodation" sidebar, page 480). There are hundreds of *sobe* in the
Dubrovnik area, including many actually inside the Old Town walls.
For more peace, modern comforts, and a better price, I'd opt for one
near (but not in) the Old Town. Prices vary, depending on time of
year (most expensive July–Aug), how long you stay (often 20–30 percent more for stays shorter than 3 nights), and amenities like a private
bathroom or air-conditioning. For a basic double with shared bathroom in peak season, figure around 300 kn; add about 100 kn for a
private bathroom.

You can book a room at one of the several fine *sobe* listed here
(or find your own online); book through an agency (which charges a
premium, but still offers far better value than hotels); or make a deal
with a *soba* hustler on the street upon arrival.

Booking *Sobe* through an Agency: Several travel agencies in
Dubrovnik can find you a room for a fee. You book through them,
and their handy offices serve as a kind of reception desk. **Atlas** is
professional and well-organized (see "Helpful Hints," page 465).

Finding Your Own *Sobe*: It seems locals you encounter on the
street don't say "Hello"—they say, "Room?" While the town is pretty
tight from mid-July through August, you can generally find a €40
double if you're nervy enough to just show up. It's actually fun to
visit a few homes and make a deal. If prowling on your own for a
room (look for *sobe* signs), check out the Pile neighborhood, above
Pile Gate just outside the Old Town (especially Strednji Kono
street). Also look for locals with signs advertising rooms (they hang

out at bus and boat terminals to meet backpackers arriving without reservations).

My Recommended *Sobe:* The first *soba* listed here is a chic yuppie haven a five-minute hike above the Pile Gate. The next three are near a quiet cove just outside the Old Town walls, within 50 yards of Restaurant Orhan (a good breakfast spot—omelet, coffee, and juice for 50 kn). To reach this neighborhood, leave the Pile Gate TI to the right, then go down the first flight of stairs on your right; wind down the lanes to the little bay and the lane called Od Tabakarije. The last one listed here is farther from the Old Town, near Dubrovnik's Youth Hostel. The first four places all speak English.

$$ Jadranka and Milan Benussi, a young professional couple, rent four rooms in their stony-chic home in a quiet, traffic-free setting with a leafy terrace a five-minute hike above the Old Town. Jadranka speaks excellent English and gives her place modern Croatian class (Db-€60, apartment for up to 4-€90–100, 20 percent more for 1-night stays, no breakfast, cash only, family deals, all rooms have air-con and kitchenettes; go 2 blocks up busy Dr. Ante Starčevića street from the TI and follow tiny Miha Klaica lane to the right steeply above a small church to Miha Klaica 10, tel. 020/429-339, mobile 098/928-1300, mbenussi@inet.hr).

$ Paulina Čumbelić is a kind, gentle woman renting four rooms in her homey, clean, and quiet house. You'll feel like you're visiting your Croatian grandma (S-160 kn, D-240 kn, T-300 kn; July–Aug: S-190 kn, D-280 kn, T-400 kn; 20 percent more for fewer than 3 nights, cash only, closed in winter, Od Tabakarije 2, tel. 020/421-327, mobile 091/530-7985).

$ Dubravka Matić is a charming, young, English-speaking mom renting out three woody, tidy, and simple rooms in her cozy home. You'll truly feel you're sharing her house, but thanks to friendly Dubravka, that's not a problem (S-130 kn, D-260 kn; July–Aug: S-150 kn, D-300 kn; 2-night minimum, Frana Antice 2, tel. 020/311-904, mobile 098/938-8281).

$ At Restaurant Orhan Guest House, you'll pay near-hotel prices and get impersonal, guest-house service. But the 11 simple rooms are new, air-conditioned, well-located, and quiet, with modern bathrooms (Sb-200 kn, Db-400 kn, Tb-600 kn, same prices year-round, no extra charge for 1-night stays, consider the restaurant your reception desk, Od Tabakarije 1, tel. 020/414-183).

$ Dubravka Vnučec, who lives next to Dubrovnik's Youth Hostel, rents three forgettable, cheap, basic rooms to hostelers who'd rather have a double. Dubravka speaks German and a tiny bit of English, but knows how to communicate (S-100 kn, D-200 kn, T-300 kn, rental bikes, tel. 020/425-145). To get here, follow the directions up to the Youth Hostel (see "Hotels—Near Boninovo Bay," below).

Dalmatian Accommodation

Even though they were communists, Yugoslavs were savvy business-men. To maximize beach-tourism occupancy in the 1960s and 1970s, they razed charming Old World buildings to make way for new, big resort hotels. Now, throughout Dalmatia, it's very hard to find midsize, characteristic pensions; your choices are basically these hulking complexes or a room in a private home...and little in between.

Today, the resort hotels, no longer new, usually have faded communist-era furnishings, "beach" access (often on a concrete pad), a travel-agency desk selling tours in the lobby, and a seaview apéritif bar. The rooms are unremarkable, with a moldy-college-dorm ambience. And they're expensive—you'd pay less for the same room in the center of a Western European capital. These hotels are just fine with the busloads of German, Austrian, British, and Slovene tourists who head south for the European answer to Cancún or Acapulco.

If that doesn't appeal to you, consider a room in a private home (*soba*, plural *sobe*). *Sobe* (SOH-bay), usually run by empty-nesters, offer travelers a characteristic and money-saving alternative for a quarter of the price of a hotel. Guests are welcome to use the kitchen and cozy dining room and settle in to their own private bedroom

Hotels

The frustrating hotel scene is Dubrovnik's biggest downside. There are only two hotels inside the Old Town walls—and one of them charges $500 a night (Pucić Palace, www.thepucicpalace.com). Any big, resort-style hotel near the Old Town will run you at least €130. These inflated prices drive most visitors to the Lapad Peninsula, a 15-minute bus ride (or 60-kn taxi ride) west of the Old Town. Though it lacks Old World ambience, Lapad is surprisingly charming—most hotels cluster around beautiful coves that would be a fine place to vacation, even if the Dubrovnik Old Town weren't around the bend.

I've listed the shoulder-season prices (June and Sept), and noted how much of an increase you can expect for July and August. Off-season prices are much lower. Air-conditioning, which generally adds substantially to the hotel price, is rarely necessary on breezy Dubrovnik evenings.

In the mass-tourism tradition, most European visitors choose to take the half-board option at their hotel (i.e., dinner in the hotel restaurant). This can be a good value, but I've listed several fine places with great food for you to enjoy on your own (see "Eating," below).

In the Old Town

$$$ **Hotel Stari Grad,** the only affordable Old Town hotel option, is a good splurge. Its eight rooms are nothing special, but the location is

(bathroom often down the hall). You'll give up some privacy and the comforts of a big hotel, but you'll have a better chance of connecting with the locals.

Registered *sobe* have been rated by the government using a system—sometimes arbitrary—that assigns stars based on amenities. There are generally three tiers: deluxe room with private bathroom and breakfast included; standard room with bathroom and no breakfast; and rock-bottom room with a bathroom down the hall and no breakfast.

At any boat dock or bus station in Dalmatia, you'll encounter pushy locals trying to get you to stay in their *soba*. Many of these *sobe* have not been classified by the government, but they can sometimes turn out to be a good deal. If you trust the sales pitch, and the location seems convenient, give it a look.

I've listed a few *sobe* in this chapter, but to get a wider range of options, wander the streets looking for *sobe* signs. You can also enlist the help of a travel agency, but you'll pay 10–30 percent extra. (To search from home, see www.adriatica.net.) The prices fluctuate with the seasons—just like those of the big hotels—and stays of less than three nights almost always come with a 20–30 percent surcharge.

ideal: a block off the main drag (Sb-€95, Db-€136, extra bed-€40, same prices year-round, air-con, Od Sigurate 4, tel. 020/321-373, fax 020/321-256, www.hotelstarigrad.com, hotelstarigrad@yahoo.com).

Near Boninovo Bay

These places cluster around Boninovo Bay, a 15-minute walk from the Old Town (straight up Dr. Ante Starčevića). Once you're comfortable with the buses, the location is excellent (from Pile Gate, take #1a, #3, #4, #5, #6, #8, or #9). From the Boninovo bus stop, go down Pera Čingrije (the road running parallel to the cliff overlooking the sea). There's a super little 24-hour bakery across the street from Hotel Bellevue, and a funky cliffside view café/bar across the parking lot 30 yards uphill.

$$$ **Hotel Bellevue,** backed up against the cliff rising up from Boninovo Bay, has a striking location—with an elevator plunging directly to its own pebbly beach. They have 50 basic rooms in a three-building complex with a proficient and friendly staff. This place is slated for renovation in 2005, which will bump up the following prices considerably (main building rooms all have sea views and balconies: Sb-580 kn, Db-760 kn; more for air-con—rarely necessary—and July-Aug; less off-season and in their simpler annex buildings—Villa Florida and Villa Miramare; non-view rooms come with street noise, elevator, free and easy parking, half board-€12,

Pera Čingrije 7, tel. 020/413-095, fax 020/414-058, www.hotel-bellevue.hr, sales@hotel-bellevue.hr).

$$ Hotel Lero, 200 yards up the hill from Hotel Bellevue, is modern and fresh, but without the exotic cliffside setting. Its 160 reasonably priced, new-feeling rooms come with small sea views and access to Hotel Bellevue's beach (Sb-€60, Db-€80, 15 percent more mid-July–mid-Sept, cheaper off-season, air-con, elevator, Internet access, half-board-€5, Iva Vojnovića 14, tel. 020/332-122, fax 020/332-123, www.hotel-lero.hr, info@hotel-lero.hr).

$ Dubrovnik's fine Youth Hostel is a quiet, modern, and well-run, but fairly stark place with fresh, woody dorms (82 beds in 19 rooms; bed in 4- to 6-bed dorm: 110 kn July–Aug, 95 kn June and Sept, 85 kn May and Oct, 75 kn Nov–April, 10 kn more for non-members, includes sheets and breakfast, open daily 7:00–2:00—that's A.M.—ulica bana Jelačića 15–17, tel. 020/423-241, tel. & fax 020/412-592, www.hfhs.hr, dubrovnik@hfhs.hr). From the Boninovo bus stop, go down Pera Čingrije towards Hotel Bellevue, but take the first right uphill onto ulica bana Jelačića and look for signs up to the hostel on your left.

Near Lapad Bay

These hotels cluster around Lapad Bay, a 15-minute bus ride from the Old Town (from the bus stop in front of Pile Gate, take #5 to Pošta Lapad). There are about a dozen different hotels within walking distance around the bay, but the following places are the best values. For dinner in this area, consider Casa Bar and Restaurant (see page 484). For after-hours ideas, see "Nightlife," page 476.

$$$ Hotel Villa Wolff, a small boutique hotel at the gorgeous end of the road, has three suites, three doubles, and a generous view terrace. It's enthusiastically run by an Austrian named Gonzalas, who fell in love with Dubrovnik (and one of its women) and moved here just months before the war. The rooms are plush, mod, and spacious (Db-€160, suite-€225, slightly cheaper off-season, air-con, Pučića 1, tel. 020/438-710, fax 020/435-350, www.villa-wolff.hr, info@villa-wolff.hr).

$$$ Hotel Kompas, your big-hotel option, has 117 plush rooms right across the street from the beach (June–Sept: seaview Db-1,100 kn, non-view Db-900 kn, less off-season, non-smoking rooms, air-con, elevator, Internet access, Šetalište Kralja Zvonimira 56, tel. 020/352-000, fax 020/435-877, www.hotel-kompas.hr, sales@hotel-kompas.hr).

$$ Hotel Zagreb is a rarity among Dubrovnik hotels: small and quaint, in an elegant old villa surrounded by a lush garden. The 25 rooms are basic but comfortable (Db-600 kn, prices 30 percent higher July–Aug, prices lower off-season, Šetalište Kralja Zvonimira 27, reception tel. 020/436-146). Hotel Zagreb is slated for renovation and may increase its prices in 2005. Still, its charm and location make it worth considering. Hotel Zagreb is technically an annex of **Hotel Sumratin,** just down the street, which has lower rates for 44 not-nearly-as-nice rooms in a less charming setting (Db-460 kn, prices 30 percent higher July–Aug, prices lower off-season, elevator, Šetalište Kralja Zvonimira 31, reception tel. 020/436-333). To reserve at either hotel: tel. 020/436-500, fax 020/436-006, hot -sumratin@du.htnet.hr.

EATING

In the Old Town

While the Old Town is packed with busy restaurants, my first three recommendations distinguish themselves by providing quality as if there were no easy tourist buck. This makes them very popular with locals and in-the-know visitors—expect lines throughout normal dining hours.

Konoba Kamenice, a no-frills fish restaurant, is the locals' unanimous choice for Dubrovnik's best eatery. This place offers inexpensive, fresh, and delicious seafood dishes on a charming market square, as central as can be in the Old Town. Arrive early, or you'll have to wait (most main dishes 35–45 kn, huge splittable plates, daily 7:00–24:00, Gundulićeva poljana 8, tel. 020/421-499, no reservations).

Lokanda Peskarija, facing the old port, is popular for its fine seafood and harborside setting—so close to all the tourism, yet still peaceful. Servings are hearty and come in a pot, "homestyle." The 40-kn seafood risotto easily feeds two, and sharing is no problem. The menu's tiny—not much in the way of vegetables other than potatoes—but the value is appreciated (daily 12:00–24:00, Ribarnica, tel. 020/324-750, no reservations). This is a good place to try the typical Dubrovnik desert, *rozata* (crème caramel).

Mea Culpa is a popular spot for cheap and tasty pizza (pizzas 25–40 kn, salad bar, takeout available, daily 8:00–24:00, just off the main drag at Za Rokom 3, tel. 020/323-430).

Gavun Sandwich Bar serves the best sandwiches in town, specializing in seafood. The photo menu makes ordering easy. Get your sandwich toasted and wrapped to go, or—for the same price—eat it at a wooden streetside table (with a bowl of cake-like homemade bread). A sit-down sandwich here gives you a quick and inexpensive, but high-quality meal without having to spend the time and money to dine at a restaurant (20-kn sandwiches, daily 10:00–15:00 & 18:00–23:00; 50 yards off main drag at Siroka 3—the widest side street, midway up the Stradun; tel. 020/323-206). Compared to Gavun, other sandwich places are a bad value.

The Old Town's "Restaurant Row": **Prijeko street,** a block towards the mainland from the Stradun promenade, is lined with outdoor, tourist-oriented eateries—each one with a huckster out front trying to lure in diners. This is hardly a local scene, but a stroll along here is fun, the atmosphere is lively, the sales pitches are entertainingly desperate, and the food is generally good.

Picnic in the Old Town: Pick up picnic grub at Konzum (the cheapest grocery store in town, just outside Pile Gate), at the open-air produce market (each morning near the cathedral), or at the Gavun Sandwich Bar (see above). Good picnic spots include the shady benches overlooking the old port; the Porporela breakwater (beyond the old port and fort; comes with a swimming area, sunny, no-shade benches, views of Lokrum Island, and tenders fetching cruisers); and the green, welcoming park in what was the moat just under the Pile Gate entry to the Old Town.

Drinks with a View: **Cold Drinks "Buža"** offers, without a doubt, the most scenic spot for a drink. Perched on a cliff above the sea, clinging like a barnacle to the outside of the city walls, this is a peaceful, shaded getaway from the bustle of the Old Town...the perfect place to watch cruise ships sail into the horizon. Filled with mellow tourists and bartenders pouring wine from tiny screw-top bottles into plastic cups, it comes with castaway views and Frank Sinatra ambience (drinks only, 20 kn, summer daily 9:00–24:00, closed mid-Nov–Jan, find doorway in city wall marked *Cold Drinks* just up from cathedral, behind St. Ignatius' Church).

Ice Cream: There's lots of great gelato in Dubrovnik; one of the best places is **Dolce Vita** (daily 9:00–24:00, a half block off Stradun at Nalješkovićeva 1A, tel. 020/321-666).

Near Lapad Bay

If you're staying on the Lapad Peninsula and don't want to venture into the Old Town for dinner, consider strolling down the tree-shaded Šetalište Kralja Zvonimira promenade, lined with touristy but acceptable cafés and restaurants. **Casa Bar and Restaurant** provides the best romantic, harborside, candlelit dining in the area, with a straightforward, user-friendly menu offering traditional cooking with fresh ingredients. Tables overlook Lapad Bay, and English-speaking owner Gonzalas enjoys exploring the menu with his diners (80 kn per fish plate, daily, on the bay just beyond Hotel Kompas' restaurant, tel. 020/438-710).

TRANSPORTATION CONNECTIONS

From Dubrovnik by Jadrolinija ferry: The big boat leaves Dubrovnik in the morning (usually around 8:00 or 10:00) and goes to **Korčula** (3–4 hrs), **Split** (8–10 hrs), and other coastal destinations (including Stari Grad on Hvar Island and the big northern port city of Rijeka). The boat generally cruises four times each week June–Sept, twice weekly off-season. For schedules, see Jadrolinija's user-friendly Web site, www.jadrolinija.hr.

By bus to: Split (almost hrly, 5 hrs), **Korčula** (1/day, 4 hrs), **Zagreb** (4/day, 11 hrs).

By plane: To quickly connect this remote destination with the rest of your trip, consider a cheap flight (see "Getting Around the Dalmatian Coast," above.)

Split

Dubrovnik is the darling of the Dalmatian Coast, but Split is Croatia's second city (after Zagreb), bustling with a quarter of a million people. If you've been hopping along the coast, landing in urban Split feels like a return to civilization. While most Dalmatian coastal towns seem made for tourists, Split is real and vibrant—a shipbuilding city with an ugly sprawl surrounding an atmospheric Old Town, teeming with Croatians living life to the fullest. Though Split throbs to a modern, young beat, its history goes way back—all the way to the Roman Empire. Along with all the trappings of a modern city, Split has some of the best Roman ruins this side of Italy.

In the 4th century, the Roman Emperor Diocletian wanted to retire in his native Dalmatia, so he built a huge palace here. Eventually, the palace was abandoned. Then locals, fleeing 7th-century Slavic invaders, moved in and made themselves at home, and a medieval town sprouted from the rubble of the old palace. In the 15th century, the Venetians took over the Dalmatian Coast, adding on to the city and building several small palaces. But even as Split grew, the nucleus remained the ruins of Diocletian's Palace. To this day, 2,000 people live or work inside the former palace walls. A maze of narrow alleys is home to fashionable boutiques and galleries, wonderfully atmospheric cafés, and Roman artifacts around every corner.

Planning Your Time

Many visitors to Dalmatia only change boats in Split, but the city is the perfect real-life contrast to the tackiness of Dalmatian beach resorts—it deserves a full day. Begin by strolling the remains of Diocletian's Palace, then have lunch or a coffee break along the Riva promenade. After lunch, browse the shops or visit a couple of Split's museums (the Meštrović Gallery is tops). Promenading along the Riva with the natives is *the* evening activity.

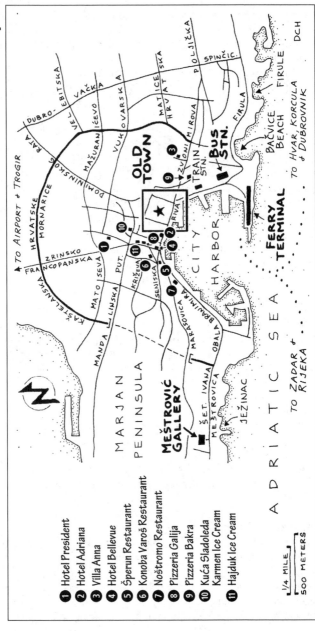

Split

1. Hotel President
2. Hotel Adriana
3. Villa Anna
4. Hotel Bellevue
5. Šperun Restaurant
6. Konoba Varoš Restaurant
7. Noštromo Restaurant
8. Pizzeria Galija
9. Pizzeria Bakra
10. Kuća Sladoleda Karmen Ice Cream
11. Hajduk Ice Cream

ORIENTATION

(area code: 021)

Split sprawls, but almost everything of interest to travelers is around the City Harbor (Gradska Luka). At the top of this port is the Old Town (Stari Grad). Between the Old Town and the sea is the Riva—the waterfront pedestrian promenade lined with cafés and shaded by palm trees. The main ferry terminal (Trajektni Terminal) juts out into the harbor from the east side of the port. Between the ferry terminal and the Old Town are the long-distance bus station (Autobusni Kolodvor) and forlorn little train station (Željeznička Stanica). West of the Old Town, poking into the Adriatic, is the lush and hilly Marjan peninsula.

Split's domino-shaped Old Town is made up of two square sections. The east half was once Diocletian's Palace, and the west half is the medieval town that sprang up next door. The shell of Diocletian's ruined palace provides a checkerboard street plan, with a gate at each end. At the center of the former palace is the Peristyle square (Peristil), where you'll find the TI, cathedral, and highest concentration of Roman ruins.

Tourist Information

Split's TI is on the Peristyle square, in the very center of Diocletian's Palace (Mon–Fri 8:00–20:00, Sat–Sun 9:00–13:00, tel. 021/345-606). Pick up the free town map and *Welcome to Split* magazine. The TI also sells books, maps, and the Splitcard (museum discount card, not worth considering for most visits).

The helpful **Turistički Biro** travel agency, between the two halves of the Old Town on the Riva, books *sobe* and hotels, sells guidebooks and maps, rents scooters and cars, and sells tickets for excursions (mid-July–mid-Aug Mon–Fri 8:00–21:00, Sat 8:00–20:00, Sun 8:00–13:00; off-season Mon–Fri 8:00–20:00, Sat 8:00–14:00, closed Sun, Riva 12, tel. & fax 021/347-100, turist-biro-split@st.htnet.hr).

Arrival in Split

Split's boat, bus, and train terminals share a busy and very practical strip of land called Obala Kneza Domagoja, on the east side of the City Harbor (Gradska Luka), just in front of the Old Town. Along here, you'll find travel agencies, baggage-check offices, hustlers trying to rent rooms, the post office, and a fine Internet point (Backpacker C@fé—see "Helpful Hints," below). Arriving or leaving from this central location, you never need to deal with the concrete, exhaust-stained sprawl of Split.

By Boat: Split's ferry terminal (Trajektni Terminal) is a 10-minute walk from the center around the east side of the City Port.

Split Landmarks

English	Croatian	Pronounced
Old Town	**Stari Grad**	STAH-ree grahd
City Harbor	**Gradska Luka**	GRAHD-skah LOO-kah
Harborfront Promenade	**Riva**	REE-vah
Peristyle (old Roman square)	**Peristil**	PEH-ree-steel
Adriatic Sea	**Jadran**	YAH-drahn

After leaving the boat, wade through the *sobe* hucksters to the main terminal building, where you'll find ATMs, WCs, a grocery store, and offices for all of the main ferry companies, including Jadrolinija (open long hours daily). You can see the Old Town and Riva from the boat dock; just walk around the port towards the big bell tower.

By Bus or Train: Split's long-distance bus station (Autobusni Kolodvor) and little train station (Željeznička Stanica) are along the east side of the City Port between the ferry terminal and the Old Town. To reach the center, exit to the right and walk along the waterfront toward the big bell tower.

By Plane: Split's airport (Zračna Luka Split-Kaštela) is across the big bay (Kaštelanski Zaljev), 15 miles northwest of the center, near the town of Trogir. A Croatia Airlines bus leaves Split 90 minutes before each flight from the small Air Terminal near the southeast corner of Diocletian's Palace, and meets each arriving flight at the airport (30 kn, 40 min). Figure on paying 300 kn for a taxi to the center. Airport info: tel. 021/203-506, www.split-airport.hr.

By Car: Split is split by its Old Town, which is welded to the harbor by the pedestrian-only Riva promenade. This means drivers needing to get 300 yards from one side of the Old Town to the other must drive about 15 minutes entirely around the center, which can be miserably clogged with traffic. A semicircular ring road makes this better than it might be. To get to the west end, you'll go through a tunnel under the Marjan peninsula. To reach the ferry terminal (east side), follow signs to *Trajektni* (look for the tiny ferry).

Helpful Hints

Baggage Check: Both the train and the bus stations have safe and efficient baggage-check services (20 kn/day). If one is very crowded, the other may be empty—check both before waiting in a long line.

Sightseeing Schedules: Things close down for a long siesta in the afternoon, then stay open late. The market thrives in the morning.

Internet Access: Backpacker C@fé is smartly run by an Australian (daily 8:00–21:00, next to bus station on Obala Kneza Domagoja, tel. 021/338-548).

Post Office: The modern little post office is next to the bus station (daily 7:00–21:00, on Obala Kneza Domagoja).

Laundry: Croatia's "only automatic launderette" offers self- and full-service washing and drying just off the harbor (40 kn/load, daily 10:00–20:00, air-con, next to recommended Šperun Restaurant—handy if multitasking is your style, on Šperun street).

Folk Dancing: Each Saturday morning in the summer, there's a folk-dancing show in Diocletian's Palace (generally 11:00–13:00 in the cellars, details at TI).

Local Guides: The guide association, with an office on the Old Town's Peristyle square, has a list of local English-speaking guides who'd love to give you a two-hour tour for 300 kn (this price for 2 tourists, 50 kn per person after that, tel. 021/346-267, mobile 098/361-936).

Getting Around Split

Most of what you'll want to see is within walking distance, but some hotels and sights (such as the Meštrović Gallery) are a bit farther out.

By Bus: Local buses, run by Promet, cost 8 kn per ride (or 7 kn if you buy ticket from a kiosk; ask for a *putna karta*). Validate your ticket as you board the bus. Suburban buses to towns near Split (like Salona or Trogir) leave from two different stations: Some use the Air Terminal at the southeast corner of Diocletian's Palace, but most use the Suburban Bus Station (Prigradski Autobusni Kolodvor), a 15-minute walk due north of the Old Town on Domovinskog rata.

By Taxi: Taxis start at 18 kn, then cost around 8 kn per kilometer. Figure 50–60 kn for most rides within the city (for example, from the ferry terminal to most hotels). To call for a taxi, try Radio Taxi (tel. 021/970).

SIGHTS AND ACTIVITIES

Diocletian's Palace (Dioklecijanova Palača)

Split's only ▲▲▲ sight is the remains of Roman Emperor Diocletian's enormous retirement palace, sitting on the harbor in the heart of the city. Since the ruins themselves are now integrated into the city's street plan, exploring them is free (though you'll pay to enter a few parts—such as the cellars and the cathedral/mausoleum). As fragments of the palace are poorly marked, and there's not yet any good guidebook or audioguide for tracking down the remains, Split is a good place to hire a local guide (300 kn/2 hrs; see "Helpful Hints," above). This self-guided tour explains the basics. To begin the tour, stand in front of the Palace (at the east end of the Riva, at the corner with the yellow information pillar) to get oriented.

Background: Diocletian grew up just inland from Split, in the town of Salona (*Solin* in Croatian)—which was then the capital of Dalmatia. He worked his way up the Roman hierarchy and became emperor (A.D. 284–305). Despite all of his achievements, Diocletian is best remembered for two questionable legacies: dividing the huge empire among four emperors (arguably leading to its decline); and torturing and executing Christians—thousands of them, here on the Dalmatian Coast.

As Diocletian grew older, he decided to return to his homeland for retirement (since he was in poor health, the medicinal sulfur spring here was another plus). His massive palace took only 11 years to build—and this fast pace required a big push (over 2,000 slaves died during construction). Huge sections of his palace still exist, modified by medieval and modern developers alike.

Palace Facade: The "front" of today's Split—facing the harbor— was actually the back door of Diocletian's Palace. The water level was much higher back then, and this part of the palace could be reached only by boat—sort of an emergency exit.

Visually trace the outline of the gigantic palace, which was more than 600 feet long on each side. On the corner to the right stands a big, rectangular guard tower (one of the original 16). To the left, the tower is gone and the corner is harder to pick out (look for the beginning of the newer-looking buildings). Erase in your mind the ramshackle two-story buildings added 200 years ago, which obscure the grandness of the palace wall.

Halfway up the facade, notice the row of 42 arched window frames (mostly filled in today). Diocletian and his family lived in the seaside half of the palace; imagine him strolling back and forth along this fine arcade, enjoying the views of his Adriatic homeland. The inland, non-view half of the palace was home to 700 servants, body-guards, and soldiers.

Now go through the poorly marked, low-profile door in the middle of the palace (known as the "Brass Gate"; look for the *i* sign pointing to the TI). Just inside the door is the entrance to...

Diocletian's Cellars (Podrum): Since the palace was built on land that sloped down to the sea, these chambers were built to level out the main floor (like a modern "daylight basement"). The cellars weren't used for storage; they were filled with water from three different sources: a freshwater spring, a sulfur spring, and the sea. Later, medieval residents used them as a dump. Rediscovered only in the last century, the cellars enabled archaeologists to derive the floor plan of the long-gone palace. Today, these underground chambers are used for art exhibits and a little strip of souvenir stands. But before you go shopping, explore the cellars at this end (8 kn, June–Aug daily 9:00–21:00, May daily 10:00–17:00, Sept–mid-Oct daily

Diocletian's Palace

1 Palace Facade View
2 Cellar Entrance
3 Underground Passage to Peristyle
4 Peristyle Square
5 Entry Vestibule
6 Cathedral of St. Dominus
7 Jupiter's Temple/St. John's Baptistery
8 View down Cardo Street
9 Bishop Gregory of Nin Statue
10 City Museum
11 Turistički Biro Travel Agency
12 Hotel Slavija
13 Restoran Sarajevo
14 Sara Mari Ice Cream
15 Air Terminal Bus Stop
16 To Internet Café

10:00–18:00, April and late Oct daily 10:00–14:00, Nov–March Mon–Sat 10:00–14:00, closed Sun).

Wander through the labyrinthine area beyond the ticket desk (on the left, or west, side of the palace). When those first villagers took refuge in the abandoned palace from the rampaging Slavs in 641, the elite lived upstairs, grabbing what was once the emperor's wing. They carved the rough holes you see in the ceiling to dump their garbage and sewage. Over the generations, the basement (where you're standing) actually filled up with waste and solidified, ultimately becoming a once-stinky, then-precious bonanza for 20th-century archaeologists. Notice the unexcavated wings—a compost pile of ancient lifestyles, awaiting the tiny shovels and toothbrushes of future archaeologists. Today, this huge, vaulted hall is used for everything from flower and book shows to fashion catwalks. The headless black granite sphinx is one of 13 Diocletian brought home from Egypt. The two beams on display once supported floorboards overhead (see the holes on either side of the vaults).

The cellars on the east side can also be explored (same ticket). Here you'll find a semicircular marble table used by the Romans, who—as shown in Hollywood movies—ate lying down (3 would lounge and feast, while servants dished things up from the straight side).

When you're finished, head back to the main gallery, where you can shop your way down the passage and up the stairs into the...

Peristyle (Peristil): This square was the centerpiece of Diocletian's Palace. As you walk up the stairs, the entry vestibule into the residence is above your head, Diocletian's mausoleum (today's Cathedral of St. Dominus) is to your right, and the street to Jupiter's Temple is on your left. The little chapel straight ahead houses the TI, and beyond that is the narrow street to the former main entrance to the palace, the Golden Gate.

Go to the middle of the square and take it all in. The red granite pillars—which you'll see all over Diocletian's Palace—are from Egypt (the café in the square is called Luxor, where Diocletian spent many of his preretirement years). Imagine the pillars defining fine arcades—now obliterated by medieval houses. The black sphinx is the only one of Diocletian's collection of 13 that's still intact.

Diocletian's Entry Vestibule: Climb the stairs (above where you came in) into the domed, open-ceiling entry vestibule. Impressed? That's the idea. This was the grand entry to Diocletian's living quarters, meant to wow visitors. Emperors were believed to be gods. Diocletian called himself Jovius—the son of Jupiter, the most powerful of all gods. Four times a year (at the change of the seasons), Diocletian would stand here and overlook the Peristyle. His subjects would lie on the ground in worship, praising his name. Notice the four big niches at floor level, which once held statues of the four tetrarchs who ruled the unwieldy empire after Diocletian retired. The ceiling was covered with frescoes and mosaics. Wander out back to the harbor side through medieval buildings (some with 7th-century foundations), which evoke the way local villagers came in and took over the once spacious and elegant palace.

Now go back into the Peristyle square and turn right, climbing the steps to the...

Cathedral of St. Dominus (Katedrala Sv. Duje): The original octagonal structure was Diocletian's elaborate mausoleum, built in the 4th century. But after the fall of Rome, it was converted into the town's cathedral. Construction on the bell tower began in the 13th century and took 300 years to complete. Before you go inside, notice the sarcophagi ringing the cathedral. In the late Middle Ages, this was prime post-mortem real estate, since being buried closer to a cathedral improved your chances of getting to heaven.

Step inside the oldest building used as a cathedral anywhere in Christendom (5 kn, get the 10-kn combo-ticket includes Jupiter's Temple—see below, daily 7:00–12:00 & 17:00–19:00, Kraj Sv. Duje 5, tel. 021/345-602). Imagine the place in pre-Christian times, with Diocletian's tomb in the center. The only surviving decor from those days are the granite columns and the relief circling the base of the dome (about 50 feet up)—a ring of carvings heralding the greatness of the emperor. The small, multicolored marble pillars around the top of the pulpit were scavenged from Diocletian's sarcophagus. These are all that remains of Diocletian's remains...he was a pretty unpopular guy. What happened to the rest of him is anyone's guess—but it's certainly not a pretty picture.

Diocletian brutally persecuted his Christian subjects, sometimes in the crypt of this very building. To kick off his retirement upon his arrival on the Dalmatian Coast, he had Bishop Dominus of Salona killed, along with several thousand Christians. When Diocletian died, there were riots of happiness. In the 7th century, his mausoleum became a cathedral dedicated to the martyred bishop. The extension behind the altar was added in the 9th century, and the doors are 12th-century walnut originals. The sarcophagus of St. Dominus (to the right of the altar, with early Christian carvings) was once the cathedral's high altar. To the left of today's main altar is the altar of St. Anastasius—lying on a millstone, which is tied to his neck. On Diocletian's orders, this Christian martyr was drowned in Adriatic. Posthumous poetic justice: Now Christian saints are entombed in Diocletian's mausoleum...and Diocletian is nowhere to be found.

Jupiter's Temple/St. John's Baptistery: Diocletian believed himself to be Jovius (that's Jupiter, Junior). On exiting the mausoleum of Jovius, worshippers would look straight ahead to the temple of Jupiter. (Back then, of course, all of these medieval buildings weren't cluttering up the view.) Make your way through the narrow alley, past another headless, pawless sphinx, to explore the small temple (using the 10-kn combo-ticket you bought at the cathedral; same hours as cathedral).

The temple has long since been converted into a baptistery—with a big 12th-century baptismal font and a statue of St. John by the great Croatian sculptor Ivan Meštrović (EE-vahn MESH-troh-veech; see page 496). The half-barrel vaulted ceiling is considered the best preserved of its kind anywhere. Every face and each patterned box is different.

Back at the Peristyle square, stand in front of the TI with your back to the entry vestibule (and harbor). The little street just beyond the TI (going left to right) connects the east and west gates. If you've had enough Roman history, head right (east) to go through the "Silver Gate" and find Split's bustling, open-air Green Market. Or, to the left (west), you'll wind up at the "Iron Gate" and People's Square (see "More Sights in Split," below), and, beyond that, the fresh-and-smelly fish market. But if you want to see one last bit of Roman history, continue straight ahead up the...

Cardo: This street—literally, "Hot Street"—was the most important in Diocletian's Palace, connecting the main entry with the heart of the complex. As you walk, you'll pass a bank with modern computer gear all around its exposed Roman ruins (on the right 10 yards from the TI, look through window); a Venetian merchant's palace (a reminder that Split was dominated by Venice from the 15th century on; step into his courtyard, first gate on left); and an alley to the City Museum (on the right—see "More Sights in Split," below). Before long, you'll pass through the...

Golden Gate (Zlatna Vrata): This great gate was the main entry of Diocletian's Palace. Its name came from the golden statues of Diocletian and other Roman VIPs that adorned it. Straight ahead from here is Salona (Solin), which was a bustling city of 60,000 (and Diocletian's hometown) before there was a Split. The big statue by Ivan Meštrović is **Bishop Gregory of Nin,** a 10th-century Croatian priest who convinced the Vatican to allow sermons during Mass to be said in Croatian, rather than Latin. People rub his toe for good luck (though only non-material wishes are given serious consideration).

More Sights in Split

▲▲**The Riva (Obala Hrvatskog Narodnog Preporoda)**—The official name for this seaside pedestrian drag is the "Croatian National Revival Embankment," but locals just call it "Riva" (Italian for "harbor"). This is the town's promenade, an integral part of Mediterranean culture. After dinner, Split residents collect their families and friends for a stroll on the Riva. This offers some of the best people-watching in Eastern Europe; make it a point to be here for an hour or two after dinner. At the west end of the Riva, the people parade of Croatian culture turns right and heads away from the water, up Marmontova. The stinky smell that sometimes accompanies the stroll isn't a sewer. It's sulfur—a reminder that the town's medicinal sulfur spas have attracted people here since the days of Diocletian.

▲People's Square (Narodni Trg)—The lively square at the center of the Old Town is called by locals simply *Pjaca*, pronounced the same as the Italian *piazza*. Stand in the center (find your own little inlaid square) and enjoy the bustle. Look around for a quick lesson in Dalmatian history. When Diocletian lived in his palace, a Roman village sprouted here just outside the wall. Face the former wall of Diocletian's Palace (behind and to the right of the clock tower). This was the western gate, or so-called Iron Gate. By the 14th century, the medieval town had developed, making this the main square of Split. The city's grand old café, Gradska Kavana, has been the Old Town's venerable meeting point for generations (daily 9:00–23:00). To the left, the white building jutting out into the square is the Ethnographic Museum (see below). Once the City Hall, the loggia is all that remains of the original Gothic building. Directly to your left as you face the museum is the Nakić House, built in Viennese Secession style—a reminder that Dalmatia was part of the Hapsburg Empire, ruled by Vienna, from Napoleon's downfall through World War I. The lane on the right side of this building leads to Split's fish market (Ribarnica).

Ethnographic Museum (Etnografski Muzej)—The museum shows off the colorful art and dress of Dalmatian villages (10 kn, Mon–Fri 10:00–15:00, Sat 10:00–13:00, closed Sun, Narodni Trg 1, tel. 021/344-164).

City Museum (Muzej Grada)—This small museum, housed in the 15th-century Papalić Palace, displays fragments of Split's Roman and medieval past—including another beheaded sphinx (10 kn, mid-May–mid-Sept Tue–Fri 9:00–12:00 & 18:00–21:00, Sat–Sun 10:00–13:00, closed Mon, no lunch break July–Aug; off-season Tue–Fri 9:00–16:00, Sat–Sun 10:00–13:00, closed Mon; Papalićeva 1, tel. 021/344-917).

Radić Brothers Square (Trg Braće Radića)—A Venetian citadel watches over this square, just off the Riva between the two halves of the Old Town. After Split became part of the Venetian Republic, there was a serious danger of attack by the Turks, so octagonal towers like this were built all along the coast. But this imposing tower had a second purpose—to encourage citizens of Split to forget about any plans of rebellion. In the middle of the square is a sculpture by Ivan Meštrović of the poet Marko Marulić, considered to be the father of the Croatian language.

On the downhill (harbor) side of the square is **Croata,** a necktie boutique that loves to tell how Croatian soldiers who fought with the French in the Thirty Years' War (1618–1648) had a distinctive way of tying their scarves. The French found it stylish, adopted it, and called it *à la Croate*—or eventually, *cravate*—thus creating the modern tie that many people wear to work every day throughout the world.

Split's Outskirts and Beyond

▲▲Meštrović Gallery (Galerija Meštrović)—This museum is dedicated to sculptor Ivan Meštrović (1883–1962), the most important and famous of all Croatian artists. Split's best art museum is housed in a palace designed by the sculptor himself; if you have time, it's worth the 20-minute walk or short bus or taxi ride from the Old Town.

Meštrović grew up in a family of poor, nomadic farm workers just inland from Split. At an early age, his drawings and wooden carvings showed promise, and a rich family took him in and made sure he was properly trained. He eventually went off to school in Vienna, where he fell in with the Secession movement and found fame and fortune. Later in life—like Diocletian before him—Meštrović returned to Split and built a huge seaside mansion (today's Meštrović Gallery). During World War II, Meštrović moved abroad to escape the Nazi puppet government and lectured at Notre Dame (in Indiana, not France) and Syracuse (in New York, not Italy).

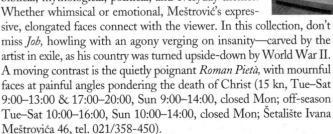

You'll see Meštrović's works all over Split and throughout Croatia. Most are cast bronze, depicting biblical, mythological, political, and everyday themes. Whether whimsical or emotional, Meštrović's expressive, elongated faces connect with the viewer. In this collection, don't miss *Job*, howling with an agony verging on insanity—carved by the artist in exile, as his country was turned upside-down by World War II. A moving contrast is the quietly poignant *Roman Pietà*, with mournful faces at painful angles pondering the death of Christ (15 kn, Tue–Sat 9:00–13:00 & 17:00–20:00, Sun 9:00–14:00, closed Mon; off-season Tue–Sat 10:00–16:00, Sun 10:00–14:00, closed Mon; Šetalište Ivana Meštrovića 46, tel. 021/358-450).

If you enjoy the gallery, continue five more minutes down Šetalište Ivana Meštrovića to **Kaštelet Chapel,** a 16th-century fortified palace Meštrović bought to display his wooden carvings of Jesus' life. The centerpiece is a powerful wooden crucifix (same ticket and hours as gallery).

Marjan Peninsula—This long, hilly peninsula extends west from the center of Split. This is where Split goes to relax, with out-of-the-way beaches and lots of hiking trails (great views and a zoo on top).

Hit the Beach—Since it's more of a big city than a resort, Split's beaches aren't as scenic (and the water not as clean) as towns farther south. The beach that's most popular—and crowded—is Bačvice, in a sandy cove just east of the main ferry terminal. You'll find less crowded beaches just to the east of Bačvice. Locals like to hike around Marjan, the peninsular city park (see above), ringed with several sunbathing beaches.

Trip to Trogir—Just 12 miles northwest of Split is Trogir, a tiny, art-and-medieval-architecture-packed town surrounded by water. It has a bustling market, a wonderfully carved old cathedral, and medieval ambience that can only really be appreciated from an outdoor café with a honey-drenched piece of baklava and a Turkish coffee. Get details at the Split TI.

Other Excursions—Consider one of many half-day and full-day excursions: a tour of Split and Trogir (180 kn, half day, 1/week), whitewater rafting on the nearby Cetina River (360 kn, full day, 2/week), the island of Brač (350 kn, full day, 1/week), the island of Hvar (330 kn, full day, 1/week), Brač and Hvar together (450 kn, full day, 1/week), Plitvice Lakes National Park (460 kn, full day, 1/week; see Zagreb and the Plitvice Lakes chapter), or even Dubrovnik (320 kn, full day, 1/week). Get information and tickets at the Turistički Biro on the Riva (see "Tourist Information," above).

NIGHTLIFE

Bačvice Beach—A family-friendly beach by day, it's a throbbing party zone for young locals late at night. All Old Town bars have to close by 1:00 in the morning. This is when night owls hike on over to the Bačvice crescent of clubs. The three-floor club complex is a cacophony of music, with each club's beat melting into the next's—all with breezy terraces overlooking the harbor.

SLEEPING

(€1 = about $1.20, 6 kn = about $1, country code: 385, area code: 021)
Since Split is a big city with more options, the accommodations situation isn't quite as dismal here as in other Dalmatian destinations. There are actually a few good values hiding between the expensive, new, business-class hotels and the rotting, old, communist-style places (many of which are slated for reconstruction—or a visit from the wrecking ball).

Hotels
To locate these hotels, see the map on page 486.

$$$ **Hotel President** is a slick, new place offering 40 plush, business-class rooms with all the comforts, overlooking a dreary parking lot a 10-minute walk north of the Old Town (Sb-€100,

Db-€130, non-smoking rooms, air-con, elevator, garage-€10/day, parking lot-€3.50/day, Starčevićeva 1, tel. 021/305-222, fax 021/305-225, www.hotelpresident.hr, hotel.president@st.htnet.hr).

$$$ **Hotel Adriana** has seven new rooms perched right above the bustling Riva. Choose between harborview front rooms or quieter back rooms. Though the rooms are good, they're an afterthought to the busy restaurant (Sb-600 kn, Db-750–850 kn, 10 percent less with cash off-season, prices include tax, air-con, elevator, Riva 8, tel. 021/340-000, fax 021/340-008, www.hotel-adriana.hr, info@hotel-adriana.hr).

$$ **Villa Ana** may just be the best value on the Dalmatian Coast, with five modern, comfortable rooms in a smart, little, newly renovated house a five-minute walk from the Old Town. This delightful, free-standing stone home, while surrounded by modern urban muck, is pristine and welcoming inside (Sb-550 kn, Db-690 kn, Tb-790 kn, 10 percent off with cash, air-con, street parking or a tight little parking spot, 2 blocks east of Old Town up busy Kralja Zvonimira, follow the driveway-like lane opposite the "skyscraper" 30 yards to Vrh Lučac 16, tel. 021/482-715, fax 021/482-721, www.villaana-split.hr, info@villaana-split.hr).

$$ **Hotel Bellevue** used to be the grande dame of Split. It's wonderfully central, at the west end of the Riva, but its 50 rooms are outmoded and extremely tired...as is the staff. Still, the great location and low prices make it worth considering (Sb-440 kn, Db-610–682 kn depending on season, Tb-810 kn, breakfast-40 kn, rooms overlooking the square have no traffic noise, third-floor rooms are quietest, but come with tiny portholes for windows, fans, a few handy parking spots, bana Josipa Jelačića 2, tel. 021/347-499, fax 021/362-383, www.hotel-bellevue-split.hr).

$$ **Hotel Slavija** is the only real hotel inside Diocletian's Palace. It's newly renovated and comfortable, but very noisy—especially on weekends—as it's surrounded by trendy cafés with late-night house music (25 rooms, new Db-550 kn, older Db-460 kn, Buvinina 2, tel. 021/323-840, fax 021/323-868, www.hotelslavija.com, info @hotelslavija.com).

Lower-Priced *Sobe* (Private Rooms)

Booking *Sobe* through an Agency: Though there are no *sobe* inside Split's Old Town, there are plenty within a 10-minute walk. **Turistički Biro,** a booking agency for locals with rooms to rent, helps you find the best fit. Make your reservation in advance; then, on arrival, drop by their office (which serves as a reception desk for the scattered rooms), pick up your welcome packet, pay, and head off to your awaiting landlady (figure S-€25, Sb-€28, D-€32, Db-€46, a few euros more July–Aug, 30 percent less for stays of 4 nights or more; office open mid-July–mid-Aug Mon–Fri 8:00–21:00, Sat

8:00–20:00, Sun 8:00–13:00; off-season Mon–Fri 8:00–20:00, Sat 8:00–14:00, closed Sun; Riva 12, tel. & fax 021/347-100, turist-biro -split@st.htnet.hr).

Going Direct: In addition to the government-regulated *sobe* administered by room-finding agencies, there is also an abundance of unregulated, cash-only rooms within a 10-minute walk of the Old Town (about €35 for a double). Locals hawking rooms meet each arrival at the boat, bus, and train terminals. The person generally shows photos of her place, you haggle for a price, then she escorts you to your new home in Split. While it takes nerve to just show up without a room, this is standard operating procedure for backpackers (who spend a third of what others do for the same comfort and a more memorable experience).

EATING

Split's Old Town has oodles of atmosphere, but places to eat are limited mostly to cafés and fast-food joints (Restoran Sarajevo is one exception). There's just one touristy place on the Riva, with a glorious harborfront setting (Restaurant Adriana). My favorite three spots (Šperun, Konoba Varoš, and Buffet Fife) are within 200 yards of each other just west of the Old Town.

Šperun Restaurant is a tiny place with a passion for good Dalmatian food. Zdravko Banović and his son serve a mix of Croatian and "eclectic Mediterranean," offering a good value and a warm welcome in a charming setting (most main dishes 30–50 kn, plus seafood splurges, air-con interior, a few sidewalk tables, daily 11:00–23:00, Šperun 3, tel. 021/346-999).

Konoba Varoš, though pricier than Šperun and a bit impersonal, seems to be everyone's choice for the best restaurant near the Old Town. It's so popular that reservations are virtually required for dinner. Vest-wearing, unsmiling waiters serve typical dishes under droopy fishnets (most main dishes 35–70 kn, daily 9:00–24:00, ban Mladenova 7, tel. 021/396-138).

Buffet Fife is your cheap, dream-come-true fish joint, where a colorful local crowd shares rough wood tables, and the waitstaff seem cold until you crack them up. Their tiny menu is ignored, as Zvonko (the charming-as-a-cartoon waiter) tells you what's available today— dictated by what they found at the market. The front room comes with a TV and a little bar action. It's quieter in the back. If you ask, they'll grill your fish rather than fry it, and bring a little plate of chopped garlic to doll up your bread with oil (daily, grilled fish plate- 40 kn, walk 200 yards along the waterfront west of Old Town to Trumbičeva obala 11, tel. 021/345-223). When you ask for dessert, they say, "Go 20 meters to the pastry shop next door" (good suggestion—that's Delta Matejuška, below).

Delta Matejuška, a handy little bakery, sells great pies and cakes by the slice, sandwiches, and pizza to go (daily 7:00–24:00, fine-print English menu on the wall, next door to Buffet Fife at Trumbičeva obala 13). After dining at Buffet Fife (above), drop by here for a special treat, and enjoy it on a bench overlooking the harbor.

In the Old Town: **Restoran Sarajevo,** a block off People's Square in the Old Town, serves good Dalmatian meat dishes under old arches (grilled meats-50–80 kn, Italian dishes-35–45 kn, better for meat than for seafood, can be smoky, daily 7:00–24:00, Domaldova 6, tel. 021/347-454).

On the Riva: **Restaurant Adriana** is your only choice for dining on the harborfront promenade. It's packed with tourists, so you'll get mediocre food and service for top prices. But the people-watching ambience couldn't be better. It's not a bad place for a slow meal or scenic drink (open long hours daily, Riva 8, tel. 021/340-000).

Pizza: **Ristorante Pizzeria Galija** has good wood-fired pizza, pasta, and salads at the west end of the Old Town (35–45 kn, air-con, Mon–Sat 9:00–23:00, Sun 12:00–23:00, Tončićeva 12, tel. 021/347-932). At the east end of the Old Town, you'll find good pizza at **Pizzeria Bakra** (25-40 kn, daily 9:00–23:00, Radovanova 2, tel. 021/488-488).

Gelato: Split has several spots for Italian-gelato-style ice cream *(sladoled).* Convenient and tasty is **Sara Mari,** just inside the west gate of Diocletian's Palace (steps from People's Square). But locals swarm a few blocks northwest of the Old Town to **Kuća Sladoleda Karmen** (daily 8:00–24:00, Slastičarna 2) and **Hajduk** (daily 8:00–24:00, Matošićeva 4).

TRANSPORTATION CONNECTIONS

From Split by Jadrolinija ferry: The boat generally leaves Split at 6:30 in the morning (sometimes 7:00) and heads south, stopping at **Korčula** (3.5–6 hrs, 5/week in summer, less off-season), **Dubrovnik** (7–10.5 hrs, generally around 8 hrs, 3–4/week in summer, less off-season), and sometimes other coastal destinations. Regional ferries also connect Split to **Korčula Island** via the town of Vela Luka (35 kn per person, 312 kn per car)—a long bus trip across the island from Korčula town (see page 510; if taking a car, there are no reservations—just show up an hour early and you should be fine). Split's **Jadrolinija office** is in the main ferry terminal (see "Arrival in Split," page 487), with several smaller branch offices between there and the Old Town (tel. 021/338-333). For details on boats to Italy, see "Getting Around the Dalmatian Coast," page 458.

By bus to: Zagreb (at least hrly, 6.5–8 hrs, depending on route, 115–135 kn), **Dubrovnik** (12/day—about every 2 hrs, including several very early—4.5 hrs, 100 kn), **Korčula** (1 night bus leaves 24:45 and arrives 6:00, 100 kn), **Zadar** (at least hrly, 3 hrs, 70 kn). Zagreb-bound buses sometimes also stop at **Plitvice** (confirm with driver and ask him to stop; 4–6 hrs, 70–80 kn). Reservations for buses are generally not necessary, but always ask about the fastest option—which can save hours of bus time. Bus info: tel. 021/338-483 or toll tel. 060/327-327.

By train to: Zagreb (3/day, 7.25–9 hrs, including 2 night trains), **Budapest** (1 direct night train/day, 17 hrs; or transfer in Zagreb). Train info: tel. 021/338-525 or toll tel. 060/333-444.

Korčula

To get a break from the Dalmatian Coast's two bustling cities, consider a sleepy island getaway in Korčula (KOHR-choo-lah). In Korčula's medieval quarter—poking out into the sea on a picture-perfect peninsula—tiny lanes branch off the humble main drag like ribs on a fishbone. This street plan is designed to catch both the breeze and the shade.

Korčula was founded by ancient Greeks, became part of the Roman Empire, and was eventually a key southern outpost of the Venetian Republic. Four centuries of Venetian rule left Korčula with a quirky Gothic-Renaissance mix and a strong siesta tradition. Though the Venetians also claim him, Korčula insists that the great explorer Marco Polo was born here in 1254. The town's other claims to fame include shipbuilding and the traditional *Moreška* sword dance. This laid-back island village is an ideal place to take a vacation from your busy vacation.

Planning Your Time

Korčula offers little to do besides taking it easy. Wander the medieval Old Town, explore the handful of tiny museums, kick back at a café or restaurant, or bask on the beach. If you're here on a Thursday, be sure to catch the performance of the *Moreška* dance (also Mon July–Aug). One day is more than enough for Korčula—but because of sometimes sparse ferry schedules, you may end up stranded here for longer. With the extra time, consider a one-day package excursion to Mljet Island and its National Park.

Korčula has a couple of fun annual festivals. The "Return to the Age of Marco Polo" festival is the last week of May, with lots of exhibitions, concerts, dances, and a parade with a costumed Marco

Polo returning to his native Korčula after his long visit to China. For 10 days at the beginning of September, Korčula remembers the great 1298 naval battle that took place just offshore, when the Genoese captured Marco Polo. The festivities culminate in a 14-ship reenactment, complete with smoke and sound effects.

ORIENTATION

(area code: 020)
The long, skinny island of Korčula runs alongside the even longer, skinnier Pelješac Peninsula. The main town and best destination on the island—just across a narrow strait from Pelješac—is also called Korčula.

Korčula's compact, highly fortified Old Town (Stari Grad) is on a little peninsula jutting into the Adriatic. Most tourist facilities—ATMs, travel agencies, Jadrolinija ferry office, Internet cafés—are where the Old Town peninsula meets the mainland.

Tourist Information
Korčula's we-try-harder TI is on the west side of the Old Town waterfront, next to Hotel Korčula (mid-June–Sept Mon–Sat 8:00–15:00 & 16:00–22:00, Sun 9:00–14:00; Oct–mid-June Mon–Sat 8:00–15:00, closed Sun; tel. 020/715-701, www.korcula.net). Pick up the free *Korčula* magazine, with maps, pictures, hotel listings, and other town information.

Arrival in Korčula
By Boat: Jadrolinija ferries usually arrive on the east side of town. As you exit the boat, the fortified Old Town is on your right. To reach the hotels on the far side of Shell Bay (Liburna, Park, Marko Polo), exit left and walk around the bay (about a 10-min walk). To get to the Old Town, Hotel Korčula, and recommended Depolo *soba*, go straight ahead from the boat landing. In two minutes, you'll come to a big staircase (the Old Town's main entrance gate). On the square in front of these steps, you'll find an ATM, the Atlas travel agency (room booking), a colorful outdoor produce market, and the Jadrolinija office.

Sometimes the Jadrolinija ferry arrives on the west side of town, by Hotel Korčula (also used by Orebić passenger ferry). To reach the center, walk with the Old Town on your left-hand side and turn left around the big round tower. In two minutes, you'll reach the staircase described above.

A few boats (car ferries from Orebić and Drvenik) come to the Dominče dock two peninsulas east of Korčula (near Hotel Bon Repos). Hourly buses connect this dock with Korčula.

By Bus: The bus station is at the southeast corner of Korčula's

Korčula

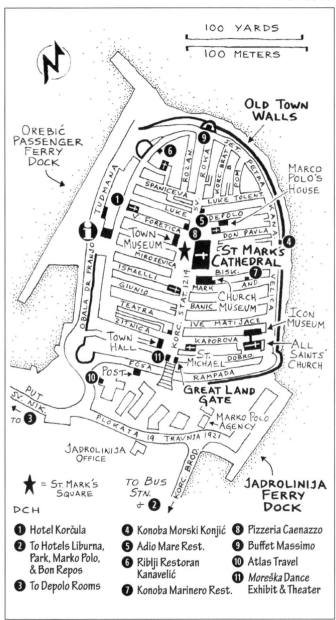

100 YARDS

100 METERS

OLD TOWN WALLS

OREBIĆ PASSENGER FERRY DOCK

MARCO POLO'S HOUSE

TUDMANA

SPANICEVA

ROZANA

SV. ROKA

SV. PETRA

KORC. BRAT. B

POM

SET.

LUKE

LUKE TOLENT.

V. FORETICA

DEPOLO

DON PAVLA

KANZA

TOWN MUSEUM

MIROSEVICA

St MARK'S CATHEDRAL

BISK.

ISMAELLI

OBALA DR. FRANJO

MARK

AND.

CHURCH MUSEUM

VELICA

GIUNIO

BANIC

KORC. STAT. 1214

TEATRA

IVE MATIJACE

ICON MUSEUM

ZITNICA

KAPOROVA

TOWN HALL

FOSA

ST. MICHAEL

ST. DOBRO

ALL SAINTS' CHURCH

POST→

RAMPADA

PUT SV. NIK.

TO ❸

PLOKATA 19 TRAVNJA 1921

GREAT LAND GATE

MARKO POLO AGENCY

KORC. BROD.

JADROLINIJA OFFICE

TO BUS STN.

❷

JADROLINIJA FERRY DOCK

★ = ST. MARK'S SQUARE

DCH

❶ Hotel Korčula

❷ To Hotels Liburna, Park, Marko Polo, & Bon Repos

❸ To Depolo Rooms

❹ Konoba Morski Konjić

❺ Adio Mare Rest.

❻ Riblji Restoran Kanavelić

❼ Konoba Marinero Rest.

❽ Pizzeria Caenazzo

❾ Buffet Massimo

❿ Atlas Travel

⓫ Moreška Dance Exhibit & Theater

Shell Bay. If you leave the station with the bay on your left, you'll get to hotels Liburna, Park, and Marko Polo. If you leave with the bay on your right, you'll get to the Old Town, Hotel Korčula, Depolo *soba,* and the main ferry terminal (see "By Boat," above).

By Car: See "Transportation Connections," below.

SIGHTS

Korčula's few sights cluster within a few yards of each other in the Old Town. Aside from the *Moreška* dance, I've listed them roughly in order from the Great Land Gate (the Old Town's main entry) to the tip of the Old Town peninsula.

▲▲**Moreška Dance**—Lazy Korčula snaps to life when locals perform a medieval folk dance called the *Moreška* (moh-REHSH-kah). The plot helps Korčulans remember their hard-fought past: A bad king takes the good king's bride, the dancing forces of good and evil battle, and there's always a happy ending (60 kn, June–mid-Oct every Thu at 21:00, July–Aug also Mon at 21:00, in Gradska Vijećnica theater next to Great Land Gate, or in movie theater if bad weather; buy tickets from local travel agency, at your hotel, or at the door).

▲**Great Land Gate (Veliki Revelin)**—An impres-  sive staircase leads up to the main entrance to the Old Town. Like all of the town's towers, it's adorned with the Venetian winged lion and the coats-of-arms of the doge of Venice (left) and the rector of Korčula (right; the offset coat of arms below was the rector who renovated the gate later). You can climb up the tower to visit a small exhibit on the *Moreška* dance and enjoy panoramic town views (10 kn, daily 9:30–21:30, less off-season, English descriptions).

Just inside the gate is **Franjo Tuđman Square**—recently (in 2001) renamed for the controversial first president of an independent Croatia (see page 454). During the war, Tuđman was considered a hero. In later years, he grew power-hungry and held secret negotiations with the merciless Serbian leader, Slobodan Milošević. But members of his party are still in power and hold local offices throughout the country, sometimes adorning a square or street with his name. (Many locals think—or hope—these names will be changed again before too long.)

On the left inside the gate is the 16th-century **Town Hall and Rector's Palace.** The seal of Korčula symbolizes the town's importance as the southernmost bastion of the Venetian Republic: St. Mark standing below three defensive towers. The little church on the other side of the square is dedicated to **St. Michael** (Crkva Sv. Mihovila). Throughout Croatia, you'll often find churches to

St. Michael just inside the town gates, as he is believed to offer saintly protection from enemies. Notice that a passageway connects the church to the building across the street—home to the Brotherhood of St. Michael, one of Korčula's many religious fraternal organizations (see "Icon Museum," below).

Now continue up the...

▲Street of the Korčulan Statute of 1214 (Ulica Korčulanskog Statuta 1214)—This street is Korčula's backbone...literally (the street plan is designed as a fish skeleton). While most medieval towns slowly evolved with twisty, mazelike lanes, Korčula was carefully planned. The streets to the west (left) of this one are straight, to allow the refreshing west winds *(maestral)* into town. To the east (right), they're curved (notice you can't see the sea)—to keep out the bad-vibe southeast winds.

The street's complicated name honors a 1214 statute, the oldest known written law in Central Europe, with regulations about everyday life and instructions on maintaining the walls, protecting nature, keeping animals, building a house, and so on.

If you continue a few steps up the street, you'll reach **St. Mark's Square** (Trg Sv. Marka). From here, you're a few steps from the next four sights.

▲St. Mark's Cathedral (Katedrala Sv. Marka)—Korčula became a bishopric in the 14th century. In the 19th century—36 bishops later—the Hapsburgs decided to centralize ecclesiastical power in their empire, and removed Korčula's bishop. The town still has this beautiful "cathedral"—but no bishop. On the facade, you'll see another Venetian statue of St. Mark (flanked by Adam and Eve). Inside, above the main altar, is an original Tintoretto painting (recently restored in Zagreb). As you leave, notice the weapons on the back wall, used in some of the pivotal battles that have taken place near strategically situated Korčula.

▲Church Museum (Opatska Riznica)—This small museum has an unusual and fascinating collection. Try to find the following: a ceremonial necklace from Mother Teresa (which she gave to a friend from Korčula), some old 12th-century hymnals, two tiny drawings by Leonardo da Vinci, a coin collection, including a 2,400-year-old Greek coin minted here in Korčula, some Croatian modern paintings, and two framed reliquaries with dozens of miniscule relics (10 kn, 40-kn English guidebook; June–Aug Mon–Sat 8:00–21:00, closed Sun; May and Sept–Oct Mon–Sat 10:00–13:00, closed Sun; closed Nov–April).

▲Town Museum (Gradski Muzej)—Housed in an old mansion, this museum does a fine job of bringing together Korčula's eclectic claims to fame. It's arranged like a traditional Dalmatian home: shop on the ground floor, living quarters in the middle floors, kitchen on top. Notice that many of the interior walls are not finished (including just inside the entry). Archaeologists are continually doing actual "digs" into these walls to learn how medieval houses here were built.

On the ground floor is an exhibit on stonemasonry, displaying some 1st-century Roman jugs. Upstairs is a display on Korčula's long-standing shipbuilding industry, including models of two modern steel ships built here (the town still builds ship parts today). There's also a furnished living room and, in the attic, a kitchen. This was a smart place for the kitchen—if it caught fire, it was less likely to destroy the whole building. Notice the little WC in the corner. A network of pipes took kitchen and other waste through town and out to sea (10 kn, 40-kn English book, mid-June–Aug Mon–Sat 9:30–21:00, closed Sun; May–mid-June and Sept–Oct Mon–Sat 10:00–13:00, closed Sun; closed Nov–April).

▲**Marco Polo's House (Kuća Marka Pola)**—Korčula's favorite son is the great 13th-century explorer Marco Polo. Though Polo sailed under the auspices of the Venetian Republic, and technically was a Venetian (since the Republic controlled this region), Korčulans proudly claim him as their own. Marco Polo was the first Westerner to sail to China, bringing back amazing stories and goods, like silk, that Europeans had never seen before. After his trip, Marco Polo fought in an important naval battle against the Genoese near Korčula. He was captured, taken to Genoa, and imprisoned. He told his story to a cellmate, who wrote it down, published it, and made the explorer a world-class and much-in-demand celebrity. To this day, kids in swimming pools around the world try to find him with their eyes closed.

Today, Korčula is the proud home to "Marco Polo's House"— actually a more recent building on the site of what may or may not have been his family's property—with a modest exhibit about the explorer's life. The house is in poor repair, and is closed indefinitely while the city haggles with the private owners to renovate and reopen it to the public (just north of cathedral on—where else?— ulica Depolo).

▲**Icon Museum (Zbirka Ikona)**—Korčula is known for its many brotherhoods—centuries-old fraternal organizations that have sprung up around churches. The Brotherhood of All Saints has been meeting every Sunday after Mass since the 14th century, and they run a small but interesting museum of icons. These golden religious images were brought back from Greece in the 17th century by Korčulans who had been fighting the Turks on a Venetian warship (8 kn, May–Oct Mon–Sat 10:00–13:00 & 18:00–20:00, closed Sun and Nov–April, on Kaprova ulica at the Old Town's southeast tip).

Brotherhoods' meeting halls are often connected to their church by a second-story walkway. Use this one to step in to the Venetian-style **All Saints' Church** (Crkva Svih Svetih). Under the loft in the back of the church, notice the models of boats and tools—donated by Korčula's shipbuilders. Look closely at the painting to the right of the altar. See the guys in the white robes kneeling under Jesus? That's the Brotherhood, who commissioned this painting.

▲**Old Town Walls**—For several centuries, Korčula held an crucial strategic position: This was the southernmost border of the Venetian Republic (the Republic of Dubrovnik started at the Pelješac Peninsula, just across the sea). The original town walls around Korčula date from at least the 13th century, but the fortifications were extended (and new towers built) over several centuries to defend against various foes of Venice—mostly Turks and pirates.

The most recent tower dates from the 16th century, when the Turks attacked Korčula. The rector and other VIPs fled to the mainland, but a brave priest remained on the island and came up with a plan. All of the women of Korčula dressed up as men, and then everybody in town peeked over the wall—making the Turks think they were up against a huge army. The priest prayed for help, and a strong north wind *(bora)* blew. Not wanting to take their chances with the many defenders and the weather, the Turks sailed away, and Korčula was saved.

By the late 19th century, Korčula was an unimportant Hapsburg beach town, and the walls had no strategic value. The town decided to quarry the top half of its old walls to build new homes (and to improve air circulation inside the city). While today's walls are half as high as they used to be, the town has restored many of the towers, giving Korčula its fortified feel today. Each one has a winged lion—a symbol of Venice—and the seal of the rector of Korčula when the tower was built.

ACTIVITIES

Excursions—Local travel agencies offer day-long excursions to nearby destinations. The most popular options are Dubrovnik (320 kn, 3/week) and the National Park on Mljet Island (190 kn, 2/week). You can buy tickets at any local travel agency (try Atlas or Marko Polo, both listed under "Booking *Sobe* Through an Agency," below).

Swimming—The water around Korčula is clean and popular for swimming. You'll find pebbly beaches strewn with holiday-goers all along Sv. Nikola, the street that runs west from the Old Town. Another popular swimming spot is at the very end of the Old Town peninsula.

SLEEPING

(€1 = about $1.20, 6 kn = about $1, country code: 385, area code: 020)
Korčula's accommodations options are extremely limited. There are five hotels in town—all decaying, overpriced, resort-style hotels, and

all owned by the same company (which is, in turn, government-run). The lack of competition keeps prices high and quality low—and makes *sobe* a particularly good alternative.

$ Lower-Priced *Sobe*

Rezi and Andro Depolo, probably distant relatives of Marco, rent four wonderful rooms on a bay five minutes by foot from the Old Town. English-speaking Rezi is very friendly and works to make her guests comfortable. Her rooms are better by far than the big hotels, go for a quarter of the price, and are the only air-conditioned rooms in town to boot (Db-200 kn, or 240 kn July–Aug, room with kitchen-40 kn more, 30 percent more for 1- or 2-night stays, breakfast extra, cash only, Sv. Nikola 43; walk along waterfront from Old Town with bay on your right, look for *sobe* sign at the yellow house set back from the street, just before the 2 monasteries; tel. 020/711-621, tereza.depolo@du.t-com.hr). If Rezi is full, she's well-connected with neighbors also renting private rooms.

Booking *Sobe* through an Agency: While you can walk along Sv. Nikola and generally find a fine deal on a private room, you can also book one through one of Korčula's travel agencies (for an additional 20 percent). **Marko Polo Tours** books private rooms from their selection of 20 places. You'll use their office as a kind of reception desk (Db-340 kn in high season, 250 kn in shoulder season, daily in summer 8:00–20:00, off-season 8:00–14:00 & 17:00–19:00, located just outside the Old Town gate at Biline 5, tel. 020/715-400, fax 020/715-800, marko-polo-tours@du.htnet.hr). **Atlas Travel** is another option (daily in summer 7:00–20:30, off-season Mon–Sat 8:00–12:00, closed Sun, Trg 19. Travnja, tel. 020/711-060, fax 020/715-580).

$$ Moderately-Priced Hotels

All five of Korčula's hotels are owned by HTP Korčula. If you don't want to stay in a *soba*, these are the only game in town. You can reserve rooms at any of them through the main office (tel. 020/726-336, fax 020/711-746, www.korcula.net, htp-korcula@du.htnet.hr; at all hotels, credit cards are accepted, there is no air-con, and there are no non-smoking rooms; you'll pay 10 percent more for a seaview room, more July–Aug, and less off-season).

The handiest is **Hotel Korčula,** centrally located in the Old Town. It has a fine seaside terrace restaurant and friendly staff, even if the 20 rooms are outmoded and overpriced (Sb-€58, Db-€90, July–Aug: Sb-€73, Db-€102, less off-season, reception tel. 020/711-078).

Three more hotels cluster around the far side of Shell Bay. All are poorly maintained and overpriced, but share a nice beach. **Hotel Liburna** has 83 rooms—some of them accessible by elevator—and the same prices as Hotel Korčula (reception tel. 020/726-006). **Hotel Park** has 153 rooms, some of them lightly renovated (old rooms: Sb-315 kn, Db-480 kn, July–Aug: Sb-395 kn, Db-560; newer rooms: Sb-365 kn, Db-560 kn, July–Aug: Sb-460 kn, Db-750 kn, reception tel. 020/726-100). **Hotel Marko Polo** has 109 rooms and an elevator (Sb-365 kn, Db-560 kn, July–Aug: Sb-460 kn, Db-750 kn, reception tel. 020/726-100). The fifth hotel, **Hotel Bon Repos**—another 15 minutes by foot from the Old Town—is, in every sense, the last resort.

EATING

Korčula has plenty of tasty seafood restaurants. Try these suggestions, or follow your nose through the Old Town.

Konoba Morski Konjić ("Moorish Seahorse") is a tourist-friendly restaurant with tables spilling along the seawall, offering atmospheric dining with salty views and jaded service. If you want romantic harborside dining, this is your best option (50- to 60-kn plates, daily 8:00–24:00, tel. 020/711-878).

Adio Mare offers fine seafood and pleasant, cave-like, Old World atmosphere near Marco Polo's House (daily 18:00–24:00, also 12:00–14:00 in peak season, tel. 020/711-253).

Riblji Restoran Kanavelić, near the far end of the Old Town peninsula, serves good seafood in a fancier setting (non-seafood dishes 20–45 kn, plus seafood splurges, daily 18:00–24:00, tel. 020/711-800).

Konoba Marinero has nautical decor on a peaceful alley just two blocks from the main street in the Old Town (most dishes 35–60 kn, daily 11:00–15:00 & 18:00–24:00, Marka Andrijića 13, tel. 020/711-170).

Pizzeria Caenazzo is hard to miss, serving decent pizza right on St. Mark's Square (daily 9:00–24:00).

Picnics: Just outside the main gate, you'll find a lively produce market and a big, modern, air-conditioned supermarket (next to Marko Polo Tours). A short stroll from there, down Sv. Nikola, takes you to beach perches with the best Korčula views. Otherwise, there are plenty of picnic spots along the Old Town embankment.

A Scenic Drink: The best setting for drinks is at **Buffet "Massimo,"** in a city-wall tower at the tip of the Old Town peninsula. The main dining room is just inside the top of the tower, but if you're just having drinks, climb the ladder and sit up top with wonderful views (pizzas 30–45 kn, otherwise just drinks, daily 17:00–2:00, tel. 020/715-073).

TRANSPORTATION CONNECTIONS

Korčula is reasonably well-connected to the rest of the Dalmatian Coast by boat—though service becomes sparse in the off-season. It's smart to carefully study boat schedules when planning your itinerary. There are plans in the near future for a more frequent high-speed hydrofoil connecting Korčula town with Split; ask a local TI for details.

From Korčula by boat: Most travelers get to Korčula by Jadrolinija ferry (docks right at Old Town). You can take it to **Split** (5/week in summer, less off-season, stops at Stari Grad on Hvar Island en route) or **Dubrovnik** (3–4/week in summer, less off-season). The Jadrolinija office is located where the Old Town meets the mainland (mid-June–Sept Mon–Fri 8:00–20:00, Sat–Sun 8:00–14:00; Oct–mid-June Mon–Fri 8:00–14:00, Sat–Sun 8:00–13:00, tel. 020/715-410, www.jadrolinija.hr).

There's another way to **Split,** but it requires a very early bus from Korčula to the port at **Vela Luka,** an hour away at the other end of the island. Every day, a local Jadrolinija ferry and a faster hydrofoil leave from the Vela Luka dock and go to Hvar, then on to Split (ferry: Mon–Sat at 6:30, Sun at 9:30, 1.5 hrs to Hvar, 3 hrs to Split; hydrofoil: Mon–Sat at 5:30, Sun at 8:00, 30 min to Hvar, 1.5 hrs to Split; bus for Mon–Sat boats leaves Korčula at 4:10, bus for Sun boats leaves Korčula at 7:45). Confirm these schedules carefully at the Korčula TI or Jadrolinija office before you get up early to make the trip. Each ferry arriving at Vela Luka is met by a bus waiting to whisk arriving travelers to Korčula town.

By bus to: Dubrovnik (2/day, 3 hrs; off-season 1/day, early departure), **Zagreb** (1/day, 9–12 hrs depending on route), **Split** (1/day, 5 hrs, same bus goes to Zagreb), **Vela Luka** (at far end of island, Mon–Fri 7/day, Sat 6/day, Sun 4/day, first bus at 4:10 gets you to the early-morning ferries—see above).

By car: The island of Korčula is connected to the mainland by a small ferry between Orebić and Dominče (1 mile from Korčula town, 50 kn/car, 10 kn/passenger, 15-min ride, departs Dominče at the top of most but not all hours—check carefully in Korčula, departs Orebić at :30 past most hours).

Rather than take this shorter ferry and then drive the rest of the way between Korčula and Split, I prefer to take the longer ferry the whole way. There are several each day between Split and Vela Luka (at the far end of Korčula Island—see above) for a reasonable price (312 kn/car, 35 kn/passenger). The scenic and relaxing four-hour boat ride saves you about that much driving time. Once in Korčula town, there's plenty of free parking at the bus station along the marina.

ZAGREB and the PLITVICE LAKES

Croatia is known for its idyllic coastline, but there are also worthwhile stops in the interior. The underrated capital, Zagreb—with good museums, interesting streets, and a thriving café culture—is worth exploring. Just to the south are the Plitvice Lakes—Croatia's first and most important national park, and one of Europe's best back-to-nature experiences.

Zagreb

While Zagreb doesn't have the world-class sights of Budapest or the stay-awhile charm of Ljubljana, the city offers historic neighborhoods, offbeat museums, and an illuminating contrast to Croatia's coast. As a tourist destination, Zagreb pales in comparison to the sparkling coastal towns. But you can't get a complete picture of modern Croatia without a visit here—away from the touristy resorts, in the lively and livable city that is home to one out of every five Croatians (population around 1 million).

Zagreb began as two walled medieval cities, Gradec and Kaptol, separated by a river. As Croatia fell under the control of various foreign powers—Budapest, Vienna, Berlin, and Belgrade—the two hill towns that would become Zagreb gradually took on more religious and civic importance. Kaptol became a bishopric in 1094, and it's still home to Croatia's most important church. In the 16th century, the *Ban* (Croatia's governor) and the *Sabor* (parliament) called Gradec home. The two towns officially merged in 1850, and soon after, the railroad connecting Budapest with the Adriatic port city of Rijeka was built through the city. Zagreb prospered.

After centuries of being the de facto religious, cultural, and political capital of Croatia, Zagreb officially became a European

Zagreb

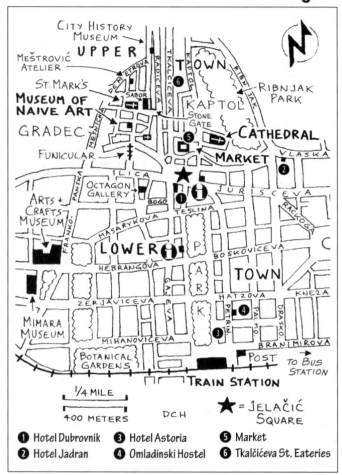

CITY HISTORY MUSEUM
UPPER TOWN
MEŠTROVIĆ ATELIER
ST. MARK'S
MUSEUM OF NAIVE ART
GRADEC
FUNICULAR
PETROVA
RADIĆEVA
TKALČIĆEVA
KAPTOL
SABOR
MESNIČKA
STONE GATE
KAPTOL
RIBNJAK
RIBNJAK PARK
CATHEDRAL
MARKET
VLAŠKA
ILICA
PANSKA
OCTAGON GALLERY
BOGO
FRANKO
MASARYKOVA
TESLINA
JURIŠIĆEVA
RAČKOGA
ARTS & CRAFTS MUSEUM
LOWER TOWN
HEBRANGOVA
BOŠKOVIĆEVA
KNEZA
ZERJAVIĆEVA
PARK
HATZOVA
PETRINJSKA
PALMOTIĆEVA
DRAŠKO
MIMARA MUSEUM
MIHANOVIĆEVA
BRANIMIROVA
BOTANICAL GARDENS
POST
TO BUS STATION
TRAIN STATION

¼ MILE
400 METERS
DCH

★ = JELAČIĆ SQUARE

❶ Hotel Dubrovnik ❸ Hotel Astoria ❺ Market
❷ Hotel Jadran ❹ Omladinski Hostel ❻ Tkalčićeva St. Eateries

capital when the country declared its independence in 1991. In the ensuing war with Serbia, Zagreb was hardly damaged—Serbian bombs hit only a few strategic targets (the bloodiest fighting was to the east and south of here).

Today, just a decade later, Zagreb has long since repaired the minimal damage, and the capital feels safe, modern, accessible, and forward-looking.

Planning Your Time

Most American visitors just pass through Zagreb, but the city is worth a look. Check your bag at the station and zip into the center for a quick visit—or consider spending the night.

You can get a decent sense of the Croatian capital in just a few short hours. With whatever time you have, make a beeline for Jelačić Square to visit the TI and get oriented. If you arrive midday, get to the market before it closes up at 14:00. If you're in town earlier (or too late for the market), take the funicular up to Gradec, visit the Museum of Naive Art, and stroll St. Mark's Square before heading down through the Stone Chapel to the lively Tkalčićeva scene (good for a drink or meal), through the market, and on to Kaptol and the cathedral. With more time, visit some of Zagreb's museums or wander the "Green Horseshoe" (a series of parks—described below). Note that virtually all Zagreb museums are closed on Monday.

ORIENTATION

(area code: 01)

Zagreb, just 30 minutes from the Slovenian border, stretches from the foothills of Medvednica ("Bear Mountain") to the Sava River. In the middle of the sprawl, you'll find the modern **Lower Town** (Donji Grad, centered on **Jelačić Square**) and the historic **Upper Town** (Gornji Grad—comprising the original hill towns of **Gradec** and **Kaptol**). To the south is a U-shaped belt of parks, squares, and museums that make up "Lenuci's Green Horseshoe." The east side of the U is a series of three parks, with the train station at the bottom (south) and Jelačić Square at the top (north).

Zagrebians have devised a brilliant scheme for confusing tourists: Street names can be depicted several different ways. For example, the street that is signed as ulica Kralja Držislava ("King Držislav Street") is often called by locals simply Držislavova ("Držislav's"). So if you're looking for a street, don't search for an exact match—be willing to settle for something that just has a lot of the same letters.

Tourist Information

Zagreb has two TIs—the handier one is at **Jelačić Square** (Mon–Fri 8:30–20:00, Sat 9:00–17:00, Sun 10:00–14:00, sometimes longer hours in summer, Trg bana Jelačića 11, tel. 01/481-4051, www.zagreb-touristinfo.hr), and the other is just a few blocks south, along the west side of **Zrinjevac Park** (Mon, Wed, and Fri 9:00–17:00, Tue and Thu 9:00–18:00, closed Sat–Sun, Trg Nikole Šubića Zrinskoga 14, tel. 01/492-1645). Zagreb's TIs are helpful, with piles of well-produced tourist brochures that desperately try to convince visitors to do more than just pass through. Pick up the one-page city map (with handy transit map and regional map on back), the *Zagreb Info A–Z* booklet (including accommodations listings), and the great *City Walks* brochure—with a couple of easy, self-guided walking tours (all free).

The **Zagreb Card** gives you free transportation and discounts

Zagreb Landmarks

English	Croatian	Pronounced
Jelačić Square	Trg bana Jelačića	turg BAH-nah YEH-lah-chee-chah
Gradec (original civic hill town)	Gradec	GRAH-dehts
Kaptol (original religious hill town)	Kaptol	KAHP-tohl
Café street between Gradec and Kaptol	Tkalčićeva	tuh-kahl-chee-CHAY-vah
Train station	Glavni Kolodvor	GLAHV-nee KOH-loh-dvor
Bus station	Autobusni Kolodvor	OW-toh-boos-nee KOH-loh-dvor

on Zagreb sights for 72 hours (60 kn, sold at TI). This usually doesn't make sense for folks who are day-tripping here, but it's a good deal for longer stays, or if you're taking a city tour.

To get oriented, consider the fun daily **city tours,** led by local guides dressed up as important historical Zagrebians (2-hr walking tour: €13, 4/week; 3-hr bus-plus-walking tour: €20, 3/week; 50 percent discount on either tour with Zagreb Card—a great deal; call TI 1 day ahead to reserve and request English guide, tel. 01/481-4051).

Arrival in Zagreb

By Train: Zagreb's train station (Glavni Kolodvor) is conveniently located a few blocks south of Jelačić Square on the "Green Horseshoe." Good signage will direct you to the arrival hall, information desk, ticket windows, ATMs, WCs, and kiosks. The left-luggage office is at the left end of the station, with your back to the tracks (open daily 24 hrs). To reach the center, go straight out the front door. You'll run into a taxi stand, and then the tracks for tram #6 (direction Črnomerec zips you to Jelačić Square; direction Sopot takes you to the bus station). If you walk straight ahead through the long, lush park, you'll wind up at the bottom of Jelačić Square in 10 minutes.

By Bus: The user-friendly bus station (Autobusni Kolodvor) is southeast of the center. The station has all the essentials—ATMs, post office, mini-grocery store, left-luggage counter, and even a chapel. Upstairs, you'll find ticket windows and access to the buses (follow signs to *perone;* wave ticket in front of turnstile to open gate). Tram #6 (in direction Črnomerec) takes you to the train station, then on to Jelačić Square.

By Plane: Zagreb's airport is about 10 miles south of the center (tel. 01/626-5222, www.zagreb-airport.hr). The Croatia Air bus connects the airport to Zagreb's bus station (25 kn, every 30 min, 25-min trip). Figure 180 kn for a taxi from the airport to the center.

Getting Around Zagreb

The main mode of public transportation is the **tram,** operated by ZET (Zagreb Electrical Transport, www.zet.hr). A single ticket (good for 90 min in one direction, including transfers) costs 6 kn if you buy it from the driver (5.50 kn at kiosk, ask for *ZET karta*). A day ticket *(dnevna karta)* costs 15 kn. The most useful tram for tourists is #6, connecting Jelačić Square with the train and bus stations.

Taxis start at 25 kn, then run 7 kn per kilometer (more expensive at night; as always, there are corrupt cabbies—ask for an estimate up front, or call Radio Taxi, tel. 01/970).

SIGHTS

The following sights are listed in the order of a handy one-way circular orientation walk, starting at Jelačić Square. The entire route will take you about an hour at a leisurely pace (not counting museum stops).

▲**Jelačić Square (Trg bana Jelačića)**—Zagreb's main square bustles with life. It's lined with cafés, shops, trams, Baroque buildings, and the TI. When Zagreb consisted of the two hill towns of Gradec and Kaptol, this Donji Grad ("lower town") held the townspeople's farm fields. Today, it features a prominent equestrian statue of national hero **Josip Jelačić** (YEH-lah-cheech, 1801–1859), a 19th-

century governor who extended citizens' rights and did much to unite the Croats within the Hapsburg Empire. In Jelačić's time, the Hungarians were exerting a lot of control over Croatia, even trying to make Hungarian the official language. Meanwhile, Budapesters revolted against Hapsburg rule in 1848. Jelačić, ever mindful of the need to protect Croatian cultural autonomy, knew that he'd have a better shot at getting his way from Austria than from Hungary. Jelačić chose the lesser of two evils, and fought alongside the Hapsburgs to put down the Hungarian uprising. In the Yugoslav era, Jelačić was considered dangerously nationalistic, and this statue was taken down. But when Croatia broke away in 1991, Croatian patriotism was in the air, and Jelačić returned. Though Jelačić originally faced his Hungarian foes to the north, today he's staring down the Serbs to the south.

Get oriented. If you face Jelačić's statue, a long block to your left is a funicular that takes you up to one of Zagreb's original villages, Gradec. To the right, look for the TI. If you leave the square ahead and to the right, you'll reach the other original village, Kaptol, and the cathedral. If you leave the square ahead and to the left, you'll come to the market (Dolac) and the café street, Tkalčićeva.

▲▲**Gradec**—Eventually absorbed by Zagreb, the city of Gradec (GRAH-dehts) was granted status as a free royal state by the 1242 Golden Bull—meaning that the town answered only and directly to the Holy Roman Emperor (not that pesky nobility bureaucracy). In later years, Gradec became the seat of Croatia's government—including its *Sabor*, or parliament, and *Ban*, or governor.

To reach Gradec from Jelačić Square, go a long block down the busy Ilica. On the way, duck inside the big shopping gallery on the left (at #5, called the Octagon). If you go down the first passage, you'll come to a beautiful stained-glass ceiling and a tie store called **Croata.** This is a reminder that the French may have "invented" the tie, but they were inspired by Croatian soldiers, who wore jaunty scarves into battle when they went to fight in the Thirty Years' War. The French even named the new accessory *cravate*—after "Croat."

Continue up Ilica and turn right on Tomičeva, where you'll see a small **funicular** (ZET Uspinjača) crawling up the hill. Dating from the late 19th century, this funicular is looked upon fondly by Zagrebians—both as a bit of nostalgia and as a way to avoid some steps. You can walk up if you want, but the ride is more fun and takes only 55 seconds (3 kn, leaves every 10 min daily 6:30–21:00).

From the top of the funicular, you'll enjoy a fine panorama over Zagreb. The tall tower you face as you exit is one of Gradec's original watchtowers, the **Burglars' Tower** (Kula Lotrščak). After the Tartars ransacked Central Europe in the early 13th century, King Béla IV decreed that towns be fortified—so, Gradec built a wall and guard towers (just like Kraków and Buda did). Look for the little cannon in the top-floor window. Every day at noon, this cannon fires a shot, supposedly to commemorate a 15th-century victory over the besieging Turks. (Zagrebians hold on to other traditions, too—the lamps on this hill are still gas-powered, lit by a city employee every evening.)

Head up the street next to the tower. Little remains of medieval Gradec. When the Turks overran Europe, they never managed to take Zagreb—but the threat was enough to scare the nobility into the countryside. When the Turks left, the nobles came back, and replaced the medieval buildings here with Baroque mansions. At the first square, to the right, you'll see the Jesuit **Church of Saint Catherine.** It's not much to look at from outside, but the interior is intricately decorated. The same applies to several mansions on Gradec. This simple-outside, ornate-inside style is known as "Zagreb Baroque."

As you continue up the street, you'll see the excellent **Croatian**

Museum of Naive Art (Hrvatski Muzej Naivne Umjetnosti) on the left. This remarkable museum, rated ▲▲, collects paintings and sculptures by untrained peasant artists. These stirring images—including several by the movement's star, Ivan Generalić—are well worth a look (10 kn, Tue–Fri 10:00–18:00, Sat–Sun 10:00–13:00, closed Mon, ulica Sv. Čirila i Metoda 3, tel. 01/485-1911, www.hmnu.org).

At the end of the block, you'll come to the low-key **St. Mark's Square** (Markov trg), centered on the **Church of St. Mark.** The original church here was from the 12th century, but only a few fragments remain. The colorful tile roof, from 1880, depicts two coats of arms. On the left, the red-and-white checkerboard symbolizes north-central Croatia, the three lions' heads stand for the Dalmatian Coast, and the marten (*kuna,* like the money) running between the two rivers (Sava and Drava) represent Slavonia—Croatia's northern, inland panhandle. On the right is the seal of Zagreb: a walled city with wide-open doors (welcoming in visitors...like you).

As you face the church, to the right is the *Sabor,* or parliament. From the 12th century, Croatian noblemen would gather to make important decisions regarding their territories. This gradually evolved into today's modern parliament (original building around the corner). Across the square (to your left as you face the church) is the **Ban's Palace** (Banski Dvori), today the offices for the president and prime minister. This was one of the few buildings in central Zagreb destroyed in the recent war. In October of 1991, the Serbs shelled it from afar, knowing that Croatian President Franjo Tuđman was inside...but Tuđman survived.

Walk from Gradec to Kaptol: For an interesting stroll from St. Mark's Square to the cathedral, head down the street (Kamenita ulica) to the right of the parliament building. Near the end of the street, you'll see the oldest pharmacy in town (c. 1350, on the right) before coming to Gradec's oldest surviving gate, the **Stone Gate** (Kamenita Vrata). Inside is a moving chapel. The focal point is a painting of Mary that miraculously survived a major fire in 1731. When this medieval gate was reconstructed in the Baroque style, they decided to turn it into a makeshift chapel. The candles represent Zagrebians' prayers, and the stone plaques on the wall give thanks *(Hvala)* for prayers that were answered. Mary was made official patron saint of Zagreb in 1990.

As you leave the Stone Gate and come to Radićeva, turn right. Take the next left, onto the street called Krvavi Most—literally, "Blood Bridge." At the end of Krvavi Most, you'll come to **Tkalčićeva.** This lively café-and-restaurant street used to be a river—the natural boundary between Gradec and Kaptol. The two towns did not always get along, and sometimes fought against each other. Blood was spilled, and the bridge that once stood here between them became known as Blood Bridge. By the late 19th century, the towns had united, and the river began to stink—so they covered it over with this street.

As you cross Tkalčićeva, you enter the old town of Kaptol. You'll come to the **market** (Dolac), packed with colorful stalls selling produce of all kinds (usually open daily 7:00–14:00). Underneath you is an underground, indoor part of the market, where farmers sell farm-fresh eggs and dairy products (same hours as outdoor market, entrance down below in the direction of Jelačić Square).

On the other side of the market, visit the...

▲Cathedral (Katedrala)—In 1094, when a diocese was established at Kaptol, this church quickly became a major center of high-ranking church officials—and it's still Croatia's most important church. (The country is 90 percent Catholic...though the percentage was lower before the conflict with the Orthodox Serbs.) In the mid-13th century, the original cathedral was destroyed by invading Tartars, who actually used it as a stable. It was rebuilt, only to be destroyed again by an earthquake in 1880. The current version is neo-Gothic. Surrounding the church are Renaissance towers (part of a larger archbishop's palace) that were built for protection against the Turks. The full name is the Cathedral of the Assumption of the Blessed Virgin Mary and the Saintly Kings Stephen and Ladislav (whew!)— but most locals just call it "the cathedral."

Step inside (free, Mon–Sat 10:00–17:00, Sun 13:00–17:00). Look closely at the silver relief on the first altar: a scene of the Holy Family doing chores around the house (Mary sewing, Joseph and Jesus building a fence...and angels helping out). In the back left corner, find the tombstone of Alojzije Stepinac. He was the Archbishop of Zagreb in World War II, during which time he shortsightedly supported the Nazis—thinking, like many Croatians, that this was the ticket to greater independence from Serbia. When Tito came to power, he put Stepinac on trial and sent him to jail for five years. But Stepinac never lost his faith, and remains to many the most important inspirational figure of Croatian Catholicism.

As you leave the church, look to the back of the left apse. This strange script is the Glagolitic alphabet *(glagoljca),* invented by Byzantine missionaries Cyril and Methodius in the 9th century to translate the Bible into Slavic languages. Though these missionaries worked mostly in Moravia (today's eastern Czech Republic), their alphabet caught on only here, in Croatia. (Glagolitic was later adapted in Bulgaria to become the Cyrillic alphabet—still used in Serbia, Russia, and other parts east.) In 1991, when Croatia became its own country and nationalism surged, the country flirted with the idea of making this the official alphabet (to differentiate Croatian from the very similar Serbian, and to revive old Croat tradition).

Other Zagreb Museums—Zagreb has lots of forgettable museums, but a few others are worth checking out.

The **Mimara Museum** (Muzej Mimara) houses the eclectic

collection of a wealthy Dalmatian, ranging from ancient artifacts to paintings by Peter Paul Rubens, Rembrandt, Pierre-Auguste Renoir, and Edouard Manet (25 kn, Tue–Sat 10:00–17:00, Thu until 19:00, Sun 10:00–14:00, closed Mon, Rooseveltov trg 5, tel. 01/482-8100).

The **Ivan Meštrović Atelier** features works by the 20th-century Croatian sculptor—see page 496 for more information on this prolific, thoughtful artist (10 kn, Tue–Fri 9:00–14:00, Sat 10:00–18:00, Sun 10:00–14:00, closed Mon, behind St. Mark's Square at Mletačka 8, tel. 01/485-1123).

The **Arts and Crafts Museum** (Muzej za Umjetnost i Obrt) has an excellent decorative arts collection—mostly furniture, ceramics, and clothes—from the Gothic age to the present (20 kn, Tue–Sat 10:00–19:00, Sun 10:00–14:00, closed Mon, Trg Maršala Tita 10, tel. 01/488-2111, www.muo.hr).

And the **Zagreb City History Museum** (Muzej Grada Zagreba) covers just that (20 kn, Tue–Fri 10:00–18:00, Sat–Sun 10:00–13:00, closed Mon, at north end of Gradec at Opatička 20, tel. 01/485-1358, www.mdc.hr/mgz).

SLEEPING

$$$ Plush **Hotel Dubrovnik** has an ideal location (at the bottom of Jelačić Square) and 268 fine business-class rooms (Sb-€91–105, Db-€130–150, Tb-€180, suite-€180, prices soft, non-smoking floors, elevator, Gajeva 1, tel. 01/487-3555, fax 01/481-8447, www.hotel-dubrovnik.htnet.hr, hotel-dubrovnik@hotel-dubrovnik.tel.hr).

$$ **Hotel Jadran** has 48 good rooms near the cathedral, a few blocks east of Jelačić Square (Sb-490 kn, Db-680 kn, Tb-855 kn, some street noise—ask for quiet room, elevator, Vlaška 50,

---

Sleep Code

(€1 = about $1.20, 6 kuna = about $1, country code: 385, area code: 01)
S = Single, **D** = Double/Twin, **T** = Triple, **Q** = Quad, **b** = bathroom, **s** = shower only. English is spoken at each place. Unless otherwise noted, credit cards are accepted, breakfast is included, and the modest tourist tax (7 kn/€1 per person, per night) is not.

To help you sort easily through these listings, I've divided the rooms into three categories based on the price for a standard double room with bath:

$$$ **Higher Priced**—Most rooms 700 kn (€97) or more.
$$ **Moderately Priced**—Most rooms between 400–700 kn (€55–97).
$ **Lower Priced**—Most rooms 400 kn (€55) or less.

tel. 01/455-3777, fax 01/461-2151, www.hup-zagreb.hr, jadran
@hup-zagreb.hr).

$$ Hotel Astoria has 60 drab, old, socialist-era rooms near the
train station (Sb-330 kn, Db-500 kn, Tb-600 kn, elevator, closed in
winter, Petrinjska ulica 71, tel. 01/484-1222, fax 01/484-1212,
hotel-astoria@zg.htnet.hr).

$ Omladinski Hostel Zagreb, ramshackle and desperate for
renovation, has the cheapest beds in the center (€10-dorm bed, S-
€22, Sb-€30, D-€29, Db-€40, more for non-members, cash only,
elevator, handy to the train station at Petrinjska ulica 77, tel. 01/484-
1261, fax 01/484-1269, www.hfhs.hr, zagreb@hfhs.hr).

EATING

You'll find lots of good and handy cafés and restaurants along
Tkalčićeva, behind Jelačić Square. For something quicker and even
more local, grab a bite at the **market.**

TRANSPORTATION CONNECTIONS

From Zagreb by train to: Rijeka (3/day, 4 hrs), **Split** (3–4/day,
7.5–9 hrs, including direct night trains), **Zadar** (1/day, 9-hr night
train with transfer in Knin), **Ljubljana** (8/day, 2.5 hrs), **Vienna**
(2/day, 6.5 hrs), **Budapest** (2/day, 5–7 hrs).

By bus to: Plitvice Lakes National Park (2 hrs, frequency likely
to change in 2005 due to new expressway—see "Getting to Plitvice,"
below), **Split** (2/hr until 18:00, then hrly, 6–9 hrs), **Dubrovnik** (2 in
the early morning, then 4–6 overnight, 11–12.5 hrs), **Korčula**
(1/night, 14 hrs). Bus info: www.akz.hr.

Plitvice Lakes National Park
(Nacionalni Park Plitvička Jezera)

Plitvice (PLEET-veet-seh) is one of Europe's most spectacular nat-
ural wonders. Imagine Niagara Falls diced and sprinkled over a
heavily forested Grand Canyon. There's nothing like this lush valley
of 16 terraced lakes, laced together by waterfalls and miles of pleas-
ant plank walks. Countless cascades and strangely clear and colorful
water make this park a misty natural wonderland. Years ago, after
eight or nine visits, I thought I really knew Europe. Then I discov-
ered Plitvice, and realized you can never exhaust Europe's surprises.

Planning Your Time
Plitvice deserves at least a few good hours. Since it takes some time
to get to the park (2 hrs by car or bus from Zagreb), the most

sensible plan is to spend the night in one of the park's hotels (no character, but comfortable and convenient) or a nearby private home (cheaper, but practical only if you're driving). If you're coming from the north (e.g., Ljubljana), head to Zagreb in the morning, spend a few hours seeing the Croatian capital, then take the bus or drive to Plitvice in the early evening to spend the night at the park. Get up early and hit the trails; by early afternoon, you'll be ready to move

on (perhaps by bus to the coast, or back to Zagreb). Two nights and a full day at Plitvice is probably overkill for all but the most avid hikers.

Getting to Plitvice

Plitvice Lakes National Park, a few miles from the Bosnian border, is two hours by car south of Zagreb on National Road #1 (a.k.a. D1).

By **car** from Zagreb, you'll take the expressway south for about an hour, exiting at Karlovac (marked for 1 and *Plitvice*). From here, D1 takes you directly south about another hour to the park.

Buses leave from Zagreb's main bus station in the direction of Plitvice. Various bus companies handle the route; just go to the ticket window and ask for the next departure (65 kn, trip takes 2–2.5 hrs). With the opening of the new freeway connecting Zagreb and Split, many buses now bypass the park altogether. Confirm that your bus actually will stop at Plitvice (the driver may stop at your specific hotel, or, for the worst-case scenario, he'll drop you at the official Plitvice bus stop, which is a 10-min walk beyond the hotels). Confirm the schedule online (www.akz.hr) or at the Plitvice office in Zagreb (Trg Kralja Komislava 19, tel. 01/461-3586).

By car or bus, you'll see some thought-provoking terrain between Zagreb and Plitvice. As you leave Karlovac, you'll pass through the village of **Turanj,** part of the war zone just a decade ago. It's safe to assume that the destroyed, derelict houses belonged to Serbs who have not come back to reclaim and repair them. Farther along, about 25 miles before Plitvice, you'll pass through the striking village of **Slunj,** picturesquely perched on travertine formations (like Plitvice's) and surrounded by sparkling streams and waterfalls. If you're in a car, this is worth a photo stop. This town, too, looks very different than it did before the war—when it was 30 percent Serb. As in countless other villages in the Croatian interior, the Orthodox church has been destroyed...and locals still seethe when they describe how occupying Serbs "defiled" the town's delicate beauty.

ORIENTATION

(area code: 053)

Plitvice's 16 lakes are divided into the Upper Lakes *(gornja jezera)* and the Lower Lakes *(donja jezera)*. The park officially has two entrances *(ulaz)*, each with ticket windows and snack and gift shops. Entrance 1 is at the bottom of the Lower Lakes, across the busy D1 road from the park's best restaurant, Lička Kuća (see "Eating," page 528). Entrance 2 is about 1.5 miles south, at the cluster of Plitvice's three hotels (Jezero, Plitvice, and Bellevue; see "Sleeping," page 527). There is no town at Plitvice. The nearest village, Mukinje, is a residential community mostly for park workers (boring for tourists, but has some good private room options).

Cost and Hours: The price to enter the park varies by season (July–Aug 95 kn, May–June and Sept–Oct 75 kn, Nov–April 50 kn; ticket good for entire stay, including park entry, boat, shuttle bus, and parking). Park hours are also changeable (generally from 7:00 in summer, 8:00 in spring and fall, and 9:00 in winter; closes at dusk). Night owls should note that the park never "closes"; these hours are for the ticket booths and the boat and shuttle bus system. You can just stroll right into the park at any time, provided that you aren't using the boat or bus. For fewer tour-group crowds, visit early or late in the day.

Tourist Information

A handy map of the trails is on the back of your ticket, and big maps are posted all over the park. The big 20-kn map is a good investment; the 60-kn English-language guidebook is poorly translated and not very helpful (both sold at entrances, hotels, and shops throughout the park). The park has a good Web site: www.np -plitvice.com.

Getting Around Plitvice

Of course, Plitvice is designed for hikers. But the park has a few ways (included in the cost of entry) to help you connect the best parts.

By Shuttle Bus: Buses connect the hotels at Entrance 2 (stop ST2, below Hotel Jezero) with the top of the Upper Lakes (stop ST4) and roughly the bottom of the Lower Lakes (stop ST1, a 10-min walk from Entrance 1). Between Entrance 2 and the top of the Upper Lakes is an intermediate stop (ST3, at Galovac lake)—designed for tour groups, available to anyone, and offering a convenient way to skip the less interesting top half of the Upper Lakes. Buses start running early and continue until late afternoon (frequency depends on demand—generally 3–4/hr; buses run from March until the first snow—often Dec). Note that the park refers to its buses as "trains," which confuses some visitors. Also note that

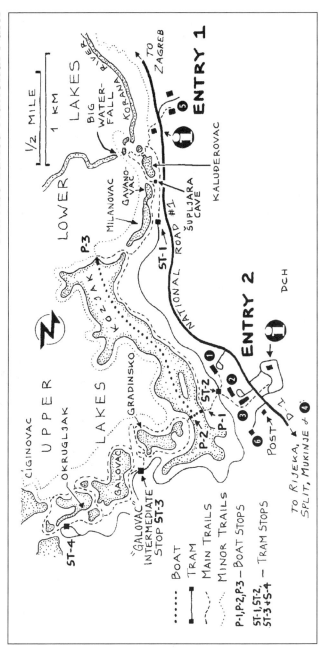

no local buses take you along the major road (D1) that connects the entrances. The only way to get between them without a car is by shuttle bus (within the park) or by foot (about a 40-min walk).

By Boat: Low-impact electric boats ply the waters of the biggest lake, Kozjak, with three stops: below Hotel Jezero (stop P1), the bottom of the Upper Lakes (P2), and at the far end of Kozjak, at the top of the Lower Lakes (P3). From Hotel Jezero to the Upper Lakes is a quick five-minute ride; the boat goes back and forth continuously. From the Upper Lakes to the Lower Lakes takes closer to 20 minutes, and the boat goes about twice per hour—often at the top and bottom of every hour. (With up to 10,000 people a day visiting the park, you might have to wait for a seat on this boat.) Unless the lake freezes (about every 5 years), the boat runs in the off-season, too—though frequency drops to hourly, and it stops running earlier. At P1, you can also rent rowboats (50 kn/hr).

SIGHTS AND ACTIVITIES

Plitvice is a refreshing playground of 16 terraced lakes, separated by natural limestone dams and connected by countless waterfalls. Over time, the water has simultaneously carved out, and, with the help of mineral deposits, built up this fluid landscape.

Plitvice became Croatia's first national park in 1949. On Easter Sunday in 1991, the first shots of Croatia's war with Yugoslavia were fired right here—in fact, the war's first casualty was a park policeman, Josip Jović. The Serbs occupied Plitvice until 1995, and many of the Croatians you'll meet here were evacuated and lived near the coastline as refugees. Today, the war is a  fading memory, and the park is again a popular tourist destination, with 700,000 visitors each year. But Americans are still needlessly wary about coming here; in 2004, only 1.5 percent of the park's visitors came from the United States.

Hiking the Lakes

Plitvice's system of trails and boardwalks makes it possible for visitors to get up close to the park's beauty. (In some places, the paths literally lead right up the middle of a waterfall.) The official park map and signage recommend a variety of hikes, but there's no need to adhere strictly to these suggestions; invest in the big 20-kn map and make your own route.

I like hiking uphill, from Lower to Upper, which offers slightly better head-on views of the best scenery. (Even though this route has a gradual uphill slope, remember that if you go the other way—

The Science of Plitvice

Nearly everyone is impressed by Plitvice, and eventually asks the same question: How did it happen?

Plitvice's magic ingredient is calcium carbonate ($CaCO_3$), which interacts with the plants, algae, and moss in a unique way to create the park's beauty. Remarkably clear water flows into the park from nearby mountains. Minerals coat the vegetation on the bottom of the lakes, reflecting the sunlight to create a striking blue-green coloration. Eventually, this coating becomes thicker, travertine limestone barriers are formed, and waterfalls gradually emerge. The ongoing process means that Plitvice's landscape is always changing.

Wildlife found in the park includes deer, wolves, wildcats, wild boar, and more than 160 species of birds (from eagles to herons to owls). The lakes (and local menus) are full of trout. Perhaps most importantly, Plitvice is home to the brown bear—now extremely endangered in Europe. You'll see bears, the park's mascot, plastered all over tourist literature (and in the form of a scary representative in the lobby of Hotel Jezero).

downhill—there's a steep climb back up at the end.) Below, I've described a one-way hiking route (going uphill), divided between Upper and Lower. Walking briskly and with a few photo stops, figure on an hour for the Lower Lakes, an hour for the Upper Lakes, and a half hour to connect them by boat.

Start at the...

Lower Lakes (Donja Jezera)—The lower half of Plitvice's lakes are accessible from Entrance 1. If you start here, the route marked *G2* (intended for groups, but doable for anyone) leads you along the boardwalks to Kozjak, the big lake that connects the Lower and the Upper Lakes (see below).

From the entrance, you'll descend down a steep path with lots of switchbacks, as well as thrilling views over the canyon of the Lower Lakes. As you reach water level and begin to follow the boardwalks, you'll have great up-close views of the travertine formations that make up Plitvice's many waterfalls. See any trout? If you're tempted to throw in a line, don't. Fishing is strictly forbidden. (Besides, they're happy.)

Near the beginning of the Lower Lakes trails, a 10-minute detour takes you down to the **Big Waterfall** (Veliki Slap). It's the biggest of Plitvice's waterfalls, where the Plitvica River plunges 250 feet over a cliff into the valley below. Depending on recent rainfall, the force of the Big Waterfall varies from a light mist to a thundering deluge.

After seeing the Big Waterfall, continue on the boardwalks. On the left, a smaller trail branches off towards **Šupljara Cave.** You can actually climb through this slippery cave all the way up to the trail overlooking the Lower Lakes (not recommended). This unassuming cavern is a surprisingly big draw. In the 1960s, several German and Italian Spaghetti Westerns were filmed at Plitvice and in other parts of Croatia (which, to European eyes, has terrain similar to the American West). The most famous, *Der Schatz im Silbersee (The Treasure in Silver Lake)*, was filmed here at Plitvice, and the treasure was hidden in this cave. The movie is still a favorite in Germany—complete with *Deutsch*-speaking "Native Americans"—and popular theme tours bring German tourists to movie locations here in Croatia.

After the cave, you'll stick to the east side of the lakes, then cross over one more time to the west, where you'll cut though a comparatively dull forest. You'll emerge at a pit-stop-perfect clearing with squat-and-aim WCs, picnic tables, a souvenir shop, and a self-service restaurant. This is where you can catch the shuttle boat across Lake Kozjak to the bottom of the Upper Lakes (see "Getting Around Plitvice," above). While you're waiting for the next boat (usually every 30 min), visit the friendly old ladies in the kiosks selling wheels of cheese and a variety of strudel (10 kn per piece).

Lake Kozjak (Jezero Kozjak)—The park's biggest lake, Kozjak, connects the Lower and Upper Lakes. The 20-minute boat ride between Plitvice's two halves offers a great chance for a breather. You can hike between the lakes along the west side of Kozjak, but the scenery's not nearly as good as the rest of the park.

Upper Lakes (Gornja Jezera)—Focus on the lower half of the Upper Lakes. That's where nearly all the exotic beauty is. From the boat dock, signs for *C* and *G2* direct you up to Gradinsko Lake through the most striking scenery in the whole park. Enjoy the stroll, take your time, and be thankful you remembered to bring extra film.

At the top of Galovac Lake, you'll have three options: Make your hike a loop by continuing around the lake (following *H* and *G1* signs back to the P2 boat dock); hike a few steps up to the ST3 bus stop to catch the shuttle bus back to the hotel; or continue up to the top of the lakes. For a short visit, I'd return to the P2 boat dock by foot. For a really short visit—or a lazy one—catch the bus. To get away from the crowds and feel like you've covered the lakes thoroughly, continue to the top of the park. From here on up, the scenery is less stunning, the waterfalls are fewer and farther between, and the crowds thin out. If you do continue up to the top of the Upper Lakes, you'll finish at shuttle bus stop ST4 (with food stalls and a WC), where you can easily get a short ride back to Entrance 2. Nice work.

Sleep Code

(€1 = about $1.20, country code: 385, area code: 053)
English is spoken, credit cards are accepted, and breakfast is included at each place. The tourist tax (€1 per person, per day) is not included in these prices.

To help you sort easily through these listings, I've divided the rooms into three categories based on the price for a standard double room with bath in peak season:

$$$ **Higher Priced**—Most rooms €85 or more.
$$ **Moderately Priced**—Most rooms between €65–85.
$ **Lower Priced**—Most rooms €65 or less.

SLEEPING

At the Park

The most convenient way to sleep at Plitvice is to use the park's lodges. Book any of these hotels through the same office (reservation tel. 053/751-015, fax 053/751-013, www.np-plitvice.com, reservations@np-plitvice.com; reception numbers are listed below for each hotel in case you need to be reached, or to reach a guest at a particular hotel).

$$$ Hotel Jezero is big and modern, with all the comfort—and charm—of a Holiday Inn. It's well-located right at the park entrance, and offers 200 rooms that feel newish, but generally have at least one thing that's broken. Parkside rooms have big glass doors and balconies (July–Aug: Sb-€76, Db-€104; May–June and Sept–Oct: Sb-€69, Db-€94; Nov–April: Sb-€54, Db-€72, elevator, reception tel. 053/751-400).

$$ Hotel Plitvice, a little less plush than Jezero, offers 50 rooms and mod, wide-open public spaces on two floors with no elevators (reception tel. 053/751-100). For rooms, choose from economy (fine, older-feeling; July–Aug: Sb-€60, Db-€78; May–June and Sept–Oct: Sb-€52, Db-€70; Nov–April: Sb-€45, Db-€60), standard (just a teeny bit bigger; July–Aug: Sb-€62, Db-€84; May–June and Sept–Oct: Sb-€58, Db-€76; Nov–April: Sb-€46, Db-€62), or superior (bigger still, with a sitting area; July–Aug: Sb-€70, Db-€90; May–June and Sept–Oct: Sb-€65, Db-€84; Nov–April: Sb-€50, Db-€70).

$$ Hotel Bellevue is simple and bare-bones (no TVs or elevator). It has an older feel to it, but the price is right and the 80 rooms are sleepable (July–Aug: Sb-€54, Db-€74; May–June and Sept–Oct: Sb-€48, Db-€66; Nov–April: Sb-€40, Db-€52, reception tel. 053/751-700).

Near the Park

While the park's lodges are the easiest choice for non-drivers, those with a car should consider these cheaper alternatives.

$ Knežević Guest House, with 11 bright, modern rooms, is a new family-run hotel a five-minute drive south of the park in the nondescript workers' town of Mukinje. The street is new, but the yard is peaceful, with an inviting hammock (Db-€33, breakfast-€5, family rooms; driving south from the park, take first right turn into Mukinje and you'll see #57; tel. 053/774-081, mobile 098/168-7576, daughter Christina SE).

$ *Sobe:* Drivers looking for character and preferring to spend €40, rather than €80, should simply find a room in a private home, advertised with *sobe* signs for miles on either side of the park. For details, see "Dalmatian Accommodation," page 480.

EATING

The park runs all of the restaurants at Plitvice. These places are handy, and the food is tasty and affordable. If you're staying at the hotels, you have the option of paying for **half-board** with your room (lunch or dinner, €11 each May–Oct, €8 each Nov–April). This is designed to be used with the restaurants inside hotels Jezero and Plitvice, but you can also use the voucher at other park eateries (you'll pay the difference if the bill is more). The half-board option is worth doing if you're here for dinner, but don't lock yourself in for lunch—you'll want more flexibility as you explore Plitvice (excellent picnic spots and decent food stands abound inside the park).

Hotel Jezero and **Hotel Plitvice** both have big restaurants with good food and friendly, professional service (half-board for dinner, described above, is a good deal; or order à la carte: fish 50–60 kn, meat dishes 80–100 kn; both open daily until 23:00).

Lička Kuća, across the pedestrian overpass from Entrance 1, has a wonderfully dark and smoky atmosphere around a huge open-air wood-fired grill (grilled trout-50 kn, more elaborate dishes up to 100 kn, daily 11:00–24:00, tel. 053/751-024).

Restaurant Poljana, behind Hotel Bellevue, has the same boring, park-lodge atmosphere in both of its sections: cheap, self-service cafeteria (25–40 kn) and sit-down restaurant with open wood-fired grill (same choices and prices as the better-atmosphere Lička Kuća, above; both parts open daily but closed in winter, tel. 053/751-092).

For **picnic** fixings, there's a small supermarket across road D1 from Entrance 2. The boat docks come with a few eating options. At the P3 boat dock, locals sell homemade goodies, and at the P1 boat dock, you can buy grilled meat and drinks.

TRANSPORTATION CONNECTIONS

To reach the park, see "Getting to Plitvice," above. Moving on from Plitvice is trickier. Buses pass by the park in each direction—northbound (to **Zagreb,** 2–2.5 hrs) and southbound (to coastal destinations such as **Split,** 4–7 hrs, and **Dubrovnik,** 9–10 hrs).

There is no bus station—just a low-profile *Plitvice Center* bus stop shelter: To reach it from the park, go out to the main road from either Hotel Jezero or Hotel Plitvice, then turn right; the bus stops are just after the pedestrian overpass. The one on the hotel side of the road is for buses headed for the coast; the stop on the opposite side is for Zagreb. But here's the catch: Many buses that pass through Plitvice don't stop (either because they're full, or because they don't have anyone to drop off there). You can stand at the bus stop and try to flag one down, but it's safer to get help from the park's hotel staff. They can help you figure out which bus suits your schedule, then they'll call ahead to be sure the bus stops for you. If you don't want to make the 10-minute walk out to the bus stop, someone at the hotel can usually drive you out for a modest fee.

GATEWAYS
to EASTERN EUROPE
Vienna, Berlin, and Dresden

In this guidebook designed to help you explore the "Best of Eastern Europe," I've included three gateway cities—Vienna, Berlin, and Dresden—that are actually part of Western Europe, but serve as logical springboards into the East.

Vienna is one of the grandest cities of Europe, very reasonably called the "eastern Paris." It was built to rule the vast, multinational Hapsburg Empire, which once included nearly all of the destinations in this book...but it started and lost World War I, and consequently, its holdings. Today, Vienna is the capital of Austria—small, landlocked, and relatively insignificant. In its heyday, the Hapsburg Empire (later called the Austro-Hungarian Empire) was Europe's superpower, and most of its citizens were Slavic, rather than German. Vienna's influence is particularly strong in Prague, Budapest, and Slovenia. Historically and culturally, it makes sense to splice Vienna into any eastern adventure. And logistically, Vienna is a natural gateway to Slovenia, Budapest, and Prague.

Berlin, the capital of a newly united Germany, was also the capital of East Germany before 1989. For a generation, it was cut off from the West, accessible only by a thin ground and air corridor to the rest of Germany and Western Europe. Today, it's a thriving cultural and economic powerhouse, as well as a prime gateway to Poland and the Czech Republic.

Dresden is most famous today for its utter destruction by Allied bombing in World War II. Having been buried behind the Iron Curtain for a generation, it's generally not even considered when Americans plan a German vacation. But it's a cultural capital with a fascinating history and world-class museums, and it makes for an easy stop between Berlin and Prague. Along with Berlin, Dresden is the most important destination in what used to be the communist German Democratic Republic.

Hurdling the Language Barrier
German is the predominant language in this book's gateway cities. German—like English, Dutch, Swedish, and Norwegian—is a Germanic language, making it easier on most American ears than Slavic languages (such as Czech and Polish) or the mysterious Hungarian tongue. While many people in Eastern Europe speak

at least some English, those who don't are likely to know German (especially in Croatia, a favorite vacation destination for Germans and Austrians).

Key German Phrases

English	German	Pronounced*
Hello.	Guten Tag.	GOO-tehn tahg
Do you speak English?	Sprechen Sie Englisch?	SHPREHKH-ehn zee ENG-lish
yes / no	ja / nein	yah / nīn
Please. / You're welcome. / Can I help you?	Bitte.	BIT-teh
Thank you.	Danke.	DAHNG-keh
I'm sorry.	Es tut mir leid.	ehs toot meer līt
Excuse me. (to pass or to get attention)	Entschuldigung.	ehnt-SHOOL-dig-oong
Good.	Gut.	goot
Goodbye.	Auf Wiedersehen.	owf VEE-der-zayn
one / two	eins / zwei	īns / tsvī
three / four	drei / vier	drī / feer
five / six	fünf / sechs	fewnf / zehks
seven / eight	sieben / acht	ZEE-behn / ahkht
nine / ten	neun / zehn	noyn / tsayn
hundred	hundert	HOON-dert
thousand	tausend	TOW-sehnd
How much?	Wie viel?	vee feel
local currency	euro (€)	OY-roh
Where is...?	Wo ist...?	voh ist
...the toilet	...die Toilette	dee toy-LEH-teh
men	Herren	HEHR-ehn
women	Damen	DAH-mehn
water / coffee	Wasser / Kaffee	VAH-ser / kah-FAY
beer / wine	Bier / Wein	beer / vīn
Cheers!	Prost!	prohst
the bill	die Rechnung	dee REHKH-noong

* When using the phonetics, pronounce ī as the long i sound in "light."

VIENNA
(Wien)

Vienna is a head without a body. For 640 years the capital of the once-grand Hapsburg Empire, she started and lost World War I, and with it her far-flung holdings. Today, you'll find an elegant capital of 1.6 million people (one-fifth of Austria's population) ruling a small, relatively insignificant country. Culturally, historically, and from a sightseeing point of view, this city is the sum of its illustrious past. The city of Freud, Brahms, Maria Theresa's many children, a gaggle of Strausses, and a dynasty of Holy Roman Emperors ranks right up there with Paris, London, and Rome.

Vienna has always been the easternmost city of the West. In Roman times, it was Vindobona, on the Danube facing the Germanic barbarians. In the Middle Ages, Vienna was Europe's bastion against the Ottoman Turks—a Christian breakwater against the riding tide of Islam (hordes of up to 200,000 Turks were repelled in 1529 and 1683). During this period, as the Turks dreamed of conquering what they called "the big apple" for their sultan, Vienna lived with a constant fear of invasion (and the Hapsburg court ruled from safer Prague). You'll notice none of Vienna's great palaces were built until after 1683, when the Turkish threat was finally over. While Vienna's old walls held out the Turks, World War II bombs destroyed nearly a quarter of the city's buildings. In modern times, neutral Austria and Vienna took a big bite out of the USSR's Warsaw Pact buffer zone. And today, Vienna is a springboard for newly popular destinations in Eastern Europe.

The truly Viennese person is not Austrian, but a second-generation Hapsburg cocktail, with grandparents from the distant corners of the old empire—Hungary, the Czech Republic, Slovakia, Poland, Slovenia, Croatia, Bosnia, Serbia, Romania, and Italy. Vienna is the melting-pot capital of a now-collapsed empire that, in its heyday, consisted of 60 million people—only eight million of whom were Austrian.

Greater Vienna

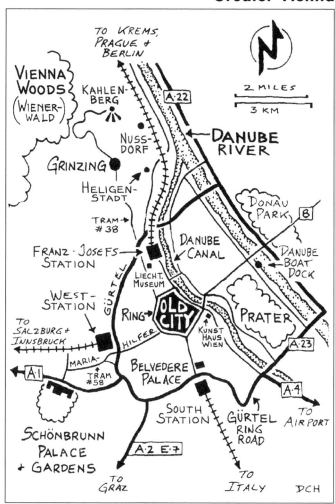

TO KREMS, PRAGUE & BERLIN

VIENNA WOODS (WIENER-WALD)

KAHLEN-BERG

A-22

N

2 MILES
3 KM

NUSS-DORF

DANUBE RIVER

GRINZING

HELIGEN-STADT

DONAU PARK

B

TRAM #38

FRANZ·JOSEFS STATION

DANUBE CANAL

DANUBE BOAT DOCK

GÜRTEL

LIECHT. MUSEUM

WEST-STATION

RING→

OLD CITY

PRATER

TO SALZBURG & INNSBRUCK

HILFER

KUNST HAUS WIEN

A-23

MARIA-

TRAM #58

A-1

BELVEDERE PALACE

SOUTH STATION

GÜRTEL RING ROAD

A-4

TO AIRPORT

SCHÖNBRUNN PALACE & GARDENS

A-2 E-7

TO GRAZ

TO ITALY

DCH

In 1900, Vienna's 2.2 million inhabitants made it the world's fifth-largest city (after New York, London, Paris, and Berlin). But these days—with dogs being the preferred "child" and the average Viennese mother having only 1.3 children—the population is down to around 1.6 million.

The Hapsburgs, who ruled the enormous Austrian Empire from 1273 to 1918, shaped Vienna. Some ad agency has convinced Vienna to make Elisabeth, wife of Emperor Franz Josef—with her narcissism and struggles with royal life—the darling of the local tourist scene. You'll see "Sissy" all over town. But stay focused on the Hapsburgs who mattered: Maria Theresa (r. 1740–1780, see page 546) and Franz Josef (r. 1848–1916, see page 556) are the most important.

After the defeat of Napoleon and the Congress of Vienna in 1815 (which shaped 19th-century Europe), Vienna enjoyed its violin-filled belle époque, which shaped our romantic image of the city—fine wine, chocolates, cafés, and waltzes.

Planning Your Time

For a big city, Vienna is pleasant and laid-back. Packed with sights, it's worth two days and two nights on the speediest trip. To be grand-tour efficient, you could sleep in and sleep out on the train (Berlin, Kraków, Venice, Rome, the Swiss Alps, Paris, and the Rhine are each handy night trains away). But then you'd miss the Danube and Melk. I'd come in from Salzburg via Hallstatt, Melk, and the Danube and spend two days this way:

Day 1: 9:00–Circle the Ring by tram, following my "Do-It-Yourself Ringstrasse Tram Orientation Tour" (page 542); 10:00–Drop by TI for any planning and ticket needs, then see the sights in Vienna's old center (using my self-guided commentary)—Monument Against War and Fascism, Kaisergruft crypt, Kärntner Strasse, St. Stephan's Cathedral, and Graben; 12:00–Finger sandwiches for lunch at Buffet Trzesniewski; 13:00–Tour the Hofburg and treasury; 16:00–Hit one more museum or shop, or browse and people-watch; 19:30–Choose classical music (concert or opera), House of Music museum, or *Heurige* wine garden.

Day 2: 9:00–Schönbrunn Palace (drivers: This is conveniently on the way out of town toward Salzburg; horse-lovers: You'll need to rearrange—or rush the palace—to see the Lipizzaner stallions' morning practice); 12:00–Back in central Vienna for lunch at Naschmarkt or Rosenberger Markt; 13:00–Tour the Opera; 14:00–Kunsthistorisches Museum; 16:00–Your choice of the many sights left to see in Vienna; Evening–See Day 1 evening options.

ORIENTATION

(area code: 01)

Vienna—Wien in German (pronounced "veen")—sits between the Vienna Woods (Wienerwald) and the Danube (Donau). To the southeast is industrial sprawl. The Alps, which arc across Europe from Marseille, end at Vienna's wooded hills, providing a popular playground for walking and sipping new wine. This greenery's momentum carries on into the city. More than half of Vienna is parkland, filled with ponds, gardens, trees, and statue-maker memories of Austria's glory days.

Think of the city map as a target. The bull's-eye is the cathedral, the first circle is the Ringstrasse, and the second is the Gürtel outer-belt. The old town—snuggling around towering St. Stephan's Cathedral south of the Danube—is bound tightly by the Ringstrasse. The Ring, marking what was the city wall, circles the first district (or *Bezirk*). The Gürtel, a broader ring road, contains the rest of downtown (*Bezirkes 2–9*).

Addresses start with the *Bezirk,* followed by street and building number. Any address higher than the ninth *Bezirk* is beyond the Gürtel, far from the center. The middle two digits of Vienna's postal codes show the *Bezirk*. The address "7, Lindengasse 4" is in the seventh district, #4 on Linden Street. Its postal code would be 1070. Nearly all your sightseeing will be done in the core first district or along the Ringstrasse. As a tourist, concern yourself only with this compact old center. When you do, sprawling Vienna suddenly becomes manageable.

Tourist Information

Vienna's one real tourist office is a block behind the Opera House at Albertinaplatz (daily 9:00–19:00, tel. 01/24555, press 2 for English info, www.info.wien.at). Confirm your sightseeing plans and pick up the free and essential city map with a list of museums and hours (also available at most hotels), the monthly program of concerts (called *Wien-Programm*—includes daily calendar and information on the contemporary cultural scene, including live music, jazz, walks, expositions, and evening museum options), the biannual city guide *(Vienna Journal),* and the youth guide *(Vienna Hype).* The TI also books rooms for a €2.90 fee. While hotel and ticket-booking agencies at the train stations and airport can answer questions and give out maps and brochures, I'd rely on the TI if possible.

Consider the TI's handy €3.60 ***Vienna from A to Z*** booklet. Every important building sports a numbered flag banner that keys into this guidebook. *A to Z* numbers are keyed into the TI's city map. When lost, find one of the "famous-building flags" and match its number to your map. If you're at a famous building, check the map to see which other key numbers are nearby, then check the *A to Z* book description to see if you want to go in. This system is especially helpful for those just wandering aimlessly among Vienna's historic charms.

The much-promoted €17 **Vienna Card** might save the busy sightseer a few euros. It gives you a 72-hour transit pass (worth €12.50) and discounts of 10–50 percent at the city's museums. (Note: Seniors and students will do better with their own discounts.)

Arrival in Vienna

By Train at the West Station (Westbahnhof): Train travelers arriving from Munich, Salzburg, and Melk land at the Westbahnhof.

The *Reisebüro am Bahnhof* books hotels (for a €4 fee), has maps, answers questions, and has a train info desk (daily 7:30–21:00). The Westbahnhof also has a grocery store (daily 5:30–23:00), ATMs, Internet access, change offices, and storage facilities. Airport buses and taxis wait in front of the station.

To get to the city center (and most likely, your hotel), take the U-3 metro (buy your ticket or transit pass—described below—from a *Tabak* shop in the station or from a machine). Blue *U-3* signs lead down to the metro tracks (direction: Simmering for Mariahilfer Strasse hotels or the center). If your hotel is along Mariahilfer Strasse, your stop is on this line (see page 581). If you're sleeping in the center or just sightseeing, ride five stops to Stephansplatz, escalate in the exit direction: Stephansplatz, and you'll hit the cathedral. The TI is a five-minute stroll down the busy Kärntner Strasse pedestrian street.

By Train at the South Station (Südbahnhof): Those arriving from Italy and Prague land here. The Südbahnhof has all the services, left luggage, and a TI (daily 9:00–19:00). To reach Vienna's center, follow the S *(Schnellbahn)* signs to the right and down the stairs, and take any train in the direction: Floridsdorf; transfer in two stops (at Landsstrasse/Wien Mitte) to the U-3 line, direction Ottakring, which goes directly to Stephansplatz and Mariahilfer Strasse hotels. Tram D also goes to the Ring, and bus #13A goes to Mariahilfer Strasse.

By Train at Franz Josefs Station: If you're coming from Krems (in the Danube Valley), you'll arrive at Vienna's Franz Josefs station. From here, take tram D into town. Better yet, get off your train at Spittelau (the stop before Franz Josefs) and use its handy U-Bahn station.

By Plane: Vienna's airport is 12 miles from the center (tel. 01/7007-22233, www.viennaairport.com). It's connected to the very central Wien-Mitte station by S-Bahn (S-7 yellow, €3, 2/hr, 24 min). A speedier new City Airport Train (CAT) connects the airport to Wien-Mitte (green signs, €9, 2/hr, 16 min, www.cityairporttrain.com). Express airport buses (parked immediately in front of the arrival hall, €6, 3/hr, 30 min, buy ticket from driver) go conveniently to Schwedenplatz, Westbahnhof, and Südbahnhof, from where it's easy to continue by subway. Taxis into town cost about €35 (including €10 airport surcharge). Hotels arrange for fixed-rate car service to the airport (€30, 30-min ride).

Helpful Hints

Banking: ATMs are everywhere. Banks are open weekdays roughly from 8:00 to 15:00 (until 17:30 on Thu). After hours, you can change money at train stations, the airport, post offices, or the American Express office (Mon–Fri 9:00–17:30, Sat 9:00–12:00, closed Sun, Kärntner Strasse 21–23, tel. 01/5154-0456).

Internet Access: The TI has a list of Internet cafés. BigNet is the dominant outfit (www.bignet.at), with lots of stations at Kärntner Strasse 61 (daily 10:00–24:00) and Höher Markt 8–9 (daily 10:00–24:00). Surfland Internet Café is near the Opera (daily 10:00–23:00, Krugerstrasse 10, tel. 01/512-7701).

Post Offices: Choose from the main post office (Postgasse in center, open 24 hrs daily, handy metered phones), Westbahnhof (daily 6:00–23:00), Südbahnhof (daily 7:00–22:00), or near the Opera (Mon–Fri 7:00–19:00, closed Sat–Sun, Krugerstrasse 13).

English Bookstores: Consider the **British Bookshop** (Mon–Fri 9:30–18:30, Sat 9:30–17:00, closed Sun, at corner of Weihburggasse and Seilerstätte, tel. 01/512-1945; same hours at branch at Mariahilfer Strasse 4, tel. 01/522-6730) or **Shakespeare & Co.** (Mon–Sat 9:00–19:00, closed Sun, north of Höher Markt square, Sterngasse 2, tel. 01/535-5053).

Travel Agency: Intropa is convenient at Neuer Markt 8, with good service for flights and train tickets (Mon–Fri 9:00–18:00, Sat 10:00–13:00, closed Sun, tel. 01/513-4000). Train tickets come with a €2 service charge when purchased from an agency, rather than at the station—a great convenience.

Getting Around Vienna

By Bus, Tram, and Metro: Take full advantage of Vienna's simple, cheap, and super-efficient transit system, which includes trams, buses, subway (U-Bahn), and faster suburban trains (S-Bahn, or *Schnellbahn*). I use the tram mostly to zip around the Ring (tram #1 or #2) and take the U-Bahn to outlying sights or hotels. Numbered lines (such as #38) are trams, and numbers followed by an *A* (such as #38A) are buses. The smooth, modern trams are Porsche-designed, with "backpack technology" locating the engines and mechanical hardware on the roofs for a lower ride and easier entry. Lines that begin with *U* (e.g., U-3) are U-Bahn lines (these metro routes are designated by the end-of-the-line stops). Blue lines are the speedier S-Bahns. Take a moment to study the eye-friendly city-center map on metro station walls to internalize how the transit system can help you. The free tourist map has essentially all the lines marked, making the too-big €1.50 transit map unnecessary (information tel. 01/790-9105).

Trams, buses, and the metro all use the same tickets. Buy your tickets from *Tabak* shops, station machines, *Vorverkauf* offices in the station, or on board (just on trams, single tickets only, more expensive). You have lots of choices:

- Single tickets (€1.50, €2 if bought on tram, good for 1 journey with necessary transfers)
- 24-hour transit pass (€5)
- 72-hour transit pass (€12)

- 7-day transit pass (€12.50, pass always starts on Mon)
- "8-day card" *(Acht Tage Karte)*—eight full days of free transportation for €24 (can be shared—for example, 4 people for 2 days each). With a per-person cost of €3/day (compared to €5/day for a 24-hour pass), this can be a real saver for groups. Kids under 15 travel free on Sundays and holidays.

Stamp a time on your ticket as you enter the metro system, tram, or bus (stamp it only the first time for a multiple-use pass). Cheaters pay a stiff €44 fine if caught—and then they make you buy a ticket. Rookies miss stops because they fail to open the door. Push buttons, pull latches—do whatever it takes. Study the excellent wall-mounted street map before you exit the metro. Choosing the right exit—signposted from the moment you step off the train—saves lots of walking.

By Taxi: Vienna's comfortable, civilized, and easy-to-flag-down taxis start at €2.50. You'll pay about €7 to go from the Opera to the Westbahnhof. Pay only what's on the meter—any surcharges (other then the €2 fee added to fares when you telephone them) are just crude cabbie rip-offs.

By Car with Driver: Consider the luxury of having your own car and driver. Johann (John) Lichtl is a kind, honest, English-speaking cabbie who can take up to four passengers in his car (€25/1 hr, €20/hr for 2 or more hours, mobile 0676/670-6750). Consider using Johann to day-trip to the Wachau Valley (see previous chapter, €100, up to 8 hrs), or to drive you to Salzburg, with Wachau sightseeing en route (€180, up to 12 hours; other trips by negotiation).

By Bike: Vienna is a great city for biking—*if* you own a bike. Bike rental is a hassle (get list at TI). There are no bike-rental options in the center; the nearest is out at Prater Park (see page 570). The bikes you'll see parked in public racks all over town are part of a loaner system that is only workable for locals with mobile phones. The bike path along the Ring is wonderfully entertaining.

By Buggy: Rich romantics get around by traditional horse and buggy. The horse buggies, called *Fiakers,* clip-clop tourists on tours lasting 20 minutes (€40—old town), 40 minutes (€65—old town and the Ring), or one hour (€95—all of the above, but more thorough). You can share the ride and cost with up to five people. Because it's a kind of guided tour, before settling on a carriage, talk to a few drivers and pick one who's fun and speaks English.

TOURS

Walks—The TI's *Walks in Vienna* brochure describes Vienna's many guided walks. The basic, 90-minute "Vienna First Glance" introductory walk is given daily throughout the summer (€11, 14:00 from near the Opera, in English and German, tel. 01/894-5363, www.wienguide.at).

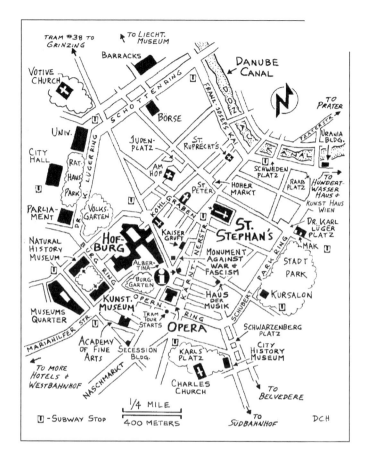

Bus Tours—Yellow Cab Sightseeing offers a one-hour, €12, quickie double-decker bus tour with recorded commentary, departing at the top of each hour (10:00–17:00) from in front of the Opera (corner of Operngasse). Vienna Sightseeing offers hop-on, hop-off tours covering 13 predictable sightseeing stops (departures from Opera at top of each hour 10:00–17:00, recorded commentary). Given Vienna's excellent public transportation and this outfit's meager one-bus-per-hour frequency, I'd take this not to hop on and off, but only to get the narrated orientation drive through town (€20 for 24-hr ticket, or €12 if you stay on for the full 60-minute circular ride—skipping the hop-on, hop-off privileges). Their 3.5-hour Vienna city sights tour includes a visit to Schönbrunn Palace and a bus tour around town (€34; April–Oct 3/day—9:45, 10:30, and 14:00; Nov–March 2/day—9:45 and 14:00; call 01/7124-6830 to book this or get info on other tours). These leave from the Südbahnhof or, 30 minutes earlier, from the Opera.

ℓnna at a Glance

ng, world-famous opera house. **Hours:** Visit by
only, daily in English; July–Aug at 11:00, 13:00,
often at 10:00 and 16:00; Sept–June fewer tours,
ar…… …ll ahead to confirm tour times.

▲▲▲**Hofburg Treasury** The Hapsburgs' collection of jewels, crowns, and other valuables—the best on the Continent. **Hours:** Wed–Mon 10:00–18:00, closed Tue.

▲▲▲**Kunsthistorisches Museum** World-class exhibit of the Hapsburgs' art collection, including Raphael, Titian, Caravaggio, Bosch, and Brueghel. **Hours:** Tue–Sun 10:00–18:00, Thu until 21:00, closed Mon.

▲▲▲**Schönbrunn Palace** Spectacular summer residence of the Hapsburgs, similar in grandeur to Versailles. **Hours:** April–Oct daily 8:30–17:00, July–Aug daily until 18:00, Nov–March daily 8:30–16:30, reservations recommended.

▲▲**Albertina Museum** Newly opened Hapsburg residence with ho-hum apartments and world-class permanent and temporary exhibits. **Hours:** Daily 10:00–18:00, Wed until 21:00.

▲▲**St. Stephan's Cathedral** Beautiful, enormous Gothic cathedral in the center of Vienna. **Hours:** Church doors open Mon–Sat 6:00–22:00, Sun 7:00–22:00, officially only open for tourists Mon–Sat 8:30–11:30 & 13:00–16:30, Sun 13:00–16:30.

▲▲**Stephansplatz, Graben, and Kohlmarkt** Atmospheric pedestrian squares and streets around the cathedral. **Hours:** Always open.

▲▲**Hofburg Imperial Apartments** Lavish main residence of the Hapsburgs. **Hours:** Daily 9:00–17:00.

▲▲**Hofburg New Palace Museums** Uncrowded collection of armor, musical instruments, and ancient Greek statues in the elegant halls of a Hapsburg palace. **Hours:** Wed–Mon 10:00–18:00, closed Tue.

▲▲**Kaisergruft** Crypt for the Hapsburg royalty. **Hours:** Daily 9:30–16:00.

▲▲**Belvedere Palace** Elegant palace of Prince Eugene of Savoy, with a collection of 19th- and 20th-century Austrian art (including Klimt). **Hours:** Tue–Sun 10:00–18:00, closed Mon.

▲▲Haus der Musik Modern musuem with interactive exhibits on Vienna's favorite pastime. **Hours:** Daily 10:00–22:00.

▲Monument Against War and Fascism Powerful four-part statue remembering victims of the Nazis. **Hours:** Always open.

▲Kärntner Strasse Vienna's lively main pedestrian drag, connecting the Opera with the cathedral. **Hours:** Always open.

▲Lipizzaner Museum Displays dedicated to the regal Lipizzaner Stallions; horse-lovers should check out their practice sessions. **Hours:** Museum open daily 9:00–18:00, stallions practice across the street roughly Feb–June and Sept–Oct, Tue–Sat 10:00–12:00 when the horses are in town, call to confirm.

▲Augustinian Church Hapsburg marriage church, now hosting an 11:00 Sunday Mass with wonderful music. **Hours:** Open daily.

▲Imperial Furniture Collection Eclectic collection of Hapsburg furniture. **Hours:** Tue–Sun 10:00–18:00, closed Mon.

▲Naschmarkt Sprawling, lively, people-filled outdoor market. **Hours:** Mon–Fri 7:00–18:00, Sat 6:00–18:00, closed Sun, closes earlier in winter.

▲Natural History Museum Big building facing Kunsthistorisches Museum, featuring the ancient *Venus of Willendorf*. **Hours:** Wed–Mon 9:00–18:30, Wed until 21:00, closed Tue.

▲Academy of Fine Arts Small but exciting collection with works by Bosch, Botticelli, Rubens, Guardi, and Van Dyck. **Hours:** Tue–Sun 10:00–18:00, closed Mon.

▲Liechtenstein Museum Recently reopened Baroque art collection. **Hours:** Wed–Mon 9:00–20:00, closed Tue.

▲KunstHausWien Modern art museum dedicated to zany local artist/environmentalist Hundertwasser. **Hours:** Daily 10:00–19:00.

▲Dorotheum Vienna's highbrow auction house. **Hours:** Mon–Fri 10:00–18:00, Sat 9:00–17:00, closed Sun.

Local Guides—The tourist board Web site (www.info.wien.at) has a long list of local guides with specialties and contact information. Lisa Zeiler is a good English-speaking guide (2-hr walks for €120—if she's booked, she can set you up with another guide, tel. 01/402-3688, lisa.zeiler@gmx.at). Ursula Klaus, an art scholar specializing in turn-of-the-20th-century Vienna, enjoys tailoring tours to specific interests (especially music, art, and architecture). She does half-day tours for €120 (tel. 01/522-8556, mobile 0676/421-4884, ursula.klaus@aon.at).

Do-It-Yourself Ringstrasse Tram Orientation Tour

In the 1860s, Emperor Franz Josef had the city's ingrown medieval wall torn down and replaced with a grand boulevard 190 feet wide. The road, arcing nearly three miles around the city's core, predates all the buildings that line it—so what you'll see is very "neo": neo-classical, neo-Gothic, and neo-Renaissance. One of Europe's great streets, it's lined with many of the city's top sights. Trams #1 and #2 and a great bike path circle the whole route—and so should you.

This self-guided tram tour, rated ▲▲, gives you a fun orientation and a ridiculously quick glimpse of the major sights as you glide by (€1.50, 30-min circular tour). Tram #1 goes clockwise; tram #2, counterclockwise. Most sights are on the outside, so use tram #2 (sit on the right, ideally in the front seat of the front car; or—for maximum view and minimum air—sit in the bubble-front seat of the second car). Start immediately across the street from the Opera House. You can jump on and off as you go (trams come every 5 min). Read ahead and pay attention—these sights can fly by. Let's go:

➲ Immediately on the left: The city's main pedestrian drag, Kärntner Strasse, leads to the zigzag roof of **St. Stephan's Cathedral.** This tram tour makes a 360-degree circle around the cathedral, staying about this same distance from it.

➲ At first bend (before first stop): Look right, toward the tall fountain and the guy on a horse. Schwarzenberg Platz shows off its **equestrian statue** of Prince Charles Schwarzenberg, who fought Napoleon. Behind that is the Russian monument (behind the fountain), which was built in 1945 as a forced thanks to the Soviets for liberating Austria from the Nazis. Formerly a sore point, it's now just ignored. Beyond that (out of sight, on tram D route) is Belvedere Palace (see page 567).

➲ Going down Schubertring, you reach the huge **Stadtpark** (City Park) on the right, which honors many great Viennese musicians and composers with statues. At the beginning of the park, the gold-and-cream concert hall behind the trees is the **Kursalon,** opened in 1867 by the Strauss brothers, who directed many waltzes here. The touristy Strauss concerts are held in this building (see "Summer Music Scene," page 572).

⊃ Immediately after next stop, look right: In the same park, the gilded statue of "Waltz King" **Johann Strauss** holds a violin as he did when he conducted his orchestra, whipping his fans into a three-quarter-time frenzy.

⊃ At next stop at end of park: On the left, a green statue of Dr. Karl Lüger honors the popular man who was mayor of Vienna until 1910.

⊃ At next bend: On the right, the quaint white building with military helmets decorating the windows was the **Austrian ministry of war**—back when that was a big operation. Field Marshal Radetzky, a military big shot in the 19th century under Franz Josef, still sits on his high horse. He's pointing toward the post office, the only Art Nouveau building facing the Ring. Locals call the architecture along the Ring "**historicism**" because it's all neo-this and neo-that—generally fitting the purpose of the particular building (for example, farther along the Ring, we'll see the neo-Gothic City Hall—recalling when medieval burghers ran the city government in Gothic days; a neoclassical parliament building—celebrating ancient Greek notions of democracy; and a neo-Renaissance opera house—venerating the high culture filling it).

⊃ At next corner: The white-domed building over your right shoulder as you turn is the Urania, Franz Josef's 1910 **observatory.** Lean forward and look behind it for a peek at the huge red cars of the giant, 100-year-old Ferris wheel in Vienna's Prater Park (fun for families, described on page 570).

⊃ Now you're rolling along the **Danube Canal.** This "Baby Danube" is one of the many small arms of the river that once made up the Danube at this location. The rest have been gathered together in a mightier modern-day Danube, farther away. This neighborhood was thoroughly bombed in World War II. The buildings across the canal are typical of postwar architecture (1960s). They were built on the cheap, and are now being replaced by sleek, futuristic buildings. This was the site of the original Roman town, Vindobona. In three long blocks, on the left (opposite the BP station, be ready—it passes fast), you'll see the ivy-covered walls and round Romanesque arches of St. Ruprecht's, the oldest church in Vienna (built in the 11th century on a bit of Roman ruins). Remember, medieval Vienna was defined by that long-gone wall that you're tracing on this tour. Across the river is an OPEC headquarters, where oil ministers often meet to set prices. Relax for a few stops until the corner.

⊃ Leaving canal, turning left up Schottenring, at first corner: A block down on the right, you can see a huge, red-brick **castle**—actually a high-profile barracks built here at the command of a nervous Emperor Franz Josef (who found himself on the throne as an 18-year-old in 1848, the same year people's revolts against autocracy were sweeping across Europe).

⊃ At next stop: On the left, the orange-and-white, neo-Renaissance temple of money—the **Börse**—is Vienna's stock exchange.

◉ Next stop, at corner: The huge, frilly, neo-Gothic church on the right is a "**votive church**," built as a thanks to God when an 1853 assassination attempt on Emperor Franz Josef failed. Ahead on the right (in front of tram stop) is the **Vienna University** building (established in 1365, it has no real campus as the buildings are scattered around town). It faces (on the left, behind a gilded angel across the Ring) a chunk of the old **city wall.**

◉ At next stop, on right: The neo-Gothic City Hall, flying the flag of Europe, towers over **Rathaus Platz,** a festive site in summer, with a huge screen showing outdoor movies, operas, and concerts and a thriving food circus (see page 589—if you're hungry and it's thriving, hop off now). In the winter, the building becomes a huge Advent calendar, with 24 windows opening—one each day—as Christmas approaches. Immediately across the street (on left) is the **Burgtheater,** Austria's national theater.

◉ At next stop, on right: The neo-Greek temple of democracy houses the **Austrian Parliament.** The lady with the golden helmet is Athena, goddess of wisdom. The big construction mess is for the restoration of the building's grand ramp. Across the street (on left) is the imperial park called the **Volksgarten.**

◉ After the next stop on the right is the **Natural History Museum,** the first of Vienna's huge twin museums. It faces the **Kunsthistorisches Museum,** containing the city's greatest collection of paintings. The **MuseumsQuartier** behind them completes the ensemble with a collection of mostly modern art museums. A hefty statue of Empress Maria Theresa squats between the museums, facing the grand gate to the **Hofburg,** the emperor's palace (on left, across the Ring). Of the five arches, only the center one was used by the emperor. (Your tour is essentially finished. If you want to jump out here, you're at many of Vienna's top sights.)

◉ Fifty yards after the next stop, on the left through a gate in the black-iron fence, is a statue of Mozart. It's one of many charms in the **Burggarten,** which until 1918 was the private garden of the emperor. Vienna had more than its share of intellectual and creative geniuses. A hundred yards farther along (on left, just out of the park), the German philosopher Goethe sits in a big, thought-provoking chair playing trivia with Schiller (across the street on your right). Behind the statue of Schiller is the Academy of Fine Arts.

◉ Hey, there's the **Opera** again. Jump off the tram and see the rest of the city.

SIGHTS

Vienna's Old Center
These sights, in the heart of Vienna, are listed in the order of a convenient self-guided walking tour through town.

▲▲▲**Opera (Staatsoper)**—The Opera, facing the Ring and near the TI, is a central point for any visitor. While the critical reception of the building 130 years ago led the architect to commit suicide, and though it's been rebuilt since the WWII bombings, it's still a dazzling place (€4.50, by guided 35-min tour only, daily in English; July–Aug at 11:00, 13:00, 14:00, 15:00, and often at 10:00 and 16:00; Sept–June fewer tours, afternoon only). Tours are often canceled for rehearsals and shows, so check the posted schedule or call 01/514-442-613.

The Vienna State Opera—with musicians provided by the Vienna Philharmonic Orchestra in the pit—is one of the world's top opera houses. There are 300 performances a year, but in July and August, the singers rest their voices. Since there are different operas nearly nightly, you'll see big trucks out back and constant action backstage—all the sets need to be switched each day. Even though the expensive seats normally sell out long in advance, the opera is perpetually in the red and subsidized by the state.

Tickets for Seats: For ticket information, call 01/513-1513 (phone answered daily 10:00–21:00, www.wiener-staatsoper.at). If seats aren't sold out, last-minute tickets (for pricey seats—up to €100) are sold for €30 from 9:00 to 14:00 only the day before the show.

Standing Room: Unless Placido Domingo is in town, it's easy to get one of 567 *Stehplätze* (standing-room spots, €2 at the top or €3.50 downstairs). While the front doors open 60 minutes early, a side door (on the Operngasse side, the door under the portico nearest the fountain) is open 80 minutes before curtain time, giving those in the know an early grab at standing-room tickets. Just walk in straight, then head right until you see the ticket booth marked *Stehplätze* (tel. 01/5144-42419). If fewer than 567 people are in line, there's no need to line up early. You can even buy standing-room tickets after the show has started—in case you want only a little taste of opera. Dress is casual (but do your best) at the standing-room bar. Locals save their spot along the rail by tying a scarf to it.

Rick's Crude Tip: For me, three hours is a lot of opera. But just to see and hear the Opera House in action for half an hour is a treat. You can buy a standing-room spot and just drop in for part of the show. Ushers don't mind letting tourists with standing-room tickets in for a short look. Ending time is posted in the lobby—you could stop by for just the finale. If you go at the start or finish, you'll see Vienna dressed up. With all the time you save, consider stopping by...

Sacher Café—The home of every chocoholic's fantasy, the *Sachertorte,* faces the rear of the Opera. While locals complain that the cakes have gone downhill (and many tourists are surprised how dry they are), a coffee and slice of cake here can be €8 well invested. For maximum elegance, sit inside (daily 8:00–23:30, Philharmoniker Strasse 4, tel. 01/51456).

Empress Maria Theresa (1717–1780) and Son Josef II (1741–1790)

Maria Theresa was the only woman to officially rule the Hapsburg Empire in that family's 700-year reign. She was a strong and effective empress (r. 1740–1780). People are quick to remember Maria Theresa as the mother of 16 children (10 survived). Imagine that the most powerful woman in Europe either was pregnant or had a newborn for most of her reign. Maria Theresa ruled after the Austrian defeat of the Turks, when Europe recognized Austria as a great power. (Her rival, the Prussian emperor, said, "When at last the Hapsburgs get a great man, it's a woman.")

The last of the Baroque imperial rulers, and the first of the modern rulers of the Age of Enlightenment, Maria Theresa marked the end of the feudal system and the beginning of the era of the grand state. She was a great social reformer. During her reign, she avoided wars and expanded her empire by skillfully marrying her children into the right families. For instance, after daughter Marie Antoinette's marriage into the French Bourbon family (to Louis XVI), a country that had been an enemy became an ally. (Unfortunately for Marie, her timing was off. Arriving in time for the Revolution, she lost her head.)

The U-Bahn station in front of the Opera is actually a huge underground shopping mall with fast food, newsstands, lots of pickpockets, and even an Opera Toilet Vienna experience (€0.50, *mit Musik*).

▲**Monument Against War and Fascism**—A powerful four-part statue stands behind the Opera House on Albertinaplatz. The split white monument, *The Gates of Violence,* remembers victims of all wars and violence, including the 1938–1945 Nazi rule of Austria. A montage of wartime images—clubs and WWI gas masks, a dying woman birthing a future soldier, chained slave laborers—sits on a pedestal of granite cut from the infamous quarry at Mauthausen, a nearby concentration camp. The hunched-over figure on the ground behind is a Jew forced to wash anti-Nazi graffiti off a street with a toothbrush. The statue with its head buried in the stone (Orpheus entering the underworld) reminds Austrians of the consequences of not keeping their government on track. Behind that, the 1945 declaration of Austria's second republic—with human rights built into it—is cut into the stone. This monument stands on the spot where several hundred people were buried alive while hiding in the cellar of a building demolished in a WWII bombing attack (see photo to right of park).

Austria was pulled into World War II by Germany, which annexed the country in 1938, saying Austrians were wannabe Germans, anyway. But Austrians are not Germans—never were, never will be. They're quick to tell you that while Austria was

Maria Theresa was a great reformer and in tune with her age. She taxed the Church and the nobility, provided six years of obligatory education to all children, and granted free health care to all in her realm. Maria Theresa also welcomed the boy genius Mozart into her court.

The empress' legacy lived on in her son, **Josef II,** who ruled as emperor himself for a decade (1780–1790). He was an even more avid reformer, building on his mother's accomplishments. An enlightened monarch, Josef mothballed the too-extravagant Schönbrunn, secularized the monasteries, established religious tolerance within his realm, freed the serfs, made possible the founding of Austria's first general hospital, and promoted relatively enlightened treatment of the mentally ill. Josef was a model of practicality (for example, reusable coffins à la *Amadeus,* and no more than 6 candles at funerals)—and very unpopular with other royals. But his policies succeeded in preempting the revolutionary anger of the age, enabling Austria to avoid the turmoil that shook so much of the rest of Europe.

founded in the 10th century, Germany wasn't born until 1870. For seven years during World War II (1938–1945), there was no Austria. In 1955, after 10 years of joint occupation by the victorious Allies, Austria regained total independence on the condition that it would be forever neutral (and never join NATO or the Warsaw Pact). To this day, Austria is outside of NATO (and Germany).

Across the square from the TI, you'll see what looks like a big terrace overlooking the street. This was actually part of Vienna's original defensive rampart. Above it is the sleek, controversial titanium canopy (called the "diving board" by locals) that welcomes visitors to the newly restored...

▲▲**Albertina Museum**—This building was the residence of Maria Teresa's favorite daughter, Maria Christina, who was the only one allowed to marry for love rather than political strategy. Her many sisters were jealous. (Marie Antoinette had to marry the French king...and wound up beheaded.) Maria Christina's husband, Albert of Saxony, was a great collector of original drawings. He amassed an enormous assortment of works by Dürer, Rembrandt, Rubens, and others. Today, the Albertina presents wonderful exhibitions of these fine works, as well as allowing visitors to tour its elegant state rooms and enjoy temporary exhibits of other artists (€9, audioguide also available for both permanent and temporary exhibits, daily 10:00–18:00, Wed until 21:00, overlooking Albertinaplatz across from TI and Opera House, tel. 01/534-830, www.albertina.at).

The Albertina consists of three components. First, stroll through the Hapsburg state rooms (French classicism—lots of white marble). Top-quality facsimiles of the collection's greatest pieces hang in these rooms. Then browse the modern gallery, featuring special exhibitions of world-famous artwork; in 2005, you'll see Marc Chagall (through March 13), Piet Mondrian (March–June), and Paul Klee (fall)—for specific dates and works to be displayed, visit www.albertina.at. Finally, the Albertina also displays selections from its own spectacular collection of works by Michelangelo, Rubens, Rembrandt, and Raphael, plus a huge sampling of precise drawings by Albrecht Dürer. Of Dürer's 400 original drawings that survived, Albert collected 300 of them. Most were sold or stolen over the ages, and today, the collection is down to about 100. As the Albertina's collection is made up of fragile sketches and exquisite drawings—very sensitive to light—they are kept mostly in darkness and shown only rarely in rotation. The collection is vast, so you'll always see exciting originals, thoughtfully described in English.

▲▲**Kaisergruft (Remains of the Hapsburgs)**—The crypt for the Hapsburg royalty, a block down the street from the Monument Against War and Fascism, is covered in detail on page 561.

▲**Kärntner Strasse**—This grand, mall-like street (traffic-free since 1974) is the people-watching delight of this in-love-with-life city. While it's mostly a crass, commercial pedestrian mall with its famed elegant shops now long gone, locals know it's the same road crusaders marched down as they headed off for the Holy Land in the 12th century. Its name indicates that it points south, in the direction of the Austrian state of Kärnten.

Starting from the Opera, you'll find lots of action—shops, street music, the city casino (at #41), the venerable Lobmeyr Crystal shop (#26), American Express (#21), the Loos American bar (dark, plush, small, great €8 cocktails, Kärntnerdurchgang 10, tel. 01/512-3283), and then, finally, the cathedral. Where Kärntner Strasse hits the Graben (at #3), the Equitable Building (filled with lawyers, bankers, and insurance men) is a fine example of historicism from the turn of the 20th century. Step in, climb the stairs, and imagine how slick the courtyard must have felt in 1900.

▲▲**St. Stephan's Cathedral (Stephansdom)**—This massive church is the Gothic needle around which Vienna spins. It has survived Vienna's many wars and symbolizes the city's freedom (church doors open Mon–Sat 6:00–22:00, Sun 7:00–22:00; officially only open for tourists Mon–Sat 8:30–11:30 & 13:00–16:30, Sun 13:00–16:30, otherwise closed for services; during services, you can enter back of church and get to north tower elevator, but unless you're attending Mass, you cannot enter main nave; entertaining €4 English tours April–Oct daily at 15:45, information board inside entry has tour schedules).

Adolf Loos
(1870–1933)

Adolf Loos—Vienna's answer to Frank Lloyd Wright—famously condemned needless ornamentation, declaring, "Decoration is a crime." You can see three good examples of his work (all c. 1900 and described in this chapter) as you stroll the old center. Just off Kärntner Strasse is the Loos American Bar (Kärntnerdurchgang 10). On the Graben, you can descend into the finest public toilets in town. And facing Michaelerplatz, in front of the Hofburg entrance, is the Loos House (a.k.a. the "house without eyebrows").

This is the third church to stand on this spot. The church survived the bombs of World War II, but, in the last days of the war, fires from the street fighting between Russian and Nazi troops leapt to the rooftop. The original timbered Gothic rooftop burned, and

the cathedral's huge bell crashed to the ground. Thanks to a financial outpouring of civic pride, the roof of this symbol of Austria was rebuilt in its original splendor by 1952. The ceramic tiles are purely decorative (locals who contributed to the postwar reconstruction each "own" one for their donations).

The **grounds** around the church were a cemetery until Josef II emptied it as an "anti-plague" measure. (Inside, a few of the most important tombstones decorate the church walls.) You can still see the footprint of the old cemetery church in the pavement, today ignored by the human statues. Remains of the earlier Virgil Chapel (dating from the 13th century) are immediately under this (on display in the subway).

Study the church's **west end** (main entrance). You can see the original Romanesque facade (c. 1240), with classical Roman statues imbedded in it. Above are two stubby towers nicknamed "pagan towers" because they are built with Roman stones (with inscriptions just flipped around to expose the smooth sides). Two 30-foot-tall columns flank the main entry. If you stand back and look at the tops, you'll see that they symbolize creation (one's a penis, the other's a vagina).

Go inside. See the dramatic photos of **WWII damage** (with bricks neatly stacked and ready) in glass cases 20 yards opposite the south entrance (on the wall near 3a).

The nave is ringed with **chapels.** The church once had over a hundred. This was typical of Catholic churches, as each guild and leading family had their own chapel. The Tupperware-colored glass windows date from 1950. Before WWII, the entire church was lit with windows like the ones behind the altar. Those, along with the city's top art treasures, were hidden safely from the Nazis and bombs in salt mines. The altar painting of the stoning of St. Stephan is early Baroque, painted on copper.

St. Stephan's is proud to be Austria's national church. A **plaque** explains how each region contributed to the rebuilding after World War II: windows from Tirol, furniture from Vorarlberg, the floor from Lower Austria, and so on.

The Gothic sandstone **pulpit** in the middle of the nave (on left) is a realistic masterpiece carved from three separate blocks (find the seams). A spiral stairway winds up to the lectern, surrounded and supported by the four Latin Church fathers: Saints Ambrose, Jerome, Gregory, and Augustine. The railing leading up swarms with symbolism: lizards (animals of light) and battle toads (animals of darkness). The "Dog of the Lord" stands at the top, making sure none of those toads pollutes the sermon. Below the toads, wheels with three parts (the Trinity) roll up, while wheels with four parts (the four seasons, symbolizing mortal life) roll down. This work, by Anton Pilgram, has all the elements of the Flamboyant Gothic style in miniature. Gothic art was done for the glory of God. Artists were anonymous. But this was around 1500, and the Renaissance was going strong in Italy. While Gothic persisted in the North, the Renaissance spirit had already arrived. In the more humanist Renaissance, man was allowed to shine—and artists became famous. So, Pilgram included a rare self-portrait bust in his work (the guy with sculptor's tools, in the classic "artist observing the world from his window" pose under the stairs).

You can ascend both **towers,** the north (via crowded elevator inside on the left) and the south (outside right transept, by spiral staircase). The north shows you a mediocre view and a big bell: the 21-ton Pummerin, cast from the cannon captured from the Turks in 1683, and supposedly the second biggest bell in the world that rings by swinging (locals know it as the bell that rings in the Austrian New Year; €4, daily 8:30–17:30, July–Aug until 18:00, Nov–March until 17:00). The 450-foot-high south tower, called St. Stephan's Tower, offers a far better view—343 tightly wound steps up the spiral staircase (€3, daily 9:00–17:30, this hike burns about 1 *Sachertorte* of calories). From the top, use your *Vienna from A to Z* to locate the famous sights.

The forlorn **Cathedral Museum** (Dom Museum, outside left transept past horses) gives a close-up look at piles of religious paintings, statues, and a treasury (€5, Tue–Sat 10:00–17:00, closed Sun–Mon, Stephansplatz 6, tel. 01/515-523-560).

▲▲**Stephansplatz, Graben, and Kohlmarkt**—The atmosphere of the church square, Stephansplatz, is colorful and lively. At nearby

Graben Street (which was once a *Graben,* or ditch—originally the moat for the Roman military camp), top-notch street entertainers dance around an extravagant **plague monument** (at Bräuner Strasse). In medieval times, people did not understand the causes of plagues and figured they were a punishment from God. It was common for survivors to bribe or thank God with a monument like this one (c. 1690). Find Emperor Leopold, who ruled during the plague and made this statue in gratitude. (Hint: The typical inbreeding of royal families left him with a gaping underbite.) Below Leopold, Faith (with the help of a disgusting little cupid) tosses old naked women—symbolizing the plague—into the abyss.

Just before the plague monument is Dorotheergasse, leading to the Dorotheum auction house (see page 568). Just beyond the monument, you'll pass a fine set of **public WCs.** Around 1900, a local chemical-maker needed a publicity stunt. He purchased two wine cellars under the Graben and hired Adolf Loos to design classy WCs in the Modernist style (complete with chandeliers and finely crafted mahogany) to prove that his chemicals really got things clean. The restrooms are clean to this day—so clean that they're used for poetry readings. Locals and tourists happily pay €0.50 for a quick visit. The Graben dead-ends at the aristocratic supermarket Julius Meinl am Graben (see page 588).

Turning left on **Kohlmarkt,** you enter Vienna's most elegant shopping street (except for "American Catalog Shopping" at #5, second floor), with the emperor's palace at the end. Strolling Kohlmarkt, daydream about the edible window displays at **Demel** (#14). Demel is the ultimate Viennese chocolate shop. During the summer, when the tables are moved outside, a room is filled with Art Nouveau boxes of Empress Sissy's choco-dreams come true: *Kandierte Veilchen* (candied violet petals), *Katzenzungen* (cats' tongues), and so on. The cakes here are moist (compared to the dry *Sachertortes*). The delectable window displays change about weekly, reflecting current happenings in Vienna. Inside, an impressive can-can of cakes is displayed to tempt visitors into springing for the €10 cake and coffee deal (point to the cake you want). You can sit inside, with a view of the cake-making, or outside, with the street action. Shops like this boast "K. u. K."—good enough for the *König und Kaiser* (king and emperor—same guy).

Just beyond Demel and across the street, at #1152, you can pop into a charming little Baroque **carriage courtyard,** with the surviving original carriage garages.

Kohlmarkt ends at **Michaelerplatz,** with a scant bit of Roman Vienna exposed at its center. On the left are the fancy Loden Plankl shop, with traditional formal wear, and the stables of the Spanish Riding School. Study the grand entry facade to the Hofburg Palace—it's neo-Baroque from around 1900. The four heroic giants illustrate Hercules wrestling with his great challenges (much like the Hapsburgs, I'm sure). Opposite the facade, notice the modern Loos House (now a bank), which was built at about the same time. It was nicknamed the "house without eyebrows" for the simplicity of its windows. An anti–Art Nouveau statement (inspired by Frank Lloyd Wright and considered Vienna's first "modern" building), this was actually shocking at the time. To quell some of the outrage, the architect added flower boxes.

Enter the Hofburg Palace by walking through the gate, under the dome, and into the first square (In der Burg).

Vienna's Hofburg Palace

The complex, confusing, and imposing Imperial Palace, with 640 years of architecture, demands your attention. This first Hapsburg residence grew with the family empire from the 13th century until 1913, when the last "new wing" opened. The winter residence of the Hapsburg rulers until 1918, it's still the home of the Spanish Riding School, the Vienna Boys' Choir, the Austrian president's office, 5,000 government workers, and several important museums.

Rather than lose yourself in its myriad halls and courtyards, focus on three sections: the Imperial Apartments, Treasury, and Neue Burg (New Palace).

Hofburg Orientation from In der Burg Square: The statue is of Emperor Franz II, grandson of Maria Theresa, grandfather of Franz Josef, and father-in-law of Napoleon. Behind him is a tower with three kinds of clocks (the yellow disk shows the stage of the moon tonight). On the right, a door leads to the Imperial Apartments. Franz faces the oldest part of the palace. The colorful gate, which used to have a drawbridge, leads to the 13th-century Swiss Court (named for the Swiss mercenary guards once stationed here), the Schatzkammer (treasury), and the Hofburgkapelle (palace chapel, where the Boys' Choir sings the Mass). For the Heroes' Square and the New Palace, continue opposite the way you entered In der Burg, passing through the left-most tunnel (with a tiny but handy sandwich bar—Hofburg Stüberl, Mon–Sat 7:00–17:00, Sun 10:00–15:00, your best bet if you need a bite or drink before touring the Imperial Apartments).

▲▲▲**Imperial Apartments (Kaiserappartements)**—These lavish, Versailles-type, "wish-I-were-God" royal rooms are the downtown version of the grander Schönbrunn Palace. If you're rushed and have time for only one palace, do this (€7.50, daily 9:00–17:00, last entry 16:30, from courtyard through St. Michael's Gate, just off Michaelerplatz, tel. 01/533-7570). Palace visits are a one-way romp through 20 rooms. You'll find some helpful English information

Vienna's Hofburg Palace

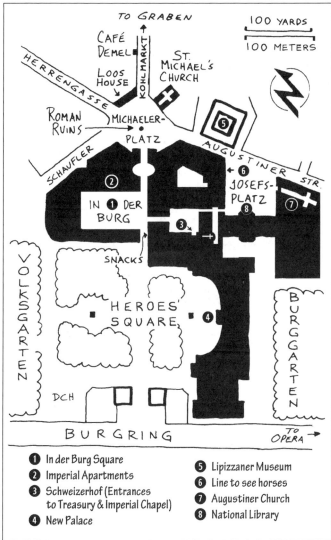

1. In der Burg Square
2. Imperial Apartments
3. Schweizerhof (Entrances to Treasury & Imperial Chapel)
4. New Palace
5. Lipizzaner Museum
6. Line to see horses
7. Augustiner Church
8. National Library

within, and, with that and the following description, you won't need the €7.50 *Imperial Apartments and Sissy* museum guidebook. The included audioguide brings the exhibit to life. Tickets include the royal silver and porcelain collection *(Silberkammer)* near the turnstile. If touring the silver and porcelain, do it first to save walking.

Self-Guided Tour: Get your ticket, tour the silver and porcelain collection, climb the stairs, go through the turnstile, study the family tree tracing the Hapsburgs from 1273 to their messy WWI demise, and use the big model of the palace complex to understand the complex lay of the imperial land. Then head into the...

Sissy Museum: The first six rooms tell the life story of Empress Elisabeth's fancy world—her luxury homes and fairytale existence. While Sissy's life story is the perfect stuff of legends, the exhibit tries to keep things from getting too giddy, and doesn't add to the sugary, kitschy image that's been created. The exhibit starts with her assignation and traces the development of her legend, analyzing how her fabulous but tragic life could create a 19th-century Princess Diana from a rocky start (when she was disdained for abandoning Vienna and her husband, the venerable Emperor Franz Josef). You'll read bits of her poetic writing, catch snatches of movies made about her, see exact copies of her now lost jewelry, and learn about her escapes, dieting mania, and chocolate bills. Admire Sissy's hard-earned thin waist (20 inches at age 16, 21 inches at age 50...after giving birth to 4 children). The black statue in the dark room represents the empress after the suicide of her son—aloof, thin, in black, with her back to the world.

After the Sissy rooms, a one-way route takes you through a series of royal rooms.

Waiting Room for the Audience Room: A map and mannequins from the many corners of the Hapsburg realm illustrate the multiethnicity of the vast empire. Every citizen had the right to meet privately with the emperor. Three huge paintings entertained guests while they waited. They were propaganda, showing crowds of commoners enthusiastic about their Hapsburg royalty. On the right: An 1809 scene of the emperor returning to Vienna, celebrating news that Napoleon had begun his retreat. Left: The return of the emperor from the 1814 Peace of Paris, the treaty that ended the Napoleonic wars. (The 1815 Congress of Vienna that followed was the greatest assembly of diplomats in European history. Its goal: to establish peace through a "balance of power" among nations. While rulers ignored nationalism in favor of continued dynastic rule, this worked for about 100 years, until a colossal war—World War I— wiped out the Hapsburgs and the rest of Europe's royal families.) Center: Less important, the emperor makes his first public appearance to adoring crowds after recovering from a life-threatening illness (1826). The chandelier—considered the best in the palace—is Baroque, made of Bohemian crystal.

Sissy

Empress Elisabeth—Franz Josef's mysterious, narcissistic, and beautiful wife—is in vogue. Sissy was mostly silent. Her main goals in life seem to have been preserving her reputation as a beautiful empress, maintaining her Barbie Doll figure, and tending to her fairytale, ankle-length hair. In spite of severe dieting and fanatic exercise, age took its toll. After turning 30, she allowed no more portraits to be painted and was generally seen in public with a delicate fan covering her face (and bad teeth). Complex and influential, she was adored by Franz Josef, whom she respected. Her personal mission and political cause was promoting Hungary's bid for nationalism. Her personal tragedy was the death of her son Rudolf, the crown prince, by suicide. Disliking Vienna and the confines of the court, she traveled more and more frequently. Over the years, the restless Sissy and her hardworking husband became estranged. In 1898, while visiting Geneva, Switzerland, she was murdered by an Italian anarchist. Sissy has been compared to Princess Diana because of her beauty, bittersweet life, and tragic death. Her story is wonderfully told in the new Sissy Museum, now part of the Hofburg Imperial Apartments tour.

Audience Room: Suddenly, you were face-to-face with the emp. The portrait on the easel shows Franz Josef in 1915, when he was over 80 years old. Famously energetic, he lived a spartan life dedicated to duty. He'd stand at the high table here to meet with commoners, who came to show gratitude or make a request. (Standing kept things moving.) On the table, you can read a partial list of 56 appointments he had on January 3, 1910 (family name and topic of meeting).

Conference Room: The emperor presided here over the equivalent of cabinet meetings. After 1867, he ruled the Austro-Hungarian Empire, so Hungarians sat at these meetings. The paintings on the wall show the military defeat of a popular Hungarian uprising...subtle.

Emperor Franz Josef's Study: The desk was originally between the windows. Franz Josef could look up from his work and see his lovely, long-haired, tiny-waisted Empress Elisabeth's reflection in the mirror. Notice the trompe l'oeil paintings above each door, giving the believable illusion of marble relief. Notice also all the family photos—the perfect gift for the dad/uncle/hubby who has it all.

The walls between the rooms are wide enough to hide servants' corridors (the door to his valet's room is in the back left corner). The emperor lived with a personal staff of 14: "three valets, four lackeys, two doormen, two manservants, and three chambermaids."

Emperor Franz Josef

Franz Josef I—who ruled for 68 years (1848–1916)—was the embodiment of the Hapsburg Empire as it finished its six-century-long ride. Born in 1830, Franz Josef had a stern upbringing that instilled in him a powerful sense of duty and—like so many men of power—a love of things military. His uncle, Ferdinand I, was a dimwit, and, as the revolutions of 1848 were rattling royal families throughout Europe, the Hapsburgs replaced him, putting 18-year old Franz Josef on the throne. FJ put down the revolt with bloody harshness and spent the first part of his long reign understandably paranoid, as social discontent simmered. FJ was very conservative. But worse, he figured wrongly that he was a talented military tactician, leading Austria into disastrous battles against Italy (which was fighting for its unification and independence) in the 1860s. His army endured severe, avoidable casualties. It was clear: FJ was a disaster as a general. Wearing his uniform to the end, he never saw what a dinosaur his monarchy was becoming, and never thought it strange that the majority of his subjects didn't even speak German. He had no interest in democracy and pointedly never set foot in Austria's parliament building. But, like his contemporary, Queen Victoria, he was the embodiment of his empire—old-fashioned, but sacrosanct. His passion for low-grade paperwork earned him the nickname "Joe bureaucrat." Mired in these petty details, he missed the big picture. He helped start a Great War that ultimately ended the age of monarchs. The year 1918 marked the end of Europe's big royal families: Hohenzollerns (Prussia), Romanovs (Russia), and Hapsburgs (Austria).

Emperor's Bedroom: This features his famous no-frills iron bed and portable washstand (necessary until 1880, when the palace got running water). While he had a typical emperor's share of mistresses, his dresser was always well-stocked with photos of Sissy. Franz Josef lived here after his estrangement from Sissy. An etching shows the empress—a fine rider and avid hunter—riding sidesaddle while jumping a hedge. The big, ornate stove in the corner was fed from behind. Through the 19th century, this was a standard form of heating.

Small Salon: This is dedicated to the memory of the assassinated Emperor Maximilian of Mexico (bearded portrait, Franz Josef's brother, killed in 1867). This was also a smoking room—necessary in the early 19th century, when smoking was newly fashionable (but only for men—never in the presence of women). Left of the door is a small button the emp had to buzz before entering the quarters of his estranged wife. You can go right in.

Empress' Bedroom and Drawing Room: This was Sissy's,

refurbished neo-rococo in 1854. She lived here—the bed was rolled in and out daily—until her death in 1898.

Sissy's Dressing/Exercise Room: Servants worked two hours a day on Sissy's famous hair here. She'd exercise on the wooden structure. While she had a tough time with people, she did fine with animals. Her favorite dogs hang adorably on the wall.

Sissy's Bathroom: Detour into the behind-the-scenes palace. In the narrow passageway, you'll walk by Sissy's hand-painted-porcelain, dolphin-head WC (on the right). In the main bathroom, you'll see her huge copper tub (with the original wall coverings behind it). Sissy was the first Hapsburg to have running water in her bathroom (notice the hot and cold faucets). You're walking on the first linoleum ever used in Vienna—from around 1880. Next, enter the servants' quarters, with tropical scenes painted by Bergl in 1766. As you leave these rooms and reenter the imperial world, look back to the room on the left.

Empress' Great Salon: The room is painted with Mediterranean escapes, the 19th-century equivalent of travel posters. The statue is of Elisa, Napoleon's oldest sister (by the neoclassical master, Canova). Turn the corner and pass through the anterooms of Alexander's apartments.

Red Salon: The Gobelin wall hangings were a 1776 gift from Marie Antoinette and Louis XVI in Paris to their Viennese counterparts.

Dining Room: It's dinnertime, and Franz Josef has called his extended family together. The settings are modest...just silver. Gold was saved for formal state dinners. Next to each name card was a menu with the chef responsible for each dish. (Talk about pressure.) While the Hofburg had tableware for 4,000, feeding 3,000 was a typical day. The cellar was stocked with 60,000 bottles of wine. The kitchen was huge—50 birds could be roasted on the hand-driven spits at once.

Through the shop, you're back on the street. Two quick lefts take you back to the palace square (In der Burg), where you can pass through the black, red, and gold gate and to the treasury.

▲▲▲**Treasury (Weltliche und Geistliche Schatzkammer)**—This "Secular and Religious Treasure Room" contains the best jewels on the Continent. Slip through the vault doors and reflect on the glitter of 21 rooms filled with scepters, swords, crowns, orbs, weighty robes, double-headed eagles, gowns, gem-studded bangles, and an eight-foot-tall, 500-year-old unicorn horn (or maybe the tusk of a narwhal)—which was considered incredibly powerful in the old days, giving its owner the grace of God. These were owned by the Holy Roman Emperor—a divine monarch. The well-produced, included audioguide provides a wealth of information (€8, Wed–Mon 10:00–18:00, closed Tue, follow *Schatzkammer* signs to the Schweizerhof, tel. 01/52524).

Room 2: The personal crown of Rudolf II has survived since 1602—it was considered too well-crafted to cannibalize for other crowns. This crown is a big deal because it's the adopted crown of the Austrian Empire, established in 1806 after Napoleon dissolved the Holy Roman Empire (an alliance of Germanic kingdoms so named because it tried to be the grand continuation of the Roman Empire). Pressured by Napoleon, the Austrian Francis II—who had been Holy Roman Emperor—became Francis I, Emperor of Austria. Francis I/II (the stern guy on the wall, near where you entered) ruled from 1792 to 1835. Look at the crown. Its design symbolically merges the typical medieval king's crown and a bishop's miter.

Rooms 3 and 4: These contain some of the coronation vestments and regalia needed for the new Austrian emperor.

Room 5: Ponder the Throne Cradle. Napoleon's son was born in 1811 and made king of Rome. The little eagle at the foot is symbolically not yet able to fly, but glory-bound. Glory is symbolized by the star, with Dad's big *N* raised high.

Room 11: The collection's highlight is the 10th-century crown of the Holy Roman Emperor. The imperial crown swirls with symbolism "proving" that the emperor was both holy and Roman. The jeweled arch over the top is reminiscent of the parade helmet of ancient Roman emperors whose successors the HRE claimed to be. The cross on top says the HRE ruled as Christ's representative on earth. King Solomon's portrait (on the crown, right of cross) is Old Testament proof that kings can be wise and good. King David (next panel) is similar proof that they can be just. The crown's eight sides represent the celestial city of Jerusalem's eight gates. The jewels on the front panel symbolize the twelve apostles.

The nearby 11th-century Imperial Cross preceded the emperor in ceremonies. Encrusted with jewels, it carried a substantial chunk of *the* cross and *the* holy lance (supposedly used to pierce the side of Jesus while on the cross; both items displayed in the same glass case). This must be the actual holy lance, as Holy Roman Emperors actually carried this into battle in the 10th century. Look behind the cross to see how it was actually a box that could be clipped open and shut. You can see bits of the "true cross" anywhere, but this is a prime piece—with the actual nail hole.

The other case has jewels from the reign of Karl der Grosse (Charlemagne), the greatest ruler of medieval Europe. Notice Charlemagne modeling the crown (which was made a hundred years after he died) in the tall painting adjacent.

Room 12: The painting shows the coronation of Maria Theresa's son Josef II in 1764. He's wearing the same crown and royal garb you've just seen.

Room 16: Most tourists walk right by perhaps the most exquisite workmanship in the entire treasury, the royal vestments

(15th century). Look closely—they are painted with gold and silver threads.

▲Heroes' Square (Heldenplatz) and the New Palace (Neue Burg)—This last grand addition to the palace, from just before World War I, was built for Franz Ferdinand, but never used. (It was tradition for rulers not to move into their predecessor's quarters.) Its grand facade arches around Heroes' Square. Notice statues of the two great Austrian heroes on horseback: Prince Eugene of Savoy (who beat the Turks who had earlier threatened Vienna) and Archduke Charles (first to beat Napoleon in a battle, breaking Nappy's image of invincibility and heralding the end of the Napoleonic age). The frilly spires of Vienna's neo-Gothic City Hall break the horizon, and a line of horse-drawn carriages awaits customers.

▲▲New Palace Museums: Armor, Music, and Ancient Greek Statues—The Neue Burg—technically part of the Kunsthistorisches Museum across the way—houses three fine museums (same ticket): an armory (with a killer collection of medieval weapons), historical musical instruments, and classical statuary from ancient Ephesus. The included audioguide brings the exhibits to life and lets you actually hear the fascinating old instruments in the collection being played. An added bonus is the chance to wander all alone among those royal Hapsburg halls, stairways, and painted ceilings (€7.50, Wed–Mon 10:00–18:00, closed Tue, almost no tourists, tel. 01/5252-4484).

More Hapsburg Sights near the Hofburg

Central Vienna has plenty more sights associated with the Hapsburgs. With the exception of the last one (on Mariahilfer Strasse), these are all near the Hofburg. Remember that the biggest Hapsburg sight of all, Schönbrunn Palace, makes a great half-day trip (4 miles from the center—see page 570).

Palace Garden (Burggarten)—This greenbelt, once the back yard of the Hofburg and now a people's park, welcomes people to loiter on the grass and is lively with office workers enjoying a break on nice days. The statue of Mozart facing the Ringstrasse is popular. The iron-and-glass pavilion now houses the recommended Palmenhaus Restaurant (see "Eating," page 588) and a small but fluttery butterfly exhibit (€5, daily 10:00–17:00). The butterfly zone is delightfully muggy on a brisk, off-season day, but trippy any time of year. If you tour it, notice the butterflies hanging out on the trays with rotting slices of banana. They lick the fermented banana juice as it beads, and then just hang out there in a stupor...or fly in anything but a straight line.

▲Lipizzaner Museum—A must for horse-lovers, this tidy museum in the Renaissance Stallburg Palace shows (and tells in English) the 400-year history of the famous riding school. Lipizzaner fans have a warm spot in their hearts for General Patton, who, at the end of World War II—knowing that the Soviets were about to take control of Vienna—ordered a raid on the stable to save the horses and ensure the survival of their fine old bloodlines. Videos show the horses in action on TVs throughout the museum. The "dancing" originated as battle moves: *pirouette* (quick turns) and *courbette* (on hind legs to make a living shield for the knight). The 45-minute movie in the basement theater also has great horse footage (showings alternate between German and English). These are very special horses—you'll notice they actually have "surnames," as all can be traced to the original six 16th-century stallions (€5, daily 9:00–18:00, Reitschulgasse 2 between Josefsplatz and Michaelerplatz, tel. 01/533-8658). Any time of day, you can see the horses prance on video in the museum's window. In 2005, they plan to install video cameras, so visitors can "peek in" on the horses live.

Seeing the Lipizzaner Stallions: Seats for performances by Vienna's prestigious Spanish Riding School book up months in advance, but standing room is often available the same day (tickets-€35–105, standing room-€24–28, March–June and Sept–Oct Sun at 11:00, sometimes also Fri at 18:00, tel. 01/533-9031, www.srs.at). Luckily for the masses, training sessions with music in a chandeliered Baroque hall are open to the public (€11.50 at the door, roughly Feb–June and Sept–Oct, Tue–Sat 10:00–12:00 when the horses are in town). Tourists line up early at Josefsplatz, gate 2. Save money and avoid the wait by buying the €14.50 combo-ticket that covers both the museum and the training session (and lets you avoid that ticket line). Or, better yet, simply show up late. If you want to hang out with Japanese tour groups, get there early and wait for the doors to open at 10:00. But almost no one stays for the full two hours—except for the horses. As people leave, new tickets are printed continuously, so you can just waltz in with no wait at all. If you arrive at 10:45, you'll see the best action, as one group of horses finishes and two more perform before they call it a day.

▲**Augustinian Church (Augustinerkirche)**—This is the Gothic and neo-Gothic church where the Hapsburgs latched, then buried, their hearts (weddings took place here, and the royal hearts are in the vault). Don't miss the exquisite, tomb-like Canova memorial (neoclassical, 1805) to Maria Theresa's favorite daughter, Maria Christina, with its incredibly sad, white-marble procession. The church's 11:00 Sunday Mass is a hit with music-lovers—both a Mass and a concert, often with an orchestra accompanying the choir. To pay, contribute to the offering plate and buy a CD afterwards. (Programs are available at the table by the entry all week.)

The church faces Josefsplatz, with its statue of the great reform emperor Josef II. The National Library (€3, next to the Augustinian Church) is worth a look.

▲▲**Kaisergruft, the Remains of the Hapsburgs**—Visiting the imperial remains is not as easy as you might imagine. These original organ donors left their bodies—about 150 in all—in the unassuming Kaisergruft (Capuchin Crypt), their hearts in the Augustinian Church (church open daily, but to see the goods, you'll have to talk to a priest; Augustinerstrasse 3), and their entrails in the crypt below St. Stephan's Cathedral. Don't tripe.

Upon entering the Kaisergruft (€4, daily 9:30–16:00, last entry 15:40, behind Opera on Neuer Markt), buy the €0.50 map with a Hapsburg family tree and a chart locating each coffin.

The double coffin of Maria Theresa (1717–1780) and her husband is worth a close look for its artwork. Maria Theresa outlived her husband by 15 years—which she spent in mourning. Old and fat, she installed a special lift enabling her to get down into the crypt to be with her dead husband (even though he had been far from faithful). The couple recline—Etruscan-style—atop their fancy lead coffin. At each corner are the crowns of the Hapsburgs—the Holy Roman Empire, Hungary, Bohemia, and Jerusalem. Notice the contrast between the rococo splendor of Maria Theresa's tomb and the simple box holding her more modest son, Josef II (at his parents' feet; for more on Joe II, see page 546).

Franz Josef (1830–1916) is nearby, in an appropriately austere military tomb. Flanking Franz Josef are the tombs of his son, the archduke Rudolf, and Empress Elisabeth. Rudolf and his teenage love committed suicide together in 1898, and—since the Church figured he forced her and was therefore a murderer—it took considerable legal hair-splitting to win Rudolf this spot (after examining his brain, it was determined that he was physically retarded and therefore incapable of knowingly killing himself and his girl). *Kaiserin* Elisabeth (1837–1898), a.k.a. Sissy, always gets the "Most Flowers" award.

In front of those three is the most recent Hapsburg tomb. Empress Zita was buried in 1989. Her burial procession was probably the last such Old Regime event in European history. The monarchy died hard in Austria.

While it's fun to chase down all these body parts, remember that the *real* legacy of the Hapsburgs is the magnificence of this city. Step outside. Look up. Watch the clouds glide by the ornate gables of Vienna.

▲**Imperial Furniture Collection (Kaiserliches Hofmobiliendepot)**— Bizarre, sensuous, eccentric, or precious, this is the Hapsburgs' furniture—from grandma's wheelchair to the emperor's spittoon—all thoughtfully described in English. Take a peek. The Hapsburgs had many palaces, but only the Hofburg was permanently furnished. The rest were furnished on the fly—set up and taken down by a gang of royal roadies called the "Depot of Court Movables"

(Hofmobiliendepot). When the monarchy was dissolved in 1918, the state of Austria took possession of the Hofmobiliendepot's inventory—165,000 items. Now this royal storehouse is open to the public in a fine, new, sprawling museum. Don't go here for the *Jugendstil* furnishings. The older Baroque, rococo, and Biedermeier pieces are the most impressive and tied most intimately to the royals. Combine a visit to this museum with a stroll down lively shopping boulevard Mariahilfer Strasse (€7, Tue–Sun 10:00–18:00, closed Mon, Mariahilfer Strasse 88, tel. 01/5243-3570).

Near Karlsplatz

These sights cluster around Karlsplatz, just southeast of Ringstrasse (U-1, U-2, or U-4: Karlsplatz).

Karlsplatz—This fine and picnic-friendly square, with its Henry Moore sculpture in the pond, is ringed with sights. The Art Nouveau station pavilions—from the 19th-century municipal train system—are textbook *Jugendstil* by Otto Wagner (steel frame and decorative marble slabs with painted gold ornaments). One of Europe's first subway systems, it was built with a military purpose in mind: to move troops quickly in time of civil unrest—specifically, out to Schönbrunn Palace.

Charles Church (Karlskirche)—Charles Borromeo, a 16th-century bishop from Milan, was an inspiration during plague times. This "votive church" was dedicated to him in 1713, when an epidemic spared Vienna. The church offers the best Baroque in Vienna, with a unique combination of columns (showing scenes from the life of Charles Borromeo, à la Trajan's Column in Rome), a classic pediment, and an elliptical dome. But it's especially worthwhile for the chance (probably through 2005) to see restoration work in progress and up close (€6, includes a skippable 1-room museum, audioguide, and visit to renovation site; Mon–Sat 9:00–12:30 & 13:00–18:00, Sun 13:00–18:00). The entry fee may seem steep, but remember that it funds the restoration.

Visitors ride the industrial lift to a platform at the base of the dome. Consider that the church was built and decorated with essentially the same scaffolding system. From there, you'll climb stairs to the steamy lantern at the extreme top of the church. At that dizzying height, you're in the clouds with cupids and angels. Many details that appear smooth and beautiful from ground level—such as gold leaf, rudimentary paintings, and fake marble—look rough and sloppy up close. It's surreal to observe the 3-D figures from an unintended angle. Faith, Hope, Charity, and Borromeo triumph and inspire while Protestants and their stinkin' books are trashed. Borromeo lobbies heaven for plague relief. At the very top, you'll see the tiny dove representing the Holy Ghost, surrounded by a cheering squad of nipple-lipped cupids.

Historical Museum of the City of Vienna (Wien Museum Karlsplatz)—This underappreciated museum walks you through the history of Vienna with fine historic artifacts. You'll work chronologically from the ground floor (Roman artifacts, original statues from St. Stephan's Cathedral—c. 1350, with various Hapsburgs showing off the slinky, hip-hugging fashion of the day) to the first floor (old city maps, booty from the Turkish siege, 1850 city model showing the town just before the wall was replaced by the Ring), to the second floor (city model from 1898 with new Ringstrasse, sentimental Biedermeier paintings and objets d'art, plus early-20th-century paintings, including some by Gustav Klimt). The museum is worth the €4 admission (free Sun and Fri morning, open Tue–Sun 9:00–18:00, closed Mon, www.wienmuseum.at).

The Secession—This building, nicknamed the "golden cabbage" today (and "a temple for bullfrogs" when it was first built around the turn of the 20th century), was created by the Vienna Secession movement, a group of nonconformist artists led by Gustav Klimt, Otto Wagner, and friends. The Secession, whose slogan was "To each age its art, and to art its liberty," first exhibited their "liberty-style" art here in 1897.

The young trees carved into the walls and its bushy "cabbage" rooftop are symbolic of the renewal cycle. That spirit of turning away from traditions survives today, and the Secession still gives cutting-edge art a platform. While the staff hopes that you take a look at the temporary exhibits (and the ticket includes them, whether you like it or not), most tourists head for the basement, home to a small exhibit about the history of the building and the museum's highlight: Klimt's classic *Beethoven Frieze* (a.k.a. the "searching souls"). One of the masterpieces of Viennese Art Nouveau, this 105-foot-long fresco was the centerpiece of a 1902 homage to Beethoven exhibition. Sit down and read the free flier, which explains Klimt's still-powerful work. The theme, inspired by Beethoven's *Ninth Symphony*, features floating female figures "yearning for happiness." They drift and weave and search—like most of us do—through internal and external temptations and forces, falling victim to base and ungodly temptations, and losing their faith. Then, finally, they become fulfilled by poetry, music, and art as they reach the "Ideal Kingdom" where "True Happiness, Pure Bliss and Absolute Love" are found in a climactic embrace (€6, Tue–Sun 10:00–18:00, Thu until 20:00, closed Mon).

▲Naschmarkt—In 1898, the city decided to cover up its Vienna River. The resulting long, wide square was filled with a lively produce market that still bustles daily. From near the Opera, the Naschmarkt (roughly, "Munchies Market") stretches along Wienzeile Street. The "belly of Vienna" comes with two parallel lanes—one lined with fun and reasonable eateries, and the other lined with the town's top-end produce and gourmet goodies. This is where top chefs

Art Nouveau Sights

Vienna gave birth to its own curvaceous brand of Art Nouveau around the early 1900s: *Jugendstil* ("youth style"). The TI has a brochure laying out Vienna's 20th-century architecture. The best of Vienna's scattered *Jugendstil* sights: the Belvedere Palace collection, the clock on Höher Markt (which does a musical act at noon), and the gilded, cabbage-domed Secession building at the Ring end of the Naschmarkt (see page 563).

like to get their ingredients. At the gourmet vinegar stall, you sample the vinegar like perfume—with a drop on your wrist. Farther from the center, the Naschmarkt becomes likeably seedy and surrounded by sausage stands, Turkish *döner kebab* stalls, cafés, and theaters. Each Saturday, it's infested by a huge flea market, where, in olden days, locals would come to hire a monkey to pick little critters out of their hair (Mon–Fri 7:00–18:00, Sat 6:00–18:00, closed Sun, closes earlier in winter, U-4: Kettenbruckengasse). For a picnic park, pick up your grub here and walk over to Karlsplatz (described above).

More Sights in Vienna

▲▲▲Kunsthistorisches Museum—This exciting museum, across the Ring from the Hofburg Palace, showcases the grandeur and opulence of the Hapsburgs' collected artwork in a grand building (built as a museum in 1888). There are European masterpieces galore, all well-hung on one glorious floor, plus a fine display of Egyptian, classical, and applied arts.

Starting with the Italian wing of the museum, you get an immediate sense of the richness of this collection—you've walked right into the High Renaissance. Here, you'll see Raphael's graceful *Madonna of the Meadow* and Correggio's voluptuous *Jupiter and Io*. Meander through the Venetian Renaissance rooms to spend time with Titian, and land (with a thud) in the heart of Realism. (Caravaggio's still-shocking *David with the Head of Goliath* shows the artist was distinctly "a head" of his time.)

The Baroque rooms offer pudgy winged babies galore—quite a contrast to the simple, direct, and down-to-earth Northern paintings by Dutch and Flemish artists, only steps away. Enjoy Hieronymus Bosch's bizarrely crowded work and linger at the paintings by Peter Brueghel, the undisputed master of the slice-of-life village scene. Giuseppe Arcimboldo's *Summer* and *Winter* (with faces made of produce and fish, respectively) are always crowd-pleasers. Try the helpful, included audioguide for the full picture. Sadly, one of the jewels in the museum's crown is now missing. Cellini's *Salt Cellar,* a divine golden salt bowl valued at €50 million, was stolen in

2003 by expert thieves—to the anguish of the Vienna art world (€10, Tue–Sun 10:00–18:00, Thu until 21:00, closed Mon, tel. 01/525-240, www.khm.at; for my more detailed description of the top artwork, download www.ricksteves.com/kunst).

▲**Natural History Museum**—In the twin building facing the art museum, you'll find moon rocks, dinosaur stuff, and the fist-sized *Venus of Willendorf*—at 30,000 years old, the world's oldest sex symbol, found in the Danube Valley. This museum is a hit with children (€6.50, Wed–Mon 9:00–18:30, Wed until 21:00, closed Tue, tel. 01/521-770).

MuseumsQuartier—The vast grounds of the former imperial stables now corral several impressive, cutting-edge museums. Walk into the complex from the Hofburg side, where the main entrance (with visitors center) leads to a big courtyard with cafés, fountains, and revolving "installation lounge furniture," all surrounded by the quarter's various museums.

The **Leopold Museum** features modern Austrian art, including the largest collection of works by Egon Schiele (1890–1918) and a few drawings by Kokoschka and Klimt (€9, Wed–Mon 10:00–19:00, Thu until 21:00, closed Tue, behind Kunsthistorisches Museum, U-2 or U-3: Volkstheater/Museumsplatz, Museumsplatz 1–5, tel. 01/525-700, www.leopoldmuseum.org). Note that for these three artists, you'll do better in the Belvedere Palace (see below).

The **Museum of Modern Art** (Museum Moderner Kunst Stiftung Ludwig, a.k.a. "Mumok") is Austria's leading modern art gallery. It's the striking, lava-paneled building—three stories tall and four stories deep, offering seven floors of far-out art encased in very young stone. This huge, state-of-the-art museum displays revolving exhibits showing off art of the last generation—including Klee, Picasso, and Pop (€8, Tue–Sun 10:00–18:00, Thu until 21:00, closed Mon, tel. 01/525-001-440, www.mumok.at).

Rounding out the sprawling MuseumsQuartier are an architecture museum, Transeuropa, Electronic Avenue, children's museum, and the Kunsthalle Wien—an exhibition center for contemporary art (€7). Various combo-tickets are available for those interested in more than just the Leopold and Modern Art museums (visit www.mqw.at).

▲**Academy of Fine Arts (Akademie der Bildenden Künste)**—This small but exciting collection includes works by Bosch, Botticelli, and Rubens (quick, sketchy cartoons used to create his giant canvases); a Venice series by Guardi; and a self-portrait by a 15-year-old Van Dyck. It's all magnificently lit and well-described by the €2 audio-guide, and comes with comfy chairs (€5, Tue–Sun 10:00–18:00, closed Mon, 3 blocks from Opera at Schillerplatz 3, tel. 01/5881-6225, www.akademiegalerie.at). The fact that this is a working art academy gives it a certain realness. As you wander the halls of the academy, ponder how history might have been different if Hitler—

who applied to study architecture here, but was rejected—had been accepted as a student. Before leaving, peek into the ground floor's central hall—textbook historicism, the Ringstrasse style of the late 1800s.

▲**Liechtenstein Museum**—The noble Liechtenstein family (who own only a tiny country, but whose friendship with the Hapsburgs goes back generations) amassed an incredible private art collection. Their palace was long a treasure for Vienna art-lovers. Then, in 1938—knowing Hitler was intent on plundering artwork to create an immense "Führer Museum"—the family fled to their tiny homeland with their best art. Only in March 2004 was the collection reestablished in Vienna, and opened again to the adoring public. The Liechtensteins' "world of Baroque pleasures" includes the family's rare French rococo carriage (which was used for the family's grand entry into Paris—after being carted to the edge of town and assembled there; nearly all such carriages were destroyed in the French Revolution), a plush Baroque library, an inviting English Garden, and an impressive collection of paintings, including a complete cycle of early Rembrandts (€10, €4 audioguide, Wed–Mon 9:00–20:00, closed Tue, tram D to Bauernfeldplatz, Fürstengasse 1, tel. 01/319-5767-252, www.liechtensteinmuseum.at).

▲**KunstHausWien: Hundertwasser Museum**—This "make yourself at home" museum is a hit with lovers of modern art. It mixes the work and philosophy of local painter/environmentalist Hundertwasser. Stand in front of the colorful checkerboard building and consider Hundertwasser's style. He was against "window racism." Neighboring houses allow only one kind of window. But $100H_2O$'s windows are each different—and he encouraged residents to personalize them. He recognized "tree tenants," as well as human tenants. His buildings are spritzed with a forest and topped with dirt and grassy little parks—close to nature, good for the soul. Floors and sidewalks are irregular—to "stimulate the brain" (although current residents complain it just causes wobbly furniture and sprained ankles). Thus $100H_2O$ waged a one-man fight—during the 1950s and 1960s, when concrete and glass ruled—to save the human soul from the city. (Hundertwasser claimed that "straight lines are godless.") Inside the museum, start with his interesting biography (which ends in 2000). His fun-loving paintings are half *Jugendstil* ("youth style") and half just kids' stuff. Notice the photographs from his 1950s days as part of Vienna's bohemian scene. Throughout the museum, notice the fun philosophical quotes from an artist who believed, "If man is creative, he comes nearer to his creator" (€8 for Hundertwasser Museum, €14 combo-ticket includes special exhibitions, half price on Mon, open daily 10:00–19:00, extremely fragrant and colorful garden café, U-3: Landstrasse, Weissgerberstrasse 13, tel. 01/712-0491).

The KunstHausWien provides by far the best look at Hundertwasser. For an actual lived-in apartment complex by the green master, walk five minutes to the one-with-nature **Hundertwasserhaus** (free, at Löwengasse and Kegelgasse). This complex of 50 apartments, subsidized by the government to provide affordable housing, was built

in the 1980s as a breath of architectural fresh air in a city of boring, blocky apartment complexes. While not open to visitors, it's worth visiting for its fun-loving and colorful patchwork exterior and the Hundertwasser festival of shops across the street. Don't miss the view from Kegelgasse to see the "tree tenants" and the internal winter garden residents enjoy.

Hundertwasser detractors—of which there are many—remind visitors that $100H_2O$ was a painter, not an architect. They describe the Hundertwasserhaus as a "1950s house built in the 1980s," and colorfully painted with no real concern for the environment, communal living, or even practical comfort. Nearly all the original inhabitants got fed up with the novelty and moved out.

▲▲**Belvedere Palace**—This is the elegant palace of Prince Eugene of Savoy—the still much-appreciated conqueror of the Turks. Eugene, a Frenchman considered too short and too ugly to be in the service of Louis XIV, offered his services to the Hapsburgs. While he was indeed short and ugly, he became the greatest military genius of his age. When you conquer cities, as Eugene did, you get really rich. He had no heirs, so the state got his property, and Josef II established the Belvedere as Austria's first great public art gallery. Today, his palace boasts sweeping views and houses the Austrian gallery of 19th- and 20th-century art (€7.50, €2.50 audioguide, Tue–Sun 10:00–18:00, closed Mon, entrance at Prinz-Eugen-Strasse 27, tel. 01/7955-7134, www.belvedere.at). To get here from the center, catch tram D at the Opera (direction Südbahnhof, it stops at the palace gate).

Belvedere means "beautiful view." Sit at the top palace and look over the Baroque gardens, the mysterious sphinxes (which symbolized solving riddles and the finely educated mind of your host, Eugene), the lower palace, and the city. The spire of St. Stephan's Cathedral is 400 feet tall, and no other tall buildings are allowed within the first district. The hills—covered with vineyards—are where locals love to go to sample the new wine. (You can see Kahlenberg, from where you can walk down to several recommended *Heurigen* beyond the spire—see page 575.) These are the first of the Alps, which stretch from here all the way to Marseilles, France. The square you're overlooking was filled with people on May 15, 1955, as local leaders stood on the balcony of the Upper Palace (behind you) and proclaimed Austrian independence.

The Upper Palace was Eugene's party house. Today, like the

Louvre in Paris (but much easier to enjoy), this palace contains a fine collection of paintings. The collection is arranged chronologically: On the first floor, you'll find historicism, Romanticism, Impressionism, Realism, tired tourism, expressionism, Art Nouveau, and early modernism. Each room tries to pair Austrian works from that period with much better-known European works. It's fun to see the work of artists like van Gogh, Munch, and Monet hung with their lesser-known Austrian contemporaries. As Austria became a leader in art around 1900, the collection from that period gets stronger, with fine works by Gustav Klimt, Oskar Kokoschka, and Egon Schiele. The Klimt room shows how even in his early work, the face was vivid and the rest dissolved into decor. During his "golden period," this background became his trademark gold leaf studded with stones. The corner room shows a small exhibit on Prince Eugene, Archduke Franz Ferdinand, and the signing of the state treaty in 1955. Don't miss the poignant Schiele family portrait from 1918. His wife died while he was still working on it. (He and his child were also soon taken by the influenza epidemic that swept through Europe after World War I.)

The upper floor shows off early-19th-century Biedermeier paintings (hyper-sensitive, super-sweet, uniquely Viennese Romanticism—the poor are happy, things are lit impossibly well, and folk life is idealized). Your ticket also includes the Austrian Baroque and Gothic art in the Lower Palace. Prince Eugene lived in that palace, but he's long gone, and I wouldn't bother to visit.

▲▲Haus der Musik—Vienna's House of Music has a small first-floor exhibit on the Vienna Philharmonic, and upstairs you'll enjoy fine audiovisual exhibits on each of the famous hometown boys (Haydn, Mozart, Beethoven, Strauss, and Mahler). But the museum is unique for its effective use of interactive touch-screen computers and headphones to actually explore the physics of sound. You can twist, dissect, and bend sounds to make your own musical language, merging your voice with a duck's quack or a city's traffic roar. Wander through the "sonosphere" and marvel at the amazing acoustics—I could actually hear what I thought only a piano tuner could hear. Pick up a virtual baton to conduct the Vienna Philharmonic Orchestra (each time you screw up, the musicians put their instruments down and ridicule you). A computer will help you compose your own waltz by throwing dice. Really experiencing the place takes time. It's open late and makes a good evening activity (€10, daily 10:00–22:00, 2 blocks from Opera at Seilerstatte 30, tel. 01/51648, www.hdm.at).

▲Vienna's Auction House, the Dorotheum—For an aristocrat's flea market, drop by Austria's answer to Sotheby's, the Dorotheum. Its five floors of antique furniture and fancy knickknacks have been put up either for immediate sale or auction, often by people who inherited old things they don't have room for (Mon–Fri

10:00–18:00, Sat 9:00–17:00, closed Sun, classy little café on second floor, between Graben and Hofburg at Dorotheergasse 17, tel. 01/515-600). Fliers show schedules for actual auctions, which you are welcome to attend.

Judenplatz Memorial and Museum—The square called Judenplatz marks the location of Vienna's 15th-century Jewish community, one of Europe's largest at the time. The square, once filled with a long-gone synagogue, is now dominated by a blocky memorial to the 65,000 Austrian Jews killed by the Nazis. The memorial—a library turned inside out—symbolizes Jews as "people of the book" and causes one to ponder the huge loss of culture, knowledge, and humanity that took place between 1938 and 1945.

The Judenplatz Museum, while sparse, has displays on medieval Jewish life and a well-done video re-creating community scenes from five centuries ago. Wander the scant remains of the medieval synagogue below street level—discovered during the construction of the Holocaust memorial. This was the scene of a medieval massacre. Since Christians weren't allowed to lend money, Jews were Europe's moneylenders. As so often happened in Europe, when Christian locals fell too deeply into debt, they found a convenient excuse to wipe out the local ghetto—and their debts at the same time. In 1421, 200 of Vienna's Jews were burned at the stake. Others who refused a forced conversion committed mass suicide in the synagogue (€3, €7 combo-ticket includes a synagogue and Jewish Museum of the City of Vienna—see below, Sun–Thu 10:00–18:00, Fri 10:00–14:00, closed Sat, Judenplatz 8, tel. 01/535-0431).

Honorable Mentions—There's much, much more. The city map lists everything. If you're into Esperanto, undertakers, tobacco, clowns, firefighting, Freud, or the homes of dead composers, you'll find them all in Vienna. Several good museums that try very hard, but are submerged in the greatness of Vienna include: **Jewish Museum of the City of Vienna** (€5, or €7 combo-ticket includes synagogue and Judenplatz Museum—listed above, Sun–Fri 10:00–18:00, Thu until 20:00, closed Sat, Dorotheergasse 11, tel. 01/535-0431, www.jmw.at), **Folkloric Museum of Austria** (Tue–Sun 10:00–17:00, closed Mon, Laudongasse 15, tel. 01/406-8905), and **Museum of Military History**, one of Europe's best if you like swords and shields (Heeresgeschichtliches Museum, Sat–Thu 9:00–17:00, closed Fri, Arsenal district, Objekt 18, tel. 01/795-610). The vast **Austrian Museum of Applied Arts** (Österreichisches Museum für Angewandte Kunst, or "MAK") is Vienna's answer to London's Victoria and Albert collection. The museum shows off the fancies of local aristocratic society, including a fine *Jugendstil* collection (€8, free Sat, open Tue–Sun 10:00–18:00, Tue until 24:00, closed Mon, Stubenring 5, tel. 01/711-360, www.mak.at).

Top People-Watching and Strolling Sights

▲**City Park (Stadtpark)**—Vienna's City Park is a waltzing world of gardens, memorials to local musicians, ponds, peacocks, music in bandstands, and locals escaping the city. Notice the *Jugendstil* entrance at the Stadtpark U-Bahn station. The Kursalon, where Strauss was the violin-toting master of waltzing ceremonies, hosts daily touristy concerts in three-quarter time.

▲**Prater**—Since the 1780s, when the reformist Emperor Josef II gave his hunting grounds to the people of Vienna as a public park, this place has been Vienna's playground. While tired and a bit run-down these days, Vienna's sprawling amusement park still tempts visitors with its huge 220-foot-tall, famous, and lazy Ferris wheel *(Riesenrad),* roller coaster, bumper cars, Lilliputian railroad, and endless eateries. Especially if you're traveling with kids, this is a fun, goofy place to share the evening with thousands of Viennese (daily 9:00–24:00 in summer, but quiet after 22:00, U-1: Praterstern). For a local-style family dinner, eat at Schweizerhaus (good food, great beer) or Wieselburger Bierinsel.

Sunbathing—Like most Europeans, the Austrians worship the sun. Their lavish swimming centers are as much for tanning as swimming. To find the scene, follow the locals to their "Danube Sea" and a 20-mile, skinny, man-made beach along Danube Island. The stretch of traffic-free concrete and grass is packed with in-line skaters and bikers, and includes rocky river access and a fun park (easy U-Bahn access on U-1 to Donauinsel).

A Walk in the Vienna Woods (Wienerwald)—For a quick side-trip into the woods and out of the city, catch the U-4 to Heiligenstadt, then bus #38A to Kahlenberg, where you'll enjoy great views and a café overlooking the city. From there, it's a peaceful, 45-minute, downhill hike to the *Heurigen* of Nussdorf or Grinzing to enjoy some new wine (see "Vienna's Wine Gardens," page 575).

City Hall (Rathaus) Food Circus and Open-Air Cinema—A thriving people scene erupts each evening through the summer in front of the City Hall (Rathaus) on the Ring. You'll find lots of colorful, food circus–type eateries and free movies of excellent concerts (see "Eating" and "Summer Music Scene," below).

Naschmarkt—Vienna's busy produce market is a great place for people-watching (see page 563).

Near Vienna: Schönbrunn Palace

Among Europe's palaces, only Schönbrunn Palace (Schloss Schönbrunn) rivals Versailles. Worth ▲▲▲ and located four miles from the center, it was the Hapsburgs' summer residence. It's big (1,441 rooms), but don't worry—only 40 rooms are shown to the public. (Today, the families of 260 civil servants rent simple apartments in the rest of the palace.)

While the exterior is Baroque, the interior was finished under Maria Theresa in let-them-eat-cake rococo. The chandeliers are either of hand-carved wood with gold-leaf gilding, or of Bohemian crystal. Thick walls hid the servants as they ran around stoking the ceramic stoves from the back, and so on. Most of the public rooms are decorated in neo-Baroque, as they were under Franz Josef (r. 1848–1916). When WWII bombs rained on the city and the palace grounds, the palace itself took only one direct hit. Thankfully, that bomb, which crashed through three floors—including the sumptuous central ballroom—was a dud.

Reservations and Hours: Schönbrunn suffers from crowds. To avoid the long delays in July and August (mornings are worst), make a reservation by telephone (tel. 01/8111-3239, answered daily 8:00–17:00). You'll get an appointment time and a ticket number. Check in at least 30 minutes early. Upon arrival, go to the group desk, give your number, pick up your ticket, and jump in ahead of the masses. If you show up in peak season without calling first, you deserve the frustration. Wait in line, buy your ticket, and wait until the listed time to enter (which could be tomorrow). Kill time in the gardens or coach museum (palace open April–Oct daily 8:30–17:00, July–Aug daily until 18:00, Nov–March daily 8:30–16:30). Crowds are worst from 9:30 to 11:30, especially on weekends and in July and August; it's least crowded from 12:00 to 14:00 and after 16:00.

Cost and Tours: The admission price is based on the tour you select. Choose between two audioguide tours: the Imperial Tour (22 rooms, €8, 35 min, Grand Palace rooms, plus apartments of Franz Josef and Elisabeth—mostly 19th-century, and therefore least interesting) or the Grand Tour (40 rooms, €10.50, 50 min, adds apartments of Maria Theresa—18th-century rococo). The Schönbrunn Pass Classic includes the Grand Tour, Gloriette viewing terrace, maze, privy garden, and the court bakery—complete with *Apfelstrudel* demo and tasting (€15, available April–Oct only; more info: www.schoenbrunn.at). I'd go for the Grand Tour.

Getting to the Palace: Take tram #58 from Westbahnhof directly to the palace, or ride U-4 to Schönbrunn and walk 400 yards. The main entrance is in the left side of the palace as you face it.

Palace Gardens—After strolling through all the Hapsburgs tucked neatly into their crypts, a stroll through the emperor's garden with countless commoners is a celebration of the natural evolution of civilization from autocracy into real democracy. As a civilization, we're doing well.

The sculpted **gardens** (with a palm house, €3.50, May–Sept daily 9:30–18:00, Oct–April daily 9:30–17:00) lead past Europe's oldest **zoo** (*Tiergarten,* built by Maria Theresa's husband for the entertainment and education of the court in 1752; €12, May–Sept daily 9:00–18:30, less off-season, tel. 01/877-9294) up to the

Gloriette, a purely decorative monument celebrating an obscure Austrian military victory and offering a fine city view (viewing terrace–€2.30, included in €15 Schönbrunn Pass Classic, April–Sept daily 9:00–18:00, July–Aug daily until 19:00, Oct daily until 17:00, closed Nov–March). The park itself is free (daily sunrise–dusk, entrance on either side of the palace). A touristy choo-choo train makes the rounds all day, connecting Schönbrunn's many attractions.

Coach Museum Wagenburg—The Schönbrunn coach museum is a 19th-century traffic jam of 50 impressive royal carriages and sleighs. Highlights include silly sedan chairs, the death-black hearse carriage (used for Franz Josef in 1916, and most recently for Empress Zita in 1989), and an extravagantly gilded imperial carriage pulled by eight Cinderella horses. This was rarely used other than for the coronation of Holy Roman Emperors, when it was disassembled and taken to Frankfurt for the big event (€4.50; April–Oct daily 9:00–18:00; Nov–March Tue–Sun 10:00–16:00, closed Mon; last entry 30 min before closing, 200 yards from palace, walk through right arch as you face palace, tel. 01/877-3244).

ACTIVITIES

Summer Music Scene

As far back as the 12th century, Vienna was a mecca for musicians—both sacred and secular (troubadours). The Hapsburg emperors of the 17th and 18th centuries were not only generous supporters of music, but also fine musicians and composers themselves. (Maria Theresa played a mean double bass.) Composers like Haydn, Mozart, Beethoven, Schubert, Brahms, and Mahler gravitated to this music-friendly environment. They taught each other, jammed together, and spent a lot of time in Hapsburg palaces. Beethoven was a famous figure, walking—lost in musical thought—through Vienna's woods. In the city's 19th-century belle époque, "Waltz King" Johann Strauss and his brothers kept Vienna's 300 ballrooms spinning.

This musical tradition has continued into modern times, leaving some prestigious Viennese institutions for today's tourists to enjoy: the Opera, the Boys' Choir, and the great Baroque halls and churches, all busy with classical and waltz concerts.

Vienna is Europe's music capital. It's music *con brio* from October through June, reaching a symphonic climax during the Vienna Festival each May and June. Sadly, in July and August, the Boys' Choir, the Opera, and many more music companies are—like you—on vacation. But Vienna hums year-round with live classical music. In the summer, you have these basic choices:

Touristy Mozart and Strauss Concerts—If the music comes to you, it's touristy—designed for flash-in-the-pan Mozart fans. Powdered-wig orchestra performances are given almost nightly in grand traditional settings (€25–50). Pesky wigged-and-powdered Mozarts peddle tickets in the streets. They rave about the quality of the musicians, but you'll get second-rate chamber orchestras, clad in historic costumes, performing the greatest hits of Mozart and Strauss. These are casual, easygoing concerts with lots of tour groups. While there's not a local person in the audience, tourists generally enjoy the evening. To sort through all your options, check with the ticket office in the TI (same price as on the street but with all venues to choose from). Savvy locals suggest getting the cheapest tickets, as no one

seems to care if cheapskates move up to fill unsold pricier seats. Critics explain that the musicians are actually very good (often Hungarians, Poles, and Russians working a season here to fund an entire year of music studies back home), but that they haven't performed much together, so aren't "tight." The Mozarthaus is a small room richly decorated in Venetian Renaissance style with intimate chamber-music concerts (€30, almost nightly at 19:30, near St. Stephan's Cathedral at Singerstrasse 7, tel. 01/911-9077).

Strauss Concerts in the Kursalon—For years, Strauss concerts have been held in the Kursalon, where the "Waltz King" himself directed wildly popular concerts 100 years ago (€32–49, 4 concerts nightly April–Oct, 1 concert nightly other months, tel. 01/512-5790). Shows are a touristy mix of ballet, waltzes, and a 15-piece orchestra in wigs and old outfits. For the cheap option, enjoy a summer-afternoon coffee concert (free if you buy a drink, weekends and maybe also weekdays July–Aug 15:00–17:00).

Serious Concerts—These events, including the Opera, are listed in the monthly *Wien-Programm* (available at TI). Tickets run from €36 to €75 (plus a stiff 22 percent booking fee when booked in advance or through a box office, like the one at the TI). While it's easy to book tickets online long in advance, spontaneity is also workable, as there are invariably people with tickets they don't need selling them at face value or less outside the door before concert time. If you call a concert hall directly, they can advise you on the availability of (cheaper) tickets at the door. Vienna takes care of its starving artists (and tourists) by offering cheap standing-room tickets to top-notch music and opera (1 hr before showtime).

Vienna's **Summer of Music Festival** (a.k.a. "KlangBogen") assures that even from June through September, you'll find lots of great concerts, choirs, and symphonies (special *KlangBogen* brochure at TI; get tickets at Wien Ticket pavilion off Kärntner Strasse next to Opera House, or go directly to location of particular event; Summer of Music tel. 01/42717, www.klangbogen.at).

Musicals—The Wien Ticket pavilion sells tickets to contemporary American and British musicals done in German language (€10–95 with €2.50 standing room), and offers these tickets at half price from 14:00 until 17:00 on the day of the show. Or you can reserve (full-price) tickets for the musicals by calling up to one day ahead (call combined office of the 3 big theaters at tel. 01/58885).

Vienna Boys' Choir—The boys sing (heard but not seen, from a high balcony) at Mass in the Imperial Chapel (Hofburgkapelle) of the Hofburg (entrance at Schweizerhof, from Josefsplatz go through tunnel) 9:15–10:30 on Sundays, except in July and August. While seats must be reserved two months in advance (€5–29, reserve by fax, e-mail, or mail: fax from the U.S. 011-43-1/533-992-775, hmk@aon.at, or write Hofmusikkapelle, Hofburg-Schweizerhof, 1010 Wien; tel. for information only—cannot book tickets—01/533-9927), the standing room inside is free and open to the first 60 who line up. Rather than line up early, you can simply swing by and stand in the narthex just outside, where you can hear the boys and see the Mass on a TV monitor. Boys' Choir concerts (on stage at the Musikverein) are also given Fridays at 16:00 in May, June, September, and October (€35–48, standing room goes on sale at 15:30 for €15, Karlsplatz 6, U-1, U-2, or U-4: Karlsplatz, tel. 01/5880-4141). They're nice kids, but, for my taste, not worth all the commotion. Remember, many churches have great music during Sunday Mass. Just 200 yards from the Boys' Choir chapel, Augustinian Church has a glorious 11:00 service each Sunday (see page 560).

Summer Music and Film Festival at the City Hall (Rathaus)—The park in front of the City Hall thrives nightly in July and August, as a huge screen is set up with top-end speakers to show films of great concerts. While it's not live, the quality is excellent, and it's free—and single locals know this is the best pickup place in town. Classical, opera, or jazz, there's a different concert every night. Go early to enjoy dinner in the park, as there are countless (mostly ethnic) stalls serving fun and cheap meals to the youthful gang (daily from 11:00 until late in July and Aug). Film schedules are at the TI.

2006: The Year of Mozart—Mozart, born in 1756, would be turning 250 years old in 2006 if he had taken better care of himself. Vienna and Salzburg will celebrate the occasion with a busy schedule of Mozart concerts (details at TI).

Classical Music to Go—To bring home Beethoven, Strauss, or the Wiener Philharmonic on a top-quality CD, shop at Gramola on the Graben, Emi on Kärntner Strasse, or Virgin Megastore on Mariahilfer Strasse.

EXPERIENCES

Vienna's Cafés

In Vienna, the living room is down the street at the neighborhood coffeehouse. This tradition is just another example of Viennese expertise in good living. Each of Vienna's many long-established (and sometimes even legendary) coffeehouses has its individual character (and characters). These classic cafés are a bit tired, with a shabby patina and famously grumpy waiters who treat you like an uninvited guest invading their living room. Still, they're welcoming places. They offer newspapers, pastries, sofas, quick and light workers' lunches, elegance, smoky ambience, and "take all the time you want" charm for the price of a cup of coffee. Order it *melange* (like a cappuccino), *brauner* (strong coffee with a little milk), or *schwarzer* (black). Americans who ask for a latte are mistaken for Italians and given a cup of hot milk. Rather than buy the *Herald Tribune* ahead of time, spend the money on a cup of coffee and read it for free, Vienna-style, in a café.

My favorites are: **Café Hawelka,** with a dark, "brooding Trotsky" atmosphere, paintings by struggling artists who couldn't pay for coffee, a saloon-wood flavor, chalkboard menu, smoked velvet couches, an international selection of newspapers, and a phone that rings for regulars (Wed–Mon 8:00–2:00, Sun from 16:00, closed Tue, just off Graben, Dorotheergasse 6); **Café Central,** with *Jugendstil* decor and great *Apfelstrudel* (high prices and stiff staff, Mon–Sat 8:00–22:00, Sun 10:00–18:00, Herrengasse 14, tel. 01/533-376-326); the **Café Sperl,** dating from 1880 with furnishings identical to the day it opened, from the coat tree to the chairs (Mon–Sat 7:00–23:00, Sun 11:00–20:00 except closed Sun July–Aug, just off Naschmarkt near Mariahilfer Strasse, Gumpendorfer 11, tel. 01/586-4158); and the basic, untouristy **Café Ritter** (daily 7:30–23:30, Mariahilfer Strasse 73, U-3: Neubaugasse, near several recommended hotels, tel. 01/587-8237).

If **Starbucks** seems big in Vienna, it's because the Seattle-based coffee firm has decided to test the Euro-waters here. Apparently, they figured that Vienna—with its love of fine coffee—would be a tough market to crack...and if they could succeed here, they could take Europe. Locals report that Starbucks is popular with teenagers and tourists, but the coffee is overpriced, and flavored coffee is nonsense to Viennese connoisseurs. Even so, the "coffee to go" trend has been picked up by many bakeries and other joints.

Vienna's Wine Gardens (Heurigen)

The uniquely Viennese institution of *Heurige* is two things: a wine, and a place to drink it. When the Hapsburgs let Vienna's vintners sell their own new wine *(Heurige)* tax-free, several hundred families opened *Heurigen* (wine-garden restaurants clustered around the edge of town)—and a tradition was born. Today, they do their best to maintain the old-village atmosphere, serving the homemade new wine (the last vintage, until November 11, when a new vintage year begins) with light meals and strolling musicians. Most *Heurigen* are decorated with enormous antique presses from their vineyards. Wine gardens might be closed on any given day; if you have your heart set on a particular place, always call ahead to confirm. (For a near-*Heurige* experience right downtown, drop by Gigerl Stadtheuriger—see "Eating," page 586.)

At any *Heurige,* fill your plate at a self-serve, cold-cut buffet (€6–9 for dinner). Food is sold by the *"10 dag"* unit. (A *dag* is a decigram, so *10 dag* is 100 grams...about a quarter pound.) Dishes to look out for: *Stelze* (grilled knuckle of pork), *Fleischlaberln* (fried ground-meat patties), *Schinkenfleckerln* (pasta with cheese and ham), *Schmalz* (a spread made with pig fat), *Blunzen* (black pudding...sausage made from blood), *Presskopf* (jellied brains and innards), *Liptauer* (spicy cheese spread), *Kornspitz* (whole-meal bread roll), and *Kummelbraten* (crispy roast pork with caraway). Waitresses will then take your wine order (€2.20 per quarter liter, about 8 oz). Many locals claim it takes several years of practice to distinguish between *Heurige* and vinegar.

There are more than 1,700 acres of vineyards within Vienna's city limits, and countless *Heurige* taverns. For a *Heurige* evening, rather than go to a particular place, take a tram to the wine-garden district of your choice and wander around, choosing the place with the best ambience.

Getting to the Heurigen: You have three options: a 15-minute taxi ride, trams and buses, or a goofy tourist train.

Trams make a trip to the Vienna Woods quick and affordable. The fastest way is to ride U-4 to its last stop, Heiligenstadt, where trams and buses in front of the station fan out to the various neighborhoods. Ride tram D to its end point for Nussdorf. Ride bus #38A for Grinzing and on to the Kahlenberg viewpoint—#38A's end station. (Note that tram #38—different from bus #38A—starts at the Ring and finishes at Grinzing). To get to Neustift am Walde, ride U-6 to Nussdorfer Strasse and catch bus #35A. Connect Grinzing and Nussdorf with bus #38A and tram D (transfer at Grinzingerstrasse).

The **Heuriger Express** train is tacky, but handy and relaxing, chugging you on a hop-on, hop-off circle from Nussdorf through Grinzing and around the Vienna Woods with a light narration (€7.30, buy ticket from driver, 60 min, April–Oct daily 12:00–19:00, departs from end station of tram D in Nussdorf at the top of every hr, tel. 01/479-2808).

Here are a couple good *Heurige* neighborhoods:

Grinzing: Of the many *Heurige* suburbs, Grinzing is the most famous, lively...and touristy. Many people precede their visit to Grinzing by riding tram #38A from Schottentor (on the Ring) to its end (up to Kahlenberg for a grand Vienna view), and then ride 20 minutes back into the *Heurige* action. From the Grinzing tram stop, follow Himmelgasse uphill toward the onion-top dome. You'll pass plenty of wine gardens—and tour buses—on your way up. Just past the dome, you'll find the heart of the *Heurige.*

Heiligenstadt (Pfarrplatz): Between Grinzing and Nussdorf, this area features several decent spots, including the famous and touristy Mayer am Pfarrplatz (a.k.a **Beethovenhaus,** Mon–Sat 16:00–23:00, Sun 11:00–23:00, bus #38A stop: Fernsprechamt/ Heiligenstadt, walk 5 min uphill on Dübling Nestelbachgasse to Pfarrplatz 2, tel. 01/370-3361). This place has a charming inner courtyard with an accordion player, and a sprawling backyard with a big children's play zone. Beethoven lived—and composed his *Sixth Symphony*—here in 1817. He hoped the local spa would cure his worsening deafness. **Weingut and Heuriger Werner Welser,** a block uphill from Beethoven's place, is lots of fun, with music nightly from 19:00 (open daily 15:30–24:00, Probusgasse 12, tel. 01/318-9797).

Nussdorf: A less touristy district—characteristic and popular with locals—Nussdorf has plenty of *Heurige* ambience. Right at the end station of tram D, you'll find three long and skinny places side by side: **Schübel-Auer Heuriger** (Tue–Sat 16:00–24:00, closed Sun–Mon, Kahlenbergerstrasse 22, tel. 01/370-2222) is my favorite. Also consider **Heuriger Kierlinger** (daily 15:30–24:00, Kahlenbergerstrasse 20, tel. 01/370-2264) and **Steinschaden** (daily 15:00–24:00, Kahlenbergerstrasse 18, tel. 01/370-1375). Walk through any of these and you pop out on Kahlenbergerstrasse, where a walk 20 yards uphill takes you to some more eating and drinking fun: **Bamkraxler** ("Tree Jumper"), the only beer garden amid all these vineyards. It's a fun-loving, youthful place with fine keg beer and a regular menu—traditional, ribs, veggie, kids' menu—rather than the *Heurige* cafeteria line (€6–10 meals, kids' playground, Tue–Sat 16:00–24:00, Sun 11:00–24:00, closed Mon, Kahlenbergerstrasse 17, tel. 01/318-8800).

Sirbu Weinbau Heuriger is actually in the vineyards, high above Vienna with great city and countryside views, a top-notch buffet, a glass veranda, and a traditional interior for cool weather. This place is a bit more touristy, since it's more upmarket and famous as "the ultimate setting" (from 15:00, closed Sun, big children's play zone, Kahlenbergerstrasse 210, tel. 01/320-5928). It's high above regular transit service, but fun to incorporate into a little walking. Ideally, ride bus #38A to the end at Kahlenberg, and ask for directions to the Heuriger (a 20-min walk downhill).

NIGHTLIFE

If old music and new wine aren't your thing, Vienna has plenty of alternatives. For an up-to-date rundown on fun after dark, get the TI's free *Vienna Hype* booklet.

Bermuda Triangle (Bermuda Dreieck)—The area known as the "Bermuda Triangle"—north of St. Stephan's Cathedral, between Rotenturmstrasse and Judengasse—is the hot local nightspot. You'll find lots of music clubs and classy pubs, or *Beisl* (such as Krah Krah, Salzamt, Bermuda Bräu, and First Floor—for cocktails with live fish). The serious-looking guards have nothing to do with the bar scene—they're guarding the synagogue nearby.

Gürtel—The Gürtel is Vienna's outer ring road. The arches of a lumbering viaduct (which carries a train track) are now filled with trendy bars, dance clubs, antique shops, and restaurants. To experience—or simply see—the latest scene in town, head out here. The people-watching—the trendiest kids on the block—makes the trip fun, even if you're looking for exercise, rather than a drink. Ride U-6 to Nussdorfer Strasse or Thaliastrasse and hike along the viaduct.

English Cinema—Two great theaters offer three or four screens of English movies nightly (€6–9): **English Cinema Haydn,** by my recommended hotels on Mariahilfer Strasse (Mariahilfer Strasse 57, tel. 01/587-2262, www.haydnkino.at); and **Artis International Cinema,** right in the town center a few minutes from the cathedral (Schultergasse 5, tel. 01/535-6570).

SLEEPING

My recommendations stretch mainly from the center (figure at least €100 for a decent double), along the likeable Mariahilfer Strasse (around €80), to the Westbahnhof (around €60). While few places in Vienna are air-conditioned (they are troubled by the fact that, per person, Las Vegas expends more energy keeping people cool than arctic Norway does to keep people warm), you can generally get fans on request. Even places with elevators often have a few stairs to climb, too.

These hotels lose big—and you pay more—if you find a room through Internet booking sites. Book direct by phone, fax, or e-mail and save. Most places will hold a room without a deposit if you promise to arrive before 17:00.

Within the Ring, in the Old City Center

You'll pay extra to sleep in the atmospheric old center, but if you can afford it, staying here gives you the best classy Vienna experience.

$$$ **Pension Pertschy** circles an old courtyard and is bigger and more hotelesque than the others listed here. Its 50 rooms are huge, but well-worn and a bit musty. Those on the courtyard are quietest (Sb-€77, small Db-€117, large Db-€170, cheaper off-season, extra bed-€30, non-smoking rooms, elevator, U-1 or U-3: Stephansplatz, Habsburgergasse 5, tel. 01/534-490, fax 01/534-4949, www.pertschy.com, pertschy@pertschy.com).

$$$ **Pension Neuer Markt** is a four-star place that feels like

Sleep Code

(€1 = about $1.20, country code: 43, area code: 01)
S = Single, **D** = Double/Twin, **T** = Triple, **Q** = Quad,
b = bathroom, **s** = shower only. English is spoken at each place.
Unless otherwise noted, credit cards are accepted and breakfast is
included.

To help you sort easily through these listings, I've divided
the rooms into three categories, based on the price for a standard
double room with bath:

  $$$ **Higher Priced**—Most rooms €115 or more.
    $$ **Moderately Priced**—Most rooms between €75–115.
     $ **Lower Priced**—Most rooms €75 or less.

it's family-run, with 37 quiet, comfy, old-feeling rooms in a very central locale (Ss-€85, Sb-€105, smaller Ds-€96, Db-€125, prices can vary with season and room size, extra bed-€20, elevator, Seilergasse 9, tel. 01/512-2316, fax 01/513-9105, www.hotelpension.at/neuermarkt, neuermarkt@hotelpension.at).

$$$ Pension Aviano is another peaceful four-star place, with 17 comfortable rooms on the fourth floor above lots of old center action (Sb-€85, Db-€125–145 depending on size, 15 percent cheaper Nov–March, extra bed-€30, elevator, non-smoking rooms, between Neuer Markt and Kärntner Strasse at Marco d'Avianogasse 1, tel. 01/512-8330, fax 01/5128-3306, www.pertschy.com, aviano @pertschy.com).

$$$ Hotel Schweizerhof is a classy, 55-room place with big rooms, three-star comforts, and a more formal ambience. It's centrally located midway between St. Stephan's Cathedral and the Danube canal (Sb-€84–88, Db-€109–131, Tb-€131–146, low prices are for July–Aug and slow times; with cash and this book, get your best price and then claim a 10 percent discount in 2005, elevator, can be noisy on weekends, Bauernmarkt 22, U-1 or U-3: Stephansplatz, tel. 01/533-1931, fax 01/533-0214, www.schweizerhof.at, office@schweizerhof.at).

$$$ Hotel zur Wiener Staatsoper, the Schweizerhof's sister hotel, is quiet and rich. Its 22 tight rooms come with high ceilings, chandeliers, and fancy carpets on parquet floors—ideal for people whose hotel tastes are a cut above mine. The singles are tiny, with beds too short for anyone over six feet tall (Sb-€76–88, Db-€111–126, Tb-€133–148, extra bed-€22, cheaper prices are for July–Aug and Dec–March, fans on request, elevator, U-1, U-2, or U-4: Karlsplatz, a block from Opera at Krugerstrasse 11, tel. 01/513-1274, fax 01/513-127-415, www.zurwienerstaatsoper.at, office @zurwienerstaatsoper.at, manager Claudia).

Hotels and Restaurants in Central Vienna

1. Pension Pertschy
2. Pension Neuer Markt
3. Pension Aviano
4. To Hotel Schweizerhof & Pension Dr. Geissler
5. Hotel zur Wiener Staatsoper
6. Pension Nossek
7. Pension Suzanne
8. To Schweizer Pension Solderer
9. Restaurant Rosenberger Markt
10. Restaurant Gigerl Stadtheuriger
11. To Restaurants Brezel-Gwölb, Ofenloch & Beisl Zum Scherer
12. To Zu den Drei Hacken
13. Wrenkh Vegetarian Restaurant
14. Buffet Trzesniewski
15. Café Rest. Palmenhaus & BBQ
16. Julius Meinl am Graben Deli
17. Café Hawelka
18. Rest. Esterhazykeller
19. To Café Central & Restaurant Melker Stiftskeller
20. Sacher Café
21. Zanoni & Zanoni Ice Cream
22. Plachutta Restaurant
23. Ferdinandt Zwickl-Beisl
24. Loos American Bar

$$ At **Pension Nossek,** an elevator takes you above any street noise into Frau Bernad's and Frau Gundolf's world, where the children seem to be placed among the lace and flowers by an interior designer. Right on the wonderful Graben, this is a particularly good value (30 rooms, S-€46–54, Ss-€58, Sb-€69–73, Db-€110, €25 extra for sprawling suites, extra bed-€35, cash only, elevator, U-1 or U-3: Stephansplatz, Graben 17, tel. 01/5337-0410, fax 01/535-3646, www.pension-nossek.at, reservation@pension-nossek.at).

$$ Pension Suzanne, as Baroque and doily as you'll find in this price range, is wonderfully located a few yards from the Opera. It's small, but run with the class of a bigger hotel; the 26 rooms are packed with properly Viennese antique furnishings. Streetside rooms come with some noise (Sb-€76, Db-€94–115 depending on size, 4 percent discount with cash, extra bed-€30, spacious apartment for up to 6 also available, discounts in winter, fans on request, elevator, a block from Opera, U-1, U-2, or U-4: Karlsplatz and follow signs for *Opera* exit, Walfischgasse 4, tel. 01/513-2507, fax 01/513-2500, www.pension -suzanne.at, info@pension-suzanne.at, manager Michael).

$$ Schweizer Pension Solderer, family-owned for three generations, is run by Anita. She runs an extremely tight ship, offering 11 homey rooms, parquet floors, and lots of tourist info (S-€38–42, Sb-€55–65, D-€58–65, Db-€78–87, Tb-€102–109, Qb-€126–131, prices depend on season and room size, cash only, entirely non-smoking, elevator, laundry-€11/load, U-2 or U-4: Schottenring, Heinrichsgasse 2, tel. 01/533-8156, fax 01/535-6469, www.schweizerpension.com, schweizer.pension@chello.at).

$$ Pension Dr. Geissler has 23 comfortable rooms on the eighth floor of a modern building about 10 blocks northeast of St. Stephan's, near the canal (S-€48, Ss-€68, Sb-€76, D-€60, Ds-€77, Db-€95, 20 percent less in winter, elevator, U-1 or U-4: Schwedenplatz, Postgasse 14, tel. 01/533-2803, fax 01/533-2635, www.hotelpension.at/dr-geissler, dr.geissler@hotelpension.at).

Hotels and Pensions along Mariahilfer Strasse

Lively Mariahilfer Strasse connects the Westbahnhof (West Station) and the city center. The U-3 line, starting at the Westbahnhof, goes down Mariahilfer Strasse to the cathedral. This very Viennese street is a tourist-friendly and vibrant area filled with local shops and cafés. Most hotels are within a few steps of a U-Bahn stop, just one or two stops from the Westbahnhof (direction from the station: Simmering).

$$$ NH Hotels, a Spanish chain, runs two stern, passionless business hotels a few blocks apart on Mariahilfer Strasse. Both rent ideal-for-families suites, each with a living room, two TVs, bathroom, desk, and kitchenette (rack rate: Db suite-€155, going rate usually closer to €100, plus €13 per person for optional breakfast, apartments for 2–3 adults, kids under 12 free, non-smoking rooms, elevator). The 78-room **NH Atterseehaus** is at Mariahilfer Strasse 78 (U-3: Zieglergasse, tel. 01/5245-6000, fax 01/524-560-015, nhatterseehaus@nh-hotels.com), and the **NH Wien** has 106 rooms at Mariahilfer Strasse 32 (U-3: Neubaugasse, tel. 01/521-720, fax 01/521-7215, nhwien@nh-hotels.com). The Web site for both is www.nh-hotels.com.

$$ **Pension Corvinus** is bright, modern, and warmly run by a Hungarian family: Miklos, Judit, and Zoltan. Its eight comfortable rooms are spacious, with small, yacht-type bathrooms (Sb-€58, Db-€91, Tb-€105, extra bed-€26, non-smoking rooms, portable air-con-€10, elevator, free Internet access, parking garage-€11/day, on the third floor at Mariahilfer Strasse 57–59, tel. 01/587-7239, fax 01/587-723-920, www.corvinus.at, hotel@corvinus.at).

$$ **Pension Mariahilf** is a four-star place offering a clean, aristocratic air in an affordable and cozy pension package. Its 12 rooms are spacious but outmoded, with an Art Deco flair (Sb-€59–66, Db-€95–102, Tb-€124, lower prices are for longer stays, elevator, U-3: Neubaugasse, Mariahilfer Strasse 49, tel. 01/586-1781, fax 01/586-178-122, penma@inode.at).

$$ **Haydn Hotel,** in the same building as the Pension Corvinus (listed above), is a big, fancy, dark place with 40 spacious rooms that have seen better days (Sb-€58–70, Db-€90–100, 10 percent discount with cash and this book in 2005, suites and family apartments, extra bed-€30, air-con, elevator, free Internet access, Mariahilfer Strasse 57–59, tel. 01/587-44140, fax 01/586-1950, www.haydn-hotel.at, info@haydn-hotel.at, Nouri).

$$ **Hotel Admiral** is huge, quiet, and practical, with 80 large, comfortable rooms (Sb-€66, Db-€91, extra bed-€23, manager Alexandra promises these prices through 2005 with this book and cash, cheaper in winter, breakfast-€5 per person, free Internet access, free parking, U-2 or U-3: Volkstheater, a block off Mariahilfer Strasse at Karl Schweighofer Gasse 7, tel. 01/521-410, fax 01/521-4116, www.admiral.co.at, hotel@admiral.co.at).

$ **Pension Hargita** rents 24 generally small, bright, and tidy rooms (mostly twins) with Hungarian decor. This spick-and-span, well-run, well-located place is an excellent value (S-€35, Ss-€40, Sb-€52, D-€48, Ds-€55, Db-€63, Ts-€70, Tb-€76, Qb-€87, breakfast-€3, U-3: Zieglergasse, corner of Mariahilfer Strasse and Andreasgasse, Andreasgasse 1, tel. 01/526-1928, fax 01/526-0492, www.hargita.at, pension@hargita.at, classy Amalia). As the place has street noise, request a room in the back.

$ **Pension Lindenhof** rents 19 worn but clean rooms and is filled with plants (S-€29, Sb-€36, D-€49, Db-€65, cash only, elevator, U-3: Neubaugasse, Lindengasse 4, tel. 01/523-0498, fax 01/523-7362, pensionlindenhof@yahoo.com, Gebrael family, Zara and Keram SE).

Hotels and Restaurants Outside the Ring

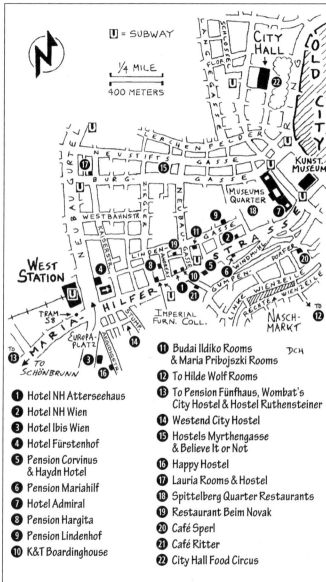

U = SUBWAY

¼ MILE

400 METERS

CITY HALL

OLD CITY

KUNST. MUSEUM

MUSEUMS QUARTER

WEST STATION

WESTBAHNSTR.

STRASSE

WINDMÜHL

DORFER

WENZEILE

LINKE WIENZEILE

RECHTE WIENZEILE

NASCH-MARKT

TRAM 58

MARIA-HILFER

EUROPA-PLATZ

TO SCHÖNBRUNN

IMPERIAL FURN. COLL.

DCH

1 Hotel NH Atterseehaus

2 Hotel NH Wien

3 Hotel Ibis Wien

4 Hotel Fürstenhof

5 Pension Corvinus & Haydn Hotel

6 Pension Mariahilf

7 Hotel Admiral

8 Pension Hargita

9 Pension Lindenhof

10 K&T Boardinghouse

11 Budai Ildiko Rooms & Maria Pribojszki Rooms

12 To Hilde Wolf Rooms

13 To Pension Fünfhaus, Wombat's City Hostel & Hostel Ruthensteiner

14 Westend City Hostel

15 Hostels Myrthengasse & Believe It or Not

16 Happy Hostel

17 Lauria Rooms & Hostel

18 Spittelberg Quarter Restaurants

19 Restaurant Beim Novak

20 Café Sperl

21 Café Ritter

22 City Hall Food Circus

$ K&T Boardinghouse rents four big, comfortable rooms facing the bustling Mariahilfer Strasse above a sex shop (Db-€65, Tb-€85, Qb-€105, 2-night minimum, no breakfast, air-con-€10, cash only, non-smoking, free Internet access, 3 flights up, no elevator, Mariahilfer Strasse 72, tel. 01/523-2989, fax 01/522-0345, www.kaled.at, kaled@chello.at, Tina SE).

$ *Private Rooms:* Two women rent rooms out of their dark and homey apartments in the same building at Lindengasse 39 (classic old elevator). Each has high ceilings and Old World furnishings, with two cavernous rooms sleeping two to four and a skinny twin room, all sharing one bathroom. These places are great if you're on a tight budget and wish you had a grandmother to visit in Vienna: **Budai Ildiko** lives on the mezzanine level and speaks English (S-€32, D-€45, T-€64, Q-€82, no breakfast but free coffee, cash only, laundry, apt. #5, tel. 01/523-1058, tel. & fax 01/526-2595, budai@hotmail.com). **Maria Pribojszki** lives on the first floor (D-€50, T-€66, Q-€88, breakfast-€4, cash only, apt. #7, tel. 01/523-9006, http://members.aon.at/bnb, bnb@aon.at).

$ Hilde Wolf, with the help of her grandson, Patrick, shares her homey apartment with travelers. Her four huge but stuffy rooms are like old libraries (S-€33, D-€48, T-€70, Q-€90, breakfast-€4, cash only, U-2: Karlsplatz, 3 blocks below Naschmarkt at Schleifmühlgasse 7, tel. 01/586-5103, fax 01/689-3505, www.schoolpool.at/bb). There's no sign or name at the street—she's on the first floor.

Near the Westbahnhof (West Station)

$$ Hotel Ibis Wien, a modern, high-rise hotel with American charm, is ideal for anyone tired of quaint old Europe. Its 340 cookie-cutter rooms are bright, comfortable, and modern, with all the conveniences (Sb-€64, Db-€79, Tb-€94, €5 more per room May–June and Aug–Oct, breakfast-€9, non-smoking rooms, air-con, elevator, parking garage-€10/day, exit Westbahnhof to the right and walk 400 yards, Mariahilfer Gürtel 22-24, tel. 01/59998, fax 01/597-9090, h0796@accor.com).

$$ Hotel Fürstenhof, right across from the station, rents 58 spacious but borderline-musty rooms. This venerable hotel has an Old World, maroon-velvet feel (S-€44, Sb-€67–92, D-€62, small Db-€95, Db-€108, Tb-€114, Qb-€120, elevator, Internet access, Europaplatz 4, tel. 01/523-3267, fax 01/523-326-726, www.hotel-fuerstenhof.com, reception@hotel-fuerstenhof.com).

$ Pension Fünfhaus is big, clean, stark, and quiet—almost institutional. Although the neighborhood is run-down and comes with a few ladies loitering late at night, this 47-room place is a good value (S-€32, Sb-€40, D-€44, Db-€52, T-€66, Tb-€78, 4-person apartments-€90, prices promised with this book in 2005, cash only, closed mid-Nov–Feb, Sperrgasse 12, tel. 01/892-3545 or 01/892-0286, fax 01/892-0460, www.pension5haus.at, Frau Susi Tersch). Half the rooms are in the fine main building and half are in the annex, which has good rooms, but is near the train tracks and a bit scary on the street at night. From the station, ride tram #52 or #58 two stops down Mariahilfer Strasse to the Kranzgasse stop, then backtrack two blocks to Sperrgasse.

Cheap Dorms and Hostels near Mariahilfer Strasse

$ **Believe It or Not** is a tiny, basic place with about the cheapest bunk beds in town, in two coed rooms for up to 10 travelers. Hardworking and friendly Heny requires a minimum two-night stay and warns that this place is appropriate only for the young at heart (bed-€13.50, €10 Nov–Easter, cash only, locked up 10:00–12:30, no curfew, kitchen facilities, Myrthengasse 10, ring apt. #14, tel. 01/526-4658, www.believe-it-or-not-vienna.at, believe_it_or_not _vienna@hotmail.com).

$ **Jugendherberge Myrthengasse** is a well-run youth hostel (260 beds, €16–18 each in 3- to 6-bed rooms, includes sheets and breakfast, non-members pay €3.50 extra, always open, no curfew, lockers and lots of facilities, Myrthengasse 7, tel. 01/523-6316, fax 01/523-5849, hostel@chello.at).

$ **Westend City Hostel,** just a block from the Westbahnhof and Mariahilfer Strasse, is well-run and well-located, with 180 beds in 4- to 12-bed dorms (€17/bed including sheets, breakfast, and a locker, cash only, laundry, Internet access, Fügergasse 3, tel. 01/597-6729, fax 01/597-672-927, www.westendhostel.at, westendcityhostel@aon.at).

$ **Happy Hostel** rents five ramshackle yet homey apartments for two to five people, beautifully located on a quiet street a couple blocks from the Westbahnhof and Mariahilfer Strasse (€25/person, Db-€50, no breakfast, Aegidigasse 19, tel. 01/208-2618, www.happyhostel.at, info@happyhostel.at).

$ **Lauria Rooms and Hostel** is a creative little place run by friendly Gosha, with two 10-bed dorms (boys and girls mixed, with lockers) and several other rooms sleeping two to six each (€13 dorm beds, around €20/person in other rooms, Kaiserstrasse 77, tram #5 or a 10-minute walk from Westbahnhof, tel. 01/522-2555, www .panda-vienna.at).

$ Other hostels with €16 beds and €40 doubles near Mariahilfer Strasse are **Wombat's City Hostel** (Grangasse 6, tel. 01/897-2336, www.wombats-hostels.com, wombats@chello.at) and **Hostel Ruthensteiner** (Robert-Hamerling-Gasse 24, tel. 01/893-4202, www.hostelruthensteiner.com, info@hostelruthensteiner.com).

EATING

The Viennese appreciate the fine points of life, and right up there with waltzing is eating. The city has many atmospheric restaurants. As you ponder the Eastern European specialties on menus, remember that Vienna's diverse empire may be gone, but its flavor lingers.

While cuisines are routinely named for countries, Vienna claims to be the only *city* with a cuisine of its own: Vienna soups come with fillings (semolina dumpling, liver dumpling, or pancake slices). *Gulasch* is a beef ragout of Hungarian origin (spiced with onion and paprika). Of course, Viennese schnitzel (Wiener schnitzel) is a breaded and fried veal cutlet. Another meat specialty is boiled beef *(Tafelspitz)*. While you're sure to have *Apfelstrudel*, try the sweet cheese strudel, too (*Topfenstrudel*—wafer-thin strudel pastry filled with sweet cheese and raisins).

On nearly every corner, you can find a colorful *Beisl*. These uniquely Viennese taverns are a characteristic cross between an English pub and a French brasserie—filled with poetry teachers and their students, couples loving without touching, housewives on their way home from cello lessons, and waiters who enjoy serving hearty food and good drinks at an affordable price. Ask at your hotel for a good *Beisl*.

Wherever you're eating, some vocabulary helps. Try the *grüner Veltliner* (dry white wine), *Traubenmost* (a heavenly grape juice—alcohol-free, but on the verge of wine), *Most* (the same thing, but lightly alcoholic), and *Sturm* (stronger than *Most*, autumn only). The local red wine (called *Portugieser*) is pretty good. Since Austrian wine is often sweet, remember the word *trocken* (dry). You can order your wine by the *Viertel* (quarter liter, 8 oz) or *Achtel* (eighth liter, 4 oz). Beer comes in a *Krügel* (half liter, 17 oz) or *Seidel* (0.3 liter, 10 oz). The *dag* you see in some prices stands for "decigram" (10 grams). Therefore, *10 dag* is 100 grams, or about a quarter pound.

Near St. Stephan's Cathedral

All of these places are within a five-minute walk of the cathedral.

Gigerl Stadtheuriger offers a near-*Heurige* experience (à la Grinzing, see "Vienna's Wine Gardens," page 575)—often with accordion or live music—without leaving the city center. Just point to what looks good. Food is sold by the weight; 100 grams *(10 dag)* is about a quarter pound (cheese and cold meats cost about €3 per 100 grams, salads are about €2 per 100 grams; price sheet is posted on the wall to right of buffet line). They also have menu entrées, along with spinach strudel, quiche, *Apfelstrudel*, and, of course, casks of new and local wines. Meals run €7–11 (daily 15:00–24:00, indoor/outdoor seating, behind cathedral, a block off Kärntner Strasse, a few cobbles off Rauhensteingasse on Blumenstock, tel. 01/513-4431).

Am Hof square (U-3: Herrengasse) is surrounded by a maze of atmospheric medieval lanes; the following places are all within a block of the square. **Restaurant Ofenloch** serves good, old-fashioned Viennese cuisine with friendly service, both indoors and out. This 300-year-old eatery, with great traditional ambience, is central, but not overrun with tourists (€12–18 main dishes, Tue–Sat 11:30–24:00, Mon 18:00–24:00, closed Sun, Kurrentgasse 8, tel. 01/533-8844). **Brezel-Gwölb,** a wonderfully atmospheric wine cellar with outdoor dining on a quiet square, serves delicious light meals, fine *Krautsuppe,* and old-fashioned local dishes. It's ideal for a romantic, late-night glass of wine (daily 11:30–1:00, leave Am Hof on Drahtgasse, then take first left to Ledererhof 9, tel. 01/533-8811). Around the corner, **Beisl "Zum Scherer"** is just as untouristy and serves traditional plates for €10. Sitting outside, you'll face a stern Holocaust memorial. Inside comes with a soothing woody atmosphere and intriguing decor (Mon–Sat 11:00–24:00, closed Sun, Judenplatz 7, tel. 01/533-5164). Just below Am Hof, the ancient and popular **Esterhazykeller** has traditional fare deep underground or outside on a delightful square (Mon–Fri 11:00–23:00, Sat–Sun 16:00–23:00, self-service buffet in lowest cellar or from menu, Haarhof 1, tel. 01/533-2614).

These wine cellars are fun and touristy, but typical, in the old center, with reasonable prices and plenty of smoke: **Melker Stiftskeller,** less touristy, is a *Stadtheurige* in a deep and rustic cellar, with hearty, inexpensive meals and new wine (Tue–Sat 17:00–24:00, closed Sun–Mon and most of July, between Am Hof and Schottentor U-Bahn stop at Schottengasse 3, tel. 01/533-5530). **Zu den Drei Hacken** is famous for its local specialties (€10 plates, Mon–Sat 11:00–23:00, closed Sun, indoor/outdoor seating, Singerstrasse 28, tel. 01/512-5895).

Ferdinandt Zwickl-Beisl is an inviting little place with a user-friendly menu featuring the classic traditional *Beisl* plates, plus salads and vegetarian dishes. Choose between Old World, woody, indoor seating and pleasant streetside seating (€7–10 plates, a block off the Kärntner Strasse mob scene at Neuer Markt 2, tel. 01/513-8991).

Wrenkh Vegetarian Restaurant and Bar is popular for its high vegetarian cuisine. Chef Wrenkh offers daily €8–10 lunch *menus* and €8–13 dinner plates in a bright, mod bar or a dark, smoke-free, fancier restaurant (daily 11:30–24:00, Bauernmarkt 10, tel. 01/533-1526).

Buffet Trzesniewski is an institution—justly famous for its elegant and cheap finger sandwiches and small beers (€0.80 each). Three different sandwiches and a *kleines Bier (Pfiff)* make a fun, light lunch. Point to whichever delights look tasty (or grab the English translation sheet and take time to study your options). Pay for your sandwiches and a drink. Take your drink tokens to the lady on the right. Sit on the bench, and scoot over to a tiny table when a spot opens up

(Mon–Fri 8:30–19:30, Sat 9:00–17:00, closed Sun, 50 yards off Graben, nearly across from brooding Café Hawelka, Dorotheergasse 2, tel. 01/512-3291). This is a good opportunity (in the fall) to try the fancy grape juices—*Most* or *Traubenmost* (see above).

Julius Meinl am Graben, a posh supermarket right on the Graben, has been famous since 1862 as a top-end delicatessen with all the gourmet fancies. Along with the picnic fixings on the shelves, there's a café with light meals and great outdoor seating, a stuffy and pricey restaurant upstairs, and a take-away counter (shop open Mon–Fri 8:30–19:30, Sat 8:30–18:00, closed Sun; restaurant open Mon–Sat until 24:00, closed Sun; Am Graben 19, tel. 01/532-3334).

Akakiko Sushi: If you're just schnitzeled out, this small chain of Japanese restaurants with an easy sushi menu may suit you. The bento box meals are tasty. Its three locations have no charm, but are fast, reasonable, and convenient (€7–10 meals, all open daily 10:00–24:00): Singerstrasse 4 (a block off Kärntner Strasse near the cathedral), Heidenschuss 3 (near other recommended eateries just off Am Hof), and Mariahilfer Strasse 42–48 (fifth floor of Kaufhaus Gerngross, near many recommended hotels).

Plachutta Restaurant, with a stylish, green-and-crème, elegant-but-comfy interior and breezy covered terrace, is famous for the best beef in town. You'll find an enticing menu with all the classic Viennese beef dishes, fine desserts, attentive service, and an enthusiastic local clientele. They've developed the art of beef to the point of producing popular cookbooks (€15–20 meals, daily 11:30–23:00, U-3: Stubentor, 10-min walk from St. Stephan's Cathedral, Wollzeile 38, tel. 01/512-1577).

Ice Cream!: **Zanoni & Zanoni** is a very Italian *gelateria* run by an Italian family. They are mobbed by happy Viennese for their huge €2 cones to go, and for their fun outdoor seating (daily 7:00–24:00, 2 blocks up Rotenturmstrasse from cathedral at Lugeck 7, tel. 01/512-7979).

Near the Opera

Café Restaurant Palmenhaus, overlooking the Palace Garden (Burggarten—see page 559), tucked away in a green and peaceful corner two blocks behind the Opera in the Hofburg's backyard, is a world apart. If you want to eat modern Austrian cuisine with palm trees rather than tourists, this is the place. And located at the edge of a huge park, it's great for families (€8 2-course lunches available Mon–Fri, €15 dinners, open daily 10:00–2:00, serious vegetarian dishes, fish, extensive wine list, indoors in greenhouse or outdoors, tel. 01/533-1033). While nobody goes to the Palmenhaus for good prices, the **Palmenhaus BBQ,** a cool, parkside outdoor pub just below that uses the same kitchen, is a wonderful value with more casual service (summer Wed–Sat from 20:00, closed Sun–Tue, open in good weather only, informal with €8 BBQ and meals posted on chalkboard).

Rosenberger Markt Restaurant is my favorite for a fast, light, and central lunch. Just a block toward the cathedral from the Opera, this place—while not cheap—is brilliant. Friendly and efficient, with special theme rooms for dining, it offers a fresh, smoke-free, and healthy cornucopia of food and drink (daily 10:30–23:00, lots of fruits, veggies, fresh-squeezed juices, addictive banana milk, ride the glass elevator downstairs, Maysedergasse 2, tel. 01/512-3458). You can stack a small salad or veggie plate into a tower of gobble for €2.80.

City Hall (Rathaus) Food Circus: During the summer, scores of outdoor food stands and hundreds of picnic tables are set up in the park in front of the City Hall. Local mobs enjoy mostly ethnic meals on disposable plates for decent-but-not-cheap prices. The fun thing here is the energy of the crowd, and a feeling that you're truly eating as the locals do...not schnitzel and quaint traditions, but trendy "world food" with people out having pure and simple fun in a fine Vienna park setting (July–Aug daily from 11:00 until late, in front of City Hall on the Ringstrasse).

Spittelberg Quarter

A charming, cobbled grid of traffic-free lanes and Biedermeier apartments has become a favorite place for Viennese wanting a little dining charm between the MuseumsQuartier and Mariahilfer Strasse (handy to many recommended hotels; take Stiftgasse from Mariahilfer Strasse, or wander over here after you close down the Kunsthistorisches or Leopold Museum). Tables tumble down sidewalks and into breezy courtyards filled with appreciative locals enjoying dinner or a relaxing drink. Stroll Spittelberggasse, Schrankgasse, and Gutenberggasse and pick your favorite place. Don't miss the vine-strewn wine garden at Schrankgasse 1. **Amerlingbeisl,** with a casual atmosphere both on the cobbled street and in its vine-covered courtyard, is a great value (€7 plates, salads, veggie dishes, traditional specialties, long hours daily, Stiftgasse 8, tel. 01/526-1660). The neighboring **Plutzer Bräu** is also good (ribs, burgers, traditional dishes, Tirolean beer from the keg, daily 11:00–2:00, Schrankgasse 4, tel. 01/526-1215). For traditional Viennese cuisine with tablecloths, consider the classier **Witwe Bolte** (daily 11:30–15:00 & 17:30–23:30, Gutenberggasse 13, tel. 01/523-1450).

Near Mariahilfer Strasse

Mariahilfer Strasse is filled with reasonable cafés serving all types of cuisine. **Restaurant Beim Novak** serves tasty and well-presented Viennese cuisine away from the modern rush. While this small and intimate place, thoughtfully run by Maximilian, has no outdoor seating, the charming back room offers a relaxing atmosphere (€7 lunch specials, €10–15 plates, Mon–Fri 11:30–15:00 & 18:00–22:00, open Sat for dinner Sept–March, closed Sun and in Aug, a block down Andreasgasse from Mariahilfer Strasse at Richtergasse 12, tel. 01/523-3244).

Naschmarkt (described on page 563) is Vienna's best Old World market, with plenty of fresh produce, cheap, local-style eateries, cafés, *döner kebab* and sausage stands, and the best-value sushi in town (Mon–Fri 7:00–18:00, Sat 6:00–18:00, closed Sun, closes earlier in winter, U-4: Kettenbrückengasse). Survey the lane of eateries at the end of the market nearest the Opera. The circa-1900 pub is inviting. Picnickers can buy their goodies at the market and eat on nearby Karlsplatz (plenty of chairs facing Charles Church).

TRANSPORTATION CONNECTIONS

Vienna has two main train stations: the Westbahnhof (West Station), serving Munich, Salzburg, Melk, and Budapest; and the Südbahnhof (South Station), serving Italy, Budapest, Prague, Poland, Slovenia, and Croatia. A third station, Franz Josefs, serves Krems and the Danube Valley (but Melk is served by the Westbahnhof). Metro line U-3 connects the Westbahnhof with the center, tram D takes you from the Südbahnhof and the Franz Josefs station to downtown, and tram #18 connects West and South stations. Train info: tel. 051-717 (to get an operator, dial 2, then 1).

From Vienna by train to: Melk (hrly, 75 min, sometimes change in St. Pölten), **Krems** (hrly, 1 hr), **Salzburg** (hrly, 3 hrs), **Innsbruck** (every 2 hrs, 5.5 hrs), **Budapest** (6/day, 3 hrs), **Prague** (6/day, 4.5 hrs), **Český Krumlov** (5/day, 6–7 hrs, up to 3 changes), **Munich** (hrly, 5.25 hrs, change in Salzburg, a few direct trains), **Berlin** (2/day, 10 hrs, longer on night train), **Zürich** (3/day, 9 hrs), **Ljubljana** (7/day, 6–7 hrs, convenient early-morning direct train, others change in Villach or Maribor), **Zagreb** (8/day, 6.5–10.5 hrs, 3 direct, others with up to 3 changes including Villach and Ljubljana), **Kraków** (4/day, 6.5–9 hrs, 2 direct including a night train departing at about 22:00, arriving around 6:00), **Warsaw** (4/day, 7.5–10 hrs, 2 direct including a night train), **Rome** (1/day, 13.5 hrs), **Venice** (3/day, 7.5 hrs, longer on night train), **Frankfurt** (4/day, 7.5 hrs), **Amsterdam** (1/day, 14.5 hrs).

Excursions with car and driver: Those wishing they had wheels may consider hiring Johann (see page 538) for Danube excursions from Vienna or en route to Salzburg (particularly economic for groups of 3–4).

To Eastern Europe: Vienna is the springboard for a quick trip to Prague and Budapest—three hours by train from Budapest (€40 one-way, €50 round-trip if you stay 4 days or less, free with Eurail) and four hours from Prague (€42 one-way, €84 round-trip,

€53 round-trip with Eurail). Americans and Canadians do not need visas to enter the Czech Republic or Hungary. Purchase tickets at most travel agencies. Eurail passholders bound for Prague must pay to ride the rails in the Czech Republic; for details, see "Transportation Connections" in the Berlin chapter.

Route Tips for Drivers

Driving in and out of Vienna: Navigating in Vienna isn't bad. Study the map. As you approach from Krems, you'll cross the North Bridge and land on the Gürtel, or outer ring. You can continue along the Danube canal to the inner ring, called the Ringstrasse (clockwise traffic only). Circle around either thoroughfare until you reach the "spoke" street you need.

Vienna West to Munich, Salzburg, and Hall in Tirol: To leave Vienna, follow the signs past the Westbahnhof to Schloss Schönbrunn (Schönbrunn Palace), which is directly on the way to the West A-1 autobahn to Linz. Leave the palace by 15:00, and you should beat rush hour.

BERLIN

No tour of Germany is complete without a look at its historic and reunited capital, a construction zone called Berlin. Stand over ripped-up tracks and under a canopy of cranes and watch the rebirth of a European capital. Enjoy the thrill of walking over what was the Wall and through the Brandenburg Gate.

Berlin has had a tumultuous recent history. After the city was devastated in World War II, it was divided by the Allied powers: The American, British, and French sectors became West Berlin, and the Soviet sector, East Berlin. The division was set in stone when the East built the Berlin Wall in 1961. The Wall lasted 28 years. In 1990, less than a year after the Wall fell, the two Germanys officially became one. When the dust settled, Berliners from both sides of the once divided city faced the monumental challenge of reunification.

The last decade has taken Berlin through a frenzy of rebuilding. And while there's still plenty of work to be done, a new Berlin is emerging. Berliners joke they don't need to go anywhere, because the city's always changing. Spin a postcard rack to see what's new. A five-year-old guidebook on Berlin covers a different city.

Reunification has had its negative side, and locals are fond of saying, "The Wall survives in the minds of some people." Some "Ossies" (impolite slang for Easterners) miss their security. Some "Wessies" miss their easy ride (military deferrals, subsidized rent, and tax breaks). For free spirits, walled-in West Berlin was a citadel of freedom within the East.

The city government has been eager to charge forward with little nostalgia for anything that was Eastern. Big corporations and the national government have moved in, and the dreary swath of land that was the Wall and its notorious "death strip" has been transformed. City planners are boldly taking Berlin's reunification and the return of the national government as a good opportunity to make Berlin a great capital once again.

Planning Your Time

Because of Berlin's inconvenient location, try to enter and/or leave by either night train or plane. On a three-week trip through Germany and Austria, I'd give Berlin two days and spend them this way:

Day 1: Begin your day getting oriented to this huge city: Either take the 10:00 "Discover Berlin" guided walking tour offered by Original Berlin Walks (see page 599); or follow my "Do-It-Yourself Orientation Tour" by bus to the Reichstag (page 603), then continue by foot down Unter den Linden (page 610). Focus on sights along Unter den Linden today, including the Reichstag dome (most crowded 10:00–16:00) and Pergamon Museum.

Day 2: Today, concentrate on the sights in central Berlin, and in eastern Berlin south of Unter den Linden. Spend the morning lost in the paintings at the Gemäldegalerie. After lunch, hike via Potsdamer Platz to the *Topography of Terror* exhibit and along the surviving Zimmerstrasse stretch of Wall to the Museum of the Wall at Checkpoint Charlie. With extra time, consider visiting the Jewish Museum.

If you are maximizing your sightseeing, you could squeeze a hop-off, hop-on bus tour into Day 1 and start Day 2 with a visit to the Egyptian and Picasso museums near Charlottenburg Palace. Remember that the Reichstag dome and the Museum of the Wall are open late.

ORIENTATION

(area code: 030)
Berlin is huge, with nearly four million people. But the tourist's Berlin can be broken into four digestible chunks:

1. Eastern Berlin: The former East Berlin has the highest concentration of worthwhile sights and colorful neighborhoods. The main sightseeing artery is the famous ***Unter den Linden*** boulevard: Reichstag building, Brandenburg Gate, Museum Island (Pergamon and Berlin Cathedral), and Alexanderplatz (TV Tower). ***South of Unter den Linden,*** you'll find the delightful Gendarmenmarkt square, most Nazi sights (including the *Topography of Terror* exhibit), the Jewish Museum, the best Wall-related sights (Museum of the Wall at Checkpoint Charlie and East Side Gallery), and the colorful Turkish neighborhood of Kreuzberg. ***North of Unter den Linden*** are these worth-a-wander neighborhoods: around Oranienburger Strasse (New Synagogue), Hackescher Markt, and Prenzlauer Berg (several recommended hotels).

Berlin Sightseeing Modules

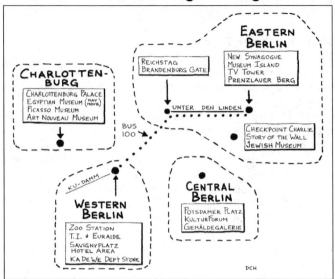

2. Central Berlin: The new city center—Potsdamer Platz, Kulturforum museums, and the giant Tiergarten park.

3. Western Berlin: The area around the Bahnhof Zoo train station and the grand Kurfürstendamm Boulevard, nicknamed "Ku'damm" (transportation hub, tours, information, shopping, and recommended hotels).

4. Charlottenburg Palace Area: The palace and nearby museums (Egyptian, Picasso, Art Nouveau), on the western edge of the city center.

Tourist Information

Berlin's TIs are run by a for-profit agency working for the city's big hotels, which colors the information they provide. The main TI is five minutes from Bahnhof Zoo, in the Europa Center (with Mercedes symbol on top, enter outside to left at Budapester Strasse 45, Mon–Sat 10:00–19:00, Sun 10:00–18:00, tel. 030/250-025, www.berlin-tourism.de). Smaller TIs are in the Brandenburg Gate (daily 10:00–18:00, longer in summer) and at the base of the TV Tower at Alexanderplatz (daily 10:00–18:00, longer in summer).

The TIs sell a good city map (€0.50), the *Berlin Programm* (a €1.60 comprehensive German-language monthly that lists upcoming events and museum hours, www.berlin-programm.de), the Museumspass (a.k.a. *Schaulust*, €12/3 days—see "Helpful Hints," below), and the German-English bimonthly *Berlin Calendar* magazine (€1.60, with timely features on Berlin and a partial calendar of events). The TIs also

Berlin

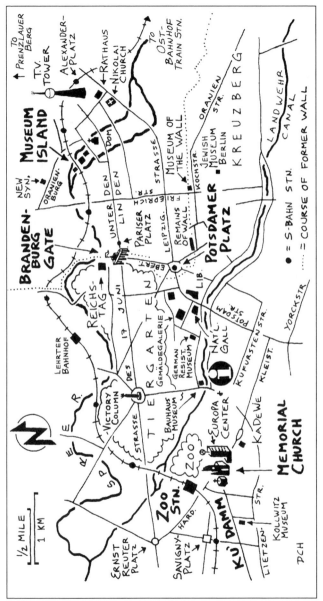

offer a €3 room-finding service (but only to hotels that give them kick-backs—many don't). Most hotels have free city maps.

EurAide's information office, located in the Bahnhof Zoo Reisezentrum (in front of train station, by taxi stand), provides an excellent service. They have answers to all your questions about Berlin or train travel around Europe. It's staffed by Americans (so communication is simple), and they have a knack for predicting your needs, then publishing free fliers to serve them (Mon–Fri 9:00–12:30 & 13:30–17:00, closed Sat–Sun and all Jan, great opportunity to get future *couchette* reservations nailed down ahead of time, Prague Excursion passes available—see "Transportation Connections" on page 641, www.euraide.com). EurAide also gives out a good, free city map and sells all public-transit tickets (including the €5.60 day pass) and the Welcome Card (see "Getting Around Berlin," page 598)—making a trip to the TI probably unnecessary. To get the most out of EurAide, have your questions ready before your visit.

Arrival in Berlin

By Train at Bahnhof Zoo: Berlin's central station is called Bahnhof Zoologischer Garten (because it's near Berlin's famous zoo), or "Zoo" for short (rhymes with "toe"). Coming from Western Europe, you'll probably land at Zoo. It's small, well-organized, and handy (lockers and baggage check available in back of station).

Upon arrival by train, orient yourself like this: Inside the station, follow signs to Hardenbergplatz. Step into this busy square filled with city buses, taxis, the transit office, and derelicts. The Original Berlin Walks start from the curb immediately outside the station at the top of the taxi stand (see "Tours," page 599). Between you and the McDonald's across the street is the stop for bus #100 (departing to the right for my "Do-It-Yourself Orientation Tour," below). Turn right and tiptoe through the riffraff to the eight-lane highway, Hardenbergstrasse. Walk to the median strip and stand with your back to the tracks. Ahead you'll see the black, bombed-out hulk of the Kaiser Wilhelm Memorial Church and the Europa Center (Mercedes symbol spinning on roof), which houses the main TI. Just ahead on the left, amid the traffic, is the BVG transport information kiosk (where you can buy a €5.60 day pass covering the subway and buses, and pick up a free subway map). If you're facing the church, my recommended western Berlin hotels are behind you to your right (see page 632).

If you're staying at my western Berlin hotels, but you arrive at one of Berlin's other train stations (trains from most of Eastern Europe arrive at Ostbahnhof), no problem: Ride another train (fastest option) or the S-Bahn or U-Bahn (runs every few min) to Bahnhof Zoo, and pretend you arrived there.

By Plane: See "Transportation Connections," page 641.

Helpful Hints

Monday Activities: Most museums are closed on Monday. Save Monday for Berlin Wall sights, the Reichstag dome, my "Do-It-Yourself Orientation Tour" and strolling Unter den Linden (see below), walking/bus tours, the Jewish Museum, churches, the zoo, or shopping along Kurfürstendamm (Ku'damm) Boulevard or at the Kaufhaus des Westens (KaDeWe) department store. (When Monday is a holiday—as it is several times a year—museums are open then and closed Tuesday.)

Museums: All **state museums,** including the Pergamon and Gemäldegalerie (plus others as noted in "Sights," page 605), are free for the last four hours on Thursdays (that is, if it closes at 18:00, it's free from 14:00 on; www.museen-berlin.de). There are two different types of discount passes for Berlin's state museums (different from the mostly private museums and sights covered by the WelcomeCard—see "Getting Around Berlin," below). The state museums are covered by a **one-day ticket** (*Tageskarte*, €10, not valid for special exhibitions, purchase at participating museums, not sold at TI). Entry to most of these museums costs €6–8, so the day ticket pays for itself if you visit at least two museums. Even better, consider the three-day **"Schaulust" Museumspass,** which covers most of the state museums (including the Pergamon and Gemäldegalerie), as well as several others (including the Jewish Museum). Only €2 more than the day ticket, it's valid for three times as long and is an excellent value if you'll be doing at least two days of museum-hopping (€12, not valid for special exhibitions, purchase at TI or participating museums). Note that if a museum is closed on one of the days of your Museumspass, you have access to that museum on the fourth day to make up for lost time.

Medical Help: If you need to see a doctor, dial "Call a Doc" at tel. 01804-2255-2362 (www.calladoc.com), a non-profit referral service designed for tourists. Payment is arranged between you and the doctor, and is likely far more affordable than similar care in the United States.

Travel Agency: Last Minute Flugbörse can help you find a flight in a hurry (next to TI in Europa Center, tel. 030/2655-1050, www.lastminuteflugboerse.de).

Addresses: Many Berlin streets are numbered with odd and even numbers on the same side of the street, often with no connection to the other side (for example, Ku'damm #212 can be across the street from #14). To save steps, check the white street signs on curb corners; many list the street numbers covered on that side of the block.

Internet Access: You'll find cheap, fast Internet access at easyInternetcafé (daily 24 hrs, Ku'damm 224, 10-min walk from

Bahnhof Zoo and near recommended western Berlin hotels, buy ticket at self-service machines, instructions in English).

Laundry: Schnell und Sauber Waschcenter is a handy launderette near my recommended western Berlin hotels (daily 6:00–23:00, €5–9 wash and dry, Leibnizstrasse 72, 4 blocks west of Savignyplatz, near intersection with Kantstrasse). Near my recommended hotels in Prenzlauer Berg, try Holly's Wasch-Theke (€5–9 wash and dry, includes detergent, daily 7:00–23:00, last load in at 21:30, attached café, Kollwitzstrasse 93, tel. 030/443-9210).

Festival: Be aware of the Love Parade, a huge techno-Woodstock that overwhelms the city with (mostly gay) love in mid-July—you'll either love it or hate it.

Getting Around Berlin

Berlin's sights spread far and wide. Right from the start, commit yourself to the fine public-transit system.

By Subway and Bus: The U-Bahn (*Untergrund-Bahn,* Berlin's subway), S-Bahn (*Schnell-Bahn,* or "fast train," mostly above ground and with fewer stops), *Strassenbahn* (streetcars), and all buses are consolidated into one "BVG" system that uses the same tickets. Here are your options:

- Basic ticket *(Einzel Fahrschein)* for two hours of travel in one direction on buses or subways—€2 (*Erwachsener* means adult—anyone 14 or older).
- A cheap short-ride ticket *(Kurzstrecke Erwachsener)* for a single short ride of six bus stops or three subway stations, with one transfer—€1.20.
- A day pass *(Tageskarte)* covering zones A and B, the city proper—€5.60 (good until 3:00 the morning after). To get out to Potsdam, you need a ticket covering zone C—€6. (For longer stays, a 7-day *Tageskarte* is also available—€22, or €28 including zone C; or buy 2 WelcomeCards, see below.)
- The Berlin/Potsdam **WelcomeCard** gives you three days of transportation in zones A, B, and C, and those same three days of minor discounts on lots of minor and a few major museums (including Checkpoint Charlie), sightseeing tours (including the recommended Original Berlin Walks), and music and theater events (€21, valid for an adult and up to 3 kids younger than 14). The WelcomeCard is a good deal for a three-day visit (since 3 1-day transit passes alone cost only €4.20 less than the WelcomeCard) and worth considering for a two-day visit.
- The **CityTourCard** covers public transportation in zones A and B, plus some museum discounts (€14.50/48 hrs, €18.90/72 hrs, www.citytourcard.com). While it's cheaper than the WelcomeCard, it doesn't include zone C (which most visitors don't need unless they're going to Potsdam), and the discounts

are not quite as good as the WelcomeCard's—for example, the CityTourCard doesn't include discounts to the Checkpoint Charlie Museum or Original Berlin Walks.

Buy your U- or S-Bahn tickets from machines at stations or at the BVG pavilion in front of Bahnhof Zoo (English instructions). To use the machine, first select the type of ticket you want, then load in the coins or paper. Punch your ticket in a red or yellow clock machine to validate it (or risk a €40 fine). The double-decker buses are a joy (can buy ticket on bus), and the subway is a snap. The S-Bahn (but not U-Bahn) is free with a validated Eurailpass (but it uses a flexi-day).

Sections of the U- or S-Bahn sometimes close temporarily for repairs. In this situation, a bus route replaces the train (*Ersatzverkehr*, or "replacement transportation").

By Taxi: Taxis are easy to flag down, and taxi stands are common. A typical ride within town costs €10–16, and a cross-town trip (for example, Zoo to Alexanderplatz) will run you around €25. A local law designed to help people get safely and affordably home from their subway station late at night is handy for tourists any time of day: A short ride of no more than two kilometers (1.25 miles) is a flat €3. (Ask for *"Kurzstrecke, drei euro, bitte."*) To get this cheap price, you must hail a cabbie on the street, rather than go to a taxi stand (from a stand, it's a minimum €5 charge). Cabbies aren't crazy about the law, so insist on the price and be sure to keep the ride short.

By Bike: Be careful—in Berlin, motorists don't brake for bikers (and bikers don't brake for pedestrians). Fortunately, some roads and sidewalks have special red-painted bike lanes. Just don't ride on the regular sidewalk—it's *nicht erlaubt* (not allowed—that's *verboten* to you and me).

In western Berlin, you can rent good bikes at the **Bahnhof Zoo** left-luggage counter (in back of station, next to lockers; comes with lock, air pump, and mounted basket, €10/day, €23/3 days, €35/7 days, daily 6:15–21:00, passport required, €50 cash deposit); in the east, go to **Fahrradstation** at Hackesche Höfe (€15/day, Mon–Fri 8:00–20:00, Sat 10:00–16:00, closed Sun, Rosenthaler Strasse 40, tel. 030/2045-4500) or at the Friedrichstrasse S-Bahn station (same hours, but also open Sun 10:00–18:00).

TOURS

▲▲▲**City Walking Tours**—The Original Berlin Walks offers a variety of worthwhile tours led by enthusiastic guides who are native English speakers. The company, run by Englishman Nick Gay, offers a three-hour **Discover Berlin** introductory walk daily year-round at 10:00, and also at 14:30 from April through October, for €12 (€9 if you're under 26 or with WelcomeCard). Just show up at the taxi rank in front of Bahnhof Zoo (or 20 min later in eastern Berlin's

Berlin at a Glance

▲▲▲**Reichstag** Germany's historic Parliament building, topped with a striking dome you can ascend. **Hours:** Daily 8:00–24:00, last entry 22:00.

▲▲▲**Museum of the Wall at Checkpoint Charlie** Moving museum near the former site of the famous border checkpoint between the American and Soviet sectors, with stories of brave escapes during the Cold War and the gleeful days when the wall fell. **Hours:** Daily 9:00–22:00.

▲▲▲**Gemäldegalerie** Germany's top collection of 13th- through 18th-century European paintings, featuring Dürer, Van Eyck, Rubens, Titian, Raphael, Caravaggio, and more. **Hours:** Tue–Sun 10:00–18:00, Thu until 22:00, closed Mon.

▲▲**Brandenburg Gate** One of Berlin's most famous landmarks, a multi-arched gateway, at the former border of East and West. **Hours:** Always open.

▲▲**Unter den Linden** Leafy boulevard through the heart of former East Berlin, lined with some of the city's top sights. **Hours:** Always open.

▲▲**Pergamon Museum** The only essential museum on Museum Island (just off Unter den Linden), featuring the fantastic 2nd-century B.C. Greek Pergamon Altar. **Hours:** Tue–Sun 10:00–18:00, Thu until 22:00, closed Mon.

▲▲**Berlin Wall** Mostly gone, but parts of the wall are still visible, including the East Side Gallery and a chunk near the Topography of Terror (former SS and Gestapo headquarters). **Hours:** Always open.

▲▲**Jewish Museum Berlin** User-friendly museum celebrating Jewish culture, in a highly conceptual building. **Hours:** Daily 10:00–20:00, Mon until 22:00.

▲▲**Gendarmenmarkt** Inviting square bounded by twin churches, a chocolate shop, and a concert hall. **Hours:** Always open.

▲▲**New Synagogue** Largest prewar synagogue in Berlin, destroyed by Nazis, with a facade that has since been rebuilt. **Hours:** Sun–Thu 10:00–18:00, Fri 10:00–14:00, closed Sat, May–Aug Sun–Mon until 20:00 and Fri until 17:00.

▲▲**Egyptian Museum** Proud home of the exquisite 3,000-year-old bust of Queen Nefertiti. **Hours:** Daily 10:00–18:00.

▲**Kaiser Wilhelm Memorial Church** Evocative destroyed church in the heart of the former West Berlin, with a modern annex. **Hours:** Church open Mon–Sat 10:00–16:00, closed Sun, annex open daily 9:00–19:00.

▲**Kurfürstendamm** West Berlin's main boulevard (nicknamed Ku'damm), packed with tourists and upscale shops. **Hours:** Always open.

▲**Käthe Kollwitz Museum** Features the black-and-white art of the local artist who conveyed the suffering of Berlin's stormiest century. **Hours:** Wed–Mon 11:00–18:00, closed Tue.

▲**Kaufhaus des Westens (KaDeWe)** The "department store of the West"—the biggest on the Continent—is where East Berliners flocked when the wall came down. **Hours:** Mon–Fri 10:00–20:00, Sat 9:30–20:00, closed Sun.

▲**Potsdamer Platz** The Times Square of old Berlin, long a postwar wasteland, now rebuilt with huge glass skyscrapers (can ascend 300-foot-tall Kollhoff tower), an underground train station, and—covered with a huge canopy—the Sony Center mall, with eateries. **Hours:** Always open.

▲**Musical Instruments Museum** Impressive collection of historic instruments. **Hours:** Tue–Fri 9:00–17:00, Sat–Sun 10:00–17:00, closed Mon.

▲**Charlottenburg Palace** Baroque Hohenzollern palace on the edge of town, across the street from Egyptian Museum. **Hours:** Tue–Sun 10:00–17:00, closed Mon.

▲**Berggruen Collection** Notable works by Picasso, Matisse, van Gogh, Cézanne, and Paul Klee. **Hours:** Tue–Fri 10:00–18:00, Sat–Sun 11:00–18:00, closed Mon.

▲**Bröhan Museum** Collection of Art Nouveau and Art Deco furnishings. **Hours:** Tue–Sun 10:00–18:00, closed Mon.

Hackescher Markt S-Bahn station, outside Häagen-Dazs). Their high-quality, high-energy guides also offer other tours: **Infamous Third Reich Sites** (€12, €9 with WelcomeCard, at 10:00 May–Sept Wed, Fri, and Sat–Sun; March–April and Oct Sat–Sun only; departs from Bahnhof Zoo meeting point only), **Jewish Life in Berlin** (€12, €9 with WelcomeCard, Mon at 10:00 May–Sept), **Potsdam** (€15, €11.20 with WelcomeCard, see page 628), and **Nightlife** (€9, see page 631). Many of the Third Reich and Jewish history sights are difficult to pin down without these excellent walks. Also consider their six-hour trip to the **Sachsenhausen Concentration Camp,** intended "to challenge preconceptions," according to Nick (€15, €11.20 with WelcomeCard, at 10:15 May–Sept Tue, Thu, and Sat–Sun; March–April and Oct Tue and Sat; departs from Bahnhof Zoo meeting point only, requires transit day ticket with zone C—or buy from guide, call office for specifics). Confirm tour schedules at EurAide or by phone with Nick or his wife and partner, Serena (private tours also available, tel. 030/301-9194, www.berlinwalks.com, berlinwalks@snafu.de).

For a more exhaustive (or, for some, exhausting) walking tour of Berlin, consider **Brewer's Berlin Tours,** run by Terry, a former British embassy worker in East Berlin, and his well-trained staff. These daily tours—especially the in-depth Total version—are legendary for their length, and best for those with a long attention span and a serious interest in Berlin (€10 for either tour, all-day Total Berlin starts at 10:30 and can last 5–8 hrs, 4-hr Classic Berlin starts at 12:30, both meet at New Synagogue, Oranienburger Strasse 28/30, U-Bahn: Oranienburger Tor, look for red sign, also does Potsdam tours twice weekly, mobile 0179-739-5389, www.brewersberlin.com).

▲**City Bus Tours**—For bus tours, you have two choices:

1. Full-blown bus tours. Contact Severin & Kühn (€22, 3 hrs, daily at 10:00 and 14:00, live guides in 2 languages, from Ku'damm 216, tel. 030/880-4190), or take BVG buses from Ku'damm 18 (€20, 2.5 hrs, leave every 30–60 min daily 10:00–17:00, tel. 030/885-9880).

2. Hop-on, hop-off circle tours. Several companies make a circuit of the city (City-Circle Sightseeing is good, offered by Severin & Kühn). The TI has all the brochures. The tours offer unlimited hop-on, hop-off privileges for their routes (about 14 stops) with a good recorded commentary (€18, daily 10:00–18:00, last bus leaves from Ku'damm at 16:00, 2–4/hr, 2-hr loop). Just hop on where you like, and pay the driver. On a sunny day, when some double-decker buses go topless, these are a photographer's delight, cruising slowly by just about every top sight in town.

Do-It-Yourself Orientation Tour:
Bus #100 from Bahnhof Zoo to the Reichstag

This tour narrates the route of convenient bus #100, which connects my recommended hotel neighborhood in western Berlin with the sights in eastern Berlin. If you have the €18 and two hours for a hop-on, hop-off bus tour (described above), take that instead. But this short €2 bus ride is a fine city introduction. Bus #100 is a sightseer's dream, stopping at Bahnhof Zoo, Europa Center/Hotel Palace, Victory Column (Siegessäule), Reichstag, Brandenburg Gate, Unter den Linden, Pergamon Museum, and ending at Alexanderplatz. While you could ride it to the end, it's more fun to get out at the Reichstag and walk down Unter den Linden at your own pace (using my self-guided commentary on page 610). When combined with the self-guided stroll down Unter den Linden, this tour merits ▲▲▲. Before you take this bus into the East, consider checking out the sights in the West (see page 624).

The Tour Begins: Buses leave from Hardenbergplatz, in front of the Bahnhof Zoo (and nearly next door to the Europa Center TI, in front of Hotel Palace; take it in the direction of Mollstrasse and Prenzlauer Allee). Buses come every 10 minutes, and single tickets are good for two hours—so take advantage of hop-on-and-off privileges. Climb aboard, stamp your ticket (giving it a time), and grab a seat on top. This is about a 10-minute ride. Note: The upcoming stop will light up on the reader board inside the bus.

❍ On your left and then straight ahead, before descending into the tunnel, you'll see the bombed-out hulk of the **Kaiser Wilhelm Memorial Church,** with its postwar sister church (described below) and the **Europa Center.** This is the west-end shopping district, a bustling people zone with big department stores nearby. When the Wall came down, East Berliners flocked to this area's department stores (especially KaDeWe, described below). Soon after, the biggest, swankiest new stores were built in the East. Now the West is trying to win those shoppers back by building even bigger and better shopping centers around Europaplatz. Across from the Zoo station, the under-construction Zoofenster tower will be taller than all the buildings you see here.

Emerging from the tunnel, on your immediate right you'll see the Berlin tourist information office.

❍ At the stop in front of Hotel Palace: On the left, the elephant gates mark the entrance to the **Berlin Zoo** and its aquarium (described on page 626).

❍ Driving down Kurfürstenstrasse, you'll pass several Asian restaurants—a reminder that, for most, the best food in Berlin is not German. Turning left, with the huge Tiergarten park in the distance ahead, you'll cross a canal and see the famous **Bauhaus Archive** (an off-white, blocky building) on the right. The Bauhaus movement ushered in a new age of modern architecture that emphasized function over beauty, giving rise to the blocky steel-and-glass skyscrapers in big cities around the world. On the left is Berlin's new embassy row. The big turquoise wall marks the communal home of all five Nordic embassies.

● The bus enters a 400-acre park called the **Tiergarten,** packed with cycling paths, joggers, and nude sunbathers. The **Victory Column** (Siegessäule, with the gilded angel, described on page 621) towers above this vast city park that was once a royal hunting grounds, now nicknamed the "green lungs of Berlin."

● On the left, a block after leaving the Victory Column: The 18th-century, late rococo **Bellevue Palace** is the German White House. Formerly a Nazi VIP guest house, it's now the residence of the federal president (whose power is mostly ceremonial). If the flag's out, he's in.

● Driving along the Spree River: This park area was a residential district before World War II. Now, on the left-hand side, it's filled with the buildings of the **national government.** The huge, brick "brown snake" complex was built to house government workers—but it didn't sell, so now its apartments are available to anyone. A Henry Moore sculpture entitled *Butterfly* floats in front of the slope-roofed House of World Cultures (Berliners have nicknamed this building "the pregnant oyster"). The modern tower (next on left) is a carillon with 68 bells (1987).

● While you could continue on bus #100, it's better on foot from here. Leap out at the **Platz der Republik.** Through the trees on the left, you'll see Germany's new and sprawling chancellery. Started during the more imperial rule of Helmut Kohl, it's now considered overly grand. The big park is the Platz der Republik, where the Victory Column stood until Hitler moved it. The gardens were recently dug up to build underground train tracks to serve Berlin's new main train station (the Lehrter Bahnhof, across the field). Watch your step—excavators found a 250-pound undetonated American bomb.

● Just down the street stands the **Reichstag.** As you approach the old building with the new dome, look for the row of slate slabs imbedded in the ground (looks like a fancy slate bicycle rack). This is a memorial to the 96 politicians who were murdered and persecuted because their politics didn't agree with Chancellor Hitler's. Each slab is marked with a name and the party that politician belonged to—mostly KPD (Communists) and SPD (Socialists).

Throughout Berlin, you'll see posters advertising a play called *Ich bin's nicht, Adolf Hitler es gewesen* ("It wasn't me, Adolf Hitler did it"). The photo is of a model by Hitler's architect Albert Speer of what Berlin was to look like when the Nazis controlled the planet. Hitler planned to rename his capital city "Germania Metropolis." The enormous dome is the Great Hall of the People. Below it and to the right is the tiny Reichstag. Imagine this huge 950-foot-high dome dwarfing everything in Berlin (in the field to your left as you face the Reichstag).

Now visit the Reichstag (open late, no lines in evening), described below.

SIGHTS

Eastern Berlin

Along Unter den Linden

These sights line the famous Unter den Linden—the main boulevard that leads through the heart of former downtown East Berlin. I've arranged them in the order of a convenient self-guided orientation walk, picking up where my "Do-It-Yourself Orientation Tour" (above) leaves off. Allow a comfortable hour for this walk from the Reichstag to Alexanderplatz, including time for lingering (but not museum stops).

▲▲▲**Reichstag Building**—The Parliament building—the heart of German democracy—has a short but complicated and emotional history. When it was inaugurated in the 1890s, the last emperor, Kaiser Wilhelm, disdainfully called it the "house for chatting." It was from here that the German Republic was proclaimed in 1918. In 1933, this symbol of democracy nearly burned down. While the Nazis blamed a Communist plot, some believe that Hitler himself planned the fire, using it as a handy excuse to frame the Communists and grab power. As World War II drew to a close, Stalin ordered his troops to take the Reichstag from the Nazis by May 1 (the workers' holiday). More than 1,500 Nazis made their last stand here—extending World War II by two days. On April 30, 1945, it fell to the Allies. It was hardly used from 1933 to 1999. For the building's 101st birthday in 1995, the Bulgarian-American artist Christo wrapped it in silvery-gold cloth. It was then wrapped again in scaffolding, rebuilt by British architect Lord Norman Foster, and turned

into the new parliamentary home of the Bundestag (Germany's lower house). To many Germans, the proud resurrection of the Reichstag—which no longer has a hint of Hitler—symbolizes the end of a terrible chapter in German history.

The **glass cupola** rises 155 feet above the ground, and a double staircase winds 755 feet to the top for a grand view. Inside the dome, a cone of 360 mirrors reflects natural light into the legislative chamber below. Lit from inside at night, this gives Berlin a memorable nightlight. The environmentally friendly cone also helps with air circulation, drawing hot air out of the legislative chamber and pulling in cool air from below.

Unter den Linden

NOT TO SCALE

① Pariser Platz
② Future U.S. Embassy & Holocaust Memorial
③ Hotel Adlon
④ Russian Embassy
⑤ Komische Oper
⑥ Frederick II Statue
⑦ Bebelplatz
⑧ Humboldt University
⑨ Book Burning Memorial
⑩ Neue Wache
⑪ German History Museum
⑫ Berlin Cathedral
⑬ Palace of the Republic
⑭ Pergamon Museum
⑮ Marien Church
⑯ City Hall
⑰ TV Tower
⑱ Alexanderplatz
⑲ Gendarmenmarkt
⑳ German Cathedral

Ⓢ S-BAHN
Ⓤ U-BAHN

Hours: Free, daily 8:00–24:00, last entry 22:00, most crowded 10:00–16:00 (wait in line to go up—good street musicians, metal detectors, no big luggage allowed, some hour-long English tours when parliament is not sitting, tel. 030/2273-2152, www.bundestag.de).

Line-Beating Tip: Those with table reservations at the Dachgarten rooftop restaurant don't wait in the long lines. Go straight to the front and tell them you have a reservation. Reserve in advance by phone or e-mail (€15–26 entrées with a view, daily 9:30–16:30 & 18:30–24:00, tel. 030/2262-9933, kaeferreservierung.berlin@feinkost -kaefer.de).

Self-Guided Tour: As you approach the building, look above the door, surrounded by stone patches from WWII bomb damage, to see the motto and promise: *Dem Deutschen Volke* ("to the German people"). The open, airy lobby towers 100 feet high, with 65-foot-tall colors of the German flag. Glass doors show the **central legislative chamber.** The message: There will be no secrets in government. Look inside. The seats are "Reichstag blue," a lilac-blue color designed by the architect to brighten the otherwise gray interior. The German eagle (a.k.a. the "fat hen") spreads his wings behind the podium. Notice the doors marked "Yes," "No," and "Abstain"...the

Bundestag's traditional "sheep jump" way of counting votes (for critical and close votes, all 669 members leave and vote by walking through the door of their choice).

Ride the elevator to the base of the glass **dome.** Take time to study the photos and read the circle of captions—an excellent exhibit telling the Reichstag story. Then study the surrounding architecture: a broken collage of old on new, like Germany's history. Notice the dome's giant and unobtrusive sunscreen, which moves as necessary with the sun. Peer down through the skylight to look over the shoulders of the elected representatives at work. For Germans, the best view is down—keeping a close eye on their government.

Start at the ramp nearest the elevator and wind up to the top of the **double ramp.** Take a 360-degree survey of the city as you hike: First, the big park is the **Tiergarten,** the "green lungs" of Berlin. Beyond that is the **Teufelsberg,** or Devil's Hill (built of rubble from the bombed city in the late 1940s and famous during the Cold War as a powerful ear of the West—notice the telecommunications tower on top). Given the violent and tragic history of Berlin—a city blown apart by bombs and covered over by bulldozers—locals say, "You have to be suspicious when you see the nice, green park."

Find the **Victory Column** (Siegessäule, moved by Hitler in the 1930s from in front of the Reichstag to its present position in the Tiergarten). Next, scenes of the new Berlin spiral into your view— **Potsdamer Platz,** marked by the conical glass tower that houses Sony's European headquarters. The yellow building to the right is the Berlin Philharmonic Concert Hall. Continue circling left, and find the green chariot atop the **Brandenburg Gate.** A monument to Gypsy victims of the Holocaust will be built between the Reichstag and Brandenburg Gate. (Gypsies, as disdained by the Nazis as were the Jews, lost the same percentage of their population to Hitler.) Another Holocaust memorial will be built just south of Brandenburg Gate.

Next, you'll see **former East Berlin** and the city's next huge construction zone, with a forest of 300-foot-tall skyscrapers in the works. Notice the TV Tower (with the Pope's Revenge—explained on page 614), the Berlin Cathedral's massive dome, the red tower of the city hall, the golden dome of the New Synagogue, and the Reichstag's **Dachgarten Restaurant** ("Roof Garden"—see above). Follow the train tracks in the distance to the left toward a huge construction zone marking the future central Berlin train station, Lehrter Bahnhof. Just in front of it, alone in a field, is the Swiss Embassy. This used to be surrounded by buildings, but now it's the only one left. Complete your spin tour with the blocky **Chancellery,** nicknamed "the washing machine" by locals. It may look like a pharaoh's tomb, but it's the office and home of Germany's most powerful person, the chancellor.

Let's continue our walk and cross what was the Berlin Wall.

Leaving the Reichstag, turn left around the building. You'll see the Brandenburg Gate ahead on your right. Stay on the park side of the street for a better view of the gate. As you cross at the light, look down and notice the double row of cobblestones—this marks where the Wall used to be.

▲▲**Brandenburg Gate (Brandenburger Tor)**—The historic Brandenburg Gate (1791) is the last survivor of 14 gates in Berlin's old city wall (this one led to the city of Brandenburg). The gate was the symbol of Prussian Berlin...and later the symbol of a divided Berlin. It's crowned by a majestic four-horse chariot with the Goddess of Peace at the reins. Napoleon took this statue to the Louvre in Paris in 1806. When the Prussians got it back, she was renamed the Goddess of Victory.

The gate sat unused, part of a sad circle dance called the Wall, for more than 25 years. Now postcards all over town show the ecstatic day—November 9, 1989—when the world enjoyed the sight of happy Berliners jamming the gate like flowers on a parade float. Pause a minute and think about struggles for freedom—past and present. (There's actually a "quiet room" built into the gate for this purpose, daily 11:00–18:00.) Around the gate, look at the information boards with pictures of how much this area changed throughout the 20th century. The latest chapter: The shiny white gate was completely restored in 2002. The TI within the gate is open daily 10:00–18:00.

Ponder the fact that you're standing in what was the so-called death strip. Now cross through the gate, into...

▲**Pariser Platz**—This "Paris Square" was once filled with important government buildings—all bombed to smithereens in World War II. For decades, it was an unrecognizable, deserted no-man's-land. But now, sparkling new banks, embassies (the French Embassy rebuilt where it was before World War II), and a swanky hotel have filled the void.

Face the gate and look to your left. The **U.S. Embassy** once stood here, and a new one will stand in the same spot (due to be completed in 2006). This new embassy has been controversial; for safety's sake, Uncle Sam wanted it away from other buildings, but the Germans preferred it in its original location. A compromise was reached, building the embassy by the gate—but rerouting several major roads to reduce the security risk. The new **Holocaust memorial,** consisting of more than 2,500 gravestone-like pillars, will be completed in 2005 and will stand behind the new embassy.

Just to the left, the **DZ Bank building** is by Frank Gehry, the unconventional American architect famous for Bilbao's golden

The Berlin Wall

The 100-mile "Anti-Fascist Protective Rampart," as it was called by the East German government, was erected almost overnight in 1961 to stop the outward flow of people (3 million leaked out between 1949 and 1961). The 13-foot-high Wall *(Mauer)* had a 16-foot tank ditch, a no-man's-land (or "death strip") that was 30 to 160 feet wide, and 300 sentry towers. During its 28 years, there were 1,693 cases when border guards fired, 3,221 arrests, and 5,043 documented successful escapes (565 of these were East German guards).

The carnival atmosphere of those first years after the Wall fell is gone, but hawkers still sell "authentic" pieces of the Wall, DDR (East German) flags, and military paraphernalia to gawking tourists. When it fell, the Wall was literally carried away by the euphoria. What managed to survive has been nearly devoured by a decade of persistent "Wall-peckers."

Americans—the Cold War victors—have the biggest appetite for Wall-related sights, and a few bits and pieces remain for us to seek out. Pick up the free brochure *Berlin: The Wall*, available at EurAide or the TI, which traces the history of the Wall and helps you find the remaining chunks and other Wall-related sights in Berlin. You can also rent a *Hear We Go* audioguide about the Wall at Checkpoint Charlie, which guides you from the Checkpoint along Zimmerstrasse to Potsdamer Platz, and then brings you back via Leipziger Strasse and Mauerstrasse (€7, 80 min).

Guggenheim, Prague's Dancing House, and Seattle's Experience Music Project. Gehry fans might be surprised at the DZ Bank building's low profile. Structures on Pariser Platz are expected to be bland, so as not to draw attention away from the Brandenburg Gate. (The glassy facade of the Academy of Arts, next to Gehry's building, is controversial for that very reason.) For your fix of good old Gehry, step into the lobby and check out its undulating interior.

Brandenburg Gate, the center of old Berlin, sits on a major boulevard, running east–west through Berlin. The western segment, called Strasse des 17. Juni, stretches for four miles from the Victory Column (past the flea market—see page 621) to the Olympic Stadium. But we'll follow this city axis in the opposite direction, east, up what is known as Unter den Linden—into the core of old imperial Berlin and past what was once the palace of the Hohenzollern family who ruled Prussia and then Germany. The palace—the reason for just about all you'll see—is a phantom sight, long gone (though some Berliners hope to rebuild it). Alexanderplatz, which marks the end of this walk, is near the base of the giant TV Tower hovering in the distance.

▲▲**Unter den Linden**—This is the heart of former East Berlin. In Berlin's good old days, Unter den Linden was one of Europe's grand boulevards. In the 15th century, this carriageway led from the palace to the hunting grounds (today's big Tiergarten). In the 17th century, Hohenzollern princes and princesses moved in and built their palaces here so they could be near the Prussian emperor.

Named centuries ago for its thousand linden trees, this was the most elegant street of Prussian Berlin before Hitler's time and the main drag of East Berlin after his reign. Hitler replaced the venerable trees—many 250 years old—with Nazi flags. Popular discontent actually drove him to replant linden trees. Today, Unter den Linden is no longer a depressing Cold War cul-de-sac, and its pre-Hitler, strolling café ambience is returning.

As you walk toward the giant TV Tower, the big building you see jutting out into the street on your right is the **Hotel Adlon.** It hosted such notables as Charlie Chaplin, Albert Einstein, and Greta Garbo. (This is where Garbo said, "I want to be alone," during the filming of *Grand Hotel*.) Destroyed in World War II, the grand Adlon was rebuilt in 1996. See how far you can get inside.

The Unter den Linden S-Bahn station ahead of you is one of Berlin's former **ghost subway stations.** During the Cold War, most underground train tunnels were simply blocked at the border. But a few Western lines looped through the East. To make a little hard Western cash, the Eastern government rented the use of these tracks to the West, but the stations (which happened to be in East Berlin) were strictly off-limits. For 28 years, the stations were unused, as Western trains slowly passed through, seeing only eerie DDR (East German) guards and lots of cobwebs. Literally within days of the fall of the Wall, these stations were reopened, and today they are a time warp (with dreary old green tiles and original signage). Go down into the station, walk along the track, and exit on the other side, following signs to *Russische Botschaft*...the Russian Embassy.

The **Russian Embassy** was the first big postwar building project in East Berlin. It's built in the powerful, simplified, neoclassical style Stalin liked. While not as important now as it was a few years ago, it's immense as ever. It flies the Russian white, red, and blue. Find the hammer-and-sickle motif decorating the window frames. Continuing past the Aeroflot Airline offices, look across the street to the right to see the back of the **Komische Oper** (Comic Opera; program and view of ornate interior posted in window). While the exterior is ugly, the fine old theater interior—amazingly missed by WWII bombs—survives. The shop ahead on your right is an amusing mix of antiques, local guidebooks, knickknacks, and East Berlin nostalgia souvenirs.

The West lost no time in consuming the East; consequently, some are feeling a wave of nostalgia—or *Ost*-algia—for the old days of East Berlin. In recent local elections, nearly half of East Berlin's voters—and 6 percent of West Berliners—voted for the old Communist Party. One symbol of that era has been given a reprieve. As you continue to Friedrichstrasse, look at the DDR-style pedestrian lights, and you'll realize that someone had a sense of humor back then. The perky red and green men—*Ampelmännchen*—were under threat of replacement by the far less jaunty Western signs. Fortunately, the DDR signals will be kept after all.

At **Friedrichstrasse,** look right. Before the war, the Unter den Linden/Friedrichstrasse intersection was the heart of Berlin. In the 1920s, Berlin was famous for its anything-goes love of life. This was the cabaret drag, a springboard to stardom for young and vampy entertainers like Marlene Dietrich. (Born in 1901, Dietrich starred in the first German "talkie," and then headed straight to Hollywood.) Over the last few years, this boulevard—lined with super department stores (such as Galeries Lafayette, with its cool marble-and-glass, waste-of-space interior, Mon–Sat 9:30–20:00, closed Sun; belly up to its amazing ground-floor viewpoint) and big-time hotels (such as the Hilton and Four Seasons)—has slowly begun to replace Ku'damm as the grand commerce and café boulevard of Berlin. (More recently, the West is retaliating with some new stores of its own.) Across from Galeries Lafayette is American Express (handy for any train-ticket needs, Mon–Fri 9:00–19:00, Sat 10:00–13:00, closed Sun, travel agency tel. 030/201-7400; for traveler's checks, call tel. 0800-185-3100).

If you continued down Friedrichstrasse, you'd wind up at the sights listed in "South of Unter den Linden," below—including the Museum of the Wall at Checkpoint Charlie (a 10-min walk from here). But for now, continue along Unter den Linden. You'll notice big, colorful **water pipes** around here, and throughout Berlin. As long as the city remains a big construction zone, it will be laced with these drainage pipes—key to any building project. Berlin's high water table means any new basement comes with lots of pumping out.

Continue down Unter den Linden a few more blocks, past the large equestrian statue of Frederick II ("the Great"), and turn right into the square called **Bebelplatz.** Stand on the glass window in the center. (Construction of an underground parking lot might prevent you from reaching the glass plate.)

Frederick the Great—who ruled from 1740 to 1786—established Prussia as a military power. This square was the center of the "new Rome" Frederick envisioned. Much of Frederick's palace actually survived World War II, but was torn down by the communists, since it symbolized the imperialist past. Now some Berliners want to rebuild the palace, from scratch, exactly as it once was. Other Berliners insist that what's done is done.

Bebelplatz is bounded by great buildings. The German State

Opera was bombed in 1941, rebuilt to bolster morale and to celebrate its centennial in 1943, and bombed again in 1945. The former state library is where Lenin studied much of his exile away (climb to the second floor of the library to see a stained-glass window depicting his life's work with almost biblical reverence; there's a good café with light food, Tim's Canadian Deli, downstairs). The round Catholic St. Hedwig's Church—nicknamed the "upside-down teacup"—was built to placate the subjects of Catholic lands Frederick added to his empire. (Step inside to see the cheesy DDR government renovation.)

Humboldt University, across Unter den Linden, was one of Europe's greatest. Marx and Lenin (not the brothers or the sisters) studied here, as did Grimm (both brothers) and more than two dozen Nobel Prize winners. Einstein, who was Jewish, taught here until taking a spot at Princeton in 1932 (smart guy).

Look down through the glass you're standing on: The room of empty bookshelves is a memorial to the notorious Nazi **book burning.** It was on this square in 1933 that staff and students from the university threw 20,000 newly forbidden books (like Einstein's) into a huge bonfire on the orders of Nazi propaganda minister Joseph Goebbels.

Continue down Unter den Linden. The next square on your right holds the Opernpalais' restaurants (see page 640). On the university side, the Greek temple–like building is the **Neue Wache** (the emperor's "New Guardhouse," from 1816). When the Wall fell, this memorial to the victims of fascism was transformed into a new national memorial. Look inside, where a replica of the Käthe Kollwitz statue, *Mother with Her Dead Son,* is surrounded by thought-provoking silence. This marks the tombs of Germany's unknown soldier and the unknown concentration camp victim. The inscription in front reads, "To the victims of war and tyranny." Read the entire statement in English (on wall, right of entrance).

After the Neue Wache, the next building you'll see is the **German History Museum** (Deutsches Historisches Museum, €2, daily 10:00–18:00, tel. 030/203-040, www.dhm.de). I find its I. M. Pei–designed annex with a spiraling glass staircase more interesting than the collection (to find the annex, go down the street—Hinter dem Giesshaus—to the left of the museum).

Just before the bridge, wander left along the canal through a tiny but colorful arts-and-crafts market (weekends only, a larger flea market is just outside the Pergamon Museum; see page 613). Canal tour boats leave from here. Then go back out to the main road and cross the bridge to...

Museum Island (Museumsinsel)—This island, home of Germany's first museums, is gradually being renovated to consolidate the art collections of East and West Berlin (see below). For 300 years, the island's big square, the **Lustgarten,** has flip-flopped between being a military parade ground and a people-friendly park, depending upon the political tenor of the time. In 1999, it was made into a park again (read the history posted in corner opposite church). On a sunny day, it's packed with relaxing locals and is one of Berlin's most enjoyable public spaces.

The towering church is the century-old **Berlin Cathedral** (Berliner Dom, €4, €5 includes access to dome gallery, Mon–Sat 9:00–19:00, Sun 12:00–19:00, on summer Thu church—but not dome gallery—open until 22:00, www.berliner-dom.de; May–Sept organ concerts offered most Wed–Fri at 15:00, free with regular admission; for other concerts, visit ticket office on Lustgarten side, Mon–Fri 10:00–17:30, closed Sat–Sun, tel. 030/2026-9136). Inside, the great reformers (Luther, Calvin, and company) stand around the brilliantly restored dome like stern saints guarding their theology. Frederick I rests in an ornate tomb (right transept, near entrance to dome). The 270-step climb to the outdoor dome gallery is tough, but offers pleasant, breezy views of the city at the finish line (last entry 30 min before closing, dome closes in bad weather and at 17:00 in winter). The crypt downstairs is not worth a look.

Across Unter den Linden is the decrepit **Palace of the Republic** (with the copper-tinted windows). A symbol of the communist days, it was East Berlin's parliament building and futuristic entertainment complex. Although it officially has a date with the wrecking ball, many Easterners want it saved, and its future is still uncertain.

Berlin hopes to make Museum Island into one of the finest museum complexes in the world. They've got a good head start with the excellent Pergamon Museum (see below). Berlin's Egyptian Museum, with the famous bust of Queen Nefertiti, is due to move here sometime in 2005 (see page 627). You could visit either of the two following museums—the Pergamon or Old National Gallery—before continuing our walk. Once you're finished, skip down to "Museum Island to Alexanderplatz," below, to resume the walk.

▲▲**Pergamon Museum**—Of all the island's museums, the Pergamon is the best (and, until the Egyptian Museum moves here, the only one that's essential). Its highlight is the fantastic Pergamon Altar. From a 2nd-century B.C. Greek temple, the altar shows the Greeks under Zeus and Athena beating the giants in a dramatic pig pile of mythological mayhem. Check out the action spilling onto the stairs. The Babylonian Ishtar Gate (glazed blue tiles from the 6th century B.C.) and many ancient Greek and Mesopotamian treasures are also impressive (€8, covered by Museumspass, free Thu after 18:00, open Tue–Sun 10:00–18:00, Thu until 22:00, closed Mon, courtyard café, behind Museum Island's red-stone museum of antiquities, Am Kupfergraben, tel. 030/2090-5577 or 030/209-050). The excellent audioguide (free with admission, but €4 during free Thu extended hours) covers the museum's highlights. Don't mind the scaffolding. Renovation projects (due to last until 2008) may cause small sections of the museum to close temporarily in 2005, but the museum will remain open.

Old National Gallery (Alte Nationalgalerie)—This gallery shows 19th-century German Romantic art: man against nature, Greek ruins dwarfed in enchanted forests, medieval churches, and powerful mountains (€8, covered by Museumspass, free Thu after 18:00, open Tue–Sun 10:00–18:00, Thu until 20:00, closed Mon, tel. 030/2090-5801).

Museum Island to Alexanderplatz: Continue walking down Unter den Linden. Before crossing the bridge (and leaving Museum Island), look right. The pointy twin spires of the 13th-century Nikolai Church mark the center of medieval Berlin. This Nikolai-Viertel (district) was restored by the DDR and was trendy in the last years of socialism. Today, it's dull and, with limited time, not worth a visit.

As you cross the bridge, look left in the distance to see the gilded **New Synagogue,** rebuilt after WWII bombing (see page 620). Across the river to the left of the bridge is the construction site of a new shopping center with a huge aquarium in the center. The elevator will go right through the middle of an undersea world.

Walk toward **Marien Church** (from 1270, interesting but very faded old *Dance of Death* mural inside door) at the base of the TV Tower. The big, red-brick building past the trees on the right is the **City Hall,** built after the revolution of 1848 and arguably the first democratic building in the city. In the park are grandfatherly statues of Marx and Engels (nicknamed "the old pensioners" by locals). Surrounding them are stainless-steel monoliths depicting the struggles of the workers of the world.

The 1,200-foot-tall **TV Tower** (Fernsehturm) offers a fine view from halfway up (€7, daily March–Oct 9:00–1:00, Nov–Feb 10:00–24:00, tel. 030/242-3333). The tower offers a handy city orientation and an interesting view of the flat, red-roofed sprawl of Berlin—including a peek inside the city's many courtyards *(Höfe).* Consider a kitschy trip to the observation deck for the view and lunch in its revolving restaurant (reservations smart for dinner, same phone number). Built (with Swedish know-how) in 1969, the tower was meant to show the power of the atheistic state at a time when DDR leaders were having the crosses removed from church domes and spires. But when the sun shined on their tower, the greatest spire in East Berlin, a huge cross, reflected on the mirrored ball. Cynics called it "The Pope's Revenge." East Berliners dubbed the tower the "Big Asparagus." They joked that if it fell over, they'd have an elevator to the West.

Farther east, pass under the train tracks into **Alexanderplatz.** This area—especially the Kaufhof department store—was the commercial pride and joy of East Berlin. Today, it's still a landmark, with a major U- and S-Bahn station.

Our orientation stroll is finished. For a ride through workaday eastern Berlin, with its Lego-hell apartments (dreary even with their new face-lifts), hop back on bus #100 from here. It loops five minutes to the end of the line and then, after a couple of minutes' break, heads on back. (This bus retraces your route, finishing at Bahnhof Zoo.) Or consider extending this foray into eastern Berlin, to...

Karl-Marx-Allee—The buildings along Karl-Marx-Allee in East Berlin (just beyond Alexanderplatz) were completely leveled by the Red Army in 1945. When Stalin decided this main drag should be a showcase street, he had it rebuilt with lavish Soviet aid and named it Stalin Allee. Today, this street, done in the bold "Stalin Gothic" style so common in Moscow in the 1950s, has been restored (and named after Karl Marx)—providing a rare look at Berlin's communist days. Cruise down Karl-Marx-Allee by taxi, or ride the U-Bahn to Strausberger Platz and walk to Schillingstrasse. There are some fine Social Realist reliefs on the buildings, and the lampposts incorporate the wings of a phoenix (rising from the ashes) in their design.

South of Unter den Linden

The following sights—heavy on Nazi and Wall history—are listed roughly north to south (as you reach them from Unter den Linden).

▲▲**Gendarmenmarkt**—This delightful and historic square is bounded by twin churches, a tasty chocolate shop, and the concert hall (designed by Schinkel, the man who put the neoclassical stamp on Berlin and Dresden) for the Berlin symphony. In summer, it hosts a few outdoor cafés, *Biergartens*, and sometimes concerts. The name of the square—part French and part German—reminds us that in the 17th century, a fifth of all Berliners were French émigrés, Protestant Huguenots fleeing Catholic France. Back then, tolerant Berlin was a magnet for the persecuted. The émigrés vitalized the city with new ideas and know-how.

The German Cathedral (described below) on the square has an exhibit worthwhile for history buffs. The French Cathedral (Franzosischer Dom) offers a humble museum on the Huguenots (€1.50, Tue–Sun 12:00–17:00, closed Mon) and a chance to climb 254 steps to the top for a grand city view (€1.50, daily 9:00–19:00).

Fassbender & Rausch, on the corner near the German Cathedral, is Europe's biggest chocolate store. After 150 years of chocolate-making, this family-owned business proudly displays its sweet delights—250 different kinds—on a 55-foot-long buffet. Truffles are sold for about €0.50 each. The shop's evangelical Herr Ostwald (a.k.a. Benny) would love you to try his best-seller: tiramisu (Mon–Fri 10:00–20:00, Sat 10:00–18:00, Sun 12:00–20:00, corner of Mohrenstrasse at Charlottenstrasse 60, tel. 030/2045-8440).

German Cathedral (Deutscher Dom)—This cathedral houses the thought-provoking *Milestones, Setbacks, Sidetracks (Wege, Irrwege, Umwege)* exhibit, which traces the history of the German

Eastern Berlin

WHAT WAS THE WALL 1961–1989

LEHRTER Ⓢ

TIER-

CHANCEL-LORY

REICHS-TAG

Bus 100 TO ZOO

STR. DES 17 JUNI

TO VICTORY COLUMN

GARTEN

TIERGARTENSTRASSE

GEMÄLDE-GALERIE

NAT'L. GALL.

PHIL-HARMONIE.

POTSDAM.

TOPOGRAPHY OF TERROR

CITY LIBRARY

SCHÖNEBERGSTRASSE

BUS 129 TO KU'DAMM

FRIEDRICH-STRASSE

BRANDEN-BURG GATE

Bus 100 TO ALEX. PLATZ

POTSDAMER PLATZ

EB.STR.

PORTION OF WALL STILL STANDING

FORMER LUFTWAFFE

BUS 129 TO KU'DAMM

ANHALTER BAHNHOF (RUINS)

NEW SYNAGOGUE

ORANIENBURGER Ⓤ

PERGAMON MUSEUM

GER. HIST. MUSEUM

NEUE WACHE

UNTER DEN LINDEN

PALACE OF REP.

FRIEDRICHSTRASSE

GENDARMEN-MARKT

LEIPZIGER STR.

KOCHSTRASSE

BUS 129 KOCH-STRASSE

Ⓤ Ⓢ

HACK. MARKT.

MUSEUM ISLAND

MARIEN CHURCH

Dom

MARX-ENGELS PLATZ

MÜHL. BR.

FORMER "CHECKPOINT CHARLIE"

■ MUSEUM OF THE WALL

TO PRENZLAUER BERG

T.V. TOWER

ALEXANDER-PLATZ

RATHAUS STR.

RATHAUS

NIKOLAI CHURCH & OLD TOWN

SPREE

"EAST" "WEST"

ORANIEN STR.

LINDEN STR.

JEWISH MUSEUM BERLIN

TO OST-BAHN-HOF

KREUZBERG

Ⓢ S-BAHN
Ⓤ U-BAHN

NOT ALL STATIONS ARE SHOWN

DCH

NOTE: MAP NOT TO SCALE
BRAND. GATE TO T.V. TOWER IS A **15**-MIN. WALK

---

parliamentary system. The exhibit is well done and more interesting than it sounds. There are no English descriptions, but you can follow a fine and free 90-minute audioguide (passport required for deposit) or buy the detailed €10 guidebook (free, June–Aug Tue–Sun 10:00–19:00, Tue until 22:00, closed Mon; Sept–May Tue–Sun 10:00–18:00, Tue until 22:00, closed Mon; on Gendarmenmarkt just off Friedrichstrasse, tel. 030/2273-0431).

▲▲▲**Museum of the Wall at Checkpoint Charlie (Mauermuseum Haus am Checkpoint Charlie)**—While the famous border check-point between the American and Soviet sectors is long gone, its memory is preserved by one of Europe's most interesting museums: the House at Checkpoint Charlie. During the Cold War, it stood defiantly—spitting distance from the border guards—showing off all the clever escapes over, under, and through the Wall.

Today, while the drama is over and hunks of the Wall stand like victory scalps at its door, the museum still tells a gripping history of the Wall, recounts the many ingenious escape attempts (early years—with a cruder wall—saw more escapes), and includes plenty of video and film coverage of those heady days when people-power tore down the Wall (€9.50, assemble 10 tourists and get in for €5.50 each, €3 audioguide, discount with WelcomeCard, but not covered by Museumspass, cash only, daily 9:00–22:00, U-6 to Kochstrasse or—better from Zoo—U-2 to Stadtmitte, Friedrichstrasse 43–45, tel. 030/253-7250, www.mauermuseum.de). If you're pressed for time, this is a good after-dinner sight. With more time, consider the €7 *Hear We Go* audioguide about the Wall that takes you on a walk outside the museum (80 min).

Where Checkpoint Charlie once stood, notice the thought-provoking post with larger-than-life posters of a young American soldier facing east and a young Russian soldier facing west. Around you are reconstructions of the old checkpoint. It's not named for a person, but for Number Three—as in Alpha (at the East–West German border, a hundred miles west of here), Bravo (as you enter Berlin proper), and Charlie (the most famous because it was the only place where foreigners could pass). A few yards away (on Zimmerstrasse), a glass panel describes the former checkpoint. From there, a double row of cobbles in Zimmerstrasse traces the former path of the Wall (these innocuous cobbles run throughout the city). Follow it one very long block to Wilhelmstrasse, a surviving stretch of Wall, and the...

Topography of Terror (Topographie des Terrors)—The park behind the Zimmerstrasse/Wilhelmstrasse bit of the Wall marks the site of the command center of Hitler's Gestapo and SS. Because of the horrible things planned here, the rubble of these buildings will always be left as rubble. The SS, Hitler's personal bodyguards, grew to become a state-within-a-state, with talons in every corner of German society. Along an excavated foundation of the building, an exhibit tells the story of National Socialism and its victims in Berlin (free, info booth open May–Sept daily 10:00–20:00, Oct–April daily 10:00–18:00 or until dark, free English audioguide, requires passport as a deposit, available only until 18:45 in summer, tel. 030/2548-6703, www.topographie.de).

Across the street (facing the Wall) is the **German Finance Ministry** (Bundesministerium der Finanzen). Formerly the head-quarters of the Nazi Luftwaffe (Air Force), this is the only major Hitler-era government building that survived the war's bombs. The communists used it to house their—no joke—Ministry of Ministries.

Hitler and the Third Reich

While many come to Berlin to see Hitler sights, these are essentially invisible. The German Resistance Museum is in German only and difficult for the tourist to appreciate (see page 622). The *Topography of Terror* (SS and Gestapo headquarters) is a fascinating exhibit but—again—only in German, and all that remains of the building is its foundation (see page 617). (Both museums have helpful audioguides in English.) Hitler's bunker is completely gone (near Potsdamer Platz). Your best bet for "Hitler sites" is to take the Infamous Third Reich Sites walking tour offered by Berlin Walks (see "Tours," page 599). EurAide has a good flier listing and explaining sites related to the Third Reich.

Walk up Wilhelmstrasse (to the north) to see an entry gate (on your left) that looks much like it did when Germany occupied nearly all of Europe. On the north side of the building (farther up Wilhelmstrasse, at corner with Leipziger Strasse) is a wonderful example of communist art. The mural (from the 1950s) is classic Social Realism, showing the entire society—industrial laborers, farm workers, women, and children—all happily singing the same patriotic song. This was the communist ideal. For the reality, look at the ground in the courtyard in front of the mural to see an enlarged photograph from a 1953 uprising here against the communists—quite a contrast.

▲▲**Jewish Museum Berlin (Jüdisches Museum Berlin)**—This museum is one of Europe's best Jewish sights. The highly conceptual building is a sight in itself, and the museum inside—an overview of the rich culture and history of Europe's Jewish community—is excellent. The Holocaust is appropriately remembered, but it doesn't overwhelm this celebration of Jewish life.

Designed by American architect Daniel Libeskind (who is redeveloping New York City's World Trade Center site), the zinc-walled building's zigzag shape is pierced by voids symbolic of the irreplaceable cultural loss caused by the Holocaust. Enter the museum through the 18th-century Baroque building next door, then go through an underground tunnel to reach the main exhibit. While underground, you can follow the Axis of Exile to a disorienting slanted garden with 49 pillars, or to the Axis of Holocaust, an eerily empty tower shut off from the outside world.

When you emerge from underground, climb the stairs to the engaging, thought-provoking, and accessible museum. There are many interactive exhibits (spell your name in Hebrew) and pieces of artwork (the *Fallen Leaves* sculpture in the building's largest void is especially powerful), and it's all very kid-friendly (peel the giant garlic and climb through a pomegranate tree). English explanations interpret both the exhibits and the design of the very symbolic building. The museum is in a nondescript residential neighborhood a 10-minute walk from the Checkpoint Charlie museum, but it's well worth the trip (€5, covered by Museumspass, discount with WelcomeCard, daily 10:00–20:00, Mon until 22:00, closed on Jewish holidays, tight security includes bag check and metal detectors; U-Bahn line 1, 6, or 15 to HalleschesTor, take exit marked Jüdisches Museum, exit straight ahead, then turn right on Franz-Klühs-Strasse, museum is 5 min ahead on your left at Lindenstrasse 9; tel. 030/2599-3300, www.jmberlin.de). The museum has a good café/restaurant (€9 daily specials, lunch 12:00–16:00, snacks at other times, tel. 030/2593-9760).

East Side Gallery—The biggest remaining stretch of the Wall is now "the world's longest outdoor art gallery." It stretches for nearly a mile and is covered with murals painted by artists from around the world. The murals are routinely whitewashed, so new ones can be painted. This segment of the Wall makes a poignant walk. For a quick look, take the S-Bahn to Ostbahnhof station (follow signs to Stralauerplatz exit; once outside, TV Tower will be to your right; go left, and at next corner, look to your right—Wall is across the busy street). The gallery only survives until a land-ownership dispute can be solved, when it will likely be developed like the rest of the city. (Given the recent history, imagine the complexity of finding rightful owners of all this suddenly very valuable land.) If you walk the entire length, you'll find a small Wall souvenir shop at the end (they'll stamp your passport with the former East German stamp) and a bridge crossing the river to a subway station at Schlesisches Tor (in Kreuzberg).

Kreuzberg—This district—once abutting the dreary Wall and inhabited mostly by poor Turkish guest laborers and their families—is still run-down, with graffiti-riddled buildings and plenty of student and Turkish street life. It offers a gritty look at melting-pot Berlin in a city where original Berliners are as rare as old buildings. Berlin is the fourth-largest Turkish city in the world, and Kreuzberg is its "downtown." But to call it a "little Istanbul" insults the big one. You'll see *döner kebab* stands, shops decorated with spray paint, and mothers wearing scarves. For a dose of Kreuzberg without getting your fingers dirty, joyride on bus #129 (catch it near Jewish Museum). For a colorful stroll, take the U-Bahn to Kottbusser Tor and wander—ideally on Tuesday and Friday between 12:00 and 18:00, when the Turkish Market sprawls along the Maybachufer riverbank.

North of Unter den Linden

While there are few major sights to the north of Unter den Linden, this area has some of Berlin's trendiest, most interesting neighborhoods.

▲▲**New Synagogue (Neue Synagogue)**—A shiny gilded dome marks the New Synagogue, now a museum and cultural center on Oranienburger Strasse. Only the dome and facade have been restored, and a window overlooks a vacant field marking what used to be the synagogue. The largest and finest synagogue in Berlin before World War II, it was desecrated by Nazis on "Crystal Night" (Kristallnacht) in 1938, bombed in 1943, and partially rebuilt in 1990. Inside, past tight security, there's a small but moving exhibit on the Berlin Jewish community through the centuries, with some good English descriptions (ground floor and first floor). On its facade, the *Vergesst es nie* message—added by East Berlin Jews in 1966—means "Never forget." East Berlin had only a few hundred Jews, but now that the city is united, the Jewish community numbers about 12,000 (€3, Sun–Thu 10:00–18:00, Fri 10:00–14:00, closed Sat, May–Aug Sun–Mon until 20:00 and Fri until 17:00, last entry 30 min before closing, U-Bahn: Oranienburger Tor, Oranienburger Strasse 28/30, tel. 030/8802-8300 and press 1, www.cjudaicum.de).

A block from the synagogue, walk 50 yards down Grosse Hamburger Strasse to a little park. This street was known for 200 years as the "street of tolerance," because the Jewish community donated land to Protestants so that they could build a church. Hitler turned it into the "street of death" *(Todes Strasse),* bulldozing 12,000 graves of the city's oldest Jewish cemetery and turning a Jewish nursing home into a deportation center. Note the two memorials—one erected by the former East Berlin government and one built later by the city's unified government. Somewhere nearby, a plainclothes police officer keeps watch over this park.

▲**Oranienburger Strasse**—Berlin is developing so fast, it's impossible to predict what will be "in" next year. The area around Oranienburger Strasse is definitely trendy (but is being challenged by hip Friedrichshain, farther east, and Prenzlauer Berg, described below).

While the area immediately around the synagogue is dull, 100 yards away things get colorful. The streets behind Grosse Hamburger Strasse flicker with atmospheric cafés, *Kneipen* (pubs), and art galleries.

At night, techno-prostitutes line Oranienburger Strasse. Prostitution is legal here, but there's a big debate about taxation. Since they don't get unemployment insurance, why should they pay taxes?

Hackescher Markt—This neighborhood, near Oranienburger Strasse, is worth exploring. A block in front of the Hackescher Markt S-Bahn station is **Hackesche Höfe,** with eight courtyards bunny-hopping through a wonderfully restored 1907 *Jugendstil* building. It's full of trendy restaurants, theaters, and cinema (playing movies in their original languages). This is a fine example of how to make huge city blocks livable—Berlin's apartments are organized around courtyard after courtyard off the main roads.

Prenzlauer Berg—Young, in-the-know locals agree that this is one of Berlin's most colorful up-and-coming neighborhoods (roughly between Helmholtzplatz and Kollwitz Platz and along Kastanien-allee, U-Bahn: Senefelderplatz and Eberswalder Strasse). This part of the city was largely untouched during World War II, but its buildings slowly rotted away under the communists. Since the Wall fell, it's been overrun with laid-back hipsters, energetic young families, and clever entrepreneurs who are breathing life back into its classic old apartment blocks, deserted factories, and long-forgotten breweries. Though it's a few blocks farther out than the neighborhoods described above, it's a fun place to explore and have a meal (see page 640) or spend the night (see page 636).

Natural History Museum (Museum für Naturkunde)—This place is worth a visit just to see the largest dinosaur skeleton ever assembled. While you're there, meet "Bobby," the stuffed ape (€3.50, Tue–Fri 9:30–17:00, Sat–Sun 10:00–18:00, closed Mon, last entry 30 min before closing, U-Bahn line 6 to Zinnowitzer Strasse, Invalidenstrasse 43, tel. 030/2093-8591).

Central Berlin

Tiergarten Park and Victory Column (Siegessäule)—Berlin's "Central Park" stretches two miles from Bahnhof Zoo to Brandenburg Gate. Its centerpiece, the Victory Column, was built to commemorate the Prussian defeat of France in 1870. The pointy-helmeted Germans rubbed it in, decorating the tower with French cannons and paying for it all with francs received as war reparations. The three lower rings commemorate Bismarck's victories. I imagine the statues of Moltke and other German military greats—which lurk in the trees nearby—goose-stepping around the floodlit angel at night. Originally standing at the Reichstag, the immense tower was actually moved to this position by Hitler in 1938 to complement his anticipated victory parades. At the first level, notice how WWII bullets chipped the fine marble columns. Climbing its 285 steps earns you a breathtaking Berlin-wide view and a close-up look at the gilded angel made famous in the U2 video (€2.20, April–Sept Mon–Thu 9:30–18:30, Fri–Sun 9:30–19:00, Oct–March daily 9:30–17:30, closes in the rain, WCs for paying guests only, no elevator, bus #100, tel. 030/8639-8560). From the tower, the grand Strasse des 17. Juni (named for a workers' uprising against the DDR government in the 1950s) leads east to the Brandenburg Gate.

Flea Market—A colorful flea market with great antiques, more than 200 stalls, collector-savvy merchants, and fun German fast-food stands thrives weekends beyond the Victory Column on Strasse des 17. Juni (S-Bahn: Tiergarten).

German Resistance Memorial (Gedenkstätte Deutscher Widerstand)—This memorial and museum tells the story of the German resistance to Hitler. The Benderblock was a military headquarters where an ill-fated attempt to assassinate Hitler was plotted (the actual attempt occurred in Rastenburg, eastern Prussia). Stauffenberg and his co-conspirators were shot here in the courtyard. While posted explanations are in German only, the spirit that haunts the place is multilingual (free, Mon–Fri 9:00–18:00, Thu until 20:00, Sat–Sun 10:00–18:00, free and good English audioguide with passport, €3 printed English translation, no crowds, near Kulturforum just south of Tiergarten at Stauffenbergstrasse 13, enter in courtyard, door on left, main exhibit is on third floor, bus #129, tel. 030/2699-5000).

▲**Potsdamer Platz**—The Times Square of Berlin, and possibly the busiest square in Europe before World War II, Potsdamer Platz was cut in two by the Wall and left a deserted no-man's-land for 40 years. Today, this immense commercial/residential/entertainment center, sitting on a futuristic transportation hub, is home to the European corporate headquarters of several big-league companies. The new Potsdamer Platz was a vision begun in 1991, when it was announced that Berlin would resume its position as capital of Germany. Sony, Daimler-Chrysler, and other major corporations have turned it once again into a center of Berlin. While most of the complex just feels big (the arcade is like any huge, modern, American mall), the entrance to the complex and Sony Center Platz are worth a visit.

For an overview of the new construction, and a scenic route to Sony Center Platz, go to the east end of Potsdamer Strasse, facing the skyscrapers (the opposite end from Kulturforum, at main intersection of Potsdamer Strasse/Leipziger Strasse and Ebert Strasse/Stressemanstrasse, U-Bahn: Potsdamer Platz). Find the green, hexagonal clock tower with the traffic lights on top. This is a replica of the first automatic **traffic light** in Europe, which once stood at the six-street intersection of Potsdamer Platz. On either side of Potsdamer Strasse, you'll see enormous cubical entrances to the brand-new underground Potsdamer Platz train station (due to open in 2005). Near these entrances, notice the **glass cylinders** sticking out of the ground. The mirrors on the tops of the tubes move with the sun to collect light and send it underground. Now go in one of the train station entrances and follow signs to *Sony Center*. (While you're down there, look for the other ends of the big glass tubes.)

You'll come up the escalator into **Sony Center** under a grand canopy. At night, multicolored floodlights play on the underside of this tent. Office workers and tourists eat here by the fountain, enjoying the parade of people. The modern Bavarian Lindenbrau beer hall— the Sony boss wanted a *Bräuhall*—serves good traditional food

(€5–16, big salads, 3-foot-long taster boards of 8 different beers, daily 11:00–24:00, tel. 030/2575-1280). The adjacent Josty Bar is built around a surviving bit of a venerable hotel that was a meeting place for Berlin's rich and famous before the bombs (daily 9:00–24:00, tel. 030/2575-9702). You can browse the futuristic Sony Style Store, visit the Filmhaus (a museum with an exhibit on Marlene Dietrich), and do some surfing at Web Free TV (on the street).

Across Potsdamer Strasse, you can ride what's billed as "the fastest elevator in Europe" to skyscraping rooftop **views.** You'll travel at nearly 30 feet per second to the top of the 300-foot-tall Kollhoff tower (€3.50, Tue–Sun 11:00–20:00, closed Mon, in redbrick building at Potsdamer Platz 1, tel. 030/2529-4372, www.panoramapunkt.de).

Kulturforum

Just west of Potsdamer Platz, with several top museums and Berlin's concert hall, is the city's cultural heart (admission to all sights covered by €10 state museums day ticket, or 3-day €12 Museumspass; phone number for all museums: tel. 030/266-2951). Of its sprawling museums, only the Gemäldegalerie is a must. To reach the Kulturforum, take the S- or U-Bahn to Potsdamer Platz, then walk along Potsdamer Platz and Potsdamer Strasse. From the Zoo station, you can also take bus #200 to Philharmonie. Across Potsdamer Strasse from the Kulturforum is the huge National Library (free English periodicals).

▲▲▲**Gemäldegalerie**—Germany's top collection of 13th- through 18th-century European paintings (more than 1,400 canvases) is beautifully displayed in a building that's a work of art in itself. Follow the excellent free audioguide. The North Wing starts with German paintings of the 13th to 16th centuries, including eight by Dürer. Then come the Dutch and Flemish—Jan Van Eyck, Brueghel, Rubens, Van Dyck, Hals, and Vermeer. The wing finishes with German, English, and French 18th-century art, such as Gainsborough and Watteau. An octagonal hall at the end features a fine stash of Rembrandts. The South Wing is saved for the Italians—Giotto, Botticelli, Titian, Raphael, and Caravaggio (€6, free Thu after 18:00, open Tue–Sun 10:00–18:00, Thu until 22:00, closed Mon, clever little loaner stools, great salad bar in cafeteria upstairs, Matthäikirchplatz 4).

New National Gallery (Neue Nationalgalerie)—This features 20th-century art, with ever-changing special exhibits (€6–8, depending on exhibit, free Thu after 18:00, open Tue–Fri 10:00–18:00, Thu until 22:00, Sat–Sun 11:00–18:00, closed Mon, café downstairs).

Museum of Arts and Crafts (Kunstgewerbemuseum)—Wander through a thousand years of applied arts—porcelain, fine *Jugendstil*

(Art Nouveau) furniture, Art Deco, and reliquaries. There are no crowds and no English descriptions (€3, free Thu after 14:00, open Tue–Fri 10:00–18:00, Sat–Sun 11:00–18:00, closed Mon).

▲Musical Instruments Museum (Musikinstrumenten Museum)— This impressive hall is filled with 600 exhibits from the 16th century to modern times. Wander among old keyboard instruments and funny-looking tubas. There's no English, aside from a €0.10 info sheet, but it's fascinating if you're into pianos (€3, free Thu after 13:00, Tue–Fri 9:00–17:00, Sat–Sun 10:00–17:00, closed Mon, low-profile white building east of the big, yellow Philharmonic Concert Hall, tel. 030/254-810).

Poke into the lobby of Berlin's **Philharmonic Concert Hall** and see if there are tickets available during your stay (ticket office open Mon–Fri 15:00–18:00, Sat–Sun 11:00–14:00, must purchase tickets in person, box office tel. 030/2548-8132).

Western Berlin

Western travelers still think of Berlin's "West End" as the heart of the city. While it's no longer that, the West End still has the best infrastructure to support your visit and works well as a home base. Here are a few sights within an easy walk of your hotel and the Zoo station.

▲Kurfürstendamm—West Berlin's main drag, Kurfürstendamm boulevard (nicknamed "Ku'damm"), starts at Kaiser Wilhelm Memorial Church and does a commercial cancan for two miles. In the 1850s, when Berlin became a wealthy and important capital, her new rich chose Kurfürstendamm as their street. Bismarck made it Berlin's Champs-Elysées. In the 1920s, it became a chic and fashionable drag of cafés and boutiques. During the Third Reich, as home to an international community of diplomats and journalists, it enjoyed more freedom than the rest of Berlin. Throughout the Cold War, economic subsidies from the West made sure that capitalism thrived on Ku'damm. And today, while much of the old charm has been hamburgerized, Ku'damm is still a fine place to feel the pulse of the city and enjoy the elegant shops (around Fasanenstrasse), department stores, and people-watching.

▲Kaiser Wilhelm Memorial Church (Gedächtniskirche)—The church was originally a memorial to the first emperor of Germany, who died in 1888. Its bombed-out ruins have been left standing as a memorial to the destruction of Berlin in World War II. Under a fine mosaic ceiling, a small exhibit features interesting photos about the bombing and before-and-after models of the church (free, Mon–Sat 10:00–16:00, closed Sun, www.gedaechtniskirche.com).

After the war, some Berliners wanted to tear the church down and build it anew. Instead, it was decided to keep the ruin as a memorial, and stage a competition to design a modern add-on section. The winning selection—the short, modern building (1961)

Western Berlin

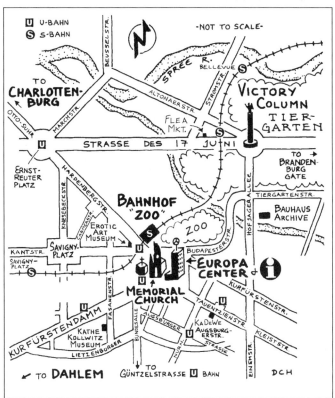

U-BAHN
S S-BAHN

-NOT TO SCALE-

N

SPREE R.
BELLEVUE
S

BEUSSELSTR.

TO
CHARLOTTEN-
BURG

ALTONAER STR.

STROMSTR.

VICTORY
COLUMN
TIER-
GARTEN

OTTO-SUHR

MARCHSTR.

FLEA
MKT.

STRASSE   DES   17   JUNI
S

U

TO
BRANDEN-
BURG
GATE

ERNST-
REUTER
PLATZ

HARDENBERGSTR.

KNESEBECKSTR.

CARMERSTR.

TIERGARTENSTR.

BAHNHOF
"ZOO"

BAUHAUS
ARCHIVE

HOFJÄGERALLEE

EROTIC
ART
MUSEUM

S

ZOO

KANT-STR.
SAVIGNY-
PLATZ

U

BUDAPESTER STR.

EUROPA
CENTER
i

SAVIGNY-
PLATZ
S

U

KURFÜRSTENSTR.

FASANENSTR.

MEMORIAL
CHURCH

U

KURFÜRSTENDAMM

TAUENTZIENSTR.

U

KÄTHE
KOLLWITZ
MUSEUM

BUNDESALLEE

AUGSBURGER
KADEWE
AUGSBURG-
ERSTR.

KLEIST STR.

TO DAHLEM

LIETZENBURGER

TO
GÜNTZELSTRASSE U BAHN

2

STRASSE

EINEMSTR.

DCH

next to the church—offers a world of 11,000 little blue windows (free, daily 9:00–19:00). The blue glass was given to the church by the French as a reconciliation gift. For more information on both churches, pick up the English booklet (€2.60).

The lively square between the churches and the Europa Center (a shiny high-rise shopping center built as a showcase of Western capitalism during the Cold War) usually attracts street musicians.

▲**Käthe Kollwitz Museum**—This local artist (1867–1945), who experienced much of Berlin's stormiest century, conveys some powerful and mostly sad feelings about motherhood, war, and suffering through the black-and-white faces of her art (€5, €1 pamphlet has English explanations of a few major works, Wed–Mon 11:00–18:00, closed Tue, a block off Ku'damm at Fasanenstrasse 24, tel. 030/882-5210, www.kaethe-kollwitz.de).

▲Kaufhaus des Westens (KaDeWe)—The "department store of the West," with a staff of 2,100 to help you sort through its vast selection of 380,000 items, claims to be the biggest department store on the Continent. You can get everything from a haircut and train ticket (basement) to souvenirs (third floor). The theater and concert box office on the sixth floor charges an 18 percent booking fee, but they know all your options (cash only). The sixth floor is also a world of gourmet taste treats. The biggest selection of deli and exotic food in Germany offers plenty of classy opportunities to sit down and eat. Ride the glass elevator to the seventh floor's glass-domed Winter Garden self-service cafeteria—fun but pricey (Mon–Fri 10:00–20:00, Sat 9:30–20:00, closed Sun, U-Bahn: Wittenbergplatz, tel. 030/21210, www.kadewe.com). The Wittenbergplatz U-Bahn station (in front of KaDeWe) offers a unique opportunity to see an old-time station. Enjoy its interior.

Berlin Zoo—More than 1,400 different kinds of animals call Berlin's famous zoo home—or so the zookeepers like to think. Germans enjoy seeing the pandas at play (straight in from the entrance). I enjoy seeing the Germans at play (€10 for zoo or world-class aquarium, €15 for both, children half price, daily 9:00–18:30, Nov–Feb until 17:00, aquarium closes at 18:00, feeding times—*Fütterungszeiten*—posted on map just inside entrance, enter near Europa Center in front of Hotel Palace or opposite Bahnhof Zoo on Hardenbergplatz, Budapester Strasse 34, tel. 030/254-010).

Erotic Art Museum—This offers three floors of graphic (mostly 18th-century) Oriental art, a tiny theater showing erotic silent movies from the early 1900s, and a special exhibit on the queen of German pornography, the late Beate Uhse. This amazing woman, a former test pilot for the Third Reich and groundbreaking purveyor of condoms and sex ed in the 1950s, was the female Hugh Hefner of Germany and CEO of a huge chain of porn shops. If you're traveling far and are sightseeing selectively, the sex museums in Amsterdam or Copenhagen are much better. This one, though well-described in English, is little more than prints and posters (€5, daily 9:00–24:00, last entry 23:00, hard-to-beat gift shop, at corner of Kantstrasse and Joachimstalerstrasse, a block from Bahnhof Zoo, tel. 030/886-0666). If you just want to see sex, you'll see much more for half the price in a private video booth next door.

Charlottenburg Palace Area

The Charlottenburg district—with a cluster of fine museums across the street from a grand palace—makes a good side-trip from downtown. (Note that the neighborhood's best sight, the Egyptian Museum, is scheduled to move to Museum Island in 2005—confirm it's still here before making the trip.) Ride U-2 to Sophie-Charlotte Platz and walk 10 minutes up the tree-lined boulevard Schlossstrasse

Charlottenburg Palace Area

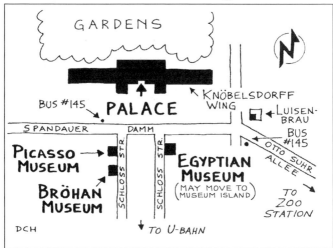

GARDENS

N

BUS #145

PALACE

KNÖBELSDORFF WING

LUISEN-BRAU

BUS #145

SPANDAUER DAMM

OTTO SUHR ALLEE

PICASSO MUSEUM →

SCHLOSS STR.

EGYPTIAN MUSEUM (MAY MOVE TO MUSEUM ISLAND)

SCHLOSS STR.

TO ZOO STATION

BRÖHAN MUSEUM

DCH

↓ TO U-BAHN

(following signs to *Schloss*), or—much faster—catch bus #145 (direction Spandau) direct from Bahnhof Zoo.

For a Charlottenburg lunch, the **Luisen Bräu** is a comfortable brewpub restaurant with a copper and woody atmosphere, good local "microbeers" (*dunkles* means "dark," *helles* means "light"), and traditional German grub (€5–8 meals, daily 9:00–24:00, fun for groups, across from palace at Luisenplatz 1, tel. 030/341-9388).

▲**Charlottenburg Palace (Schloss Charlottenburg)**—If you've seen the great palaces of Europe, this Baroque Hohenzollern palace comes in at about number 10 (behind Potsdam, too). It's even more disappointing since the main rooms can be toured only with a German guide (€8 includes 50-min tour, €2 to see just upper floors without tour, €7 to see palace grounds excluding tour areas, last tour 1 hour before closing, cash only, Tue–Sun 10:00–17:00, closed Mon, tel. 030/320-911).

The **Knöbelsdorff Wing** features a few royal apartments. Go upstairs and take a substantial hike through restored-since-the-war, gold-crusted, white rooms (€5, depending on special exhibitions, free English audioguide, Tue–Fri 10:00–18:00, Sat–Sun 11:00–18:00, closed Mon, last entry 30 min before closing, when facing the palace walk toward the right wing, tel. 030/3209-1202).

▲▲**Egyptian Museum (Ägyptische Museum)**—Across the street from the palace, the Egyptian Museum offers one of the great thrills in art appreciation—gazing into the still-young and beautiful face of 3,000-year-old Queen Nefertiti, the wife of King Akhenaton (€6, covered by Museumspass, free Thu after 14:00, open daily 10:00–18:00, free English audioguide, Schlossstrasse 70, tel. 030/343-5730). Remember that the museum is slated to move to Museum Island on Unter den Linden sometime in 2005.

This bust of Queen Nefertiti (c. 1340 B.C.) is perhaps the most famous piece of Egyptian art in Europe. Discovered in 1912, it shows the Marilyn Monroe of the early 20th century, with all the right beauty marks: long neck, symmetrical face, and just the right makeup (she's called "Berlin's most beautiful woman"). The bust never left its studio, but served as a master model for all other portraits of the queen. (That's probably why the left eye was never inlaid.) Buried for over 3,000 years, she was found by a German team who, by agreement with the Egyptian government, got to take home any workshop models they found. Although this bust is not representative of Egyptian art, it has become a symbol for Egyptian art by popular acclaim. Don't overlook the rest of the impressive museum, which is wonderfully lit and displayed, but with little English aside from the audioguide.

▲**Berggruen Collection: Picasso and His Time**—This tidy little museum is a pleasant surprise. Climb three floors through a fun and substantial collection of Picassos. Along the way, you'll see plenty of notable works by Matisse, van Gogh, and Cézanne. Enjoy a great chance to meet Paul Klee (€6, covered by Museumspass, free Thu after 14:00, open Tue–Fri 10:00–18:00, Sat–Sun 11:00–18:00, closed Mon, Schlossstrasse 1, tel. 030/326-9580).

▲**Bröhan Museum**—Wander through a dozen beautifully furnished *Jugendstil* (Art Nouveau) and Art Deco living rooms, a curvy organic world of lamps, glass, silver, and posters. English descriptions are posted on the wall of each room on the main floor. While you're there, look for the fine collection of Impressionist paintings by Karl Hagemeister (€4–6 depending on special exhibits, covered by Museumspass excluding special exhibits, Tue–Sun 10:00–18:00, closed Mon, Schlossstrasse 1A, tel. 030/3269-0600, www.broehan -museum.de).

Near Berlin

▲**Potsdam Palaces**—Featuring a lush park strewn with the extravagant whimsies of Frederick the Great, the sleepy town of Potsdam has long been Berlin's holiday retreat. Frederick's super-rococo Sanssouci Palace is one of Germany's most dazzling. His equally extravagant New Palace, built to disprove rumors that Prussia was running out of money after the costly Seven Years' War, is on the other side of the park (it's a 30-min walk between palaces). The Potsdam **TI** is a fine source of information (April–Oct Mon–Fri 9:00–19:00, Sat–Sun 10:00–16:00, less off-season, 5-min walk from Potsdam S-Bahn station, walk straight out of station and take first right onto An der Orangerie, Friedrich-Ebert Strasse 5, tel. 0331/275-5850).

Your best bet for seeing Sanssouci Palace is to take the Potsdam

TI's walking tour (see below). Otherwise, to make sense of all the ticket and tour options for the two palaces, stop by the palaces' information office (across the street from windmill near Sanssouci entrance, helpful, English-speaking staff, tel. 0331/969-4202).

Sanssouci Palace: Even though *sans souci* means "without a care," it can be a challenge for an English-speaker to have an enjoyable visit here. The palaces of Vienna, Munich, and even Würzburg offer equal sightseeing thrills with far fewer headaches. While the grounds are impressive, the interior of Sanssouci Palace can be visited only by a one-hour tour in German (with a borrowed English text), and these tours get booked up quickly. The only English option is the Potsdam TI's tour (see below).

If you take a German tour of Sanssouci, you must be at the palace in person to get your ticket and the appointment time for your tour. In the summer, if you arrive by 9:00, you'll get right in. If you arrive after 10:00, plan on a wait. If you arrive after 12:00, you may not get in at all (€8, April–Oct Tue–Sun 9:00–17:00, closed Mon, Nov–March Tue–Sun 9:00–16:00, closed Mon).

New Palace (Neues Palais): Use the English texts to tour Frederick's New Palace (€5, plus €1 for optional live tour in German, April–Oct Sat–Thu 9:00–17:00, closed Fri, Nov–May Sat–Thu 9:00–16:00, closed Fri). If you also want to see the king's apartments, you must take a required 45-minute tour in German (€6, offered May–Oct daily at 11:00 and 14:00). Off-season (Nov–April), the king's apartments are closed, and you can visit the rest of the New Palace only on a German tour (€5); it can take up to an hour for enough people to gather.

Walking Tours: The Potsdam TI's handy walking tour includes Sanssouci Palace, offering the only way to get into the palace with an English-speaking guide (€26 covers walking tour, palace, and park, 11:00 daily except Mon, 3.5 hrs, departs from Film Museum across from TI—walk straight out of Potsdam S-Bahn station and take first right onto An der Orangerie, reserve by phone, in summer reserve at least 2 days in advance, tel. 0331/275-5850).

A "Discover Potsdam" walking tour (which doesn't include Sanssouci Palace) is offered by Original Berlin Walks and led by a native English-speaking guide. The tour leaves from Berlin's Zoo station at 9:40 on Saturdays May through October (€15, or €11.20 if under age 26 or with WelcomeCard, meet at taxi stand at Zoo station, public transportation not included, but can buy ticket from guide, no booking necessary, tel. 030/301-9194). The guide takes you to Cecilienhof Palace (site of postwar Potsdam conference attended by Churchill, Stalin, and Truman), through pleasant green landscapes to the historic heart of Potsdam for lunch, and to Sanssouci Park.

What to Avoid: Potsdam's much-promoted Wannsee boat rides are torturously dull.

Greater Berlin

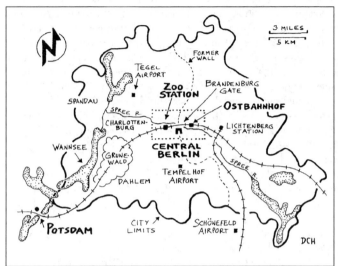

Getting to Potsdam: Potsdam is easy to reach from Berlin (17 min on direct Regional Express/RE trains from Bahnhof Zoo every 30 min, or 30 min direct on S-Bahn line 7 from Bahnhof Zoo to Potsdam station; round-trip covered by €6 transit day pass with zones A, B, and C). If you're taking the Potsdam TI's tour, walk to the Film Museum from the Potsdam S-Bahn stop (see "Walking Tours," above). If not taking the TI tour, catch bus #695 from the Potsdam station to the palaces (3/hr, 20 min). Use the same bus #695 to shuttle between the sights in the park. For a more scenic approach, take tram #96 or #X98 from the Potsdam station to Luisenplatz, then walk 15 minutes through the park and enjoy a classic view of Sanssouci Palace.

Other Day Trips—EurAide has researched and printed a *Get Me Outta Here* flier describing good day trips to small towns, and another flier on the nearby Sachsenhausen Concentration Camp (which many think is as interesting as Dachau; a Sachsenhausen day trip is also offered by The Original Berlin Walks—see "City Walking Tours," page 599).

NIGHTLIFE

Berlin is a happening place for nightlife—whether it's nightclubs, pubs, jazz music, cabaret, hokey-but-fun German variety shows, theater, or concerts. Tourists stroll the Ku'damm after dark.

Berlin Programm lists a nonstop parade of concerts, plays, exhibits, and cultural events (€1.60, in German, www.berlin-programm.de); the

Ex-Berliner (€2, www.ex-berliner.com) and the TI-produced *Berlin Calendar* (€1.60) have less information, but are in English (all sold at kiosks and TIs). For the young and determined sophisticate, *Zitty* and *Tip* are the top guides to alternative culture (in German, sold at kiosks). Also pick up the free schedules *Flyer* and *030* in bars and clubs. The free *New Berlin* magazine—available at EurAide, Starbucks, and hostels—provides the English-language inside scoop on nightlife, cheap eats, and hostels (www.newberlinmagazine.com).

Visit KaDeWe's ticket office for your music and theater options (sixth floor, 18 percent fee but access to all tickets, see page 626). Ask about "competitive improvisation" and variety shows.

Jazz—For jazz (blues and boogie, too) near my recommended Savignyplatz hotels in western Berlin, consider **A Trane Jazz Club** (daily, 21:00–2:00, Bleibtreustrasse 1, tel. 030/313-2550) and **Quasimodo Live** (Kantstrasse 12a, under Delphi Cinema, tel. 030/312-8086). For quality blues and New Orleans–style jazz, stop by **Ewige Lampe** (from 21:00, Niebuhrstrasse 11a).

Cabaret—Bar Jeder Vernunft offers modern-day cabaret a short walk from the recommended hotels in western Berlin. This variety show, under a classic old tent perched atop a modern parking lot, is a hit with German-speakers, but can still be worthwhile for those who don't speak the language (as some of the music shows are in a sort of "Dinglish"). Even some Americans perform here periodically. Tickets are generally around €15, and shows change regularly (performances start at 20:30, closed Sun, seating can be a bit cramped, south of Ku'damm at Schaperstrasse 24, tel. 030/883-1582, www .bar-jeder-vernunft.de).

German Variety Show—To spend an evening enjoying Europe's largest revue theater, consider Revue Berlin at the Friedrichstadt Palast. The show basically depicts the history of Berlin, and is choreographed in a funny and musical way that's popular with the Lawrence Welk–type German crowd. It's even entertaining for your entire English-speaking family (€13–51, Tue–Sat 20:00, also Sat–Sun at 16:00, U-Bahn: Oranienburger Tor, tel. 030/284-8830, www.friedrichstadtpalast.de).

Nightclubs and Pubs—Oranienburger Strasse's trendy scene (page 620) is being eclipsed by the action at Friedrichshain (farther east). To the north, you'll find the hip Prenzlauer Berg neighborhood, packed with everything from smoky pubs to small art bars and dance clubs (best scene is around Helmholtsplatz, U-Bahn: Eberswalder Strasse; see page 621).

Tour—Original Berlin Walks offers a Nightlife Berlin tour that goes beyond just a pub crawl, since the guides offer history along the way (€9, May–Sept on Tue, Thu, Sat, and Sun at 22:30, meet at Häagen-Dazs at Hackescher Markt S-Bahn station).

SLEEPING

When in Berlin, I sleep in the former West, on or near Savignyplatz. While Bahnhof Zoo and Ku'damm are no longer the center of Berlin, the trains, TI, and walking tours are all still handy to Zoo. And the streets around the tree-lined Savignyplatz (a 10-min walk behind the station) have a neighborhood charm. While towering new hotels are being built in the new center, simple, small, friendly, good-value places abound here. My listings are generally located a couple of flights up in big, run-down buildings. Inside, they're clean, quiet, and spacious enough that their well-worn character is actually charming. Rooms in back are on quiet courtyards.

As an alternative, I've also listed some suggestions in eastern Berlin's youthful and increasingly popular Prenzlauer Berg neighborhood, as well as a couple other possibilities elsewhere.

Berlin is packed and hotel prices go up on holidays, including Green Week in mid-January, Easter weekend, the first weekend in May, Ascension weekend in May, the Love Parade (mid-July), Germany's national holiday (Oct 2–4), Christmas, and New Year's.

During slow times, the best values are actually business-class rooms on the push list booked through the TI. But as the world learns what a great place Berlin is to visit, a rising tide of tourists will cause these deals to fade away.

Western Berlin

Near Savignyplatz and Bahnhof Zoo

These hotels and pensions are a 5- to 15-minute walk from Bahnhof Zoo (or take S-Bahn to Savignyplatz). Hotels on Kantstrasse have street noise. Ask for a quieter room in back. The area has an artsy charm going back to the cabaret days in the 1920s, when it was the center of Berlin's gay scene. Of the accommodations listed in this area, Pension Peters offers the best value for budget travelers.

$$$ **Hotel Askanischerhof** is the oldest *Zimmer* in Berlin, posh as can be, with 16 sprawling, antique-furnished rooms. Photos on the walls brag of famous movie-star guests. Frau Glinicke offers Old World service and classic Berlin atmosphere (Sb-€95–110, Db-€117–145, extra bed-€25, free parking, non-smoking rooms, elevator, Ku'damm 53, tel. 030/881-8033, fax 030/881-7206, www.askanischer-hof.de, info@askanischer-hof.de).

$$$ **Hecker's Hotel** is an ultramodern, four-star business hotel with 69 rooms and all the sterile Euro-comforts (Sb-€125, Db-€150, breakfast-€15, weekend breakfasts included, all rooms €200 during conferences, non-smoking rooms, elevator, parking-€9-12/day, between Savignyplatz and Ku'damm at Grolmanstrasse 35, tel. 030/88900, fax 030/889-0260, www.heckers-hotel.com, info@heckers-hotel.com).

Sleep Code

(€1 = about $1.20, country code: 49, area code: 030)
S = Single, **D** = Double/Twin, **T** = Triple, **Q** = Quad,
b = bathroom, **s** = shower only, **SE** = Speaks English, **NSE** = No
English. Unless otherwise noted, credit cards are accepted,
English is spoken, and breakfast is included.

To help you sort easily through these listings, I've divided
the rooms into three categories, based on the price for a standard
double room with bath:

$$$ **Higher Priced**—Most rooms €120 or more.
  $$ **Moderately Priced**—Most rooms between €85–120.
    $ **Lower Priced**—Most rooms €85 or less.

$$$ Hotel Astoria is a friendly, three-star, business-class hotel
with 32 comfortably furnished rooms and affordable summer and
weekend rates (high season Db-€117–128; prices drop to Sb-
€86–97, Db-€94–118 during low season of July–Aug, Nov–Feb, for
any 2 weekend nights or if slow; breakfast-€10 extra, rooms with
showers are cheaper than rooms with baths, non-smoking floors,
elevator, free Internet access, parking-€13/day, around corner from
Bahnhof Zoo at Fasanenstrasse 2, tel. 030/312-4067, fax 030/312-
5027, www.hotelastoria.de, info@hotelastoria.de).

$$ Hotel Pension Savoy, under new ownership, rents 16 comfortable and colorfully decorated rooms with all the amenities. You'll
love the cheery old pastel breakfast room. Most rooms overlook a
quiet courtyard (Sb-€69–79, Db-€99–109, extra person-€34–46, elevator, Meinekestrasse 4, tel. 030/881-3700, fax 030/8847-1610,
www.hotel-pension-savoy.de, info@hotel-pension-savoy.de).

$$ Hotel Atlanta has 30 newish rooms in an older building with
big leather couches, half a block south of Ku'damm. It's next to Gucci,
on an elegant shopping street (Ss-€40–70, Sb-€60–99, Db-€80–120,
Tb-€100–140, Qb-€120–160, non-smoking rooms, Fasanenstrasse
74, tel. 030/881-8049, fax 030/881-9872, www.hotelatlanta.de, mail
@hotelatlanta.de).

$$ Hotel Carmer 16, with 30 bright, airy rooms, feels like a
big, professional hotel with all the comfy extras, but a cold reception
staff (Sb-€72, Db-€93–122, extra person-€20, some rooms have balconies, elevator and a few stairs, beauty parlor and mini-spa upstairs,
Carmerstrasse 16, tel. 030/3110-0500, fax 030/3110-0510,
carmer16@t-online.de).

$$ Hotel-Pension Funk, the former home of a 1920s silent-
movie star, is delightfully quirky. Kind manager Herr Michael
Pfundt offers 14 elegant old rooms with rich Art Nouveau

Berlin's Savignyplatz Neighborhood

S S-BAHN
U U-BAHN

¼ MILE
400 METERS

POST

GOETHE STRASSE

ZOO STN.

S-BAHN

ZOO

PESTALOZZISTR.

BUS STOP

KANT STRASSE

SAVIGNY PLATZ

TAXI

NIEBUHR STR.

TAUEN.

MOMMSEN STR.

MEMORIAL CHURCH

KU'FU

LIETZENBURGER

DCH

1 Hotel Pension Savoy
2 Hotel Astoria
3 Hecker's Hotel
4 Hotel Askanischerhof
5 Hotel Atlanta
6 Hotel-Pension Funk
7 Hotel Bogota

8 Hotel Carmer 16
9 Hotel Pension Columbus
10 Pension Peters
11 Pension Alexis
12 Hotel Crystal Garni
13 Hotel Pension Alexandra
14 To Hotels Austriana, Insel Rügen, Bella & Curtis; To Weyers Café Rest.

15 Dicke Wirtin Pub
16 Restaurant Die Zwölf Apostel
17 Ristorante San Marino
18 Restaurant Zillemarkt
19 Quasimodo Live
20 A Trane Jazz Club
21 Käthe Kollwitz Museum
22 To Launderette

furnishings (S-€34–57, Ss-€41–72, Sb-€52–82, D-€52–82, Ds-€72–93, Db-€82–113, extra person-€23, prices guaranteed through 2005 with this book, cash preferred, Fasanenstrasse 69, a long block south of Ku'damm, tel. 030/882-7193, fax 030/883-3329, www.hotel-pensionfunk.de, berlin@hotel-pensionfunk.de).

$$ Hotel Bogota has 125 unique rooms and several large lounges in a sprawling old maze of a building that once housed the Nazi Chamber of Culture. (After the war, German theater stars were "de-Nazified" here before they could go back to work.) Photographer Helmut Newton lived here for two years, and Benny Goodman is rumored to have played here in the 1920s. Today, pieces of the owner's modern art collection lurk around every corner. Take a peek at the bizarre collage in the atrium, with mannequins suspended from the ceiling (S-€44, Ss-€55–57, Sb-€66–72, D-€66–69, Ds-€74–77, Db-€94–98, extra bed-€20, children under 12 free, prices guaranteed through 2005 with this book, non-smoking rooms, elevator, bus #109 from Bahnhof Zoo to Schlüterstrasse 45, tel. 030/881-5001, fax 030/883-5887, www.hotelbogota.de, hotel .bogota@t-online.de).

$$ Hotel Pension Alexandra has 10 pleasant rooms on a tree-lined street between Savignyplatz and Ku'damm. Expect the usual high ceilings and marble entryway found in these turn-of-the-20th-century buildings, but with added touches—most rooms and the elegant breakfast room are decorated with original antique furniture (Ss-€50–72, Sb-€58–82, Ds-€63–82, Db-€65–99, extra bed-€25–35, Wielandstrasse 32, tel. 030/881-2107, fax 030/885-7780, www.alexandra-berlin.de, mail@alexandra-berlin.de).

$ Pension Peters, run by a German-Swedish couple, is sunny and central, with a cheery breakfast room. Decorated sleek Scandinavian, with every room renovated, it's a winner (S-€36, Ss-€47, Sb-€58, D-€51, Ds-€68, Db-€78-83, extra bed-€10, prices guaranteed through 2005 with this book, kids under 12 free, family room, cash preferred, Internet access, 10 yards off Savignyplatz at Kantstrasse 146, tel. 030/3150-3944, fax 030/312-3519, www.pension-peters -berlin.de, penspeters@aol.com, Annika and Christoph SE). The same family also runs a larger hotel just outside of Berlin (see Hotel Pankow on page 638) and rents apartments (ideal for small groups and longer stays).

$ Hotel Pension Columbus, run by the König family, fills a sprawling floor of a grand building with modest and well-worn, but clean rooms (S-€40–45, Ss-€55, Sb-€65, D-€65, Ds-€75, Db-€85, elevator, Meinekestrasse 5, tel. 030/881-5061, fax 030/881-3200, www.columbus-berlin.de, info@columbus-berlin.de).

$ Pension Alexis is a classic, Old World, four-room pension in a stately 19th-century apartment run by Frau and Herr Schwarzer. The shower and toilet facilities are old and cramped, but this, more than any other Berlin listing, has you feeling at home with a faraway aunt (S-€43, D-€65, T-€97, Q-€128, cash only, big rooms, handheld showers, Carmerstrasse 15, tel. 030/312-5144, enough English spoken).

$ Hotel Crystal Garni is professional and offers small, well-worn, comfortable rooms and a *vollkorn* breakfast room (S-€36, Sb-€41, D-€47, Ds-€57, Db-€66–77, elevator, a block past Savignyplatz at Kantstrasse 144, tel. 030/312-9047, fax 030/312-6465, run by John and Dorothy Schwarzrock and Herr Vasco Flascher).

South of Ku'damm

Several small hotels are nearby in a charming, café-studded neighborhood 300 yards south of Ku'damm (near intersection of Sächsische Strasse and Pariser Strasse, bus #109 from Bahnhof Zoo, direction: Airport Tegel). They are less convenient from the station than most of the Savignyplatz listings above. The last three places are all in the same building and run by the same family (the Visnaps).

$$ Hotel-Pension Bella, a clean, simple place with high ceilings, rents nine big, comfortable rooms, but is a lesser value (Ss/Sb-€45–65, Ds-€70–85, Db-€80–90, extra person-€10, apartment also available, elevator, bus #249 from Zoo, Ludwigkirchstrasse 10a, tel. 030/881-6704, fax 030/8867-9074, www.pension-bella.de, info @pension-bella.de).

$$ Hotel Austriana, with 25 modern and bright rooms, is energetically run by the Visnap family (S-€33–43, Ss-€41–48, Sb-€49–67, Ds-€62–69, Db-€78–89, Ts-€78–96, Qs-€96–104, prices higher for holidays and conferences, half the rooms have balconies, elevator, Pariser Strasse 39, tel. 030/885-7000, fax 030/8857-0088, www.hotel-pension-austriana.de, austriana@t-online.de).

$ Insel Rügen Hotel has 31 rooms and ornate Eastern decor (S-€29–35, Ss-€34–40, D-€40–50, Ds-€55–65, Db-€65–85, elevator, Pariser Strasse 39, tel. 030/884-3940, fax 030/8843-9437, www.insel-ruegen-hotel.de, info@insel-ruegen-hotel.de).

$ Hotel-Pension-Curtis offers 10 hip, piney, basic rooms (S-€25–30, Ds-€50–60, Ts-€70–80, Qs-€72–90, cash only, elevator, Pariser Strasse 39, tel. 030/883-4931, fax 030/8843-9437, www.insel-ruegen-hotel.de, info@insel-ruegen-hotel.de).

Eastern Berlin

In Prenzlauer Berg

If you want to sleep in the former East Berlin, set your sights on the youthful, colorful, fun Prenzlauer Berg district. After decades of neglect, this corner of the East has quickly come back to life. Gentrification has brought Prenzlauer Berg great hotels, fine ethnic and German eateries (see page 621), and a happening nightlife scene. Prenzlauer Berg is about a mile and a half north of Alexanderplatz, roughly between Kollwitz Platz and Helmholtzplatz, and to the west, along Kastanienallee (known affectionately as "Casting Alley" for its share of beautiful people). The handiest U-Bahn stops are Senefelderplatz at the south end of the neighborhood and Eberswalder Strasse at the north end. For more on Prenzlauer Berg, see page 621.

$$$ Myer's Hotel is a boutique-hotel splurge offering simple and small, but elegant rooms and gorgeous public spaces, including a patio and garden. Details done right and impeccable service set this place apart. This peaceful hub—off a quiet courtyard and tree-lined street just a 10-minute walk from Kollwitz Platz or the nearest U-Bahn stop (Senefelderplatz)—makes it hard to believe you're in a capital city (Sb-€80–130, Db-€100–165, Metzer Strasse 26, tel. 030/440-140, fax 030/4401-4104, www.myershotel.de, info@myershotel.de).

$$ Hotel Jurine (yoo-REEN) is a pleasant, business-style hotel with a friendly staff that aims to please. Enjoy the breakfast buffet surrounded by modern art, or relax in the lush backyard (Sb-€75, Db-€90, Tb-€130, extra bed-€35, prices can double during conventions, breakfast-€13, parking garage-€12/day, 10-min walk to U-Bahn: Senefelderplatz, Schwedter Strasse 15, tel. 030/443-2990, fax 030/4432-9999, www.hotel-jurine.de, mail@hotel-jurine.de).

$$ Hotel Kastanienhof is a simple place offering fine but slightly overpriced rooms. The hotel is centrally located, making getting around Berlin a cinch, and it's near the hip Eberswalder Strasse bar scene (Sb-€73–93, Db-€98–108, Kastanienallee 65, tel. 030/443-050, fax 030/4430-5111, www.hotel-kastanienhof-berlin.de, info@hotel-kastanienhof-berlin.de).

$$ Apartments am Kollwitz Platz is typical of Prenzlauer Berg: an old, decrepit building that was gutted and remodeled, resulting in bright, clean, new-feeling spaces. It's in a quiet courtyard off a charming street speckled with cafés and shops; each room comes with a small kitchenette (Sb-€60, Db-€90, cash only, minimum 2-night stay, no breakfast, most rooms non-smoking, Wörther Strasse 20, tel. 030/4404-3641, fax 030/442-6433, www.hvp-pensionen.de, info@hvp-pensionen.de).

$ Transit Loft is technically a hostel, but feels more like an upscale budget hotel. Located in a refurbished factory, it offers clean, bright, modern, new-feeling, mostly-blue rooms with an industrial touch. The reception—staffed by friendly, hip Berliners—is open 24 hours, with a bar serving drinks all night long (dorm bed-€19, Sb-€59, Db-€69, Tb-€90, sheets and breakfast included, no age limit, cheap Internet access, fully wheelchair-accessible, Greifswalder Strasse 219; U-Bahn: Alexanderplatz, then tram #2, #3, or #4 to Hufelandplatz; tel. 030/4849-3773, fax 030/4405-1074, www.transit-loft.de, loft@hotel-transit.de).

$ Lette'm Sleep is a typical 50-bed youth hostel. It's not going to win any awards for cleanliness, but it's funky and relaxed, and fronts Helmholtzplatz—smack in the middle of Berlin's coolest neighborhood (dorm beds-€15–19, D with small kitchen area-€48, Db apartment-€66, sheets-€3 extra, no breakfast but communal kitchen, lockers, free Internet access, bike rental, Lettestrasse 7, tel. 030/4473-3623, fax 030/4473-3625, www.backpackers.de, info@backpackers.de).

On Unter den Linden

$$$ Hotel Unter den Linden is ideal for those nostalgic for the days of Soviet rule—although nowadays, at least the management tries to be efficient and helpful. Formerly one of the best hotels in the DDR, this huge, blocky place, right on Unter den Linden in the heart of what was East Berlin, is reasonably comfortable and reasonably priced. Built in 1966, with prison-like corridors, it has 331 modern, plain, and comfy rooms (Sb-€67–87, Db-€109–123, non-smoking rooms, Unter den Linden 14, at intersection with Friedrichstrasse, tel. 030/238-110, fax 030/2381-1100, www.hotel-unter-den-linden.de, reservation@hotel-unter-den-linden.de).

Away from the Center

$ **Hotel Pankow** is a fresh, colorful 43-room place run by friendly Annika and Christoph (from the Pension Peters, above). It's a 30-minute commute north of downtown, but a good value (S-€31, Sb-€46, D-€41, Db-€61, T-€51, Tb-€71, Q-€61, Qb-€81, family rooms, 2 children under 16 free in room with parents, elevator, Internet access, free parking in lot or €3/day in garage, tram in front of hotel takes you to the center in 30 min, Pasewalker Strasse 14-15, tel. 030/486-2600, fax 030/4862-6060, www.hotel-pankow -berlin.de, hotelpankow@aol.com).

Hostels

Berlin is known among budget travelers for its fun, hip hostels. Here are four good bets (all prices listed per person): **Studentenhotel Meininger 10** (€23/person, includes sheets and breakfast, cash only, no curfew, elevator, free parking, near City Hall on JFK Platz, Meiningerstrasse 10, U-Bahn: Rathaus Schoneberg, tel. 030/7871-7414, fax 030/7871-7412, www.meininger-hostels.de), **Mitte's Backpacker Hostel** (€15 dorm beds, S-€30–35, D-€23–28, T-€21, Q-€20, sheets-€2.50, no breakfast, could be cleaner, no curfew, Internet access, laundry, bike rental, English newspapers, U-Bahn: Zinnowitzerstrasse, Chauseestrasse 102, tel. 030/2839-0965, fax 030/2839-0935, www.backpacker.de, info@backpacker.de), **Circus** (dorm bed-€15–18, S-€28–32, D-€21–24, T-€18–20, Q-€16–18, 2-person apartment with kitchen-€65–75, 4-person apartment-€115–130, breakfast-€4, sheets-€2, cash only, no curfew, Internet access, 2 locations, U-Bahn: Rosa-Luxemburg Platz, Rosa-Luxemburg Strasse 39, or U-Bahn: Rosenthaler Platz, Weinbergsweg 1a, both tel. 030/2839-1433, fax 030/2839-1484, www.circus-berlin.de, info@circus-berlin.de), or **Clubhouse** (dorm bed-€14, bed in 5- to 7-bed room-€17, S-€32, D-€23, T-€20, breakfast-€3, sheets-€2, cash only, Internet access, on second floor, nightclub below, in hip Oranien-burger Strasse area, S- or U-Bahn: Friedrichstrasse, Kalkscheunen-strasse 4-5, tel. 030/2809-7979, fax 030/2809-7977, www.clubhouse -berlin.de, info@clubhouse-berlin.de).

EATING

Don't be too determined to eat "Berlin-style." The city is known only for its mildly spicy sausage. Still, there is a world of restaurants in this ever-changing city to choose from. Your best approach may be to choose a neighborhood, rather than a particular restaurant.

For quick and easy meals, colorful pubs—called *Kneipen*—offer light meals and the fizzy local beer, *Berliner Weiss*. Ask for it *mit Schuss* for a shot of fruity syrup in your suds. If the kraut is getting wurst, try one of the many Turkish, Italian, or Balkan restaurants.

Eat cheap at *Imbiss* snack stands, bakeries (sandwiches), and falafel/kebab places. Bahnhof Zoo has several bright and modern fruit-and-sandwich bars and a grocery (daily 6:00–24:00).

Western Berlin

Near Savignyplatz

Several good places are on or within 100 yards of Savignyplatz. Take a walk and survey these: **Dicke Wirtin** is a smoky old pub with traditional old-Berlin *Kneipe* atmosphere, famously cheap *Gulaschsuppe,* and salads (daily 12:00–4:00, just off Savignyplatz at Carmerstrasse 9, tel. 030/312-4952). **Die Zwölf Apostel** is trendy for leafy, candlelit ambience and Italian food. A dressy local crowd packs the place for €10 pizzas and €15–30 meals. Late-night partygoers appreciate Apostel's great breakfast (daily, 24 hrs, cash only, outside seating in summer until 10:00, immediately across from Savignyplatz S-Bahn entrance, Bleibtreustrasse 49, tel. 030/312-1433). **Ristorante San Marino,** on the square, is another good Italian place, serving cheaper pasta and pizza (daily 11:00–1:00, Savignyplatz 12, tel. 030/313-6086). **Zillemarkt Restaurant,** which feels like an old-time Berlin beer garden, serves traditional Berlin specialties in the garden or in the rustic candlelit interior (€10 meals, daily 10:00–24:00, near the S-Bahn tracks at Bleibtreustrasse 48a, tel. 030/881-7040).

Weyers Café Restaurant, serving quality international and German cuisine, is a great value and worth a short walk. It's sharp, with white tablecloths, but not stuffy. On a sunny day, its patio is packed with locals (€10 dinner plates, daily 8:00–2:00, seating indoors or outside on the leafy square, Pariser Strasse 16, reservations smart after 20:00, tel. 030/881-9378).

Ullrich Supermarkt is the neighborhood grocery store (Mon–Sat 9:00–22:00, closed Sun, Kantstrasse 7, under the tracks near Bahnhof Zoo). There's plenty of fast food near Bahnhof Zoo and on Ku'damm.

Near Bahnhof Zoo

Self-Service Cafeterias: The top floor of the famous department store, **KaDeWe,** holds the Winter Garden Buffet view cafeteria, and its sixth-floor deli/food department is a picnicker's nirvana. Its arterials are clogged with more than 1,000 kinds of sausage and 1,500 types of cheese (Mon–Fri 10:00–20:00, Sat 9:30–20:00, closed Sun, U-Bahn: Wittenbergplatz). **Wertheim** department store, a half-block from the Kaiser Wilhelm Church, has cheap food counters in the basement and a city view from its fine self-service cafeteria, Le Buffet, located up six banks of escalators (Mon–Sat 9:30–20:00, closed Sun, U-Bahn: Ku'damm). **Marche,** a chain that's popped up in big cities all over Germany, is another inexpensive, self-service cafeteria within a half block of the Kaiser Wilhelm

Church (Mon–Thu 8:00–22:00, Fri–Sat 8:00–24:00, Sun 10:00–22:00, plenty of salads, fruit, made-to-order omelettes, Ku'damm 14, tel. 030/882-7578).

At Bahnhof Zoo: **Terrassen am Zoo** is a good restaurant right in the station, offering peaceful decency amidst a whirlwind of travel activity (daily 6:00–22:00, upstairs, next to track 1, tel. 030/315-9140).

Eastern Berlin

Along Unter den Linden

The Opernpalais, preening with fancy prewar elegance, hosts a number of pricey restaurants. Its **Operncafé** has the best desserts and the longest dessert bar in Europe (daily 8:00–24:00, across from university and war memorial at Unter den Linden 5, tel. 030/202-683); sit down and enjoy perhaps the classiest coffee stop in Berlin. The beer and tea garden in front has a cheap food counter (from 10:00, depending on weather).

Near Pergamon Museum

Deponie3 is a trendy Berlin *Kneipe* usually filled with students from nearby Humboldt University. Garden seating in the back is nice, if you don't mind the noise of the S-Bahn passing directly above you. The interior is a cozy, wooden wonderland of a bar, serving basic sandwiches, salads, and daily specials (€3–7 breakfasts, €5–11 lunches and dinners, sometimes with live music, open Mon–Fri from 9:00, Sat–Sun from 10:00, Georgenstrasse 5, 1 block from Pergamon under S-Bahn tracks, tel. 030/2016-5740). Georgenstrasse is home to other good restaurants, including a branch of Die Zwölf Apostel (daily until 24:00, described under "Near Savignyplatz," above).

Near Checkpoint Charlie

Lekkerbek, a busy little bakery and cafeteria, sells inexpensive and tasty salads, soups, pastas, and sandwiches (Mon–Fri 6:00–18:00, Sat 7:00–13:00, closed Sun, a block from Checkpoint Charlie museum at U-Bahn: Kochstrasse, Friedrichstrasse 211, tel. 030/251-7208). For a classier sit-down meal, try **Café Adler,** across the street from the museum (€4–9, Mon–Sat 10:00–24:00, Sun 10:00–19:00, Friedrichstrasse 20b, tel. 030/251-8965).

In Prenzlauer Berg

Prenzlauer Berg is packed with fine restaurants—German, ethnic, and everything in between. (For more on this district, see page 621.) If you want to just wander, plenty of good places cluster around Helmholtzplatz. Otherwise, here are a few suggestions.

The **KulturBrauerei** complex of buildings offers a smorgasbord of eateries and activities. This former home to the Schultheiss brewery hosts a pool hall, concert venues, nightclubs, and restaurants (open daily, Knaackstrasse 97, U-Bahn: Eberswalder Strasse, tel. 030/4431-5152, www.kulturbrauerei-berlin.de).

Prater Biergarten offers a mellower outdoor ambience. This self-service place isn't the typical yodeling-and-lederhosen Bavarian beer garden—in addition to the wurst and beer, you'll find fine wine and snacks like olives, nuts, and pickles (Mon–Sat 18:00–24:00, Sun 10:00–24:00, just around the corner from KulturBrauerei at Kastanienallee 7, tel. 030/448-5688).

Knoppke's Imbiss has been a Berlin institution for over 70 years—it was family-owned even during DDR times. Locals say Knoppke's cooks up the best *Currywurst* (grilled hot dog with curry-infused ketchup) in town (Mon–Fri 4:30–20:00, closed Sat–Sun, Schönhauser Allee 44A). Don't be fooled by the Currystation at the foot of the stairs coming out of the Eberswalder Strasse U-Bahn station; Knoppke's is actually across the street, under the tracks.

TRANSPORTATION CONNECTIONS

Berlin has three train stations (with more on the way). Bahnhof Zoo was the West Berlin train station and still serves Western Europe: Frankfurt, Munich, Hamburg, Paris, and Amsterdam. The Ostbahnhof (former East Berlin's main station) still faces east, serving Prague, Warsaw, Vienna, and Dresden. The Lichtenberg Bahnhof (eastern Berlin's top U- and S-Bahn hub) also handles a few eastbound trains. Expect exceptions. All stations are conveniently connected by subway, and even faster by train. Train info: tel. 11861 (€0.46/min).

From Berlin by train to: Dresden (every 2 hrs, 2.25 hrs), **Frankfurt** (14/day, 5 hrs), **Munich** (14/day, 7 hrs, 10 hrs overnight), **Köln** (hrly, 6.5 hrs), **Amsterdam** (4/day, 7 hrs), **Budapest** (2/day, 13 hrs; 1 goes via Czech Republic and Slovakia, so Eurail is not valid), **Copenhagen** (4/day, 8 hrs, change in Hamburg), **London** (4/day, 15 hrs), **Paris** (6/day, 13 hrs, change in Köln, 1 direct night train), **Zürich** (12/day, 10 hrs, 1 direct night train), **Prague** (4/day, 5 hrs, no overnight trains), **Warsaw** (4/day, 8 hrs, 1 night train from Lichtenberg station; reservations required on all Warsaw-bound trains), **Kraków** (2/day, 10 hrs), **Vienna** (2/day, 12 hrs via Czech Republic; for second-class ticket, Eurailers pay an extra €23 if under age 26 or €31 if age 26 or above; otherwise, take the Berlin–Vienna via Passau train—nightly at 20:00).

Eurailpasses don't cover the Czech Republic. The **Prague Excursion pass** picks up where Eurail leaves off, getting you from any border into Prague and then back out to Eurail country again within seven days (first class-€50, second class-€40, youth second class-€30, buy from EurAide at Berlin's Bahnhof Zoo or Munich's Hauptbahnhof and get reservations—€3—at the same time).

There are **night trains** from Berlin to Amsterdam, Munich, Köln, Brussels, Paris, Vienna, Budapest, Kraków, Warsaw, Stuttgart, Basel, and Zürich, but there are no night trains from Berlin to anywhere in Italy or Spain. A *Liegeplatz*, or berth (€15–36), is a great deal; inquire at EurAide at Bahnhof Zoo for details. Beds cost the same whether you have a first- or second-class ticket or railpass. Trains are often full, so reserve your bed a few days in advance from any travel agency or major train station in Europe. Note: Since the Paris–Berlin night train goes through Belgium, railpass holders cannot use a Eurail Selectpass to cover this ride unless they've selected Belgium.

Berlin's Three Airports

Allow €20 for a taxi ride to or from any of Berlin's airports. **Tegel Airport** handles most flights from the United States and Western Europe (4 miles from center, catch the faster bus #X9 to Bahnhof Zoo, or bus #109 to Ku'damm and Bahnhof Zoo for €2; bus TXL goes to Alexanderplatz in East Berlin). Flights from the east and on Buzz Airlines usually arrive at **Schönefeld Airport** (12.5 miles from center, short walk to S-Bahn, catch S-9 to Zoo station). **Templehof Airport**'s future is uncertain (in Berlin, bus #119 to Ku'damm or U-Bahn 6 or 7). The central telephone number for all three airports is 01805-000-186. Call British Air at 01805-266-522, Delta at 01803-337-880, SAS at 01803-234-023, or Lufthansa at 01803-803-803.

DRESDEN

Dresden, the capital of Saxony, surprises visitors with fine Baroque architecture and impressive museums. It's historical, intriguing, and fun. While the city is packed with tourists, 85 percent of them are German. Until Americans rediscover Dresden's Baroque glory, you'll feel like you're in on a secret.

At the peak of its power in the 18th century, the capital of Saxony ruled most of present-day Poland and Eastern Germany from the bank of the Elbe River. Dresden's "Louis XIV" was Augustus the Strong. Both prince elector of Saxony and king of Poland, he imported artists from all over Europe, peppering his city with stunning Baroque buildings. Dresden's grand architecture and dedication to the arts—along with the gently rolling hills surrounding the city—earned it the nickname "Florence on the Elbe."

Sadly, Dresden is better known for its destruction in World War II. American and British pilots firebombed the city on the night of February 13, 1945. More than 25,000 people were killed, and 75 percent of the historical center was destroyed. (American Kurt Vonnegut, who was a POW in Dresden during the firebombing, later memorialized the event in his novel *Slaughterhouse-Five.*)

When Germany was divvied up at the end of World War II, Dresden wound up in the Soviet sector. Forty years of communist rule left the city in an economic hole—even today, Saxony's unemployment rate hovers around 19 percent. Some older Dresdeners feel nostalgia for the Red old days, when "everyone had a job." But in the decade and a half since the Berlin Wall fell, Dresden has made real progress in getting back on its feet—and most locals are enjoying capitalism with gusto. Today's Dresden is a young and vibrant city, crawling with happy-go-lucky students who barely remember communism.

Under the communists, Dresden patched up some of its damaged buildings, left many others in ruins, and replaced even more with huge, modern, pedestrian-unfriendly sprawl. But today, Dresden seems to be all about rebuilding. Circa-1946 photos are on walls everywhere, and the city's most important and beautiful historic buildings in the Old Town have been restored. Across the river, the New Town was missed by the bombs. While well-worn, it has retained its prewar character and is emerging as the city's fun and lively people zone. Most tourists never cross the bridge away from the famous Old Town museums...but a visit to Dresden isn't complete without a wander through the New Town.

Planning Your Time

Dresden, conveniently located halfway between Prague and Berlin, is well worth even a quick stop. If you're short on time, Dresden's top sights can be seen in a midday break on your Berlin–Prague train ride (it's about 2.5 hours from both). Catch the early train, throw your bag in a locker at the station (€2), follow my self-guided tour (below), and visit some museums before taking an evening train out. If you have more time, Dresden merits an overnight stay.

Many of Dresden's museums (including all Zwinger museums and Watchman's Tower) are closed on Monday. The Royal Palace and Albertinum are closed on Tuesday. The Hofkirche hosts free pipe-organ concerts twice a week (April–Dec on Wed and Sat at 11:30).

ORIENTATION

(area code: 0351)

Dresden's city center hugs a curve on the Elbe River. The Old Town (Altstadt) stretches along the south bank, and the New Town (Neustadt) is to the north. Dresden is big, with half a million residents, but virtually all of its sights are within easy strolling distance along the south bank of the Elbe in the Old Town. The main train station (Hauptbahnhof) is a five-minute tram ride or a 15-minute walk south of the historical center, partly along the heavily communist-influenced Prager Strasse. The New Town, to the north of the river, is more residential. While it boasts virtually no sights, it's lively, colorful, and fun to explore—day or night—and has some recommended hotels and restaurants.

Tourist Information

Dresden has two TIs: in the heart of the Old Town at **Theaterplatz** (in neoclassical Schinkelwache building, next to Zwinger), and in a freestanding kiosk at the train-station end of **Prager Strasse** (both TIs open Mon–Fri 10:00–18:00, Sat 10:00–16:00, closed Sun, general TI tel. 0351/491-920, www.dresden-tourist.de). Both tourist offices book rooms (€3/person), sell concert and theater tickets, and operate travel agencies. Get the handy, free one-page map of

Dresden

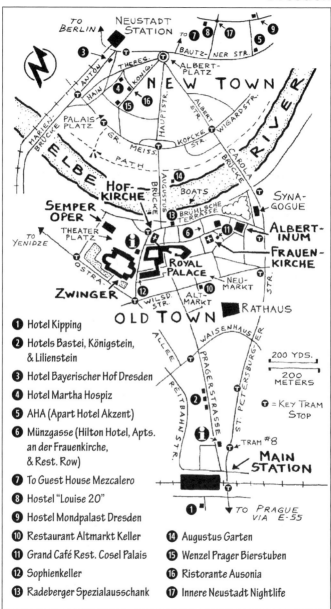

1. Hotel Kipping
2. Hotels Bastei, Königstein, & Lilienstein
3. Hotel Bayerischer Hof Dresden
4. Hotel Martha Hospiz
5. AHA (Apart Hotel Akzent)
6. Münzgasse (Hilton Hotel, Apts. an der Frauenkirche, & Rest. Row)
7. To Guest House Mezcalero
8. Hostel "Louise 20"
9. Hostel Mondpalast Dresden
10. Restaurant Altmarkt Keller
11. Grand Café Rest. Cosel Palais
12. Sophienkeller
13. Radeberger Spezialausschank
14. Augustus Garten
15. Wenzel Prager Bierstuben
16. Ristorante Ausonia
17. Innere Neustadt Nightlife

Dresden with a listing of key sights, hours, and prices on the back. For live entertainment and cultural events, study the monthly *Theater Konzert Kunst* (free, in German only).

The **Dresden City Card** (sold at both TIs) gives you admission to all of Dresden's top museums, discounts on some lesser museums, and unlimited use of the city's transit system (€18/48 hrs, €29 for 72-hr "Regional" version that includes outlying areas). If you're only here for the day, skip it—instead, buy a one-day museum pass, called a *Tageskarte* (€10, covers all state museums, including all listed below; available at participating museums). The Web site for all Dresden museums is www.skd-dresden.de.

Local Guide: Maren Koban is a genteel local woman who loves sharing the story of her hometown, as she has since 1991 (€100/half day, tel. 0351/311-1315).

Arrival in Dresden

Dresden has two major train stations. If you're coming for the day and want the easiest access to the sights, use the **Hauptbahnhof (Main Train Station),** just south of the Old Town. Exit the station following signs for the city, taxis, and trams. Cross Wiener Platz and veer right to find tram #8 or #11 (departing to your left), which zips you to the historical center (Theaterplatz or Postplatz). The walk to the Old Town (15 min) offers an enjoyable dose of the communist era as you stroll down Prager Strasse (from the station, continue straight through Wiener Platz, under and past the towering Mercure Hotel).

The **Neustadt** station serves the New Town north of the river, near some recommended hotels. From the Neustadt station, tram #11 runs to Am Zwingerteich, a park in the center of the Old Town right next to the sights.

Trains run between the Hauptbahnhof and Neustadt station every 10 minutes (€1.60, 10-min ride, most trains stop at each station—ask; the stations are also connected by slower tram #3).

Getting Around Dresden

Dresden's slick new trams and buses work well for the visitor. Buy tickets at the machines in the backs of trams (€1.60 per ride or €1 for a *Kurzstrecke*—short stretch—of fewer than 4 stops). A day ticket *(Tageskarte)* is good until 4:00 the next morning (the 1-zone, €4 version works for sightseeing within the city). Free use of public transit is included with the City Card (see above). Taxis are handy and generally honest (€2 drop, €1.10 per kilometer). The Hilton Hotel (across from the Frauenkirche) rents bikes to guests and non-guests (€8/5 hrs, €12/day, leave ID for security deposit).

SIGHTS AND ACTIVITIES

Do-It-Yourself Dresden Baroque Blitz Tour

Dresden's main sights are conveniently clustered along a delightfully strollable promenade next to the Elbe. Though Dresden has a long and colorful history, focus on the three eras that have shaped it the most: Dresden's golden age in the mid-18th century under Augustus the Strong; the city's WWII destruction by firebombs; and the communist regime that took over at the war's end and continued until 1989.

The following walk laces together Dresden's top sights in about an hour, not counting museum stops. Unless otherwise noted, Dresden's museums are light on English information (no audioguides), but heavy on sightseeing value.

Theaterplatz: Begin at Theaterplatz (convenient drop-off point for tram #8 from Hauptbahnhof). Face the equestrian statue (King John, an unimportant, mid-19th-century ruler) in the middle of the

square. In front of you, behind the statue, is the Saxon State Opera House—nicknamed the **Semper Oper** after its architect, Gottfried Semper (visits only with a tour, see page 655).

When facing the Opera House, on your left stands the neoclassical Schinkelwache (Guardhouse, houses the TI). The big building behind it and to the right is the Semper Gallery, the east wing of the Zwinger (your next stop). Across the square from the Opera House is the Hofkirche, with its distinctive open-work steeple, and behind that is the sprawling Royal Palace (both described below). All the buildings you see here—Dresden's Baroque treasures—are replicas. The originals were destroyed by American and British bombs in a single night. For over 60 years, Dresden has been rebuilding—and there's lots more work to do.

Walk through the passageway into the Zwinger courtyard (to your left as you face the Opera House), noticing the Crown Gate on the opposite side lowering majestically into view. Stop in the middle of the courtyard, where we'll survey all four wings.

The Zwinger: This palace complex, worth ▲▲, is a Baroque masterpiece—once the pride and joy of the Wettin dynasty, and today filled with fine museums. The Wettins ruled Saxony for over 800 years, right up until the end of the First World War. Saxony wasn't ruled by a king, but by a prince elector—one of a handful of nobles who elected the Holy Roman Emperor. The prince elector of Saxony was one of Germany's most powerful people, and the 18th century was Saxony's golden age. Friedrich Augustus I, prince elector of Saxony, wheeled and dealed—and converted from his Saxon Protestantism to a more Polish-friendly Catholicism—to become

Central Dresden

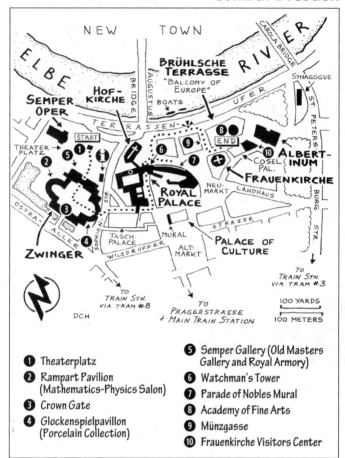

① Theaterplatz
② Rampart Pavilion (Mathematics-Physics Salon)
③ Crown Gate
④ Glockenspielpavillon (Porcelain Collection)
⑤ Semper Gallery (Old Masters Gallery and Royal Armory)
⑥ Watchman's Tower
⑦ Parade of Nobles Mural
⑧ Academy of Fine Arts
⑨ Münzgasse
⑩ Frauenkirche Visitors Center

King Augustus II of Poland. Legends paint Augustus as a macho, womanizing, powerful, ambitious, properly Baroque man—a real Saxon superstar. A hundred years after his death, historians dubbed him "the Strong." Today, tour guides love to impart silly legends about Augustus, who supposedly fathered 365 children and could break a horseshoe in half with his bare hands. Like most Wettins, Augustus the Strong was unlucky at war, but a clever diplomat and a lover of the arts. We can thank Augustus and the rest of the Wettins—and the nobles who paid taxes—for Dresden's rich architectural and artistic heritage.

"Zwinger" means the no-man's land just outside the city wall. Gradually, this empty space evolved into the complex of buildings you see today. By Augustus' time, the Zwinger was used for celebrations of Saxon royalty. Imagine an over-the-top royal wedding in this complex.

Let's get oriented. Face the north wing (with the Crown Gate on your left). You're looking at the **Rampart Pavilion** (Wallpavillon)**,** the first wing of the palace—an orangery built for Augustus' fruit trees. Stairs lead to a fine Zwinger view from the terrace above. This wing of the Zwinger houses the fun **Mathematics-Physics Salon** (see page 654). Turn to the left, facing the **Crown Gate** (Kronentor); its golden crown is topped by four eagles, symbolizing Polish royalty (remember that Augustus was also king of Poland). Turn again to the left to see the **Glockenspielpavillon.** The glockenspiel near the top of the gate has 40 bells made of Meissen porcelain (bells chime every 15 min and play melodies at 11:15, 14:15, and 17:15). Above the glockenspiel stands Atlas, with the earth on his back—a fitting symbol for Augustus the Strong. This wing of the Zwinger also houses Augustus the Strong's **Porcelain Collection** (see page 654). Turn once more to the left (with the Crown Gate behind you) to see the **Semper Gallery.** This Zwinger wing was added to the original courtyard a hundred years later by Gottfried Semper (of Opera House fame). It houses Dresden's best museum, the **Old Masters Gallery,** as well as the **Royal Armory** (see page 653).

Throughout the city, you'll see the local sandstone looking really sooty. Locals claim that it's not pollution, but natural oxidation that turns the stone black in about 30 years.

Take time to enjoy some of the Zwinger's excellent museums. Ponder this: Anticipating WWII bombs, Dresdeners preserved their town's art treasures by storing them in underground mines and cellars in the countryside. This saved these great works from Allied bombs...but not from the Russians. Nearly all of the city's artwork ended up in Moscow until after Stalin's death in 1953, when the art was returned by the communist regime to win over their East German subjects.

When you're finished with the museums, exit the Zwinger through the Glockenspielpavillon (south gate). Halfway through the corridor, look for the timelines telling the history of the Zwinger in German: to the right, its construction, and to the left, its destruction and reconstruction. Notice the Soviet spin: On May 8, 1945, the Soviet army liberated Dresden from "fascist tyranny" *(faschistischen Tyrannei),* and from 1945 to 1964, the Zwinger was rebuilt with the "power of the workers and peasants" *(Arbeiter- und Bauern-Macht).*

As you exit the corridor, jog to the left, cross the street and the tram tracks, and walk down the perpendicular Taschenberg Strasse with the yellow Taschenberg Palace on your right (ruined until 1990, today the city's finest 5-star hotel). Go under the passageway between the Royal Palace and the yellow palace. Ahead of you and to the right, the blocky modern building is the...

Palace of Culture (Kulturpalast): This theater, built by the communist government in 1969, is still used for concerts today. Notice the mural depicting communist themes: workers; strong women; care for the elderly; teachers and students; and, of course, the red star and the seal of the former East Germany.

Now turn left (with the Palace of Culture behind you). Walk toward the tallest tower ahead on the left (the climbable **Watchman's Tower**). On your left is the east wing of the sprawling...

Royal Palace (Residenzschloss): The palace is still being repaired from the WWII firebombing; the farther you walk, the more destruction you'll see. Its reconstruction is expected to last until 2010, when the Royal Palace will house civic offices and the city's massive art collection—only one-third of which is currently in museums. Much of the palace is already open, with a fine collection—consider stopping in now to see the sumptuous **Green Vault** (see page 655).

Just before you reach the big passageway, look for the bombed-out gap in the wall to your left. This was the palace's **Great Courtyard.** Across the courtyard, you see the black-and-white decoration on the inside of the western wing. These images, called sgraffito, are scratched into plaster over charcoal. Look halfway up the Watchman's Tower at the tourists, enjoying the best viewpoint in town (to get up there, find the entrance on the right-hand side of the big passageway; see page 655).

Continue through the passageway into the **Palace Square.** Ahead of you and to the left is the...

Hofkirche (Cathedral): Why does Dresden, a stronghold of local-boy Martin Luther's Protestant Reformation, boast such a beautiful Catholic cathedral? When Augustus the Strong died, his son wanted to continue as king of Poland, like his father. The pope would allow it only if Augustus Junior built a Catholic church in Dresden. Thanks to Junior's historical kissing-up, the mere 5 percent of locals who are Catholic get to enjoy this fine church. The elevated passageway connecting the church with the palace allowed the royal family to avoid walking in the street with commoners.

Step inside (free, enter through side door facing palace, Sat–Thu 8:00–19:00, Fri 13:00–19:00, tel. 0351/484-4712, www.kathedrale -dresden.de). The fine Baroque pulpit—hidden by locals in the countryside during World War II—is carved out of linden wood. The glorious 3,000-pipe organ filling the back of the nave is played for the public on Wednesdays and Saturdays at 11:30 (free, April–Dec only).

The Memorial Chapel (facing the rear of the church, on the left) is dedicated to those who died in the WWII firebombing and to all victims of violence. Its evocative *pietà* altarpiece was made in 1973 of Meissen porcelain. Mary offers the faithful the crown of thorns, as if to remind us that Jesus—on her lap, head hanging lifeless on the left—died to save humankind. The altar (freestanding, in front) shows five flaming heads. It seems to symbolize how Dresdeners suffered...in the presence of their suffering savior. The dates on the altar (30-1-33 and 13-2-45) mark the dark period between Hitler's rise to power and the night Dresden was destroyed.

The basement houses the royal crypt, including the heart of still-virile Augustus the Strong—which, according to legend, beats when a pretty woman comes near (crypt only open for one 45-min German tour each day).

As you leave the Hofkirche, look back at the palace. To the left, next to the palace's main entrance, you'll see a long, yellow mural called the...

Parade of Nobles (Fürstenzug): This mural—worth ▲—is painted on 24,000 tiles of Dresden porcelain. Longer than a football field, it illustrates 700 years of Saxon royalty. It was created out of the Saxons' need to commemorate their heritage after Saxony became a part of Germany in 1871. The artist carefully studied armor and clothing through the ages, allowing you to accurately

trace the evolution of weaponry and fashions for seven centuries. (This is great for couples: men watch the fashions, women the weaponry.)

The very last figure (or the first one you see, coming from this direction) is the artist himself, Wilhelm Walther. Then come commoners (miner, farmer, carpenter, teachers, students, artists), and then the royals, with 35 names and dates marking over 700 years of Wettin rule. Stop at 1694. That's August II (Augustus the Strong), the most important of the Saxon kings. He stomps on the rose (symbol of Martin Luther, the Protestant movement, and the Lutheran church today) to gain the Polish crown. The first Saxon royal is Konrad der Grosse ("the Great"). And waaay up at the very front of the parade, an announcer with a band and 12th-century cheerleaders excitedly herald the arrival of this wondrous procession. The porcelain tiles, originals from 1907, survived the bombing. When created, they were fired three times at 2,400 degrees Fahrenheit...and then fired again during the 1945 firestorm at only 1,800 degrees.

When you're finished looking at the mural, return to the Palace Square, face the river, and climb the big staircase on your right, up to the...

Brühlsche Terrasse: This "Balcony of Europe," a delightful ▲▲ promenade, was once Dresden's defensive rampart. Look ahead along the side of the terrace facing the river to see openings for cannons and other weapons. By Baroque times, fortresses were no longer necessary, and this became one of Europe's most charming promenades. Stroll and enjoy the leafy canopy of linden trees. Past the first fountain and the café, belly up to the railing facing the Elbe River.

Dresden claims to have the world's largest and oldest fleet of historic **paddleboat steamers:** nine riverboats from the 19th century (some of which still have plaques promising a "10-year warranty"). The hills in the distance (to left) are home to Saxon vineyards, producing Germany's northernmost wine. Because only a small amount of the land is suitable for vineyards, Saxon wine is expensive and enjoyed mostly by locals.

Below you to the left is the **Augustus Bridge** (Augustusbrücke), connecting Dresden's Old Town with the New Town. The water during the massive floods of August, 2002, filled about two-thirds of the arches. Notice how the raging floodwaters actually cleaned the sandstone inside the bridge's arches. At the far end of the Augustus Bridge, look for the golden equestrian statue, a symbol of Dresden. It's Augustus the Strong, the **Goldene Reiter** (Golden Rider), facing east to his kingdom of Poland.

The area across the bridge is the **New Town** (Neustadt). While three-quarters of Dresden's Old Town was decimated by Allied firebombs, much of the New Town survived. The 18th-century apartment buildings here were restored—giving the area a Baroque look instead of the blocky Soviet style predominant on the Old Town side of the river. The New Town is a trendy district today, and well worth exploring (see page 656). The **Three Kings Church** (Dreikönigskirche, steeple visible above the Goldene Reiter) marks a neighborhood with some recommended restaurants (see page 660).

The interesting, mosque-shaped building in the distance to the far left (marked Yenidze), originally a tobacco factory designed to advertise Turkish cigarettes, is now an office building with restaurants and nightclubs. A few steps to your left is the recommended Radeberger Spezialausschank café—the best place for a drink or meal with a river view (see page 661).

Continue walking along the Brühlsche Terrasse. Ahead on the right, you'll see the glass domes of the **Academy of Fine Arts.** (Locals call the big dome on the right "the lemon juicer.") At the modern globe sculpture on the terrace, go down the stairs on your right and head toward the huge rebuilt Frauenkirche. You'll walk along **Münzgasse,** lined with trendy restaurants (see page 661). This street re-creates the lively café scene of prewar Dresden. With the newly rebuilt Frauenkirche (ahead of you) as a centerpiece, this district will teem with more restaurants and cafés like these.

At the end of Münzgasse, you'll see reconstructed...

Frauenkirche (Church of Our Lady): This church, rated ▲▲, is the heart and soul of the city. Augustus the Strong grew jealous of the mighty Catholic domes of Venice and London, and demanded that a proper Lutheran church be built in Dresden. Completed in 1743, this was Germany's biggest Protestant church (310 feet high). Its unique central stone cupola design gave it the nickname "handbell church." While a great church, this building garners the world's attention because of its tragic history. On the night of February 13, 1945, the firebombs came. When the smoke cleared the next morning, the Frauenkirche was still standing. It burned for two days before finally collapsing. After the war, the Frauenkirche was kept in rubble as a peace monument and the site of many memorial vigils.

In 1992, the reconstruction of the church began. The restorers used as many of the church's original stones as possible, fitting it together like a giant jigsaw puzzle. About a third of the church is original stones (notice the dark ones, placed in their original spots), and new pieces were custom-made to fill in the gaps. The reconstruction has cost more than €100 million, 90 percent of which came from donors around the world. The year 2005 sees the rebuilt church's grand opening—a year before the city's 800th anniversary.

When the church reopens in 2005, guests will be welcome to come inside and to climb the dome (for the latest, see www .frauenkirche-dresden.de). Inside, you'll find the tangled, battered original cross that stood at the top of the dome until 1945. The copy capping the new church was built by an English coppersmith whose father actually dropped bombs on the church during that fateful night.

But until the grand reopening, groups are admitted on the hour only to be locked in the basement for 50 minutes to watch a German-language video. Don't bother. Instead, wander around the site and read the various signs. The nearby **Frauenkirche Visitors Center** will likely be left after the church reopens to tell the story of the bombing and rebuilding (Mon–Fri 10:00–18:00, Sat–Sun until 17:00, grayish-green building beyond yellow palace at Georg-Treu-Platz 3, tel. 0351/486-7757).

Your tour is over. Enjoy the bustle of Münzgasse, and consider taking in more museums, such as the nearby Albertinum (sculpture and modern art—see page 655).

In the Zwinger

All museums in the Zwinger palace complex have the same hours: Tue–Sun 10:00–18:00, closed Mon (tel. 0351/491-4678 or 0351/491-4622). All of these sights are covered by the €10 *Tageskarte* museum pass (buy at any sight).

▲▲▲**Old Masters Gallery (Gemäldegalerie Alte Meister)**—Dresden's best museum features works by Raphael, Titian, Rembrandt, Rubens, Vermeer, and more. It's particularly enjoyable for its "quality, not quantity" approach to showing off great art.

Locals remember this buildings as the first big public building reopened after the war, in 1956.

Entering, you'll pass a small room with portraits of the Wettin kings who patronized the arts and founded this collection. The next room shows five cityscapes of Dresden, painted during its golden age by Canaletto. These paintings of mid-18th-century Dresden—showing the Hofkirche (still under construction) and the newly completed Frauenkirche—offer a great study of the city. Next, you enter a world of Rubens and Belgian Baroque. This high-powered Catholic art is followed by humbler, quieter Protestant art of the Dutch Masters, including a fine collection of Rembrandts (don't miss his jaunty self-portrait—with Saskia on his lap and a glass of ale held aloft) and a pristine Vermeer *(Girl at a Window Reading a Letter)*. The German late Gothic/early Renaissance rooms include exquisite canvases by Cranach and Dürer. Farther on, the Venetian masters include a sumptuous *Slumbering Venus* by Giorgione (1510). He died while still working on this, so Titian stepped in to finish it. Giorgione's idealized Venus isn't asleep, but deeply restful—at peace with the plush nature.

The collection's highlight: Raphael's masterful *Sistine Madonna*. The portrait features the Madonna and Child, two early Christian martyrs (Saints Sixtus and Barbara), and wispy angel faces in the clouds. Mary is in motion, offering the savior to a needy world. But recently, the stars of this painting are the pair of whimsical angels in the foreground. These lovable tykes—of T-shirt and poster fame—are bored...just hanging out, oblivious to the exciting arrival of the Messiah just behind them. They connect the heavenly world of the painting with you and me (€6, includes Royal Armory entry, no English explanations, so consider the good €13 English guidebook, in Zwinger's Semper Gallery, tel. 0351/491-4678).

Royal Armory (Rüstkammer)—One big room packed with swords and suits of armor, the armory is especially interesting for its tiny children's armor and the jousting exhibit in the back (€3 alone, or included with €6 ticket to Old Masters Gallery, across passage from Old Masters Gallery).

Mathematics-Physics Salon (Mathematisch-Physikalischer Salon)—This fun collection features globes, lenses, and clocks from the 16th–19th centuries (€3, north end of Zwinger courtyard).

▲**Porcelain Collection (Porzellansammlung)**—Every self-respecting European king had a porcelain works, and the Wettins had the most famous: Meissen. The Saxon prince electors went beyond producing, and also collected other porcelain—from France to Japan and China. Augustus the Strong was obsessed with this stuff... he liked to say he had "porcelain sickness." Here you can enjoy some of his symptoms, under chandeliers in elegant Zwinger galleries (€5, good English descriptions, south end of Zwinger courtyard).

More Sights in the Old Town

These sights are listed in the order you'll encounter them on my self-guided walking tour (above).

Semper Opera—Three opera houses have stood in this spot: The first was destroyed by a fire in 1869, the second by firebombs in 1945. The Semper Oper continues to be a world-class venue, and tickets for the Saxon State Orchestra (the world's oldest) are hard to come by (on sale a year in advance; box office in Schinkelwache TI across the square, Mon–Fri 10:00–18:00, Sat 10:00–13:00, closed Sun, tel. 0351/491-1705, fax 0351/491-1700, www.semperoper.de).

The opulent opera house is great for concerts and performances, but not for touring. It can only be visited with a German-speaking guide and English handouts (€5, 1 hr, enter on right side, tel. 0351/491-1496).

▲▲Royal Palace (Residenzschloss)—This Renaissance palace was once the residence of the Saxon prince elector. Formerly one of the finest Renaissance buildings in Germany, it's slowly being rebuilt after the destruction of World War II. In 2005 and 2006, the grand halls and audience chambers of Augustus the Strong will be reopened. Until then, it holds a coin collection, a print collection, and the lavish Green Vault treasure chamber.

The famed **Green Vault (Grünes Gewölbe),** which finally returned to the palace in 2004, is a glittering treasury collection conceived as a Baroque synthesis of the arts by Augustus the Strong in the early 1700s. It evolved as the royal family's extravagant treasure trove of ivory, silver, and gold knickknacks. Gawk at the incredibly elaborate diorama of the Delhi Court birthday celebration of a mogul (a thinly veiled stand-in for Augustus the Strong). In 2005, half of the collection is viewable (€6, covered by €10 *Tageskarte* museum pass, Wed–Mon 10:00–18:00, closed Tue). In 2006, the entire collection should be on display in its historic rooms on the ground floor of the west wing.

▲Watchman's Tower (Hausmannsturm)—This tower is worth the 160 steps for a panoramic view of Dresden. On the way up, you'll see exhibits (in German, but with interesting photos and blueprints) about the tower's construction, destruction, and reconstruction (€2.50 for tower, if just going up for the view don't buy the €5 ticket for tower and temporary exhibit, covered by €10 *Tageskarte* museum pass, Wed–Mon 10:00–18:00, closed Tue, entrance inside Royal Palace's Georgenbau passageway next to Parade of Nobles mural—follow signs for Hausmannsturm, tel. 0351/491-4678).

Albertinum—This historic building houses the **Sculpture Collection** (Skulpturensammlung) and the **New Masters Gallery** (Gemälde-galerie Neue Meister), which features works by 19th- and 20th-century greats such as Renoir, Rodin, van Gogh, Degas, and Klimt. Don't miss Otto Dix's moving triptych, *War* (painted between the world wars), Gustav Klimt's *Buchenwald,* and a Rodin *Thinker* at the top of the main stairwell (€6, covered by €10 *Tageskarte* museum pass, Wed–Mon 10:00–18:00, closed Tue, at far end of Brühlsche Terrasse, tel. 0351/491-4714 or 0351/491-4622).

Away from the Old Town

The first sight is near the Hauptbahnhof; the other is across the Augustus Bridge from the Old Town.

Prager Strasse—This communist-built pedestrian mall, connecting the train station and the historic center, was ruins until the 1960s. Even today, "Prague Street" reflects Soviet ideals: big, blocky, functional buildings without extraneous ornamentation. As you stroll down Prager Strasse, imagine these buildings without any of the color or advertising. (Stores "advertised" with simple signs reading "Milk," "Bread," or simply "Products.") Today, the street is filled with corporate logos, shoppers with lots of choices, and a fun summertime food circus. When all the construction is finished, this will be an impressive people zone.

▲New Town (Neustadt)—A big sign across the river from the old center declares, "Dresden continues here." This seems directed at tourists who visit the city and stay exclusively in the Old Town. Don't be one of them—make it a point to explore Dresden's New Town, too.

While there are no famous sights in the New Town, it's the only part of Dresden that predates World War II. Today, it's thriving with cafés, shops, clubs, and—most important—just regular people. I've listed several hotels and restaurants worth considering in the neighborhood (see "Sleeping" and "Eating," below).

Near Dresden: Saxon Switzerland National Park

Consider a break from big-city sightseeing to spend a half day taking a *wunderbar* hike through this scenic national park.

Twenty miles southeast of Dresden (an easy 45-min S-Bahn ride away), the Elbe River cuts a scenic swath through the beech forests and steep cliffs of Saxon Switzerland (Sächsische Schweiz) National Park. You'll share the trails with serious rock climbers and equally serious Saxon grandmothers. Allow five hours (including lunch) to enjoy this day trip.

Take the S-Bahn line 1 from either the Hauptbahnhof or the Neustadt station (a €9 *Verbundraum Tageskarte*—regional day ticket—covers the whole trip, direction: Schandau, departs hourly). Get off at the Kurort Rathen stop, follow the road downhill five minutes through town to the dock, and take the ferry across the Elbe (€1.30 round-trip, buy on board, crossing takes 2 min, runs continuously). When the ferry docks on the far (north) side of the river, turn your back on the river and walk 100 yards through town, with the little creek on your right. Turn left after the Sonniges Eck

Restaurant (tasty lunch option, check out the 2002 flood photos in their front dining room) and walk up the lane. The trail begins with stairs on your left just past Hotel Amselgrundschlösschen (follow *Bastei* signs).

A 45-minute walk uphill through the woods leads you to the Bastei Bridge and stunning views of gray sandstone sentries rising several hundred feet from forest ridges. Elbe Valley sandstone was used to build Dresden's finest buildings (including the Frauenkirche and Zwinger), as well as Berlin's famous Brandenburg Gate. The multiple-arch bridge looks straight out of Oz—built in 1851 specifically for Romantic Age tourists, and scenic enough to be the subject of the first landscape photos ever taken in Germany. Take the time to explore the short 50-yard spur trails that reward you with classic views down on the Elbe 900 feet below. Watch the slow-motion paddle steamers leave V-shaped wakes as they chug upstream toward the Czech Republic, just around the next river bend. If you're not afraid of heights, explore the maze of catwalks through the scant remains of the Neue Felsenberg, a 13th-century Saxon fort once perched precariously on the bald, stony spires (€1.50, entrance 50 yards before Bastei Bridge).

Just a five-minute uphill hike beyond the bridge is the Berg Hotel Panorama Bastei, with a fine restaurant, a quick snack bar, and memorable views. Return back down to the Elbe ferry via the same trail.

NIGHTLIFE

To really connect with Dresden as it unfolds, you need to go to the **Innere Neustadt** ("Inner New Town," a 10-min walk from Neustadt station). This area was not bombed in World War II, and after 1989, it sprouted the first entrepreneurial cafés and bistros. While eateries are open long hours, the action picks up after 22:00. The clientele is young, hip, pierced, and tattooed.

Rather than seek out particular places in this continuously evolving scene, I'd just get to the epicenter (corner of Görlitzer Strasse and Louisenstrasse) and wander. Pop through the Kunsthofpassage, a Hundertwasser-type apartment block with some fun spots (Görlitzer Strasse 23). At Bohmischestrasse 34 (a half block off Lutherplatz), a Russian-flavored *Kneipe* has an imported beach, giving it a Moscow/Maui ambience. The Carte Blanche Transvestite Bar is a hoot for some (€22, most nights from 20:00, Priessnitzstrasse 10, tel. 0351/204-720).

For more sedate entertainment, stroll along the New Town's riverbank after dark for fine floodlit views of the Old Town.

SLEEPING

Dresden is packed with big, conference-style hotels. Characteristic, family-run places are harder to come by. (The communists weren't fans of quaint.) The TI has a room-booking service (€3/person). Peak season for big business-class hotels is May, June, September, and October. Peak season for hostels is July and August (especially weekends).

In the Old Town

$$$ **Hilton Dresden** has 340 luxurious rooms (some with views of the Frauenkirche) in the heart of the Old Town, one block from the river. Complete with porters, fitness club, pool, and several restaurants, it's everything you would expect from a four-star chain hotel (Sb-€155–190, Db-€170–205, breakfast-€19, An der Frauenkirche 5, tel. 0351/864-2777, fax. 0351/864-2889, www.hilton.de, info .dresden@hilton.com).

$$ **Hotel Kipping,** with 20 tidy rooms a hundred yards behind the Hauptbahnhof, is professionally run by the friendly and proper Kipping brothers (Rainer and Peter). The building was one of few in this area to survive the firebombing—in fact, people took shelter here during the attack (Sb-€70–95, Db-€85–115, 1-person suite-€115–130, 2-person suite-€130–145, child's bed-€20; higher prices are for weekends, May–June, and Sept–Oct; elevator, free parking, Winckelmannstrasse 6, tram #8 whisks you to the center, tel. 0351/478-500, fax 0351/478-5090, www.hotel-kipping.de, reception @hotel-kipping.de). Their restaurant serves international cuisine and Saxon specialties (entrées €9–12, Mon–Sat 18:00–22:30, closed Sun).

$$ **Apartments an der Frauenkirche** rents 24 new units just above all the restaurant action on Münzgasse. Designed for longer stays, but also welcoming one-nighters, these modern, comfortable apartments come with kitchens and the lived-in works (Db-€80–95, extra bed-€15, breakfast not included, cheaper for longer stays and off-season, Münzgasse 6, tel. 0351/438-1111, www.dresden-tourismus.de, info@dresden-tourismus.de).

$ **Hotels Bastei, Königstein, and Lilienstein** are cookie-cutter members of the Ibis chain, goose-stepping single-file up Prager Strasse (listed in order from the station to the center). Each is practically identical, with 360 rooms (newly renovated Bastei is a couple euros more in high season). Though utterly lacking in charm, they are an excellent value in a convenient location between the Hauptbahnhof and the Old Town (Sb-€55–65, Db-€65–74, apartment-€80 for a family of 3 or 4, breakfast-€9/person, air-con, elevator, Internet access, parking-€6.50/day, can't miss them on Prager Strasse; Bastei reservation tel. 0351/4856-6661, fax 0351/4856-5555, hotel-bastei@ibis-dresden.de; Königstein reservation tel. 0351/4856-6662, fax 0351/4856-6666,

Sleep Code

(€1 = about $1.20, country code: 49, area code: 0351)
S = Single, **D** = Double/Twin, **T** = Triple, **Q** = Quad, **b** = bathroom, **s** = shower only. All of these places speak English and accept credit cards. Unless otherwise noted, breakfast is included.

To help you sort easily through these listings, I've divided the rooms into three categories, based on the price for a standard double room with bath:

$$$ **Higher Priced**—Most rooms €120 or more.
$$ **Moderately Priced**—Most rooms between €80–120.
$ **Lower Priced**—Most rooms €80 or less.

hotel-koenigstein@ibis-dresden.de; Lilienstein reservation tel. 0351/4856-6663, fax 0351/4856-7777, hotel-lilienstein@ibis -dresden.de; Web site for all three: www.ibis-hotel.de). Skip their overpriced hotel restaurants. Instead, eat at the nearby Hotel Kipping (see above) or in the Old Town (see "Eating," page 660).

In the New Town
The first two hotels are fancy splurges in a tidy residential neighborhood a three-minute walk from the Neustadt train station. The rest are cheap and funky, buried in the trendy, newly happening café and club zone called the Innere Neustadt ("Inner New Town," about a 10-min walk from Neustadt station—see page 646).

$$$ Hotel Bayerischer Hof Dresden, a hundred yards toward the river from the Neustadt train station, offers 50 rooms and elegant and inviting public spaces in a grand old building (Sb-€85–95, Db-€110–130, pricier suites, non-smoking rooms, elevator, free parking, Antonstrasse 33–35, yellow building across from station, tel. 0351/829-370, fax 0351/801-4860, www.bayerischer-hof -dresden.de, info@bayerischer-hof-dresden.de).

$$ Hotel Martha Hospiz, with 50 rooms near the recommended restaurants on Königstrasse, is bright and cheery. The two old buildings that make up the hotel have been smartly renovated and connect in back with a glassed-in winter garden and an outdoor breakfast terrace in a charming garden. It's a 10-minute walk to the historical center, and a five-minute walk to the Neustadt station (S-€54, Sb-€72–84, Db-€102–118, extra bed-€26, elevator; leaving Neustadt station, turn right on Hainstrasse, left on Theresenstrasse, and then right on Nieritzstrasse to #11; tel. 0351/81760, fax 0351/8176-222, www.vch.de/marthahospiz.dresden, marthahospiz .dresden@vch.de).

$$ AHA (Apart Hotel Akzent), on a big, noisy street, has a homey and welcoming ambience. The 29 simple but neat apartments all come with kitchens; all except the top floor have balconies. It's a bit farther from the center—10 minutes by foot east of Albertplatz, a 20-minute walk or a quick ride on tram #11 from the center—but its friendliness, coziness, and good value make it a winner (Sb-€60–65, Db-€70–90, small Db about €10 cheaper, twins about €10 more, request back side to avoid street noise, elevator, Bautzner Strasse 53, tel. 0351/800-850, fax 0351/8008-5114, www .aha-hotel-dresden.de, kontakt@aha-hotel-dresden.de).

$ Guest House Mezcalero, decorated Mexican from top to bottom, is a 22-room place a 10-minute walk from the Neustadt station at the edge of the lively Innere Neustadt zone. It feels classy and comfy, with an adobe ambience (S-€30, Sb-€45, D-€50, Db-€60, dorm bed-€17, breakfast extra, from either station catch tram #7 to Bischofsweg, Königsbrücker Strasse 64, tel. 0351/810-770, fax 0351/810-7711, www.mezcalero.de, info@mezcalero.de).

$ Hostel "Louise 20" rents 83 beds in the heart of the Innere Neustadt. Though located in the wild-and-edgy nightlife district, it feels safe, solid, clean, and comfy. The newly furnished rooms, guests' kitchen, cozy common room, and friendly staff make it the best place in town for cheap beds (S-€29, D-€42, small dorm-€17/bed, 20-bed dorm-€12.50/bed, €2.50 less if you have sheets, breakfast extra, no lockers, generally booked up on summer weekends, Louisenstrasse 20, tel. 0351/8894-894, www.louise20.de, info@louise20.de).

$ Hostel Mondpalast Dresden is young and hip, in the heart of the Innere Neustadt above a cool bar. It's good for backpackers with little money and an appetite for late-night fun (D-€37, Db-€50, dorm bed-€16, lockers, kitchen, lots of facilities, tram #7 from Hauptbahnhof or #11 from Neustadt station, near Kamenzer Strasse at Louisenstrasse 77, tel. 0351/563-4050, www.mondpalast.de, info @mondpalast.de).

EATING

Dresden's ancient beer halls were destroyed in the firebombing and not replaced by the communists. As the city comes back to life, nearly every restaurant seems bright, shiny, and modern. While Old Town restaurants are touristy, the prices are reasonable, and it's easy to eat for €10–15 just about anywhere. For cheaper prices and authentic local character, leave the famous center, cross the river, and wander through the New Town.

The special local dessert is *Dresdner Eierschecke,* an eggy cheesecake with vanilla pudding, raisins, and almond shavings, sold all over town.

In the Old Town

Münzgasse, the busy and touristy street that connects the Brühlsche Terrasse promenade and the Frauenkirche, is the liveliest street in the Old Town, with a fun selection of eateries. Choose from tapas, Aussie, goulash, crêpes, and even antiques (Kunst Café Antik scatters its tables among a royal estate sale of fancy furniture and objets d'art). Service is a necessary evil, the clientele is international, and the action spills out onto the cobbled pedestrian lane on balmy evenings. Towering high above you is the newly rebuilt Frauenkirche.

Altmarkt Keller, a few blocks farther from the river on Altmarkt square, is a festive beer cellar that serves nicely presented Saxon and Bohemian food and has good Czech beer on tap. The lively crowd, cheesy music (live Fri–Sat from 20:00), and jolly murals add to the fun. While the on-square seating is fine, the vast-but-stout, air-conditioned cellar offers your best memories. The giant mural inside the entryway—representing the friendship between Dresden and Prague—reads, "The sunshine of life is drinking and being happy" (entrées €8–10, daily 11:00–24:00, Altmarkt 4, to right of McDonald's, tel. 0351/481-8131).

Grand Café Restaurant Cosel Palais serves Saxon and French cuisine in the shadow of the newly rebuilt Frauenkirche. This is a Baroque, chandeliered dining experience with fine courtyard seating—great for an elegant meal or tea and pastries (€10–15 meals, daily specials, open daily 10:00–24:00, An der Frauenkirche 12, tel. 0351/496-2444).

Erlebnisgastronomie (**"Experience Gastronomy"**): All the rage among Dresdeners (and German tourists in Dresden) is *Erlebnisgastronomie.* Elaborately decorated theme restaurants have sprouted next to the biggest-name sights around town, with over-the-top, theme-park decor and historically costumed waitstaff. These can offer a fun change of pace, and aren't the bad value you might suspect. The best is **Sophienkeller.** It does its best to take you to the 18th century and the world of Augustus the Strong. The king himself, along with his countess, musicians, and magicians, stroll and entertain, while court maidens serve traditional Saxon food from "ye olde" menu. Read their colorful brochure to better understand the place. It's big (400 seats), and even has a rotating carousel table with suspended swing-chairs that you sit in while you eat (€10–15 plates, daily 11:00–24:00, under the 5-star Taschenberg Palace Hotel, Taschenberg 3, tel. 0351/497-260, www.sophienkeller -dresden.de).

With a River View: **Radeberger Spezialausschank** is dramatically situated on the Brühlsche Terrasse promenade with a rampart-hanging view terrace and three levels taking you down to river level. For river views from the "Balcony of Europe," this is your spot. The inviting-yet-simple menu includes daily Saxon specials and cheap wurst and kraut. The cool, river-level bar comes with big copper brewery vats and good beer (daily 10:00–24:00, reservations smart for view terrace, Terrassenufer 1, tel. 0351/484-8660).

In the New Town

Venture to these eateries—across Augustus Bridge from the Old Town—for lower prices and a more local scene. I've listed them from nearest to farthest from the Old Town.

Just across Augustus Bridge

Augustus Garten is a lazy, crude-yet-inviting beer garden with super-cheap, self-service food (pork knuckle, kraut, cheap beer, and lots of mustard). You'll eat among big bellies—and no tourists—with a fun city-skyline-over-the-river view (daily 11:00–24:00, good weather only, Wiesentorstrasse 2, tel. 0351/404-5854). Walk across the bridge from the Old Town, and it's on your immediate right.

On Königstrasse

For trendy elegance without tourists, have dinner on Königstrasse. After crossing the Augustus Bridge, hike five minutes up the obviously communist-built main drag of the New Town, then turn left to find this charming Baroque street. As this is a fast-changing area, you might survey the other options on and near Königstrasse before settling down.

Wenzel Prager Bierstuben serves country Bohemian cuisine in a woodsy bar that spills out into an airy, glassed-in gallery—made doubly big by its vast mirror (entrées €8–10, daily 11:00–24:00, Königstrasse 1, tel. 0315/804-2010).

Ristorante Ausonia, with Italian cuisine, comes with fine outdoor seating. Luigi Murolo and his family will give you a break from mustard and kraut (€7–9 pizza or pasta, daily 11:30–23:30, Königstrasse 9, tel. 0351/803-3123). While you're here, the breezy beer garden in the churchyard across the street is worth a look.

TRANSPORTATION CONNECTIONS

From Dresden Hauptbahnhof by train to: Berlin (every 2 hrs, 2.25 hrs), **Prague** (7/day, 3 hrs), **Munich** (every 2 hrs, 7 hrs, transfer in Leipzig, Nürnberg, or Fulda), **Frankfurt** (every 2 hrs, 4.5 hrs), **Nürnberg** (every 2 hrs, 4.5 hrs), **Vienna** (1/day, 7 hrs), Budapest (1/day, 9 hrs). There are overnight trains from Dresden to Zürich, the Rhineland, and Munich. Train info: tel. 11861 (€0.46/min).

UNDERSTANDING YUGOSLAVIA

Americans struggle to understand the complicated breakup of Yugoslavia, which was a largely artificial union of the South Slavic peoples. During the Yugoslav era, it was no less confusing—as the old joke went, Yugoslavia had seven distinct peoples in six republics, with five languages, three religions (Orthodox, Catholic, and Muslim), and two alphabets (Roman and Cyrillic), but only one Yugoslav—Tito.

Here's an oversimplified, boiled-down-to-the-basics history to get you started as you begin your own exploration of Slovenia and Croatia, two of the six countries that were briefly called Yugoslavia.

Who's Who

For starters, it helps to have a handle on the Balkans—the southeastern European peninsula between the Adriatic and the Black Sea, stretching from Hungary to Greece. The Balkan Peninsula has always been a crossroads of cultures. The Illyrians, Greeks, and Romans had settlements here before the Slavs moved into the region from the north around the 7th century. During the next millennium and a half, the western part of the peninsula—which would become Yugoslavia—became divided by a series of cultural, ethnic, and religious fault lines that separate the Christian West, the Orthodox East, and the Muslim south.

The most important Balkan influences were **Western Christianity** (Roman Catholicism, primarily brought to the region by Charlemagne, and later reinforced by the Austrian Hapsburgs), **Eastern Orthodox Christianity** (from the Byzantine Empire), and **Islam** (from the invading Ottoman Turks).

Two major historical factors made the Balkans what they are today: The first was the **split of the Roman Empire** in the 4th century A.D., dividing the Balkans down the middle into west (Catholic/Roman) and east (Orthodox/Byzantine)—roughly along today's Bosnian-Serbian border. The second was the **invasion of the**

Yugoslav Succession

Islamic Ottoman Turks in the 14th century. The Turkish victory at the Battle of Kosovo (1389) began five centuries of Islamic influence in Bosnia-Herzegovina and Serbia (less in other parts of the region), dividing the Balkans into north (Christian) and south (Islam). These two key events essentially divided the Balkans into quarters.

Over the years, several ethnic identities (defined by religion) emerged: the Christian **Croats** and **Slovenes** (mostly west of the Dinaric Mountains, along the Adriatic coast and north, towards Austria); the Orthodox **Serbs** (mostly east of the Dinaric range); and the Muslim **Bosniaks** (who converted to Islam under the Turks, mostly living in the Dinaric Mountains). To complicate matters, the region is also home to several non-Slavic groups—such as **Hungarians** (in the northern province of Vojvodina) and **Albanians,** concentrated in the southern province of Kosovo (descended from the Illyrians, who lived here long before the Greeks and Romans).

Of course, these geographic divisions are extremely general. The groups overlapped a lot—which is exactly why the breakup of Yugoslavia was so contentious. One of the biggest causes of this ethnic mixing came in the 16th century. The Ottoman Turks were threatening to overrun Europe, and the Austrian Hapsburgs wanted a buffer zone—a "human shield." The Hapsburgs encouraged Serbs who were fleeing from Turkish invasions to settle along the frontier (along today's Croatian-Bosnian border—known as *Vojna Krajina*, or "Military Frontier"). The Serbs stayed after the Turks had left, establishing homes in predominantly Croat communities.

After the Turkish threat subsided in the late 17th century, some of the Balkans (basically today's Slovenia and Croatia) became part of the Austrian Hapsburg Empire. The Turks stayed longer in the south and east (today's Bosnia-Herzegovina and Serbia)—making the cultures in these regions even more different. Serbia finally gained its independence from the Ottomans in the mid-19th century, but it wasn't too long before World War I started...after a disgruntled Serbian nationalist killed the Austrian archduke.

South Slavs Unite

When the Austro-Hungarian Empire fell at the end of World War I, the European map was redrawn for the 20th century. After centuries of being governed by foreign powers, the South Slavs began to see their shared history as more important than their minor differences. A tiny country of two million Slovenes or four million Croats couldn't have survived. Rather than be absorbed by a non-Slavic power, the South Slavs decided that there was safety in numbers, and banded together as a single state—first called the "Kingdom of the Serbs, Croats, and Slovenes" (1918), later known as Yugoslavia (literally, "Union of the South Slavs"—*yugo* means "south"). "Yugoslav unity" was in the air, but this new union was artificial and ultimately bound to fail (not unlike the partnership between the Czechs and Slovaks, formed at the same time and for much the same reasons).

From the very beginning, the Serbs, Croats, and Slovenes struggled for power within the new union. Serbia already had a very strong king, Alexander Karađorđević, who immediately made attempts to give his nation a leading role in the federation. A nationalistic Croatian politician named Stjepan Radić, pushing for a more equitable division of powers, was shot by a Serb during a parliament session in 1928. Karađorđević abolished the parliament and became dictator. Six years later, infuriated Croatian separatists killed him.

Many Croat nationalists sided with the Nazis in World War II in the hopes that it would be their ticket to independence from Serbia. The Nazi puppet government in Croatia (called Ustaše) conducted an extermination campaign, murdering many Serbs (along with Jews and Gypsies) living in Croatia—the first use of ethnic cleansing in Yugoslavia. To this day, Serbs and Croats squabble over whether the number of Serb deaths at the hands of the Ustaše was in the tens of thousands or the hundreds of thousands.

At the end of World War II, the rest of Eastern Europe was "liberated" by the Soviets—but the Yugoslavs regained their independence on their own, as their communist partisan army forced out the Nazis. After the short but rocky Yugoslav union between the World Wars, it seemed that no one could hold the southern Slavs together in a single nation. But there was one man who could, and did: Tito.

Tito

Communist Party president and war hero Josip Broz—who dubbed himself with the simple nickname Tito—emerged as a political leader after World War II. With a Slovene mother, a Croatian father, a Serbian wife, and a home in Belgrade, Tito was a true Yugoslav. For the next three decades, he managed to keep Yugoslavia intact—essentially by the force of his own personality.

Tito's new incarnation of Yugoslavia aimed for a more equitable division of powers. It was made up of six republics, each with its own parliament and president: **Croatia** (mostly Catholic Croats), **Slovenia** (mostly Catholic Slovenes), **Serbia** (mostly Orthodox Serbs, with some Hungarians in the northern province of Vojvodina and Albanians in the southern province of Kosovo), **Bosnia-Herzegovina** (the most diverse—Muslims, Serbs, and Croats), **Macedonia** (with about 25 percent Albanians and 75 percent Macedonians—who are claimed variously by Bulgarians and Serbs), and **Montenegro** (mostly Serb-like Montenegrins). Each republic managed its own affairs...but always under the watchful eye of president-for-life Tito, who said that the borders between the republics should be like "white lines in a marble column."

Tito walked the walk. He was unquestionably a political genius. Every Yugoslav had to serve in the National Army, and Tito made sure that each unit was a microcosm of the complete Yugoslavia—with equal representation from each ethnic group. (Allowing an all-Slovene unit, stationed in Slovenia, would be begging for trouble.) There was also a dark side to Tito, who resorted to violent, Stalinist measures to assert his power—especially early in his reign. He staged brutal, Soviet-style "show trials" to intimidate potential dissidents, and imprisoned church leaders, such as Alojzije Stepinac (see page 518). Nationalism was strongly discouraged, and this tight control—though sometimes oppressive—kept the country from unraveling. In retrospect, most former Yugoslavs forgive Tito for governing with an iron fist, believing that this was necessary for keeping the country strong and united. Today, most of them consider Tito more of a hero than a villain, and usually speak of him with reverence.

Tito's Yugoslavia was communist, but it wasn't Soviet communism; you'll find no statues of Lenin or Stalin here. Despite strong pressure from Moscow, Tito refused to ally himself with the Soviets—and therefore received good will (and $2 billion) from the United States. Tito's vision was for a "third way," where Yugoslavia could work with both East and West, without being dominated by either. Yugoslavia was the most free of the communist states: While large industry was nationalized, Tito's system allowed for small businesses. This experience with market economy benefited Yugoslavs when Eastern Europe's communist regimes eventually fell. And even during the communist era, Yugoslavia remained a popular tourist destination, keeping its standards more in line with the West than the Soviet states.

Things Fall Apart

With Tito's death in 1980, Yugoslavia's six constituent republics gained more autonomy, with a rotating presidency. But before long, the delicate union Tito had held together began to unravel. In the late 1980s, Serbian President Slobodan Milošević took advantage of ethnic-motivated conflicts in the province of Kosovo to grab more centralized power. Other republics (especially Slovenia and Croatia) feared that he would gut their nation to create a "Greater Serbia," instead of a friendly coalition of diverse Yugoslav republics. Over the next decade, Yugoslavia broke apart, with much bloodshed.

The Slovene Secession: Slovenia was the first Yugoslav republic to hold free elections, in the spring of 1990. The voters wanted their own nation. After months of stockpiling weapons, Slovenia closed its borders and declared independence from Yugoslavia on June 25, 1991. Along with being the most ethnically homogeneous of the Yugoslav nations, Slovenia was also the most Western-oriented, most prosperous, most geographically isolated, and smallest. Belgrade briefly fought the Slovenes, but after 10 days and only 66 deaths, Yugoslavia decided to let Slovenia have its independence.

The Croatian Conflict: As Slovenia geared up for independence, Croatia decided it would follow suit. But in the months leading up to Croatia's secession, the 600,000 Serbs living in Croatia—especially those in the city of Knin—saw the writing on the wall and began to rise up. Inspired by Slobodan Milošević's rhetoric, Croatian Serbs began the so-called "tree trunk revolution"—blocking important tourist roads with logs and other barriers. Tensions escalated, and the first shots of the conflict were fired on Easter Sunday of 1991 at Plitvice Lakes National Park, between Croatian policemen and Serb irregulars from Knin.

By the time Croatia declared its independence (on the same day as Slovenia), it was already embroiled in the beginnings of a bloody war. The new nation of Croatia did not address the status of its more than half-million Serb residents. So Croatian Serbs, nervous about their rights and backed by the Serbian-dominated Yugoslav Army, in turn declared independence from Croatia. The Yugoslav National Army swept in, supposedly to keep the peace between Serbs and Croats—but it soon became obvious that they were there to support the Serbs. The ill-prepared Croatian resistance, made up mostly of policemen and a few soldiers who defected from the Yugoslav National Army, were quickly overwhelmed. The Serbs gained control over a large swathe of inland Croatia, mostly around the Bosnian border (including Plitvice) and in Croatia's inland panhandle (the region of Slavonia). They called this territory—about a quarter of Croatia—the **Republic of Serbian Krajina** (*krajina* means "border"). This new "country" (hardly recognized by any other nations) minted its own money and had its own army, much to the consternation of Croatia—which was now worried about the safety of Croats living in Krajina.

As the Serbs advanced, hundreds of thousands of Croats fled to the coast and lived as refugees in resort hotels. (Many of these hotels—such as the prominent Marjan in Split—are still being refurbished.) The Serbs began a campaign of **ethnic cleansing,** systematically removing Croatians from their territory—often by murdering them. The bloodiest siege was at the town of **Vukovar,** which the Yugoslav army surrounded and shelled relentlessly for three months. At the end of the siege, thousands of Croat soldiers and civilians mysteriously disappeared. Many of these people were later discovered in mass graves; hundreds are still missing, and bodies are still continually being found. In a surprise move, Serbs also attacked the tourist capital of **Dubrovnik** (see page 468). By early 1992, both Croatia and the Republic of Serbian Krajina had established their borders, and a tense ceasefire fell over the region.

The standoff lasted until 1995, when the now well-equipped Croatian Army retook the Serbian-occupied areas in a series of two offensives—**"Lightning"** *(Bljesak),* in the northern part of the country (Slavonia), and **"Storm"** *(Oluja),* further south. Some Croats retaliated for earlier ethnic cleansing by doing much of the same to Serbs—torturing them, killing them, and dynamiting their homes. Croatia quickly established the borders that exist today, and the Erdut Agreement brought peace to the region—but most of the 600,000 Serbs who once lived in Croatia/Krajina were forced into Serbia or were killed. Today, only a few thousand Serbs remain in Croatia. While Serbs have long since been legally invited back to their ancestral Croatian homes, few have returned—afraid of the "welcome" they might receive from the Croat neighbors who killed their relatives or blew up their houses just a few years ago.

The War in Bosnia-Herzegovina: The situation was even more complicated in Bosnia-Herzegovina (which I'll refer to as

"Bosnia" for simplicity). Bosnia declared its independence from Yugoslavia four months after Croatia and Slovenia did. But Bosnia was always at the crossroads of Balkan culture, and therefore even more diverse than Croatia—predominantly Muslim Bosniaks (mostly in the cities), but also with large Serb and Croat populations (often farmers), as well as Albanian Kosovars. In the spring of 1992, Serbs within Bosnia (with the support of Serbia) began a campaign of ethnic cleansing against the Bosniaks and Croats. Before long, the Croats did the same against the Serbs. The three groups fought a brutal war for the next three years, until the 1995 Dayton Peace Accords carefully divided Bosnia among the different ethnicities. Today, Bosnia continues to work on its tenuous peace, rebuild its devastated country, and bring its infrastructure up to its neighbors' standards.

Kosovo: The ongoing Yugoslav crisis finally reached its peak in the Serbian province of Kosovo. After years of poor treatment by the Serbs, Kosovars rebelled in 1998. The Yugoslav National Army moved in, and in March 1999, they began a campaign of ethnic cleansing. Thousands of Kosovars were murdered, and hundreds of thousands fled into Albania and Macedonia. NATO planes, under the command of U.S. General (and Supreme Allied Commander) Wesley Clark, bombed Serb positions for two months, forcing the Serb army to leave Kosovo in the summer of 1999.

The Fall of Milošević: After years of bloody conflicts, Serbian public opinion had clearly swung against their president. The transition began gradually in early 2000, spearheaded by Otpor and other nonviolent, grassroots, student-based opposition movements. These organizations used clever PR strategies to gain support and convince Serbians that real change was possible. As anti-Milošević sentiments gained momentum, opposing political parties banded together and got behind one candidate, Vojislav Koštunica. Public support for Koštunica mounted, and when the arrogant Milošević called an early election in September 2000, the Serbian strongman was soundly defeated. Though Milošević tried to claim that the election results were invalid, determined Serbs streamed into their capital, marched on their parliament, and—like the Czechoslovaks a decade before—peacefully took back their nation.

Today's "Yugoslavia": The nation of "Yugoslavia" no longer exists, having been officially renamed "Serbia and Montenegro"—after the only two republics that remain in the union of South Slavs. Though the Montenegrins wanted independence, Serbia made concessions to keep the nations loosely united. While they share an army, each country has its own government and currency (Montenegro officially uses the euro, even though it's not in the EU).

Finding Their Way:
The Former Yugoslav Republics

Today, Slovenia and Croatia are as stable as Western Europe, Bosnia-Herzegovina is slowly putting itself back together, and an ailing Slobodan Milošević is on trial for war crimes in The Hague.

But these South Slav neighbors—once countrymen—still don't get along. Croatians still smolder when they talk about the Serbs. In Dubrovnik, travel agencies reluctantly admit that a day trip to Montenegro is the most popular excursion, but are quick to mention that they personally have no interest in visiting this Serb stronghold. Silly border disputes belie lingering grudges. For example, in an ongoing feud, Croatia insists Slovenia should not be allowed to operate its only port, Koper. According to a technicality of international law, Slovenia's tiny, 29-mile-long coastline shouldn't have a port because it's between peninsulas belonging to other nations (Italy and Croatia)—but until now, everyone looked the other way. Of course, shutting down Koper would conveniently force more business to nearby Croatian ports.

It's important to remember that there were no "good guys" and no "bad guys" in these wars—just a lot of ugliness on all sides. If there were any victims, they were the Muslim Bosniaks and the Kosovars—but even they were not blameless. When considering specifically the war between the Croats and the Serbs, it's tempting for Americans to take Croatia's "side"—because we saw them in the role of victims first; because they're Catholic, so they feel more "like us" than the Orthodox Serbs; and because we admire their striving for an independent nation. But in the streets and the trenches, it was never that clear-cut. When Croatians retook the Serb-occupied areas in 1995, they were every bit as brutal as the Serbs had been a few years before. Both sides resorted to ethnic cleansing, both sides had victims, and both sides had victimizers.

Perhaps the only "easy" villains in this conflict were Serbian President Slobodan Milošević and Croatian President Franjo Tuđman. As Milošević's trial in The Hague drags on (and on... and on...), information continually emerges that makes these two leaders out to be even more ruthless than once thought. It's increasingly clear that Tudjman and Milošević secretly orchestrated the whole brutal war in close association with each other, using their citizens as pawns in a giant war game. (It seems their ultimate plan was to partition Bosnia between their newly independent countries, much as Hitler and Stalin secretly plotted to divide Poland.)

It's easy for us to simply blame these conflicts on some deep-seated, inevitable cultural hatred among the Yugoslav ethnic groups. This is an oversimplification, and ignores the fact that Serbs, Croats, Bosniaks, and Kosovars coexisted more or less peacefully and happily during the Tito era. While some long-standing tensions and misunderstandings did exist, it wasn't until Milošević and Tuđman expertly colluded to manipulate them that the country fell into war. By vigorously fanning the embers of ethnic grudges, and carefully controlling media coverage of the escalating violence, these two leaders turned a healthy political debate into a holocaust.

Tension still exists throughout the former Yugoslavia—especially areas that were most war-torn. When Serbs or Croats encounter other Yugoslavs in their travels, they immediately evaluate each other's accent to determine: Are they one of us, or one of them?

But, with time, these hard feelings are fading. The younger generations don't look back—teenaged Slovenes no longer learn Serbo-Croatian, can't imagine not living in an independent little country, and get bored (and a little irritated) when their old-fashioned parents wax nostalgic about the days of a united Yugoslavia. While Croatians are (understandably) relieved to have the Yugoslav period—and the bloody war—behind them, many other former Yugoslavs recall better days. A middle-aged Slovene friend of mine thinks fondly of his months of voluntary service in the Yugoslav National Army, when his unit was made up of Slovenes, Croats, Serbs, Bosniaks, Macedonians, and Montenegrins—all of them countrymen, and all good friends. To these young Yugoslavs, nationalism didn't matter. He still often visits with his army buddy from Dubrovnik—600 miles away, not long ago part of the same nation—and wishes there had been a way to keep it all together. But he says, optimistically, "I look forward to the day when the other former Yugoslav republics also join the European Union. Then, in a way, we will all be united once again."

APPENDIX

Let's Talk Telephones

To make international calls, you need to break the codes: the international access codes and country codes (see below). For specifics on making local, long-distance, and international calls, please see the "European Calling Chart" in this appendix. You'll find more information on telephones in the introduction on page 31.

Country Codes

After you've dialed the international access code (011 if you're calling from the United States or Canada; 00 if you're calling from Europe), dial the code of the country you're calling.

Austria—43	Italy—39
Belgium—32	Morocco—212
Britain—44	Netherlands—31
Canada—1	Norway—47
Croatia—385	Poland—48
Czech Rep.—420	Portugal—351
Denmark—45	Slovakia—421
Estonia—372	Slovenia—386
Finland—358	Spain—34
France—33	Sweden—46
Germany—49	Switzerland—41
Gibraltar—350	Turkey—90
Greece—30	U.S.A.—1
Ireland—353	

European Calling Chart

Just smile and dial, using this key:
AC = Area Code, LN = Local Number.

European Country	Calling long distance within …	Calling from the U.S.A./ Canada to …	Calling from a European country to …
Austria	AC + LN	011 + 43 + AC (without the initial zero) + LN	00 + 43 + AC (without the initial zero) + LN
Belgium	LN	011 + 32 + LN (without initial zero)	00 + 32 + LN (without initial zero)
Britain	AC + LN	011 + 44 + AC (without initial zero) + LN	00 + 44 + AC (without initial zero) + LN
Croatia	AC + LN	011 + 385 + AC (without initial zero) + LN	00 + 385 + AC (without initial zero) + LN
Czech Republic	LN	011 + 420 + LN	00 + 420 + LN
Denmark	LN	011 + 45 + LN	00 + 45 + LN
Finland	AC + LN	011 + 358 + AC (without initial zero) + LN	00 + 358 + AC (without initial zero) + LN
France	LN	011 + 33 + LN (without initial zero)	00 + 33 + LN (without initial zero)
Germany	AC + LN	011 + 49 + AC (without initial zero) + LN	00 + 49 + AC (without initial zero) + LN
Greece	LN	011 + 30 + LN	00 + 30 + LN
Hungary	06 + AC + LN	011 + 36 + AC + LN	00 + 36 + AC + LN
Ireland	AC + LN	011 + 353 + AC (without initial zero) + LN	00 + 353 + AC (without initial zero) + LN
Italy	LN	011 + 39 + LN	00 + 39 + LN

European Country	Calling long distance within...	Calling from the U.S.A./ Canada to...	Calling from a European country to...
Netherlands	AC + LN	011 + 31 + AC (without initial zero) + LN	00 + 31 + AC (without initial zero) + LN
Norway	LN	011 + 47 + LN	00 + 47 + LN
Poland	AC + LN	011 + 48 + AC (without initial zero) + LN	00 + 48 + AC (without initial zero) + LN
Portugal	LN	011 + 351 + LN	00 + 351 + LN
Slovakia	AC + LN	011 + 421 + AC (without initial zero) + LN	00 + 421 + AC (without initial zero) + LN
Slovenia	AC + LN	011 + 386 + AC (without initial zero) + LN	00 + 386 + AC (without initial zero) + LN
Spain	LN	011 + 34 + LN	00 + 34 + LN
Sweden	AC + LN	011 + 46 + AC (without initial zero) + LN	00 + 46 + AC (without initial zero) + LN
Switzerland	LN	011 + 41 + LN (without initial zero)	00 + 41 + LN (without initial zero)
Turkey	AC (if no initial zero is included, add one) + LN	011 + 90 + AC (without initial zero) + LN	00 + 90 + AC (without initial zero) + LN

- The instructions above apply whether you're calling a fixed phone or mobile phone.

- The international access codes (the first numbers you dial when making an international call) are 011 if you're calling from the U.S.A./Canada, or 00 if you're calling from anywhere in Europe.

- To call the U.S.A. or Canada from Europe, dial 00, then 1 (the country code for the U.S.A. and Canada), then the area code and number. In short, 00 + 1 + AC + LN = Hi, Mom!

U.S. Embassies

Austria: Boltzmanngasse 16, Vienna, tel. 01/313-390, www.usembassy.at
Croatia: Ulica Thomasa Jeffersona 2, Zagreb, tel. 01/661-2200, consular services tel. 01/661-2300, www.usembassy.hr
Czech Republic: Tržiště 15, Prague, tel. 257-530-663, www.usembassy.cz
Germany: Clayallee 170, Berlin, tel. 030/832-9233, www.usembassy.de
Hungary: Szabadság tér 12, Budapest, tel. 1/475-4400, after hours tel. 1/475-4703 or 1/475-4924, www.usembassy.hu
Poland: Aleja Ujazdowskie 29/31, Warsaw, tel. 022/504-2000, www.usinfo.pl; also a U.S. Consulate in Kraków at ulica Stolarska 9, tel. 012/424-5100, fax 012/424-5103
Slovakia: Bratislava, tel. 02/5443-3338, www.usis.sk
Slovenia: Prešernova 31, Ljubljana, tel. 01/200-5500, fax 01/200-5555, www.usembassy.si

Eastern European Festivals and Holidays in 2005

Jan 1	New Year's Day, all countries
Jan 6	Epiphany, Poland and Croatia
Feb 8	National Day of Culture, Slovenia (celebrates Slovenian culture and national poet France Prešeren)
March 15	National Day, Hungary (celebrates 1848 Revolution)
March 18–April 3	Budapest Spring Festival, Budapest, Hungary (www.festivalcity.hu)
March 19–20	Ski Flying World Championships, Planica, Slovenia (www.fis-ski.com)
March 27	Easter Sunday, all countries
March 28	Easter Monday, all countries
April 27	National Resistance Day, Slovenia
May 1	Labor Day, all countries
May 3	Constitution Day, Poland (celebrates Europe's first constitution)
May 8	Liberation Day, Czech Republic
May 12–June 4	"Prague Spring" Music Festival, Prague, Czech Republic (www.festival.cz)
May 16	Whitmonday, Hungary
May 26	Corpus Christi, Poland and Croatia
1 week in May	Juvenalia, Kraków, Poland (student festival, costumes, and parties)
late May	Dance Week Festival, Zagreb, Croatia (www.danceweekfestival.com)

2005

JANUARY

S	M	T	W	T	F	S
						1
2	3	4	5	6	7	8
9	10	11	12	13	14	15
16	17	18	19	20	21	22
23/30	24/31	25	26	27	28	29

FEBRUARY

S	M	T	W	T	F	S
		1	2	3	4	5
6	7	8	9	10	11	12
13	14	15	16	17	18	19
20	21	22	23	24	25	26
27	28					

MARCH

S	M	T	W	T	F	S
		1	2	3	4	5
6	7	8	9	10	11	12
13	14	15	16	17	18	19
20	21	22	23	24	25	26
27	28	29	30	31		

APRIL

S	M	T	W	T	F	S
					1	2
3	4	5	6	7	8	9
10	11	12	13	14	15	16
17	18	19	20	21	22	23
24	25	26	27	28	29	30

MAY

S	M	T	W	T	F	S
1	2	3	4	5	6	7
8	9	10	11	12	13	14
15	16	17	18	19	20	21
22	23	24	25	26	27	28
29	30	31				

JUNE

S	M	T	W	T	F	S
			1	2	3	4
5	6	7	8	9	10	11
12	13	14	15	16	17	18
19	20	21	22	23	24	25
26	27	28	29	30		

JULY

S	M	T	W	T	F	S
					1	2
3	4	5	6	7	8	9
10	11	12	13	14	15	16
17	18	19	20	21	22	23
24/31	25	26	27	28	29	30

AUGUST

S	M	T	W	T	F	S
	1	2	3	4	5	6
7	8	9	10	11	12	13
14	15	16	17	18	19	20
21	22	23	24	25	26	27
28	29	30	31			

SEPTEMBER

S	M	T	W	T	F	S
				1	2	3
4	5	6	7	8	9	10
11	12	13	14	15	16	17
18	19	20	21	22	23	24
25	26	27	28	29	30	

OCTOBER

S	M	T	W	T	F	S
						1
2	3	4	5	6	7	8
9	10	11	12	13	14	15
16	17	18	19	20	21	22
23/30	24/31	25	26	27	28	29

NOVEMBER

S	M	T	W	T	F	S
		1	2	3	4	5
6	7	8	9	10	11	12
13	14	15	16	17	18	19
20	21	22	23	24	25	26
27	28	29	30			

DECEMBER

S	M	T	W	T	F	S
				1	2	3
4	5	6	7	8	9	10
11	12	13	14	15	16	17
18	19	20	21	22	23	24
25	26	27	28	29	30	31

late May	Return to the Age of Marco Polo Festival, Korčula, Croatia (concerts, folk dancing, parades)
June 18–19	Celebration of the Rose, Český Krumlov, Czech Republic (medieval festival, music, theater, dance, knights' tournament)
June 22	Antifascist Struggle Day, Croatia
June 25	National Day, Slovenia; Statehood Day, Croatia
June 25–July 3	Jewish Culture Festival, Kraków, Poland (www.jewishfestival.pl)
June 28–29	Budapest Farewell, Budapest, Hungary (celebrates last Soviet soldier leaving; parades, costumes, music)

June	Dance Prague, Czech Republic (modern dance festival, www.tanecpha.cz)
July 5	Sts. Cyril and Methodius Day, Czech Republic
July 6	Jan Hus Day, Czech Republic
July 10–Aug 25	Dubrovnik Summer Festival, Croatia (www.dubrovnik-festival.hr)
July 15–Aug 27	International Music Festival, Český Krumlov, Czech Republic (www.czechmusicfestival.com)
July 20–24	International Folklore Festival, Zagreb, Croatia (costumes, songs, dances from all over Croatia; www.msf.hr)
July 29–31	Formula 1 races, Budapest, Hungary (www.hungaroinfo.com/formel1)
July	"Budafest" Summer Opera and Ballet Festival, Budapest, Hungary (www.viparts.hu)
early July–late Aug	Ljubljana Summer Festival, Slovenia (www.festival-lj.si)
mid-July	Visegrád International Palace Games, Visegrád, Hungary (archery, jousting, medieval arts; www.palotajatekok.hu)
mid-July–mid-Aug	Summer Festival, Split, Croatia (music and theater; www.splitsko-ljeto.hr)
Aug 5	National Thanksgiving Day, Croatia
Aug 10–17	Sziget Festival, Budapest, Hungary (rock and pop music, www.sziget.hu)
Aug 15	Assumption of Mary, Poland, Slovenia, and Croatia
Aug 20	Constitution Day and St. Stephen's Day, Hungary (fireworks, celebrations)
Aug 20–21	Jazz at Summer's End Festival, Český Krumlov, Czech Republic
late Aug–early Sept	Jewish Summer Festival, Budapest, Hungary (www.jewishfestival.hu)
Sept 12–Oct 2	Prague Autumn Music Festival, Czech Republic (www.pragueautumn.cz)
Sept 28	St. Wenceslas Day, Czech Republic (celebrates national patron saint and Czech statehood)
early Sept	Marco Polo Naval Battle Reenactment, Korčula, Croatia
late Sept	Warsaw Autumn, Poland (contemporary music festival, www.warsaw-autumn.art.pl)

Oct 23	Republic Day, Hungary (remembrances of 1956 Uprising)
Oct 28	Independence Day, Czech Republic
Oct 31	Reformation Day, Slovenia
late Oct	Budapest Autumn Festival, Budapest, Hungary (music, www.festivalcity.hu)
late Oct–early Nov	International Jazz Festival, Prague, Czech Republic (www.jazzfestivalpraha.cz)
Nov 1	All Saints' Day, Poland, Slovenia, and Croatia (religious festival, some closures)
Nov 11	Independence Day, Poland; St. Martin's Day (official first day of wine season), Slovenia and Croatia
Nov 17	Velvet Revolution Anniversary, Czech Republic
Dec 5	St. Nicholas Eve, Prague, Czech Republic (St. Nick gives gifts to children in town square)
Dec 25	Christmas Day, all countries
Dec 26	Boxing Day, Hungary; Independence Day, Slovenia; St. Stephen's Day, Croatia
Dec 31	St. Sylvester's Day, Prague, Czech Republic (fireworks)

Numbers and Stumblers

- Europeans write a few of their numbers differently than we do: 1 = 1, 4 = 4, 7 = 7. Learn the difference or miss your train.
- Europeans write dates as day/month/year (Christmas is 25/12/05).
- Commas are decimal points, and decimals are commas. A dollar and a half is 1,50. There are 5.280 feet in a mile.
- When counting with fingers, start with your thumb. If you hold up your first finger to request one item, you'll probably get two.
- What we Americans call the second floor of a building is the first floor in Europe.
- Europeans keep the left "lane" open for passing on escalators and moving sidewalks. Keep to the right.

Climate

Here is a list of average temperatures (first line—average daily low; second line—average daily high; third line—days of rain). This can be helpful in planning your itinerary, but I have never found European weather to be particularly predictable, and these charts ignore humidity.

	J	F	M	A	M	J	J	A	S	O	N	D
AUSTRIA • Vienna												
	25°	28°	30°	42°	50°	56°	60°	59°	53°	44°	37°	30°
	34°	38°	47°	58°	67°	73°	76°	75°	68°	56°	45°	37°
	15	14	13	13	13	14	13	13	10	13	14	15
CROATIA • Dubrovnik												
	42°	43°	57°	52°	58°	65°	69°	69°	64°	57°	51°	46°
	53°	55°	58°	63°	70°	78°	83°	82°	77°	69°	62°	56°
	13	13	11	10	10	6	4	3	7	11	16	15
CZECH REPUBLIC • Prague												
	23°	24°	30°	38°	46°	52°	55°	55°	49°	41°	33°	27°
	31°	34°	44°	54°	64°	70°	73°	72°	65°	53°	42°	34°
	13	11	10	11	13	12	13	12	10	13	12	13
GERMANY • Berlin												
	23°	23°	30°	38°	45°	51°	55°	54°	48°	40°	33°	26°
	35°	38°	48°	56°	64°	70°	74°	73°	67°	56°	44°	36°
	17	15	12	13	12	13	14	14	12	14	16	15
HUNGARY • Budapest												
	25°	28°	35°	44°	52°	58°	62°	60°	53°	44°	38°	30°
	34°	39°	50°	62°	71°	78°	82°	81°	74°	61°	47°	39°
	13	12	11	11	13	13	10	9	7	10	14	13
POLAND • Kraków												
	22°	22°	30°	38°	48°	54°	58°	56°	49°	42°	33°	28°
	32°	34°	45°	55°	67°	72°	76°	73°	66°	56°	44°	37°
	16	15	12	15	12	15	16	15	12	14	15	16
SLOVENIA • Ljubljana												
	25°	25°	32°	40°	48°	54°	57°	57°	51°	43°	36°	30°
	36°	41°	50°	60°	68°	75°	80°	78°	71°	59°	47°	39°
	13	11	11	13	16	16	12	12	10	14	15	15

Temperature Conversion: Fahrenheit and Celsius

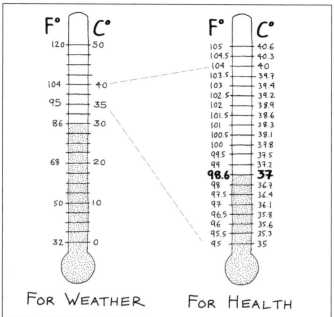

For Weather   For Health

Metric Conversion (approximate)

1 inch = 25 millimeters	32 degrees F = 0 degrees C
1 foot = 0.3 meter	82 degrees F = about 28 degrees C
1 yard = 0.9 meter	1 ounce = 28 grams
1 mile = 1.6 kilometers	1 kilogram = 2.2 pounds
1 centimeter = 0.4 inch	1 quart = 0.95 liter
1 meter = 39.4 inches	1 square yard = 0.8 square meter
1 kilometer = 0.62 mile	1 acre = 0.4 hectare

Making Your Hotel Reservation

Most hotel managers know basic "hotel English." Faxing or e-mailing are the preferred methods for reserving a room. They're more accurate than telephoning and much faster than writing a letter. Use this handy form for your fax or find it online at www.ricksteves.com/reservation. Photocopy and fax away.

One-Page Fax

To: _____ @ _____
             hotel   **fax**

From: _____ @ _____
               name   **fax**

Today's date: _____ / _____ / _____
                   day   month   year

Dear Hotel _____ ,
Please make this reservation for me:

Name: _____

Total # of people:_____ # of rooms: _____ # of nights: _____

Arriving: _____ / ____ / ____   My time of arrival (24-hr clock): _____
              day   month   year   (I will telephone if I will be late)

Departing: ____ / ____ / ____
                day   month   year

Room(s): Single _____ Double ___ Twin _____ Triple ___ Quad _____

With: Toilet _____ Shower _____ Bath _____ Sink only _____

Special needs: View ___ Quiet ___ Cheapest ___ Ground Floor ___

Please fax, mail, or e-mail confirmation of my reservation, along with the type of room reserved and the price. Please also inform me of your cancellation policy. After I hear from you, I will quickly send my credit-card information as a deposit to hold the room. Thank you.

_____
Signature

_____
Name

_____
Address

_____
City   **State**   **Zip Code   Country**

_____
E-mail Address

INDEX

Start your trip at
www.ricksteves.com

Rick Steves' website is packed with over 3,000 pages of timely travel information. It's also your gateway to getting FREE monthly travel news from Rick — and more!

Free Monthly European Travel News

Fresh articles on Europe's most interesting destinations and happenings. Rick will even send you an e-mail every month (often direct from Europe) with his latest discoveries!

Timely Travel Tips

Rick Steves' best money-and-stress-saving tips on trip planning, packing, transportation, hotels, health, safety, finances, hurdling the language barrier…and more.

Travelers' Graffiti Wall

Candid advice and opinions from thousands of travelers on everything listed above, plus whatever topics are hot at the moment (discount flights, packing tips, scams…you name it).

Rick's Annual Guide to European Railpasses

The clearest, most comprehensive guide to the confusing array of railpass options out there, and how to choo-choose the railpass that best fits your itinerary and budget. Then you can order your railpass (and get a bunch of great freebies) online from us!

Great Gear at the Rick Steves Travel Store

Enjoy bargains on Rick's guidebooks, planning maps and TV series DVDs—and on his custom-designed carry-on bags, wheeled bags, day bags and light-packing accessories.

Rick Steves Tours

Every year more than 5,000 lucky travelers explore Europe on a Rick Steves tour. Learn more about our 26 different one-to-three-week itineraries, read uncensored feedback from our tour alums, and sign up for your dream trip online!

Rick on TV

Read the scripts and see video clips from the popular Rick Steves' Europe TV series, and get an inside look at Rick's 13 newest shows.

Respect for Your Privacy

Ordering online from us is secure. When you buy something from us, join a tour, or subscribe to Rick's free monthly travel news e-mails, we promise to never share your name, information, or e-mail address with anyone else. You won't be spammed!

Have fun raising your Travel I.Q. at
www.ricksteves.com

Travel smart...carry on!

The latest generation of Rick Steves' carry-on travel bags is easily the best—benefiting from two decades of on-the-road attention to what really matters: maximum quality and strength; practical, flexible features; and no unnecessary frills. You won't find a better value anywhere!

Convertible, expandable, and carry-on-size:

Rick Steves' Back Door Bag $99

This is the same bag that Rick Steves lives out of for three months every summer. It's made of rugged water-resistant 1000 denier Cordura nylon, and best of all, it converts easily from a smart-looking suitcase to a handy backpack with comfortably-curved shoulder straps and a padded waistbelt.

This roomy, versatile 9" x 21" x 14" bag has a large 2600 cubic-inch main compartment, plus three outside pockets (small, medium and huge) that are perfect for often-used items. And the cinch-tight compression straps will keep your load compact and close to your back—not sagging like a sack of potatoes.

Wishing you had even more room to bring home souvenirs? Pull open the full-perimeter expando-zipper and its capacity jumps from 2600 to 3000 cubic inches. When you want to use it as a suitcase or check it as luggage (required when "expanded"), the straps and belt hide away in a zippered compartment in the back.

Attention travelers under 5'4" tall: This bag also comes in an inch-shorter version, for a compact-friendlier fit between the waistbelt and shoulder straps.

Convenient, durable, and carry-on-size:

Rick Steves' Wheeled Bag $119

At 9" x 21" x 14" our sturdy Rick Steves' Wheeled Bag is rucksack-soft in front, but the rest is lined with a hard ABS-lexan shell to give maximum protection to your belongings. We've spared no expense on moving parts, splurging on an extra-long button-release handle and big, tough inline skate wheels for easy rolling on rough surfaces.

This bag is not convertible! Our research tells us that travelers who've bought convertible wheeled bags never put them on their backs anyway, so we've eliminated the extra weight and expense.

Rick Steves' Wheeled Bag has exactly the same three-outside-pocket configuration as our Back Door Bag, plus a handy "add-a-bag" strap and full lining.

Our Back Door Bags and Wheeled Bags come in black, navy, blue spruce, evergreen and merlot.

For great deals on a wide selection of travel goodies, begin your next trip at the Rick Steves Travel Store!

Visit the Rick Steves Travel Store at
www.ricksteves.com

Rick Steves

COUNTRY GUIDES 2005

France
Germany & Austria
Great Britain
Ireland
Italy
Portugal
Scandinavia
Spain
Switzerland

CITY GUIDES 2005

Amsterdam, Bruges & Brussels
Florence & Tuscany
London
Paris
Prague & The Czech Republic
Provence & The French Riviera
Rome
Venice

BEST OF GUIDES

Best European City Walks & Museums
Best of Eastern Europe
Best of Europe

More *Savvy*. More *Surprising*. More *Fun*.

PHRASE BOOKS & DICTIONARIES

French
French, Italian & German
German
Italian
Portuguese
Spanish

MORE EUROPE FROM RICK STEVES

Easy Access Europe
Europe 101
Europe Through the Back Door
Postcards from Europe

DVD
RICK STEVES' EUROPE

Rick Steves' Europe All Thirty
   Shows 2000–2003
Britain & Ireland
Exotic Europe
Germany, The Swiss Alps
   & Travel Skills
Italy

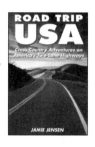

For a complete listing of Rick Steves' books, see page 10.

Avalon Travel Publishing
1400 65th Street, Suite 250
Emeryville, CA 94608

Avalon Travel Publishing
An Imprint of Avalon Publishing Group

Printed in the U.S.A. by Worzalla
First printing February 2005

Special thanks to Ian Watson for his innumerable contributions, from sharing his linguistic and map-making skills to writing about Polish and Hungarian cuisine. Many thanks also to Honza Vihan for his help with all things Czech (including writing the Czech food section).

Portions of this book were originally published in *Rick Steves' Germany & Austria* © 2005, by Rick Steves; in *Rick Steves' Germany, Austria & Switzerland* © 2004, 2003, 2002, 2001, 2000, 1999, by Rick Steves; and in *Rick Steves' Prague & the Czech Republic* © 2005, by Rick Steves and Honza Vihan.

For the latest on Rick Steves' lectures, guidebooks, tours, and public television series, contact Europe Through the Back Door, Box 2009, Edmonds, WA 98020, tel. 425/771-8303, fax 425/771-0833, www.ricksteves.com, rick@ricksteves.com.

ISBN 1-56691-786-7
ISSN 1547-8505

Europe Through the Back Door Managing Editor: Risa Laib
ETBD Editors: Cameron Hewitt, Jennifer Hauseman
Avalon Travel Publishing Editor and Series Manager: Roxanna Font
Avalon Travel Publishing Project Editor: Patrick Collins
Research Assistance: Ian Watson (Danube Bend)
Copy Editor: Mia Lipman
Production & Typesetting: Patrick David Barber
Cover Design: Kari Gim, Laura Mazer
Interior Design: Laura Mazer, Jane Musser, Amber Pirker
Maps & Graphics: David C. Hoerlein, Zoey Platt, Lauren Mills, Mike Morgenfeld
Indexer: Kevin Millham
Photography: Cameron Hewitt, Rick Steves
Front Matter Color Photos: page i: Krakow © Cameron Hewitt; page ii: Wawel Cathedral, Krakow, Poland © Cameron Hewitt; page xii: City Wall, Dubrovnik, Croatia © Cameron Hewitt
Cover Photos: front: Széchenyi Baths, Budapest, Hungary © Cameron Hewitt; back: Predjama Castle, Slovenia © Cameron Hewitt

Distributed to the book trade by Publishers Group West, Berkeley, California